Lecture Notes in Computer Science

Lecture Notes in Artificial Intelligence 15877

Founding Editor

Jörg Siekmann

The series Lecture Notes in Artificial Intelligence (LNAI) was established in 1988 as a topical subseries of LNCS devoted to artificial intelligence.

The series publishes state-of-the-art research results at a high level. As with the LNCS mother series, the mission of the series is to serve the international R & D community by providing an invaluable service, mainly focused on the publication of conference and workshop proceedings and postproceedings.

Alexandra I. Cristea · Erin Walker · Yu Lu ·
Olga C. Santos · Seiji Isotani
Editors

Artificial Intelligence in Education

26th International Conference, AIED 2025
Palermo, Italy, July 22–26, 2025
Proceedings, Part I

Springer

Editors
Alexandra I. Cristea
Durham University
Durham, UK

Yu Lu
Beijing Normal University
Beijing, China

Seiji Isotani
University of São Paulo
São Carlos, Brazil

Erin Walker
University of Pittsburgh
Pittsburgh, PA, USA

Olga C. Santos
UNED
Madrid, Spain

ISSN 0302-9743 ISSN 1611-3349 (electronic)
Lecture Notes in Artificial Intelligence
ISBN 978-3-031-98413-6 ISBN 978-3-031-98414-3 (eBook)
https://doi.org/10.1007/978-3-031-98414-3

LNCS Sublibrary: SL7 – Artificial Intelligence

This Springer imprint is published by the registered company Springer Nature Switzerland AG
The registered company address is: Gewerbestrasse 11, 6330 Cham, Switzerland

Preface

Welcome to the 26th International Conference on Artificial Intelligence in Education, taking place from July 22–26, 2025 in the vibrant city of Palermo, Italy. AIED 2025 is ranked A in ICORE[1], in the top 14.92% of all 784 ranked venues, and clearly growing and attracting more submissions, this year with over 800 initial submissions. Thus, as we celebrate over a quarter of a century of advancing the science and engineering of intelligent human-technology ecosystems that support learning, this edition marked a significant evolution in our conference structure, with the introduction of a dedicated track-based system. This new format was designed to capture the growth of the area, as well as the dynamic and multifaceted nature of research in educational AI, reflecting the rapid pace and expanding impact of the field.

The theme for AIED 2025—"AI as a Catalyst for Inclusive, Personalised, and Ethical Education: Empowering Teachers and Students for an Equitable Future"—embodies our vision for a transformative future in education. Artificial Intelligence is progressing at an unprecedented rate, with generative AI and related technologies spearheading this transformative shift. As these innovations reshape both teaching and learning processes, they unlock novel opportunities for creating personalised and dynamic learning experiences. Even as traditional AI techniques continue to evolve and enrich our understanding, true change lies in leveraging these advancements to provide educators with powerful tools for deeper insights, tailored instruction, and increased student engagement.

At the heart of this transformation is the commitment to equity and ethical practice. By harnessing AI's capacity to personalise learning experiences, we can address the diverse needs of students and reduce educational disparities, especially among underserved and marginalised communities. Equally important is the need to integrate AI responsibly, ensuring that fairness, transparency, and privacy remain paramount in our educational practices. This dual commitment—to innovation and to ethical inclusion—was the cornerstone of our conference theme.

The conference program comprised seven thematic tracks:

- **Track 1 – AIED Architectures and Tools:** This track highlighted innovative engineering advances, from multi-agent systems and tangible interfaces to scalable, domain-specific applications across a variety of educational contexts.
- **Track 2 – Machine Learning and Generative AI:** Emphasising data-driven techniques and generative models, this track explored novel algorithms and computational approaches that enhance predictive and adaptive functionalities in educational environments.
- **Track 3 – Learning, Teaching, and Pedagogy:** Focusing on empirical and theoretical work, this track examined the impact of AI on teaching practices, learner engagement, and the evolution of both formal and informal learning experiences.

[1] https://portal.core.edu.au/conf-ranks.

- **Track 4 – Human-Centred Design and Design-Based Research:** This track addressed the design principles and interactive strategies that place educators and learners at the centre, fostering collaborative human-AI partnerships to promote agency and effective decision-making.
- **Track 5 – Teaching AI:** Dedicated to advancing AI literacy, the research in this track explored methods and technologies that demystify AI, empowering individuals to understand, utilise, and critically evaluate its capabilities.
- **Track 6 – Ethics, Equity, and AIED in Society:** This track delved into the societal dimensions of AI in education, with an emphasis on fairness, transparency, privacy, and strategies to mitigate educational disparities.
- **Track 7 – Theoretical Aspects of AIED and AI-Based Modeling for Education:** This track emphasised conceptual and theoretical contributions providing deeper insights into cognitive, motivational, and socio-cognitive processes, underpinning rigorous models of learning and teaching.

AIED 2025 attracted an exceptionally broad range of submissions. We received over 800 submissions across all tracks, of which 711 met the eligibility criteria and were accepted for review. From the full paper submissions, 130 were accepted as full papers, and an additional 129 were accepted as short papers. The acceptance rates for both full and short papers were 18%, respectively.

Every paper and presentation at AIED 2025 underwent a rigorous, double-blind peer-review process designed to ensure the highest scholarly standards and fair evaluation, with an average of three reviews per submission. This meticulous process—drawing on the expertise of leading researchers, seasoned reviewers, and senior committee members—culminated in an outstanding program that spanned the full spectrum of AIED research and practice.

Beyond the scholarly sessions and paper presentations compiled in these LNCS volumes, AIED 2025 offered a rich program of keynote addresses, panel discussions, interactive demonstrations, and specialised sessions which are compiled in the CCIS volumes of the conference. Specifically, this year had both a general AIED panel as well as a joint panel with sister conferences, Educational Data Mining (EDM 2025) and ACM Learning @ Scale (L@S 2025), which were co-located in Palermo with AIED 2025. Attendees had the opportunity to participate in the Doctoral Consortium, Workshops and Tutorials, Late-Breaking Results sessions, and dedicated tracks for practitioners, industry, and policy. Notably, the BlueSky track invited visionary reflections on past progress and future trajectories in AIED, while the WideAIED track amplified perspectives from under-represented regions and communities. Additionally, the conference offered presentations on the latest publication in IJAIED[2], the journal associated with the conference. As a member of the International Alliance to Advance Learning in the Digital Era (IAALDE)[3] alliance, AIED 2025 hosted, last but not least, presentations of the best papers from other IAALDE conferences (in particular, ICCE 2024 and LAK 2025).

[2] https://link.springer.com/journal/40593.

[3] https://alliancelss.com/.

This conference would not have been possible without the unwavering commitment of the International Artificial Intelligence in Education Society, the Organising Committee, the Program and Senior Program Committees, and the sponsors and partners who support our mission. Their passion and dedication to advancing intelligent educational systems is the foundation of AIED's continued success and innovation.

We invite you to engage wholeheartedly in the exchange of ideas, to challenge conventional paradigms, and to forge new collaborations that will shape the future of education. Together, we will explore how artificial intelligence can act as a true catalyst for creating more inclusive, personalised, and ethical learning environments for teachers and students around the world. Welcome to AIED 2025 — where the future of education is actively being reimagined, one innovative idea at a time.

July 2025

Alexandra I. Cristea
Erin Walker
Yu Lu
Olga C. Santos
Seiji Isotani

Organization

Conference General Co-chairs

Olga C. Santos	UNED, Spain
Seiji Isotani	University of São Paulo, Brazil

Program Co-chairs

Alexandra I. Cristea	Durham University, UK
Erin Walker	Arizona State University, USA
Yu Lu	Beijing Normal University, China

Local Organising Co-chairs

Davide Taibi	Institute for Educational Technology, National Research Council, Italy
Giusuè Lo Bosco	University of Palermo, Italy

Doctoral Consortium Co-chairs

Zitao Liu	Jinan University, China
Carla Limongelli	University of Roma Tre, Italy
Sergey Sosnovsky	Utrecht University, Netherlands

Workshop and Tutorials Co-chairs

Gabriella Casalino	University of Bari, Italy
Tanja Mitrovic	University of Canterbury, New Zealand
Sebastiane Lalle	Sorbonne University, France

Practitioners, Industry, and Policy Co-chairs

Sreecharan Sankaranarayanan	Amazon, USA
Penghe Chen	Beijing Normal University, China
Emmanuel G. Blanchard	Le Mans University, France
Christian M. Stracke	University of Bonn, Germany

Posters and Late Breaking Results Co-chairs

Jingyun Wang	Durham University, UK
Ilona Buchem	Berliner Hochschule für Technik, Germany

AIED Mentoring Fellowship Co-chairs

Vania Dimitrova	University of Leeds, UK
Ig Ibert Bittencourt	Universidade Federal de Alagoas, Brazil

Panel Co-chairs

Ryan Baker	University of Pennsylvania, USA
Marta Cimitile	UnitelmaSapienza, Italy

Blue Sky Co-chairs

Stamos Katsigiannis	Durham University, UK
Bruce M. McLaren	Carnegie Mellon University, USA

WideAIED Co-chairs

Isabel Hilliger	Pontificia Universidad Católica, Chile
Giovanni Fulantelli	Institute for Educational Technology, National Research Council, Italy
Ilaria Torre	University of Genoa, Italy

Diversity and Inclusion Co-chairs

Valery Psyché	TÉLUQ University, Canada
Kaska Porayska-Pomsta	UCL Institute of Education, UK

Interactive Events Co-chairs

Leonardo B. Marques	Federal University of Alagoas, Brazil
Emmanuel G. Blanchard	LIUM, Le Mans Université, France

Proceedings Co-chairs

Paraskevi Topali	Radboud University, Netherlands
Rafael D. Araújo	Universidade Federal de Uberlândia, Brazil
Elaine Harada	Universidade Federal do Amazonas, Brazil

International Journal of AIED Chair

Conrad Borchers	Human-Computer Interaction Institute, USA

Virtual Experiences Co-chairs

Teng Guo	Jinan University, China
Salvatore Calderaro	University of Palermo, Italy

Publicity Co-chairs

Miguel Portaz	UNED, Spain
Xinyuan Hao	University College London, UK
Mariella Farella	Institute for Educational Technology, National Research Council, Italy

Volunteer Co-chairs

Lele Sha	Monash University, Australia
Domenico Amato	University of Palermo, Italy

Sponsorship Chair

Pietro Paolo Corso	University of Palermo, Italy

Scholarship Chair

Michele Tumminello	University of Palermo, Italy

Website Chair

Andrea Nelson Mauro	Institute for Educational Technology, National Research Council, Italy

Research Track Junior Advisory Board

Conrad Borchers	Human-Computer Interaction Institute, USA
Amine Hatun Ataş	Galatasaray University, Turkey
Krishna Chaitanya Rao Kathala	University of Massachusetts, USA
Guher Gorgun	IPN – Leibniz Institute for Science and Mathematics Education, Germany
Isaac Alpizar-Chacon	Utrecht University, Netherlands

Research Track 1 – AIED Architectures and Tools

Senior Program Committee Members

Ig Ibert Bittencourt	Federal University of Alagoas, Brazil
Emmmanuel G. Blanchard	LIUM, Le Mans Université, France
François Bouchet	Sorbonne Université - LIP6, France
Julien Broisin	IRIT, Université Toulouse III - Paul Sabatier, France

Vania Dimitrova	University of Leeds, UK
Ralph Ewerth	L3S Research Center, Leibniz Universität Hannover, Germany
Sébastien George	LIUM, Le Mans Université, France
Srecko Joksimovic	University of South Australia, Australia
Mirko Marras	University of Cagliari, Italy
Riichiro Mizoguchi	Japan Advanced Institute of Science and Technology, Japan
Andrew Olney	University of Memphis, USA
Craig Stewart	Durham University, UK

Program Committee Members

Pablo Arnau-González	Universidad de Valencia, Spain
Juan I. Asensio-Pérez	Universidad de Valladolid, Spain
Aneesha Bakharia	University of Queensland, Australia
Beata Beigman Klebanov	Educational Testing Service, USA
Anis Bey	Higher School of Management Sciences - Annaba, Algeria
Anthony F. Botelho	University of Florida, USA
Anis Boubaker	École de Technologie Supérieure (ETS), Canada
German Capdehourat	Ceibal, Uruguay
Alberto Casas-Ortiz	Universidad Nacional de Educación a Distancia, Spain
Eason Chen	Carnegie Mellon University, Taiwan
Jiahao Chen	TAL, China
Penghe Chen	Beijing Normal University, China
Pei Hua Cher	National University of Singapore, Singapore
Sergio Chevtchenko	Western Sydney University, Australia
Maria González	Tecnológico de Monterrey Campus Laguna, Mexico
Rafael D. Araújo	Universidade Federal de Uberlândia, Brazil
Barbara Ericson	University of Michigan, USA
Effat Farhana	Vanderbilt University, USA
Brendan Flanagan	Kyoto University, Japan
Kaushik Gopalan	FLAME University, India
Cyril Goutte	National Research Council Canada, Canada
Jiangang Hao	Educational Testing Service, USA
Elaine Harada	Universidade Federal do Amazonas, Brazil
Yann Hicke	Cornell University, USA
Ruikun Hou	University of Tübingen, Germany
Wanqing Hu	Beijing Normal University, China

Eleni Ilkou	Leibniz University Hannover, Germany
Patricia Jaques	PPGC/UFPEL, Brazil
Yeo Jin Kim	North Carolina State University, USA
Vasily Konovalov	AIRI, Russia
Salima Lamsiyah	Université Sidi Mohamed Ben Abdellah Fès, Morocco
Juho Leinonen	Aalto University, Finland
Zachary Levonian	University of Minnesota, USA
Hang Li	Michigan State University, USA
Zhaohui Li	Penn State University, USA
Siaw Ling Lo	Singapore Management University, Singapore
James Martin	University of Colorado Boulder, USA
Sungjin Nam	ACT, Inc., USA
Seyed Parsa Neshaei	EPFL, Switzerland
Hiran Nonato Macedo Ferreira	Universidade Federal de Uberlândia, Brazil
Narges Norouzi	UC Berkeley, USA
Pedro Orvalho	University of Oxford, UK
Tadachika Ozono	Nagoya Institute of Technology, Japan
Ulrike Pado	HFT Stuttgart, Germany
Eduard Pogorskiy	Open Files Ltd., UK
Valéry Psyché	Université TÉLUQ, Canada
Mitra Purandare	Eastern Switzerland University of Applied Sciences, Switzerland
Manikandan Ravikiran	Hitachi India Pvt Ltd, India
Luiz Rodrigues	Federal University of Alagoas, Brazil
Hannes Rosenbusch	University of Amsterdam, Netherlands
Anirban Roy	SRI International, USA
José A. Ruipérez Valiente	University of Murcia, Spain
Stefan Ruseti	University "Politehnica" of Bucharest, Romania
Ana Serrano-Mamolar	Universidad de Burgos, Spain
Mahsa Sheikhi Karizaki	Penn State University, USA
Atsushi Shimada	Kyushu University, Japan
Siddharth Siddharth	Plaksha University, India
Aakash Soni	ECE Paris, France
Vinitra Swamy	EPFL, Switzerland
Liang Zhang	University of Memphis, USA
Qi Zhou	University College London, UK
Xiaofei Zhou	University of Rochester, USA

Research Track 2 – Machine Learning and Generative AI

Senior Program Committee Members

Ayan Banerjee	Arizona State University, USA
Abhinava Barthakur	University of South Australia, Australia
Gautam Biswas	Vanderbilt University, USA
Nigel Bosch	University of Illinois Urbana-Champaign, USA
Dan Carpenter	North Carolina State University, USA
Guanliang Chen	Monash University, Australia
Ricardo Conejo	Universidad de Málaga, Spain
Mingyu Feng	WestEd, USA
Dragan Gasevic	Monash University, Australia
Johan Jeuring	Utrecht University, Netherlands
Yang Jiang	Columbia University, USA
Irena Koprinska	University of Sydney, Australia
Vitomir Kovanovic	University of South Australia, Australia
Sébastien Lallé	Sorbonne University, France
Andrew Lan	University of Massachusetts Amherst, USA
Mikel Larrañaga	University of the Basque Country UPV/EHU, Spain
Hady Lauw	Singapore Management University, Singapore
Nguyen-Thinh Le	Humboldt Universität zu Berlin, Germany
James Lester	North Carolina State University, USA
Fuhua Lin	Athabasca University, Canada
Zitao Liu	Jinan University, China
Jeffrey Matayoshi	McGraw Hill ALEKS, USA
Noboru Matsuda	North Carolina State University, USA
Wookhee Min	North Carolina State University, USA
Antonija Mitrovic	University of Canterbury, New Zealand
Huy Nguyen	Carnegie Mellon University, USA
Roger Nkambou	Université du Québec à Montréal, Canada
Radek Pelánek	Masaryk University, Czechia
Rinat B. Rosenberg-Kima	Technion - Israel Institute of Technology, Israel
Sreecharan Sankaranarayanan	Carnegie Mellon University, USA
Filippo Sciarrone	Universitas Mercatorum, Italy
Maomi Ueno	University of Electro-Communications, Japan

Program Committee Members

Seth Adjei	Northern Kentucky University, USA
Itziar Aldabe	University of the Basque Country (UPV/EHU), Spain
Manar Alkhatib	British University in Dubai, United Arab Emirates
Samah Alkhuzaey	University of Liverpool, UK
Isaac Alpizar-Chacon	Utrecht University, Netherlands
Antonio R. Anaya	Universidad Nacional de Educacion a Distancia, Spain
Eduardo Aranha	UFRN, Brazil
Pasquale Ardimento	University of Bari Aldo Moro, Italy
Miguel Arevalillo-Herráez	University of Valencia, Spain
Vedant Bahel	University of British Columbia, Canada
Aneesha Bakharia	University of Queensland, Australia
Tiffany Barnes	North Carolina State University, USA
Alex Barrett	Florida State University, USA
Idir Benouaret	Epita Research Laboratory, France
Kamal Berahmand	Queensland University of Technology, Australia
Yoav Bergner	New York University, USA
Mario Luca Bernardi	University of Sannio, Italy
Maria Bolsinova	Tilburg University, Netherlands
Rex Bringula	University of the East, Philippines
Okan Bulut	University of Alberta, Canada
Tyler Burleigh	Khan Academy, USA
Jie Cao	University of Colorado Boulder, USA
Paulo Carvalho	Carnegie Mellon University, USA
Alberto Casas-Ortiz	Universidad Nacional de Educación a Distancia, Spain
Binglin Chen	University of Illinois Urbana-Champaign, USA
Jiahao Chen	TAL, China
Li Chen	Kyushu University, Japan
Wei-Peng Chen	Fujitsu Labs of America, USA
Keith Cochran	DePaul University, USA
Jade Mai Cock	EPFL, Switzerland
Lea Cohausz	University of Mannheim, Germany
Maria González	Tecnológico de Monterrey Campus Laguna, Mexico
Mark G. Core	University of Southern California, USA
Jeffrey Cross	Tokyo Institute of Technology, Japan
Yuan Cui	Northwestern University, USA
Sidney D'Mello	University of Colorado Boulder, USA

Marcos Da Silveira	Luxembourg Institute of Science and Technology, Luxembourg
Mihai Dascalu	University Politehnica of Bucharest, Romania
Pasquale De Meo	University of Messina, Italy
Hannah Deininger	Eberhard-Karls-Universität Tübingen, Germany
Michel Desmarais	Polytechnique Montréal, Canada
Emmanuel Dorley	University of Florida, USA
Junlei Du	Beijing Normal University, Beijing, China
Jamie Duell	Nanyang Technological University, Singapore
Cristina Dumdumaya	University of Southeastern Philippines, Philippines
Andrew Emerson	National Board of Medical Examiners, USA
Wicaksono Febriantoro	University College London, UK
Shihui Feng	University of Hong Kong, China
Nigel Fernandez	University of Massachusetts Amherst, USA
Alessio Ferrato	Roma Tre University, Italy
Rafael Ferreira Mello	Cesar School, Brazil
Joyce Fonteles	Vanderbilt University, USA
Cristiano Galafassi	Universidade Federal do Rio Grande do Sul, Brazil
Wenbin Gan	National Institute of Information and Communications Technology, Japan
Ananya Ganesh	University of Colorado, Boulder, USA
Oscar Garces	University of Technology Sydney, Australia
Alireza Gharahighehi	imec - KU Leuven, Belgium
Guher Gorgun	University of Alberta, Canada
Sabine Graf	Athabasca University, Canada
Wolfgang Gritz	TIB – Leibniz Information Centre for Science and Technology, Germany
Quanlong Guan	Jinan University, China
Haoyu Han	Michigan State University, USA
Jieun Han	KAIST, South Korea
Elaine Harada	Universidade Federal do Amazonas, Brazil
Peng He	Washington State University, USA
Hasnain Heickal	University of Massachusetts Amherst, USA
Anett Hoppe	Leibniz Universität Hannover, Germany
Shuyan Huang	TAL Education Group, China
Yu-Kai Huang	Carnegie Mellon University, USA
Corina Ilinca	University of Bucharest, Romania
Tsunenori Ishioka	National Center for University Entrance Examinations, Japan
Hamid Karimi	Utah State University, USA

Matthew C. Kelley	George Mason University, USA
Rene Kizilcec	Cornell University, USA
Ali Koksal	A*STAR, Singapore
Sotiris Kotsiantis	University of Patras, Greece
Charles Koutcheme	Aalto University, Finland
Udo Kruschwitz	University of Regensburg, Germany
Andrey Kuznetsov	AIRI, Russia
Chahrazed Labba	Université de Lorraine, France
Chandra Shekar Lakshminarayanan	Indian Institute of Technology Madras, India
Ehsan Latif	University of Georgia, USA
Tai Le Quy	University of Koblenz, Germany
Gayoung Lee	Baekseok University, South Korea
Wee Leong Lee	Singapore University of Social Sciences, Singapore
Haiying Li	University of Pennsylvania, USA
Hongming Li	University of Florida, USA
Huiyong Li	Kyushu University, Japan
Juanhui Li	Michigan State University, USA
Shan Li	Lehigh University, USA
Xinyu Li	Monash University, Australia
Zhi Li	University of California, Berkeley, USA
Jionghao Lin	University of Hong Kong, China
Siyuan Liu	Nanyang Technological University, Singapore
Feng Liu	Drexel University, USA
Guimei Liu	A*STAR, Singapore
Naiming Liu	Rice University, USA
Ninghao Liu	University of Georgia, USA
Ziyuan Liu	Singapore Management University, Singapore
Rose Luckin	University College London, UK
Jakub Macina	ETH Zurich, Switzerland
Christopher MacLellan	Georgia Institute of Technology, USA
George Magoulas	University of London, UK
Subhankar Maity	IIT Kharagpur, India
Talles Medeiros	Federal University of Ouro Preto, Brazil
Guilherme Medeiros Machado	ECE Paris, France
Paolo Mengoni	Hong Kong Baptist University, China
Eva Millan	Universidad de Málaga, Spain
Tsunenori Mine	Kyushu University, Japan
Sein Minn	Inria, France
Yoshimitsu Miyazawa	National Center for University Entrance Examinations, Japan

Mehrnoush Mohammadi Bolbanabad	University of Queensland, Australia
Mukesh Mohania	IIIT Delhi, India
Pedro J. Muñoz-Merino	Universidad Carlos III de Madrid, Spain
Takashi Nagai	Institute of Technologists, Japan
Vinay Namboodiri	University of Bath, UK
Hung Tuan Nguyen	Tokyo University of Agriculture and Technology, Japan
Ange Adrienne Nyamen Tato	Université Laval, Canada
Hilário Oliveira	Instituto Federal do Espírito Santo - Campus Serra, Brazil
Luc Paquette	University of Illinois Urbana-Champaign, USA
Zach Pardos	University of California, Berkeley, USA
Rebecca Passonneau	Pennsylvania State University, USA
Tung Phung	MPI-SWS, Germany
Yang Pian	Beijing Normal University, China
Juan Pinto	University of Illinois Urbana-Champaign, USA
Valentina Poggioni	Università di Perugia, Italy
Marjana Prifti Skenduli	University of New York Tirana, Albania
Ratnavel Rajalakshmi	VIT University, Chennai Campus, India
Mladen Rakovic	Monash University, Australia
Erik Rodner	Hochschule für Technik und Wirtschaft, Germany
Oleg Rogov	AIRI, Russia
José Raúl Romero	University of Córdoba, Spain
Lu Rong	Tianjin University, China
Leo Sylvio Rüdian	Humboldt-Universität zu Berlin, Germany
Rohit Saluja	IIT Mandi, India
Batuhan Sayis	Universitat Pompeu Fabra, Spain
Alexander Scarlatos	University of Massachusetts, USA
Kshitij Sharma	Norwegian University of Science and Technology, Norway
Mahsa Sheikhi Karizaki	Penn State University, USA
Leixian Shen	Tsinghua University, China
Bruce Sherin	Northwestern University, USA
Andy Smith	North Carolina State University, USA
Hyun-Je Song	Jeonbuk National University, South Korea
Francesco Sovrano	ETH Zurich, Switzerland
Sebastian Strauß	Ruhr University Bochum, Germany
Man Su	Saarland University, Germany
Zhongtian Sun	University of Kent, UK
Abhijit Suresh	University of Colorado Boulder, USA
Cheng Tang	Kyushu University, Japan

Patricia Tedesco	Universidade Federal de Pernambuco, Brazil
Khushboo Thaker	University of Pittsburgh, USA
Danielle R Thomas	Carnegie Mellon University, USA
Becky Tomaso	University of South Alabama, USA
Rodothea Myrsini Tsoupidi	Independent Researcher, Sweden
Emiko Tsutsumi	University of Electro-Communications, Japan
Miriam Ugarte Querejeta	Mondragon Unibertsitatea, Spain
Josh Underwood	Independent, Spain
Masaki Uto	University of Electro-Communications, Japan
Kirk Vanacore	Worcester Polytechnic Institute, USA
Maureen Villamor	University of Southeastern Philippines, Philippines
Sree Aurovindh Viswanathan	Infosys Technologies Limited, India
Alessandro Vivas	UFVJM, Brazil
Marco Volpe	University of Leicester, UK
Christabel Wayllace	New Mexico State University, USA
Daniel Weitekamp	Carnegie Mellon University, USA
Jinta Weng	University of Chinese Academy of Sciences, China
Chris Wong	University of Technology Sydney, Australia
Tat Wing Wong	Chinese University of Hong Kong, China
Anna Wróblewska	Warsaw University of Technology, Poland
Bo Wu	Colorado School of Mines, USA
Jinran Wu	University of Queensland, Australia
Zihan Wu	University of Michigan, USA
Jinjun Xiong	University at Buffalo, USA
Yaping Xu	Beijing Normal University, China
Takayoshi Yamashita	Chubu University, Japan
Xi Yang	IBM Research, USA
Calvin Yeung	Nagoya University, Japan
Guoxian Yu	Shandong University, China
Jifan Yu	Tsinghua University, China
Rajamanickam Yuvaraj	Anna University, India
Andres Felipe Zambrano	University of Pennsylvania, USA
Jiayi Zhang	University of Pennsylvania, USA
Rui Zhang	Tongji University, China
Shugang Zhang	Ocean University of China, China
Yupei Zhang	Northwestern Polytechnical University, China
Nina Zhou	A*STAR, Singapore

Research Track 3 – Learning, Teaching, and Pedagogy

Senior Program Committee Members

Bita Akram	North Carolina State University, USA
Laura Allen	University of Minnesota, USA
Ivon Arroyo	University of Massachusetts Amherst, USA
Ryan Baker	University of Pennsylvania, USA
Ig Ibert Bittencourt	Federal University of Alagoas, Brazil
Jesus G. Boticario	UNED, Spain
Irene-Angelica Chounta	University of Duisburg-Essen, Germany
Floriana Grasso	University of Liverpool, UK
Beate Grawemeyer	Coventry University, UK
Jason Harley	McGill University, Canada
Srecko Joksimovic	University of South Australia, Australia
Akihiro Kashihara	University of Electro-Communications, Japan
Amruth Kumar	Ramapo College of New Jersey, USA
Tanja Käser	EPFL, Switzerland
Roberto Martinez-Maldonado	Monash University, Australia
Gordon McCalla	University of Saskatchewan, Canada
Kathryn McCarthy	Georgia State University, USA
Bruce McLaren	Carnegie Mellon University, USA
Tomohiro Nagashima	Saarland University, Germany
Ido Roll	Technion - Israel Institute of Technology, Israel
Nikol Rummel	Ruhr-Universität Bochum, Germany
Craig Stewart	Durham University, UK
Marco Temperini	Università di Roma, Italy
Diego Zapata-Rivera	Educational Testing Service, USA

Program Committee Members

Adetunji Adeniran	Carnegie Mellon University, USA
Daniele Agostini	University of Trento, Italy
Azza Abdullah S. Alghamdi	KAU, Saudi Arabia
Manal Alhathli	Princess Nourah bint Abdulrahman University, Saudi Arabia
Ioannis Anastasopoulos	University of California, Berkeley, USA
Ella Anghel	Rutgers University, USA
David Arnau	University of Valencia, Spain
Burcu Arslan	Educational Testing Service, USA

Lili Aunimo	Haaga-Helia University of Applied Sciences, Finland
Miriam Celia Bergue Alves	Naval Postgraduate School, USA
Nirav Bhatt	IIT Madras, India
Conrad Borchers	Carnegie Mellon University, USA
Kristy Elizabeth Boyer	University of Florida, USA
Maria Concetta Carruba	Università Telematica Pegaso, Italy
Omar D. Castrillon	Universidad Nacional de Colombia, Colombia
Silvio César Cazella	UFCSPA, Brazil
Li Chen	Kyushu University, Japan
Si Chen	University of Notre Dame, USA
Jennifer Cromley	University of Illinois Urbana-Champaign, USA
Sidney D'Mello	University of Colorado Boulder, USA
Rafael D. Araújo	Universidade Federal de Uberlândia, Brazil
Cesar Delgado	North Carolina State University, USA
Diego Dermeval	Federal University of Alagoas, Brazil
Blaženka Divjak	University of Zagreb, Croatia
Isabela Dramnesc	West University of Timisoara, Romania
Benedict du Boulay	University of Sussex, UK
Nghia Duong-Trung	German Research Centre for Artificial Intelligence, Germany
Barbara Ericson	University of Michigan, USA
Cassia Fernandez	USP, Brazil
Carol Forsyth	Educational Testing Service, USA
Selen Galiç	Hacettepe University, Turkey
Andrea Garavaglia	Università degli Studi di Milano, Italy
Francisco José García-Peñalvo	University of Salamanca, Spain
Jan-Martin Geiger	University of Münster, Germany
Ralucca Gera	Naval Postgraduate School, USA
Lucia Giraffa	Pontificia Universidade Católica do Rio Grande do sul, Brazil
Jiesi Guo	Australian Catholic University, Australia
Shivang Gupta	Carnegie Mellon University, USA
Ashish Gurung	Carnegie Mellon University, USA
Songhee Han	Florida State University, USA
Elaine Harada	Universidade Federal do Amazonas, Brazil
Yugo Hayashi	Ritsumeikan University, Japan
Yusuke Hayashi	Hiroshima University, Japan
Davinia Hernández-Leo	Universitat Pompeu Fabra, Barcelona, Spain
László Horváth	Eötvös Loránd University, Hungary
Xiangen Hu	Hong Kong Polytechnic University, China
Stephen Hutt	University of Denver, USA

Paul Inventado	California State University Fullerton, USA
Jennifer Jacobs	University of Colorado Boulder, USA
Enkelejda Kasneci	Technical University of Munich, Germany
Hassan Khosravi	University of Queensland, Australia
Elizabeth Koh	Nanyang Technological University, Singapore
Kazuaki Kojima	Teikyo University, Japan
Harsh Kumar	University of Toronto, Canada
Eleni Kyza	Cyprus University of Technology, Cyprus
Élise Lavoué	Université Jean Moulin Lyon 3, LIRIS, France
Tobias Ley	University for Continuing Education Krems, Austria
Liang-Yi Li	National Taiwan Normal University, Taiwan
Shan Li	Lehigh University, USA
Tingting Li	Washington State University, USA
Chang-Yen Liao	National Central University, Taiwan
Amna Liaqat	University of Toronto, Canada
Boxuan Ma	Kyushu University, Japan
Uwe Maier	University of Education Schwäbisch Gmünd, Germany
Vasco Manquinho	Universidade de Lisboa, Portugal
Michele Marangi	eCampus University, Italy
Leonardo Brandão Marques	Universidade Federal de Alagoas, Brazil
Ruben Martins	Carnegie Mellon University, USA
Alejandra Martínez-Monés	Universidad de Valladolid, Spain
D. Moritz Marutschke	Kyoto University of Advanced Science, Japan
Ana Mouta	Universidad de Salamanca, Portugal
Michael Mrazek	University of Texas Health Science Center, USA
Nidhi Nasiar	University of Pennsylvania, USA
Allen Nie	Stanford University, USA
Abbie Olszewski	University of Nevada, Reno, USA
Ranilson Paiva	Universidade Federal de Alagoas, Brazil
Abelardo Pardo	University of Adelaide, Australia
Terry Payne	University of Liverpool, UK
Livia Petti	University of Molise, Italy
Federica Picasso	University of Trento, Italy
Oleksandra Poquet	University of South Australia, Australia
Liu Qiang	Sichuan Chengdu Shude High School, China
Ilana Ram	Technion Israel Institute of Technology, Israel
Sowmya Ramachandran	Stottler Henke Associates Inc., USA
J. Elizabeth Richey	University of Pittsburgh, USA
Maren Scheffel	Ruhr University Bochum, Germany
Tami Seifert	Kibbutzim College of Education, Israel

Research Track 4 – Human-Centered Design and Design-Based Research

Senior Program Committee Members

David Joyner	Georgia Institute of Technology, USA
Simon Knight	University of Technology Sydney, Australia
Maria Mercedes T. Rodrigo	Ateneo de Manila University, Philippines
Stefan Trausan-Matu	University Politehnica of Bucharest, Romania

Program Committee Members

Yusuf Akemoğlu	Duzce University, Turkey
Sihem Amer-Yahia	CNRS - LIG, France
Yuya Asano	University of Pittsburgh, USA
Jordan Barria-Pineda	University of Pittsburgh, USA
Sarah Bichler	Ludwig Maximilian University of Munich, Germany
Carmen Bisogni	Università degli Studi di Salerno, Italy
Minghao Cai	University of Alberta, Canada
Hyunjin Cha	Soonchunhyang University, South Korea
Eason Chen	Carnegie Mellon University, USA
Elaine Chen	Nottingham Trent University, UK
Thomas K. F. Chiu	Chinese University of Hong Kong, China
M. Ali Akber Dewan	Athabasca University, Canada
Rahul Divekar	Rensselaer Polytechnic Institute, USA
Martin Ebner	Graz University of Technology, Austria
Ann-Christin Falhs	Ruhr-Universität Bochum, Germany
Gloria Fernandez	Universidad Distrital Francisco José de Caldas, Colombia
Reva Freedman	Northern Illinois University, USA
Nikki G. Lobczowski	University of Pittsburgh, USA
Kobi Gal	University of Edinburgh, UK
Shivang Gupta	Carnegie Mellon University, USA
Ella Haig	University of Portsmouth, UK
Songhee Han	Florida State University, USA
Peng He	Washington State University, USA
John Hollander	Arkansas State University, USA
Xinying Hou	University of Michigan, USA
Xiaoshan Huang	McGill University, Canada
Xinyue Jiao	New York University, USA
Dorota Kamińska	Instytut Mechatroniki i Systemów Informatycznych Politechniki Łódzkiej, Poland
Yoon Jeon Kim	University of Wisconsin-Madison, USA
Harsh Kumar	University of Toronto, Canada
Seiyon Lee	University of Florida, USA

Bibeg Limbu	University of Duisburg-Essen, Germany
Xinyi Lu	University of Michigan, USA
Linda Mannila	University of Helsinki, Finland
Leonardo Brandão Marques	University of São Paulo, Brazil
Wannisa Matcha	Prince of Songkla University, Thailand
Jennifer Olsen	University of San Diego, USA
Fatiha Sadat	UQAM, Canada
Jerry Schnepp	Roosevelt University, USA
Ratan Sebastian	TIB Leibniz Information Centre for Science and Technology, Germany
Lei Shi	Newcastle University, UK
Valerie Shute	Florida State University, USA
Sri Yash Tadimalla	University of North Carolina Charlotte, USA
Marwa Trabelsi	L3i Laboratory, La Rochelle University, France
Alyssa Van Camp	TeachFX, USA
Alexandra Sasha Vassar	UNSW, Sydney, Australia
Jayakrishnan Warriem	IIT Madras, India
Beverly Woolf	University of Massachusetts, USA
Grzegorz Zwoliński	Lodz University of Technology, Poland

Research Track 5 – Teaching AI

Senior Program Committee Members

Bert Bredeweg	University of Amsterdam, Netherlands
Floriana Grasso	University of Liverpool, UK
Carla Limongelli	Università Roma Tre, Italy
Benjamin Nye	University of Southern California, USA
Mohammed Saqr	University of Eastern Finland, Finland
Craig Stewart	Durham University, UK
Rosa Vicari	Universidade Federal do Rio Grande do Sul, Brazil

Program Committee Members

Azza Abdullah S. Alghamdi	King Abdulaziz University, Saudi Arabia
Mario Luca Bernardi	University of Sannio, Italy
Alka Bhushan	Indian Institute of Technology Madras, India
Ilona Buchem	Berlin University of Applied Sciences, Germany
William Cain	University of Wyoming, USA

Gaowei Chen	University of Hong Kong, China
Penghe Chen	Beijing Normal University, China
Si Chen	University of Notre Dame, USA
Chih-Yueh Chou	Yuan Ze University, Taiwan
Yo Ehara	Tokyo Gakugei University, Japan
Manuel Freire Morán	Universidad Complutense de Madrid, Spain
Bruno Galmar	National Central University, Taiwan
Sai Gattupalli	University of Massachusetts Amherst, USA
Jeff Ginger	University of Illinois Urbana-Champaign, USA
Arto Hellas	Aalto University, Finland
Iris Howley	Williams College, USA
Xinyue Jiao	New York University, USA
Judy Kay	University of Sydney, Australia
Marie Lefevre	LIRIS - Université Lyon 1, France
Nicholas Lytle	Georgia Institute of Technology, USA
Michael Mrazek	University of Texas Health Science Center, USA
Kasia Muldner	Carleton University, Canada
Andrew Olney	University of Memphis, USA
Livia Petti	University of Molise, Italy
Marcela Pianucci	COGNA, Brazil
Liu Qiang	Sichuan Chengdu Shude High School, China
Angelo Rega	Pegaso Telematic University, Italy
Daniela Rotelli	Sorbonne Université, France
Mika Saari	Tampere University of Technology, Finland
Isabella Saccardi	Utrecht University, Netherlands
Sabine Seufert	University of St. Gallen, Switzerland
Christian M. Stracke	University of Bonn, Germany
Vidya Sudarshan	Nanyang Technological University, Singapore
Lars-Jochen Thoms	Thurgau University of Teacher Education, Switzerland
Xiaoyi Tian	North Carolina State University, USA
Maya Usher	Technion, Israel
Ruiwei Xiao	Carnegie Mellon University, USA
Pingjing Yang	University of Illinois Urbana-Champaign, USA
Jianwei Zhang	University at Albany, USA
Yingbin Zhang	South China Normal University, China
Jia Zhu	Zhejiang Normal University, China
Meina Zhu	Wayne State University, USA

Research Track 6 – Ethics, Equity, and AIED in Society

Senior Program Committee Members

Armelle Brun	LORIA - Université de Lorraine, France
Isabela Gasparini	Santa Catarina State University, Brazil
Monique Grandbastien	LORIA, Université de Lorraine, France
Peter Hastings	DePaul University, USA
Vanda Luengo	Sorbonne Université - LIP6, France
Collin Lynch	North Carolina State University, USA
Roberto Martinez-Maldonado	Monash University, Australia
Craig Thompson	University of British Columbia, Canada

Program Committee Members

Meital Amzalag	Holon Institute of Technology, Israel
Clara Belitz	University of Illinois Urbana-Champaign, USA
Susan Beudt	Deutsches Forschungszentrum für Künstliche Intelligenz, Germany
William Cain	University of Wyoming, USA
Francisco Enrique Vicente Castro	New York University, USA
Chelsea Chandler	University of Colorado Boulder, USA
Irene-Angelica Chounta	University of Duisburg-Essen, Germany
Markus Christen	University of Zurich, Switzerland
Lea Cohausz	University of Mannheim, Germany
Jeanine DeFalco	University of New Haven, USA
Diego Dermeval	Federal University of Alagoas, Brazil
Aniket Deroy	IIT Kharagpur, India
Yannis Dimitriadis	University of Valladolid, Spain
Konomu Dobashi	Aichi University, Japan
Juan Manuel Dodero	Universidad de Cádiz, Spain
Deborah Fields	Utah State University, USA
Kobi Gal	University of Edinburgh, UK
Andrew Gibson	Queensland University of Technology, Australia
Daniela Inclezan	Miami University, USA
Kirsty Kitto	University of Technology, Sydney, Australia
Rene Kizilcec	Cornell University, USA
Gayoung Lee	Baekseok University, South Korea
Haejin Lee	University of Illinois Urbana-Champaign, USA
Seiyon Lee	University of Florida, USA
Chenglu Li	University of Utah, USA

Tingting Li	Washington State University, USA
Elisa Marengo	University of Torino, Italy
Goran Martinovic	J.J. Strossmayer University of Osijek, Croatia
Jon Mason	Charles Darwin University, Australia
Hagit Meishar-Tal	Holon Institute of Technology, Israel
Roberto Micalizio	Università di Torino, Italy
Audrey Michal	University of Michigan, USA
Iulia Mihalache	Université du Québec en Outaouais, Canada
Phaedra Mohammed	University of the West Indies, Trinidad and Tobago
Patrick Ocheja	Kyoto University, Japan
Martha Palmer	University of Colorado Boulder, USA
Viktoria Pammer-Schindler	Graz University of Technology, Austria
Dimitra Pappa	NCSR Demokritos, Greece
Giorgio Pedrazzi	University of Brescia, Italy
Bruno Pimentel	Universidade Federal de Alagoas, Brazil
Niels Pinkwart	Humboldt-Universität zu Berlin, Germany
Priya Sharma	Pennsylvania State University, USA
Amy Stornaiuolo	University of Pennsylvania, USA
Hiroki Tanioka	Tokushima University, Japan
Marcelo Tibau	Universidade Federal do Estado do Rio de Janeiro, Brazil
Adrienn Toth	ETH Zurich, Switzerland
Alistair Windsor	Memphis University, USA
Feiwen Xiao	Penn State University, USA
Piotr Olaf Żylicz	WSB Merito University in Poznań, Poland

Research Track 7 – Theoretical Aspects of AIED and AI-Based Modeling for Education

Senior Program Committee Members

Mohsen Dorodchi	University of North Carolina Charlotte, USA
H. Chad Lane	University of Illinois Urbana-Champaign, USA
Sergey Sosnovsky	Utrecht University, Netherlands

Program Committee Members

Stephen Aguilar	University of Southern California, USA
Yusuf Akemoglu	Duzce University, Turkey

Ahmed Al Khateeb	University of Southampton, UK
Ainhoa Alvarez	University of the Basque Country, UPV/EHU, Spain
Francisco Bellas	Universidade da Coruna, Spain
Ching-sing Chai	Chinese University of Hong Kong, China
Sidney D'Mello	University of Colorado Boulder, USA
Fabiano Dorça	Universidade Federal de Uberlândia, Brazil
Yo Ehara	Tokyo Gakugei University, Japan
Mohamed Ez-Zaouia	Université de Rennes, France
Yael Feldman-Maggor	KTH Royal Institute of Technology, Sweden
Sebastian Gombert	DIPF | Leibniz Institute for Research and Information in Education, Germany
Art Graesser	University of Memphis, USA
Jiesi Guo	Australian Catholic University, Australia
Yusuke Hayashi	Hiroshima University, Japan
Corina Ilinca	University of Bucharest, Romania
Mizue Kayama	Shinshu University, Japan
Chanmin Kim	Pennsylvania State University, USA
Armanda Lewis	New York University, USA
Jiaju Lin	Pennsylvania State University, USA
Frieder Loch	Ostschweizer Fachhochschule, Switzerland
Abbie Olszewski	University of Nevada, Reno, USA
Sebastian Strauß	Ruhr University Bochum, Germany
Mikel Villamañe	University of the Basque Country, Spain
Peter Wulff	Heidelberg University of Education, Germany
Sho Yamamoto	Kindai University, Japan
Zhiwei Yang	Jinan University, China

International Artificial Intelligence in Education (IAIED) Society

IAIED Management Board

President

Olga C. Santos	UNED, Spain

President-Elect

Seiji Isotani	University of São Paulo, Brazil

Secretary

Vania Dimitrova	University of Leeds, UK

Journal Editors

Vincent Aleven	Carnegie Mellon University, USA
Cristina Conati	University of British Columbia
Marcus Specht	Delft University of Technology

Finance Chair

Benedict du Boulay	University of Sussex, UK

Membership Chair

Benjamin D. Nye	University of Southern California, USA

IAIED Officers

Conrad Borchers	Carnegie Mellon University, USA
Xinyuan Hao	University College London, UK
Jionghao Lin	University of Hong Kong, China
Miguel Portaz	UNED, Spain

IAIED Executive Committee

Akihiro Kashihara	University of Electro-Communications, Japan
Amruth Kumar	Ramapo College of New Jersey, USA
Christothea Herodotou	Open University, UK
Jeanine A. Defalco	CCDC-STTC, USA
Judith Masthoff	Utrecht University, Netherlands
Maria Mercedes T. Rodrigo	Ateneo de Manila University, Philippines
Ning Wang	University of Southern California, USA
Olga C. Santos	UNED, Spain
Rawad Hammad	University of East London, UK
Zitao Liu	Jinan University, China
Bruce M. McLaren	Carnegie Mellon University, USA
Cristina Conati	University of British Columbia, Canada
Diego Zapata-Rivera	Educational Testing Service, Princeton, USA
Erin Walker	University of Pittsburgh, USA
Seiji Isotani	University of São Paulo, Brazil
Tanja Mitrovic	University of Canterbury, New Zealand
Noboru Matsuda	North Carolina State University, USA
Min Chi	North Carolina State University, USA

Alexandra I. Cristea	Durham University, UK
Neil Heffernan	Worcester Polytechnic Institute, USA
Andrew M. Olney	University of Memphis, USA
Irene-Angelica Chounta	University of Duisburg-Essen, Germany
Beverly Park Woolf	University of Massachusetts, USA
Ig Ibert Bittencourt	Universidade Federal de Alagoas, Brazil

International Alliance to Advance Learning in the Digital Era (IAALDE)

The IAIED Society is a member of the International Alliance to Advance Learning in the Digital Era (IAALDE) and belongs to its board. IAIED is currently represented at IAALDE by Olga C. Santos, as president of IAIED.

AIED 2025 Sponsors

Platinum

Gold

Silver

Bronze

Best Paper Award Sponsorship

Contents – Part I

Full Papers

Full Papers

Plan More, Debug Less: Applying Metacognitive Theory to AI-Assisted Programming Education

Tung Phung[1(✉)], Heeryung Choi[2], Mengyan Wu[3], Adish Singla[1], and Christopher Brooks[3]

[1] MPI-SWS, Saarbrücken, Germany
mphung@mpi-sws.org
[2] University of Minnesota, Twin Cities, USA
[3] University of Michigan, Ann Arbor, USA

Abstract. The growing adoption of generative AI in education highlights the need to integrate established pedagogical principles into AI-assisted learning environments. This study investigates the potential of metacognitive theory to inform AI-assisted programming education through a hint system designed around the metacognitive phases of planning, monitoring, and evaluation. Upon request, the system can provide three types of AI-generated hints–planning, debugging, and optimization–to guide students at different stages of problem-solving. Through a study with 102 students in an introductory data science programming course, we find that students perceive and engage with planning hints most highly, whereas optimization hints are rarely requested. We observe a consistent association between requesting planning hints and achieving higher grades across question difficulty and student competency. However, when facing harder tasks, students seek additional debugging but not more planning support. These insights contribute to the growing field of AI-assisted programming education by providing empirical evidence on the importance of pedagogical principles in AI-assisted learning.

Keywords: Programming Education · Feedback Generation · Metacognitive Theory · Generative AI

1 Introduction

Recent advancements in generative AI have sparked significant interest in the field of programming education [10,25,34,45], especially in the generation of personalized feedback [23,35,45,48]. However, existing studies often focus on technical correctness [15] or student preference [25,30] and overlook the importance of grounding AI-generated feedback in well-established pedagogical theories, potentially limiting the effectiveness of such feedback in student learning.

To address this gap, we propose enhancing AI-generated hints through the use of metacognitive scaffolds [24,40,44]. Metacognitive scaffolds are instructional support mechanisms that help students plan, monitor, and evaluate their

A. I. Cristea et al. (Eds.): AIED 2025, LNAI 15877, pp. 3–17, 2025.
https://doi.org/10.1007/978-3-031-98414-3_1

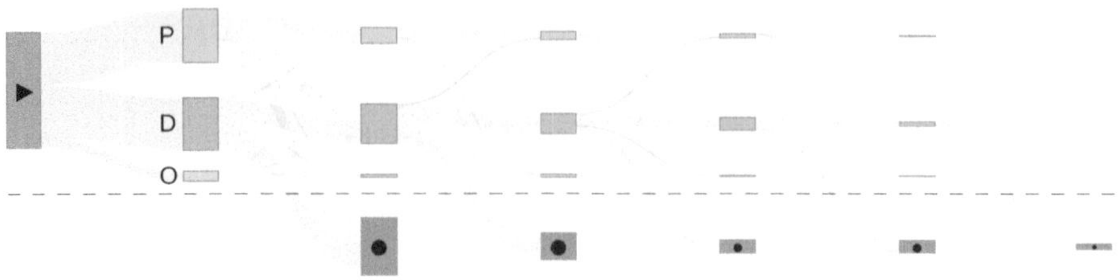

Fig. 1. Overview of requested hints (725 hints in 366 student-question pairs). Throughout the paper, P, D, and O denote a planning, debugging, and optimization hint, respectively. ▶ marks the beginning and • marks the end of problem-solving. The graph displays sequences of hints, link sizes depicting counts.

learning processes while fostering self-regulation and strengthening adaptive problem-solving skills [14,18,39]. These scaffolds are crucial in programming education, where students often struggle with structuring approaches to solving (planning) [11,32], identifying and fixing errors (monitoring) [31], and optimizing solutions (evaluation) [38]. By grounding AI-generated hints in these metacognitive phases, we aim to provide not only technical assistance but also structured yet flexible support to promote students' metacognitive development. Specifically, we design three corresponding types of hint: *planning*, *debugging*, and *optimization*, which we collectively refer to as **AI**-generated hints based on **M**etacognitive **S**caffolds (AIMS hints). To foster students' metacognitive awareness of their problem-solving stages, we adopt a learning-assisted approach in which we set a quota for total hints per question and let the students decide for themselves which hint type to request based on their needs. Figure 1 provides an overview of how students utilized these hints in our deployment of this system.

Our study is centered on the following research questions:

RQ1: How do AIMS hints impact students' help-seeking behaviors?
RQ2: How do those behaviors relate to students' problem-solving performance?

We examine these questions across all students and subsets based on question difficulty and student competency levels. Our contributions are as follows:

- **Hint and system design.** Using metacognitive theory, we design a hint system that offers three types of AIMS hints: planning, debugging, and optimization, and evaluate these hints through a classroom field study.
- **Student behavior analysis.** We analyze student help-seeking behaviors, revealing trends such as students value planning hints highly but often underutilize them in favor of debugging hints, especially when facing harder tasks.
- **Student performance analysis.** We find that planning hints are linked to better performance, notably for higher-competency students.
- **Code release.** To enhance reproducibility and aid future research, we publicly release the implementation of our AIMS hint generation techniques.

By integrating metacognitive scaffolds into AI-generated hints, this work not only contributes to a deeper understanding of how personalized AI support can enhance programming education but also provides practical insights for designing pedagogically-grounded educational AI systems.

2 Related Work

Metacognitive Scaffolds and Self-regulated Learning. Many efforts have been made to incorporate metacognitive scaffolds in programming education. The benefits of metacognition on learning behaviors and performance have been consistently shown through research [8,37,40,43,44,49]. For example, Vieira et al. [43] found that novice computer science students wrote longer self-explanation in-code comments compared to experienced peers because they saw self-explaining as a learning opportunity. Choi et al. [8] showed that prompting reflection after programming tasks was correlated with better learning perception and performance on both immediate and delayed post-tests. Yilmaz and Yilmaz [49] showed that students who received personalized metacognitive feedback weekly engaged significantly more in a Computer I course. Inspired by these insights, we ground in metacognitive theory to design AI-generated scaffolding hints.

AI-Generated Feedback in Programming Education. Recent research has explored AI-generated feedback in programming education [45,50]. Phung et al. [35] found that providing symbolic information such as the buggy output and fixed programs in prompts can improve the quality of AI-generated debugging hints. Lohr et al. [23] showed that AI can be directed to provide feedback that focuses on specific aspects, such as knowledge about task constraints or performance. Xiao et al. [48] explored students' perceptions of hints with varying detail levels, revealing that their effectiveness depends on context and that high-quality next-step and debugging hints do not always facilitate student progress. Building on this line of work, our study employs AI techniques that utilize symbolic information to generate different types of hints tailored to students' needs. Our hint system utilizes a button-based interface, as opposed to a chat-based one [25,42], since the latter's pedagogical effects are still unclear.

Students' Help-Seeking Behaviors with Automated Hints. Several studies have examined how students interact with automated hints [21,47]. Marwan et al. [28] found that data-driven next-step hints improved immediate performance, and when paired with self-explanation prompts, led to learning gains. Expanding on this, we investigate the association between AI-generated hints and student performance. Price et al. [36] found that the quality of initial hints positively correlates with help abuse. To address this, we set a fixed quota for hint use to prevent over-reliance on help. Wiggins et al. [47] characterized student's hint-seeking behavior along two axes of elapsed time and code completeness, while Bui et al. [7] explored different hint formats, including text and skeleton code. Our study extends this research by analyzing additional aspects, including engagement, perception, and hint request sequence in the context of AIMS hints.

AI Support and Metacognition. Recently, concerns have arisen that AI technologies might reduce students' engagement in metacognitive practices, a concept referred to as *Metacognitive laziness* [13]. Our work explicitly addresses this by integrating metacognitive theory into AI-generated hints, aiming to support self-regulated learning (SRL) skills development rather than replace it.

Hint type	Description
Planning	A hint aimed at helping you to identify the steps needed to solve the question.
Debugging	A hint aimed at helping you to identify and fix a bug in your current program.
Optimization	A hint aimed at helping you to optimize your current program for better performance and readability.

Fig. 2. AIMS hint types with the descriptions provided to students.

3 Study Setup

This section outlines the study context, our proposed AIMS hints, the deployment, and methods to estimate question difficulty and student competency.

3.1 Course and Students

Course Overview. This study was conducted in a Python-based introductory data science course as part of an online Master's program at the University of Michigan. The four-week course featured weekly assignments covering key topics such as regular expressions, *pandas* data frame manipulation, Excel processing, and CSV file handling. Each assignment, delivered as a Jupyter notebook, consisted of three to four programming questions (14 in total), requiring students to complete Python functions for specific tasks. Assignments were due weekly, and students could submit multiple times before the deadline, with their highest score counting toward the final grade.

Student Overview. Overall, 102 students enrolled in the course: 71 males, 27 females, and four unspecified. Their ages range from 18 to 58 (mean = 32, stddev = 8.5). Requesting hints was voluntary, with no additional incentives or penalties, and instructors were unaware of whether or how often students requested hints. Students were informed about the research aspect of the initiative, including anonymous data recording and the AI-generated nature of hints which might not always be correct. This study was deemed exempt from oversight by the Institutional Review Board under application number HUM00251143.

3.2 Hint Types and AI-Generation Techniques

AIMS Hints. We mapped the three metacognitive phases of planning, monitoring, and evaluation onto disciplinary terms of planning, debugging, and optimization. Each hint type was designed with a specific goal: planning hints assist in initial strategy formulation, debugging hints aid in issue identification and resolution, and optimization hints foster code quality reflection and improvement for students aiming to exceed assignment expectations (see Fig. 2).

Techniques for Generating AIMS Hints. Each hint type is generated by a technique, all with careful consideration of incorporating "guard-rails" instruc-

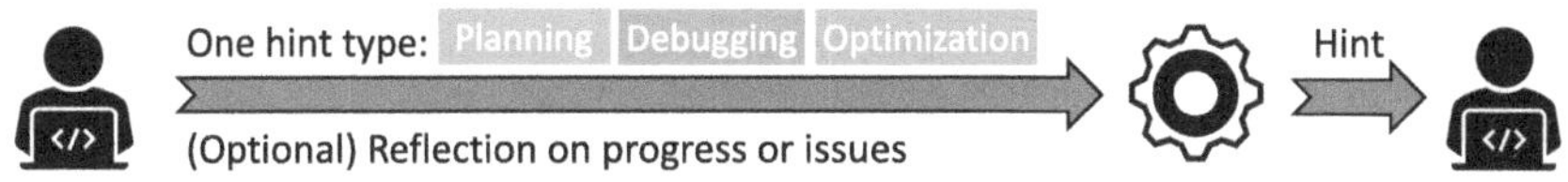

Fig. 3. Interaction between a student and our hint system for requesting a hint.

tions [22] to prevent the AI model (GPT-4o [19]) from revealing the solutions.[1] Our technique for debugging hints is adapted from previous studies that showed good performance in data science programming education [35,50]. It follows a two-phase process: First, it extracts symbolic information including (1) the buggy output (obtained from running the student's program) and (2) a repaired program (obtained from requesting the AI model). Second, it uses this information along with the student's code and any reflection (detailed in Sect. 3.3) to prompt the AI to generate an explanation (leveraging Chain-of-Thought [46]) and a Socratic-style hint for a single bug (to be provided to the student). Since there were no existing techniques for generating high-quality planning and optimization hints, we adjust this technique for the other two hint types. For planning hints, we modify the prompt's language to focus on problem-solving steps rather than debugging and remove the repaired program to shift emphasis away from errors. For optimization hints, we follow a similar two-phase process but replace the repaired program with an AI-generated optimized program–focusing on short running time while still requiring correctness.

3.3 Hint System and Student Interaction

AIMS Hint System. We develop a hint system consisting of two main components: (1) a backend server for generating hints using the techniques introduced in Sect. 3.2 and (2) a JupyterLab extension as the interface for interacting with students. To prevent over-reliance on AI and foster students' metacognitive awareness, we set a quota limit of five hints per question and allow students to choose the type of hint to request. The extension displays three buttons below each assignment question, enabling students to request planning, debugging, or optimization hints. Before the course, the instructor introduced the hint system and demonstrated how to use it to the class. Students could always click a "?" button located next to the hint buttons to view descriptions of the hint types (as in Fig. 2). The first time a student requests a hint, a "Consent" pop-up informs them about the research aspect of the system (see Sect. 3.1). Students can only proceed to request hints after agreeing to this notice. To ensure easy access to previous hints, each hint is stored in a collapsible widget below the corresponding question's hint buttons. When a student reopens a notebook, these widgets are collapsed by default and can be expanded with a click to revisit previous hints.

Student Interaction. Figure 3 demonstrates the interaction between students and our system for requesting hints. When requesting hints, students are encouraged to reflect on their progress or issues. These reflections serve dual purposes: promoting students' engagement by prompting them to articulate their

[1] https://github.com/machine-teaching-group/aied2025-plan-more-debug-less.

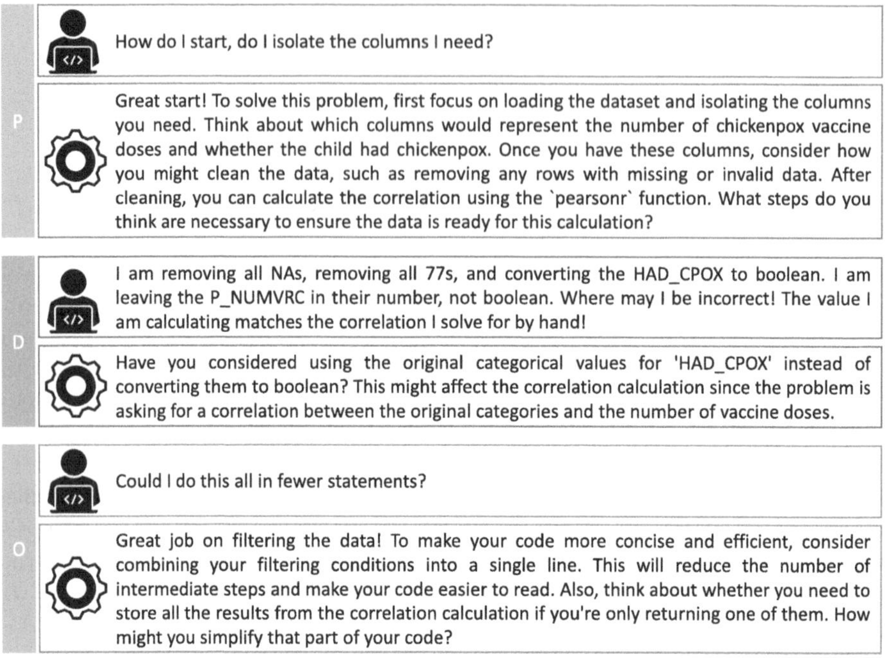

Fig. 4. Examples of hint types: student reflections and received hints in the study.

thoughts and providing the AI model with context to generate a relevant hint. Once the backend generates a hint, it is sent back to the interface and displayed to the student, accompanied by two feedback buttons: "thumb up" and "thumb down", allowing the student to rate the hint as helpful or unhelpful, respectively.

3.4 Data Collection

We collected comprehensive data on student behavior and performance, including hint requests and revisits, assignment submissions, and final solving status. Of 102 students, 101 (99%) activated the JupyterLab extension, and 76 (75%) requested at least one hint. Figure 4 shows examples of provided hints. Figure 5 provides a breakdown of students and hints across 14 assignment questions.

3.5 Question Difficulty and Student Competency

To analyze the impacts of AIMS hints across varying conditions, we categorize questions by difficulty and students by competency. Question difficulty is estimated using past student performance in two prior iterations of the same course: the easier (harder) group consists of four highest- (lowest-) scored questions, one per assignment. Student competency is approximated based on the number of attempts until solving all questions in Assignment 1: fewer attempts indicate higher competency. We designate the top third (34 students) as the higher-competency group and the bottom third (34 students) as the lower-competency group. Since Assignment 1 served as a proxy, it is excluded from competency-based analyses.

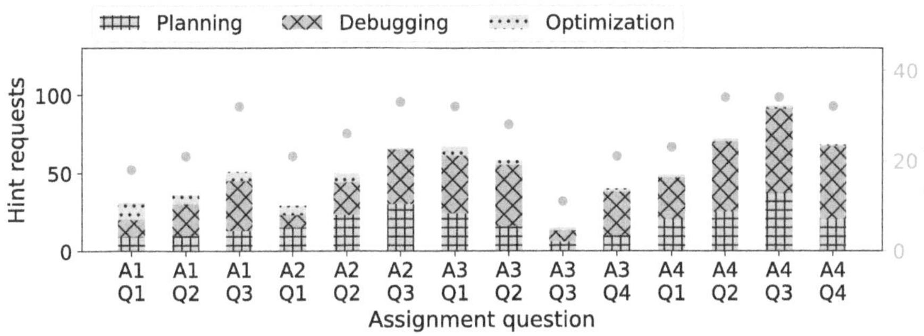

Fig. 5. Overview of students and hint requests. The orange dots and the right y-axis indicate the number of students who requested at least one hint (of any type) for each question. The stacked bars and the left y-axis represent the total number of hint requests per question, categorized by AIMS hint types. In total, students requested 258 planning, 411 debugging, and 56 optimization hints. (Color figure online)

4 RQ1: Impacts of AIMS Hints on Help-Seeking Behavior

This section addresses RQ1 by outlining our analysis setup (Sect. 4.1), presenting results (Sect. 4.2), and discussing key findings (Sect. 4.3).

4.1 Analysis Setup

To evaluate the impact of AIMS hints on student help-seeking behavior, we decompose RQ1 into three sub-questions: [RQ1a]: How do students engage with and perceive AIMS hints?, [RQ1b]: What behavioral patterns emerge in students' interactions with AIMS hints?, and [RQ1c]: How do these patterns vary based on question difficulty and student competency?

For RQ1a, engagement is measured by contemplation time and hint revisits, while perception is assessed through students' hint ratings. The contemplation time is defined as the time between receiving a hint and performing the next major action (i.e., requesting another hint or submitting a solution). To exclude irrelevant delays such as students taking a break, only durations up to $t = 1$ hour are considered for analysis.[2] Hint revisits are quantified by counting the number of times a student expands hint widgets to view previous hints.

For RQ1b, we analyze the sequence of requested hint types, the frequency of a type being present in the sequence, the first-requested type, and the most-requested type. Each of these is counted based on all student-question pairs.

For RQ1c, we examine how hint sequences and the presence of hint types vary across question difficulty and student competency (as defined in Sect. 3.5).

4.2 Results

Engagement and Perception of AIMS Hints. Figure 6 summarizes engagement and perception results. A Mood's median test [29] reveals a significant

[2] We note that other choices, such as $t = 0.5$ or $t = 2$ hours also yield similar results.

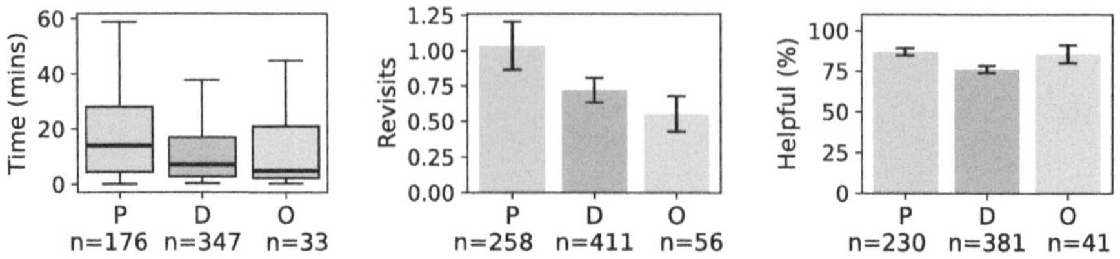

(a) Contemplation time (b) Hint revisits (c) Hint rating

Fig. 6. Results for RQ1a: Student engagement and perception of hints. (a) demonstrates the amount of time students contemplated after receiving a hint. (b) shows the number of revisits per hint. (c) presents the average rating of hints.

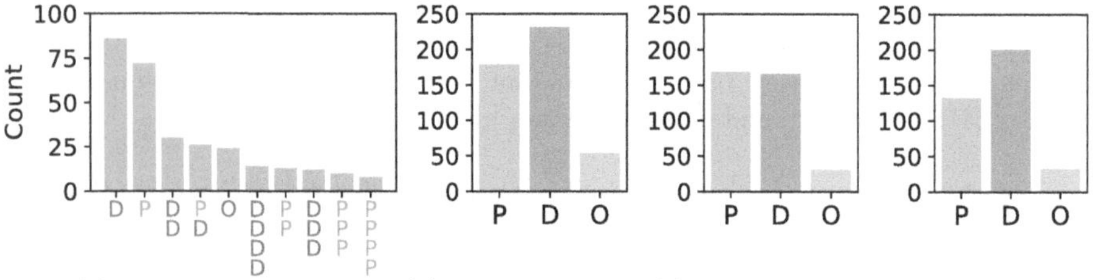

(a) Hint sequence (b) Type present (c) First type (d) Majority type

Fig. 7. Results for RQ1b: Patterns of student hint usage. In all plots, y-axis represents the counts of student-question pairs. (a) displays the most common hint sequences; (b), (c), and (d) show the number of times a hint type is present in a sequence, is the first in a sequence, and is the majority in a sequence, respectively.

difference in contemplation time across hint types ($p = 0.002$). Post hoc pair-wise comparisons with Bonferroni correction [6] confirm that the contemplation time on planning hints (median = 14.0 minutes) is longer than debugging hints (median = 7.1 minutes, $p = 0.006$). For hint revisits, a Kruskal-Wallis H test [20] indicates a significant difference ($p = 0.009$), with Dunn's post hoc tests using Bonferroni correction confirming more revisits for planning than for debugging hints ($p = 0.015$). Similarly, a χ^2 test [33] detects a significant difference in hint rating ($p = 0.003$), with pair-wise comparison using a Bonferroni correction confirming higher ratings for planning than for debugging hints ($p = 0.005$). Optimization hints, with smaller sample sizes (33–56), do not show any significant differences.

Help-seeking Patterns. Fig. 7 shows students' help-seeking patterns. Nine out of ten most frequent hint sequences consist of a single hint type, with debugging hints being requested the most, followed by planning hints, while optimization hints were rarely used. When both planning and debugging hints were sought, planning hints were more likely to be requested first, aligning with metacognitive phases [39]. Notably, 43% of optimization hints (24 out of 56) were requested in isolation. Upon investigation of students' code and reflections, these cases often belonged to high-performing students who solved without hints and then sought further improvements. However, some other students seemed to mistakenly request these optimization hints when they needed debugging support.

Behavioral Patterns by Difficulty and Competency. Figure 8 compares help-seeking behaviors based on question difficulty (Figs. 8a and 8b) and student competency (Figs. 8c and 8d). As question difficulty increases, students request more debugging hints, while planning hint usage remains constant. In contrast, optimization hints were requested more often for easier questions (in 20 student-question pairs) than harder ones (10 pairs). Regarding student competency, higher-competency students request more hints overall, particularly planning hints, compared to their lower-competency peers.

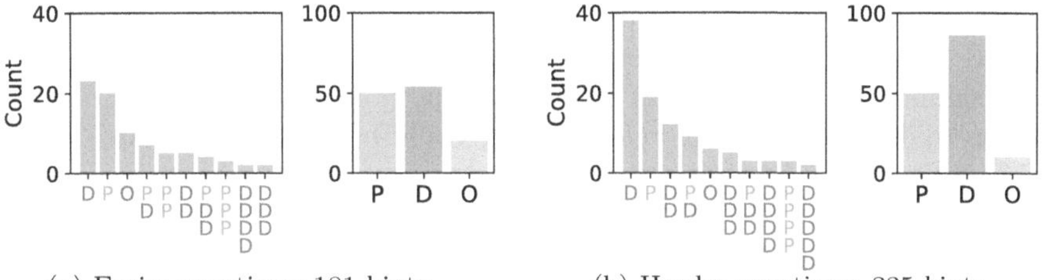

(a) Easier questions: 181 hints. (b) Harder questions: 225 hints.

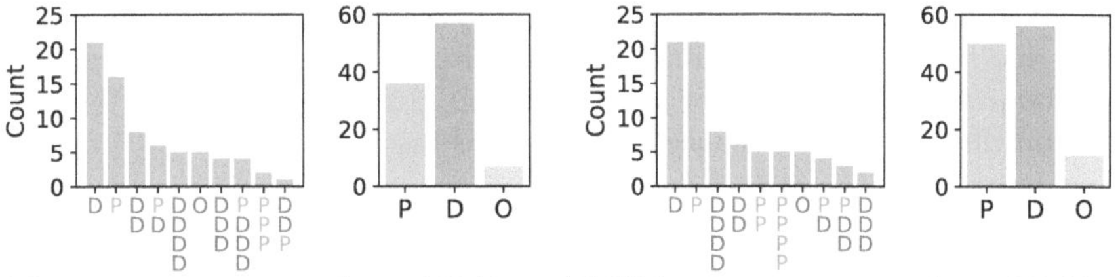

(c) Lower-competency students: 160 hints. (d) Higher-competency students: 200 hints.

Fig. 8. Results for RQ1c: Behaviors by difficulty and competency. In each subfigure, the left shows Hint sequence and the right shows Type present. (a) and (b) present results by difficulty while (c) and (d) present results by competency.

4.3 Discussions

Our findings reveal key patterns in students' help-seeking behavior and hint usage. The high engagement and positive perception of planning hints suggest that structured guidance at the planning stage can be highly beneficial. However, it remains overlooked in many existing feedback systems, which primarily focus on debugging support [30,35]. By emphasizing planning, educators and AI systems could better scaffold students' problem-solving processes and reduce inefficient trial-and-error cycles. Despite the high perceived value of planning hints, students requested debugging hints more often, especially for harder questions. This suggests reactive rather than proactive strategies [1,17,26], where students rely on troubleshooting rather than strategic planning. While debugging is an essential skill, over-reliance on it may hinder deeper conceptual understanding. Future AI-assisted learning environments should promote proactive planning, encouraging students to articulate their problem-solving strategies before coding. Optimization hints, which were aimed at mastering skills rather than improving grades, were underutilized (8% of total requests). Further research is needed to make them more attractive and effective, fostering student mastery learning [5].

Students predominantly requested a single hint type per question, indicating a potential lack of metacognitive awareness–they may not always recognize when they need planning, monitoring, or evaluation support [24,41]. The variation in hint-seeking behavior by question difficulty further reinforces this issue. While debugging hints were requested more for harder questions, planning hint usage remained unchanged, even though structured planning is particularly useful for complex tasks [12]. Intelligent tutoring systems could use adaptive prompts or reflective exercises to help students better assess their difficulties [2,8]. Additionally, designing interventions that make planning more explicit–such as requiring students to draft pseudocode before coding–could help bridge the gap.

The difference in hint usage between higher- and lower-competency students may provide further insights into how metacognition contributes to learning. While some studies reported that weaker students require more help [3,4], our results show that higher-competency students requested more hints overall, especially planning hints. This may be because they are more persistent in problem-solving and thus, are more willing to engage with available support. In contrast, lower-competency peers may be more prone to give up earlier. This difference likely contributes to performance disparities, as discussed next.

5 RQ2: AIMS Hints and Performance

Building on the behavioral patterns identified in RQ1, this section addresses RQ2: how those patterns relate to student problem-solving performance.

5.1 Analysis Setup

We break RQ2 into two sub-questions: [RQ2a]: How do students' interaction patterns with AIMS hints relate to their problem-solving performance? and [RQ2b]: How do these effects vary by question difficulty and student competency? To answer these, we focus on students' final solving rates in relation to hint usage.

5.2 Results

Hint Usage and Overall Performance. As shown in Fig. 9a, requesting planning hints is associated with significantly higher performance than no hints ($p = 0.013$). Other types (debugging, optimization) show no significant effects.

Performance Variation by Difficulty and Competency. Across all difficulty and competency conditions, planning hints are consistently (even though not always significantly) associated with higher performance than no hints (see

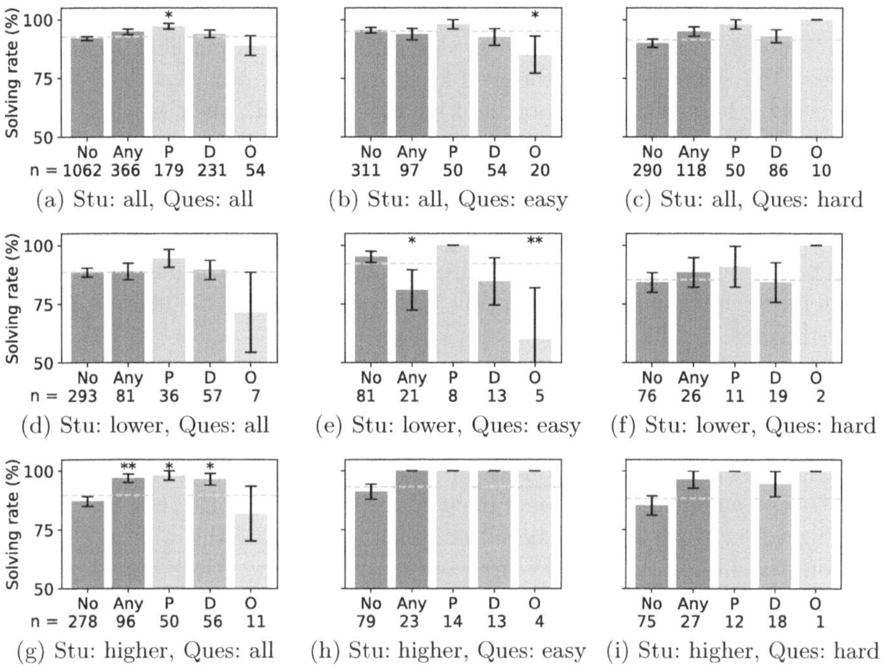

Fig. 9. Results for RQ2: Performance by help-seeking behavior. The dashed line depicts the average overall performance of the condition; the five bars represent no hint requested, any type requested, and each type present in the sequence of requested hints (i.e., Type present). The vertical lines indicate standard errors; * indicates a significant difference in performance to the 'No' group w.r.t a χ^2 test with $p < 0.05$, while ** indicates $p < 0.01$. Y-axes are plotted from 50%.

Fig. 9). In contrast, optimization hints are linked to lower performance on easier questions ($p = 0.039$), particularly by lower-competency students ($p = 0.003$). A closer examination of code and reflections reveals that in most of these cases, students misused optimization hints for debugging aid. Only higher-competency students, but not lower-competency ones, exhibit significantly better performance associated with hint use. Among higher-competency students, requesting any hints is linked to significantly higher performance ($p = 0.007$), with independent positive effects for planning ($p = 0.024$) and debugging hints ($p = 0.044$).

5.3 Discussions

Our findings underscore a consistent association between planning hints and higher performance. This aligns with metacognitive theory, which emphasizes planning as a critical step in problem-solving [9,12,16]. While the study did not establish causality (students' high intrinsic SRL skills could be a confounding factor that caused both requesting of planning hints and higher final performance), these results suggest potential instructional value from planning hints.

In contrast, optimization hints are sometimes linked to lower performance, likely due to students' misuse, despite clear descriptions and availability of reference (see Sect. 3.3). This highlights the need for AI-assisted learning systems to ensure awareness of the available support and its alignment with their issues.

Our results differ from some studies that found hints more beneficial for lower-competency students [3,4]. This may be because lower-competency students may have weaker SRL skills, making it harder to leverage hints effectively. Additionally, since our hints are purposely Socratic and non-direct, lower-competency students may learn less from them than higher-competency ones. Future research should explore varying hint detail levels to fit different student groups [27,48].

6 Limitations

This work has several limitations. First, it was conducted in a single programming course, where students could make multiple submissions, resulting in high overall grades (>92%). This makes it challenging to isolate the impacts of AIMS hints on student performance. Future work should examine AIMS hints in diverse courses with varying grading schemes. Second, students' under-utilization of optimization hints limited our ability to assess their impact on students. However, this highlights an opportunity for future work on strategies to encourage students to pursue mastery learning beyond correct solutions. Third, we did not measure long-term learning gains. Future research should evaluate the long-term effects using methods such as retention tests, delayed post-tests, or longitudinal tracking. Fourth, we focused solely on button-based hints. Future work could explore alternative interfaces, such as chatbots or voice assistants. Finally, we investigated AIMS hints in isolation from other forms of support. Future studies should investigate their integration with complementary support, such as instructor-led office hours, to create a more comprehensive learning environment.

7 Conclusions

This paper investigates the integration of metacognitive theory in AI-assisted programming education through a hint system aligned with planning, monitoring, and evaluation phases. By designing three corresponding hint types–planning, debugging, and optimization–and allowing students to select hints within a quota, our approach not only tailors the support to students' problem-solving stage but also fosters students' metacognitive awareness. A field study reveals that students engage most with planning hints, which are consistently linked to higher performance. However, students often request only one hint type per question and, when facing harder tasks, request more debugging but not more planning hints. This insight warrants future work on better metacognitive guidance in student awareness. Our findings provide empirical evidence of the synergy between AI and pedagogical theory in programming education, opening avenues for future research on pedagogically informed AI-tutoring systems.

Acknowledgments. Funded/Co-funded by the European Union (ERC, TOPS, 101039090). Views and opinions expressed are however those of the author(s) only and do not necessarily reflect those of the European Union or the European Research Council. Neither the European Union nor the granting authority can be held responsible for them.

References

1. Alasmari, N.J., Althaqafi, A.S.A.: Teachers' practices of proactive and reactive classroom management strategies and the relationship to their self-efficacy. Lang. Teach. Res. **28**, 2158–2189 (2024)
2. Alzaid, M., Hsiao, I.h.: Effectiveness of reflection on programming problem solving self-assessments. In: Frontiers in Education Conference (FIE) (2018)
3. Beal, C.R., Arroyo, I.M., Cohen, P.R., Woolf, B.P.: Evaluation of AnimalWatch: an intelligent tutoring system for arithmetic and fractions. J. Interact. Online Learn. **9**, 64–77 (2010)
4. Beal, C.R., Walles, R., Arroyo, I., Woolf, B.P.: On-line tutoring for math achievement testing: a controlled evaluation. J. Interact. Online Learn. **6**, 43–55 (2007)
5. Bloom, B.S.: Learning for mastery. Instruction and curriculum. Regional education laboratory for the Carolinas and Virginia, topical papers and reprints, number 1. Evaluation Comment **1**, n2 (1968)
6. Bonferroni, C.: Teoria statistica delle classi e calcolo delle probabilita. Pubblicazioni del R istituto superiore di scienze economiche e commericiali di firenze **8**, 3–62 (1936)
7. Bui, G., Susanto, N., Sibia, N., Zavaleta Bernuy, A., Liut, M., Petersen, A.: Do hints enhance learning in programming exercises? Exploring students' problem-solving and interactions. In: Proceedings of the Technical Symposium on Computer Science Education (SIGCSE), vol. 2 (2024)
8. Choi, H., Jovanovic, J., Poquet, O., Brooks, C., Joksimović, S., Williams, J.J.: The benefit of reflection prompts for encouraging learning with hints in an online programming course. Internet High. Educ. **58**, 100903 (2023)
9. Cohen, P.R., Feigenbaum, E.: Planning and problem solving. Stanford University, Department of Computer Science (1982)
10. Denny, P., et al.: Generative AI for education (GAIED): advances, opportunities, and challenges. CoRR abs/2402.01580 (2024)
11. Ebrahimi, A., Kopec, D., Schweikert, C.: Taxonomy of novice programming error patterns with plan, web, and object solutions. ACM Comput. Surv. **38**, 1–24 (2006)
12. Eichmann, B., Goldhammer, F., Greiff, S., Pucite, L., Naumann, J.: The role of planning in complex problem solving. Comput. Educ. **128**, 1–12 (2019)
13. Fan, Y., et al.: Beware of metacognitive laziness: effects of generative artificial intelligence on learning motivation, processes, and performance. Br. J. Educ. Technol. **56**, 489–530 (2024)
14. Flavell, J.H.: Metacognition and cognitive monitoring: a new area of cognitive-developmental inquiry. Am. Psychol. **34**, 906–911 (1979)
15. Gabbay, H., Cohen, A.: Combining LLM-generated and test-based feedback in a Mooc for programming. In: Proceedings of the Conference on Learning@ Scale (L@S) (2024)
16. Gunzelmann, G., Anderson, J.R.: Problem solving: increased planning with practice. Cognit. Syst. Res. **4**, 57–76 (2003)

17. Hoffman, H.J., Elmi, A.F.: Do students learn more from erroneous code? Exploring student performance and satisfaction in an error-free versus an error-full Sas® programming environment. J. Stat. Data Sci. Educ. **29**, 228–240 (2021)
18. Holton, D., Clarke, D.: Scaffolding and metacognition. Int. J. Math. Educ. Sci. Technol. **37**, 127–143 (2006)
19. Hurst, A., et al.: GPT-4o system card. Arxiv Preprint Arxiv:2410.21276 (2024)
20. Kruskal, W.H., Wallis, W.A.: Use of ranks in one-criterion variance analysis. J. Am. Stat. Assoc. **47**, 583–621 (1952)
21. Li, R., Che Hassan, N., Saharuddin, N.: College student's academic help-seeking behavior: a systematic literature review. Behav. Sci. **13**, 637 (2023)
22. Liffiton, M., Sheese, B.E., Savelka, J., Denny, P.: CodeHelp: using large language models with guardrails for scalable support in programming classes. In: Proceedings of the Koli Calling International Conference on Computing Education Research (2023)
23. Lohr, D., Keuning, H., Kiesler, N.: You're (not) My type-can LLMs generate feedback of specific types for introductory programming tasks? J. Comput. Assist. Learn. **41**, e13107 (2025)
24. Loksa, D., et al.: Metacognition and self-regulation in programming education: theories and exemplars of use. ACM Trans. Comput. Educ. (TOCE) **22**, 39 (2022)
25. Ma, B., Chen, L., Konomi, S.: Enhancing programming education with ChatGPT: a case study on student perceptions and interactions in a Python course. In: Proceedings of the Artificial Intelligence in Education (AIED) (2024)
26. Mallik, S., Gangopadhyay, A.: Proactive and reactive engagement of artificial intelligence methods for education: a review. Front. Artif. Intell. **6**, 1151391 (2023)
27. Mao, P., Cai, Z., Wang, Z., Hao, X., Fan, X., Sun, X.: The effects of dynamic and static feedback under tasks with different difficulty levels in digital game-based learning. Internet High. Educ. **60**, 100923 (2024)
28. Marwan, S., Jay Williams, J., Price, T.: An Evaluation of the Impact of Automated Programming Hints on Performance and Learning. In: Proceedings of the Conference on International Computing Education Research (ICER) (2019)
29. Mood, A.M.: Introduction to the Theory of Statistics. McGraw-hill (1950)
30. Pankiewicz, M., Baker, R.S.: Navigating compiler errors with AI assistance - A study of GPT hints in an introductory programming course. In: Proceedings of the Innovation and Technology in Computer Science Education (ITiCSE) (2024)
31. Park, E., Cheon, J.: Exploring debugging challenges and strategies using structural topic model: a comparative analysis of high and low-performing students. J. Educ. Comput. Res. **62**, 2104–2126 (2025)
32. parsons, R, Hao, Q., Ding, l.: exploring differences in planning between students with and without prior experience in programming. In: American Society for Engineering Education Annual Conference & Exposition (ASEE) (2023)
33. Pearson, K.: X. On the criterion that a given system of deviations from the probable in the case of a correlated system of variables is such that it can be reasonably supposed to have arisen from random sampling. London Edinburgh Dublin Philos. Mag. J. Sci. **50**, 157–175 (1900)
34. Phung, T., et al.: Generative AI for programming education: benchmarking Chatgpt, GPT-4, and human tutors. In: Proceedings of the Conference on International Computing Education Research (ICER) - Volume 2 (2023)
35. Phung, T., et al.: Automating human tutor-style programming feedback: leveraging GPT-4 tutor model for hint generation and GPT-3.5 student model for hint validation. In: Proceedings of the International Learning Analytics and Knowledge Conference (LAK) (2024)

36. Price, T.W., Zhi, R., Barnes, T.: Hint generation under uncertainty: the effect of hint quality on help-seeking behavior. In: Artificial Intelligence in Education (AIED) (2017)
37. Rum, S., Ismail, M.A.: Metacognitive support accelerates computer assisted learning for novice programmers. J. Educ. Technol. Soc. **20**, 170–181 (2017)
38. Saliba, L., Shioji, E., Oliveira, E., Cohney, S., Qi, J.: Learning with style: improving student code-style through better automated feedback. In: Proceedings of the Technical Symposium on Computer Science Education (SIGCSE) (2024)
39. Schraw, G., Moshman, D.: Metacognitive theories. Educ. Psychol. Rev. **7**, 351–371 (1995)
40. Shin, Y., Jung, J., Zumbach, J., Yi, E.: The effects of worked-out example and metacognitive scaffolding on problem-solving programming. J. Educ. Comput. Res. **61**, 073563312311744 (2023)
41. Stanton, J.D., Sebesta, A.J., Dunlosky, J.: Fostering metacognition to support student learning and performance. CBE—Life Sci. Educ. **20**, fe3 (2021)
42. Sun, D., Boudouaia, A., Yang, J., Xu, J.: Investigating students' programming behaviors, interaction qualities and perceptions through prompt-based learning in ChatGPT. Humanit. Soc. Sci. Commun. **11**, 1–14 (2024)
43. Vieira, C., Magana, A.J., Roy, A., Falk, M.: Student explanations in the context of computational science and engineering education. Cognit. Instruct. **37**, 201–231 (2019)
44. Volet, S.E., Lund, C.: Metacognitive instruction in introductory computer programming: a better explanatory construct for performance than traditional factors. J. Educ. Comput. Res. **10**, 297–328 (1994)
45. Wang, S., Mitchell, J.C., Piech, C.: A large scale RCT on effective error messages in CS1. In: Proceedings of the Technical Symposium on Computer Science Education (SIGCSE) (2024)
46. Wei, J., Wang, X., Schuurmans, D., Bosma, M., Xia, F., Chi, E., Le, Q.V., Zhou, D., et al: Chain-of-thought prompting elicits reasoning in large language models. In: Advances in Neural Information Processing Systems (NeurIPS), vol. 35 (2022)
47. Wiggins, J.B., et al.: Exploring novice programmers' hint requests in an intelligent block-based coding environment. In: Proceedings of the Technical Symposium on Computer Science Education (SIGCSE) (2021)
48. Xiao, R., Hou, X., Stamper, J.: Exploring how multiple levels of GPT-generated programming hints support or disappoint novices. In: Extended Abstracts Of The Conference On Human Factors In Computing Systems (CHI) (2024)
49. Karaoglan Yilmaz, F.G., Yilmaz, R.: Learning analytics intervention improves students' engagement in online learning. Technol. Knowl. Learn., 1–12 (2021). https://doi.org/10.1007/s10758-021-09547-w
50. Zamfirescu-Pereira, J., Qi, L., Hartmann, B., DeNero, J., Norouzi, N.: Conversational Programming with LLM-Powered Interactive Support in an Introductory Computer Science Course. NeurIPS 2023 Workshop on Generative AI for Education (GAIED) (2023)

Understanding Students' Nuanced Views on AI-Supported Classroom Learning Through Perspective Taking

Tomohiro Nagashima[1(✉)], Martina Vincoli[2], Niklas Scholz[1], and Man Su[1]

[1] Saarland University, Saarland Informatics Campus, Saarbrücken, Germany
{nagashima,mansu}@cs.uni-saarland.de,
nisc00019@stud.uni-saarland.de

[2] Department of Humanities, Social and Political Sciences, ETH Zürich, Zurich, Switzerland
martina.vincoli@gess.ethz.ch

Abstract. AI technology has progressively been integrated into school classrooms, creating a complex and dynamic environment where multiple stakeholders are involved in the decision making about students' learning experience. In such a situation, understanding stakeholder views is challenging as their views might implicitly reflect what they expect of other stakeholders. In this paper, we propose to apply *perspective taking* as an analytical lens for understanding school students' nuanced views regarding their preferences about using AI in the classroom environment. By identifying how 16 students implicitly take the perspectives of others when sharing their views, we found that students consider other stakeholders' expected roles and preferences in the classroom, providing nuanced preferences on AI use in the classroom. This work makes contributions to the AIED community by illustrating students' nuanced preferences in the complex, multi-stakeholder classroom environment supported by AI. It also demonstrates how perspective taking can be used as a human-centered methodology for uncovering nuanced perspectives in the complex classroom environment.

Keywords: Perspective taking · Human-AI interaction · K-12 Classroom · Hybrid intelligence

1 Introduction

Schools worldwide are increasingly integrating Artificial Intelligence (AI)-based technologies, such as Intelligent Tutoring Systems (ITSs), into classrooms [7, 15]. School classrooms are one major environment in which youth today interact with AI technologies more frequently than ever before. Although these systems have shown their established effectiveness in enhancing student learning outcomes and achievement [13, 15], a critical under-explored topic is how students perceive the use of AI technologies in the K-12 classroom. Prior work on AI in education has focused more on teachers as key design partners (e.g., asking teachers for their preference on how to use AI-based tutoring system [17, 20], but see [8]). However, students—another major stakeholder

A. I. Cristea et al. (Eds.): AIED 2025, LNAI 15877, pp. 18–31, 2025.
https://doi.org/10.1007/978-3-031-98414-3_2

in the K-12 classroom—also shape, and are influenced by, AI-supported environments, making their perspectives equally critical to examine.

School classrooms are complex ecosystems where multiple stakeholders (i.e., students, peers, and teachers) interact with AI technologies [5, 12, 27]. For instance, students' decision making about which content to learn in AI-based tutoring software is often influenced by teachers, who may override system recommendations based on their knowledge of individual students [27]. Furthermore, teachers and students may have conflicting expectations about AI's role in learning [5, 8]. This dynamic interplay complicates efforts to understand students' genuine desires and needs, as their responses in a research setting may reflect not only their own views but also what they expect of other stakeholders. For example, students might understate their desire for AI assistance because they think that their teacher would value students' independent problem solving over reliance on AI assistance. Capturing these nuanced perspectives requires methodological approaches that account for implicit influences [9].

To address this challenge, we employ *perspective taking* as an analytical lens. Perspective taking is a cognitive and affective process of understanding and considering others' viewpoints [16]. This approach enables us to disentangle stakeholder perspectives by identifying when participants take others' viewpoints. In this work, we re-analyzed approximately 14 h of interview data from 16 school-aged students in Germany, examining their perceptions and preferences on AI use in the classroom through the lens of perspective taking. Our research question asks: *How might we better understand students' nuanced desires and needs for decision-making control in an AI-supported classroom through the lens of perspective taking?*

Findings revealed that students have nuanced views on AI use where their shared thoughts represent the balancing of the benefits and limitations of AI, influenced by their expectations of both their teachers and AI systems. These expectations, in turn, influence how much decision-making power students desire to retain. Our contributions are twofold: (1) we provide insights into students' nuanced preferences on the use of AI in classrooms (where complex interactions happen among the stakeholders dynamically), considering the roles of both AI and teachers in supporting learning, and (2) we demonstrate that perspective taking can be used as a valuable analytical approach for examining qualitative data in a complex, multi-stakeholder environments. This human-centered approach can inform the design of future AIED systems, such as teacher dashboards that support instructional decision-making [2].

2 Background

2.1 The Use of AI-Based Technology in School Classrooms

AIED research has long focused on developing and evaluating adaptive learning systems, such as Intelligent Tutoring Systems (ITSs) [7]. ITSs detect students' knowledge state, problem-solving performance, affective state, and other fine-grained student behaviors and adapt their content, tasks, feedback/hints, and scaffolding based on the detected information [18, 19]. These systems have demonstrated effectiveness in improving student learning outcomes in classrooms [15].

Historically, classroom studies have treated teacher and peer interactions as the *natural* part of the "in-vivo" classroom research, without explicitly analyzing their influence on student-AI interactions [13]. Recent work, however, advocates for "hybrid intelligence"—a collaborative approach where AI works in conjunction with both students and teachers to support teaching and learning [11]. This approach emphasizes shared control over the learning process, enabling students and teachers to engage in co-regulated learning with AI and improving decision making in complex classroom environments [11]. Studies have increasingly recognized the importance of teachers [7–9, 12, 17, 20, 27] and peers during learning with AI-based systems [24]. For example, Karumbaiah et al. [12] found that teacher movement in a classroom using an algebra intelligent tutoring software was associated with students' subsequent positive learning behaviors. Despite this progress, most hybrid intelligence research that target K-12 classrooms still prioritizes teachers as the primary design partners, often overlooking students' voices in shaping AI use in classrooms. In particular, it is important to acknowledge that students and teachers may hold different—even conflicting—views on how AI should be used in the classroom [8].

Yet, understanding students' genuine preferences in AI-supported classrooms is challenging. When asked about their desires and needs in a multi-stakeholder environment, students may unconsciously adjust their responses based on perceived expectations of other stakeholders, rather than expressing their own views only. This tendency may be observed especially for children and youth, as classroom power dynamics might influence what and how they share their views. However, research rarely captures these influences explicitly. Creative design research methodologies, such as the "superpower" probing [9], may encourage students to imagine their ideal "superpowers" without constraints, revealing underlying preferences that might otherwise remain unspoken. Since these behaviors and perspective sharing are often unpredictable and can emerge spontaneously in design studies, a post-hoc analytical approach is also essential for capturing such nuanced insights.

2.2 Perspective Taking as an Analytical Lens

This study demonstrates the value of *perspective taking* as an analytical lens for understanding AI-infused classroom environments. Defined as the ability to perceive and interpret the world from others' point of view, perspective taking encompasses perceptual, cognitive, affective, and spatial dimensions [16]. It plays a crucial role in fostering empathy, facilitating communication, and supporting decision making [4, 6].

In human-computer interaction (HCI) and human-robot interaction (HRI) research, perspective taking has been a key focus, for instance in studies on child-robot interactions [25, 26]. Studies show that designing tasks that require children to consider a robot's perspective not only promotes cognitive development but also cultivates empathy among young learners [25, 26]. Following these approaches, our study takes a human-centered approach to understanding students' thoughts and perspectives on AI-supported classroom learning. Perspective taking serves as a pivotal framework for exploring how AI technologies can be integrated into classroom settings in an effective and empathetic manner. Considering the complexity of modern classrooms with stakeholders from multicultural backgrounds, perspective taking has also emerged as a critical skill for educators, especially those committed to culturally responsive pedagogy [1]. By applying perspective taking as an analytical lens, we gain deeper insights into the expectations, needs, and interactions of multiple classroom stakeholders, informing more inclusive and adaptive AI-based learning environments.

3 Method

We ask the following research question: *How might we better understand students' nuanced desires and needs for student agency in an AI-infused classroom through the lens of perspective taking?* We re-analyzed qualitative data from a prior study exploring students' preferences for decision-making control in AI-supported learning in the classroom. In that study, 16 school-aged students participated in one-on-one speed dating sessions using storyboards depicting various AI use cases in classrooms. The original dataset, analyzed by three researchers, contained 644 qualitative codes. In the present work, we focused on a subset of these codes relevant to perspective taking (see below).

3.1 Participants

We recruited 16 secondary school students in Germany (M = 14.19; *SD* = 2.04) since "digitalization" programs in Germany primarily target schools with this age group. Participants were recruited through prior lab contacts or school teachers. Participants could choose to participate remotely or in-person at the authors' institution. They also chose their preferred study language (German or English). The study was approved by the university's ethical review board, and each participant was given an informed consent form, with legal guardians signing on their behalf. Participants received 12 Euros for their voluntary participation.

3.2 Materials

To elicit students' preferences toward AI use in the classroom, we designed storyboards (which we call *scenarios*) depicting hypothetical AI-supported learning situations. These scenarios were introduced to students using the speed-dating method, a design research method that presents multiple possible futuristic scenarios to gather immediate participant reactions [28]. Speed dating has been widely used in AIED to capture participants' needs/desires [8, 27].

Our scenario design was informed by prior research that used storyboards to elicit insights from teachers and students [8, 27] and empirical investigations of AI-driven learning systems [18, 19, 21]. To address key decision-making aspects in AI-supported classrooms, we used Vincoli et al. [23]'s four dimensions of decision-making between students and AI systems in the classroom: *Data Sharing* (i.e., how much a student vs. AI shares data and with whom [8, 22]), *Help Seeking* (i.e., how much help a student receives vs. AI provide [3, 14, 19]), *Content Selection* (i.e., what content and problems a student chooses to learn/suggested by AI [18, 21]), and *Collaborative Learning* (i.e., with whom a student wants to be paired up with for a collaborative work vs. AI automatically assigns student groups [17, 27]). Past design-based research has typically explored these four aspects separately, but not in a systematic, holistic manner [5, 8].

For each of the four decision-making domains, we created two contrasting scenarios: one where the student retains most of the control and one where AI exercises higher decision-making authority [23]. For instance, on *Data Sharing* (Fig. 1), one scenario depicted a situation where students have more control and choose not to disclose their data to the teacher (Fig. 1a). On the other hand, another (Fig. 1b) showed a situation where students' data is automatically collected and sent to the teacher with no decision making by students [8]. In total, eight scenarios (4 domains * 2 decision-making conditions) were developed.

To further explore students' perceptions of AI's role in decision-making, each scenario included two alternative endings—one positive and one negative. For example, in Fig. 1 on *Data Sharing*, we constructed two versions. The student-controlled version (Fig. 1a) illustrates a scenario in which the student has full control over sharing of their learning data. The positive ending (4A in Fig. 1a) shows that students feel relieved, while the negative ending (4B in Fig. 1a) shows that the teacher lacks information to provide support. The AI-controlled version (Fig. 1b) illustrates a situation where the AI has greater control over data sharing. The positive ending (4A in Fig. 1b) shows that the teacher can effectively help the student because of the shared data, while the negative outcome (4B in Fig. 1b) is that students feel over-monitored.

(a) (b)

Fig. 1. (a) Scenario with greater learner control over data sharing where the student can choose not to share their data with the system/teacher and (b) a scenario where AI has more power over decision making (b). These situations were depicted based on prior work.

These dual endings were designed to encourage nuanced discussions, as student preferences might shift depending on the consequences of student-controlled or AI-controlled decision-making participants observe. Since school-aged children might not spontaneously articulate their thoughts, we intentionally structured scenarios with clear positive and negative outcomes to scaffold deeper reflections. Before data collection, the materials were pilot-tested with an 18-year-old student to ensure clarity and engagement. All materials were prepared in both German and English. All eight storyboards are available at: https://tinyurl.com/8scenariosstudents.

3.3 Procedure

We conducted the study online via a video conferencing system ($n = 13$) or in-person at a university lab ($n = 3$). Each session lasted 45–60 min. Two researchers (including one native German speaker) facilitated all sessions. In each session, participants were presented with the eight scenarios in a random order to minimize order effects. Importantly, researchers did not prompt/encourage participants to consider other stakeholders' perspectives; all perspective-taking utterances analyzed in the study emerged spontaneously. All participants were interviewed individually, except for one case where two students participated together at their request, as their parents believed it would make them more comfortable. For this special case, we alternated the order of the respondents to minimize influence between their responses. All sessions were video recorded, except for one session where the participant permitted only written notes.

3.4 Analysis

We collected about 14 h of video recordings, excluding one session. All recordings were first machine-transcribed and then manually edited, with three interviews translated from German to English. Two researchers (including one native German speaker) ensured accuracy in this process. For the session with no video recording, researchers compiled written notes and added the data to the analysis.

Four researchers performed the analysis, including the two who conducted data collection. We started with 644 codes from the original study, which were generated using bottom-up coding. Each researcher reviewed all 644 codes and identified those where perspective taking seemed to occur (e.g., "I would do XYZ if I were a teacher"). These selected codes were placed onto a Venn diagram representing the four main stakeholders in the classroom (i.e., teacher, student, peers, and AI, see Fig. 2a). Codes were placed in the corresponding stakeholder circle based on whose perspective the student adopted (e.g., if a code/quote shows student's perspective taking of a teacher, we put the code in the teacher circle, see "x" in Fig. 2a). If perspective-taking involved more than one stakeholder view, the code was placed in an overlapping area. Non-perspective-taking codes were discarded, reducing the dataset to 382 codes.

After placing all 382 codes onto the Venn diagram, we conducted Affinity Diagramming *within* each of the 11 areas in the Venn diagram separately. This process was performed to find common themes and ideas in students' utterances when they took the perspective of a particular stakeholder. Affinity Diagramming is a popular method in HCI that allows researchers to form multi-layer categories and themes through hierarchical structuring of individual codes [10]. All four researchers reviewed the codes within each of the 11 areas and formulated categories that include codes that show similar underlying themes. This process identified 82 *low-level* clusters/themes (Fig. 2b).

Following this initial phase, we then conducted *mid-level* Affinity Diagramming *across* the areas (i.e., looking for any common themes *across* different perspectives, Fig. 2c). In other words, in this phase, we looked for themes on the *same topic* from the perspectives of different stakeholders. For example, low-level themes related to data sharing from both the Student and Teacher area were clustered, so that we would get a mid-level category on data sharing when students take the perspective of multiple stakeholders (the cluster with "x" and the cluster with "y" are grouped together, in Fig. 2c). This process allowed us to see whether students' views aligned or conflicted when they took different stakeholders' perspectives, producing 21 mid-level themes. During this phase, we decided to discard the "peer student" stakeholder group, as its themes closely resembled those in the Student category (Fig. 2c). Finally, we synthesized the 21 themes into three high-level themes, forming the foundation of our findings.

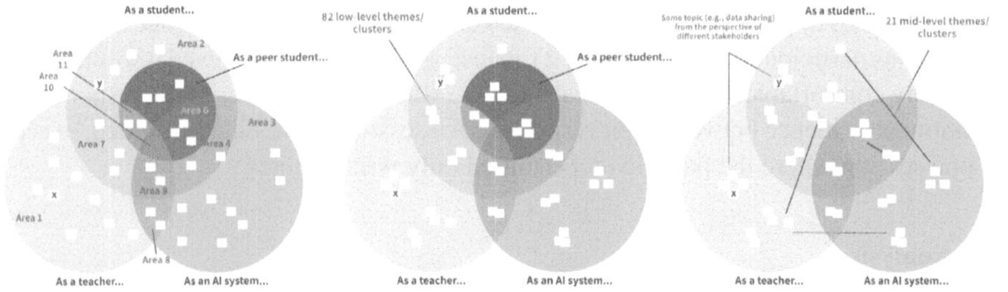

(a) First, we put perspective-taking codes into the 11 areas in the Venn diagram, resulting in 382 codes.

(b) Next we conducted Affinity Diagramming within each of the 11 areas to find common patterns when students take a particular perspective

(c) Finally, we conducted Affinity Diagramming across the 11 areas to find out, for the same topic, how students' views might look similar/different if they take perspectives of different stakeholders, finding 21 mid-level themes. After this process, we synthesized the 21 themes to form three high-level themes.

Fig. 2. Illustration of our analytical process. (a) Mapping perspective-taking utterances: 382 codes were categorized based on the stakeholder perspective adopted by students. (b) Grouping individual codes into themes: Within each of the 11 areas ("Area 1–11"), related codes were clustered, producing 82 low-level themes. (c) Cross-perspective analysis: the 82 themes were compared across stakeholder perspectives to identify shared or conflicting viewpoints, leading to 21 mid-level themes (see Table 1 below) and ultimately three high-level themes.

4 Results

4.1 Mid-Level Themes Illustrating Students' Nuanced Views on Each Agency Category

As described above, we identified 21 mid-level themes when we contrasted students' shared thoughts among different targets (e.g., teacher, AI) of their perspective taking. To present these themes, we grouped the 21 themes into the four areas of decision making (*Help Seeking, Data Sharing, Collaborative Learning,* and *Content Selection*). These themes reflect students' perspectives when speaking as themselves ("As a student…"), as teachers ("As a teacher…"), and as AI systems ("As an AI system…") (Table 1), for each of the decision-making areas. Analyzing these perspectives provides deeper insight into how students conceptualize decision-making roles in the classroom. Note that these statements are not necessarily direct quotes; many of the themes are interpretative quotes. For the presentation purpose, we use first-person sentences to emphasize the perspective-taking observed.

Help Seeking. The Help Seeking row presents students' preferred mode of receiving help when learning with AI systems in the classroom. Students generally preferred human help over AI assistance, Valuing teacher guidance for its ability to adapt to their individual needs (T1: *i would rather ask for human help instead of just following help from the system*). They acknowledged AI's potential to offer *quick, discreet help* (T15), but also recognized the risk of AI providing ineffective/excessive assistance, which could *hinder deeper understanding and independent problem-solving skills* (T16). For instance, one participant said, "[AI] should not give too many hints. Well, it should tell you how to [solve the problem], but should not show the answer," recognizing that AI systems' hint features might not help student learning well. In contrast, they consider that teachers

Table 1. The 21 mid-level themes, grouped into the stakeholder groups and decision-making areas.

	As a student...	As a teacher...	As an AI system...
Help Seeking	T1: "I would rather ask for human help instead of just following help from the system"	T6: "I would provide substantial feedback and support to students, using AI as a supplement, ensuring that the human element remains in the classroom"	T15: "I can offer quick, discreet help" T16: "I might provide ineffective or excessive assistance, potentially hindering deeper understanding and independent problem-solving skills"
Data Sharing	T2: "I would feel pressured and judged by others if they see my data" T3: "I want to make decisions about my own data"	T7: "I would be responsible for safeguarding student data privacy" T8: "It is important to see student data so that I can effectively help them" T9: "I would be concerned if my students do not share data with me"	T17: "I would invade students' privacy, but it will help students"
Collaborative Learning	T4: "I think I can benefit from getting in a group that I would not choose"	T10: "I don't really know everyone's abilities and problems" T11: "I need to be able to change group assignments, especially when students show potentials of better/worse performance when working with certain partners"	T18: "I cannot understand social dynamics of students, which are important" T19: "I should balance skill-based group formation and students' preferences as I do not understand students' social dynamics"

(*continued*)

Table 1. (*continued*)

	As a student…	As a teacher…	As an AI system…
Content Selection	T5: "I should not select what to learn because I would choose easy tasks"	T12: "I would ensure a tailored learning experience for each student, with my expertise driving the selection of content over AI" T13: "I would personally guide the choices regarding tests, exercises, group work, and homework assignments rather than leaving it to AI" T14: "I know my students the best and should make final decisions"	T20: "I can help student learning by tailoring content to each student's needs" T21: "I might assign tasks that do not match students' individual status"

would offer appropriate help that supplements AI's limited capabilities and they want to have a "human element" in the classroom (T6: *as a teacher, I would provide substantial feedback and support to students, using AI as a supplement*). Students emphasized that teachers, instead of AI, should make final decisions, as they understand students better: "I think [AI] is able to do this but i would give [the decision-making power] to the teacher…because humans are better to [make decisions] and they know you better."

Data Sharing. The Data Sharing row shows students' strong interest in maintaining the decision-making power over their own data (T3). They expressed concerns about privacy and judgment from others (T2: *I would feel pressured and judged by others if they see my data*) and viewed AI systems as potentially invasive, even when designed to help teaching and learning (T17: *As an AI system, I would invade students' privacy, but it will help students*). One student expressed concerns about data transparency in AI-supported education: "I think that AI is just checking you […] It's kind of like creepy because you don't know what is happening." However, students recognized the benefits of data sharing when considering the teacher's perspective (T8: *As a teacher, it is important to see student data so that I can effectively help them*). One student said, "So it has advantages and disadvantages if you share with someone the information. As an example with not so good grades, that you don't want to share with your teacher, then I can also understand that, because if you get trouble, then it is not so nice. But it also has a disadvantage, because, then the teacher or parents cannot help, if you just do not show where you have errors." Also, while students generally trusted their teachers to use data ethically, they wanted clear boundaries: "I think everything I do in school and only in school would be OK that my teacher can see but everything else that is out of school is my own."

Collaborative Learning. The Collaborative Learning row shows contrasting views from the perspectives of students, teachers, and AI systems, which reveal the complex process of orchestrating group formation in educational settings [5]. Students, while recognizing limitations in both teachers and AI technologies, consider that being grouped with those who they would not normally choose to work with might be beneficial (T4: *I can benefit from getting in a group that I would not choose*). From a teacher's standpoint, however, realizing the limits in understanding every student's unique ability and challenge, highlights the importance of retaining flexibility in group assignments based on observed performance and dynamics (T11: *I need to be able to change group assignments, especially when students show potentials of better/worse performance when working with certain partners*). Similarly, from the perspective of AI, realizing its lack of ability to fully grasp social nuances, such as students' friendship (T18: *I cannot understand social dynamics of students*), students emphasized the importance of adopting a balanced approach in group assignments that considers both skill levels (that AI would use) and students' preferences.

Content Selection. The Content Selection row presents distinct insights into who should hold the primary responsibility for choosing learning content and structuring educational activities. Students were reluctant to take full control of their learning choices, primarily due to self-awareness of their biases towards choosing easier tasks (T5: *I should not select what to learn because I would choose easy tasks*). They saw teachers as better suited to tailor learning experiences (T12: *As a teacher, I would ensure a tailored learning experience for each student, with my expertise driving the selection of content over AI*; T13: *I would personally guide the choices regarding test assessments rather than leaving it to AI*; T14: *I know my students the best and should make final decisions*). Also, AI was viewed as useful for personalized content recommendations (T20: *I can help student learning by tailoring content to each student's needs*). It is important to emphasize that students actually prefer guidance from AI systems as they understand what AI can do that teachers cannot do. For instance, one participant shared that students do not often tell the teacher about their struggles: "[It is good that] the topic is chosen from what the students are probably least able to because when the teacher asks, 'Did you all understand that?' then it's just usually that all people would nod or say 'yes,' even if it is not like that either." This aligns with students' broader preferences for teacher-AI collaboration in content selection: "A downside would be that [the AI's assignment may not] match perfectly [sometimes]. And I feel like sometimes teachers do have a little better connection to their students and so they understand a lot better what the student really needs."

4.2 High-Level Themes on Students' Nuanced Views on Decision Making When Using AI in the Classroom

Reviewing themes for each decision-making area shows that students hold slightly different views and preferences depending on through whose perspective they consider AI use in the classroom. Synthesizing the 21 mid-level themes, we found three high-level themes that illustrate students' nuanced views on the tensions around decision making with AI systems in the classroom. These themes highlight students' acknowledgement of AI's benefits, their trust in teachers as key decision-makers, and their varying preferences for decision-making control depending on the context.

Students Recognize AI's Benefits but Acknowledge its Limitations in Supporting Learning. Students see AI as a useful tool in the classroom but also recognize its limitations and potential pitfalls. They expressed concerns about AI's inability to fully understand social relationships, particularly in group assignment for *Collaborative Learning* [5]. Similar concerns arose in *Content Selection* and *Help Seeking,* where students acknowledged that AI could provide tailored support, yet it may misinterpret their needs or offer inappropriate assistance. This suggests that while students appreciate AI-driven personalization, they remain cautious about its imperfections and the impact of algorithmic decision making on their learning experience.

Students Trust their Teachers and See them as a "Gatekeeper" of Effective Learning. We found students' high degree of trust in their human teachers in the classroom. Many students doubted AI's capability to make truly optimal choices on its own and instead preferred a teacher-AI collaboration where teachers oversee and refine AI-generated recommendations. For instance, students valued AI's ability to generate useful learning data but felt that teachers should interpret and apply this data appropriately to ensure ethical and meaningful use. Also, students highlighted AI-driven content selection as beneficial if integrated thoughtfully, with teachers playing a supervisory role to ensure the alignment with student needs. This trust in teachers' expertise was most notably observed in *Content Selection*, *Help Seeking*, and *Data Sharing*. Rather than viewing AI as a replacement, students envisioned a complementary relationship where teachers mitigate AI's shortcomings while leveraging its strengths.

Students Prefer Strong Control on Some Aspects but Seek Teacher Guidance in Others. Students desire autonomy on certain aspects of AI-supported learning, particularly on data privacy. They were reluctant to share personal learning data with AI and expressed concerns about over-surveillance. However, they were less confident in taking full control over other aspects, such as content selection, fearing that they might choose easier exercises rather than appropriately challenging tasks. In such cases, they preferred teacher guidance, recognizing teachers' ability to ensure meaningful learning progress. This theme illustrates that students adjust their desired degree of decision-making control depending on their perceptions of other stakeholders' capabilities.

5 Discussion

Understanding students' desires in AI-supported classrooms is challenging, as their responses often reflect implicit considerations of other stakeholders' roles, particularly in environments with power dynamics, such as the teacher-student relationship. Directly analyzing students' utterance might not explicitly highlight their nuanced views as they may compromise their views considering other stakeholders' roles. We re-analyzed interview data from 16 students using perspective taking as an analytical lens.

Our findings show that students weigh the benefits and limitations of AI based on their expectations of AI capabilities and teachers' roles. This perspective-taking approach allowed us to *decompose* students' reasoning in ways that would have been difficult to capture through direct analysis of utterance without considering whose perspective students were taking. Notably, some of students' considerations align with prior research (e.g., teachers wanting to intervene in AI's grouping for collaborative learning [5, 27]).

This study contributes to two key areas in AIED. First, much of the existing research on AIED still focuses on teachers as primary design partners [17, 20], with relatively limited attention to students' perspectives in K-12 classrooms (but see [8]). Our work addresses this gap by providing important insights into how students perceive AI-supported K-12 classrooms. Our findings suggest that AI tools should be designed to foster a balanced partnership between students and teachers, ensuring that both students' needs and teachers' goals are met [8]. By understanding students' expectations of AI's role in decision-making, future AI-based educational tools can better align with learner autonomy, trust, and classroom collaboration. Second, our work shows how *perspective taking* can be used as an analytical lens to uncover stakeholders' nuanced views in complex learning environments. Students did not simply express their own desires but actively considered how teachers and AI systems would/should function in the classroom environment. For example, when adopting a teacher's perspective, students recognized the importance of data visibility for providing effective instructional support. When shifting to an AI system perspective, they recognized AI's limitations in capturing social dynamics, which could lead to inappropriate groupings or work assignments. The ability to shift perspectives demonstrates that students were not only aware of, and focused on, their own needs but also considered the broader classroom dynamics with multi-stakeholder involvement. These nuanced insights would likely have remained hidden without applying the perspective-taking approach, as students may not have explicitly expressed their views in response to direct interview questions.

We acknowledge several limitations of the study. First, while we did not explicitly prompt students to take different perspectives, the presence of a classroom teacher in some of the scenarios might have encouraged participants to consider teachers' expectations. Future research could explore whether similar patterns emerge in open-ended discussions without predefined scenarios. Second, although our scenarios were based on prior work and existing AI tutors, they may not fully represent all possible AI-supported classroom situations. Expanding the range of decision-making contexts could provide a more comprehensive understanding. Further, our sample of 16 German students would not represent school students outside of the specific study context (e.g., students in North America, where AI-based systems have been well integrated into daily instruction in some schools). Future studies should explore cross-cultural perspectives on AI-supported decision-making.

Acknowledgments. This work was supported by JST, PRESTO Grant Number JPMJPR2318, Japan. We thank all the participants in the study.

References

1. Abacioglu, C.S., et al.: Teachers' multicultural attitudes and perspective taking abilities as factors in culturally responsive teaching. Brit. J. Edu. Psychol. **90**(3), 736–752 (2020). https://doi.org/10.1111/bjep.12328
2. Aleven, V., et al.: A dashboard to support teachers during students' self-paced AI-supported problem-solving practice. In: Hilliger, I., et al. (eds.) Educating for a New Future: Making Sense of Technology-Enhanced Learning Adoption, pp. 16–30 Springer, Cham (2022). https://doi.org/10.1007/978-3-031-16290-9_2
3. Aleven, V., et al.: Help helps, but only so much: research on help seeking with Intelligent Tutoring Systems. Int. J. Artif. Intell. Educ. **26**(1), 205–223 (2016). https://doi.org/10.1007/s40593-015-0089-1
4. Cigala, A., et al.: Learning others' point of view: perspective taking and prosocial behaviour in preschoolers. Early Child Dev. Care **185**(8), 1199–1215 (2015). https://doi.org/10.1080/03004430.2014.987272
5. Echeverria, V., et al.: Designing hybrid human–AI orchestration tools for individual and collaborative activities: a technology probe study. IEEE Trans. Learning Technol. **16**(2), 191–205 (2023). https://doi.org/10.1109/TLT.2023.3248155
6. Hinnant, J., O'Brien, M.: Cognitive and emotional control and perspective taking and their relations to empathy in 5-year-old children. J. Genet. Psychol. **168**(3), 301–322 (2007). https://doi.org/10.3200/GNTP.168.3.301-322
7. Holmes, W., Tuomi, I.: State of the art and practice in AI in education. Euro. J. Educ. **57**(4), 542–570 (2022). https://doi.org/10.1111/ejed.12533
8. Holstein, K., et al.: Designing for complementarity: teacher and student needs for orchestration support in AI-enhanced classrooms. In: Isotani, S., et al. (eds.) Artificial Intelligence in Education, pp. 157–171 Springer, Cham (2019). https://doi.org/10.1007/978-3-030-23204-7_14
9. Holstein, K., et al.: Intelligent tutors as teachers' aides: exploring teacher needs for real-time analytics in blended classrooms. In: Proceedings of the Seventh International Learning Analytics & Knowledge Conference, pp. 257–266 ACM, Vancouver British Columbia Canada (2017). https://doi.org/10.1145/3027385.3027451
10. Holtzblatt, K., Beyer, H.: Consolidation and ideation: the bridge to design. In: Contextual Design, pp. 21–51 Springer, Cham (2015). https://doi.org/10.1007/978-3-031-02207-4_4
11. Järvelä, S., et al.: Human and artificial intelligence collaboration for socially shared regulation in learning. Brit. J. Educ. Tech. **54**(5), 1057–1076 (2023). https://doi.org/10.1111/bjet.13325
12. Karumbaiah, S., et al.: A spatiotemporal analysis of teacher practices in supporting student learning and engagement in an AI-enabled classroom. In: Wang, N., et al. (eds.) Artificial Intelligence in Education, pp. 450–462 Springer, Cham (2023). https://doi.org/10.1007/978-3-031-36272-9_37
13. Koedinger, K., et al.: In vivo experiments on whether supporting metacognition in intelligent tutoring systems yields robust learning. Handbook of Metacognition in Education, pp. 897–964 (2009)
14. Koedinger, K.R., Aleven, V.: Exploring the assistance dilemma in experiments with Cognitive Tutors. Educ. Psychol. Rev. **19**(3), 239–264 (2007). https://doi.org/10.1007/s10648-007-9049-0
15. Kulik, J.A., Fletcher, J.D.: Effectiveness of intelligent tutoring systems: a meta-analytic review. Rev. Educ. Res. **86**(1), 42–78 (2016)
16. Kurdek, L.A., Rodgon, M.M.: Perceptual, cognitive, and affective perspective taking in kindergarten through sixth-grade children. Dev. Psychol. **11**(5), 643–650 (1975). https://doi.org/10.1037/0012-1649.11.5.643

17. Lawrence, L., et al.: Co-designing AI-based orchestration tools to support dynamic transitions: design narratives through conjecture mapping. In: Proceedings of the 15th International Conference on Computer-Supported Collaborative Learning (CSCL) (2022)
18. Long, Y., Aleven, V.: Gamification of joint student/system control over problem selection in a linear equation tutor. In: Trausan-Matu, S. et al. (eds.) Intelligent Tutoring Systems. pp. 378–387. Springer, Cham (2014). https://doi.org/10.1007/978-3-319-07221-0_47
19. Nagashima, T., et al.: Promoting students' self-regulated learning choices with diagrams in intelligent tutoring software. Presented at the 17th International Conference of the Learning Sciences (ICLS) (2023)
20. Nazaretsky, T., et al.: Empowering teachers with AI: Co-designing a learning analytics tool for personalized instruction in the science classroom. In: LAK22: 12th International Learning Analytics and Knowledge Conference, pp. 1–12 ACM, Online USA (2022). https://doi.org/10.1145/3506860.3506861
21. Sawyer, R., et al.: Is more agency better? the impact of student agency on game-based learning. In: André, E. et al. (eds.) Artificial Intelligence in Education, pp. 335–346. Springer, Cham (2017). https://doi.org/10.1007/978-3-319-61425-0_28
22. Slade, S., Prinsloo, P.: Learning analytics: ethical issues and dilemmas. Am. Behav. Sci. **57**(10), 1510–1529 (2013). https://doi.org/10.1177/0002764213479366
23. Vincoli, M., et al.: Multidimensional student agency in learning with AI: a conceptual framework and design implications. In: Artificial Intelligence in Education. Springer, Cham (2025)
24. Walker, E., et al.: Adaptive intelligent support to improve peer tutoring in algebra. Int. J. Artif. Intell. Educ. **24**(1), 33–61 (2014). https://doi.org/10.1007/s40593-013-0001-9
25. Yadollahi, E., et al.: Can you guide me?: supporting children's spatial perspective taking through games with robots. In: Proceedings of the 2020 ACM Interaction Design and Children Conference: Extended Abstracts, pp. 217–222. ACM, London United Kingdom (2020). https://doi.org/10.1145/3397617.3397831
26. Yadollahi, E., et al.: Motivating children to practice perspective-taking through playing games with cozmo. In: 2022 31st IEEE International Conference on Robot and Human Interactive Communication (RO-MAN), pp. 1482–1489 IEEE, Napoli, Italy (2022). https://doi.org/10.1109/RO-MAN53752.2022.9900523
27. Yang, K.B., et al.: Surveying teachers' preferences and boundaries regarding human-AI control in dynamic pairing of students for collaborative learning. In: De Laet, T. et al. (eds.) Technology-Enhanced Learning for a Free, Safe, and Sustainable World, pp. 260–274. Springer, Cham (2021). https://doi.org/10.1007/978-3-030-86436-1_20
28. Zimmerman, J., Forlizzi, J.: Speed dating: providing a menu of possible futures. J. Des. Econ. Innov. **3**(1), 30–50 (2017)

Dyslexia and AI: Do Language Models Align with Dyslexic Style Guide Criteria?

Eleni Ilkou[1(✉)], Thomai Alexiou[2], Grigoris Antoniou[1,3], and Olga Viberg[4]

[1] L3S Research Center, Leibniz University Hannover, Hanover, Germany
ilkou@l3s.de
[2] Aristotle University of Thessaloniki, Thessaloniki, Greece
[3] Leeds Beckett University, Leeds, UK
[4] KTH Royal Institute of Technology, Stockholm, Sweden

Abstract. Dyslexia presents significant challenges in education for students worldwide. While assistive technologies have been used to enhance readability, no study has systematically evaluated the ability of Language Models (LMs) to generate dyslexia-friendly text aligned with established accessibility guidelines. This proof-of-concept study assesses three state-of-the-art LMs on their ability to identify and apply dyslexia-friendly text criteria. Our findings reveal that their knowledge is limited and poses potential risks. To address this, we introduce *DysText*, a novel metric that quantifies dyslexia-friendly text characteristics based on the British Dyslexia Association's Dyslexia Style Guide. Results indicate that while LMs can enhance the dyslexia-friendliness of texts, their responses should not be blindly trusted, underscoring the need for further verification.

Keywords: Special Education · Text Accessibility · Dyslexic Criteria

1 Introduction

Around 10% of the general population are people with dyslexia [48], with some suggesting that the percentage could be up to 20% [43], making it one of the predominant causes of learning difficulties. Also, among students with special education needs, about 75% face difficulties in reading [9], which can be benefited from assistive technologies used for dyslexia-friendly texts. Yet, the adoption of natural language processing (NLP) tools and Language Models (LMs) in dyslexia-friendly transformations of educational content is still limited [42].

The integration of artificial intelligence (AI) and LMs into special education settings presents both opportunities and challenges for all learners [6], and particularly those with dyslexia [20]. LMs are used to assist learners with dyslexia by simplifying text [30], and assisting in written communication [23,28]. As there is no metric for evaluating the dyslexia-friendliness of texts, the research relies on manual methods [21,24], readability indexes (i.e. LIX) [30], and lexical (i.e. BLEU) and semantic (i.e. BERTScore) metrics [44]. Although these metrics are effective for their intended tasks, they do not align with the criteria outlined

A. I. Cristea et al. (Eds.): AIED 2025, LNAI 15877, pp. 32–47, 2025.
https://doi.org/10.1007/978-3-031-98414-3_3

in dyslexia-friendly text guidelines and are limited in capturing only a few of the key characteristics of such texts. Thus, there is a need for an evaluation technique that aligns with dyslexia-friendly criteria for text.

Dyslexia-Friendly Criteria. There are plenty of criteria introduced for making a presented text friendlier to readers with dyslexia. Most of them focus on the user-interface, such as the "easy-to-read" which is supported by the United Nations [35], and the European standards for making information easy to read and understand [45]. In the web, the W3C has a Web Accessibility Initiative (WAI) [58] includes plenty of accessibility criteria, which fit the learners with dyslexia [14]. However, there is no one guideline with specific mandatory characteristics that serves as the gold-standard for dyslexia-friendly text. To overcome this obstacle, we adopt the publicly and specifically described criteria in the Dyslexia Style Guide by the British Dyslexia Association [10], which offers an overview of specific dyslexia-friendly text criteria, as we report in Table 1.

Objective and Research Questions. To the best of our knowledge, the present work is the first to quantify guidelines for dyslexia-friendly text, and investigate LMs' understanding of dyslexia-friendly text criteria and measure their ability to produce dyslexia-friendly text. We develop a proof-of-concept study centered on the Dyslexia Style Guide criteria and the LMs Gemma, Phi4 and GPT4-turbo. We summarize our inquiry into specific research questions (RQs), as following:
RQ1: Are LMs effective in recognizing the Dyslexic Style Guide criteria?
RQ2: How well can LMs generate dyslexia-friendly text according to the Dyslexia Style Guide?
RQ3: Can we improve the LMs' performance on producing dyslexia-friendly text if we provide the Dyslexic Style Guide criteria?

To tackle the RQs, we selected a diverse set of representative LMs, namely Gemma, Phi4 and GPT4-turbo, to evaluate their capacity to generate text that aligns with established dyslexia-friendly criteria. We find that LMs recognize around half of the Dyslexic Style Guide criteria (Table 2 Sect. 4.1), while their recommendations for additional criteria hinders potential risks for inclusivity (Table 3 Sect. 4.1). We introduce *DysText* (Sect. 3.4), a novel metric which quantifies the text-related criteria from the Dyslexic Style Guide. We find that the LMs can produce dyslexia-friendly text with *DysText* total scores of 2.88, 3.24, and 2.22 in Gemma, Phi4 and GPT4-turbo respectively (Table 5 Sect. 4.2). However, by analyzing the generated texts we conclude that the LMs responses require further quality control. The improvements in *DysText* total scores are significant across all prompts (Fig. 1 Sect. 4.3, and online).

2 Background

Assistive technologies and educational tools are recommended for students with dyslexia [11], as they can support in customizing text presentation

Table 1. The Dyslexia Style Guide by the British Dyslexia Association reported per computation feature. With "C", we indicate the criteria which can be computed from a JSON file, and with "O" the rest.

	Feature	Explanation
O1	Font style	Use sans serif fonts, such as Arial and Comic Sans, as letters can appear less crowded. Alternatives include Verdana, Tahoma, Century Gothic, Trebuchet, Calibri, Open Sans.
O2	Font size	Font size should be 12–14 point or equivalent (e.g. 1–1.2em / 16–19 px). Some dyslexic readers may request a larger font.
O3	Spacing inter-letters	Larger inter-letter / character spacing (sometimes called tracking) improves readability, ideally around 35% of the average letter width. If letter spacing is excessive it can reduce readability.
O4	Spacing inter-words	Inter-word spacing should be at least 3.5 times the inter-letter spacing
O5	Spacing inter-lines	Some dyslexic people find that larger line spacing improves readability. It should be proportional to inter-word spacing; 1.5 / 150% is preferable.
O6	Headings font size	For headings, use a font size that is at least 20% larger than the normal text. If further emphasis is required, then use bold.
O7	Assistive technology	Use formatting tools for text alignment, justification, indents, lists, line and paragraph spacing to support assistive technology users.
O8	Hyperlinks look	Ensure hyperlinks look different from headings and normal text.
O9	Background colour	Use single colour backgrounds. Avoid background patterns or pictures and distracting surrounds.
O10	Background contrast	Use sufficient contrast levels between background and text. Use sufficient contrast levels between background and text.
O11	No green, red/pink	Avoid green and red/pink, as these colours are difficult for those who have colour vision deficiencies (colour blindness).
O12	Alternative to white background	Consider alternatives to white backgrounds for paper, computer and visual aids such as whiteboards. White can appear too dazzling. Use cream or a soft pastel colour. Some dyslexic people will have their own colour preference.
O13	Print paper quality	When printing, use matt paper rather than gloss. Paper should be thick enough to prevent the other side showing through.
O14	Use images	Use images to support text. Flow charts are ideal for explaining procedures. Pictograms and graphics can help to locate and support information in the text
O15	Instructions	Give instructions clearly.
O16	No jargon	Avoid jargon where possible; always provide the expanded form when first used. Provide a glossary of jargon
C1	Spacing paragraphs	Use white space to remove clutter near text and group related content.
C2	No *Italics*	Avoid Underlining and italics as this can make the text appear to run
C3	No Underline	together and cause crowding.
C4	Use **Bold**	Use bold for emphasis.
C5	No uppercase	Avoid using capital letter and uppercase letters for continuous text. Lower case letters are easier to read.
C6	Left align	Left align text, without justification. This makes it easier to find the start and finish of each line and ensures even spacing between words.
C7	Short sentences	Write short simple sentences: 60 to 70 characters is optimal.
C8	Short paragraphs	Be concise; avoid using long, dense paragraphs.
C9	Section headings	Break up the text with regular section headings in long documents
C10	ToC	and include a table of contents.
C11	Active voice	Use active rather than passive voice.
C12	Simple language	Write in simple clear language using every day words.
C13	Bullets or lists	Consider using bullet points and numbering rather than continuous prose.
C14	No double negatives	Avoid double negatives.
C15	No abbreviations	Avoid abbreviations where possible.
C16	Avoid columns	Avoid multiple columns (as used in newspapers).
C17	Headings spacing	Add extra space around headings and between paragraphs.

[1,26,46,56,61], font design [27], spelling and grammar [37,55], offer game-based learning [34] and text simplification [5,53] to address the learners' needs better [3]. The research to support learners with dyslexia has focused on adaptive learning support technologies, such as audio-books [7], text-to-speech [15,16,47], interface adjustments [3], and spell checkers [12], which enable learners to bypass traditional reading and writing barriers [50].

A widely adopted approach to improve text for learners with dyslexia is the text simplification, which is used to enhance texts' accessibility and inclusion in educational settings. Schicchi and Taibi [51] introduced an automatic text simplification system using automatic text simplification and automatic text complexity evaluation. They suggest that automatic text simplification systems can be useful when limited textual resources are available for teaching a particular topic, allowing the tool to assist in creating multiple versions of the same text to assist text accessibility. AI-powered tools for content summarization condense lengthy texts into manageable summaries, empowering learners with dyslexia to grasp the main ideas efficiently [40]. Further most studies evaluate the accessibility of text based on readability indexes, such as the LIX readability index, which takes into consideration the number of words, letters and periods present in a text [8].

Madjidi and Crick [38] developed a model that modifies text based on dyslexia-friendly guidelines using transfer learning, training T5 and RoBERTa on crowdsourced data. A follow-up study enhanced this by adding syllable and morphological analysis, helping simplify complex word structures [39]. Testing undergraduates with dyslexia showed faster reading times, though comprehension varied. Meanwhile, Ayang et al. [13] created a cloud-based system that reformats Microsoft Word documents into dyslexia-friendly versions by adjusting fonts, spacing, and colors, allowing users to customize modifications for improved readability and privacy. While useful for general readability, the existing research and tools do not fully capture nor measure the features of dyslexia-friendly texts and do not incorporate specific dyslexia-friendly criteria into their approaches.

3 Methodology

3.1 Data Collection

Currently, there is no gold-standard dataset available for converting texts into both original and dyslexia-friendly formats [61]. To ensure the applicability of most dyslexia-friendly criteria which are not applicable to short texts, i.e. "C13: Bullets or lists" from Table 1, we require longer texts, hence we focus on the domain of history. Our focus is on educational text found in learning resources, and not AI-generated text to ensure the pedagogical alignment of our study. Due to licensing restrictions and copyright protections, we aimed for widely adopted textbooks with an open license to ensure broad applicability and maximize the impact of our research. Our first choice is the textbook "History Textbook: West African senior school certificate examination" which is openly available under a CC BY-NC 3.0 license [4]. The book claims that *"is aimed at West African students taking the West African Senior School Certificate Examination"*, which makes it a textbook with high impact and everyday outreach. The second choice of textbook is the "U.S. History" from openstax which is openly available under a CC BY 4.0 license [19]. We exclude texts with small paragraphs, annotations and hyperlinks as they already fulfill some of the criteria. We gather a total of 50 chapters which we manually add into JSON file while maintaining the line breaks characteristics.

3.2 Language Models and Prompts

The selection of LMs is based on their applicability to educational settings, as the smaller models have low requirements for local installation in a personal or school laptop, while GPT is a popular alternative for users around the world. Also, our choice is motivated by variations in size, and architecture, which might impact dyslexia-friendly performance. The hyper-parameters used are temperature=0 for consistent outputs, top_p=0.5 to control the diversity of outputs, repeat_penalty=1.1 and no maximum tokens prefixed to allow full paragraph-length responses without artificial thresholds. In our study, we use:

Gemma. Gemma [54], developed by Google, is a 7B parameter language model based on the transformer decoder architecture. It is pre-trained on primarily-English data, and it demonstrate strong performance across academic benchmarks for language understanding.

textbiPhi4. Phi4 [2], developed by Microsoft, is a 14B parameter language model based on a decoder-only transformer architecture. It is pre-trained on organic sources and synthetic data, and achieves state-of-the-art performance comparable to large models such as GPT 4o in STEM.

GPT4-Turbo. GPT4-turbo [41], developed by OpenAI, has hundreds of billions parameters LM based sparse attention and mixture-of-experts architecture. GPT4-turbo has a context window of 128k tokens allowing for big text inputs.

Prompt Engineering. Prompt engineering techniques in LMs are widely studied [49]. As we are limited by successful examples of text in its original form and in dyslexia-friendly format, we perform zero-shot prompting. Following a similar study's results [30], we formulate our prompts to be direct and short. To detect the LMs knowledge about the dyslexia-friendly criteria, we deploy four prompts: 1. "Which are the criteria for making a text dyslexia friendly?", 2. "Which are the principles in Dyslexia Style guide that suggests changes in written material for dyslexic readers?", 3. "What guidelines should be followed to make a text more accessible for people with dyslexia?", and 4. "How can I make a text dyslexia-friendly?". To evaluate the LMs ability to generate dyslexia-friendly text, we deploy two prompts without a guide included: 1. "Make the following text dyslexia-friendly :\n [Chapter]", and 2. "Rewrite the following text according to dyslexic style guide:\n [Chapter]". Additionally we utilize 1. the full Dyslexia Style Guide, and 2. only the JSON text related criteria as [Guide] and formulate the prompts "I will provide the Dyslexic Style Guide and a text, I want you to make the text according to the Dyslexic Style Guide. \n Here is the Dyslexic Style guide: \n [Guide]\n Here is the text: \n [Chapter]".

3.3 Data Analysis

We process the LMs responses to retain only answers related to dyslexia-friendly text, as manual cleaning proved necessary even when LMs were instructed to exclude guidelines or explanations. We report the statistics of the minimum (Min.), median (Mdn.), maximum (Max.), average (Av.) and standard deviation (SD) as the descriptive statistics are commonly used to detail the readability of the original versus the generated text by the LMs [30]. To evaluate significance, we deployed paired statistical tests to compare the generated texts of the LMs against the original dataset. The normality was assessed using the Shapiro-Wilk test, a robust method for testing departures from normality. For comparisons where the differences met the assumption of normality, a two-tailored paired t-test was performed to assess whether the mean differences were statistically significant. In cases where the differences violated the assumption of normality, the non-parametric Wilcoxon signed-rank test was utilized as a distribution-free alternative. Statistical significance was evaluated at the threshold of $p < 0.05$.

3.4 New Metric for Dyslexia-Friendly Text *DysText*

Our proposed metric, *DysText*, is theoretically grounded on the guidelines set forth by the Dyslexia Style Guide from the British Dyslexia Association. *DysText* is pioneer metric that quantifies the 17 out of the 33 criteria introduced by Dyslexia Style Guide, and is able to measure the accessibility of text based inclusivity guidelines. The metric focuses on features present in JSON formats, as extracted by LMs responses. Building on the criteria outlined in Table 1, we examine the characteristics that can be computed by the LMs JSON output marked in "C". We compute each criterion by recognizing patterns in the JSON format, and utilizing NLP libraries. Our data, further results, and the *DysText* metric are available at: https://github.com/eilkou/DysText.

Semantic Interpretation of Dyslexic Style Guide Criteria. Given that the British Dyslexia Association does not assign a priority to any individual criterion, we treat each criterion as equally significant in contributing to the dyslexia-friendliness of the text. To accurately capture the impact of each criterion on text accessibility, we map the corresponding recommendations that when present improve the accessibility to a scale ranging from 0 to 1, where values from 0 to 1 indicate improvements in dyslexia-friendly text accessibility. Conversely, recommendations to avoid are mapped to values between -1 and 0, reflecting their potential to hinder accessibility. The metric is computed as the sum of individual criterion outputs and has a range of values of [-10,11]. We assume that the criteria of left align (C6) and avoid columns (C16) are covered by default.

4 Results

4.1 LMs Knowledge of Dyslexic Style Guide Criteria

We begin our analysis with prompting LMs to provide the criteria for dyslexia-friendly texts. In Table 2, we report the scores of the LMs in recognizing the dyslexia-friendly criteria, accompanied with the wrongly reported criteria per LM. The total score is calculated based on individual criterion scores, with +1 point awarded for a correct response, +0.5 points for a partially correct response (e.g., when the LM recognizes "Font size" as a relevant criterion but fails to suggest appropriate fonts), 0 points for a missed criterion, and -1 for an incorrect answer (e.g., suggesting the use of green when the criteria advise against it). The negative score serves as a penalty, as incorrect recommendations can reduce dyslexia-friendliness and negatively impact the overall reading experience.

Table 2. The LMs knowledge scores of the Dyslexic Style Guide criteria. They recognize less than half of the 33 criteria reported in Table 1.

	Total Score		Wrongly reported
	Av.	SD	
Gemma	10.13	0.63	C2: No *Italics*, O11: No green, red/pink
Phi4	13.88	0.63	-
GPT4-turbo	13.00	0.41	-

Phi4 is more informed about the dyslexia-friendly criteria than GPT4-turbo. All LMs perform below average, as they identify less than 14 criteria from the 33 included in the Dyslexia Style Guide. A common theme that erased from the criteria the LMs recommended was the font size and style, the short sentences and simple language. Regarding the font style, the LMs recommended additionally the usage of OpenDyslexic font [27], an open-source font which is designed with distinctive letter forms. Although some studies suggest it can enhance reading accuracy and rate [18], it might not always be helpful to learners [59]. It is worth-mentioning that all the LMs included additional criteria, which are not found in the Dyslexic Style Guide, as we report in Table 3.

Potential Risks from Additional Recommended Criteria. In Table 3, we report a qualitative analysis and classification of the additional criteria provided by LMs. Although interactive elements, are not always practical in static text formats [25], they can enhance comprehension when applied judiciously [52]. Predictability in word structure enhances readability but, if oversimplified, may compromise linguistic depth [17]. Although encouragement is beneficial for all students, praise can have negative effects when not accompanied with detailed feedback [36]. This is particularly critical in students with low self-esteem, which

Table 3. The additional criteria reported by the Language Models.

Additional Criterion	LM	Risk	Example
Accessibility considerations	Gemma	Low	"Keyboard-accessible navigation with clear links and menus"
Audio support	Gemma, Phi4, GPT4-turbo	Low	"Where possible, offer audio versions of texts to provide alternative access methods."
Avoid effects	Gemma, Phi4	Low	"Avoid flickering or animated content"
Consistent layout	Phi4, GPT4-turbo	Low	"Maintain a consistent layout throughout the document to help readers establish familiarity and reduce confusion."
Feedback & Testing	Gemma, Phi4, GPT4-turbo	Medium	" "Feedback from dyslexic individuals on readability and accessibility"
Encouragement & Praise	Gemma	High	"Use of positive language and encouraging messages"
Interactive elements	Gemma, Phi4	Medium	"Interactive activities and games to promote engagement"
Predictability	Gemma	Medium	"Provide predictable syllable patterns and word structures"
Reader's Perspective	Gemma	High	"Imagine you are reading the text from the perspective of someone with dyslexia."
Summaries	Gemma, GPT4-turbo	Low	"Provide summaries or outlines at the beginning of lengthy documents to give an overview of what follows"

receive more person praise rather than process praise and ends up predisposing them for feeling failure shame [29]. Hence, excessive encouragement and praise, may be patronizing or ineffective, especially if they emphasize personal attributes rather than learning processes. Writing from the perspective of a reader with dyslexia also presents risks, as it introduces labeling concerns and may border on unintentional discrimination [57]. While considering diverse perspectives is valuable, inclusivity should be achieved through broader accessibility rather than narrowly defined reader experiences.

4.2 LMs Generating Dyslexia-Friendly Text

In Table 4, we report the statistics of the original texts and in Table 5, we present the same statistics over the LMs' generated texts. All three LMs improved their scores in *DysText* visual, content and total scores, which demonstrates their ability to improve the text into a more dyslexia-friendly format according to the Dyslexia Style Guide. However, their performance in *DysText* metric shows that there is plenty of room for improvement as their values reached a maximum of 5 (5.05 in Phi4, 5.31 in Gemma, and 5.53 in GPT4-turbo) over the maximum possible score of 11 points. Gemma produced the shorter generated text compared to Phi4 and GPT4-turbo, which could imply that Gemma missed reporting valuable information.

LIX Vs *DysText* Scores. A crucial element highlighted by the comparison between readability LIX score, in which the smaller scores indicate easier to read texts, and *DysText*. *DysText* incorporates the elements of LIX with additional criteria, and both seem to predict the LM with the better dyslexia-friendly generated texts. Gemma scores the lowest in LIX score with 43.81 on average across all generated texts, which indicates that the LMs responses are medium in difficulty to read. At the same time, Gemma gains the biggest average content score and the second biggest average total performance in *DysText*, which indicates bigger compliance to the Dyslexic Style Guide criteria and more dyslexia-friendly texts. However, since *DysText* encompasses more characteristics than just word and sentence count, it demonstrates that relying solely on the LIX score does not provide insight into the dyslexia-friendly features of a text. This is highlighted by Phi4, which shows only a modest improvement in the LIX score, from an average of 49.68 to 48.79, despite achieving the highest average *DysText* total score. The *DysText* visual score is more closely correlated with the number of paragraphs (No. Paragraphs) which includes the sum of headers and bullet points, hence, higher values in "No. Paragraphs" indicate high values in *DysText* visual score.

Table 4. Analysis of the dataset with the original texts.

	Chapters				
	Min.	Mdn.	Max.	Av.	SD
No. Sentences	8	21.5	59	24.74	1.74
No. Words	184	490	1468	538.84	39.74
No. Long Words (>6 characters)	50	127	381	145.92	10.94
No. Paragraphs	1	4	17	4.82	0.46
Readability LIX score	37.43	50.61	62.07	49.68	0.81
DysText visual score	0	0	0	0	0
DysText content score	−3.08	−0.43	0.39	−0.62	0.10

Table 5. Analysis of LMs generated dyslexia-friendly text over the dataset. The number of paragraphs (No. Paragraphs) includes the headers and bullet points.

	Gemma					Phi4					GPT4-turbo				
	Min.	Mdn.	Max.	Av.	SD	Min.	Mdn.	Max.	Av.	SD	Min.	Mdn.	Max.	Av.	SD
No. Sentences	4	17	36	17.24	6.15	9	22	40	21.37	6.62	6	15	27	15.18	3.50
No. Words	69	263.5	711	280.46	107.87	140	324.5	704	330.56	103.54	135	330.5	3041	356.11	248.48
No. Long Words	14	71	200	76.73	38.38	41	105.5	248	108.44	38.38	36	117.5	1900	140.11	158.61
No. Paragraphs	1	6	24	7.22	4.87	1	13	45	15.35	9.33	2	10	40	11.80	6.95
LIX score	24.10	44.39	81.98	43.81	10.64	33.49	48.12	67.53	48.79	6.92	35.00	57.20	265.21	60.84	21.65
DysText Visual	0	1	3	1.00	0.88	0	2	2	1.45	0.82	0	2	4	1.21	1.07
DysText Content	−1.60	1.92	3.52	1.88	0.93	−0.39	1.91	3.16	1.80	0.72	−8.26	1.25	3.27	1.02	1.37
DysText Total	−1.60	3.05	5.31	2.88	1.46	−0.39	3.44	5.05	3.24	1.08	−7.26	2.51	5.53	2.22	1.82

Qualitative Result: LMs Responses Require Verification. Our qualitative analysis reveals that the LMs responses should not be fully trusted, and a supervised or human-in-the-loop approach is suggested to validate the content of the responses. In minor consideration of the responses, the LMs might require small edits as the generated text misses spaces between words in some cases, i.e. the response contained *"butalso"* instead of *"but also"*. These cases were more often found in the end of the response rather at the first sentences. In odd observations, Gemma changed the word "the" to *"da"* in two of the chapters, and produced a few spelling mistakes, such as *"Diplomcy"* instead of *"Diplomacy"*. Also, in the one case GPT4-turbo did not provide a response, and Gemma gave as an answer only recommendations for making the text dyslexia-friendly instead of providing the text; in those cases we re-run the prompt.

Further, potential issues could be raised from specific phrasing. An example is extracted from headings proposed for different chapters by the LMs, the *"Reparation - Easier to Read"* from Gemma, and the *"Making History Easier to Read: Britain's Financial Challenges After War* and *"English Colonization in North America: A Dyslexia-Friendly Overview"* from Phi4. While the latter has a clearly positive tone, and the use of *"Making History Easier to Read"* could be seen as simplifying a complex historical topic, however, it might unintentionally suggest that the audience is incapable of understanding the historical topic unless it is made "easy". Emphasis on sensitivity of language and minor adjustments, such as in Gemma *"[Topic]- Easier to Read"*, can maintain the integrity of the content without risking demeaning the target audience. We highlight that in no prompt the word "easy" was used. Hence, that phrasing can be problematic, interpreted as insensitive and patronizing commentary, and hinder inclusivity.

In addressing more significant concerns, we turn our attention to the qualitative analysis of the generated text responses. Notably, we observe that GPT4-turbo in section "European Trading Communities in West Africa" [4] deviated from its assigned task, and transitioned mid-response into an unprompted discourse on humanity and history. This deviation raises significant concerns regarding the LLM's ability to adhere to task-specific constraints and maintain alignment with instructional prompts, underscoring potential challenges in its reliability for focused educational or research applications.

Another example related to potential risks is raised from the quality of responses. In five cases, the GPT4-turbo responses were initiated with proper context, without raising concerns, however the body context raised concerns. The five cases were split into: one case from the book "U.S. History" the chapter "The Rise of Slavery in the Chesapeake Bay Colonies", and four cases from the book "History Textbook: West African senior school certificate examination" in the sections "European Contact with West Africa" and "Trans-Saharan Trade. Origins, organization and effects in the development of West Africa". After careful consideration of the whole body of responses, we see that the GPT4-turbo repeats nonsense phrases. All these cases had in common the lengthy responses by GPT4-turbo, which could indicate a potential threshold for quality control. However, in a broader perspective, even as isolated events, these incidents highlight the need to examine the generated answers, by focusing not only on technical criteria compliance, but also on the accuracy and quality of the content. It is worth questioning why the misconduct on responses occurred on the topics about colonies and slavery, even if not all chapters on these thematics were affected. This discrepancy may indicate a potential bias or restrictions in topics of responses in GPT4-turbo, warranting further investigation is needed to understand these inconsistencies and their impact on accessibility.

4.3 LMs Improving Dyslexia-Friendliness of Texts

All LMs showed statistically significant improvements to the original texts across all prompts. In Fig. 1 are the boxplots of the *DysText* total scores differences between each generated text and its corresponding original. Phi4 improved 100% of the original texts in visual and total *DysText* score across all prompts. One of the reasons for the 100% improved *DysText* visual score could be that Phi4, unlike Gemma and GPT-4 Turbo, often provided a glossary and/or a summary.

Prompting the Dyslexic Style Guide criteria which are only applicable to text improves the performance and produces consistent good improvements. This is demonstrated by prompt 4 in Fig. 1, which provided the criteria only applicable to text in JSON format as are in the explanations of features "C" in Table 1. Prompt 4 improved the original texts *DysText* scores in 100% of visual, content and total on Phi4, in 96% of visual and 100% of content and total on Gemma, and in 100% of visual and 98% of content and total on GPT4-turbo. Gemma is reporting its second best improvements in prompt 4, which is probably due to its shorter context length of 8192 tokens, in contrast to 16k of Phi4 and 128k of GPT4-turbo. The context length refers to the maximum number of words and characters the LM can process and retain in a single pass, where exceeding this limit results in the truncation or loss of earlier input, hence,

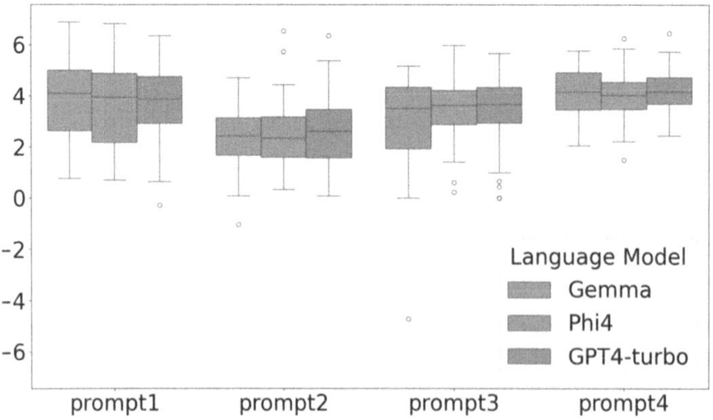

Fig. 1. The boxplots of the improvements for each text over the total DysText scores across the prompts and LMs.

affecting the LM's performance. The second best was the prompt: "Make the following text dyslexia-friendly :\n [Chapter]". The least benefited score was the *DysText* visual in prompt 2 "Rewrite the following text according to dyslexic style guide:\n [Chapter]". The biggest improvements in scores were noticed in *DysText* visual score on GPT4-turbo in prompt 4, with 2.16 points gained on average, in *DysText* content and total scores on Gemma in prompt 1, with 3.21 and 4.75 points gained on average, respectively. This analysis demonstrates the capabilities of small LMs such as Gemma and Phi4, to compete with large LMs.

5 Discussion and Conclusion

LMs Knowledge of Dyslexia-Friendly Criteria is Limited. Our results show that the LMs are not informed about most than half of the Dyslexia Style Guide criteria, as they identify 13 from the 33 criteria. Moreover, even if they are aware of a criterion, i.e. "O2: Font style", they often recommend additional features for it, which are not included in the guide, not fully supported by research findings.

LMs Significantly Improve the Dyslexia-Friendliness of Texts. Our study demonstrates that Gemma, Phi4, and GPT-4 Turbo significantly enhance original texts, making them more dyslexia-friendly, as measured by the DysText metric. This metric quantifies adherence to the Dyslexic Style Guide by detecting formatting and linguistic features in JSON-structured outputs. The results indicate that the examined LMs consistently perform better when prompted with text-only criteria alongside the corresponding chapter, suggesting that structured input helps optimize their ability to generate accessible content. This aligns with previous research highlighting the importance of explicit, well-defined constraints in guiding LMs to produce more user-friendly and readable outputs.

LMs Responses Require Verification. However, we emphasize that the findings from the qualitative analysis underscored the need to avoid automatically trusting the LMs' generated text responses. Moreover, the LMs are not a reliable source for informing the users about the dyslexia-friendly recommendations for text, as their recommendations can hinder potential risks in the documentation of reported dyslexia-friendly criteria from Gemma, the headings selection from Phi4, and generated text in historically sensitive topics from GPT4-turbo.

LIX readability score misses dyslexia-friendly features. While Gemma has the lowest LIX score, indicating medium difficulty, it achieves the highest DysText score, showing stronger compliance with the Dyslexic Style Guide. In contrast, Phi4 shows only a slight improvement in LIX despite achieving the best DysText score. This discrepancy highlights a fundamental difference between the two metrics: 1. LIX assesses readability based on sentence length and word complexity, which could be insufficient in capturing accessibility improvements tailored for dyslexic readers. 2. *DysText*, integrates a broader set of dyslexia-friendly criteria, such as the existence of bullet points, offering a more comprehensive evaluation of how well a text aligns dyslexia-friendly features.

Limitations. There are ethical and legal implications when using LMs in education [60], particularly regarding the biases, transparency, fairness, and accountability of the LM-generated content, such as the nonsensical or biased responses generated by GPT4-turbo on texts about charged themes, such as colonization and slavery, raising concerns about their reliability and potential to misinform learners. Our study highlights two key challenges. First, LMs misinterpret or omit critical information, which can compromise dyslexia-friendly content. Second, there are legal concerns about text use without proper processing rights, particularly in relation to licensing agreements and GDPR compliance [22]. The DysText metric is limited to English-language texts, restricting its applicability to other linguistic and cultural contexts and necessitating external validation for context alignment. Also, jargon detection is context- and domain-dependent. For example, such terms as *Senegambia*, require expert validation to ensure accuracy.

Future Work. Since prompting LMs performs best with quality examples, e.g. Chain of Thought reasoning [49], our aim is to develop a benchmark dataset featuring original and dyslexia-friendly texts in collaboration with experts and the DysText metric. This dataset could further support fine-tuning LMs for dyslexia-related learning practices. For multilingual adaptation, NLP libraries for non-English corpora can be utilized alongside cultural and linguistic coverage criteria to adjust language-sensitive features (e.g., C11: Active voice). In addition, DysText could be expanded to incorporate all the criteria of the Dyslexic Style Guide, including the considerations of the graphical user interface [3]. We plan to analyze which criteria LMs handle most effectively and where they struggle in generating dyslexia-friendly texts, forming further improvements in AI-driven accessibility solutions [31,32].

Conclusions. Our study is a proof-of-concept exploring LMs' awareness and application of dyslexia-friendly criteria by LMs, quantifying their ability to generate accessible text. Our findings stress both the potential and the risks of automated dyslexia-friendly text generation using LMs that can be deployed on student or school laptops. These methods could enhance text accessibility, reduce stigma in special education, and address educational inequities, aligning with global efforts towards inclusive and equitable quality education [33].

Acknowledgments. This work was partially supported by a 2024 AIED-DEIA Fellowship grant from the IAIED Society (iaied.org). Viberg was partly supported by the Future AI project by KTH.

References

1. Cambium Learning, Group: Kurzweil 3000. https://www.kurzweil3000.com/
2. Abdin, M., Aneja, J., Behl, H., et al.: Phi-4 technical report. arXiv preprint arXiv:2412.08905 (2024)

3. Abdul Aziz, N.I., Husni, H., Hashim, N.L.: Dyslexia-friendly design features for tangible user interfaces: a systematic literature review. Int. J. Inf. Learn. Technol. **39**(4), 360–372 (2022)
4. Achebe, N., Adu-Gyamfi, S., Alie, J., et al.: History textbook: West African senior school certificate examination (2018)
5. AI, Y.: Dyslexic GPT-Dyslexia-Friendly Reading Tool, empowering readability with AI. https://www.yeschat.ai/gpts-9t55QeOXpjD-Dyslexic-GPT
6. Aliu, T.V.: Artificial intelligence in special education: a literature review. Syst. Anal. **2**(2), 188–199 (2024)
7. Almgren Bäck, G., Lindeblad, E., Elmqvist, C., Svensson, I.: Dyslexic students' experiences in using assistive technology to support written language skills: a five-year follow-up. Disabil. Rehabil. Assist. Technol. **19**(4), 1217–1227 (2024)
8. Anderson, J.: LIX and RIX: variations on a little-known readability index. J. Read. **26**(6), 490–496 (1983)
9. Association, I.D.: Frequently Asked Questions how common are language-based learning disabilities? (2025). https://dyslexiaida.org/frequently-asked-questions-2/
10. Association, T.B.D.: Creating a dyslexia friendly workplace, dyslexia friendly style guide. https://www.bdadyslexia.org.uk/advice/employers/creating-a-dyslexia-friendly-workplace/dyslexia-friendly-style-guide
11. Association, T.D.: Assistive technology training (2025). https://www.dyslexia.uk.net/service/assistive-technology-training/
12. el Atawy, S.M., Ahmed, H.M.: Spelling checker for dyslexic second language ARAB learners. J. Theor. Appl. Inf. Technol. **99**, 390–402 (2021)
13. Ayang, D., et al.: Accessibility made easy: the development of a cloud-based service to make documents more dyslexia-friendly. In: EDULEARN24 Proceedings. IATED (2024)
14. Berget, G., Herstad, J., Sandnes, F.E.: Search, read and write: an inquiry into web accessibility for people with dyslexia. In: Universal Design 2016: Learning from the Past, Designing for the Future, pp. 450–460. IOS Press (2016)
15. Bhola, N.: Effect of text-to-speech software on academic achievement of students with dyslexia. Integr. J. Res. Arts Humanit. **2**, 51–55 (2022)
16. Bonifacci, P., Colombini, E., Marzocchi, M., Tobia, V., Desideri, L.: Text-to-speech applications to reduce mind wandering in students with dyslexia. J. Comput. Assist. Learn. **38**(2), 440–454 (2022)
17. Borleffs, E., Maassen, B.A., Lyytinen, H., Zwarts, F.: Cracking the code: the impact of orthographic transparency and morphological-syllabic complexity on reading and developmental dyslexia. Front. Psychol. **9**, 2534 (2019)
18. Broadbent, L.: Comparing the impact of OpenDyslexic and Arial fonts on the reading performance of Key Stage 2 readers with dyslexia. Ph.D. thesis (2023)
19. Corbett, P.S., Janssen, V., Lund, J.M., Pfannestiel, T., Waskiewicz, S., Vickery, P.: US history (2024)
20. Dawson, K., Antonenko, P., Lane, H., Zhu, J.: Assistive technologies to support students with dyslexia. Teach. Except. Child. **51**(3), 226–239 (2019)
21. De Marco, V., Sciarrone, F., Temperini, M.: TutorChat: a chatbot for the support to dyslexic learner's activity through generative AI. In: 2024 IEEE International Conference on Advanced Learning Technologies (ICALT), pp. 155–157. IEEE (2024)
22. Duncan, A., Joyner, D.A.: With or without EU: Navigating GDPR constraints in human subjects research in an education environment. In: Proceedings of the Eighth ACM Conference on Learning@ Scale, pp. 343–346 (2021)

23. D'Urso, S., Sciarrone, F.: AI4LA: an intelligent chatbot for supporting students with dyslexia, based on generative AI. In: Sifaleras, A., Lin, F. (eds.) International Conference on Intelligent Tutoring Systems, pp. 369–377. Springer, Cham (2024). https://doi.org/10.1007/978-3-031-63028-6_31
24. Eroğlu, G., Abou Harb, M.R.: Assessing ChatGPT's accuracy in dyslexia inquiry. In: 2024 Medical Technologies Congress (TIPTEKNO), pp. 1–4. IEEE (2024)
25. Fawcett, A., Nicolson, R.: Dyslexia, Learning, and the Brain. MIT Press (2008)
26. fontconverter4dyslexia@gmail.com: Font converter for dyslexia (2025). https://fontconverterfordyslexia.neocities.org/
27. Gonzalez, A.: OpenDyslexic, a typeface for dyslexia. https://opendyslexic.org/
28. Goodman, S.M., Buehler, E., et al.: Lampost: AI writing assistance for adults with dyslexia using large language models. Communications of the ACM (2024)
29. Graf-König, N., Puca, R.M.: "wow, you're really smart!"-how children's self-esteem affects teachers' praise. Educ. Psychol. **44**(6–7), 749–764 (2024)
30. Hedlin, E., Estling, L., Wong, J., Epp, C.D., Viberg, O.: Got it! prompting readability using ChatGPT to enhance academic texts for diverse learning needs. In: Proceedings of the 15th Learning Analytics and Knowledge Conference (2025)
31. Ilkou, E., Galletti, M., Dobriy, D., et al.: Edumultikg attains 92% accuracy in k-12 user profiling. In: Proceedings of the ESWC, vol. 2043 (2023)
32. Jaldi, C.D., Ilkou, E., Schroeder, N., Shimizu, C.: Education in the era of neurosymbolic AI. J. Web Semant. **85**, 100857 (2025)
33. Johnstone, C.J., Schuelka, M.J., Swadek, G.: Quality education for all? The promises and limitations of the SDG framework for inclusive education and students with disabilities. In: Grading goal four, pp. 96–115. Brill (2020)
34. Learning, N.: Dyslexia quest dyslexia quest, quickly screen and identify those children at risk for dyslexia. https://www.nessy.com/en-gb/product/dyslexia-quest-home
35. of Library Associations, I.F., Institutions: International federation of library association and institutions IFLA professional reports: guidelines for easy-to-read materials (2010). https://www.ifla.org/wp-content/uploads/2019/05/assets/hq/publications/professional-report/120.pdf
36. Lipnevich, A.A., Eßer, F.J., Park, M.J., Winstone, N.: Anchored in praise? potential manifestation of the anchoring bias in feedback reception. Assess. Educ. Principles, Policy Pract. **30**(1), 4–17 (2023)
37. ltd., G.: Ghotit, dyslexia writing & reading assistant. https://www.ghotit.com/
38. Madjidi, E., Crick, C.: Enhancing textual accessibility for readers with dyslexia through transfer learning. In: Proceedings of the 25th International ACM SIGACCESS Conference on Computers and Accessibility, pp. 1–5 (2023)
39. MADJIDI, E., CRICK, C.: Towards inclusive reading: a neural text generation framework for dyslexia accessibility (2024)
40. Nandhini, K., Balasundaram, S.: Improving readability of dyslexic learners through document summarization. In: 2011 IEEE International Conference on Technology for Education, pp. 246–249. IEEE (2011)
41. OpenAI: Introducing GPT-4 turbo (2023). https://openai.com/blog/gpt-4-turbo
42. Paudel, S., Acharya, S.: A comprehensive review of assistive technologies for children with dyslexia. arXiv preprint arXiv:2412.13241 (2024)
43. Phillips, B., Odegard, T.N.: Evaluating the impact of dyslexia laws on the identification of specific learning disability and dyslexia. Ann. Dyslexia **67**, 356–368 (2017)
44. Price, G., Wu, S.: Lost in translation: benchmarking commercial machine translation models for dyslexic-style text (2024)

45. Programme, L.L.: Information for all European standards for making information easy to read and understand. https://easy-to-read.inclusion-europe.eu/wp-content/uploads/2014/12/EN_Information_for_all.pdf
46. Reader, B.: BeeLine Reader, read faster and easier, all day long (2017). https://www.beelinereader.com/
47. Rello, L., Baeza-Yates, R., Bott, S., Saggion, H.: Simplify or help? Text simplification strategies for people with dyslexia. In: Proceedings of the 10th international cross-disciplinary conference on web accessibility, pp. 1–10 (2013)
48. Roitsch, J., Watson, S.M.: An overview of dyslexia: definition, characteristics, assessment, identification, and intervention. Sci. J. Educ. **7**(4), 81 (2019)
49. Sahoo, P., Singh, A.K., Saha, S., Jain, V., Mondal, S., Chadha, A.: A systematic survey of prompt engineering in large language models: techniques and applications. arXiv preprint arXiv:2402.07927 (2024)
50. Schaur, M., Koutny, R.: Dyslexia, reading/writing disorders: assistive technology and accessibility: Introduction to the special thematic session. In: Miesenberger, K., Peňáz, P., Kobayashi, M. (eds.) International Conference on Computers Helping People with Special Needs, pp. 269–274. Springer, Cham (2024). https://doi.org/10.1007/978-3-031-62849-8_33
51. Schicchi, D., Taibi, D.: Ai-driven inclusion: Exploring automatic text simplification and complexity evaluation for enhanced educational accessibility. In: Casalino, G., et al. (eds.) International Conference on Higher Education Learning Methodologies and Technologies Online. Springer, Cham (2023). https://doi.org/10.1007/978-3-031-67351-1_24
52. Snowling, M.J., Hulme, C.: Annual research review: reading disorders revisited-the critical importance of oral language. J. Child Psychol. Psychiatry **62**(5), 635–653 (2021)
53. Team, D.: Diffit, learning resources for all. https://web.diffit.me/
54. Team, G., et al.: Gemma: open models based on gemini research and technology. arXiv preprint arXiv:2403.08295 (2024)
55. texthelp: Claroread, help neurodiverse students to achieve more with reading and writing. https://www.texthelp.com/en-gb/solutions/dsa/claroread/
56. texthelp: Read&Write, help students understand and express themselves. https://www.texthelp.com/products/read-and-write-education/
57. Tunmer, W.E., Chapman, J.W.: Does set for variability mediate the influence of vocabulary knowledge on the development of word recognition skills? Scientific Studies of Reading (2012)
58. W3C Web Accessibility Initiative (WAI), E., (EOWG), O.W.G.: W3C web accessibility, introduction to web accessibility. https://www.w3.org/WAI/fundamentals/accessibility-intro/
59. Wery, J.J., Diliberto, J.A.: The effect of a specialized dyslexia font, opendyslexic, on reading rate and accuracy. Ann. Dyslexia **67**, 114–127 (2017)
60. Yan, L., et al.: Practical and ethical challenges of large language models in education: a systematic scoping review. Br. J. Edu. Technol. **55**(1), 90–112 (2024)
61. Yap, J.R., Aruthanan, T., Chin, M.: Artificial intelligence in dyslexia research and education: a scoping review. IEEE Access **13**, 7123–7134 (2025)

ASD-HI: A Parent-Child Interaction Dataset for Automated Assessment of Home Intervention

Zhaohui Li[1(✉)], Yusuf Akemoglu[1,2], Jincheng Lyu[3], Qingxiao Zheng[1], and Jinjun Xiong[1]

[1] Department of Computer Science and Engineering, University at Buffalo, Buffalo, USA
{zli253,qingxiao,jinjun}@buffalo.edu
[2] Department of Special Education, Duzce University, Duzce, Turkey
[3] The Pennsylvania State University, University Park, USA
jjl6992@psu.edu

Abstract. Home-based interventions are vital for supporting young children with autism spectrum disorder (ASD), yet many parents struggle to implement strategies effectively due to limited training. While specialists such as educators and speech-language pathologists provide guidance, real-time feedback outside professional settings remains scarce. To bridge this gap, we leverage advances in AI to support parents through automated assessment. However, training such AI systems requires robust data, which is currently limited. To address this, we created ASD-HI (Autism Spectrum Disorder - Home Intervention), a multimodal dataset comparing 473 real parent-child interaction videos across three families. ASD-HI supports two core tasks: 1) Strategy Detection, identifying the behavioral strategies parents use, and 2) Fidelity Assessment, assessing the fidelity with which these strategies are implemented. We also propose a prompting-based LLM pipeline as a reference approach. It achieves 74% recall and 50% precision for strategy detection and 60% accuracy for fidelity assessment. Our work lays a foundation for developing AI-driven tools to enhance home interventions and improve outcomes for children with special needs.

Keywords: Autism Spectrum Disorder · Large Language Models · Home-based Intervention · Early Intervention · Special Education

1 Introduction

Effective home-based interventions are critical in promoting the development of children with autism spectrum disorder (ASD), particularly within special education programs [19,26]. Parent participation and parent-implemented home-based interventions have been used to promote the social-emotional, social communication, and cognitive development of children with ASD [24]. However, many

A. I. Cristea et al. (Eds.): AIED 2025, LNAI 15877, pp. 48–62, 2025.
https://doi.org/10.1007/978-3-031-98414-3_4

Fig. 1. Examples of shared reading from the dataset, where parents use strategies (gestures, expressions, discussion) to engage children and build joint attention.

parents face substantial challenges implementing recommended interventions at home due to time constraints and insufficient training [4]. At the same time, special education professionals often struggle to provide continuous support beyond the classroom due to resource limitations and large caseloads [9]. These barriers highlight a critical gap in sustaining effective home-based interventions.

Educators widely use artificial intelligence (AI) tools like ChatGPT [20] to generate instructional materials, design interventions, and even conduct assessments in recent five years [14,29]. In special education, AI has been applied to automate child engagement assessment [28], create individualized interventions [17], and monitor progress for children with ASD [31,32]. Recent work also shows that LLMs can analyze ASD clinical conversations as well as, or better than, non-expert humans [12]. However, adoption in special education remains slower than in general education [16], due to the highly individualized nature of home-based interventions and the lack of high-quality data, compounded by ethical concerns in data collection [13].

To address these challenges, we introduce ASD-HI, a multi-modal dataset derived from real-world parent-child interaction videos (Fig. 1), designed to support AI-driven monitoring of home-based interventions. The data were originally collected during the i-PiECS (Internet-based Parent-implemented Early Communication Strategies-Storybook) project [1,2]. i-PiECS trained parents in naturalistic communication strategies (NCT) during storybook reading with their children with ASD. Approved by IRB, in i-PiECS, ASD experts manually evaluated parent recordings and provided detailed feedback. Building on these annotations, ASD-HI automates the process via two tasks: *Strategy Detection*, identifying NCT strategies used, and *Fidelity Assessment*, evaluating how well they are implemented. To convert i-PiECS data into AI tasks, we aligned human-annotated transcripts with video using an automatic speech recognition (ASR) model to establish ground-truth time frames for Strategy Detection. Discrepancies were resolved through additional human annotation to ensure reliability. The final ASD-HI dataset includes 478 labeled instances (4.25 h), split into 239 training, 120 validation, and 119 test samples.

We propose potential solutions for strategy detection and fidelity assessment, building on recent breakthroughs in AI and utilizing multi-modal learning techniques to integrate video, audio, and contextual data. To detect the NCT strategy, we first employed the Whisper ASR model [22] to obtain a transcript of the entire video. Next, we utilized JanusPro, a visual LLM [7], to generate a video description for each sentence in the transcript, allowing us to extract relevant visual information. We then developed a greedy search algorithm (refer to Algorithm 1) to identify all parent strategies in the video, using expert-designed LLM prompts alongside the transcripts and video descriptions. We formulated fidelity assessment as a video classification problem and designed a classification prompt using LLMs, incorporating expert-designed prompts with the transcripts and video descriptions. Our experiments assessed various pre-trained baseline approaches, including SOTA video understanding and classification models. The results demonstrate that our method, which combines transcript analysis with video description classification using GPT-4o, achieves the best performance, yielding around a 60% F1 score and accuracy. In the discussion section, we conduct an error analysis to highlight the main challenge of this task: identifying joint attention between parent and child.

ASD-HI provides training data for AI algorithms to automate the assessment of home-based interventions, enhance parental engagement, and improve educational outcomes for children with special needs. We have two main contributions: We created ASD-HI, the first large-scale, multimodal video dataset focused on assessing parent-child interactions in home-based interventions for children with ASD. The dataset includes 478 video recordings of reading sessions involving autistic children and their parents, providing high-quality, reliably annotated data. This resource is invaluable for research in computer vision and special education, facilitating advancements in AI-driven behavior analysis. We developed efficient AI pipeline solutions that utilize multimodal LLMs to automate the identification and evaluation of NCT strategies used by parents and children. By bridging the gap between AI techniques and domain expertise through LLM prompting, this pipeline supports scalable home-based ASD interventions.

2 Related Works

Recent multi-modal datasets for ASD primarily focus on AI-driven diagnosis using computer vision and machine learning techniques. [10,11] provide image-based ASD datasets for prediction using AI models. [8] introduced a dataset containing 22 h of social interaction videos for autism risk assessment, though it is not publicly available. The dataset proposed in [33] includes 1,837 video sequences for gesture analysis in ASD detection. [6] compiled a dataset of 82 children's videos, using deep learning-based head-related feature extraction for ASD diagnosis. [23] proposed a dataset with 2,467 videos, incorporating frame convolutional and attention map features for ASD classification.

Despite these advancements, there is a critical lack of datasets focusing on parent-child interactions in home-based ASD interventions. The Parent-Teacher Interaction Study [21] examines parental involvement in the education of individuals with ASD, highlighting the impact of stress and well-being, but does not include direct interaction recordings. The Engagnition Dataset [15] captures children's engagement in a serious game, incorporating physiological and behavioral data with usability assessments from parents. The DREAM dataset comprises over 3,000 robot-assisted therapy sessions, totaling more than 300 h, to assess educational and therapeutic interventions for children with ASD, though it primarily focuses on structured interactions with robots rather than human-human engagement. Most of these existing datasets emphasize child-centric behaviors, such as reactions to stimuli or motor tasks, rather than dyadic parent-child or teacher-child interactions. Additionally, studies such as [21] rely on questionnaire-based assessments rather than multi-modal recordings of real-world interactions.

There are only two video datasets that focus on parent-child interactions in ASD domain: 1. The Autism Diagnostic Observation Schedule, Second Edition (ADOS-2) Module 3 (ADOSMod3) dataset includes recordings used to assess social behaviors in verbally fluent individuals, comprising 170 people diagnosed with autism and 120 with non-ASD conditions [18]. 2. The Remote Natural Language Sampling (Remote-NLS) dataset [5] consists of 89 Zoom video recordings, each capturing a 15-minute interaction between a parent and their child, aged 4 to 7 years, with ASD. However, both of these datasets focus on clinical settings rather than home-based interventions, and they primarily target child behavior rather than parent-child interactions. To the best of our knowledge, the ASD-HI dataset is the first to provide video data of parent-child interactions specifically designed for home-based ASD interventions.

3 Dataset Creation

Since there is currently no video dataset designed explicitly for the automated evaluation of home-based interventions, and given that both parents and specialists require additional support in this area, we propose the ASD-HI dataset. This dataset features expert-labeled annotations intended to train AI algorithms that can help assess and provide feedback on parental intervention strategies. To achieve this, we have developed two tasks: Strategy Detection and Fidelity Assessment, to bridge the gap between advanced AI techniques and the expertise of special educators, aiming to facilitate research in AI-driven solutions for special education and improve outcomes (Table 1).

Table 1. Data statistics of fidelity scores across parent strategies

Fidelity	Modeling	Mand-Model	Time Delay	Summary
4	36	146	49	231
3	14	66	12	92
2	25	81	11	117
1	4	28	6	38
Summary	79	321	78	478

3.1 Backgound

The data for these two tasks were collected from real-world video recordings of parent-child interactions within the i-PiECS project, an evidence-based intervention program for children with ASD and their families [1,2]. i-PiECS stands for internet-based parent-implemented early communication interventions storybook. In the i-PiECS program, parents are trained and coached to implement NCT strategies during storybook reading sessions with their children with ASD, fostering developmental progress through structured, clinically validated evidence-based strategies. Across the i-PiECS studies, data were primarily collected through Zoom videoconferencing, where parents recorded their shared reading sessions using NCT strategies. ASD-HI focuses on three key NCT strategies: modeling, mand-model, and time delay. **Modeling** is a teaching strategy where the parent models words, phrases, or gestures, expecting the child to imitate. For example, the parent might label an object by saying *"Blue ball!"* while pointing to a picture of a blue ball, encouraging the child to respond by repeating. **Mand-Model** is similar but includes a verbal prompt in the form of a question, choice, or directive. For instance, the parent may ask, *"Is this an apple or a banana?"* or instruct *"Say 'more please."'* Unlike modeling, the mand-model approach explicitly requires a response. Simply labeling an object expecting imitation (e.g., *"Ball."*) or asking a yes/no question (e.g., *"Is this a gorilla?"*) does not fit this strategy. **Time-Delay** encourages the child to initiate communication by pausing within familiar routines or activities. For example, while reading a book, a parent may leave a sentence incomplete, such as *"Edwin dropped one large box of ___,"* and wait expectantly for the child to complete it. Similarly, during a turn-taking activity, the parent might hold a page without turning it, waiting for the child to say *"My turn!"* Each of these strategies distinctly fosters language development by shaping how children engage in communication.

3.2 Task Design

The first task in the ASD-HI dataset is **Strategy Detection**. This task serves as a foundational step, without accurate segmentation, subsequent evaluation and feedback mechanisms cannot be reliably applied. We labeled 478 parent strategy uses with *start-time*, *end-time*, and *strategy label*. The strategy label has three classes of NCT strategies we mentioned before: *Modeling*, *Mand-Model*, and *Time Delay*. The goal of the strategy detection task is to identify the use of NCT strategies in full-length reading sessions. The output consists of the session *start-time*, *end-time*, and *strategy label*. We provide a dataset from three families, with the objective of detecting all 478 parent strategy uses in 48 reading sessions, including their respective start-time, end-time, and strategy type. To evaluate performance, we propose two metrics: *Coverage*: Measures the proportion of correctly detected NCT strategies used among all labeled data; *Accuracy*: Assesses how precise the detections are.

After identifying all strategy use instances, another AI algorithm is required to evaluate how effectively parents executed the NCT strategies. This evaluation is represented by a fidelity score. To achieve this, we introduce a second task, **Fidelity Assessment**, formulating it as a four-way classification problem. For ease of machine learning model training, we separate this task from the strategy detection task. We utilize the 478 labeled parent strategy video clips from the strategy detection task (by segmenting the reading session videos by start and end time label), along with the ground truth fidelity scores provided in the i-PiECS annotations. The evaluation metrics for this task follow standard machine learning classification practices, utilizing the F1 score and Accuracy.

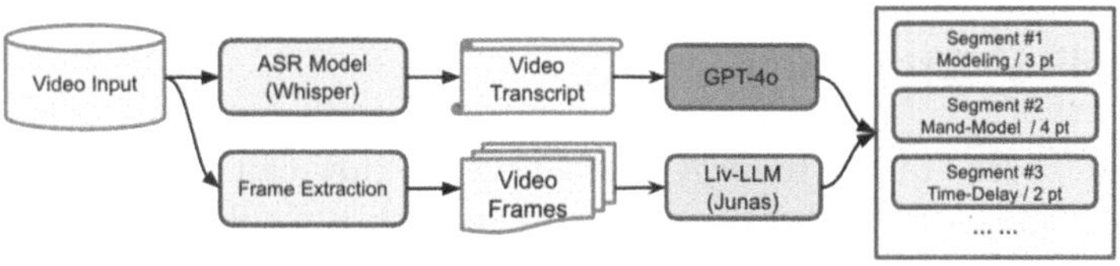

Fig. 2. Multi-modal pipeline for strategy detection.

3.3 Data Annotation

Parents in i-PiECS completed online training modules and received telepractice coaching via videoconferencing. It used a single-case multiple-baseline design and a 4-point fidelity scale to evaluate strategy implementation. Parent-child reading sessions were video recorded, and trained raters annotated strategy use and child responses by timestamp. Fidelity for modeling, mand-model, and time-delay strategies was rated from 1 (low) to 4 (high) based on criteria from [3], such as establishing joint attention, presenting the strategy, pausing, and giving feedback. Scores decreased if key steps were missed.

The original i-PiECS annotation has high reliability, primary raters annotated all assigned parent-child interaction videos by manually coding NCT strategies and child communication, while blinded secondary raters independently coded a subset, ensuring inter-rater reliability through discussions and achieving over 90% agreement. To evaluate the data reliability, the ASD-HI data annotation process begins with raw video footage paired with expert human-coded transcripts from i-PiECS. We leveraged ASR models to align i-PiECS transcripts with video timelines, segmenting recordings into shorter clips. Each clip corresponds to a NCT strategy, labeled with the specific communication strategy employed and a fidelity score reflecting adherence to i-PiECS protocols. During this step, we identified several missing lines in the i-PiECS annotated transcripts compared to ASR-generated transcripts, indicating potential inconsistencies in the original human-coded data. In addition, we conducted an additional round of human annotation. A trained computer scientist compared human annotations with machine-generated labels. If inconsistencies were detected, a separate ASD researcher reviewed and finalized the labeling. There are two main reasons for incorporating algorithmic checks in transcript validation and video segmentation: First, by using ASR models, we can assess the consistency and accuracy of human-coded transcripts from i-PiECS. If discrepancies exist, ASR can help identify them. Second, The i-PiECS dataset does not pre-segment reading session videos into labeled clips. Since video annotation is time-intensive, a hybrid approach where machine-generated labels are first applied and then verified by humans, optimizes efficiency while maintaining annotation accuracy. The data for each task is split into approximately 50% training, 25% validation, and 25% test sets. Detailed coding protocols and the dataset are available on our website[1].

4 Baseline Approach

In ASD-HI, there are two main AI challenges: 1) How can we identify strategy-specific segments within lengthy videos? This task is challenging because these segments often lack dramatic scene changes or clear verbal cues that indicate a transition. 2) How can we evaluate the fidelity of the strategies used by parents? This requires analyzing joint attention between the parent and child. However, there is no visual model that effectively captures this subtle visual pattern.

To tackle the strategy detection task, we first examined the field of video shot detection, which aims to identify and annotate distinct segments within a video by detecting abrupt shot changes [25]. The objective is to automatically pinpoint moments in a video where visual or thematic content shifts significantly, indicating the start or end of a shot. However, in our context, there are no substantial scene changes between strategies, rendering existing SOTA methods ineffective. In addition, the detection of strategy mainly relies on verbal conversation information. Consequently, we devised a baseline approach that leverages cues from the transcript and joint attention signals in the visual data. We propose a pipeline for integrated strategy detection that utilizes ASR and multi-modal LLM prompting. The pipeline comprises two stages: *Preprocessing* and *Processing* (details are provided in Algorithm 1).

In the preprocessing stage, we extract audio from the input videos to generate transcripts $T = \{s_1, s_2, \ldots, s_{|T|}\}$, where each sentence s_i is associated with a start time and an end time. This transcription is performed by the pre-trained Whisper model [22]. Meanwhile, video frames are sampled at a rate of 1 frame per second for visual analysis. Next, we employ Janus-Pro-1B [7] to generate visual descriptions for each frame by a prompt designed by ASD exert (see Table 2), $V = \{v_1, v_2, \ldots, v_{|V|}\}$. We deliberately avoid using end-to-end video understanding models (e.g., VideoLLaMA [30]) for two reasons: (1) current models struggle to capture fine-grained interaction details essential for our task, such as parent-child joint attention; and (2) the recorded sessions often exceed two minutes in duration, making it impractical to generate a single comprehensive description to check joint attention. We chose Janus-Pro-1B for its advanced performance, compact model size, and open-source availability.

[1] https://asdhi.xlabub.com/.

Table 2. Prompts for describing parent-child interaction videos and images.

Prompt A: Generate an Image Description for Video Frame

<image_placeholder>

This image is from a parent-child interaction video. Please provide a detailed description of the image, focusing on the following aspects:

- **Parent's Actions:** Describe what the parent is doing, including any notable gestures or expressions.
- **Child's Reactions:** Detail the child's behavior or reactions.
- **Joint Attention:** Identify whether the parent and child are looking at the same object. Provide evidence from the image, then explicitly state either:
  - `*Yes, they have joint attention.*`
  - `*No, they do not have joint attention.*`
- `Visual Cues: Books or toys and other visual elements present in the frame.`

Prompt B: Summarize Video Descriptions from Frame Image Descriptions

You are provided with a series of detailed frame descriptions from a parent-child interaction video. Each frame description focuses on the following key elements: **Parent's Actions:**, **Child's Reactions: Joint Attention:**, **Visual Cues:** Books or toys and other visual elements present in the frame.

Your task is to combine these individual frame descriptions into a single comprehensive summary. Present whether the parent and child are looking at the same object. Provide evidence from the descriptions, then explicitly state either:

- `'Yes, they have joint attention.'`
- `'No, they do not have joint attention.'`

Please respond **only** in the following format (without additional commentary):

1. **Reasoning**: <your reasoning based on the evidence>
2. **Fidelity**: `'Yes, they have joint attention.' | 'No, they do not have joint attention.'`

Frame Descriptions:

`<Concatenated frame descriptions here>`

In the processing stage, we apply a greedy search algorithm (Algorithm 1) to identify all *strategy groups*, i.e., sequences of sentences representing an NCT strategy instance. Typically, a strategy group comprises three main sentences: a *parenting order*, a *child response*, and *parental feedback*, although additional sentences may also be included. The greedy search operates by scanning from the first sentence; once it detects a clue sentence indicating the start of a strategy group, it continues checking subsequent sentences to see if they belong to the same group. When it encounters a sentence that does not fit, the search terminates that group and resumes from the new sentence. This approach reduces computational complexity while maintaining robust accuracy.

Recognizing that fidelity assessment is a video classification task, we reviewed several SOTA classification models as baselines, including Transformer-based classifiers and pre-trained LLMs, to evaluate performance across different modalities. However, as the results shown in the section (5), these methods did not perform well due to the lack of pre-trained parent-child interaction data. We decided to use the few-shot prompting classification method from the LLM, as described in Table 3 prompt D. We maintained the same transcript and video description that were used in the strategy detection task. This approach was chosen for its ease of use and the extensive pre-training it has undergone across various knowledge domains. Additionally, integrating fidelity assessment into the existing strategy detection pipeline allows for a seamless, fully automated system that performs both tasks simultaneously, as illustrated in Fig. 2.

5 Experiments

This section presents the results of our baseline approach on the ASD-HI evaluation set. We conducted two sets of experiments to evaluate our baseline methods. First, we assessed our strategy detection pipeline through an ablation study using two different modality approaches. Then, we evaluated our prompt-based fidelity assessment method against SOTA baseline models.

For strategy detection, we designed our pipeline as described in Sect. 4. It incorporates two modality approaches: *Transcript-only* and *Video Description+Transcript*. The *Transcript-only* method relies solely on audio transcripts to identify the strategy sentences, while the *Video Description+Transcript* method combines both the transcript and video descriptions. The video-only approach is not applicable here because it depends entirely on video descriptions without transcripts; however, identifying the strategy requires verbal communication. We utilize the GPT-4o API for classifying the strategy sentences, and Janus-Pro-1B is employed to generate the video descriptions. In all prompts, the temperature is set to zero to ensure consistency and reproducibility.

Table 4 presents the results on the ASD-HI validation set. Both pipeline methods show medium-level performance. The results indicate that the Transcript-

Algorithm 1 The Greedy Strategy Search Algorithm

1: **Input:** Transcript sentence set $T = \{s_1, s_2, \ldots, s_{|T|}\}$, every s has an start time and end time
2: **Input:** Video Frame description set $V = \{v_1, v_2, \ldots, v_{|V|}\}$
3: Initialize result set: $O \leftarrow \emptyset$, set $i \leftarrow 1$
4: **while** $i \leq |T|$ **do**
5: Compute video description d_i for sentence s_i using LLM method α (Prompt A&B, Table 2):

$$d_i = \alpha\Big(v_{s_i[\text{start\_time}]}, v_{s_i[\text{start\_time+1}]}, \ldots, v_{s_i[\text{end\_time-1}]}, v_{s_i[\text{end\_time}]}\Big)$$

6: Classify s_i into NCT strategies {Modeling, Mand-model, Time-delay, None}:

$$NCT(s_i) = \beta(s_i, d_i), \text{where } \beta \text{ is a LLM Classifier (Prompt C in Table 3)}$$

7: Skip the sentence if it does not use any strategy:

$$\text{if } NCT(s_i) = \text{None}, \quad i \leftarrow i + 1, \quad \text{continue}$$

8: If s_i is using a strategy, initialize a strategy group: $g \leftarrow [s_i]$, and set $j \leftarrow i + 1$.
9: If $\theta(g, s_j)$ is **True**, append s_j to g and increment $j = j + 1$.
10: Repeat step 9 until $\theta(g, s_j)$ returns **False**, and append $g = [s_i, \ldots, s_{j-1}]$ to O.
11: **end while**
12: **return** O

Table 3. Prompts with examples for classifying and evaluating NCT strategies. We show simplified prompts due to the space limitation.

Prompt C: Classify the NCT Strategies with Transcript and Video Description

System Prompt:

You are an expert in classifying parent-child intervention strategies. Your task is to read a line of transcript and video description and categorize the NCT strategy into one of three strategies:

1) **Modeling** - Parent demonstrates a thing in the book by saying one or two words. - Modeling can't be a sentence longer than five words. It focuses only on meaningful noun words that represent a thing in the book. - **Examples**: - Referring to a ball picture in a book, the parent says, "Blue ball!" expecting the child to imitate. - ... - **Non-Examples**: - Asking, "What do you have?" (This is a Mand-Model.) ... ... 2) **Mand-model** - ... ... 3) **Time Delay** - ... ... **User Prompt:**

Classify the following text according to the categories above:

- `Video Description: "{description}"` - `Transcript: "{text}"`

Respond only with "Modeling", "Mand-model", "Time Delay" or "None".

Prompt D: Classify NCT Strategy use into Fidelity Scores

You are a Speech-Language Pathologist evaluating a parent's use of the **Modeling** strategy in a parent-child interaction.

Fidelity Scoring (1 to 4):

Award +1 point for each of the following:

1. Presenting a verbal or gestural model; 2. Establishing joint attention; 3. Waiting ~3 s for the child's response; 4. Providing verbal feedback that is **NOT** a simple "Yes/No" question

Now, read the following **transcript**, **video description**, and **waiting time** to evaluate based on the fidelity criteria above.

Provided Information:

`{video_description} {transcript}`

Response Format:

Please respond **only** in the following format (without additional commentary):

1. **Reasoning**: `<your explanation>` 2. **Fidelity**: `<1 | 2 | 3 | 4>`

only method achieves the best performance, covering 73.68% of NCT strategies used in a reading session. This suggests that it effectively detects most strategy usages. However, its accuracy is only 50.21%, highlighting the need for more precise detection in future tasks. Comparing *Transcript-only* with *Video Description + Transcript* serves as an ablation experiment to assess the contributions of different modalities. The results support the hypothesis that strategy use primarily relies on verbal conversation. Incorporating additional visual information, such as gestures and background details, does not enhance performance within our experimental setup.

Table 4. Strategy detection performance by coverage and accuracy

Strategy Detection Method	Coverage	Accuracy
Transcript-only	73.68%	50.21%
Video Description+Transcript	68.42%	39.39%

For fidelity assessment task, we compared with SOTA video classification with our prompting method via GPT families. We employed several video classification models as baselines, including training a transformer-based classifier and video LLM prompting. Below, we provide an overview of the baselines used in our experiments: **VideoMAE**: A SOTA performance video classification model with video masked autoencoder on several benchmarks [27]. We trained this on trainset, it can only trains this masked autoencoders on video frames data. **Transcript**: This baseline follows a two-stage process. First, we use the whisper model to extract transcripts from the videos. These transcripts are then used to train a BERT-based classifier, enabling classification based on spoken content. **Video + Audio**: This baseline also follows a two-stage process. First, we use Video-LLaMA [30] to generate video descriptions. These descriptions are then combined with ASR transcripts to train a BERT-based classifier, enabling classification based on both vision and audio content. **Video-LLaMA**: The method utilizes a prompting approach with Video-LLaMA, a LLM designed for video question answering with SOTA performance. This model leverages advanced language understanding to analyze video content based on specific prompts.

For our GPT prompting method, we also employ Janus-Pro-1B to generate video descriptions. We design three classification prompts for three different strategies; here, we only show the Modeling prompt due to the space limitation (see Table 3. Additionally, we evaluate classification performance across different GPT models, including GPT-4, GPT-4o, and the latest GPT-o1. Furthermore, we investigate performance differences across different modalities, comparing Transcript-Only versus Video + Transcript conditions (Fig. 3).

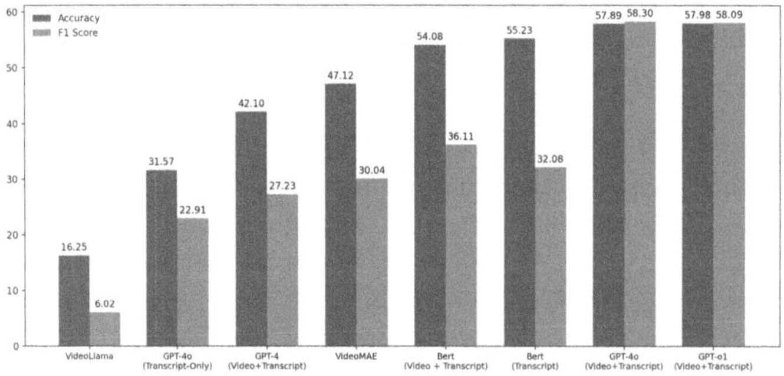

Fig. 3. Fidelity assessment: Accuracy and F1 by different baseline models

As shown by the F1 and Accuracy scores in Table 3, our prompting method using GPT models generally outperforms other SOTA classifiers, particularly when compared to Video-LLaMA. The Video-LLaMA demonstrates poor performance, achieving only 16% accuracy. This could be attributed to the fact that the model is trained on different tasks and does not generalize well to our specific task. In contrast, text-based LLMs such as GPTs exhibit strong generalization capabilities. Among the various GPT prompting methods, using video and transcript together outperforms the Transcript-Only approach, as demonstrated in the GPT-4o experiments. Both GPT-4o and GPT-o1 (Video+Transcript) achieve the highest performance levels, exceeding the strongest baseline, Bert (Video+Transcript), by at least 4% in accuracy and 12% in F1 score. These results highlight the challenges of training a four-way video classification model for this task. A future direction is fine-tuning LLMs to improve performance.

In summary, our method demonstrates competitive performance in both Strategy Detection and Fidelity Assessment tasks. Notably, our prompting method achieves significant gains in fidelity classification compared to SOTA models. Since our approach does not require additional training, it can generalize well and is readily applicable to real-world scenarios. However, its effectiveness heavily depends on expert-designed prompts, and its performance still falls short of human-level accuracy. Future work should focus on fine-tuning LLMs or optimizing prompts to achieve further improvements.

6 Discussion and Conclusion

Even though our algorithm has achieved relatively high performance in both tasks, several challenges remain for future research. In strategy detection, our algorithm struggles with accurate identification, resulting in only 50% accuracy. This limitation arises from the inherent complexity of multimodal tasks and the error accumulation of greedy search. For example, if the algorithm incorrectly identifies a strategy that is not actually present, but that misidentified instance contains part of the next strategy usage sentence, it can lead to failures in subsequent detections. In fidelity assessment, our error analysis was driven by discrepancies between predicted labels and ground truth labels. We found that, in many cases, our algorithm systematically underestimates fidelity scores, often predicting values one point lower than the ground truth. For example, a data point with a ground truth fidelity score of 4 was frequently predicted as 3. The algorithm provided the following explanation: *"Reasoning: The parent used a question prompt and waited 3 s, then provided verbal feedback beyond yes/no. However, they did not consistently maintain joint attention. Fidelity: 3."* Upon further inspection of the generated video description, we observed: *"Across most frames, the parent and child are shown looking at the same book, indicating joint attention while reading. However, in a later frame, the child focuses on a stuffed animal while the parent looks at the child, and in another frame, the child looks at the book while the parent looks at the child. These instances show that they are not always looking at the same object. No, they do not have joint attention."* The issue here is that the AI model rigidly evaluates joint attention across all video frames. If joint attention is absent in even a few frames, the AI fails to award the joint attention point. However, human raters are less strict and typically consider joint attention established if it occurs predominantly during the interaction. This error case highlights a fundamental challenge: controlling AI to apply human-like judgment criteria, especially when analyzing multi-modal data. Future work should focus on aligning AI evaluation strategies with human decision-making processes to reduce systematic discrepancies.

Our baseline approach has other limitations. First, we only tested the GPT family of LLMs, as its API is readily accessible and easy to use. Other LLMs require different formats and integrations, which we plan to explore in future work. Second, our prompt was designed by ASD experts, but we did not apply prompt optimization or fine-tune the model on the training set. Future research should investigate whether tailored fine-tuning or systematic prompt engineering could improve performance. Third, our model's accuracy remains limited, achieving only 50% in strategy detection, indicating the need for further refinement. Finally, dataset size is a constraint, limiting the ability to fully optimize our models. In fidelity classification, the LLM prompting method outperformed our trained classifier, suggesting that additional labeled data is necessary for improving model generalization. We will continue expanding and refining the dataset to establish a more robust resource for child behavior research.

Conclusion. We introduced ASD-HI, a new video dataset featuring real-world recordings of parent-child interactions during home-based interventions. The dataset includes accurately labeled data from human annotators, facilitating the study of automated evaluation and feedback for these interventions. We presented two key tasks: strategy detection and fidelity assessment, which are intended for training and evaluating AI algorithms. Furthermore, we established baseline systems for both tasks. Looking ahead, our future work will focus on refining the annotations with more detailed labels, developing a robust evaluation framework, and organizing a competition to encourage wider participation and maximize impact.

Acknowledgments. This work is supported, in part, by the National Science Foundation under Grant 2229873 (AI4ExceptionalEd) and U.S. Department of Education under Grant R305C240046 (CELaRAI). Any opinions, findings and conclusions or recommendations expressed in this material are those of the author(s) and do not necessarily reflect the views of the sponsors.

References

1. Akemoglu, Y., Hinton, V., Laroue, D., Jefferson, V.: A parent-implemented shared reading intervention via telepractice. J. Early Interv. **44**(2), 190–210 (2022)
2. Akemoğlu, Y., Laroue, D., Kudesey, C., Stahlman, M.: A module-based telepractice intervention for parents of children with developmental disabilities. J. Autism Dev. Disord. **52**(12), 5177–5190 (2022)
3. Akemoglu, Y., Tomeny, K.R.: A parent-implemented shared-reading intervention to promote communication skills of preschoolers with autism spectrum disorder. J. Autism Dev. Disord. **51**(8), 2974–2987 (2021)
4. Burke, M.M., Goldman, S.E.: Special education advocacy among culturally and linguistically diverse families. J. Res. Spec. Educ. Needs **18**, 3–14 (2018)
5. Butler, L.K., et al.: Remote natural language sampling of parents and children with autism spectrum disorder: role of activity and language level. Front. Commun. **7**, 820564 (2022)

6. Cai, M., Li, M., Xiong, Z., Zhao, P., Li, E., Tang, J.: An advanced deep learning framework for video-based diagnosis of ASD. In: Wang, L., Dou, Q., Fletcher, P.T., Speidel, S., Li, S. (eds.) International Conference on Medical Image Computing and Computer-Assisted Intervention, pp. 434–444. Springer, Cham (2022). https://doi.org/10.1007/978-3-031-16440-8_42
7. Chen, X., et al.: Janus-pro: Unified multimodal understanding and generation with data and model scaling. arXiv preprint arXiv:2501.17811 (2025)
8. Chong, E., et al.: Detecting gaze towards eyes in natural social interactions and its use in child assessment. In: Proceedings of the ACM on Interactive, Mobile, Wearable and Ubiquitous Technologies, vol. 1, no. 3, pp. 1–20 (2017)
9. Dawson-Squibb, J.J., Davids, E.L., Harrison, A.J., Molony, M.A., de Vries, P.J.: Parent education and training for autism spectrum disorders: scoping the evidence. Autism **24**(1), 7–25 (2020)
10. Duan, H., et al.: A dataset of eye movements for the children with autism spectrum disorder. In: Proceedings of the 10th ACM Multimedia Systems Conference, pp. 255–260 (2019)
11. Elbattah, M.: Visualization of eye-tracking scan path in autism spectrum disorder: image dataset. In: Proceedings of the 12th International Conference on Health Informatics, Prague, Czech Republic, pp. 22–24 (2019)
12. Feng, T., et al.: Can generic LLMs help analyze child-adult interactions involving children with autism in clinical observation? arXiv preprint arXiv:2411.10761 (2024)
13. Holmes, W.: Artificial intelligence in education: promises and implications for teaching and learning. Center for Curriculum Redesign (2019)
14. Kasneci, E., et al.: ChatGPT for good? On opportunities and challenges of large language models for education. Learn. Individ. Differ. **103**, 102274 (2023)
15. Kim, W., Seong, M., Kim, K.J., Kim, S.: Engagnition: a multi-dimensional dataset for engagement recognition of children with autism spectrum disorder. Sci. Data **11**(1), 299 (2024)
16. Kotsi, S., Handrinou, S., Iatraki, G., Soulis, S.G.: A review of artificial intelligence interventions for students with autism spectrum disorder. Disabilities **5**(1), 7 (2025)
17. Kulik, J.A., Fletcher, J.D.: Effectiveness of intelligent tutoring systems: a meta-analytic review. Rev. Educ. Res. **86**(1), 42–78 (2016)
18. Lord, C., et al.: The autism diagnostic observation schedule–generic: a standard measure of social and communication deficits associated with the spectrum of autism. J. Autism Dev. Disord. **30**, 205–223 (2000)
19. McWilliam, R.: Working with Families of Young Children with Special Needs. Guilford Press (2010)
20. OpenAI: Chatgpt: language model for natural language processing (2023). https://openai.com/chatgpt. Accessed 20 Feb 2025
21. Đorđević, M., Glumbić, N., Memisevic, H., Brojčin, B., Krstov, A.: Parent-teacher interactions, family stress, well-being, and parental depression as contributing factors to parental involvement mechanisms in education of children with autism. Int. J. Dev. Disabil. **68**(6), 838–849 (2022)
22. Radford, A., Kim, J.W., Xu, T., Brockman, G., McLeavey, C., Sutskever, I.: Robust speech recognition via large-scale weak supervision. In: International Conference on Machine Learning, pp. 28492–28518. PMLR (2023)
23. Serna-Aguilera, M., Nguyen, X.B., Seo, H.S., Luu, K.: A novel dataset for video-based autism classification leveraging extra-stimulatory behavior. arXiv preprint arXiv:2409.04598 (2024)

24. Sheridan, S.M., Knoche, L.L., Edwards, C.P., Bovaird, J.A., Kupzyk, K.A.: Parent engagement and school readiness: effects of the getting ready intervention on preschool children's social-emotional competencies. Early Educ. Dev. **21**(1), 125–156 (2010)
25. Soucek, T., Lokoc, J.: Transnet v2: an effective deep network architecture for fast shot transition detection. In: Proceedings of the 32nd ACM International Conference on Multimedia, pp. 11218–11221 (2024)
26. Sukkar, H., Dunst, C.J., Kirkby, J.: Early Childhood Intervention: Working with Families of Young Children with Special Needs. Taylor & Francis (2016)
27. Tong, Z., Song, Y., Wang, J., Wang, L.: VideoMAE: masked autoencoders are data-efficient learners for self-supervised video pre-training. Adv. Neural. Inf. Process. Syst. **35**, 10078–10093 (2022)
28. Whitehill, J., Serpell, Z., Lin, Y.C., Foster, A., Movellan, J.R.: The faces of engagement: automatic recognition of student engagement from facial expressions. IEEE Trans. Affect. Comput. **5**(1), 86–98 (2014)
29. Zawacki-Richter, O., Marín, V.I., Bond, M., Gouverneur, F.: Systematic review of research on artificial intelligence applications in higher education-where are the educators? Int. J. Educ. Technol. High. Educ. **16**(1), 1–27 (2019)
30. Zhang, H., Li, X., Bing, L.: Video-LLaMA: an instruction-tuned audio-visual language model for video understanding. In: Feng, Y., Lefever, E. (eds.) Proceedings of the 2023 Conference on Empirical Methods in Natural Language Processing: System Demonstrations, pp. 543–553. Association for Computational Linguistics, Singapore (2023). https://doi.org/10.18653/v1/2023.emnlp-demo.49
31. Zheng, Q., et al.: Towards responsible use of large multi-modal AI to analyze human social behaviors. In: Companion Publication of the 2024 Conference on Computer-Supported Cooperative Work and Social Computing, pp. 663–665 (2024)
32. Zheng, Q., Rabbani, P., Lin, Y.R., Mansour, D., Huang, Y.: Soap. AI: a collaborative tool for documenting human behavior in videos through multimodal generative AI. In: Companion Publication of the 2024 Conference on Computer-Supported Cooperative Work and Social Computing, pp. 87–90 (2024)
33. Zunino, A., et al.: Video gesture analysis for autism spectrum disorder detection. In: International Conference on Pattern Recognition (ICPR) (2018)

AIBAT: AI Behavior Analysis Tool for Teacher-Driven Contextual Evaluation of Language Models in Education

Shamya Karumbaiah(✉), Yaxuan Yin, and Aayush Bharadwaj

University of Wisconsin–Madison, Madison, WI 53706, USA
{shamya.karumbaiah,yaxuan.yin,abbharadwaj}@wisc.edu

Abstract. With the increasing reliance of AIED on opaque, black-box scaffolds such as large language models to support student learning, there is a growing concern about their limitations when used in diverse pedagogical contexts. This opacity often undermines educators' trust and shapes their perceptions, contributing to resistance toward the adoption of AI scaffolds in schools. To address these challenges, we developed AIBAT, a workflow and system designed to support educators in auditing and critically evaluating the potential benefits and harms of AI systems within their specific pedagogical contexts (e.g., subject matter, grade level, English proficiency). With AIBAT, teachers can specify expected behaviors—i.e., what they anticipate the AI scaffold should do—and test the system against those expectations. We conducted an exploratory user study with 14 teachers to examine how AIBAT facilitates the identification and sensemaking of AI-related risks, while enabling educators to use evidence to calibrate their trust in AI scaffolds. Our findings reveal that teachers valued the ability to engage with AI decisions rather than passively accepting them, describing the process as a "conversation" that enhanced transparency, trust, and a sense of control. We identify key opportunities to foster meaningful user engagement in AI auditing processes and discuss broader implications for promoting responsible and effective teacher participation in the evaluation and deployment of AI systems in educational settings.

Keywords: Large Language models · Evaluation · Teachers · Context · Behavior analysis · Scaffolds · Responsible AI in education

1 Introduction

An equitable and synergistic use of AI for scaffolding in classrooms must acknowledge differences in pedagogical contexts. In a classroom, scaffolding is often distributed across materials, peers, technology, and the teacher [16]. AI systems that scaffold student learning can free up teachers' time, allowing them to focus on students who need support the most [22,23]. Hence, AI systems designed to

A. I. Cristea et al. (Eds.): AIED 2025, LNAI 15877, pp. 63–76, 2025.
https://doi.org/10.1007/978-3-031-98414-3_5

work synergistically with teacher practices are more effective [24]. Since pedagogical contexts vary, so too do scaffolding needs and priorities—as well as teachers' definitions of system failure.

However, AI evaluation typically assumes universal deployment, ignoring differences in contexts. Indeed, the dominant approach for AI evaluation (i.e., generalization estimation on test data) often tends to be an overestimation of real-world performance [20,29]. In most cases, the test data used to evaluate generalization poorly represent the range of real-world scenarios and often contain the same biases as the training data. Even when tested with data from the deployment context, the population distribution may shift over time [17].

Recent research in natural language processing (NLP)—a kind of AI system involving computational models of text—has shown that engaging stakeholders to analyze NLP model behaviors (in conditions relevant to their context) was effective in identifying failures that are likely to go unnoticed in tests for generalization [8,9]. Stakeholders with limited prior experience in AI were able to identify failures in key capabilities such as fairness (e.g., biases against linguistic minorities), robustness to perturbations (e.g., spelling errors), and domain-specific vocabulary when evaluating NLP systems used for language translation, content moderation, and question-answering.

Although analyzing AI system behavior in context offers a promising avenue for enabling stakeholders to interrogate AI black boxes, we still don't know: (1) what value this approach holds for stakeholders of educational AI such as teachers; (2) how we could align it better with teachers' contextual needs; (3) how to build teacher expertise and agency in identifying beneficial and harmful scaffolding behaviors; and (4) how it impacts teacher trust and practices with AI scaffolds. Several forms of AI systems already exist for distributed scaffolding (e.g., NLP systems for writing feedback, conversational agents, AI tutors) and now with the advent of generative AI, teachers are faced with the difficult choice of trusting these advanced technologies to take advantage of them. Trusting such systems is especially difficult as they become less transparent and raise equity concerns for minoritized students. As learning sciences raises critical questions about student and teacher agency with technology [1], we ask: How do we equip educational stakeholders with tools that build their expertise and agency in trustworthy and equitable AI use in classrooms? Hence, the central research question in our study is:*How do teachers analyze AI system behaviors to identify the benefits and harms of using AI scaffolds with their students?*

2 Conceptual Framing

We first frame AI systems as scaffolds to support student learning and argue that human mediation is necessary for the appropriate use of AI in classrooms. Then, we show how system failures differ by pedagogical context in ways not captured by generalization estimates. Last, we explain how allowing stakeholders such as teachers to evaluate AI system behaviors in their pedagogical context fosters trust and agency for an equitable and synergistic human–AI scaffolding.

2.1 AI Systems as Scaffolds to Support Student Learning

Scaffolding is closely related to the sociocultural perspective of learning proposed by Vygotsky [2], wherein learning occurs first at the social level in interactions with others and later at an individual level. Although scaffolding was originally described as the one-on-one support an adult offers to a child in their zone of proximal development (ZPD), practical limitations of present-day classrooms pose constraints on one teacher responsible for multiple ZPDs at the same time. Hence, scaffolding is often synergistically distributed across instructional materials, peers, technology, and the teacher [22]. AI systems, designed as scaffolds [30], could anticipate students' changing needs in their ZPD and support them to reach their potential [6]. Well-designed scaffolds are sensitive to students' ZPD [16]. For example, over the past 40 years, research on AI tutors has developed models to assess students' current skill levels and adapt instructional support in the moment [12], allowing teachers to attend to students who need individualized support [18].

2.2 Human–AI Synergy in Distributed Scaffolding

Although AI systems as scaffolds may be narrowly defined to support a specific task [30], scaffolding, as a dialogic process, is theoretically grounded in the sociocultural approach [16]. Human mediation, involving interpersonal interactions within the learning environment, is key for material scaffolds or tools to be used appropriately [33]. In classrooms, social structures facilitating dialogues with peers and teachers serve as social scaffolds that enable learning with tools (e.g., [31]). Moreover, teachers play a critical role in adapting and continually adjusting scaffolding in the moment based on their students' changing needs [19], making sensitive, conscious decisions to complement the support provided by the tool. Teachers are also responsible for responsively fading scaffolds to promote student independence. Hence, a system of scaffolding (i.e., distributed scaffolding [16]), involving tools and social scaffolds, must function synergistically to effectively support students in classrooms. For instance, past research with AI tutors shows that even when technology is designed to work with minimal human intervention, teacher practices matter to student learning [7]. Moreover, adaptive experiences are jointly facilitated by both teachers and technology [14]. Hence, in contrast to an automation-first approach to AI, a more beneficial approach for AI use in classrooms could be intelligence augmentation [21,26], where AI builds on teachers' pedagogical knowledge.

2.3 The Need to Go Beyond Generalization Estimates for Equitable AI

Despite significant differences in the pedagogical contexts in which educational AI systems are used, AI evaluation is often limited to generalization estimates (e.g., overall accuracy, mean squared error) that inherently assume universal deployment [32]. Moreover, AI systems are known to systematically fail on rare groups not obvious in aggregate evaluation [27], such as minoritized student populations. Past research demonstrates how ignoring learner context in the design of AI tutors could introduce harmful biases in them [3]. Despite a recent spike in efforts to identify and mitigate bias in educational AI [10], significant challenges remain. A common approach to fairness is ensuring that the system performs well for student subgroups. In addition to oversimplified or politically influenced categorizations of student demographics, these approaches fall short in considering the myriad of ways in which student identities intersect [15]. Moreover, technical conceptions of bias are often vague, lack normative grounding, and diverge from how bias is socially understood [28]. Hence, answers to the question of "what kinds of system behaviors are harmful, in what ways, to whom, and why?" [25] need to be contextually grounded in the lived experiences of the stakeholders.

2.4 Stakeholder-Driven Contextual Evaluation of Behaviors for Human–AI Trust

There has been an increasing call for contextual evaluation [11] that recognizes differences in the lived experiences of stakeholders, which in turn define system failures differently [13]. Specifying desired system behavior serves an important role in transparency and trust, opening the AI system for stakeholder scrutiny [8]. Prior work has formalized human–AI trust as contractual, i.e., trust is built on explicit, context-specific contracts that stakeholders specify based on the expected behaviors of the AI system [5]. System *behaviors* defined through testing can act as components of such contracts—particularly when they incorporate stakeholders' contextual expertise to translate implicit expectations (e.g., fairness) into explicit, testable criteria. In addition to better-informed trust, contextual evaluation of AI scaffold behaviors can improve AI transparency [4]. With improved awareness of both the benefits and limitations of using AI scaffolds in their context—as well as the associated equity concerns—stakeholders can more effectively situate AI scaffolds within their broader system of scaffolding distributed across tools and social supports. This may involve adjusting scaffolding practices to amplify the benefits and mitigate the limitations of the AI scaffold.

3 AIBAT System Design

With AIBAT, teachers specify *behaviors* (i.e., what they expect the AI scaffold to do) and test scaffolds such as large language models (LLMs) against those expectations. For example, to analyze how fairly an LLM treats bilingual students, teachers can define a target LLM behavior (e.g., tag incorrect student response for feedback) and test whether that behavior stays invariant based on a specified condition (e.g., no change in assessment when a relevant Spanish idiom is added to the response). Although AI scaffolds may be expected to perform various tasks such as assessment, feedback, and question answering, we focus on assessment as an illustrative example in this study because it is often the first step in diagnosing students' scaffolding needs. In this section, we first describe the infrastructure and iterative workflow of AIBAT in Sect. 3.1. We then introduce three integrated design features from Sects. 3.2 to 3.4, along with the interface shown in Fig. 2, aimed at helping teachers understand the harms and benefits of AI performance and trust.

3.1 System Overview

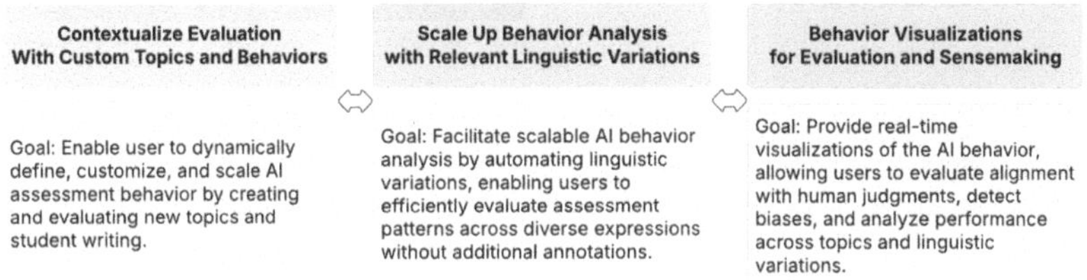

Fig. 1. AIBAT's workflow consists of Contextualized Evaluation with Custom Topics and Behaviors, Scale Up Behavior Analysis with Relevant Linguistic Variations, and Behavior Visualizations for Evaluation and Sensemaking to facilitate the sensemaking of the benefits and harms of LLM assessments..

As shown in Fig. 1, there are three key design features in AIBAT: 1) Contextualize Evaluation With Custom Topics and Behaviors, 2) Scale Up Behavior Analysis with Relevant Linguistic Variations, and 3) Behavior Visualizations for Evaluation and Sensemaking. First, teachers define expected AI behavior by providing test cases (e.g., student responses) and expected assessments (e.g., acceptable versus unacceptable). Teachers can contextualize the evaluation process by creating new topics relevant to their subject matter and adding test cases that reflect their students' writing (see Sect. 3.2). Second, the platform offers full test case management, enabling users to edit, delete, or add test cases as needed. After reviewing the AI's assessment, teachers can indicate whether they agree or disagree with it, and AIBAT visualizes these results through interactive graphs. These visualizations provide insights into AI assessment performance, potential biases, and overall consistency (see Sect. 3.4). Third, AIBAT allows teachers to introduce linguistic variations (see Sect. 3.3), such as misspellings, missing punctuation, translations, and paraphrased versions of test statements, to evaluate how the AI assessment handles the diverse ways in which their students write. AIBAT is built using Django and Next.js and hosted on Lambda Cloud GPU instances.

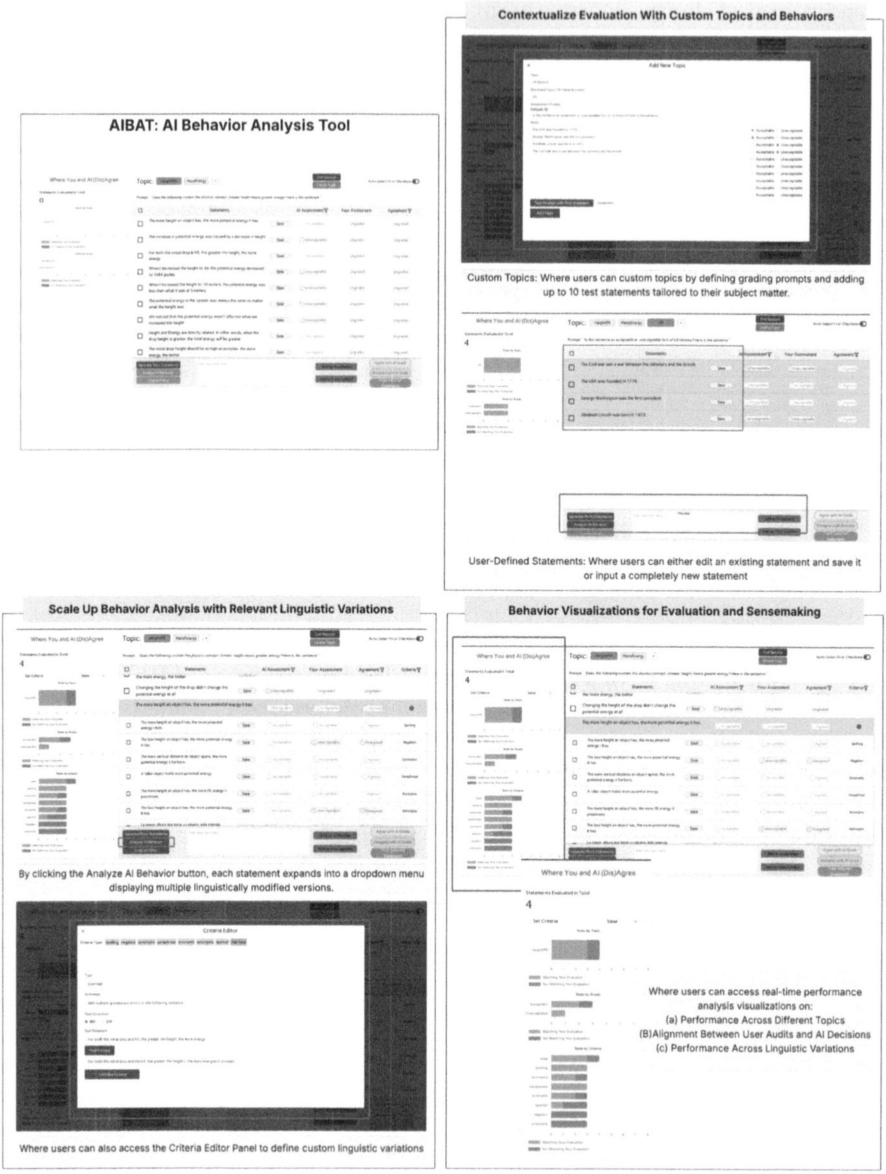

Fig. 2. AIBAT's Interface and Key Features. The interface includes default status (top left), Contextualize Evaluation with Custom Topics and Behaviors (top right), Scale Up Behavior Analysis with Relevant Linguistic Variations (bottom left), and Behavior Visualizations for Evaluation and Sensemaking (bottom right).

3.2 Contextualize Evaluation with Custom Topics and Behaviors

By default, the platform includes two sample middle-school science topics—how Potential Energy (PE) varies with height and how mass affects total energy—along with a set of predefined student responses. For each topic, users are presented with 20 predefined statements on the main panel, each accompanied by an AI-generated assessment indicating whether the statement is deemed acceptable or unacceptable. Users can review these assessments and provide feedback by agreeing or disagreeing with the AI's decision with a single click. To provide adaptability to different subject areas and grading criteria, AIBAT offers a Custom Topic Definition feature, allowing users to define and evaluate new topics dynamically.

This feature comprises two configurable options to support varied evaluation needs. First, Custom Topics allow teachers to create their own topics by defining assessment prompts and adding up to 10 test statements tailored to their subject matter. These user-defined topics function as prompts that help AIBAT generate a bookmarkable topic page, similar to the default Height/PE and Mass/Energy topics, allowing users to switch between them. If teachers wish to augment their evaluation with additional, auto-generated test statements, they can select "Generate More Statements", prompting AIBAT to produce new statements under the defined topic.

Second, User-Defined Statements allow users to manually input specific statements under an existing topic for AI evaluation. Users can either edit an existing statement and save it, prompting the LLM to regrade the modified statement, or input a completely new statement instead of modifying a predefined one, indicating whether they consider it acceptable or unacceptable. Once submitted, the statement appears in the panel under the selected topic, accompanied by the LLM-generated assessment (acceptable/unacceptable) and an indication of whether the AI's assessment aligns with the teacher's decision (agree/disagree). Together, these options allow educators to tailor AIBAT's evaluation system to a range of grading needs, ensuring flexibility beyond its default topics and statements.

3.3 Scale Up Behavior Analysis with Relevant Linguistic Variations

AIBAT incorporates a Linguistic Variation feature to account for the diverse ways a given statement can be expressed. When teachers enable this feature by clicking the Analyze AI Behavior button, each statement expands into a drop-down menu displaying multiple linguistically modified versions. These variations include adjustments such as spelling modifications, negation, synonyms, paraphrasing, acronyms, antonyms, and translations into Spanish by default. Additionally, users can access the Criteria Editor Panel to define custom linguistic variations, providing key information that helps fine-tune the model's responses. Taken holistically, this feature aims to enhance scalability by allowing teachers to assess AI-graded patterns across multiple linguistic forms with their previous decisions populated automatically, rather than manually reviewing each case in isolation. In real-world classroom settings, student responses naturally vary in wording, grammar, and phrasing, yet traditional AI evaluation methods often rely on fixed expressions, limiting the scope of assessment. By automating the generation of systematic linguistic variations, AIBAT enables educators to efficiently examine how AI models handle diverse inputs at scale.

3.4 Behavior Visualizations for Evaluation and Sensemaking

AIBAT includes a real-time AI performance analysis panel that provides dynamic insights into the AI model's evaluation accuracy through bar charts. The visualization is structured around three key dimensions: (a) Performance Across Different Topics—The system evaluates AI behaviors across various subject areas, enabling users to assess whether the model generalizes effectively or struggles with certain topics. This feature helps identify subject-specific biases and inconsistencies that may impact grading fairness. (b) Alignment Between User Audits and AI Decisions—This metric measures the extent to which users' auditing decisions align with the AI's assessment. It distinguishes between true positives (correct acceptances), true negatives (correct rejections), false positives (incorrect acceptances), and false negatives (incorrect rejections). This allows users to identify patterns in the AI's errors and assess its reliability in different grading scenarios. (c) Performance Across Linguistic Variations—AIBAT also analyzes how the AI responds to different linguistic variations, such as changes in grammar, spelling, and negation. By tracking performance across these variations, users can detect potential biases or weaknesses in the model's ability to handle diverse linguistic expressions.

3.5 LLM Model Specifications

AIBAT leverages various LLMs throughout the application to perform different tasks effectively. For grading the default topics, the platform utilizes a fine-tuned RoBERTa classification model, specifically trained to evaluate responses related to the default subjects. When it comes to grading new, user-defined topics, AIBAT switches to a general-purpose, pre-trained Llama 3 model, which provides flexibility for a broader range of grading tasks. For generating new test cases, AIBAT relies on a Mistral model, which helps create diverse and relevant test scenarios. Linguistic perturbations are generated using Mistral. Through these carefully selected models, AIBAT ensures accurate grading, efficient test case generation, and robust perturbation handling for various educational needs.

4 Method

4.1 Participant Recruitment

We recruited 14 participants (3 male, 11 female) through institutional networks to participate in this study, which was conducted under Institutional Review Board (IRB) approval. All participants had prior teaching experience, ranging from K–12 to the college level, with an average of 16 years of teaching experience. Their disciplinary backgrounds spanned various fields, including arts, history, social studies, technology, and entrepreneurship. While nine participants self-reported familiarity with LLM tools such as ChatGPT, the remaining five had no prior experience with them. We conducted the think-aloud sessions in person, with each session lasting between 58 and 110 min.

4.2 Procedure and Data Analysis

To evaluate the usability and effectiveness of AIBAT, we conducted a user study in which participants explored the tool's features while providing real-time feedback. We began by introducing the goal of AIBAT, explaining its intended application scenarios to ensure participants understood its purpose and relevance. Following this introduction, researchers guided participants through each feature, demonstrating its functionality and encouraging hands-on interaction. Participants were then given the opportunity to explore AIBAT independently while being instructed to think aloud, verbalizing their thoughts, impressions, and any challenges they encountered. To capture their real-time interactions, participants were asked to share their screens throughout the session. This enabled researchers to closely observe navigation patterns, engagement levels, and any usability issues that emerged during exploration. At the conclusion of each session, researchers conducted a brief debriefing with participants to reflect on their experiences, gather feedback, and identify areas for improvement.

To analyze the study data, we reviewed all video recordings, transcribed the discussions, and extracted relevant quotes and actions that illustrated how participants approached creating example sets and tests, as well as how they reasoned about and reflected on the model. Using affinity diagrams, we annotated and categorized these insights into thematic groups. We iteratively analyzed the transcripts, grouped interpretation notes, and identified emerging themes from the data, allowing us to discern key patterns and trends in participant interactions and reasoning.

5 Findings

5.1 Evaluation Mechanism Facilitates Human-AI Trust

Our findings indicate that AIBAT's evaluation mechanism, which allows users to audit AI-generated assessments, plays a critical role in fostering user autonomy and trust in LLM-based assessment. Specifically, participants expressed that the ability to engage with AI decisions—rather than passively accepting them—contributed to a greater sense of control over the system's outputs. As P13 noted: *"Some other tools are just like, well, I put this in, this came out, and we can only hope it's right or we have to verify it ourselves."* One participant highlighted how the ability to see AI assessments directly within the interface and compare them against their own judgments provided a clearer understanding of the model's decision-making process, stating, *"Looking at it, like we had talked about with how we know the information is accurate... now we can actually see it right there."* . Moreover, P5 described this evaluation as a "conversation" with the AI, stating, *"I generally love this tool...It kind of shows that it's a conversation almost—like a back and forth. Transparency can also be super critical in getting anybody else to accept it."* Overall, our results suggest that the ability to evaluate AI assessments empowered users to critically assess the model's outputs, aligning with the idea that AI should be a tool for collaboration rather than a source of unquestioned authority.

Additionally, participants emphasized that the ability to interactively evaluate the model increased their trust in the system. P4 explained, *"Being given the tools to kind of test it and move it and kind of train it and understand a little bit about what it's looking for gives me that stronger trust, and I would be more likely to use it."* Similarly, P11 noted *"It kind of helps you look through these lenses, if you will, to get a more accurate tool and move towards trust and reliability. If I was given the tool on my own and just told to use it, my trust would be really low."* Participants also emphasized how the evaluation process encouraged active engagement and critical thinking beyond just grading. As one P7 explained: *"One of the things I keep thinking of is how important it always has been, but even more so now, we need to teach students critical thinking. If we do not start now, they will not know what to trust and what not to trust. The evaluation in this tool is a good starting point."*

5.2 Structured Evaluation Through Custom Topics and Linguistic Variation

Participants emphasized that AIBAT's structured evaluation approach, particularly the ability to assess performance across different linguistic variations, provided a critical framework for systematic evaluation. Having a well-defined structure allowed users to effectively test and refine the tool, as P1 noted: *"It tries to come up with different ways to say the same thing so that you don't have to create that exhaustive list of what would be official."* This suggests that without structured guidance, users may struggle to generate diverse and meaningful examples, limiting their ability to thoroughly assess AI outputs. Moreover, participants agreed that AIBAT's ability to automatically generate a variety of statements significantly reduced the cognitive burden associated with manually creating test cases. As P9 observed: *"Just the way that middle school students write—it varies so much that it's hard to capture all the possibilities. Like all the different ways they could say the same thing or you know, even they can say the same thing with commas."* Similarly, P3 stated that *"Not having to use my brain power to come up with all of those statements."* Overall, participants emphasized that AIBAT's ability to systematically capture linguistic variation strengthened human-AI collaboration by reducing the manual effort required for grading while still allowing educators to apply their expertise in evaluating AI behavior.

5.3 Evaluating AI Grading Across Linguistic Variations for Inclusive and Context-Aware Assessment

The Linguistic Variation feature in AIBAT provides educators with a structured way to assess AI grading across diverse linguistic expressions, allowing for a more nuanced evaluation of student responses. Our results show that linguistic variation may serve as a parameter for aligning grading practices with pedagogical goals. Specifically, it allows educators to ensure that students are not unfairly penalized for deviations in language use when they successfully convey core concepts. As P12 described, the feature makes it possible to adjust AI grading to be *"a little bit more permissive"* under certain conditions, ensuring that rigid language rules do not obscure a student's understanding of the material. P4 also emphasized this challenge, particularly for students who struggle with writing mechanics: *"If students really struggle with writing, I can understand their reading—or their writing, rather—and know that they grasp the main idea... even though they might not be using all the correct vocabulary, they might not be using correct punctuation or any punctuation at all."* Moreover, P3 recognized the need for flexible grading criteria based on student skill levels: *"when you're dealing with certain [students'] ages, there's a more level playing field. But in middle school, you know, I have students with probably a third-grade reading and writing level all the way up to like a high, you know, middle of high school writing level...I would have different grading criteria in different grade levels."* This perspective highlights a key challenge in AI-driven assessment—balancing linguistic accuracy with instructional goals. AIBAT's scalability through linguistic variation enables teachers to see where AI applies "stricter" or more "lenient" grading, allowing them to adjust their decisions accordingly.

5.4 Interpreting Model Bias Through Visualization to Enhance Transparency and Decision-Making

Our results show that Behavior Visualizations for Evaluation and Sensemaking provided users with an intuitive means to recognize model biases, facilitating sensemaking and encouraging deeper reflection on AI decision-making processes. Beyond detecting biases, the visualization actively engaged users in deliberating their role in addressing systemic inconsistencies. As P2 reflected: *"That visualization makes me think—Do I need to do more work with the tool to get consistency across the board, or... just accept that I'm not going to track Spanish, for instance, because it's already doing a good job?"* By surfacing these discrepancies in an accessible format, AIBAT's visualization feature supported a more nuanced approach to AI trust and oversight. Furthermore, P4 recommended reorganizing the data to prioritize areas of greatest disagreement, suggesting that results be sorted *"from least agreed to most disagreed"*, which underscores the practical need for structured prioritization, enabling users to quickly identify and address problematic classifications, streamlining the auditing and decision-making process.

6 Discussion and Future Directions

We introduce AIBAT, an iterative workflow and tool designed for teacher-driven contextual evaluation of language models in education. Unlike traditional model evaluation approaches that emphasize generalization performance and quantitative benchmarks, AIBAT shifts the focus toward contextualizing model harms in the pedagogical context and instructional goals.

Our think-aloud study findings highlight the role of AIBAT's evaluation mechanism in fostering user autonomy and trust in AI-generated assessments. Participants valued the ability to engage with AI decisions rather than passively accepting them, describing the process as a "conversation" that enhanced transparency and control. This interactive approach empowered users to critically assess AI outputs, reinforcing the idea that AI should serve as a collaborative tool rather than an unquestioned authority. Additionally, AIBAT's structured evaluation framework, particularly its ability to assess linguistic variations, enabled systematic and efficient grading assessment. By generating diverse student responses automatically, the tool reduced cognitive effort while ensuring comprehensive evaluation. Participants also emphasized the importance of linguistic variation in grading fairness, noting that it helped avoid penalizing students for language differences while aligning assessments with pedagogical goals. The ability to adjust AI grading criteria based on student proficiency levels allowed for more inclusive and context-aware evaluations. Furthermore, visual representations of model behavior provided an intuitive way to detect AI biases, facilitating informed decision-making and strengthening trust. Some participants suggested prioritizing areas of greatest disagreement to streamline the auditing process. Overall, AIBAT's evaluation, linguistic flexibility, and bias visualization features enhanced human-AI collaboration, improving transparency, trust, and usability.

AIBAT also inherits limitations that we have identified as areas for future iterations. One challenge is expanding beyond single-sentence test cases to support context-aware evaluation. Currently, many AI evaluation methods assess responses in isolation, which may not fully capture how model outputs align with broader pedagogical structures, discourse patterns, and curricular themes. Another key direction is deepening AIBAT's interactive feedback mechanisms. In its current form, AIBAT enables educators to provide constructive evaluations of AI-generated responses, but future work can strengthen its iterative feedback loop, allowing teachers not only to identify issues but also receive explanations of why the model produced a particular response and make adjustments dynamically to improve alignment with pedagogical expectations.

In conclusion, we argue that current AI evaluation frameworks offer limited support for teachers to critically assess AI models based on the specific knowledge, skills, and values emphasized in their curriculum. AIBAT addresses this gap by offering a scaffolded evaluation process that enables teachers to customize evaluation topics, surface critical examples where model outputs misalign with pedagogical expectations, and engage in deeper sensemaking. This approach empowers teachers to be active participants in AI development, rather than positioning them as passive adopters.

Acknowledgments. This work was supported by the Office of the Vice Chancellor for Research and Graduate Education at the University of Wisconsin–Madison, with funding from the Wisconsin Alumni Research Foundation. We thank Nora Tseng, Lucas Anderson, Pranav Poddutoori, Aditya Anand, and Daryush Ghadiali. We also appreciate Dana Gnesdilow, Ananya Ganesh, Nate Smith, Kaycie Barron, Sandra Taylor-Marshall, Kiyo White, and all the think-aloud participants for their valuable feedback.

References

1. Vakil, S., McKinney de Royston, M.: Youth as philosophers of technology. Mind Cult. Act. **29**(4), 336–355 (2022)
2. Vygotsky, L.S.: Mind in Society: The Development of Higher Psychological Processes. Harvard University Press (1978)
3. Karumbaiah, S., Ocumpaugh, J., Baker, R.S.: Context matters: differing implications of motivation and help-seeking in educational technology. Int. J. Artif. Intell. Educ. **1**, 1–40 (2021)
4. Bommasani, R., Liang, P., Lee, T.: Holistic evaluation of language models. Ann. N. Y. Acad. Sci. **1525**(1), 140–146 (2023)
5. Jacovi, A., Marasović, A., Miller, T., Goldberg, Y.: Formalizing trust in artificial intelligence: Prerequisites, causes, and goals of human trust in AI. In: Proceedings of the ACM Conference on Fairness, Accountability, and Transparency, pp. 624–635 (2021)
6. Reiser, B.J.: Scaffolding complex learning: the mechanisms of structuring and problematizing student work. J. Learn. Sci. **13**(3), 273–304 (2004)
7. Holstein, K., Aleven, V., Rummel, N.: A conceptual framework for human-AI hybrid adaptivity in education. Artif. Intell. Educ. **12163**, 240–254 (2020)
8. Suresh, H., et al.: Kaleidoscope: semantically-grounded, context-specific ML model evaluation. ACM Hum. Factors Comput. Syst. **1**, 1–13 (2023)
9. Ribeiro, M.T., Wu, T., Guestrin, C., Singh, S.: Beyond accuracy: behavioral testing of NLP models with CheckList. arXiv preprint arXiv:2005.04118 (2020)
10. Baker, R.S., Hawn, A.: Algorithmic bias in education. Int. J. Artif. Intell. Educ. **1**, 1–41 (2021)
11. Raji, D., Denton, E., Bender, E.M., Hanna, A., Paullada, A.: AI and the everything in the whole wide world benchmark. In: Neural Information Processing Systems (2021)
12. Corbett, A.T., Anderson, J.R.: Knowledge tracing: modeling the acquisition of procedural knowledge. User Model. User-Adapt. Interact. **4**, 253–278 (1994)
13. D'Ignazio, C., Klein, L.F.: Data Feminism. MIT Press (2020)
14. Dillenbourg, P.: The evolution of research on digital education. Int. J. Artif. Intell. Educ. **26**, 544–560 (2016)
15. Crenshaw, K.W.: On Intersectionality: Essential Writings. The New Press (2017)
16. Puntambekar, S.: Distributed scaffolding: scaffolding students in classroom environments. Educ. Psychol. Rev. **34**(1), 451–472 (2022)
17. Quinonero-Candela, J., Sugiyama, M., Schwaighofer, A., Lawrence, N.D. (eds.): Dataset Shift in Machine Learning. MIT Press (2008)

18. Schofield, J.W., Eurich-Fulcer, R., Britt, C.L.: Teachers, computer tutors, and teaching: the artificially intelligent tutor as an agent for classroom change. Am. Educ. Res. J. **31**(3), 579–607 (1994)
19. van de Pol, J., Volman, M., Oort, F., Beishuizen, J.: Teacher scaffolding in small-group work: an intervention study. J. Learn. Sci. **23**(4), 600–650 (2014)
20. Recht, B., Roelofs, R., Schmidt, L., Shankar, V.: Do ImageNet classifiers generalize to ImageNet? In: International Conference on Machine Learning, pp. 5389–5400. PMLR (2019)
21. Engelbart, D.C., English, W.K.: A research center for augmenting human intellect. In: Proceedings of the 9–11 December 1968 Fall Joint Computer Conference, Part I, pp. 395–410 (1968)
22. Tabak, I.: Synergy: a complement to emerging patterns of distributed scaffolding. J. Learn. Sci. **13**(3), 305–335 (2004)
23. Koedinger, K.R., Corbett, A.T.: Cognitive Tutors: Technology bringing learning science to the classroom. In: Sawyer, K. (ed.) The Cambridge Handbook of the Learning Sciences, pp. 61–78. Cambridge University Press (2006)
24. Karumbaiah, S., et al.: A spatiotemporal analysis of teacher practices in supporting student learning and engagement in an AI-enabled classroom. Artif. Intell. Educ. **450**, 450–462 (2023)
25. Blodgett, S.L., Barocas, S., Daumé III, H., Wallach, H.: Language (technology) is power: a critical survey of "bias" in NLP. arXiv preprint arXiv:2005.14050 (2020)
26. Shneiderman, B.: Human-Centered AI. Oxford University Press (2022)
27. Rajani, N., Liang, W., Chen, L., Mitchell, M., Zou, J.: SEAL: interactive tool for systematic error analysis and labeling. arXiv preprint arXiv:2210.05839 (2022)
28. Birhane, A.: Algorithmic injustice: a relational ethics approach. Patterns **2**(2), 100205 (2021)
29. Patel, K., Fogarty, J., Landay, J.A., Harrison, B.: Investigating statistical machine learning as a tool for software development. In: Proceedings of the SIGCHI Conference on Human Factors in Computing Systems, pp. 667–676. ACM, New York (2008)
30. Pea, R.D.: The social and technological dimensions of scaffolding and related theoretical concepts for learning, education, and human activity. J. Learn. Sci. **13**(3), 423–451 (2004)
31. Martin, N.D., Tissenbaum, C.D., Gnesdilow, D., Puntambekar, S.: Fading distributed scaffolds: the importance of complementarity between teacher and material scaffolds. Instr. Sci. **47**(1), 69–98 (2019)
32. Paquette, L., Ocumpaugh, J., Li, Z., Andres, A., Baker, R.: Who's learning? Using demographics in EDM research. J. Educ. Data Min. **12**(3), 1–30 (2020)
33. Kozulin, A.: Psychological tools and mediated learning. In: Kozulin, A., Gindis, B., Ageyev, V.S., Miller, S.M. (eds.) Vygotsky's Educational Theory in Cultural Context, pp. 15–38. Cambridge University Press (2003)

Synthesizing High-Quality Programming Tasks with LLM-Based Expert and Student Agents

Manh Hung Nguyen[1(✉)], Victor-Alexandru Pădurean[1], Alkis Gotovos[1], Sebastian Tschiatschek[2], and Adish Singla[1]

[1] MPI-SWS, Saarbrücken, Germany
{manguyen,vpadurea,agkotovo,adishs}@mpi-sws.org
[2] University of Vienna, Vienna, Austria
sebastian.tschiatschek@univie.ac.at

Abstract. Generative AI is transforming computing education by enabling the automatic generation of personalized content and feedback. We investigate its capabilities in providing high-quality programming tasks to students. Despite promising advancements in task generation, a quality gap remains between AI-generated and expert-created tasks. The AI-generated tasks may not align with target programming concepts, could be incomprehensible to students, or may contain critical issues such as incorrect tests. Existing works often require interventions from human teachers for validation. We address these challenges by introducing PyTaskSyn, a novel synthesis technique that first generates a programming task and then decides whether it meets certain quality criteria to be given to students. The key idea is to break this process into multiple stages performed by expert and student agents simulated using both strong and weaker generative models. Through extensive evaluation, we show that PyTaskSyn significantly improves task quality compared to baseline techniques and showcases the importance of each specialized agent type in our validation pipeline. Additionally, we conducted user studies using our publicly available web application and show that PyTaskSyn can deliver high-quality programming tasks comparable to expert-designed ones while reducing workload and costs, and being more engaging than programming tasks that are available in online resources.

Keywords: Programming Education · Generative AI · Simulated Agents

1 Introduction

Generative AI is transforming learning and teaching in computing education [7,31]. Advanced generative models such as OpenAI's GPT-4o [26] and GitHub Copilot [9] are quickly reshaping both student and teacher experiences. For students, these models can provide personalized educational content [1], provide

A. I. Cristea et al. (Eds.): AIED 2025, LNAI 15877, pp. 77–91, 2025.
https://doi.org/10.1007/978-3-031-98414-3_6

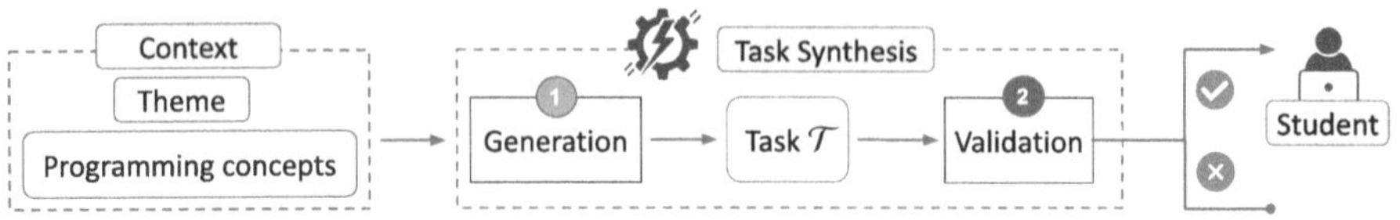

Fig. 1. Overview of contextualized programming task synthesis pipeline. Given an input context consisting of a theme and a set of programming concepts, a task $\mathcal{T}$ is first generated in Stage (1) and then validated in Stage (2). Task $\mathcal{T}$ is assigned to a student only if it meets certain quality criteria.

detailed feedback on their work [17,30], and serve as pair programmers [23]. For teachers, these models can assist in analyzing and grading student answers [29] and curriculum development [34]. A particularly promising application is their ability to generate tailored educational materials, especially in creating diverse programming exercises that target specific programming concepts.

Recent works have investigated the use of generative models for generating novel and engaging programming exercises related to a specific theme and targeting specific programming concepts [10,14,16,18,32]. While these initial efforts show promise, AI-generated tasks still fall short of human expert quality due to several issues [14,29,32]. For example, the generated programming task can contain incorrect test cases generated as part of the task or it can contain a task description that is not comprehensible [14,32]. Without an automatic validation mechanism to check these aspects of the task, human interventions would be required to validate the task's quality before they are assigned to students [11,14]. While one might consider using generative models for task validation, research has shown that they struggle with self-correction [12]. These limitations in single-agent validation motivated our multi-agent based approach.

To address these challenges, we introduce our technique, PyTaskSyn, capable of generating contextualized programming tasks and then deciding whether they meet certain quality criteria. Figure 1 depicts the overview of the pipeline implemented in PyTaskSyn. First, given a context as input, PyTaskSyn asks a simulated agent to generate a programming task composed of a description and a test suite. The generated task then goes through the second stage in the pipeline (i.e., validation), handled by multiple simulated agents with unique roles using strong (GPT-4o [26]) and weaker (GPT-4o-mini [25]) models. This validation stage is designed to provide a quality assurance mechanism and decides whether the generated task can be provided to a student or not. Our multi-agent approach builds upon research that has shown the benefit of collaborative agents [4,8,37] and used generative models to simulate humans in various roles [2,19,24,28,30]. We demonstrate the efficacy of our technique through extensive evaluation using data collected from prior works [10,11,18,32].

In summary, our main contributions are as follows.

(1) We highlight the effectiveness of decomposing the programming task synthesis into multiple stages. We introduce PyTaskSyn, a novel technique that

leverages generative models to simulate expert, tutor, and student agents, each responsible for specific stages in the synthesis process. (Sect. 4).[1]

(2) We conduct extensive evaluation of our technique for Python programming task synthesis, demonstrating significant improvements in the quality of synthesized tasks, while maintaining substantial coverage (Sect. 5).

(3) We develop a web application for Python programming task synthesis and conduct two user studies, showing that our synthesized tasks match the quality of expert-created tasks while requiring minimal cost. (Sect. 6).

2 Related Work

Programming Task Generation. With the advancement of generative models, recent studies have demonstrated the potential of using them to create natural language programming tasks [10,11,14,18,29,32]. Initial research focused on the generation of programming exercises, including sample solutions and test cases [32], while subsequent research efforts have aimed at synthesizing more diverse and contextualized programming exercises [10,11,18], as well as exercises suitable for non-English contexts [14]. A parallel line of work focused on generating programming tasks to target specific types of bugs [29], or visual programming tasks [3,27,36]. However, many of these works highlighted the significant gap between AI-generated tasks and human-crafted tasks [14,27,29,32]. Our work addresses this gap by automating the validation of programming tasks' quality.

Improving Quality of Programming Content. Recent works have focused on enhancing the quality of programming content. For example, generative models were used to generate predicates for testing a generated program [15], or to act as judges for evaluation [39]. As an enhancement, generative models can leverage their own evaluations to iteratively improve the quality of their responses [5,21]. However, prior work has shown that validating the feedback generated by one generative agent using another generative agent has proved to be more effective than using the same agent [28,30]. Similarly, in our work, we break the task synthesis process into smaller processes and assign them to different agents.

Generative Models as Simulated Agents. A recent line of research involves agents assuming different roles and collaborating to achieve a goal. For example, in AutoGen [37], multiple agents can converse, use tools, and incorporate human input. Similar studies show that simulated agents interacting with each other outperform a single agent in reasoning and planning [4,8]. Several studies have explored LLM-empowered agents for simulating classroom interactions [38], facilitating tutor training [22], and implementing learning-by-teaching environments [13,20,33]. Our work builds upon these successes by simulating experts, tutors, and students while synthesizing tasks to ensure their quality.

3 Problem Setup

We define contextualized programming tasks in Sect. 3.1, introduce a quality metric in Sect. 3.2 and technique evaluation metrics in Sect. 3.3.

[1] https://github.com/machine-teaching-group/aied2025-pytasksyn.

Theme: Superheroes

Programming concepts: Dictionaries , Classes & Objects, Strings, Arithmetic Operators

Task Description

Design and implement a Python class 'Superhero' that models a simple superhero character using the following guidelines:

1. Attributes:
   - 'name' (string) : Name of the superhero
   - 'power' (string) : A short description of their superpower
   - 'age' (integer) : Age of the superhero
   - 'world_saving_points' (integer) : Points representing the superhero's achievements.
2. Methods:
   - '__init__(self, name, power, age)' : This method should initialize a superhero with the provided name, power, and age. The 'world_saving_points' should start at 0.
   - 'save_the_day(self, difficulty)' : This method takes a difficulty level (integer) and increases the 'world_saving_points' by two times the difficulty level. If 'difficulty' is less than 1, it should not change the points.
   - 'get_description(self)' : This method returns a string describing the superhero in the format: "{name} possesses the power of {power} and is {age} years old."
3. Functions:
   - Implement a standalone function 'top_hero(hero_list)' that takes a list of 'Superhero' objects and returns the name of the superhero with the most 'world_saving_points'. If there is a tie, return the lexicographically smaller name.

Test suite

```
def test_top_hero():
  superheroes = [Superhero("Thor","thunder god",1500), Superhero("Hulk","super strength",35),
                 Superhero("Doctor Strange","magic",45)]
  superheroes[0].save_the_day(10)
  superheroes[1].save_the_day(10)
  superheroes[2].save_the_day(12)
  assert top_hero(superheroes) == "Doctor Strange"
  superheroes[1].save_the_day(4)
  assert top_hero(superheroes) == "Doctor Strange"
```

...(*other test cases are ommited for brevity*)

Validation Result

✔	✖	✖
Task description	Test suite	Context relevance

Fig. 2. Example of a contextualized programming task. This task has an incorrect test and fails to cover the "Dictionaries" concept. Our technique PyTaskSyn validates the quality of this task and abstains from outputting it to students.

3.1 Contextualized Programming Tasks

Context. We define a context ψ as a tuple $\psi = (\psi_{\text{theme}}, \psi_{\text{concepts}})$, where ψ_{theme} represents a theme of interest, and ψ_{concepts} denotes a set of target programming concepts for practicing while solving a task. The inclusion of such context aligns with prior works on generating contextualized programming tasks [10,11,18].

Programming Task. We define a programming task $\mathcal{T}$ as being composed of a task description $\mathcal{T}_{\text{desc}}$ and a test suite $\mathcal{T}_{\text{tests}}$. The task description $\mathcal{T}_{\text{desc}}$ explains what needs to be accomplished, including the requirements, expected functionality, and constraints. The test suite $\mathcal{T}_{\text{tests}}$ is a set of test cases used to verify the correctness of a code with respect to $\mathcal{T}_{\text{desc}}$. A student is given the task description $\mathcal{T}_{\text{desc}}$ to solve, while the test suite $\mathcal{T}_{\text{tests}}$ is kept hidden to verify the student's code. A student solves task $\mathcal{T}$ successfully if their code passes all test cases in $\mathcal{T}_{\text{tests}}$. Figure 2 shows an example of a contextualized programming task.

3.2 Quality of Contextualized Programming Tasks

Ensuring the quality of a contextualized programming task is crucial before giving it to students. It must be relevant to the desired theme and programming concepts while being correct and comprehensible for students to solve. We propose a systematic evaluation process for a human expert to assess the quality of task $\mathcal{T}$ created for context ψ. The process begins with the expert formulating a solution for $\mathcal{T}$, which is a natural approach to gain a thorough understanding of the task. If the expert cannot formulate a solution, this indicates a fundamental issue with the task, marking it as low-quality. Upon successfully formulating a solution code $\mathcal{C}^*$, the expert evaluates the correctness of $\mathcal{T}$ by verifying whether $\mathcal{T}_{\text{tests}}$ correctly validates $\mathcal{C}^*$, covering all base and corner cases handled by $\mathcal{C}^*$. Next, they verify whether task $\mathcal{T}$ is relevant to ψ_{theme} and whether all the programming concepts in ψ_{concepts} are required when formulating $\mathcal{C}^*$. Then, they assess whether the task description $\mathcal{T}_{\text{desc}}$ provides sufficient information for students to write solutions. We define *Q-Overall* as the overall quality metric, where an expert assigns a final numerical score at the end of the evaluation process.

3.3 Technique Evaluation Metrics

To guide our technique development and evaluate its effectiveness, we use two performance metrics: (i) *Coverage*, measuring the percentage of times a technique provides a programming task to the student, and (ii) *Precision*, measuring the percentage of times the programming task provided to the student is of high quality. Our objective is to develop a technique with high precision to ensure well-designed tasks and high coverage rate to provide tasks across diverse contexts.

4 Our Technique PyTaskSyn

In this section, we first discuss the motivation and overview of our technique in Sect. 4.1. Then, we detail each stage in our technique's pipeline, including task *generation* in Sect. 4.2 and task *validation* in Sect. 4.3.

4.1 Motivation and Overview

Common validation techniques use a single generative agent to generate both a task and its solution code for consistency checking [32] or to act as a judge for evaluating the output task [39]. However, our initial experiments revealed task quality issues when relying on a single agent (cf. Sect. 5.4). Previous research show that breaking a complex process into sub-processes and combining the capabilities of multiple agents in a modular manner significantly improves performance [4,37]. Building on this insight, we implement a multi-agent technique where each agent takes a unique role. Figure 3 presents an overview of our technique consisting of a generation stage and a validation stage. The validation aims to improve precision, but may result in less coverage. To tackle coverage drop, we use an outer loop that repeats synthesis until a task passes validation or a maximum of N trials is reached; if none pass, no task is given to the student.

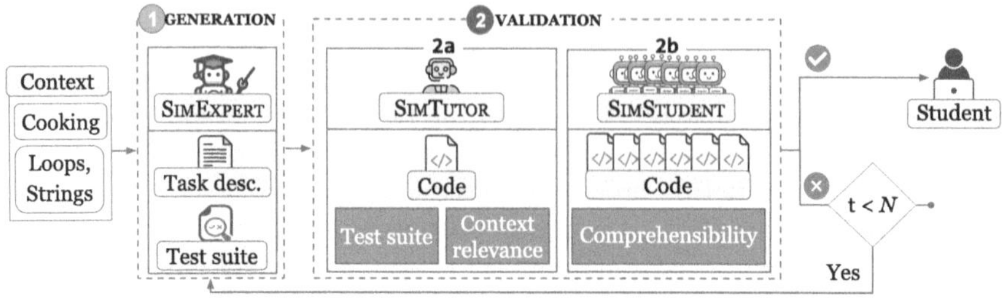

Fig. 3. Pipeline of our technique PYTASKSYN. A task candidate is generated by a SIMEXPERT agent given a theme and programming concepts (Stage 1). Then, SIMTUTOR and SIMSTUDENT agents attempt to solve the task before assessing different quality aspects of the generated task candidate (Stage 2 a-b). If the task does not pass the validation stage, our technique retries up to N times, before ultimately deciding whether or not to assign a task to the student.

4.2 Stage 1 Generation

In this stage, we aim to generate a task $\mathcal{T}$ composed of a task description $\mathcal{T}_{\text{desc}}$ and a test suite $\mathcal{T}_{\text{tests}}$ for a given input context ψ. For this, our technique uses a simulated expert agent called SIMEXPERT, implemented using the state-of-the-art generative model GPT-4o [26]. Besides asking for the components of a task $\mathcal{T}$, we also request a solution code for $\mathcal{T}$, drawing inspiration from Chain-of-thought reasoning which has proven to enhance output quality from generative models [35]. We execute this code against $\mathcal{T}_{\text{tests}}$ as a *generation consistency* check [32]. If it does not pass $\mathcal{T}_{\text{tests}}$, task $\mathcal{T}$ is considered invalid and will not go to the subsequent stages. Figure 4 (Stage 1) shows the structure of the prompt we use for this agent, with a system prompt establishing its role as a programming expert. The user prompt provides the task context ($\psi_{\text{theme}}, \psi_{\text{concepts}}$) and an instruction to generate a programming task. We use the model's default temperature of 1.0.

4.3 Stage 2 Validation

Stage 2a - Validation by SIMTUTOR. In this stage, our goal is to evaluate the test suite and contextual relevance of the task generated in Stage 1. To this end, we implement a SIMTUTOR agent to simulate a human tutor for validating the task. Figure 4 (Stage 2a) shows the prompt we use for this SIMTUTOR agent. It is assigned the role of a tutor through a system prompt, followed by a user prompt containing an input context ($\psi_{\text{theme}}, \psi_{\text{concepts}}$), and a generated task $\mathcal{T}$. First, we instruct the SIMTUTOR agent to solve the task by writing a solution code $\mathcal{C}^*$. This approach follows the Chain-of-Thought prompting strategy [35], which mimics the evaluating process of a human expert in Sect. 3.2. Solution $\mathcal{C}^*$ is then used to validate $\mathcal{T}_{\text{tests}}$. Specifically, we verify whether all test cases pass when executing $\mathcal{C}^*$ and whether every line of $\mathcal{C}^*$ is covered by $\mathcal{T}_{\text{tests}}$. Then, the agent assesses the relevance of the task to the given context. It assigns a score of 1 if task $\mathcal{T}$ effectively integrates the given theme and programming concepts, and

Stage	Prompt template
1	`[System] You are an expert in Python programming.` `[User] Given a theme of {theme} and a list of programming concepts of {concepts}, generate a Python programming task that requires only the given programming concepts to solve. The task includes a description, a test suite, and a solution program.`

2a	`[System] You are a tutor in a Python programming course.`
	`[User] The following Python programming task was created given a theme of {theme} and a list of programming concepts {concepts}.`
	`Task description: {task_description}`
	`Test suite: {testsuite}`
	`Write a program to solve the task and evaluate the context relevance of the task. The context relevance is 1 if the task is clearly relevant to the given theme and the theme is explicitly used throughout, and all given programming concepts are strictly required to solve the task; 0 otherwise.`

2b	`[System] You are a student enrolled in a Python programming course.`
	`[User] Write a program to solve the task below.`
	`Task description: {task_description}`

Fig. 4. Overview of prompt templates for each stages implemented in PyTaskSyn. {placeholders} are used to include details for concrete scenarios.

a score of 0 otherwise. We note that if the agent attempts to cheat by writing a code $\mathcal{C}^*$ that directly uses input-output pairs from $\mathcal{T}_{\text{tests}}$, the context relevance score will be 0 as it fails to use the required programming concepts. We use the GPT-4o model with its default temperature of 1.0 for our SimTutor agent.

Stage 2b - Validation by SimStudent. In this stage, we aim to evaluate the comprehensibility of the generated task $\mathcal{T}$. Specifically, the task description $\mathcal{T}_{\text{desc}}$ should provide all the necessary information for a student to write a solution code. To this end, we use a classroom-scale population of SimStudent agents (20 agents in our experiments) to simulate students' points of view and obtain their solutions. If the majority of these simulated student agents fail to solve the task, $\mathcal{T}_{\text{desc}}$ likely lacks clarity or critical information. We consider $\mathcal{T}_{\text{desc}}$ comprehensible if at least τ percent (default at 50%) of the SimStudent agents successfully solve task $\mathcal{T}$ given only $\mathcal{T}_{\text{desc}}$. To simulate students, we use a system prompt that assigns the agents the role of students, followed by a user prompt containing only the task description (see Fig. 4, Stage 2b). We use the GPT-4o-mini [25] model with a default temperature of 1.0, as prior research has shown that weaker models are better suited for simulating students' perspectives [30].

5 Evaluation

In this section, we present experimental evaluations centering around the following questions: (1) **RQ1**: How does PyTaskSyn perform compared to other existing techniques?; (2) **RQ2**: What are the contributions of different agents in PyTaskSyn?; and (3) **RQ3**: How does PyTaskSyn perform across different contexts? We present our evaluation setup in Sect. 5.1, 5.2, 5.3, followed by results in Sect. 5.4. While our evaluations focus on the Python programming language, our technique can be extended to other programming languages.

5.1 Context Selection

We evaluate the effectiveness of our technique across varied themes and programming concepts collected from prior works [10,11,18,32]. We select 5 diverse themes and uniformly sample 5 sets of 3 to 5 core Python programming concepts for each theme, resulting in 25 contexts in total (cf. Figure 7 for examples).

5.2 Evaluation Procedure

For each sampled context ψ, we generate $N = 10$ programming tasks, resulting in a pool of 250 tasks (25 contexts $\times$ 10 tasks). This is done prior to applying different validation techniques in Sect. 5.3. Two authors, with expertise in Python programming, evaluated the tasks using the Q-Overall metric introduced in Sect. 3.2 and assigned binary scores (1-High quality/0-Low quality) to each task.[2] To better understand the reasoning behind evaluations, we ask the two annotators to answer three additional Yes(1)/No(0) questions: (i) Is the test suite correct and sufficiently covering relevant cases?; (ii) Does the task accurately reflect the input context?; (iii) Is the task description comprehensible? We obtain a Cohen's Kappa agreement [6] of 0.8 for Q-Overall metric and at least 0.7 for each additional question, indicating substantial agreement between the annotators. We aggregate the two annotators' scores to obtain average quality scores for each task. Tasks passed validation of each technique in Sect. 5.3 are used for computing precision and coverage.

5.3 Techniques Evaluated

Baselines . First, BASE neither applies a consistency check during the generation stage nor uses any validation mechanisms in the validation stage. Second, GENCONSISTENCY incorporates only a consistency check during the generation stage [32]. Third, LLMJUDGE leverages an LLM as a judge [39] to validate a task in the validation stage. We prompt it with input context ψ, a task $\mathcal{T}$, then instruct it to assess the test suite, contextual relevance, and task comprehensibility. It assigns a binary Q-Overall score (1/0) for the task's overall quality.

Our Technique and Ablations. PYTASKSYN involves consistency check in Stage 1 and multiple validation mechanisms in Stage 2. It can be parameterized by τ, denoted as PYTASKSYN$_\tau$, where τ represents the threshold for the percentage of SIMSTUDENT agents that solved the task. We implement two ablation variants, each corresponding to a stage of our validation pipeline. SIMTUTORVAL relies solely on validation from the simulated tutor agent, while SIMSTUDENTVAL uses only validation from simulated student agents. The default value of τ is set to 50% for both SIMSTUDENTVAL and PYTASKSYN in our evaluation.

Oracle. To evaluate the validation efficacy, we introduce ORACLE$_p$, which has access to ground-truth quality of tasks assessed by the human experts. It can select tasks to meet any precision threshold p, serving as an upper bound.

[2] Additionally, our expert evaluation shows that 98% of the 250 generated tasks do not contain programming concepts more advanced than those in the input context.

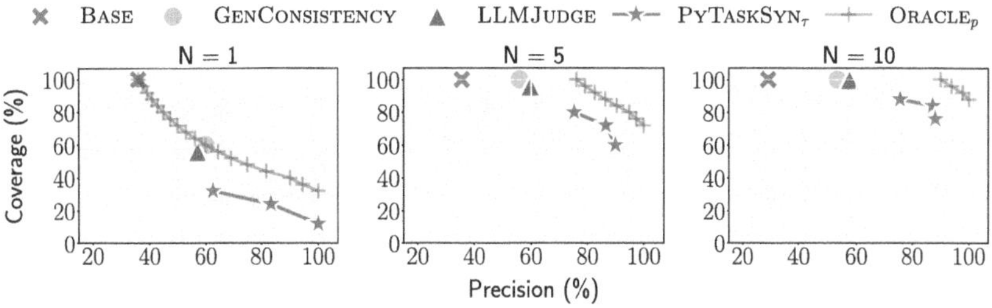

Fig. 5. Technique comparison. PYTASKSYN$_\tau$ improves task quality substantially over both baselines GENCONSISTENCY and LLMJUDGE, getting closer to the performance of ORACLE$_p$. We vary threshold $\tau \in \{0\%, 50\%, 100\}$ to showcase the tunable precision-coverage trade-off of PYTASKSYN$_\tau$.

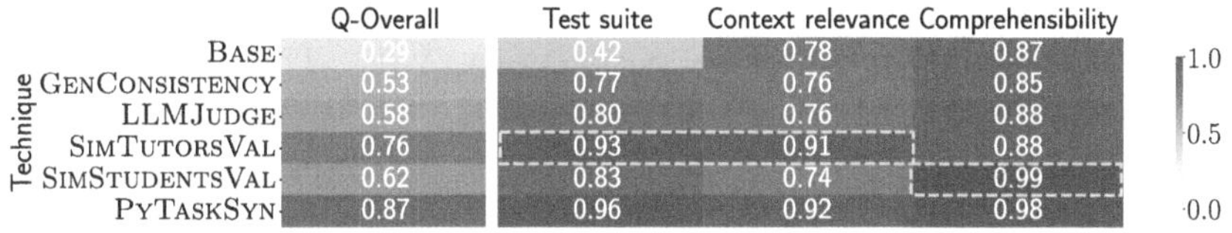

Fig. 6. Ablation study. We report average Q-Overall scores and answers for three questions answered by experts (cf. Sect. 5.2). Validation from the simulated tutor agent improves test suite quality and contextual relevance (as shown by SIMTUTORVAL), while validation from simulated student agents enhances task comprehensibility (as shown by SIMSTUDENTVAL). These agents collectively contribute to the overall quality of tasks, as demonstrated by PYTASKSYN.

5.4 Results

RQ1: How does PYTASKSYN Perform Compared to other Techniques? Figure 5 illustrates the precision and coverage of various techniques. Baseline methods including BASE, GENCONSISTENCY, and LLMJUDGE achieve high coverage but low precision ($\leq 60\%$) due to no or insufficient validation. The subpar precision of LLMJUDGE stems from a single agent's inability to thoroughly validate all aspects of task quality. Our technique PYTASKSYN$_\tau$ leveraging perspectives from different simulated tutor and student agents improves the quality of synthesized tasks. As N increases, PYTASKSYN$_\tau$ not only increases coverage but also consistently achieves the highest precision compared to baselines. At $N = 10$, PYTASKSYN demonstrates strong performance, achieving a high precision of 87.3% while maintaining substantial coverage at 84.0%. However, there is room for improvement in terms of both precision and coverage when compared to ORACLE$_p$. Finally, varying the passing threshold τ in PYTASKSYN$_\tau$ reveals a clear precision-coverage trade-off, allowing control based on requirements.

RQ2: What are the Contributions of Different Agents in PYTASKSYN? Figure 6 presents the ablation study analyzing the impact of different agent types on different task quality aspects. Our analysis reveals distinct and complemen-

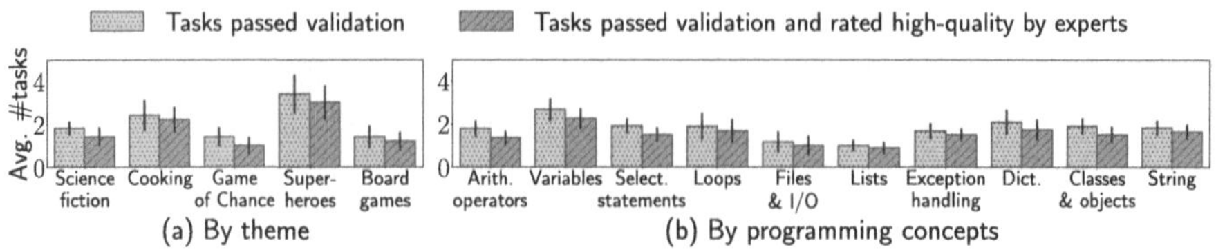

Fig. 7. Average number of tasks passed validation of PyTaskSyn out of $N = 10$ generated tasks, and average number of those rated as high-quality. PyTaskSyn could deliver high-quality tasks for any theme and programming concept.

tary contributions from the simulated agents. Simulated tutor agents enhance test suite quality notably and ensure strong context alignment (as shown by SimTutorVal), while simulated student agents substantially boost task comprehensibility (as demonstrated by SimStudentVal). Their combination in PyTaskSyn achieves the highest overall quality, with Q-Overall score of 0.87. This demonstrates how our multi-agent validation approach effectively combines different perspectives to ensure comprehensive task quality assessment.

RQ3: How does PyTaskSyn Perform Across Different Contexts? Figure 7 shows the average number of tasks synthesized by PyTaskSyn as well as how many were rated as high-quality by experts across different themes and programming concepts. We observe that our technique performs well across most themes and programming concepts. Out of $N = 10$ tasks, 1 to 3 tasks passed validation on average, with the majority rated as high-quality by human experts.

6 User Studies Using Our Web Application

We created a public web application (https://pytasksyn.netlify.app) where users can request tasks from PyTaskSyn for their chosen themes and programming concepts, write code and debug using our integrated programming environment. We conducted the following two user studies via this web application.

6.1 Comparison with Expert-Created Tasks and Online Resources

Setup. We compared tasks from PyTaskSyn against tasks created by experts and those from online resources. From 5 themes in Sect. 5.1, we re-sampled 3 to 5 programming concepts to create 5 new contexts. For each, we collected 3 tasks from: (1) an expert, (2) online resources (specifically geeksforgeeks.org), and (3) our web application.[3] We recruited 10 volunteer participants, including tutors and graduate students. They are non-native English speakers, with an average age of 28.3. Among them, 5 held Master's degrees and 5 held Bachelor's degrees in STEM fields, with an average of 6.8 years of Python experience. We assign each

[3] We made our best effort to find tasks on geeksforgeeks.org that covered programming concepts in each context. The presence of specific themes generally cannot be found.

	Theme	Concepts	Compre.	Difficulty	Interest.	Success (%)	Solving time (mins)	Creation time (mins)
Expert	0.95	0.95	0.95	0.42	0.72	84	10.82	25.20
Online resources	0.15	0.82	0.85	0.15	0.50	100	3.26	0
PyTaskSyn	0.98	0.92	0.90	0.20	0.65	100	6.66	1.29

Fig. 8. Comparison of tasks from expert, online resources, and PyTaskSyn. We report averaged participant ratings on various task aspects and other statistics. Tasks from PyTaskSyn achieved quality comparable to expert-designed ones while requiring substantially less creation time.

Statistic	Participant ID										Average
	P1	P2	P3	P4	P5	P6	P7	P8	P9	P10	
No. Requests	6	5	6	6	5	5	6	5	5	5	5.40
No. Synthesized Tasks	5	5	5	5	5	5	5	5	5	5	5.00
No. Solved Tasks	5	5	4	4	4	5	5	5	3	5	4.50
Avg. Time to Solve (mins)	4.94	12.74	12.66	13.28	5.46	8.15	10.14	6.92	7.50	6.69	8.85

Fig. 9. Statistics of each participant when they were instructed to request and solve tasks synthesized by PyTaskSyn on our web application. Our system successfully synthesized tasks for 92.6% of participant requests.

participant 2 random contexts with their corresponding 6 tasks (task sources are undisclosed). After completing each task or reaching the 20-minute limit, they provided feedback using multi-level Likert scales on: theme relevance (1-Yes/0.5-Partial/0-No), programming concepts relevance (1-Yes/0.5-Partial/0-No), task comprehensibility (1-Yes/0-No), difficulty (1-Hard/0.5-Medium/0-Easy), and interestingness (1-Interesting/0.5-Okay/0-Boring).

Results. The multi-level feedback provided by participants is mapped to scores in the range $[0.0, 1.0]$, with mean scores for each source reported in Fig. 8. Additionally, we compute averaged participant success rate, solving time, and time taken to get a task from each source. Our analysis revealed that tasks synthesized by PyTaskSyn achieved quality comparable to expert-designed tasks while requiring significantly less creation time. Moreover, PyTaskSyn has an average task creation cost of just 0.13 USD (APIs cost). Tasks from online resources, while readily available, generally lacked thematic integration and were rated as less interesting and easy. Expert-created tasks are the most challenging, resulting in longer solving times and lower success rates among participants.

6.2 Real-World Performance of Our Web Application

Setup. To evaluate our web application's real-world performance, we conducted a follow-up study with the same 10 participants. Unlike the previous study where participants solved pre-generated tasks from different sources, here each participant requested and solved 5 tasks in real-time through our web application. Participants selected their preferred contexts and made task requests until receiving a task. For each received task, we maintained the same instructions, time limits, and feedback questions as in the previous study.

Results. Our web application successfully synthesized tasks for 50/54 requests (92.6% coverage). Figure 9 provides insights into each participant's session. Participants managed to solve on average 90.0% of the synthesized tasks, with an average solving time of 8.85 minutes. When analyzing their feedback, synthesized tasks showed on average high alignment with chosen theme (1.0) and programming concepts (0.95), while maintaining good comprehensibility (0.86).

7 Concluding Discussions

We introduced PyTaskSyn, a novel synthesis technique that leverages generative models as agents simulating different classroom roles to validate generated programming tasks. Each stage in our pipeline contributes uniquely to the validation process, collectively ensuring the creation of tasks that are of high-quality and meet diverse learning objectives. Through extensive expert evaluation and user studies, we demonstrated that our approach significantly improves the quality of generated programming tasks with minimal cost, while maintaining reasonable coverage across various themes and programming concepts.

Our work brings two important implications for leveraging generative AI for computing education. First, we demonstrate how to effectively automate the quality assessment of generated programming tasks. This paves the way to reducing educator workload when designing practice exercises that target specific learning objectives in programming education. Second, our results show that by breaking down the task synthesis process into different stages, we can leverage generative models that simulate different agents for specialized roles. This agent-based approach opens up new opportunities for utilizing generative models to simulate learning analytics to generate and validate educational content.

Next, we discuss some limitations of our work and possible ways of approaching them in the future. First, we adopt an accept/reject approach during our validation; future work could employ a framework for refining programming tasks by leveraging feedback from the validation stage. Second, we do not analyze whether the passing threshold of simulated students affects the synthesized task's difficulty; it would be valuable to investigate it and see whether it aligns with difficulty assessed by experts. Third, we focus on Python programming; it would be interesting to explore whether the capabilities of generative models for validating tasks extend beyond Python. Fourth, we conducted studies with a relatively small number of participants; it would be important to conduct larger-scale studies with students and assess their learning outcomes.

Acknowledgments. Funded/Co-funded by the European Union (ERC, TOPS, 101039090). Views and opinions expressed are however those of the author(s) only and do not necessarily reflect those of the European Union or the European Research Council. Neither the European Union nor the granting authority can be held responsible for them.

References

1. Abu-Rasheed, H., Weber, C., Fathi, M.: Knowledge graphs as context sources for LLM-based explanations of learning recommendations. In: Proceedings of the Global Engineering Education Conference (EDUCON) (2024)
2. Aher, G.V., Arriaga, R.I., Kalai, A.T.: Using large language models to simulate multiple humans and replicate human subject studies. In: Proceedings of the International Conference on Machine Learning (ICML) (2023)
3. Ahmed, U.Z., et al.: Synthesizing Tasks for Block-based Programming. In: Proceedings of the Annual Conference on Neural Information Processing Systems (NeurIPS) (2020)
4. Chen, W., et al.: AgentVerse: Facilitating Multi-Agent Collaboration and Exploring Emergent Behaviors. In: International Conference on Learning Representations (ICLR) (2024)
5. Chen, X., Lin, M., Schärli, N., Zhou, D.: Teaching Large Language Models to Self-Debug. In: International Conference on Learning Representations (ICLR) (2024)
6. Cohen, J.: A coefficient of agreement for nominal scales. Educ. Psychol. Measur. **20**, 37–46 (1960)
7. Denny, P., et al.: Generative AI for Education (GAIED): Advances, Opportunities, and Challenges. CoRR **abs/2402.01580** (2024)
8. Du, Y., Li, S., Torralba, A., Tenenbaum, J.B., Mordatch, I.: Improving factuality and reasoning in language models through multiagent debate. In: International Conference on Learning Representations (ICLR) (2024)
9. GitHub: GitHub Copilot: Your AI Pair Programmer. https://github.com/features/copilot (2022)
10. Gutierrez, A.D.C., Denny, P., Luxton-Reilly, A.: Automating Personalized Parsons Problems with Customized Contexts and Concepts. In: Proceedings of the Conference on Innovation and Technology in Computer Science Education (ITiCSE) (2024)
11. Gutierrez, A.D.C., Denny, P., Luxton-Reilly, A.: Evaluating automatically generated contextualised programming exercises. In: Proceedings of the Technical Symposium on Computer Science Education (SIGCSE) (2024)
12. Huang, J., et al.: Large Language Models Cannot Self-Correct Reasoning Yet. In: The Twelfth International Conference on Learning Representations, (ICLR) (2024)
13. Jin, H., Lee, S., Shin, H., Kim, J.: Teach AI how to code: using large language models as teachable agents for programming education. In: Proceedings of the International Conference on Human Factors in Computing Systems (CHI) (2024)
14. Jordan, M., et al.: Need a Programming Exercise Generated in Your Native Language? ChatGPT's Got Your Back: Automatic Generation of Non-English Programming Exercises Using OpenAI GPT-3.5. In: Proceedings of the Technical Symposium on Computer Science Education (SIGCSE) (2024)
15. Key, D., Li, W., Ellis, K.: Toward Trustworthy Neural Program Synthesis. CoRR **abs/2210.00848** (2022)
16. Khan, M.F.A., Ramsdell, M., Nguyen, H., Karimi, H.: Human evaluation of GPT for scalable python programming exercise generation. In: International Conference on Data Science and Advanced Analytics (DSAA), pp. 1–10. IEEE (2024)

17. Leinonen, J., et al.: Using large language models to enhance programming error messages. In: Proceedings of the Technical Symposium on Computer Science Education (SIGCSE) (2023)
18. Logacheva, E., Hellas, A., Prather, J., Sarsa, S., Leinonen, J.: Evaluating contextually personalized programming exercises created with generative AI. In: Proceedings of the Conference on International Computing Education Research (ICER) (2024)
19. Lu, X., Wang, X.: Generative students: using LLM-simulated student profiles to support question item evaluation. In: Proceedings of the Conference on Learning @ Scale (L@S) (2024)
20. Ma, Q., Shen, H., Koedinger, K., Wu, S.T.: How to teach programming in the AI Era? using LLMs as a teachable agent for debugging. In: Proceeding of the International Conference on Artificial Intelligence in Education (AIED) (2024)
21. Madaan, A., et al.: Self-refine: iterative refinement with self-feedback. In: Proceedings of the Annual Conference on Neural Information Processing Systems (NeurIPS) (2023)
22. Markel, J.M., Opferman, S.G., Landay, J.A., Piech, C.: GPTeach: Interactive TA training with GPT-based students. In: Proceedings of the Conference on Learning @ Scale (L@S) (2023)
23. Mozannar, H., Bansal, G., Fourney, A., Horvitz, E.: Reading between the lines: modeling user behavior and costs in AI-assisted programming. In: proceedings of the Chi Conference on Human Factors in Computing Systems, (chi) (2024)
24. Nguyen, M.H., Tschiatschek, S., Singla, A.: Large language models for in-context student modeling: synthesizing student's behavior in visual programming from one-shot observation. In: Proceedings of the International Conference on Educational Data Mining (EDM) (2023)
25. OpenAI: GPT-4o mini: Advancing Cost-Efficient Intelligence. https://openai.com/index/gpt-4o-mini-advancing-cost-efficient-intelligence/ (2024)
26. OpenAI: Hello GPT-4o. https://openai.com/index/hello-gpt-4o/ (2024)
27. Pădurean, V.A., Tzannetos, G., Singla, A.: Neural task synthesis for visual programming. Transactions on Machine Learning Research (TMLR) (2024)
28. Phung, T., et al.: Generating high-precision feedback for programming syntax errors using large language models. In: Proceedings of the International Conference on Educational Data Mining (EDM) (2023)
29. Phung, T., et al.: Generative AI for programming education: benchmarking ChatGPT, GPT-4, and human tutors. In: Proceedings of the Conference on International Computing Education Research (ICER) - Volume 2 (2023)
30. Phung, T., et al.: Automating human tutor-style programming feedback: leveraging GPT-4 tutor model for hint generation and GPT-3.5 student model for hint validation. In: Proceedings of the Learning Analytics and Knowledge Conference (LAK) (2024)
31. Prather, J., et al.: The robots are here: navigating the generative AI revolution in computing education. In: Proceedings of the Working Group Reports of the Conference on Innovation and Technology in Computer Science Education (ItiCSE) (2023)
32. Sarsa, S., Denny, P., Hellas, A., Leinonen, J.: Automatic generation of programming exercises and code explanations using large language models. In: Proceedings of the Conference on International Computing Education Research (ICER) (2022)
33. Schmucker, R., Xia, M., Azaria, A., Mitchell, T.M.: Ruffle&Riley: towards the automated induction of conversational tutoring systems. In: NeurIPS'23 Workshop on Generative AI for Education (GAIED) (2023)

34. Sridhar, P., Doyle, A., Agarwal, A., Bogart, C., Savelka, J., Sakr, M.: Harnessing LLMs in curricular design: using GPT-4 to support authoring of learning objectives. In: AIED'23 Workshop on Empowering Education with LLMs - the Next-Gen Interface and Content Generation (2023)
35. Wei, J., et al.: Chain-of-thought prompting elicits reasoning in large language models. In: Proceedings of the Annual Conference on Neural Information Processing Systems (NeurIPS) (2022)
36. Wen, C., Ghosh, A., Staub, J., Singla, A.: Task synthesis for elementary visual programming in xlogoonline environment. In: Proceeding of the International Conference on Artificial Intelligence in Education AIED (2024)
37. Wu, Q., et al.: AutoGen: Enabling Next-Gen LLM Applications via Multi-Agent Conversation Framework. CoRR **abs/2308.08155** (2023)
38. Zhang, Z., et al.: Simulating Classroom Education with LLM-Empowered Agents. CoRR **abs/2406.19226** (2024)
39. Zheng, L., et al.: Judging LLM-as-a-judge with MT-bench and chatbot arena. In: Proceedings of the Annual Conference on Neural Information Processing Systems (NeurIPS) (2023)

Boosting Data Literacy: The Role of AI in Teaching Detection of Deceptive Charts

Konrad J. Maciborski[1(✉)], Karolina Wysocka[2], Karolina Żelazowska-Byczkowska[3], Styliani Kleanthous[4], and Adam Wierzbicki[1]

[1] Polish-Japanese Academy of Information Technology, Warsaw, Poland
{maciborski,adamw}@pja.edu.pl
[2] Catholic University of Leuven, Leuven, Belgium
[3] Institute of Literary Research of the Polish Academy of Sciences, Warsaw, Poland
[4] Open University od Cyprus, Latsia, Cyprus

Abstract. Deceptive charts can mislead viewers through design flaws or intentional manipulation, posing a challenge to data literacy. This study introduces a deep neural network model and an AI-driven Chrome plug-in: the Deceptive Chart Detector (DCD), designed to identify deceptive charts. In a randomized controlled experiment with school children (N=114) and university students (N=120), we compared AI-supported lessons using the DCD to traditional classroom and e-learning methods. Pre-intervention tests revealed high susceptibility to deceptive charts in both groups. Post-intervention results showed significant improvement across all methods, with AI-based instruction yielding similar or greater gains in detection accuracy, particularly among adults. These findings demonstrate the effectiveness of AI-supported education in enhancing data literacy and reducing vulnerability to visual misinformation.

Keywords: Data Literacy Education · Disinformation · Deceptive Charts

1 Introduction

1.1 Research Context and Purpose

While a picture may be worth a thousand words, a chart may also speak a thousand lies. Charts, though widely used and often more effective than spreadsheets or reports for communicating complex information [9], can be misleading, whether by accident or design. The distinction between *misinformation* (unintentionally misleading) and *disinformation* (intentionally misleading) is critical [7], but in practice, both can undermine trust in data. A well-designed chart based on incorrect data, or an accurate dataset visualized poorly, can both deceive. For this reason, we use the term **deceptive chart** to refer to any misleading visualization, regardless of intent.

A. I. Cristea et al. (Eds.): AIED 2025, LNAI 15877, pp. 92–105, 2025.
https://doi.org/10.1007/978-3-031-98414-3_7

Charts are ubiquitous, from journalistic outlets to social media [28], and exemplars of clear and beautiful data design can be found on platforms like David McCandless's Information is Beautiful, which aims to "distill world data into beautiful, interesting, and useful visualizations" [17]. However, not all charts live up to this goal. The WTF Visualizations website offers a humorous catalog of flawed examples, highlighting the need for better data literacy.

Our goal is to enhance data visualization literacy by developing AI tools that help users identify deceptive charts. Research shows that deceptive charts are often perceived as objective, even by well-educated audiences [14]. We propose an AI-driven browser extension that actively teaches users to detect deceptive visualizations, both in and out of classroom settings.

Using the standard data science evaluation methodology and a randomized, controlled experiment with a pre-test and post-test, we seek to answer the following **research questions**:

1. Can we design an effective AI tool to detect deceptive charts?
2. Can AI effectively teach how to detect deceptive charts?
3. What is the best method for teaching deceptive charts detection: e-learning, classroom learning, or AI-supported education?

1.2 Hypotheses

1. Students are vulnerable to the manipulation presented by deceptive charts. We expect significant differences between their pre-intervention responses to deceptive charts and those to non-deceptive charts, highlighting their inability to consistently identify misleading visualizations.
2. Lessons utilizing AI tools to teach chart manipulation detection will significantly improve students' abilities to identify deceptive charts. We anticipate a significant improvement in accuracy when comparing their pre-intervention and post-intervention responses.
3. The AI-supported lesson on deceptive chart detection will be as effective as, if not more, than a regular classroom lesson. We will compare the post-intervention accuracy of AI-taught students and those taught by a teacher, and we expect that there will be no significant differences between them, or that AI-taught students will perform significantly better.

2 Related Work

Research on chart readability dates back to the 1920 s when efforts began to standardize the selection of the best statistical visualizations [6]. These concepts evolved through research on cognitive processing of chart information [22] and preferences for which data suits which chart type [23]. In the 1960 s, the growth of data visualization software enabled the creation of outrageously deceptive charts, prompting numerous articles and books on common pitfalls and best practices of design [2,3,12–14,24]. All of this led E. R. Tufte to develop the *Lie Factor* and a formula to calculate it [27]:

$$\text{Lie Factor} = \frac{\text{Size of effect shown in the graphic}}{\text{Size of effect in data}}$$

The further the Lie Factor deviates from 1, whether above or below, the more misleading the chart is.

A crowdsourcing study of deceptive chart evaluation revealed that users are significantly vulnerable. The study found that deceptive charts were perceived as showing effects 58.5% to 129.5% larger than control charts [19]. Similarly, in a study on Covid-19 misinformation on Twitter, Lisnic et al. [15] analysed nearly 10,000 tweets with visualizations, finding over 1,000 deceptive charts. Many tweets featured correctly designed charts but included misleading text. Detecting textual manipulation and disinformation is an active research area that complements our work. In a recent large-scale study, Lo et al. [16] identified 74 types of graph design errors that can mislead readers, including new types like visual 3D illusions and colour manipulations. Our research aims to develop a tool capable of detecting 5 types of deceptive chart designs, with potential for expansion to include more manipulation types.

These findings highlight the importance of chart literacy. Chart literacy is the ability to understand and interpret data visualizations, with varying levels among individuals [5]. Human interpretation of visualized data can generally be described, in three steps [21]:

1. recognizing the visual elements like: direction, projection, colour schema
2. understanding the relationships that the visual features represent
3. connecting interpretations from the first two steps with the labelled variables

Eye-tracking studies show that people with different levels of visual data literacy focus on different components of data visualizations [18]. High visual data literacy enables focus on axes and labels, better handling of conflicting data, and improved detection of deception, unlike low-literate users who rely on visual patterns. However, recent research shows that academic training in data visualization alone is not enough to detect deceptive charts, as those are often seen as objective [14]. Thus, in this work, we aim to design an AI-driven browser extension to help users detect deceptive charts while browsing the web.

As detailed in a recent survey [4], research on chart mining involves the automatic detection, extraction, and analysis of charts to recreate underlying data. This approach allows comparison between data effects and chart visualizations, enabling Tufte's Lie Factor calculation. While many graph mining applications exist, few are concerned with detecting deceptive charts. An early example is ReVision, a system that automatically redesigns visualizations to enhance clarity [20]. ReVision classifies chart types using graph mining but lacks precise data extraction and focuses on redesign suggestions rather than detecting misinformation. VisuaLint [10] addresses errors in data visualizations, including dual axes, ineffective colours, and missing legends. Unlike ReVision, it uses Vega-Lite's JSON-based system and implements rules to capture these visualization errors, rather than extracting graph data. Fan et al. [8] focus on line charts, using graph mining to extract data and classify chart types. Their approach identifies manipulations like truncated or inverted y-axes and changed aspect ratios but is limited to line charts and has data extraction accuracy issues. An empirical study with a Web extension showed users with access to it were less deceived and answered questions more accurately.

Psychological inoculation, or *prebunking* [26], strengthens resistance to disinformation by exposing people to weakened forms of misinformation. This approach involves preemptively alerting users and debunking common misleading tactics, enhancing critical thinking skills, and reducing susceptibility to false claims. Evidence suggests that prebunking is effective and has potential applications in digital literacy initiatives. By integrating this technique into digital literacy programs, particularly on social media, we can cultivate a more informed and resilient public, offering a proactive solution to managing the modern infodemic [25]. Future research should focus on refining these methods and assessing their efficacy across diverse populations and platforms.

2.1 Conclusions from Related Work

Research shows that while users can be trained to recognize textual disinformation, deceptive charts have not been explored sufficiently. Data literacy studies reveal that many students struggle with chart analysis, raising concerns about vulnerability to deception. No prior research has explored using AI to teach deceptive chart detection or compared its effectiveness to traditional classroom methods. **This work has two main new contributions**:

- The **Deceptive Chart Detector (DCD)** is a practical browser extension, powered by deep neural networks, that automatically detects various types of deceptive charts for everyday web users.
- The finding that an **AI-supported education method can be as successful as classroom lessons in increasing the accuracy of detecting deceptive charts by students**, both in primary and university levels.

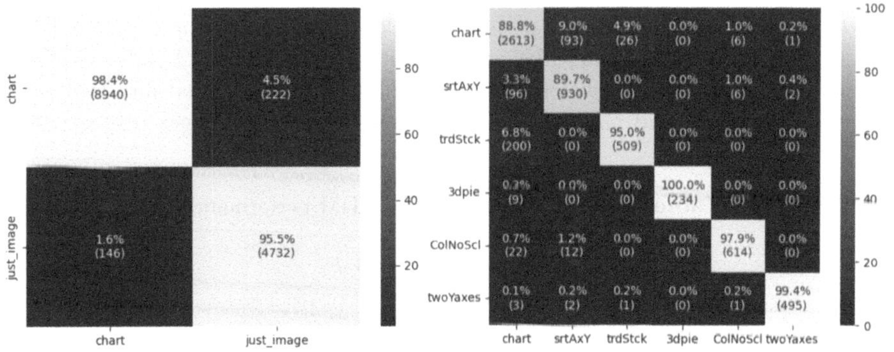

Fig. 1. CDM (left) & DCDM (right) test sets confusion matrices

3 Deceptive Chart Detector Workflow and Design

To address the deceptive chart recognition problem without employing chart mining, we utilized the CNN-based DenseNet architecture. DenseNet is effective at mitigating the vanishing gradient problem in deeper CNNs and enhancing training efficiency [1,11]. This architecture reduces the learning of redundant features, such as basic graphical elements (lines, bars, circles), and enables each layer to access the original input directly, maintaining accuracy even as parameters increase, without performance degradation or overfitting. All datasets, models, as well as the code of the Deceptive Chart Detector, are available at OSF to enable replication of our research.

3.1 Chart Deceptions Types Covered in Application Architecture

We validated our method on five common chart manipulations, demonstrating its scalable effectiveness. The selected categories are:

1. **Truncated Y axis**: common in bar charts, it starts the scale above zero, exaggerating visual differences and distorting data perception [8,15,16,19].
2. **Two Y axes**: This less common chart type manipulation, previously studied [10], is deemed illegible due to its lack of a correct interpretation.
3. **3D pie charts**: common in recent research [16], 3D pie charts distort slice sizes with tilt, and no automatic detection methods exist for this type.
4. **Bright colours and no scale**: colour manipulations in deceptive charts aim to distract attention with bright colours instead of clear data representation [16]. No automatic detection methods for this type currently exist.
5. **Trend hiding by stacking**: this category addresses intentional visual disinformation, where downward or upward trends are obscured by overlaying or rescaling data. To our knowledge, this manipulation type has not been previously documented in the literature.

3.2 Chart Detection Model (CDM)

The dataset consists of data scraped from three sources: Kaggle and USDA ERS, along with challenging chart-like images obtained using the Yandex API by labels. The collected data was manually evaluated and classified into two categories: `just_image` and `chart`, totalling 37763 and 20738 images, respectively.

Table 1. Additional metrics for CDM performance

class	precision	recall	F_1
chart	97.6%	98.4%	98.0%
just image	97.0%	95.5%	96.2%
$\bar{x}$	97.3%	97.0%	97.1%

CDM achieved 97.1–97.5% accuracy on training, 96.9–97.5% on testing, and 95.23% on unseen (appropriately relabelled) DCDM data, showing consistently high precision across classes (see Fig. 1, Table 1).

Table 2. Types of charts generated for DCDM dataset

type of chart	samples count
short y-axis	4,200
trend hiding by stacking	2,228
3D pie chart	1,016
bright colours and no scale	2,560
two Y axes	2,046
non-deceiving	12,430
=	24,480

3.3 Deceptive Chart Detection Model (DCDM)

The dataset consists of programmatically generated deceptive and non-deceptive charts. Based on numerical data generated in Python, diverse graphs with varied backgrounds, colours, and styles were created through seaborn, matplotlib, and Excel Visual Basic. Some types lack non-deceptive counterparts due to visual overlap (see Table 2).

Table 3. Additional metrics for DCDM performance

class	precision	recall	F_1
non-deceiving	95.4%	88.8%	92.0%
short y-axis	89.9%	89.7%	89.8%
trend hiding	71.8%	95.0%	81.8%
3D pie chart	96.3%	100%	98.1%
bright colours	94.8%	97.9%	96.3%
two Y axes	98.6%	99.4%	99.0%
$\bar{x}$	91.1%	95.1%	93.1%

DCDM evaluations showed accuracy between 90.5–92.1% on the training set and 89.9–91.8% on the testing set (see Fig. 1 for details). Most errors occur between the deceiving and non-deceiving classes, indicating a higher likelihood of mislabelling a deceiving chart as non-deceiving rather than as another type of deceiving chart. Expectations are met given the network's high overall performance (Table 3). We conducted a 5-fold cross-validation for a more reliable performance estimate, achieving accuracies between 88.6% and 90.8%, with an average of 89.6%.

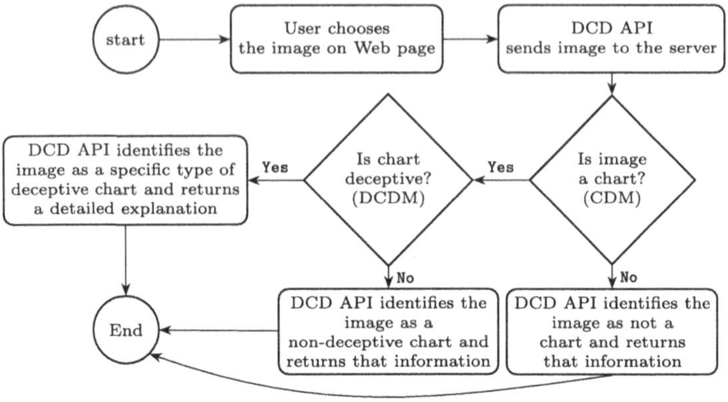

Fig. 2. Deceptive charts AI detecting application workflow logic

3.4 Deceptive Chart Detector (DCD)

We created a Chrome extension that enables users to submit deceiving charts for verification. The JavaScript front-end allows image selection on a webpage, which can be sent to a Flask-based Python back-end API. As summarized in Fig. 2: by processing the image by CDM and DCDM models, the API classifies the image. It provides one of seven possible responses, detailing whether it is a chart and if it contains deceiving visualizations. The feedback includes classification results, a detailed description, and the possibility of redirection to an educational example, as shown in Fig. 3. Since the CDM and DCMD models used by the DCD have sufficiently high accuracy, the DCD can be used as a practical tool for supporting deceiving chart detection online, for example, while browsing the Web or social media. The remainder of this paper focuses on evaluating the DCD's effectiveness in an educational setting, aiming at increasing data literacy by teaching DCD users to detect manipulated charts.

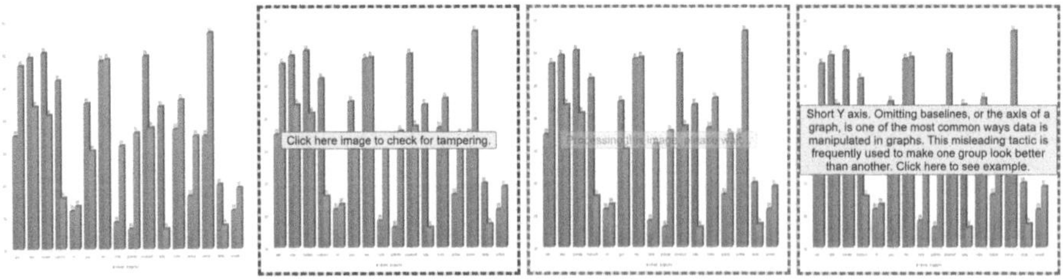

Fig. 3. Step-by-step DCD assisted interaction with deceiving chart found in Web

4 Method

4.1 Participants

The randomized, controlled experiment involved 234 participants (114 children and 120 adults) from Poland and abroad. Children participants were primary school students aged 10 to 13 ($\bar{x} = 11.41$, $\sigma = 0.867$), including 51 females and 63 males. Adult participants were computer science students aged 19 to 42 ($\bar{x} = 22.93$, $\sigma = 3.433$), including 22 females and 98 males.

Participants were informed that the study focused on critical thinking abilities, involving two questionnaires with a lesson in between. The entire experiment was anonymous. All participants could withdraw from the experiment at any time. Primary students required parental consent forms detailing the experiment. The experiment received approval from the Ethical Commission of PJAIT (decision number OKE-08-06-2024).

Children and adults were randomly assigned (in batches of 12 to 16) to one of three groups, each with different teaching methods, but with identical pre- and post-intervention questionnaires:

Group 1: Teacher-Led Group (TLG) 76 participants; 36 children (18 males), 40 adults (36 males)
Group 2: E-Learning Group (ELG) 82 participants; 42 children (15 males), 40 adults (30 males)
Group 3: AI-Supported Group (AISG) 76 participants; 36 children (18 males), 40 adults (32 males)

4.2 Materials

In every group, the experiment consisted of three stages: a pre-intervention questionnaire, a lesson (one of three types), and a post-intervention questionnaire. The full text of the questionnaires and the raw responses are available at OSF for replication of our analysis.

Pre- and Post-intervention questionnaires aimed to assess the impact of each teaching method on improving the participants' ability to recognize deceptive charts, focusing on comparing the AI-supported method with others. Both questionnaires featured six charts presenting interpretable data, each with an accompanying statement. Participants rated their agreement with the statement on a five-point Likert scale. To avoid response bias, incorrect answers could be positioned at either end of the scale (1 or 5). After data cleaning, the response scales were normalized so that the best response was always 1, and responses closer to 5 indicated an increasingly higher susceptibility to manipulation. To assess data literacy, two of the six charts were non-deceptive and easy to interpret. Questions were shuffled, and respondents completed the tests individually on Google Forms within 15 min, with the option to withdraw. Unique IDs ensured anonymity while allowing comparison of pre- and post-intervention results.

The Deception Score the mean response to questions 3–6 (deceptive charts) for each participant, pre- and post-intervention, is called the *deception score*. A higher deception score indicates greater susceptibility to manipulation. This score was used in statistical tests to verify our hypotheses.

Lesson Olans for the experiment focused on strategies for identifying deceptive charts and key data visualization concepts. The Deceptive Chart Detector could be used in a flexible lesson where students could choose their own chart examples. Such an approach would utilize the full potential of AI. Yet, this would make it impossible to compare the effectiveness of a lesson that used the DCD with an e-learning lesson that has a fixed number of examples. For that reason, all lessons used the same examples of deceptive and correct charts. The examples were chosen so that they were not part of the training or testing set of the Deceptive Chart Detection Model.

Each 20-min lesson took place in classrooms with 8–16 participants (adults and children separately), with a present (but not interfering in any way) researcher and either an active (directly interacting, engaging, and dynamically instructing) or passive (provider of pre-set content, non-interactive) teacher. The goal was to boost participants' ability to detect deceptive charts.

Lesson 1 (TLG) featured a traditional format, with an active teacher explaining deceptive techniques using deceptive chart examples (similar, but not the same, to those in the pre-intervention test) on the screen.
Lesson 2 (ELG) used an e-learning module with a passive teacher, explaining chart deceptions using text and non-interactive images.
Lesson 3 (AISG) used an e-learning module with a passive teacher, explaining chart deceptions using the interactive, AI-supported DCD plug-in.

5 Results

5.1 Pre-intervention Results

A paired-samples t-test was used to compare children's pre-intervention responses to deceptive and non-deceptive charts, showed a significant difference between deceptive charts ($M = 3.42$, $SD = 0.57$) and non-deceptive charts ($M = 2.56$, $SD = 0.94$); $t(113) = 7.22$, $p < .001$, two-tailed, indicating that **children were susceptible to deceptive charts**.

We examined the pre-intervention deception scores in each group to ensure no significant differences existed before the interventions. Due to non-normality and lack of homogeneity of variances, we conducted a non-parametric test. The mean ranks of the deception scores were 62.89 (TLG), 55.10 (ELG), and 54.92 (AISG). A Kruskal-Wallis test revealed no significant differences among groups, $H(2, N = 114) = 1.43$, $p = 0.489$, validating our group assignments.

A paired-samples t-test revealed a significant difference in adults' pre-intervention scores for deceptive vs. non-deceptive charts ($M = 3.38$, $SD = 0.71$)

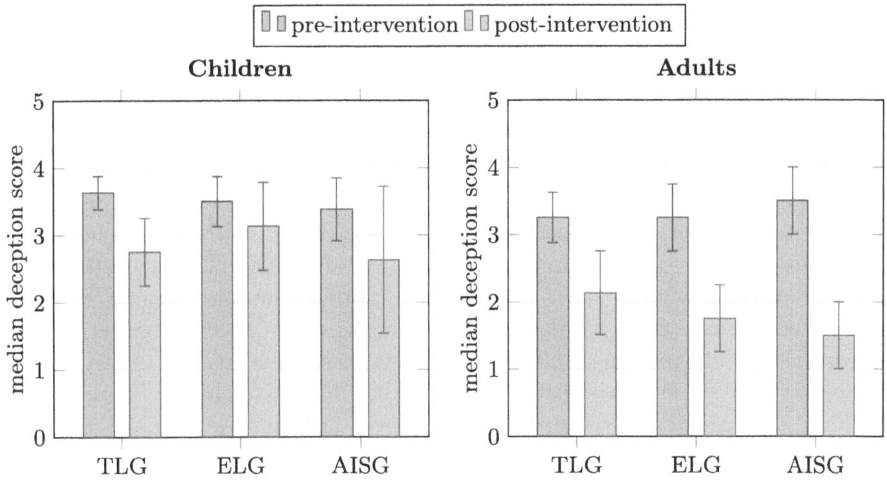

Fig. 4. Pre- and post-intervention deception score medians 4.2 for TLG, ELG and AISG

and non-deceptive charts ($M = 1.61$, $SD = 0.75$); $t(119) = 17.10$, $p < .001$, two-tailed. **Adults showed a large susceptibility to deceptive charts**, (Cohen's $d = 1.56$, 95% CI [1.29, 1.83]) with a larger manipulation effects compared to children (Cohen's $d = 0.68$, 95% CI [0.47, 0.88]).

We examined pre-intervention deception scores in adult groups using a non-parametric test due to non-normally distributed data. The mean ranks were 59.05 for TLG, 55.55 for ELG, and 66.90 for AISG. A Kruskal-Wallis test showed no significant differences between the groups ($H(2, N = 120) = 2.27$, $p = 0.322$), confirming the comparability of the groups before the lessons.

5.2 Comparison of Pre-intervention and Post-intervention Results

Figure 4 shows the median deception scores for children before and after the intervention. All groups improved after the lessons, with AISG showing the lowest median. A Wilcoxon signed-rank test revealed significant improvements for TLG ($z = -4.809$, $p < .001$) and AISG ($z = -3.161$, $p = .002$), but not for ELG ($z = -1.421$, $p = .155$). Results suggest that **e-learning is ineffective for improving children's chart literacy**, while **active teacher-led or AI-based interventions significantly reduce susceptibility to deceptive charts**.

All groups of adult students improved after the lessons, with AISG having the lowest median. The Wilcoxon signed-rank test indicated significant improvement for TLG ($z = -5.102$, $p < .001$), ELG ($z = -4.763$, $p < .001$), and AISG ($z = -5.355$, $p < .001$). These results show significant improvement in all groups post-lesson, with the lowest deception score after the AI lesson, indicating that **AI-based instruction is the most promising in reducing adults' susceptibility to deceptive charts.**

5.3 Comparison of Post-intervention Results Between Groups

Children's post-intervention deception scores were 49.69 for TLG, 67.54 for ELG, and 53.60 for AISG. A Kruskal-Wallis test showed significant differences between groups, $H(2, N = 114) = 6.44$, $p = 0.040$. Post-hoc comparisons using the Dunn method showed that TLG had a significantly lower mean rank than ELG ($p = 0.017$), indicating that an active teacher is more effective in helping participants detect deceptive charts than an e-learning lesson without a teacher. No significant differences were found between AISG and either TLG ($p = 0.615$) or ELG ($p = 0.062$). After Bonferroni correction, none of the comparisons remained significant, though the difference between active and passive teacher groups approached significance ($p = 0.051$). These results suggest that an active teacher is necessary for some children to learn to detect deceptive charts. Furthermore, the **lack of significant differences between the active teacher and AI groups** indicates that AI-supported instruction can have a similar impact.

Adults' post-intervention deception scores were 69.61 for TLG, 61.75 for ELG, and 50.14 for AISG. A Kruskal-Wallis test indicated significant differences between groups, $H(2, N = 120) = 6.42$, $p = 0.040$. Post-hoc comparisons using Dunn's method with Bonferroni correction revealed that the mean rank of AISG was significantly lower than TLG ($p = 0.035$), indicating that adults in the AI-assisted group were less susceptible to deceptive charts than those in the active teacher group. However, no significant differences were found between AISG and ELG ($p = 0.399$) or between TLG and ELG ($p = 0.927$).

These findings indicate that **for adults, AI-assisted teaching reduces susceptibility to deceptive charts more effectively than traditional methods**, even with an active teacher. The lack of significant differences between the AI-assisted and passive teacher groups suggests that adults learn better from e-learning lessons than children. However, the absence of significant differences between TLG and ELG implies that an active teacher alone may not consistently surpass passive teaching in enhancing adults' ability to detect deceptive charts (or that children learn better from a teacher than adults).

6 Discussion and Limitations

This study addressed three research questions (see 1.1), focusing on designing an AI system for detecting deceptive charts (Fig. 2). The system includes the Chart Detection Model (CDM) and the Deceptive Chart Detection Model (DCDM), achieving strong performance (CDM accuracy over 95% and DCDM averaging 89.6% after 5-fold cross-validation, see 3). These results indicate that the AI plugin with CDM and DCDM effectively identifies deceptive charts.

The experimental results show that **AI-supported lessons significantly improved test results for both primary school children and university students** (see 5.2). For primary school children, classroom lessons outperformed e-learning, while AI-supported lessons were as effective as classroom lessons. For university students, AI-supported lessons proved the most effective, indicating that younger students benefit more from human instruction, whereas adults perform well with self-guided AI learning (see 5.3).

We tested hypotheses with experiments involving school children (N=114) and university students (N=120). Pre-intervention results confirmed hypothesis 1 (see 5.1), showing that both groups are highly susceptible to deceptive charts. This aligns with prior findings [19], enhancing our study's external validity.

AI-supported lessons significantly improved students' ability to identify deceptive charts, supporting hypothesis 2. Pre- and post-intervention comparisons showed statistically significant improvements for both groups (see 5.2).

Post-intervention tests (see 5.3) indicate that, for university students, AI-supported instruction is the most effective teaching method and outperforms an active teacher. For primary school children, no significant differences emerged between the AI-supported and active-teacher groups. These findings validate hypothesis 3: **AI-supported instruction matches or exceeds the effectiveness of traditional teaching in deceptive chart detection.**

Limitations. Despite our best efforts, this study has several limitations. The smallest experimental groups had 36 participants, which, while adequate for hypothesis testing, limited our ability to account for individual differences such as IQ and numeracy skills. Although we assessed age effects by including both primary school and university students, conclusions are limited by the selection bias of predominantly male technical university students (82%), contrasting with a 45% female representation among primary school participants. We did not compare DCD to existing tools such as ReVision or VisualInt, as DCD is designed to detect different types of chart manipulations that these systems are not equipped to address.

7 Conclusion and Future Work

Our research identified a notable gap in the literature on detecting deceptive charts within data literacy education. While previous studies have concentrated on training users to recognize textual disinformation, deceptive charts have largely been overlooked, despite evidence that many students struggle with chart analysis and are vulnerable to manipulation.

Building on research showing that brief interventions can boost disinformation awareness, we demonstrate AI's potential to teach deceptive chart detection. Future work will explore integrating AI lessons into school curricula, expanding chart types, refining detection models, and testing hybrid human-AI teaching strategies to enhance digital literacy and critical thinking.

Acknowledgement. This research was supported by the EUonAIR project (number 101177370, ERASMUS-EDU-2024-EUR-UNIV-1), within the framework of the EUonAIR Centre of Excellence in Responsible AI in Education, co-funded by the European Commission.

References

1. Basodi, S., Ji, C., Zhang, H., Pan, Y.: Gradient amplification: an efficient way to train deep neural networks. Big Data Mining Anal. **3**(3), 196–207
2. Bresciani, S., Eppler, M.J.: The pitfalls of visual representations: a review and classification of common errors made while designing and interpreting visualizations. SAGE Open **5**(4), 215824401561145 (2015)
3. Cairo, A.: Graphics lies, misleading visuals. In: Bihanic, D. (ed.) New Challenges for Data Design, pp. 103–116. Springer, London, London (2015)
4. Davila, K., Setlur, S., Doermann, D., Kota, B.U., Govindaraju, V.: Chart mining: a survey of methods for automated chart analysis. IEEE Trans. Pattern Anal. Mach. Intell. **43**(11), 3799–3819 (2021)
5. Duesbery, L., Werblow, J., Yovanoff, P.: Graphical literacy moderates the interaction of decorative dimensionality and cognitive demand in computer-based graph comprehension. J. Educ. Comput. Res. **45**(1), 75–93
6. Eells, W.C.: The relative merits of circles and bars for representing component parts. J. Am. Stat. Assoc. **21**(154), 119–132 (1926)
7. European Commission. Directorate General for Communications Networks, Content and Technology.: A multi-dimensional approach to disinformation: report of the independent High level Group on fake news and online disinformation. Publications Office, LU (2018)
8. Fan, A., Ma, Y., Mancenido, M., Maciejewski, R.: Annotating line charts for addressing deception. In: CHI Conference on Human Factors in Computing Systems, pp. 1–12. ACM, New Orleans LA USA (Apr 2022)
9. Gray, J., Bounegru, L., Chambers, L., Centre, E.J., Foundation, O.K. (eds.): The data journalism handbook. O'Reilly Media, Sebastopol, CA, 1st ed edn. (2012)
10. Hopkins, A.K., Correll, M., Satyanarayan, A.: VisuaLint: sketchy in situ annotations of chart construction errors. Comput. Graph. Forum **39**(3), 219–228
11. Huang, G., Liu, Z., van der Maaten, L., Weinberger, K.Q.: Densely Connected Convolutional Networks. arXiv:1608.06993 [cs] (Jan 2018)
12. Huff, D.: How to Lie with Statistics. London, repr edn, A Penguin book mathematics, Penguin (1991)
13. Jones, G.E.: How to Lie with Charts. Sybex, San Francisco (1995)
14. Lauer, C., O'Brien, S.: How people are influenced by deceptive tactics in everyday charts and graphs. IEEE Trans. Prof. Commun. **63**(4), 327–340 (2020)
15. Lisnic, M., Polychronis, C., Lex, A., Kogan, M.: Misleading Beyond Visual Tricks: How People Actually Lie with Charts. Tech. rep., Open Science Framework
16. Lo, L.Y.H., Gupta, A., Shigyo, K., Wu, A., Bertini, E., Qu, H.: Misinformed by Visualization: What Do We Learn From Misinformative Visualizations? (2022)
17. McCandless, D.: Information is beautiful. Collins, London, new ed edn. (2012)
18. Okan, Y., Galesic, M., García-Retamero, R.: How people with low and high graph literacy process health graphs: evidence from eye-tracking. J. Behav. Decis. Mak. **29**, 271–294 (2016)
19. Pandey, A.V., Rall, K., Satterthwaite, M.L., Nov, O., Bertini, E.: How deceptive are deceptive visualizations?: an empirical analysis of common distortion techniques. In: Proceedings of the 33rd Annual ACM Conference on Human Factors in Computing Systems, pp. 1469–1478. ACM, Seoul Republic of Korea (Apr 2015)
20. Savva, M., Kong, N., Chhajta, A., Fei-Fei, L., Agrawala, M., Heer, J.: ReVision: automated classification, analysis and redesign of chart images. In: Proceedings of the 24th annual ACM symposium on User interface software and technology - UIST '11, p. 393. ACM Press, Santa Barbara, California, USA (2011)

21. Shah, P., Mayer, R.E., Hegarty, M.: Graphs as aids to knowledge construction: signaling techniques for guiding the process of graph comprehension. J. Educ. Psychol. **91**, 690–702 (1999)
22. Simkin, D., Hastie, R.: An information-processing analysis of graph perception. J. Am. Stat. Assoc. **82**(398), 454–465 (1987)
23. Spence, I., Lewandowsky, S.: Displaying proportions and percentages. Appl. Cogn. Psychol. **5**(1), 61–77 (1991)
24. Szafir, D.A.: The good, the bad, and the biased: five ways visualizations can mislead (and how to fix them). Interactions **25**(4), 26–33 (2018)
25. Traberg, C.S., et al.: Prebunking Against Misinformation in the Modern Digital Age, pp. 99–111. Springer International Publishing, Cham (2023)
26. Traberg, C.S., Roozenbeek, J., van der Linden, S.: Psychological inoculation against misinformation: current evidence and future directions. Ann. Am. Acad. Pol. Soc. Sci. **700**(1), 136–151 (2022)
27. Tufte, E.R.: The visual display of quantitative information. Graphics Press, Cheshire, Conn, 2nd ed., 8th print edn. (2013)
28. Vougiouklis, P., Carr, L., Simperl, E.P.B.: Pie chart or pizza: Identifying chart types and their virality on twitter. In: ICWSM (2020)

An End-to-End Approach for Child Reading Assessment in the Xhosa Language

Sergio Chevtchenko[1,2(✉)], Nikhil Navas[1,2], Rafaella Vale[4], Franco Ubaudi[5], Sipumelele Lucwaba[6], Cally Ardington[3], Soheil Afshar[7], Mark Antoniou[2], and Saeed Afshar[1,2]

[1] International Centre for Neuromorphic Systems, Western Sydney University, Sydney, Australia
s.chevtchenko@westernsyndey.edu.au
[2] The MARCS Institute for Brain, Behaviour and Development, Western Sydney University, Sydney, Australia
[3] University of Cape Town, Cape Town, South Africa
[4] Universidade Federal de Pernambuco, Centro de Informatica, Recife, PE, Brazil
[5] The School of Computer, Data and Mathematical Sciences, Western Sydney University, Sydney, Australia
[6] University of Pretoria, Gauteng, South Africa
[7] Macquarie University, Sydney, Australia

Abstract. Child literacy is a strong predictor of life outcomes at the subsequent stages of an individual's life. This points to a need for targeted interventions in vulnerable low and middle income populations to help bridge the gap between literacy levels in these regions and high income ones. In this effort, reading assessments provide an important tool to measure the effectiveness of these programs and AI can be a reliable and economical tool to support educators with this task. Developing accurate automatic reading assessment systems for child speech in low-resource languages poses significant challenges due to limited data and the unique acoustic properties of children's voices. This study focuses on Xhosa, a language spoken in South Africa, to advance child speech recognition capabilities. We present a novel dataset composed of child speech samples in Xhosa. The dataset is available upon request and contains ten words and letters, which are part of the Early Grade Reading Assessment (EGRA) system. Each recording is labeled with an online and cost-effective approach by multiple markers and a subsample is validated by an independent EGRA reviewer. This dataset is evaluated with three fine-tuned state-of-the-art end-to-end models: wav2vec 2.0, HuBERT, and Whisper. The results indicate that the performance of these models can be significantly influenced by the amount and balancing of the available training data, which is fundamental for cost-effective large dataset collection. Furthermore, our experiments indicate that the wav2vec 2.0 performance is improved by training on multiple classes at a time, even when the number of available samples is constrained.

A. I. Cristea et al. (Eds.): AIED 2025, LNAI 15877, pp. 106–119, 2025.
https://doi.org/10.1007/978-3-031-98414-3_8

Keywords: EGRA · Deep Learning · Speech-to-Text

1 Introduction

Reading assessment in the early grades is essential for pinpointing the difficulties children encounter while learning to read. By identifying these challenges, educators can design targeted interventions that accelerate literacy development and foster inclusion. Artificial intelligence offers a practical way to scale such assessments, providing rapid insights into children's oral-reading skills and the obstacles revealed by pronunciation tasks, even when data and resources are limited.

The motivation for this research is a pragmatic one. Good education is a crucial component for facilitating a favorable future for children. While assessing speech fluency and reading skills is a valid way to inform about the advancement of literacy acquisition in children [8], a simple approach to evaluating their aptitude to understand text in early years is to analyze their ability to correctly pronounce words [15], a key focus of this research. A poor ability to pronounce words is indicative of possible issues with hearing, understanding grammar, or other difficulties such as dyslexia [24]. As a result, uncovering these issues quickly can promote focused guidance from an early age that greatly improves a child's educational outcome [12,24].

To tackle this, the use of automatic speech recognition (ASR) can greatly assist in finding reading issues that manifest themselves in pronunciation difficulties. ASR can help automate thorough and accurate assessment of a child's ability and the determination of progress as educators seek to address problems. However, the effectiveness of ASR can be greatly impacted in the context of low-resource languages (LRL) [13,20], that is, languages with limited availability of resources, for the effective automated construction of models needed for assessing children's speech. Hence this research also focuses on languages that are characterized as LRL, an example of which is the South African language Xhosa, which also provides phonetic complexity challenges to this research [14].

This research investigates the use of state-of-the-art (SOTA) speech classification models that convert the audio of child speech into the phonetics responsible for the language of choice. The South African language Xhosa is used as the target language. Our investigation is principally focused on testing a cost-effective data-labeling method and understanding the impact of choices in model parameters, training set sizes, and model building strategies. The main goal of this research is the development of a solution that fulfills the following criteria: accurate assessment of a child's reading ability; coping with restrictions in terms of the amount of available training data; potential integration with the Early Grade Reading Assessment (EGRA) program [8], and providing a solution architecture that is easy to reuse for other speaking languages.

Accurately assessing a child's ability to pronounce words is time-consuming and prone to error, since it can be impacted by the ability and consistency of individual human assessors. As such, automation provides a way for avoiding these issues, while also reducing needed time and effort. Additionally, AI-powered assessments provide a means for consistently tracking a child's progress, while reducing the impact of confounding variables such as human assessor subjectivity and enforcing the use of an identical assessment across time and individual children.

The next problem to address is regarding LRLs. Many speaking languages are characterized as LRLs because of a lack of large text corpora or other linguistic resources that are suitable for training ASR solutions. This presents a serious barrier since it impacts solution effectiveness and greatly increases the needed effort for developing ASR solutions. Novel approaches are needed for facilitating the development of accurate models, coping with limited resources, and managing variability of human expertise across limited staff. Given these challenges, the use of self-supervised SOTA speech recognition architectures offers a promising solution by reducing the reliance on extensive labeled datasets and enabling a more detailed focus on nuanced parts of speech.

The present work makes the following contributions to automated reading assessment for LRL. First, it introduces a new, high-quality dataset of Xhosa child reading samples, specifically designed for early grade reading assessment. This dataset has been made available upon request to the community. Second, it details and validates a cost-effective online method for data labeling and verification, demonstrating its suitability for resource-constrained settings. Third, it provides a comprehensive evaluation of three fine-tuned SOTA speech classification architectures on this dataset, highlighting how variations in training set size and class balancing can significantly impact performance.

2 Related Work

Among self-supervised models, wav2vec has emerged as a state-of-the-art architecture for ASR, using self-supervised learning to extract meaningful features from raw audio and requiring minimal labeled data for fine-tuning [3]. Doumbouya et al. [7] adapted wav2vec to the West African Radio Corpus, demonstrating sensitivity to features of African languages and effective identification in noisy multilingual settings. Similarly, our work involves fine-tuning a pre-trained wav2vec 2.0 model, augmented with a classifier multilayer perceptron to classify audio recordings of early grade children learning the Xhosa language as correct or incorrect pronunciations.

Wav2vec has also been effective in detecting pronunciation errors, offering potential in language learning and pronunciation assessment [17]. Shekar et al. [22] used wav2vec to analyze speech recordings of non-native speakers, detecting mispronunciations and capturing fine-grained phonetic details for phoneme-level error diagnosis. Recent research by Jain et al. [11] examined the use of wav2vec models in pediatric learning assessment, a challenging domain due to varied speech patterns in children. Abaskohi et al. [1] further developed and adapted wav2vec with a preprocessing technique called random frequency pitch, useful for capturing the frequency characteristics of children's speech. Applied to Persian children's speech and reading recordings, the model significantly reduced word error rates compared to baselines, confirming its effectiveness in pediatric assessment tasks. Obiang et al. [16] fine-tuned wav2vec for Yoruba, a low-resourced tonal language, effectively capturing complex pitch and pronunciation variations superior to traditional methods. Similarly, Okwugbe et al. [6] developed a deep learning model combining rCNNs and BiLSTMs with CTC for speech recognition of the Fon and Igbo languages, addressing challenges due to data scarcity.

Other works have tackled the application of ASR in assessing and improving reading skills, particularly in children. Sabu and Rao [21] sought to evaluate word reading accuracy and identify prosodic elements like phrase breaks and emphasized words in children studying English as a second language. The complexities of the prosodic events were reflected in the lower precision estimation shown by the system, revealing the importance of an accurate feature extraction. Shivakumar and Georgiou [23] used transfer learning from adult ASR models as a way to circumvent the lack of extensive availability of children speech data. Strategies to adapt to varying amounts of data and children's ages were also recommended. Bai et al. [5] explored the evaluation of decoding skills in Dutch children to provide feedback meant to impact reading accuracy and speed. The study was further expanded in [4] to also highlight the most problematic words encountered by the students. Bachiri et al. [2] proposed an interactive learning system as a Moodle plugin to aid in child reading assessment in underserved educational settings. The authors make a case for the integration of AI-based speech recognition to enhance literacy development due to the positive results observed. In an attempt to investigate how AI performs in assessing students reading fluency and level compared to human experts, Yıldız et al. [25] found that AI offered reliable predictions that could contribute to lowering costs and improving efficiency.

The recent publication by Henkel et al. [9] has a significant overlap with the intended goals of the current work. The automation of reading assessment for students in a resource-constrained context is investigated to compare the potential of Whisper V2 and wav2vec 2.0 models against human raters. The models produce transcriptions of audio recordings of Ghanaian students reading to provide an estimate of the students' oral reading fluency. The fluency scores given by Whisper V2 were found to be highly correlated with assessments by human experts, even without fine-tuning. It is important to note that the way these models were used to score reading fluency in students would not be suitable for the goal of the current work, since the lack of fine-tuning may result in overcorrections that ignore mispronunciations or in the misinterpretation of accents, as demonstrated in Sect. 4.1. As the present work aims to evaluate the pronunciation of words and letters by children in the Xhosa language, fine-tuning of the models is necessary to classify samples as correct or incorrect according to the target language.

The above studies underscore the effectiveness of speech-to-text models for low-resource languages and child speech recognition. To the best of our knowledge, this is the first work to evaluate end-to-end models on words and letters for a child reading assessment problem.

3 Methodology

3.1 Dataset Description

The dataset was collected in 2024 as part of the Early Grade Reading Assessment (EGRA), conducted in grades 1 to 4 at schools in South Africa. This study focuses on the following ten letters and words in the Xhosa language: *d*, *v*, *n*, *ewe*, *hayi*, *hl*, *inja*, *kude*, *molo* and *ng*. A question is presented to the student, asking to pronounce one of these words or letters, followed by a recording. The recording stops when the student presses a button for the next question. The average duration of the recordings is around 4 s, with added variability mostly due to multiple attempts at pronouncing the same question.

A total of 14,971 recordings of the EGRA collection with over 19 h in recording time collected over 8 months are made available upon request. Each recording is labeled as correct or incorrect by three fluent Xhosa speakers, resulting in a dataset of 44,913 labeled entries. Since some recordings received conflicting labels, a validation experiment was conducted, as described in Sect. 3.2. Figure 1 illustrates the distribution of these labels by question, showing that certain items can be more challenging to classify. For example, most children correctly pronounced the letter *n*, whereas a considerable number struggled with the consonant *hl*. To enable cost-effective and efficient data collection and labeling, custom mobile and server applications were developed as part of the project. A more detailed description of these tools will be provided in a forthcoming publication.

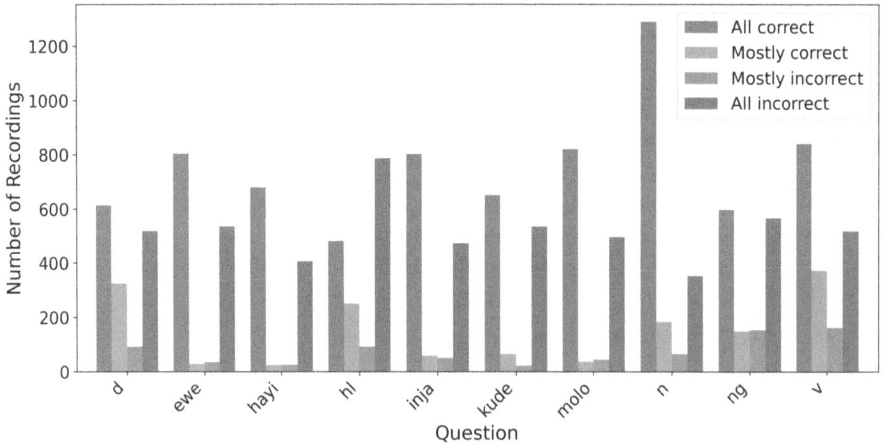

Fig. 1. Distribution of All correct, Mostly correct, Mostly incorrect, and All incorrect samples for each word and letter in the dataset.

Although each recording is intended to capture a single spoken word, even those pronounced correctly often include additional artifacts, such as classroom noise or multiple attempts at pronouncing the word on the app's screen. This variability in recording size and quality makes the classification problem more complicated and is further illustrated in Fig. 2.

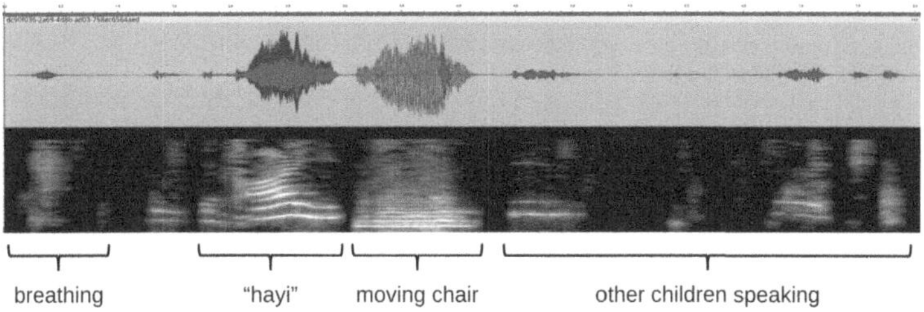

Fig. 2. A spectrogram of an eight-second recording containing a correct pronunciation of the word "hayi" and other ambient sounds.

3.2 Data Labeling and Validation

Selecting appropriate validation criteria for training data is another significant challenge. To ensure high-quality recordings, each sample is labeled by three independent markers, and only those with consensus are included in training. To validate this method, 400 recordings were randomly selected from ten words in the dataset, with each word contributing 40 samples. These were evenly distributed across four marking scenarios: (a) all three markers labeled it as correct, (b) all three labeled it as incorrect, (c) one marked it incorrect while the other two marked it correct, and (d) one marked it correct while the other two marked it incorrect. An expert in traditional EGRA marking for Xhosa language then assessed these samples, and Table 1 presents the agreement rate between the expert and the original markers. An agreement rate per question is also presented in Fig. 3. Thus, consensus-based approach retains approximately 85% of the original dataset, while maximizing data reliability. Consequently, while the provided dataset includes all 14,971 recordings, the experimental results in Sect. 4 are based only on the 12,747 consensus-marked recordings.

Table 1. Agreement rates and number of recordings for each condition.

Condition	Agreement rate	Total # of recordings
All data	71.25%	14,971
Consensus	85.00%	12,747 (85.1%)
Consensus & one incorrect	80.00%	14,235 (95.0%)
Consensus & one correct	75.00%	13,483 (90.0%)

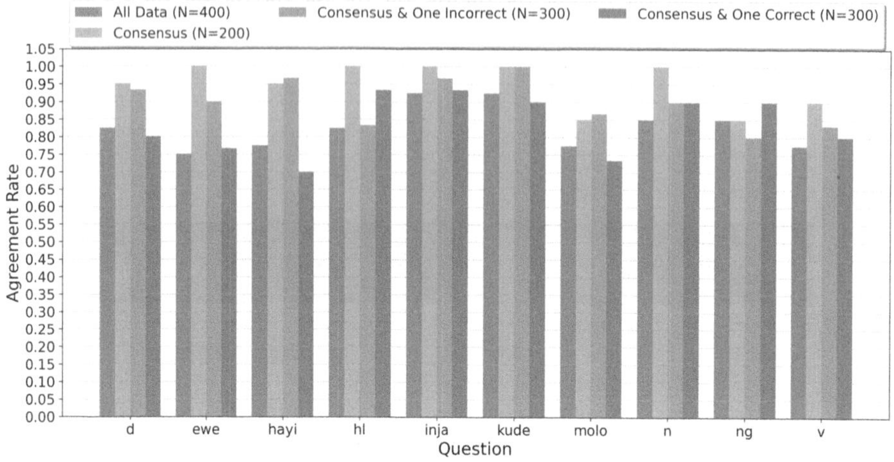

Fig. 3. Agreement rate between an expert and the reviewers, considering different validation criteria.

3.3 Fine-Tuned Classification Architectures

In this work, we consider three SOTA speech recognition architectures: wav2vec 2.0 [3], HuBERT [10] and Whisper [19]. In order to select baseline models, we conducted preliminary experiments with the pre-trained versions of these architectures and varying hyperparameters such as learning rate and batch size. While this is not meant to be an exhaustive optimization, this step is necessary to provide a good baseline for the presented dataset. The pre-trained models are fine-tuned with a learning rate of 3×10^{-5} over 1000 steps with a batch size of four and gradient accumulation of over two steps to achieve an effective batch size of eight.

This study used a snapshot of the wav2vec[1] 2.0 model which has been pre-trained on the Multilingual LibriSpeech[2], CommonVoice[3], and BABEL[4] datasets. This extensive training allows for cross-lingual representation learning via a self-supervised approach that extracts meaningful features from raw audio data. Additionally, we employed the multilingual mHuBERT 147[5] model, which was trained on 90,430 h of openly licensed audio from 147 languages across 16 independent datasets. Finally, we selected a distilled version of Whisper[6] from OpenAI, an end-to-end Transformer-based architecture for sequence-to-sequence tasks.

[1] https://huggingface.co/facebook/wav2vec2-xlsr-53-espeak-cv-ft.
[2] https://www.openslr.org/94/.
[3] https://commonvoice.mozilla.org/en/languages.
[4] https://catalog.ldc.upenn.edu/byyear.
[5] https://huggingface.co/utter-project/mHuBERT-147.
[6] https://huggingface.co/distil-whisper/distil-medium.en.

3.4 Experimental Evaluation and Metrics

A test set of 50 positive and 50 negative samples is randomly selected from the dataset for each of the ten questions, resulting in a test set of 1000 recordings. In order to produce more reliable results, we repeat this partitioning five times and evaluate each model's configuration on these five independent runs. Thus, most of the results presented in Sect. 4 are an average of 50 experiments: 5 randomly selected test sets and 10 questions from the dataset.

One of the main objectives of this work is to assess how varying amounts of training data affect the baseline models. As discussed in Sect. 3.1, certain questions often yield unbalanced samples for correct (positive) and incorrect (negative) pronunciations. To address this, we train the baseline models on 50, 100, 200, and 300 randomly selected positive and negative samples for each question, resulting in 16 distinct training configurations. Each model may be trained on a single question (as a binary classifier) or on multiple questions simultaneously, applying the same sampling strategy per question.

As each fine-tuned classifier is evaluated on a balanced set of 50 positive and 50 negative samples per question, we define the confusion matrix categories as follows:

- **True positive (TP)**: When both the ground truth label and the prediction correspond to the question.
- **True negative (TN)**: When neither the ground truth label nor the prediction correspond to the question.
- **False negative (FN)**: When the ground truth label corresponds to the question but the prediction does not.
- **False positive (FP)**: When the ground truth label does not correspond to the question but the prediction does.

We then define the false positive rate (FPR) as $FPR = \frac{FP}{FP+TN}$, the false negative rate (FNR) as $FNR = \frac{FN}{TP+FN}$, and the diagnostic efficiency (DE) as $DE = \frac{TP+TN}{TP+TN+FP+FN}$.

4 Results and Discussion

Figure 4 provides an overview of the false positive and false negative rates obtained on the test set by the three baseline architectures. As described in Sect. 3.4, the models are trained on a variable number of samples and questions at a time, while evaluated on a fixed test subset. The presented data is an average across 10 questions and 5 independent runs, making a total of 50 samples. The results indicate that changes in the training data can have a significant impact on the performance of the models and both wav2vec 2.0 and Whisper generally achieve more favorable FNR-FPR trade-offs than the HuBERT architecture.

Additionally, Table 2 compares the computational requirements of these architectures. While HuBERT is significantly more efficient in terms of training and inference, the wav2vec 2.0 model requires less computational resources for training than Whisper.

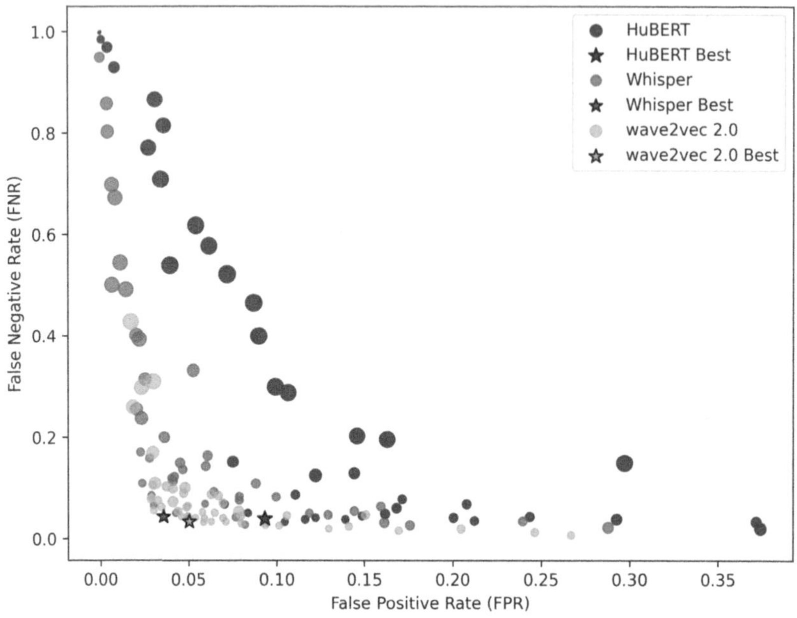

Fig. 4. Distribution of FPR and FNR for each model, averaged across ten questions. The dot size is proportional to the standard deviation over 50 samples. The highlighted results are the best ones in terms of the diagnostic efficiency.

Table 2. Comparison of training (1000 steps) and inference time (single recording) on a Google Colab L4 instance, averaged over 10 runs for each model.

Model	Training (s)	Inference (s)
HuBERT	343	0.44
wav2vec 2.0	1332	1.70
Whisper	2511	1.54

The best results obtained from each model are also presented in more detail in Table 3, considering top five configurations in terms of the diagnostic efficiency. While wav2vec 2.0 and Whisper provide mostly equivalent results in terms of DE, it should be noted that no single configuration was able to obtain the overall best performance in terms of both FPR and FNR and that wav2vec 2.0 model benefits from being trained on multiple questions at a time. This effect is further illustrated in Fig. 5, which shows how training set size influences diagnostic efficiency under a limited-data scenario (i.e., when correct and incorrect samples are restricted to 50 or 100).

A per-question breakdown of the top five models is presented in Fig. 6. This suggests that while an average diagnostic efficiency of around 91% is possible, the presented dataset is especially challenging for short sounds.

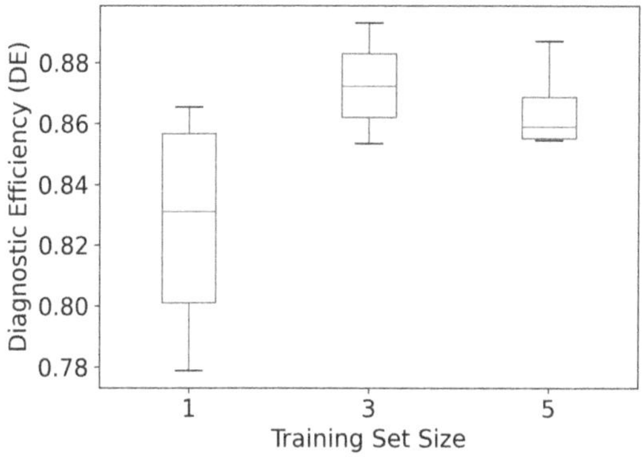

Fig. 5. The effect of training set size on the wave2vec 2.0 performance under limited data conditions.

Table 3. Top-five results per model in terms of Diagnostic Efficiency (DE). Highlighted entries are not significantly different (p>0.05) from the best value in each column. Set column indicates the number of questions used to train the model at a time.

Model	Set	Correct	Incorrect	DE % (±std)	FPR % (±std)	FNR % (±std)
HuBERT	1	200	300	87.04 (5.41)	9.32 (4.79)	**4.00 (3.64)**
HuBERT	1	100	200	86.99 (5.55)	8.40 (4.06)	5.04 (4.26)
HuBERT	1	100	300	86.66 (7.11)	7.08 (5.08)	6.76 (5.39)
HuBERT	1	300	300	86.61 (5.51)	10.44 (4.97)	**3.28 (3.42)**
HuBERT	1	200	200	85.08 (7.35)	11.60 (6.31)	**3.80 (3.57)**
W2v 2.0	3	300	200	**91.70 (5.28)**	5.04 (3.50)	**3.44 (4.10)**
W2v 2.0	3	200	300	**91.66 (6.02)**	**3.04 (2.56)**	5.48 (5.46)
W2v 2.0	5	300	200	**91.30 (5.65)**	4.60 (3.34)	4.32 (4.56)
W2v 2.0	5	300	100	**91.10 (4.88)**	5.88 (3.44)	**3.20 (3.92)**
W2v 2.0	3	200	200	**90.86 (5.62)**	4.96 (3.71)	4.40 (4.59)
Whisper	1	300	300	**92.22 (4.99)**	**3.60 (3.38)**	4.36 (3.40)
Whisper	1	300	200	**91.41 (5.22)**	4.96 (3.94)	**3.84 (3.28)**
Whisper	1	200	200	**90.89 (5.19)**	4.28 (3.33)	5.04 (4.45)
Whisper	1	200	300	**90.65 (5.40)**	**3.04 (2.84)**	6.52 (4.67)
Whisper	1	300	100	89.28 (5.75)	8.24 (4.96)	**2.72 (2.93)**

4.1 Comparison with an ASR Model

In order to highlight the advantages of the classification approach proposed in this work, we also evaluate a recently released checkpoint of the wav2vec 2.0 architecture, fine-tuned on 1,162 languages, including Xhosa, using the Massive Multilingual Speech (MMS-1B) framework [18]. For testing, we supplied the correct pronunciations of each question in our dataset as input to MMS-

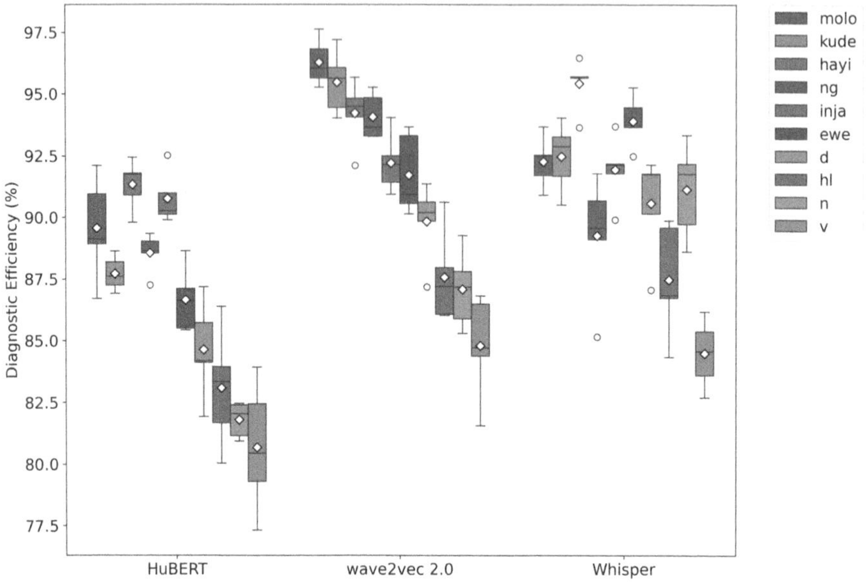

Fig. 6. Per-question average performance of the top five models from Table 3.

Table 4. Transcription accuracy by question, using the MMS-1B model for speech-to-text.

Label	Samples	Correct	Accuracy (%)
d	503	28	5.57
ewe	689	282	40.93
hayi	688	40	5.81
hl	423	1	0.24
v	796	4	0.50
n	1139	8	0.70
molo	709	177	24.96
kude	557	64	11.49
ng	538	2	0.37
inja	691	195	28.22

1B in speech-to-text mode, paired with a Xhosa tokenizer. Overall, only 6.91% of these transcriptions precisely matched the expected word or letter. Table 4 provides a breakdown of the model's performance for each question, indicating that while this approach performs better on words than on letters, it struggles significantly with noisy recordings, such as the example illustrated in Fig. 2. A sample of transcriptions[7] in different scenarios is also provided, suggesting that

[7] https://osf.io/g83vs/?view_only=19403ae222d44fe2bdd669c12fbce017.

direct multilingual ASR usage in classroom conditions may be less effective for short word- or letter-level inputs.

5 Conclusion

This paper presents a cost-effective method for collecting and labeling child speech data in a low-resource language, and for training an AI model to assess reading proficiency, tailored for early-grade learners. We introduce a challenging dataset of Xhosa child speech, recorded under realistic classroom conditions that include noise and multiple pronunciation attempts. The dataset contains 14,971 audio recordings, each containing a single word or letter, which are part of the Early Grade Reading Assessment (EGRA) system. The recordings were labeled online by three independent markers, and a sample was validated by an expert EGRA reviewer to confirm reliability.

Three state-of-the-art speech recognition architectures were fine-tuned as binary classifiers and the experimental results indicate that data balancing and multi-question training strategies substantially affect performance. In particular, wav2vec 2.0 and Whisper are generally found to outperform HuBERT, achieving lower false positive and false negative rates. Although wav2vec 2.0 and Whisper demonstrate comparable accuracy, wav2vec 2.0 demands fewer computational resources during the training phase. Further comparisons with a large-scale multilingual ASR model (MMS-1B) confirm the effectiveness of the proposed approach, especially for short, noisy speech segments in a classroom setting.

Future work is planned to focus on further improving the sample efficiency of the models, while providing a phoneme-based feedback to the user. Preliminary experiments on another LRL dataset, Sepedi, indicate similar performance for wav2vec 2.0 and this additional dataset is expected to be released in forthcoming research. Ultimately, the goal of this project is to develop a cost-effective reading tutoring system for early-grade learners, thereby supporting the preservation and educational advancement of low-resource languages.

References

1. Abaskohi, M., et al.: Automatic speech recognition for speech assessment of Persian preschool children. In: Proceedings of the International Conference on Speech and Language Processing, pp. 123–130 (2023)
2. Bachiri, Y.A., Mouncif, H., Bouikhalene, B., Hamzaoui, R.: Integrating AI-based speech recognition technology to enhance reading assessments within Morocco's tarl program. Turkish Online J. Distance Educ. **25**(4), 1–15 (2024)
3. Baevski, A., Zhou, Y., Mohamed, A., Auli, M.: wav2vec 2.0: A framework for self-supervised learning of speech representations. Adv. Neural Inform. Process. Syst. **33**, 12449–12460 (2020)
4. Bai, Y., Tejedor-García, C., Hubers, F., Cucchiarini, C., Strik, H.: Automatic speech recognition technology and reading skill development in primary school. In: ICERI2021 Proceedings, pp. 6188–6195. IATED (2021)

5. Bai, Y., Hubers, F., Cucchiarini, C., Strik, H.: ASR-based evaluation and feedback for individualized reading practice. In: Interspeech 2020, pp. 3870–3874 (2020). https://doi.org/10.21437/Interspeech.2020-2842
6. Dossou, B.F.P., Emezue, O.: Okwugbé: End-to-end speech recognition for Fon and Igbo. In: Proceedings of the 2024 International Conference on Speech and Language Technology, pp. 123–134 (2021)
7. Doumbouya, M.L., et al.: Using radio archives for low-resource speech recognition: Towards an intelligent virtual assistant for illiterate users. In: Proceedings of the IEEE International Conference on Acoustics, Speech and Signal Processing (ICASSP), pp. 1234–1238 (2021)
8. Dubeck, M.M., Gove, A.: The early grade reading assessment (EGRA): its theoretical foundation, purpose, and limitations. Int. J. Educ. Dev. **40**, 315–322 (2015)
9. Henkel, O., Horne-Robinson, H., Hills, L., Roberts, B., McGrane, J.: Supporting literacy assessment in west Africa: Using state-of-the-art speech models to assess oral reading fluency. International Journal of Artificial Intelligence in Education, pp. 1–22 (2025)
10. Hsu, W.N., Bolte, B., Tsai, Y., Lakhotia, K., Salakhutdinov, R., Mohamed, A.: Hubert: self-supervised speech representation learning by masked prediction of hidden units. IEEE/ACM Trans. Audio, Speech, Lang. Process. **29**, 3451–3460 (2021)
11. Jain, R., Barcovschi, A., Yiwere, M.Y., Bigioi, D., Corcoran, P.: CUCU: A wav2vec2-based experimental study on self-supervised learning methods to improve child speech recognition. IEEE Access **11**, 46938–46948 (2023)
12. Kim, S., Park, S., Kim, K., Jung, K., So, S., Kim, M.: Automatic pronunciation assessment using self-supervised speech representation learning. arXiv preprint arXiv:2204.03863 (2022)
13. Magueresse, A., Carles, V., Heetderks, E.: Low-resource languages: A review of past work and future challenges. arXiv preprint arXiv:2006.07264 (2020)
14. Mesham, S., Hayward, L., Shapiro, J., Buys, J.: Low-resource language modelling of south african languages. arXiv preprint arXiv:2104.00772 (2021)
15. Namasivayam, A.K., Coleman, D., O'Dwyer, A., van Lieshout, P.: Speech sound disorders in children: an articulatory phonology perspective. Front. Psychol. **10** (Jan 2020)
16. Obiang, J.P., et al.: Improving tone recognition performance using wav2vec 2.0-based learned representation in yoruba, a low-resourced language. J. Speech Lang. Technol. **37**, 101–120 (2024)
17. Peng, L., Gao, Y., Bao, R., Li, Y., Zhang, J.: End-to-end mispronunciation detection and diagnosis using transfer learning. Appl. Sci. **13**(11), 6793 (2023)
18. Pratap, V., et al.: Scaling speech technology to 1,000+ languages. arXiv (2023)
19. Radford, A., Kim, J.W., Xu, T., Brockman, G., McLeavey, C., Sutskever, I.: Robust speech recognition via large-scale weak supervision. In: International conference on machine learning, pp. 28492–28518. PMLR (2023)
20. Ranathunga, S., Lee, E.S.A., Prifti Skenduli, M., Shekhar, R., Alam, M., Kaur, R.: Neural machine translation for low-resource languages: a survey. ACM Comput. Surv. **55**(11), 1–37 (2023)
21. Sabu, K., Rao, P.: Automatic assessment of children's oral reading using speech recognition and prosody modeling. CSI Trans. ICT **6**, 221–225 (2018)
22. Shekar, J., et al.: Assessment of non-native speech intelligibility using wav2vec2-based mispronunciation detection and multi-level goodness of pronunciation transformer. J. Speech Process. **34**, 123–145 (2023)

23. Shivakumar, P.G., Georgiou, P.: Transfer learning from adult to children for speech recognition: evaluation, analysis and recommendations. Comput. Speech Lang. **63**, 101077 (2020)
24. Sobti, R., Guleria, K., Kadyan, V.: Comprehensive Literature Review on Children Automatic Speech Recognition System, Acoustic Linguistic Mismatch Approaches and Challenges. Multimed, Tools Appl (2024)
25. Yıldız, M., Keskin, H.K., Oyucu, S., Hartman, D.K., Temur, M., Aydoğmuş, M.: Can artificial intelligence identify reading fluency and level? comparison of human and machine performance. Read. Writ. Quart. **41**(1), 66–83 (2025)

Effectiveness of Forgetting and Question Difficulty in Deep Knowledge Tracing

Zhenhui Gu[1(✉)], Alyssa Sha[1], Bernardo Nunes[1], and Juan Sanguino[2]

[1] Australian National University, Acton, Australia
{zhenhui.gu,alyssa.sha,bernardo.nunes}@anu.edu.au
[2] Universidad de los Andes, Bogotá, Colombia
jc.sanguino10@uniandes.edu.co

Abstract. This study conducts an ablation analysis on existing implementations of forgetting and question difficulty in Deep Knowledge Tracing (DKT) models. Experiments with ten state-of-the-art DKT models across five prominent datasets provide insights on the effectiveness of incorporating forgetting and question difficulty components. Results indicate that modelling forgetting as an exponential decay term within self-attention mechanisms appears to be the most effective approach. Additionally, incorporating question difficulty using the Rasch model – both in input embeddings and self-attention mechanisms – yields the best results. Furthermore, datasets with long-term student interaction histories best capture the effects of forgetting and question difficulty, aligning with recent theories on human forgetting behaviour and the influence of question difficulty on learning. These insights empower Intelligent Tutoring Systems (ITSs) to leverage student cognition while learning and tailor DKT models deployed, enhancing teaching and learning.

Keywords: Ablation Study · Key Features · Deep Knowledge Tracing

1 Introduction

Deep Knowledge Tracing (DKT) has significantly advanced in the past five years, with over 13,000 conference papers and approximately 5,000 journal articles published in the ACM Digital Library[1]. These numbers highlight not only its popularity in Artificial Intelligence in Education but also underscore the need to assess the effectiveness of existing DKT models. This paper conducts an ablation study that focuses on two key features used in state-of-the-art DKT models: *forgetting* and *question difficulty*.

Forgetting accounts for the decline in students' retained knowledge over time, while question difficulty provides deeper interpretation to students' knowledge state. The selection of these two features is driven not only by their widespread implementations but also by their strong interconnection, as studies have shown

[1] https://dl.acm.org.

A. I. Cristea et al. (Eds.): AIED 2025, LNAI 15877, pp. 120–134, 2025.
https://doi.org/10.1007/978-3-031-98414-3_9

that question difficulty influences students' knowledge recall [5]. By considering the varying difficulty levels of questions and the process of forgetting, Knowledge Tracing (KT) models supposedly refine their pattern recognition capabilities and enhance predictions.

It is common that many DKT models incorporate forgetting and question difficulty features without solid theoretical support, leading to ambiguous interpretations of their impact. Psychological theories and studies related to memory discuss how forgetting manifests differently across individuals, information types and durations [24], but current implementations of forgetting are often reductive. Similarly, theories related to question difficulty encompass various cognitive dimensions that link students' knowledge state to item complexity [21], yet existing question difficulty implementations rarely connect to such theoretical foundation. This raises concerns about the validity of feature implementations like the commonly-used exponential decay function in state-of-the-art DKT models.

An overview of the KT problem, considering forgetting and question difficulty features, is shown in Fig. 1.

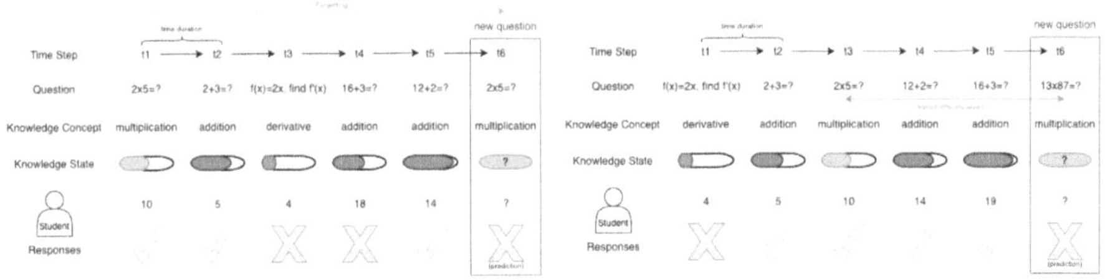

(a) Forgetting in KT

(b) Question difficulty in KT

Fig. 1. Overview of the KT problem

This study introduces a feature removal process to systematically analyse the effectiveness of forgetting and question difficulty in existing DKT models. We utilise state-of-the-art models that incorporate forgetting and question difficulty, isolate these implementations, and evaluate performance changes when these mechanisms are removed. Trained on five prominent KT datasets, our analysis reveals that the effectiveness of forgetting varies significantly across models and datasets, with some showing substantial improvements and others only marginal gains. In contrast, modelling question difficulty has shown minimal impact on model performance, suggesting it may add unnecessary complexity to the models. In some cases, removing the feature positively impacts performance, highlighting issues of theoretically poorly grounded feature implementations. Furthermore, datasets with continuous long-period student interaction sequences have shown better capability in capturing the effects of forgetting and question difficulty.

2 Related Work

Forgetting in DKT: Forgetting, a crucial aspect of student learning, has been integrated into many DKT models to account for students' loss of knowledge due to memory decay. DKT+Forgetting considers time gaps between exercises and number of exercise attempts [17], whereas SAINT+ factors in the answer time along with interval time between adjacent learning activities [26], to account for students' forgetting phenomenon. DKVMN [33] introduced a memory matrix with an erase mechanism to replicate fading of knowledge, later adopted by Deep-IRT [30]. More recent models like RKT [18] employ attention mechanisms to simulate forgetting.

A common approach among these models is the use of time-based decay functions, often inspired by Ebbinghaus's exponential forgetting curve [8]. For instance, AKT [11] applies exponential decay to model knowledge retention. Similarly, HawkesKT [28] and RKT [18] use time gaps and decaying kernel functions to reduce the influence of past learning activities. While these implementations demonstrate the importance of forgetting, they often rely on oversimplified assumptions, such as a single decay curve for all memory types, which contradicts psychological evidence [12]. This highlights a significant limitation: the lack of theoretical alignment with memory research, which distinguishes between short-term and long-term memory decay patterns [22,29].

Question Difficulty in DKT: Early DKT models often encoded questions solely based on their associated Knowledge Components (KCs), neglecting variations in difficulty. This limitation has been tackled by recent models. EKT [14] implicitly captures difficulty through advanced embeddings generated using Word2vec and Bi-LSTM. DIMKT [25] explicitly incorporates difficulty by calculating empirical success rates for questions and KCs, integrating these into embeddings. The more recent models, such as simpleKT [15] and QIKT [6], introduce difficulty vectors and dual-module approaches to better capture semantic differences and adjust knowledge states based on question difficulty.

Despite these advancements, the integration of question difficulty often remains at the representation level, ignoring its further impact on learning. Psychological studies suggest that question difficulty significantly impacts learning progression and forgetting dynamics [4,16], yet many DKT models fail to account for these perspectives. This underscores the need for a more theoretically grounded approach to modelling question difficulty, particularly in relation to its interaction with forgetting [5].

Theories on Forgetting and Question Difficulty: Forgetting is typically characterised by the gradual loss of the ability to recall previously learned information [12]. Psychological research, building on the foundational work of Ebbinghaus's forgetting curve [8], illustrates that memory decays exponentially over time unless actively revisited. This notion has been extensively adopted in DKT models to simulate the fading of knowledge over time [11,28]. However, memory is multifaceted, consisting of various types such as short-term and long-term memory, each demonstrating different decay patterns. For example, short-term memory decays quickly without consolidation, while long-term memory remains stable once consolidated [22]. Further, neurobiological studies have identified distinct brain structures associated with different memory types, indicating unique mechanisms for their encoding, storage, and retrieval [29]. This diversity in decay patterns and memory types challenges the adequacy of using a single forgetting curve to model all aspects of forgetting in KT tasks [18]. Despite the prevalent use of memory decay in DKT models, there remains a research gap in examining the robustness and theoretical grounding of them, as most rely predominantly on the classical Ebbinghaus forgetting curve.

Question difficulty also plays a critical role in the learning process. Research has shown that while easy questions have the potential to engage students, they may slow learning progression [16]. Conversely, challenging questions that require the mastery of multiple knowledge concepts can accelerate learning [23] and impact the forgetting dynamics [4]. Despite question difficulty's multifaceted impact on learning, the associated theories have rarely been applied in existing implementations.

To address these gaps, this study investigates the theoretical foundations and current implementations of forgetting and question difficulty in DKT models. We analyse these implementations in relation to model architectures and datasets used for training, aiming to offer a more theoretically grounded and practically effective approach to future modelling of forgetting and question difficulty.

3 Approach

The effectiveness of question difficulty and forgetting features modelled in DKT models is assessed systematically using a feature removal process. This process is carried out in the following steps: (i) feature identification; (ii) feature isolation and removal; and, (iii) performance evaluation. Details of the implementation of this process in the DKT models are discussed in Sect. 4.

Feature Identification: The first step identifies the specific implementation of the feature of interest (e.g., forgetting or question difficulty) within the model's architecture. This involves examining the model's mechanism, analysing the role of each component, and locating the component representing the feature.

Feature Isolation and Removal: Once identified, the feature is isolated and removed. If represented as a mathematical term, its removal depends on the operation applied. For features integrated through vector or matrix addition, both the term and its operator are eliminated. For concatenated features, adjustments to the dimensionality of associated components are made. If implemented as a neural network layer, structural modifications are required to avoid dimensional mismatches and maintain information flow.

Performance Evaluation: Finally, the performance of the modified model is evaluated and compared to that of the original model to assess the feature's contribution. This ablation process is conducted across multiple models and datasets, enabling a comprehensive comparative analysis and revealing the impact of different feature implementations on model performance.

4 Experiments

Datasets: Five educational benchmark datasets are used in performance evaluation. They all contain timestamps related to students' learning activities, which is essential in evaluating the performances of models with forgetting [24]. The varied characteristics and purposes across these datasets also help assess the robustness of the selected models. Table 1 provides an overview of the selected datasets. Datasets (and details of the feature removal process applied on each selected model) are available in our repository https://github.com/Sebotato/KT-Forgetting-QuestionDifficulty-Effectiveness.git.

- ASSISTments2012 (ASSIST12) is collected from ASSISTments' skill builder problem sets (2012–2013), with each set connected to a group of KCs. It contains student behavioural data during problem-solving, along with teacher and school identifiers.
- ASSISTments2017 (ASSIST17) comes from the ASSISTments Longitudinal Data Mining Competition 2017, containing decade-long learning activities to predict students' likelihood of securing STEM jobs post-college.
- Bridge to Algebra 2006–2007 (BA06) from KDD Cup 2010 EDM Challenge is based on the use of the "Algebra" and "Bridge to Algebra" tutoring products by 13–14 year olds (2007–2008). It is entirely mathematics-based, and each question is associated with multiple KCs.
- NeurIPS2020 Education Challenge (NIPS34) comprises multiple-choice programming questions designed to test student misconceptions.
- EdNet-KT1 (EN1) contains computing-related student activities. Due to the large magnitude of the entire EdNet dataset, only KT1 from EdNet (EN1) is used in this research. EN1 features sequences of question-response pairs and bundles questions that contain a common passage, picture or listening material.

Table 1. Details of the selected datasets

	ASSIST12 [19]	ASSIST17 [20]	BA06 [27]	NIPS34 [13]	EN1 [7]
# of questions	45,716	3162	207,856	948	13,169
# of KCs	265	102	493	57	188
# of students	27,066	1709	1,146	4,918	784,309
# of answers	2,541,201	942,816	3,656,871	1,382,727	95,293,926
Timestamp	✓	✓	✓	✓	✓
Purpose	Educational research	Longitudinal prediction	Math-focused prediction	Diagnostic questions	AI tutoring
Questions Bundling	✓	✓			✓

DKT Models: Table 2 presents the models used in this study, selected based on their incorporation of forgetting and question difficulty features, state-of-the-art

Table 2. Overview of the selected DKT models

Model	Deep Learning	Predecessor	Forgetting	QuesDiff
DKT+Forget [17]	RNN	DKT	✓	
SAINT+ [26]	Transformer	SAINT	✓	
AKT [11]	Transformer	DKVMN	✓	✓
RKT [18]	Attention	SAKT	✓	
HawkesKT [28]	Neural Network	-	✓	✓
DKVMN [33]	NTM	-	✓	
Deep-IRT [30]	Attention	DKVMN, IRT	✓	
DIMKT [25]	Adaptive Sequential NN	-		✓
SimpleKT [15]	Attention	DKVMN		✓
QIKT [6]	LSTM	IRT		✓

performance, the availability of their code for reproducibility, and the diversity in their design/technique, enabling a detailed examination in this ablation study.

We also ensure only models with separable features are selected. A separable feature is one that can be isolated as an independent term, mechanism or network layer. If an inseparable feature is removed from a model, the model may lose computational capabilities unassociated with the feature, which prevents accurate assessment of the effectiveness of the isolated feature and the model.

Experimental Setup: EduStudio (https://edustudio.ai/) – a unified library for KT benchmarking based on PyTorch – is used to ensure consistent and reproducible model performance results. K-fold cross-validation optimises training data, while an early stopping mechanism halts training after 10 consecutive checks without improvement to enhance training efficiency. Standardised metrics, including Accuracy (ACC), Area Under the Curve (AUC), and Root Mean Square Error (RMSE), are used to evaluate model performance.

Model Implementation: The feature removal process is applied on each model listed in Table 2. Details of removal are explained below separated into three groups: Forgetting-Only Implementation, Question Difficulty-Only Implementation, and Combined Implementation of Forgetting and Question Difficulty. If a DKT model incorporates forgetting, its forgetting feature is denoted as F_{model}. Likewise, QD_{model} denotes the question difficulty feature. The implementations of all models are available in our aforementioned repository for reproducibility. Details related to the feature removal process are as follows.

> **Forgetting-Only Implementation:** *DKT+Forgetting* models forgetting by integrating two multi-hot forgetting vectors into its architecture – one integrated with the input embedding and the other with the student knowledge vector – through concatenation and multiplication. Based on the linearity of vector operations, to eradicate the forgetting feature, the input embedding and student

knowledge vector remain unchanged. Subsequently, students' knowledge states are updated without forgetting effects; *SAINT+* inherits the Transformer architecture, modelling forgetting F_{SAINT+} as elapsed time and lag time embeddings within the decoder's output embedding. This output embedding is the additional combination of elapsed time, lag time, correctness, and position embeddings. Therefore, F_{SAINT+} can be removed by excluding the elapsed time and lag time embeddings; *RKT*'s forgetting vector $F_{RKT} = R^T$ comprises of exponentially decaying curve with respect to the relative time interval between the new learning interaction and every past interaction. R^T is combined with question relationship vector R^E to form relation vector R in the computation space. Removing forgetting involves replacing R with R^E; *DKVMN* and *Deep-IRT* model forgetting as an erase vector to remove memories in the external memory matrix within their Memory-Augmented Neural Networks (MANNs). Removing F_{DKVMN} and $F_{Deep-IRT}$ involves setting the erase vector to zero vector so no memory is eradicated in the write process.

> **Question Difficulty-Only Implementation:** *DIMKT* models question difficulty as a question difficulty embedding, which is concatenated with the question, KC, and KC difficulty embeddings to train the input embedding of DIMKT's Adaptive Sequential Neural Network (ASNN). QD_{DIMKT} can be removed from DIMKT by excluding the question difficulty embedding in the computation of input embedding. Since the resulting input embedding is shortened, adjustment in the dimension of the trainable weight is required to only consider the lengths of question, KC, and KC difficulty embeddings; *SimpleKT* integrates question difficulty in the input space by combining the element-wise product of a learnable question difficulty vector and a question variation representation with its latent knowledge component representation via element-wise addition. To remove $QD_{simpleKT}$, the product between the learnable question difficulty vector and the question variation representation is excluded, leaving the model input to only consider the latent knowledge component representation; In *QIKT*, question difficulty is modelled as a question-centric problem-solving neural network layer, whose output is combined with those from the question-centric knowledge acquisition layer and the question-agnostic knowledge state layer before being fed into QIKT's prediction function. Since all outputs are scalar and integrated via addition, QD_{QIKT} can be removed by excluding it from the addition operation.

> **Combined Implementation of Forgetting and Question Difficulty:** *AKT* and *HawkesKT* are the models that have both forgetting and question difficulty implementations. Forgetting is incorporated in AKT by adding an exponential term in its attention mechanism to reflect students' memory decay. The forgetting term $F_{AKT} = \exp(-\theta \cdot d(t, \tau))$ considers a scalar decay rate θ and a scalar distance measure $d(t, \tau)$, where t is the current time step and τ is a past time step. Since $\exp(-\theta \cdot d(t, \tau))$ returns a scalar, it can be removed directly from the attention mechanism to eradicate the forgetting effect. This modifies AKT's attention to become:

$$\alpha_{t,\tau} = Softmax(\frac{\mathbf{q}_t^T \mathbf{k}_\tau}{\sqrt{D_k}}), \tag{1}$$

where $\mathbf{q}_t^T$ is the query embedding layer, $\mathbf{k}_\tau$ is the key embedding layer and D_k is the dimension of keys.

AKT-R is a variant of AKT that computes context-aware question x_t and question-response embeddings y_t to be used as model input. Both x_t and y_t have question difficulty incorporated as a scalar parameter term $QD_{AKT} = \mu_{q_t}$. To remove the question difficulty characteristic from x_t and y_t, μ_{q_t} is directly removed from x_t and y_t. The updated x_t and y_t still set AKT-R apart from AKT, since contextual information other than question difficulty is reserved.

HawkesKT predicts a student's response to a new question using an intensity function comprising of base intensity and temporal cross-effects:

$$\lambda(x_i) = \lambda_0^{x_i} + \sum_{x_j \in S_{t_i}} \alpha_{x_j,x_i} \cdot \kappa_{x_j,x_i}(t_i - t_j), \tag{2}$$

where x_i is a student's i^{th} learning interaction, t_i is the timestamp of x_i for any $i < j$, S_{t_i} is the student's interaction sequence, $\lambda_0^{x_i}$ represents the difficulty level of the question and KC associated with x_i, α_{x_j,x_i} is the mutual excitation that captures cross-skill effects between x_j and x_i, and $\kappa_{x_j,x_i}(t_i - t_j)$ controls the fine-grained temporal dynamics of cross-effects between x_j and x_i [28].

$\kappa_{x_j,x_i}(t_i - t_j)$ models the forgetting behaviour of HawesKT and acts as a scaling term to α_{x_j,x_i} to provide the overall ultimate temporal cross effects. $F_{HawkesKT}$ can be removed by excluding $\kappa_{x_j,x_i}(t_i - t_j)$ in Eq. 2. With respect to question difficulty, $\lambda_0^{x_i}$ is more specifically formulated as $\lambda_0^{x_i} = \lambda_0^{q_i} + \lambda_0^{kc_i}$, in which $\lambda_0^{q_i}$ is the question difficulty parameter and $\lambda_0^{kc_i}$ is the KC difficulty parameter. Given that $QD_{HawkesKT} = \lambda_0^{q_i}$ is integrated via addition, $QD_{HawkesKT}$ can be removed by simply excluding $\lambda_0^{q_i}$ from $\lambda(x_i)$. This leaves $\lambda_0^{x_i} = \lambda_0^{kc_i}$.

5 Results

This section presents the performance of the selected models after removing F_{model} and QD_{model} (see Tables 3 and 4). Each model is compared to its original version with the feature(s) intact. For models incorporating both forgetting and question difficulty, performance is assessed with one or both features removed. Paired t-tests are used to analyse the significance of F_{model} and QD_{model} based on performance changes.

To show clear comparisons between the performances of models after feature removal, the melt function was applied to consolidate model performances across all datasets, which transforms the wide-format result data into long-format data. As shown in Fig. 2, AKT shows improved accuracy when the forgetting mechanism is included. However, other models including RKT show minimal differences after forgetting implementation, suggesting a lower sensitivity to forgetting. AKT again shows higher accuracy with the inclusion of question difficulty. In contrast, simpleKT and QIKT show marginal changes in accuracy with respect to the removal of question difficulty.

Table 3. Performance of selected models across datasets w/o forgetting

Model	Modification	ASSIST12			ASSIST17			BA06			NIPS34			EN1		
		ACC	AUC	RMSE	ACC	AUC	RMSE	ACC	AUC	RMSE	ACC	AUC	RMSE	ACC	AUC	RMSE
DKT+Forget	Original	0.7298	0.7317	0.4260	0.7088	0.7660	0.4363	0.8167	0.8139	0.3552	0.7168	0.7822	0.4336	0.6910	0.7119	0.4486
	Remove F	0.7335↑	0.7374↑	0.4233↑	0.7074↓	0.7638↓	0.4377↓	0.8153↓	0.8051↓	0.3573↓	0.7187↑	0.7836↑	0.4332↑	0.6893↓	0.7089↓	0.4501↓
SAINT+	Original	0.7198	0.6886	0.4365	0.7683	0.8336	0.3981	0.9637	0.9732	0.1799	0.8862	0.9555	0.2840	0.8388	0.8928	0.3410
	Remove F	0.7092↓	**0.6623**↓	0.4460↓	**0.7242**↓	**0.7462**↓	**0.4396**↓	0.9637	0.9655↓	0.1840↑	0.8739↓	**0.9116**↓	0.3242↓	0.8307↓	**0.8627**↓	0.3574↓
DKVMN	Original	0.7379	0.7379	0.4221	0.6958	0.7447	0.4467	0.8319	0.8078	0.3479	0.7164	0.7807	0.4345	0.7044	0.7344	0.4399
	Remove F	0.7352↓	0.7313↓	0.4238↓	0.6832↓	0.7215↓	0.4552↓	0.8286↓	0.7989↓	0.3512↓	0.7138↓	0.7782↓	0.4358↓	0.7066↑	0.7322↓	0.4404↓
Deep-IRT	Original	0.7377	0.7365	0.4224	0.6950	0.7434	0.4470	0.8346	0.8135	0.3451	0.7159	0.7808	0.4348	0.7060	0.7345	0.4401
	Remove F	0.7344↓	0.7305↓	0.4241↓	0.6784↓	0.7176↓	0.4575↓	0.8320↓	0.8048↓	0.3483↓	0.7133↓	0.7774↓	0.4363↓	0.7048↓	0.7320↓	0.4411↓
RKT	Original	0.7249	0.7000	0.4327	0.6637	0.6910	0.4624	0.8211	0.7671	0.3609	0.6882	0.7502	0.4491	0.6788	0.6738	0.4575
	Remove F	0.7254↑	0.7008↑	0.4324↑	0.6674↑	0.6924↑	0.4615↑	0.8211	0.7624↓	0.3619↓	0.6866↓	0.7484↓	0.4499↓	0.6790↑	0.6738	0.4575
AKT	Original	0.9046	0.9657	0.2594	0.9001	0.9678	0.2653	0.9752	0.9967	0.1345	0.9699	0.9968	0.1461	0.9246	0.9796	0.2307
	Remove F	**0.7533**↓	**0.7631**↓	**0.4132**↓	**0.7333**↓	**0.7819**↓	**0.4272**↓	**0.8631**↓	**0.8961**↓	**0.3223**↓	**0.7427**↓	**0.8093**↓	**0.4355**↓	**0.7817**↓	**0.8301**↓	**0.3931**↓
HawkesKT	Original	0.6945	0.6010	0.4729	0.5448	0.5239	0.6553	0.7033	0.5453	0.5438	0.5332	0.5205	0.6683	0.6467	0.5294	0.5763
	Remove F	**0.7059**↑	**0.6337**↑	**0.4474**↑	**0.6335**↑	**0.6429**↑	**0.4738**↑	**0.8032**↑	**0.7544**↑	**0.3754**↑	**0.6050**↓	**0.6443**↑	**0.4838**↓	**0.6858**↑	**0.6451**↑	**0.4551**↑

Table 4. Performance of selected models across datasets w/o question difficulty

Model	Modification	ASSIST12			ASSIST17			BA06			NIPS34			EN1		
		ACC	AUC	RMSE	ACC	AUC	RMSE	ACC	AUC	RMSE	ACC	AUC	RMSE	ACC	AUC	RMSE
AKT	Original	0.9046	0.9657	0.2594	0.9001	0.9678	0.2653	0.9752	0.9967	0.1345	0.9699	0.9968	0.1461	0.9246	0.9796	0.2307
	Remove QD	**0.8760**↓	**0.9471**↓	**0.2913**↓	**0.8540**↓	**0.9398**↓	**0.3125**↓	0.9758↑	0.9968↑	0.1330↑	0.9849↑	0.9992↑	0.1019↑	0.9377↑	0.9853↑	0.2114↑
HawkesKT	Original	0.6945	0.6010	0.4729	0.5448	0.5239	0.6553	0.7033	0.5453	0.5438	0.5332	0.5205	0.6683	0.6467	0.5294	0.5763
	Remove QD	0.6840↓	0.5834↓	0.4817↓	0.5692↑	0.5194↓	0.6340↓	0.7165↑	0.5579↑	0.5311↓	0.5188↓	0.5106↓	0.6767↓	0.6387↓	0.5190↓	0.5855↓
DIMKT	Original	0.7522	0.7671	0.4128	0.8029	0.8919	0.3602	0.9485	0.9763	0.1997	0.9211	0.9833	0.2298	0.8697	0.9459	0.2932
	Remove QD	0.7548↑	0.7728↑	0.4095↑	0.8027↓	0.8917↓	0.3596↑	0.9668↑	0.9886↑	0.1606↑	0.9192↓	0.9823↓	0.2334↓	0.8713↑	0.9471↑	0.2908↑
simpleKT	Original	0.7208	0.6848	0.4368	0.6641	0.6966	0.4606	0.9282	0.9509	0.2398	0.8103	0.8990	0.3588	0.7854	0.8372	0.3790
	Remove QD	**0.7153**↓	**0.6695**↓	0.4399↓	0.6514↓	0.6696↓	0.4686↓	0.9304↑	0.9592↑	0.2323↑	**0.7968**↓	0.8874↓	0.3696↓	0.7874↑	0.8362↓	0.3781↓
QIKT	Original	0.7530	0.7701	0.4104	0.7164	0.7767	0.4317	0.8503	0.8633	0.3244	0.7207	0.7848	0.4326	0.7089	0.7395	0.4378
	Remove QD	0.7528↓	0.7678↓	0.4113↓	0.7173↑	0.7779↑	0.4310↑	0.8498↓	0.8600↓	0.3258↓	0.7207	0.7852↑	0.4325↑	0.7089	0.7360↓	0.4391↓

Table 5 presents paired t-test results for forgetting and question difficulty. Significant changes in AKT, SAINT+, and HawkesKT indicate a notable impact of forgetting on their performance. However, DKVMN, Deep-IRT, and RKT show no statistically significant changes upon forgetting removal. The table also reveals that question difficulty modeling has no significant influence on the performance of the selected DKT models. The varying impact of forgetting and question difficulty mechanisms across DKT models underscores the need for architecture-specific feature optimisation strategies.

6 Discussion

Model Performance: Results show significant variation in forgetting effectiveness across models, despite controlled training conditions. This variation stems from differences in architecture and forgetting mechanisms. Models with self-attention achieve better forgetting when integrated directly into their mechanisms. For instance, AKT and SAINT+ embed forgetting into the query-key dot product and self-attention embeddings, respectively, yielding strong performance. In contrast, RKT models forgetting as a relation coefficient matrix independently from its self-attention mechanism, leading to weaker results. DKVMN and Deep-IRT use MANNs [33] to process students' learning interactions sequentially, making them less effective than self-attention. DKT+Forgetting and

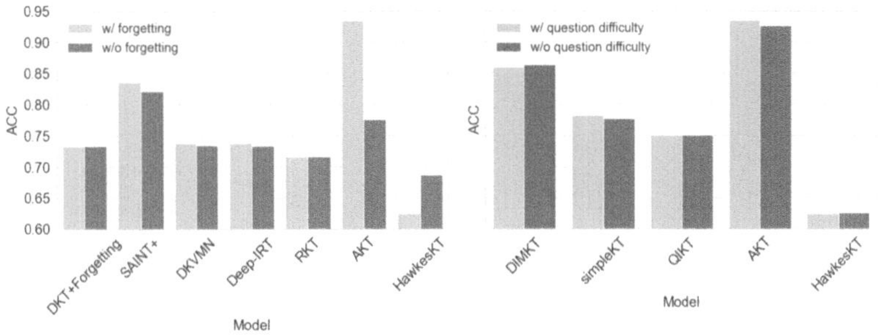

Fig. 2. Effectiveness of forgetting and question difficulty on DKT models

HawkesKT use sequential mechanisms to model forgetting, which also exhibit weaker model performance.

Our results suggest that students' forgetting behaviour may be inherently linked to long-range dependencies in input sequences, best modelled through self-attention. Such observation underscores recent breakthroughs about active forgetting processes in cognitive neurobiology, in which active forgetting mediated by a person's prefrontal cortex inherits complex associations across context representations in memory, aligning with self-attention's context aware characteristic [2]. However, without incorporating forgetting into self-attention computations, its effectiveness diminishes. For example, though MANNs implemented by DKVMN and Deep-IRT are supported by retroactive interference models, their effectiveness is limited by inherent constraints, such as the assumption that each memory has a fixed valence. [10]. Moreover, traditional RNNs, including LSTMs, may also struggle with modeling forgetting due to ineffectiveness in capturing long-range dependencies [31].

Our results also indicate that question difficulty is best captured using the Rasch model in the input space coupled with self-attention in the computation space. SimpleKT and AKT, the only models that show performance declines upon removing question difficulty, integrate it into their embeddings using the Rasch model. These embeddings are then fed into their self-attention mechanisms, suggesting a synergistic effect between the Rasch model and self-attention in enhancing performance. This reinforces the Rasch model's compatibility in automatically capturing textual difficulty within embeddings [9] and the effectiveness of self-attention in linguistical question difficulty estimation [1]. In contrast, the weaker performance of DIMKT, QIKT, and HawkesKT after incorporating question difficulty reveals the ineffectiveness of temporal recurrence mechanisms in handling question difficulty.

Datasets: Datasets with continuous longitudinal data reveal the synergy between forgetting and question difficulty. NIPS34 and EN1 span multiple years (2018–2020 and 2017–2019), enabling long-range dependencies, whereas ASSIST12, ASSIST17, and BA06 have shorter or fragmented interactions. Analysis of AKT and HawkesKT, both with forgetting and question difficulty mech-

Table 5. Paired t-tests considering forgetting and question difficulty

Model	Metric	Forgetting T-Statistic	Forgetting P-Value
DKT+Forget	ACC	-0.2014	0.8502
	AUC	1.3853	0.2382
	RMSE	-0.4338	0.6868
SAINT+	ACC	**1.9842**	**0.1182**
	AUC	**2.9182**	**0.0433***
	RMSE	**-2.8616**	**0.0459***
DKVMN	ACC	1.5756	0.1903
	AUC	2.2586	0.0868
	RMSE	-2.1332	0.0998
Deep-IRT	ACC	1.8421	0.1393
	AUC	2.1736	0.0954
	RMSE	-2.0244	0.1129
RKT	ACC	-0.6472	0.5527
	AUC	0.7813	0.4783
	RMSE	-0.3416	0.7498
AKT	ACC	**8.4215**	**0.0011***
	AUC	**8.9973**	**0.0008***
	RMSE	**-7.5697**	**0.0016***
HawkesKT	ACC	**-3.8089**	**0.0190***
	AUC	**-4.2997**	**0.0126***
	RMSE	**4.5532**	**0.0104***

Model	Metric	Question Difficulty T-Statistic	Question Difficulty P-Value
AKT	ACC	0.7618	0.4886
	AUC	1.1622	0.3098
	RMSE	-0.1695	0.8736
HawkesKT	ACC	-0.1241	0.9072
	AUC	1.1719	0.3063
	RMSE	0.2351	0.8257
DIMKT	ACC	-1.1216	0.3248
	AUC	-1.4608	0.2179
	RMSE	1.0751	0.3429
simpleKT	ACC	1.6170	0.1812
	AUC	1.5393	0.1986
	RMSE	-0.8315	0.4524
QIKT	ACC	-0.1712	0.8724
	AUC	1.5480	0.1965
	RMSE	-1.3598	0.2455

Note: p-values indicating significant changes (< 0.05) are marked with an asterisk (*)

anisms, highlights model-dependent effects. As shown in Fig. 3a, AKT's performance drops significantly on NIPS34 and EN1 when both features are removed together, compared to individual removals, while the decline is less severe on ASSIST12, ASSIST17, and BA06. Conversely, Fig. 3b shows that removing only forgetting in HawkesKT improves performance more than removing both features, particularly on NIPS34 and EN1. Since forgetting and question difficulty affect long-term learning, models leveraging long-range dependencies, like AKT, perform better on continuous datasets. Meanwhile, HawkesKT, which focuses on temporal effects, sees weaker or even negative impacts when incorporating these factors in long-period datasets. This incentivises researchers to prioritise continuity and range when developing KT datasets, especially in low-resource circumstances, which are becoming increasingly prevalent [32].

Feature Removal Process: Some models define features retrospectively as properties of implemented mechanisms, which may not be removable [14,18]. For instance, RKT derives question difficulty from the question relation vector R^E, which encodes relations between the new question and every past question using performance data (correctness) and textual similarity (cosine similarity of embeddings). Since QD_{RKT} remains as a property of R^E, it cannot be isolated or removed without disrupting other key relational information in R^E. This highlights the importance of preserving mechanisms that generate multiple

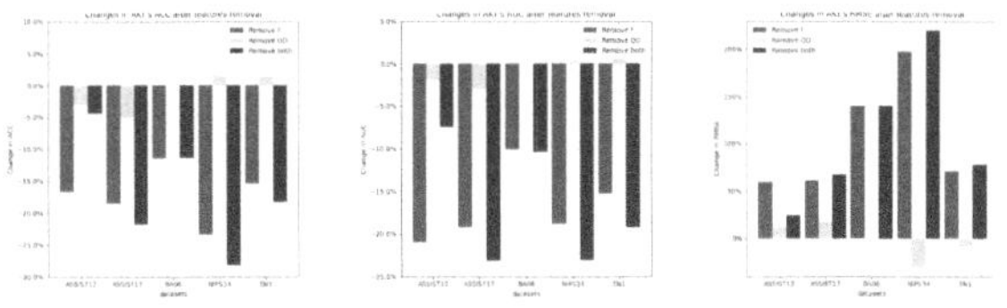

(a) AKT

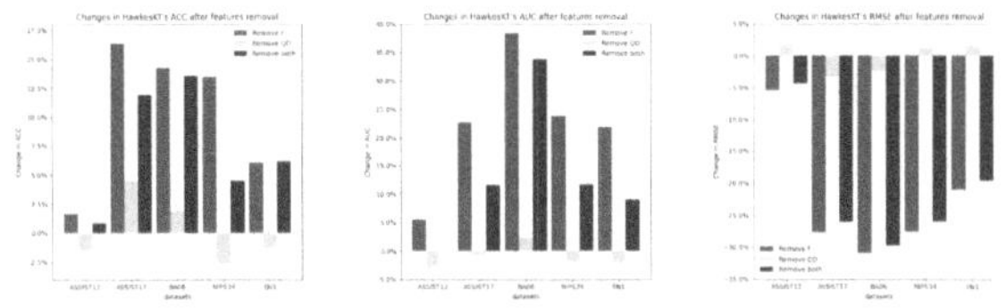

(b) HawkesKT

Fig. 3. Changes in model performance after feature removal

interdependent properties and aligns with current research in explanable KT [3] in encouraging the interpretation of latent properties in KT mechanisms.

Theoretical Interpretations: Our findings contribute to theoretical understanding in KT, tackling the research gaps in theoretical foundation of DKT models. The strong performance of self-attention in modelling forgetting aligns with recent cognitive science theories—specifically, how the human brain actively forgets information by processing relationships between different memories [2]. The effectiveness of the Rasch model combined with self-attention in capturing question difficulty supports theoretical work in automated difficulty estimation in educational contexts [1,9]. Our work uncover that there are many theoretical connections grounded in the architectural choices of DKT models, which strengthens model interpretability and accountability.

Practical Implications: Our findings also provide insights for educational AI practitioners. The weaker performance changes after removing question difficulty highlight potential for tutors to collect difficulty-related cognitive data—such as student engagement and tutor-student dialogue—which could empower more effective future implementations. Moreover, specialists in ITS could tailor models used based on the characteristics of data, for example, deploying self-attention based models if learning data tracked are continuous and longitudinal.

7 Conclusion and Future Work

This ablation study investigates two important aspects that influence knowledge tracing, *forgetting* and *question difficulty*. We adopt a unique approach to perform forgetting and question difficulty removal on state-of-the-art DKT models and evaluate their effects using benchmark KT datasets. Our findings underscore the importance of incorporating these elements with strong theoretical backing to accurately represent knowledge dynamics. Future DKT research should explore deeper integration of cognitive psychology theories, particularly in how different memory systems interact during learning and how individual student differences in cognitive processes affect knowledge retention patterns.

References

1. AlKhuzaey, S., Grasso, F., Payne, T.R., Tamma, V.: Text-based question difficulty prediction: a systematic review of automatic approaches. Int. J. Artif. Intell. Educ. **34**(3), 862–914 (2024). https://doi.org/10.1007/s40593-023-00362-1
2. Anderson, M.C., Hulbert, J.C.: Active forgetting: adaptation of memory by prefrontal control. Annu. Rev. Psychol. **72**(1), 1–36 (2021). https://doi.org/10.1146/annurev-psych-072720-094140
3. Bai, Y., Zhao, J., Wei, T., Cai, Q., He, L.: A survey of explainable knowledge tracing. Appl. Intell. 1–32 (2024). https://doi.org/10.48550/arXiv.2403.07279
4. Bjork, R.A., Bjork, E.L.: Forgetting as the friend of learning: implications for teaching and self-regulated learning. Adv. Physiol. Educ. **43**(2), 164–167 (2019). https://doi.org/10.1152/advan.00001.2019
5. Carpenter, S.K., Pashler, H., Wixted, J.T., Vul, E.: The effects of tests on learning and forgetting. Mem. Cognit. **36**(2), 438–448 (2008). https://doi.org/10.3758/mc.36.2.438
6. Chen, J., Liu, Z., Huang, S., Liu, Q., Luo, W.: Improving interpretability of deep sequential knowledge tracing models with question-centric cognitive representations. In: Proceedings of the AAAI Conference Artificial Intelligence, pp. 14196–14204 (2023). https://doi.org/10.48550/arXiv.2302.06885
7. Choi, Y., Lee, Y., Shin, D., Cho, J., Park, S., Lee, S., Baek, J., Bae, C., Kim, B., Heo, J.: EdNet: a large-scale hierarchical dataset in education. In: Bittencourt, I.I., Cukurova, M., Muldner, K., Luckin, R., Millán, E. (eds.) AIED 2020. LNCS (LNAI), vol. 12164, pp. 69–73. Springer, Cham (2020). https://doi.org/10.1007/978-3-030-52240-7_13
8. Ebbinghaus, H.: Memory: a contribution to experimental psychology. Ann. Neurosci. **20**(4), 155 (2013). https://doi.org/10.5214/ans.0972.7531.200408
9. Ehara, Y.: Neural Rasch model: how do word embeddings adjust word difficulty? In: Proceedings of the PACLING Conference, pp. 88–96. Springer (2019). https://doi.org/10.1007/978-981-15-6168-9_8
10. Georgiou, A., Katkov, M., Tsodyks, M.: Retroactive interference model of forgetting. J. Math. Neurosci. **11**(1), 1–15 (2021). https://doi.org/10.1186/s13408-021-00102-6
11. Ghosh, A., Heffernan, N., Lan, A.S.: Context-aware attentive knowledge tracing. In: Proceedings of the 26th ACM SIGKDD International Conference Knowledge Discovery Data Mining, pp. 2330–2339 (2020). https://doi.org/10.48550/arXiv.2007.12324
12. Hardt, O., Nader, K., Nadel, L.: Decay happens: the role of active forgetting in memory. Trends Cogn. Sci. **17**(3), 111–120 (2013). https://doi.org/10.1016/j.tics.2013.01.001
13. Jiang, Y., et al.: NeurIPS 2020 Competition: Predicting Generalization in Deep Learning. arXiv preprint arXiv:2012.07976 (2020)

14. Liu, Q., et al.: EKT: Exercise-aware knowledge tracing for student performance prediction. IEEE Trans. Knowl. Data Eng. **33**(1), 100–115 (2019). https://doi.org/10.48550/arXiv.1906.05658
15. Liu, Z., Liu, Q., Chen, J., Huang, S., Luo, W.: simpleKT: A Simple But Tough-to-Beat Baseline for Knowledge Tracing. arXiv preprint arXiv:2302.06881 (2023)
16. Lomas, D., Patel, K., Forlizzi, J.L., Koedinger, K.R.: Optimizing challenge in an educational game using large-scale design experiments. In: Proceedings of the CHI Conference Humand Factors Computing System, pp. 89–98 (2013). https://doi.org/10.1145/2470654.2470668
17. Nagatani, K., Zhang, Q., Sato, M., Chen, Y.Y., Chen, F., Ohkuma, T.: Augmenting knowledge tracing by considering forgetting behavior. In: Proceedings of the World Wide Web Conf. (WWW), pp. 3101–3107 (2019). https://doi.org/10.1145/3308558.3313565
18. Pandey, S., Srivastava, J.: RKT : relation-aware self-attention for knowledge tracing. In: Proceedings 29th ACM International Conference Information Knowledge Management (CIKM 2020), pp. 1205–1214 (2020). https://doi.org/10.1145/3340531.3411994
19. Pardos, Z.A., Baker, R.S.J.D., San Pedro, M.O.C.Z., Gowda, S.M., Gowda, S.M.: Affective states and state tests: Investigating how affect throughout the school year predicts end of year learning outcomes. In: Proceedings 3rd International Conference Learning Analytics Knowl. (LAK 2013), pp. 117–124 (2013). https://doi.org/10.18608/jla.2014.11.6
20. Patikorn, T., Baker, R.S., Heffernan, N.T.: ASSISTments longitudinal data mining competition special issue: a preface. J. Educ. Data Min. **12**(2), i–xi (2020). https://doi.org/10.5281/zenodo.4008048
21. Pelánek, R., Effenberger, T., Čechák, J.: Complexity and difficulty of items in learning systems. Int. J. Artif. Intell. Educ. **32**(1), 196–232 (2021). https://doi.org/10.1007/s40593-021-00252-4
22. Peterson, L., Peterson, M.J.: Short-term retention of individual verbal items. J. Exp. Psychol. **58**(3), 193 (1959). https://doi.org/10.1037/h0049234
23. Rohrer, D., Dedrick, R.F., Stershic, S.: Interleaved practice improves mathematics learning. J. Educ. Psychol. **107**(3), 900 (2015). https://doi.org/10.1037/edu0000001
24. Sha, A.S., Nunes, B.P., Haller, A.: "Forgetting" in Machine Learning and Beyond: A Survey. arXiv preprint arXiv:2405.20620 (2024)
25. Shen, S., Huang, Z., Liu, Q., Su, Y., Wang, S., Chen, E.: Assessing student's dynamic knowledge state by exploring the question difficulty effect. In: Proceedings of the 45th International ACM SIGIR Conference Research Development Information Retrieval, pp. 427–437 (2022). https://doi.org/10.1145/3477495.3531939
26. Shin, D., Shim, Y., Yu, H., Lee, S., Kim, B., Choi, Y.: SAINT+: Integrating temporal features for EdNet correctness prediction. In: Proceedings of the 11th International Conference Learning Analytics Knowledge (LAK 2021), pp. 490–496 (2021). https://doi.org/10.1145/3448139.3448188
27. Stamper, J., Pardos, Z.A.: The 2010 KDD Cup Competition Dataset: Engaging the machine learning community in predictive learning analytics. J. Learn. Anal. **3**(2), 312–316 (2016). https://doi.org/10.18608/jla.2016.32.16
28. Wang, C., et al.: Temporal cross-effects in knowledge tracing. In: Proceedings of the 14th ACM International Conference Web Search Data Mining (WSDM 2021), pp. 517–525 (2021)

29. Winters, B.D., Saksida, L.M., Bussey, T.J.: Object recognition memory: neurobiological mechanisms of encoding, consolidation and retrieval. Neurosci. Biobehav. Rev. **32**(5), 1055–1070 (2008). https://doi.org/10.1016/j.neubiorev.2008.04.004
30. Yeung, C.K.: Deep-IRT: Make Deep Learning Based Knowledge Tracing Explainable Using Item Response Theory. arXiv preprint arXiv:1904.11738 (2019)
31. Zargar, S.: Introduction to Sequence Learning Models: RNN, LSTM, GRU. Department of Mechanical and Aerospace Engineering, North Carolina State University (2021). https://doi.org/10.13140/RG.2.2.36370.99522
32. Zhang, H., Liu, Z., Huang, S., Shang, C., Zhan, B., Jiang, Y.: Improving Low-Resource Knowledge Tracing Tasks by Supervised Pre-training and Importance Mechanism Fine-tuning. arXiv preprint arXiv:2403.06725 (2024)
33. Zhang, J., Shi, X., King, I., Yeung, D.Y.: Dynamic key-value memory networks for knowledge tracing. In: Proceedings of the 26th International Conference World Wide Web (WWW 2017), pp. 765–774 (2017). https://doi.org/10.48550/arXiv.1611.08108

Embedding Ethical Awareness in Computer Science and AI Education: The PEaRCE Approach to Responsible Computing

Mohammad Hadi Nezhad[1(✉)], Francisco Enrique Vicente Castro[2], Eugene Mak[1], Peter J. Haas[1], Danielle Allessio[1], Leon Osterweil[1], Injila Rasul[1], Heather Conboy[1], and Ivon Arroyo[1]

[1] University of Massachusetts Amherst, Amherst, MA 01003, USA
{mhadinezhad,emak,phaas,allessio,ljo,irasul,hconboy,ivon}@umass.edu
[2] New York University, New York, NY 10012, USA
francisco.castro@nyu.edu

Abstract. Despite the widespread use of computer systems, their societal impacts are often poorly understood, highlighting the need for the AIED community to acknowledge and contribute to incorporating Ethical and Responsible Computing (ERC) into Computer Science (CS) education. We introduce the Platform for Ethical and Responsible Computing Education (PEaRCE), an interactive tool created to integrate ERC into post-secondary education through realistic workplace simulations. PEaRCE scenarios guide students through ERC quandaries—awareness, decision-making, feedback—during the processes of developing advanced AIED and other technologies that may have beneficial and harmful impacts. Moreover, we integrate PEaRCE into CS courses via a sequence of structured learning modules and trained "ERC Teaching Assistants (TAs)" to support the integration process. We present insights from our deployment experiences, show PEaRCE's potential to enhance ERC awareness and reasoning, and discuss the possibility of embedding PEaRCE into AI in Education courses.

Keywords: Ethics in AIED · Ethical and Responsible Computing Education · Educational Technologies · Computer Science Education

1 Introduction

Advanced computer systems have become embedded into daily life, transforming how people work, learn, and interact with societal institutions and each other. While the rapid integration of computer technologies into society offers new opportunities, their societal impacts often remain poorly understood. This raises critical questions about what consequences may arise from the use and integration of these technologies into our societal structures or how they might amplify already-existing societal concerns.

A. I. Cristea et al. (Eds.): AIED 2025, LNAI 15877, pp. 135–149, 2025.
https://doi.org/10.1007/978-3-031-98414-3_10

The use of AI-driven systems in education has highlighted these challenges. For example, England and Ireland implemented algorithmic scoring systems to standardize results and prevent grade inflation [22]. However, these systems were criticized for disproportionately downgrading students from certain groups (e.g., those attending disadvantaged schools) by overemphasizing past institutional performance, causing psychological distress, perceptions of unfairness by students and families, and legal challenges and widespread protests affecting schools and authorities. Facial recognition technology, often used for security, automated attendance, and emotion detection in schools, is often argued by experts to create surveillance environments that may undermine students' autonomy and freedom [2]. These systems have also exhibited biases related to race and gender, raising concerns about unfair treatment of certain student groups [21,27].

The AIED community acknowledges the risks of neglecting ethical considerations during the development, research, and application of AI in education, which ultimately aims for a more equitable and inclusive educational environment for the general population [19,25]. Beyond technical soundness, designing societally responsible AI technologies should not be an afterthought but a core value instilled among researchers, engineers, and developers of AI systems [17,19]. However, computing education has historically often overlooked this aspect, and researchers have noted that engineers and developers often lack systematic education on the broader societal impacts of the technologies they create [17]. In response, scholars have explored various approaches to integrating Ethical and Responsible Computing (ERC) education into computing curricula [4,5,12,20].

One approach to ERC education is to offer standalone courses that focus on ERC issues. Fiesler et al. [11], however, point out that this approach, by itself, fails to teach students that ERC considerations and technical practices are very closely intertwined. We assert, therefore, that it is crucial to embed ERC education into CS courses in a manner that deeply engages students, scales to large numbers of students and classes, and can overcome potential instructor resistance. Our approach to realizing this vision uses an educational tool—the *Platform for Ethical and Responsible Computing Education* (PEaRCE)—that immerses students in role-playing simulations.

PEaRCE is a web-based interactive simulation tool designed to embed ERC education into CS courses at post-secondary educational institutions. PEaRCE engages students in realistic workplace scenarios where they apply their technical knowledge (e.g., AI, data science) in complex, ambiguous situations involving the development of systems that may produce tangible personal or societal benefits but could potentially cause physical, economic, psychological, or societal harms. Students are presented with opportunities to explore technology's implications via conversations with simulated stakeholders, helping them increase their awareness of ERC issues they may face in the workplace and learn to seek out diverse and informative stakeholders for responsible decision-making. Reflection questions throughout the scenario deepen their engagement with the scenario as it unfolds. To further increase engagement and effectiveness, we provide supplementary curricular materials in the form of pre- and post-simulation activities.

Following prior work [11], we use trained graduate students ("ERC-TAs") to coordinate with instructors on deploying PEaRCE and its accompanying activities.

In this paper, we describe PEaRCE and examples of its simulation scenarios (Sect. 3), our protocol for integrating PEaRCE into CS classes (Sect. 4), and our experiences deploying PEaRCE over the past year in undergraduate CS courses at the University of Massachusetts Amherst, along with insights from pre- and post-test surveys and interviews on PEaRCE's impact on students ERC awareness and reasoning (Sect. 5). We conclude with a discussion of future work in the context of AI in Education. While our findings are preliminary, they inform our current perspective and motivate the suggestions we put forward in this paper. Our work thus far suggests that the PEaRCE approach has the potential to train future AIED developers and researchers on ERC education. This has critical implications for *AI education* and *AI in education* as the AIED community continues to think about what it means to design AI systems and how to prepare students to contribute to the design of socially-beneficial technologies.

2 Background and Related Work

There is a growing consensus among AI researchers that developing AI systems should be grounded on robust and ethical AI principles and universal human rights and obligations [8]. Scholars have attempted to define factors that are essential when considering designing AI for social good, including—beneficence (promoting human and planetary well-being); non-maleficence (avoiding harm, misuse, and privacy violations); autonomy (preserving human freedom in decision-making); justice (ensuring fairness, preventing discrimination, and fostering diversity); and explicability (ensuring transparency and accountability) [13]. The ethics of AI in education has also gained increased attention, seen in the recent increase in the number of articles on Ethics and AIED within the AIED community [15]. This represents a shift from the field's self-perception as inherently 'good' because of its educational purposes [25] to actively addressing the need for awareness and oversight in AIED technologies upholding the above principles.

Holmes et al. [19] claim that most AIED researchers lack the training to tackle emerging ethical challenges in AI for education. They suggested that various stakeholders—including developers, educators, and policymakers—be provided with key information about the pros and cons of specific AIED technologies, including known limitations and benefits that are likely to emerge from the use of specific AIED systems. However, for AIED developers to recognize these impacts, they must first acquire knowledge and skills about ethical awareness and reasoning. *Who* trains future AIED researchers and developers to develop such mindsets and practices thus becomes a critical point of discussion.

Several efforts have been made to integrate ethics into post-secondary computing curricula; a prevalent strategy among universities is creating stand-alone courses for teaching ethics (and AI) [16]. However, scholars also argue that separating ethics into its own courses disconnects it from the actual practice of computing; instead, ethical considerations should be integrated into technical courses to highlight their intertwined connection [11].

A review of papers on ethics education in computing courses by Brown et al. [4] found that most supported integrating ethics into existing courses. This integration ranges from a single ethics-focused module in technical courses to multiple modules. The authors suggest that the level of integration should align with learning goals, the intended conception of ethics, and context. For instance, while stand-alone courses may be better for teaching formal ethical frameworks and principles, embedding ethics in technical courses helps students identify ethical issues within specific technical implementations. While directly embedding ethics in computing courses is promising, doing this remains a challenge. A major obstacle is that many instructors lack formal ethics training and/or knowledge and may feel unqualified to teach it [4,11,23,26]. In addition, already overloaded curricula require an extensive workload to incorporate ethics. Computing educators also need expertise in pedagogical and instructional design to effectively embed ethics interventions in their coursework [4,7]—including designing suitable readings/lectures, in-class discussions, assignments and projects, and ethics awareness and reasoning assessment methods to measure learning outcomes and evaluate the effectiveness of specific interventions.

Educators have also incorporated various ethics-related content such as ethical principles [24] and frameworks (e.g., deontology, consequentialism) [9,26]. It is also argued that simply using ethical frameworks or principles does not guarantee ethical decision-making and that computing education should also consider the ways that individuals make ethical decisions (i.e., behavioral ethics) [18]. Scholars therefore advocate fostering students' critical thinking, exposing them to scenarios where computing professionals' decisions can indirectly harm individuals, building students' confidence to speak up and make their voices and values heard—especially in unsupportive organizational environments or under external pressures (see also [17]), and to help them feel comfortable navigating ethical ambiguities and to consider different aspects of a situation. The latter can be approached by having students engage with diverse technical and non-technical stakeholders to consider different viewpoints [10,20,24,26]. Researchers also stress using real-world examples—e.g., news articles and personal stories—to make ethical issues tangible. Feffer et al. [10] noted that students often struggle to envision AI system failures in real-world scenarios without prior exposure, advocating for educational tools that expose students to past incidents long before they start their careers as AI practitioners.

Student engagement with ethical topics is yet another challenge. Researchers have explored various strategies such as interactive simulations [3,6], game-based learning [14], and encouraging faculty-led discussions on responsible computing, which can help students engage more seriously with ethical content [7]. Real-world case studies can further enhance engagement by connecting ethical issues to practical and tangible applications [10,11]. Some prior work have also argued that strong technical foundations are a prerequisite for meaningful engagement with ethical topics, especially in complex computing courses [9,11]. Overall, prior studies suggest combining these strategies to optimize student engagement.

3 Platform for Ethical and Responsible Computing Education (PEaRCE)

Developed at the University of Massachusetts Amherst, PEaRCE is an interactive online platform[1] that simulates workplace scenarios involving ERC issues, where students navigate the simulation by making choices that shape the unfolding scenario. Each scenario begins by introducing a context, typically a proposed product or project whose stated goal is usually corporate profit, market positioning, or societal benefit (Fig. 1, top-left). Ethical or societal drawbacks are subtly hinted at but not emphasized. The scenario introduces the student's role, typically through a job description (Fig. 1, top-middle), and asks the student whether to accept the position or explore its ramifications by engaging in conversations with stakeholders potentially impacted by the proposed technology—such as bosses, colleagues, experts, lawyers, friends, and family members (Fig. 1, bottom-left). The simulation includes reflective prompts, encouraging students to comment on their understanding of the situation, their conversational choices, and the ethical or technical issues they face. These reflections enhance the learning experience and provide instructors with insights to gauge students' learning.

The goal is for students to sense the scenario's societal downsides and gain confirmation by engaging with stakeholders who have the most to say about those issues. Students can converse with a limited number of stakeholders (e.g., 5 out of 14), encouraging thoughtful selection of the most valuable interactions (Fig. 1, bottom-middle). A conversation is considered effective if it touches key ethical concerns, involves a directly affected stakeholder, and/or provides insights from a domain expert. During these interactive conversations, students choose questions from a list and see how the stakeholder responds (Fig. 1, bottom-right).

After the conversations, students are again given the choice of proceeding, or delaying the project for further discussion with stakeholders. Upon choosing to go ahead with the project, they receive feedback including a summary of the ethical quandary, hypothetical outcomes of proceeding, modifying, or abandoning the project, and a discussion of one's responsibility to ask critical questions and anticipate potential positive and negative consequences. Some hypothetical outcomes are intentionally unpleasant—such as public backlash over invasive data collection or biased interpretations of a foreign accent—to emphasize the seriousness of their decisions and the importance of careful consideration.

Students receive additional feedback in the form of a radar plot, showing how thoroughly their chosen conversations have touched upon the various issues and highlighting which issues are more ethically germane (e.g., user privacy concerns over promotion opportunities). The chart shows how students prioritized stakeholders within the conversation limit and what they missed by not selecting certain discussions. Finally, students are provided with links to real-world examples of similar ethical quandaries and resources such as the ACM Code of Ethics and Professional Conduct [1].

[1] Guest access available at: https://www-net.cs.umass.edu/PEaRCE/.

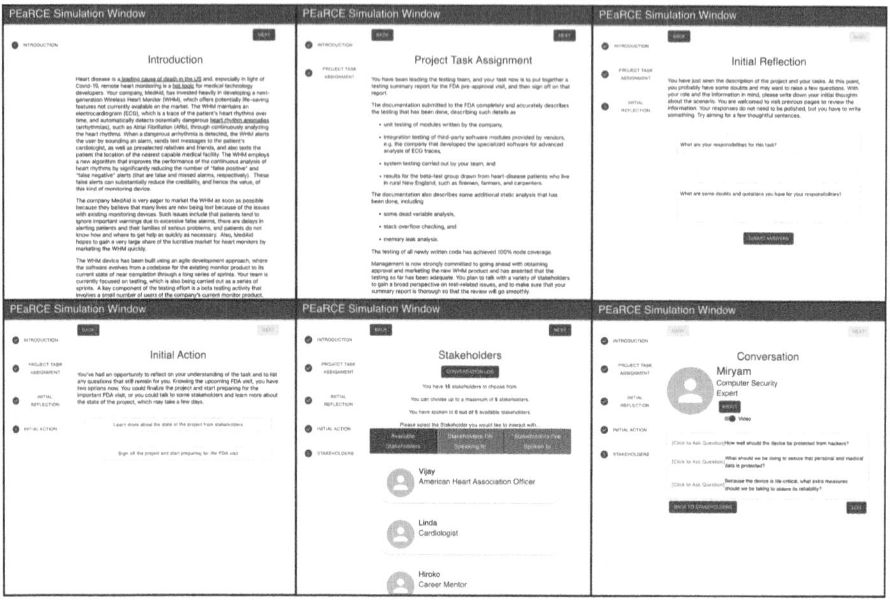

Fig. 1. Sample PEaRCE Interface Stages: (top-left) introduction to the context/technology, (top-middle) project task assignment (student role), (top-right) initial reflection on the project and tasks, (bottom-left) initial decision point, (bottom-middle) list of stakeholders, and (bottom-right) sample conversation with a stakeholder.

3.1 Examples of PEaRCE Work Scenarios

PEaRCE is a scenario-based simulation designed for scalability, allowing future expansions and updates to meet the needs and contexts of different courses across universities. The PEaRCE team collaborates with CS students to develop work scenarios that align with course content, making scenarios and ethical discussions more relevant and engaging for both students and teaching staff. Below, we present three example scenarios.

Scenario 1: Heart Monitoring Device Testability. The context of this scenario is the imminent arrival of a review team from the US Food and Drug Administration (FDA) at a company seeking FDA approval of an innovative heart monitoring device. Among the innovations is the ability of the device to not only detect heart rhythm anomalies, but then to send emails about the event to family or caregivers, to identify nearby doctors and emergency facilities and automatically send the help deemed appropriate. The student is placed as the leader of the testing team who is to make a presentation intended to convince the FDA that the device has been adequately tested. The student believes that the testing has been quite comprehensive but has qualms about the thoroughness of the testing of some of the communications capabilities. Stakeholder conversants include bosses, colleagues, testing experts, doctors, communications experts, college friends, and parents. A persuasive presentation could lead to potential improvements in patient care, as well as raises, promotions, and favorable visibility in a growing market. Downsides include violation of privacy, embarrassing and wasteful emergency calls, marketplace failure (and possible lawsuits) due to product defects that might have been detected by more thorough testing.

Scenario 2: My Medical Advisor. The context of the My Medical Advisor scenario is a company, currently operating a medical information/advice platform, that has used data gathered from customer website interactions—e.g., typing speeds, typing errors, repetitive requests—to develop a machine learning model that detects cognitive decline in older adults. The company wants to sell lists of customers flagged by the model to vendors, who can provide appropriate health products and services, and to the Department of Motor Vehicles, who can remove dangerous drivers from the road. The job description presented to the student is to lead the effort to identify and gather additional data for improving the model prior to the sales effort. Stakeholder conversants include bosses and colleagues, but also lawyers, privacy advocates, parents, and data mining experts. Doing this job well could lead to improved patient outreach and care and safer roads, as well as raises, promotions, and prestige. Downsides include violation of privacy and model biases leading to incorrect lists that could result in harassment and inappropriate revocation of drivers licenses.

Scenario 3: VR in K-12 STEM Education. This scenario is about a new marketing push by the maker of a Virtual Reality (VR) headset into the education market. The company is repurposing the VR headset and adapting it for use in schools, perhaps even in elementary schools. The student's job is to develop software to make the VR headset particularly attractive to the students in these schools by creating a recommender system aimed at bringing appropriate materials to the right students, measuring their responses to these materials, and then adjusting the recommender system to increase student and teacher satisfaction. Stakeholders include company bosses and executives, work colleagues, child education experts, recommender system experts, child psychologists, college friends, and parents. Success with this job should lead to exciting educational opportunities for students, as well as raises, promotions, admiration by colleagues, and greater job mobility. Downsides include the inadvertent inclusion of inappropriate materials in recommended lists, exacerbation of extant problems caused by excessive screen time, dizziness, and difficulty in distinguishing reality.

4 Integrating PEaRCE into Computer Science Courses

Integrating PEaRCE as a standalone assignment would dilute its impact and create a perceived disconnect between ERC education and technical material. To avoid this, we embedded PEaRCE within a series of activities across the semester, promoting deeper engagement, peer discussions, and reflection. Seamless integration into technical CS courses was a key challenge. Following Cohen et al. [7], we trained Ethical and Responsible Computing Teaching Assistants (ERC-TAs)—graduate students who supplement regular course TAs and collaborate with both the PEaRCE team and course staff to manage integration, as described later in this section.

A key advantage of using ERC-TAs is improved instructor acceptance. Prior work has highlighted that instructors' lack of training and discomfort in teaching ERC, along with reluctance to add ERC content to an already crammed syllabi, can lead to instructor resistance [4,11,23,26]. Our model eases these concerns by limiting in-class activities to a single session and shifting coordination to ERC-TAs. The specific sequence of PEaRCE activities is detailed below.

Pre-test Survey: Assessing Students' Initial Awareness. For research purposes, we collaborated with course staff and designed a pre-test survey to evaluate students' initial ERC awareness, ensuring that the survey aligns with the course schedule, workload, and timing. The survey is designed to be integrated as an early take-home course assignment and involves reading three newspaper articles (200–400 words each), adapted from the case studies of the ACM Code of Ethics and Professional Conduct [1]. Each article provides context for a publicly used technology (e.g., medical implant, internet content filtering), covering aspects such as the business project, technology features, and related incidents—all fictional and designed for educational purposes. While maintaining a balanced tone, the articles differ in emphasis: one elaborates more on the negative aspects, another on positive aspects, and the third remains neutral. Each article is followed by two open-ended questions. The first question prompts students to identify the potential parties or communities positively impacted by the technology and describe the associated possible benefits (i.e., pros). The second question follows the same format, focusing instead on the possible negative impacts (i.e., cons). The survey also asks students for feedback on the clarity of the articles and the two follow-up questions to refine future iterations.

Video Lecture: Priming Students for PEaRCE. A few weeks after the pre-test survey, students watch a recorded lecture by a PEaRCE faculty member. It emphasizes that past harmful systems have not infrequently been developed by well-meaning people, and some of those people may well have been young people, perhaps recent graduates from CS programs. The intent here is to make students aware that societally worrisome systems may arise from systems built by people like them. These points are driven home by presenting examples, such as the Volkswagen diesel engine system, whose software had been designed to deploy its pollution-suppression system only when the vehicle was being tested. While senior executives may have planned the deception, lower-level developers wrote and tested the code. The video stresses developers' responsibility to critically assess their work's impact and voice their concerns. The video ends by introducing the PEaRCE project and its goals. Overall, the lecture aims to spark curiosity around ERC and prepare students for upcoming PEaRCE activities.

Using the PEaRCE Platform. Around the mid-semester, an ERC-TA introduces students to the PEaRCE platform via a very short in-class presentation (around 5–10 min), providing an overview of its functionality to ensure they are prepared to engage with the simulation. The ERC-TA then registers students in the system (via auto-generated invitation emails) and monitors their activity for grading purposes. While students engage with the web-based PEaRCE simulation as a take-home assignment, they can report any questions or technical issues to the teaching staff through the course's communication channels.

In-Class Discussions: Reflecting on the Experience. In this phase, an ERC-TA leads a 45–75 min class session, leading a reflective discussion on students' experiences with the PEaRCE scenario. To support facilitation, the PEaRCE team provided a template slide deck that incorporates aggregated platform log data and key discussion topics, including (1) ERC issues students encountered, (2) summary statistics on decisions (e.g., stakeholder engagement rates), (3) the number of students who engaged with each of the stakeholders, and discussions on alternative choices, (4) the simulation's potential impact on students' future professional practices, and (5) students' real-life experiences where they could have evaluated the impacts of their decisions more thoroughly. The session concludes with resources to deepen learning, including the ACM Code of Ethics and Professional Conduct [1], ethics-related university courses, and student groups focused on ethics and technology.

Post-test Survey: Assessing Learning Gains. The post-test survey aims to evaluate how PEaRCE involvement influences students' awareness of ERC. Later in the semester, students complete the same assignment as the pre-test survey, allowing for a direct comparison of their responses.

5 PEaRCE Deployment Experience

This section describes our pilot deployment from Spring 2024, detailing the courses involved and the scenarios used (Sect. 5.1), followed by insights from the deployment (Sect. 5.2). Our research protocols were approved by our institutional IRB.

5.1 Courses and Scenarios

We deployed PEaRCE in two different CS courses offered in the Spring 2024 semester. One course was a 300-level undergraduate Introduction to Software Engineering course. PEaRCE was deployed in two sections, each taught by a different instructor. Participation in PEaRCE activities contributed 2–3% of the total course credit, and one ERC-TA was assigned to each section. We used the Heart Monitoring Device Testability simulation scenario (Sect. 3.1) to align with the course content. The second course was a master-level industry mentorship course offered in a single section. PEaRCE activities accounted for 5% of the total course credit, and one ERC-TA was assigned. Since the course focuses on real-world data science practices, such as data collection and use of machine-learning-based analytics, we selected the My Medical Advisor simulation scenario (Sect. 3.1) to align with the course content.

5.2 Exploration and Initial Insights

Insights from Student Responses to Pre and Post-test Surveys. We conducted a preliminary thematic analysis of 24 students' responses to pre- and post-test surveys (Sect. 4) from one section of the Software Engineering course where PEaRCE was deployed. Our analysis focused on student responses regarding the potential benefits (pros) and harms (cons) of the technology solutions presented in the newspaper articles. A primary coder identified pros and cons within the dataset, and a second coder re-coded 30% of responses to ensure high inter-rater reliability (inter-class correlation, $R = 0.98$, $p < 0.001$). A third researcher tallied the total number of potential harms and benefits in each response, and results are reported based on these averages. Figure 2 shows an increase in both the variety and quantity of potential benefits and harms that students identified. Notably, they significantly increased their recognition of the technologies' potential harms (paired samples t-test, $t(24) = -3.05$, $p < 0.006$). Overall, students' responses focused on two main areas: (1) technological aspects—e.g., privacy, security, data handling, bugs, and (2) societal impacts including health/wellness, economic/financial, legal, trust, and accessibility.

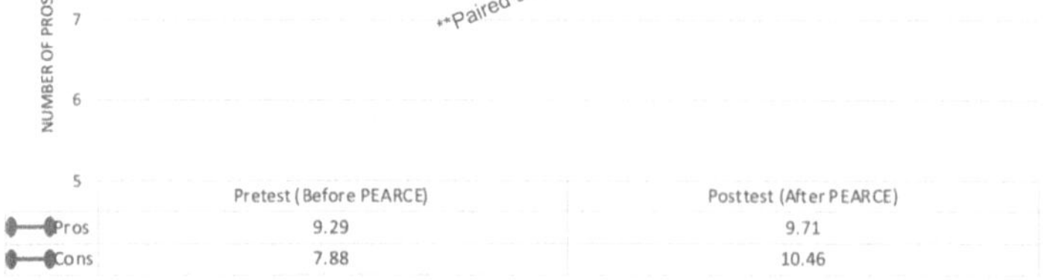

Fig. 2. Mean Pros and Cons reported by students before and after PEaRCE

Insights from Interviews. We conducted semi-structured Zoom interviews in early summer after the Spring 2024 semester with five students (from three course sections), two ERC-TAs, and one instructor. Each interview lasted 30–60 min and was led by an interviewer and a facilitator, both from the PEaRCE research team. All interviews were recorded and transcribed for analysis.

Our initial insights suggest that students and ERC-TAs viewed stakeholder conversations in the PEaRCE simulation positively. Students found them engaging: *"I was pretty engaged in [conversations] and interested in learning about what their position was on these situations"* and that they bring a broader perspective to the course content: *"[...] we usually only learn about coding it efficiently, but we don't really look at how it affects the customer [...]"*.

We also received several suggestions for making PEaRCE activities more engaging. Both ERC-TAs and students suggested more in-person involvements, with one student noting: *"in-person interaction versus a recording might've been more helpful so people could ask questions in real-time"*. While the simulation-based implementation was interesting, long texts were sometimes less engaging: *"some of the explanations [...] was a bit long and time-consuming to read every example that was given"*. An ERC-TA suggested more instructor involvement: *"[...] if it's the professor that becomes [involved], they [students] treat it a little more seriously"*. Another key insight for our multi-modular deployment was that engagement in one activity can highly depend on previous activities: *"[some students] got a lot out of PEaRCE or at least did it seriously and found it interesting, and wanted to talk about it [during in-class discussions] versus maybe [those] who didn't have much to say [...]"*.

Feedback on PEaRCE's connection to course content was mixed. Students appreciated the video lecture covering broader topics beyond CS: *"[the lecturer] did not restrict himself to just CS [...] he gave examples from different walks of life and gave us a really good idea of what to expect in real-world scenarios"*. However, they suggested deeper integration with the course: *"if it could be combined more deeply with the course, I think that would definitely be better"*. Some also recommended inviting guest speakers: *"[...] to bring in either researchers or students who have more experience introducing the ethical concepts [...]"*. One student suggested allowing scenario selection based on relevance to their work: *"[...] different scenarios and I could probably choose based on which is more relevant to me"*. ERC-TAs valued real-world connections, with one noting: *"the more relevant the content is to the real world, the more effective it can get"*, and another describing the differences between simulation and real-world complexity: *"when you're making that decision and you know that this is an ethics simulation, you kind of know what the right choice is in that sense. But in the real world, I think it's a lot more nuance, right?"*

6 Discussion, Conclusion and Future Work

We argued that AIED systems should not be assumed to be ethically designed or inherently beneficial simply because they serve an educational purpose. Instead, the AIED community should actively promote ethical and responsible computing (ERC) education for both current and future practitioners, including students, researchers, and software engineers. ERC education in any branch of Information and Computer Sciences should take place during post-secondary education to develop the practical knowledge, skills, and confidence needed to consider and voice diverse perspectives in moving forward with technology development when ethical and social concerns are overlooked or inadequately considered.

With this in mind, we introduced PEaRCE (Platform for Ethical and Responsible Computing Education), an interactive tool designed to promote ERC education through simulations of realistic workplace scenarios where advanced technologies are developed. In the simulations, users navigate complex situations, voice their opinions at reflection points, make critical decisions—e.g., engaging in conversations with a wide variety of stakeholders or proceeding with assigned jobs—and get feedback on the potential consequences of their decisions.

We also presented a multi-modular approach for integrating PEaRCE into CS courses, informed by pedagogical research, instructional design, and the expertise of our interdisciplinary team. We implemented PEaRCE in multiple undergraduate and graduate CS courses at the University of Massachusetts Amherst, with support from ERC-TAs funded by the Manning College of Information and Computer Sciences. Initial insights suggest PEaRCE's potential to enhance students' ability to recognize and articulate ethical concerns when analyzing case studies involving computing technologies. Interviews indicated that students responded positively to PEaRCE and were actively engaged with its various modules. They also offered suggestions for enhancing the experience, including increasing in-person interactions, incorporating multimedia content, and more deeply integrating PEaRCE with the content of each course.

Our approach to implementing PEaRCE at the University of Massachusetts Amherst relies on hiring an ERC-TA for every few courses to run the experience and lead discussions, which may not be feasible in settings without graduate teaching support. However, these tasks could also be handled by course instructors or trained undergraduate students, provided they receive adequate ERC training and institutional support.

Our position is that PEaRCE has the potential to train future AIED professionals on ethical aspects of developing educational systems—e.g., through our sample scenario on virtual reality headsets for K-12 children. We aim to expand PEaRCE by refining its current scenarios and developing additional ones around the ethical challenges of emerging AIED technologies, particularly those that may directly or indirectly impact key educational stakeholders (e.g., teachers, students, parents). By doing so, we seek to equip future AIED professionals with the knowledge and skills to make well-informed decisions toward ethical and responsible computing.

As we prepare to expand PEaRCE beyond our university, we invite the AIED community to collaborate with us in refining the platform, enhancing existing scenarios, creating new ones, and adapting PEaRCE for other institutions by considering their educational structures and values. The long-term goal of the

PEaRCE team is bold: We aim to make a profound impact by advancing Ethical and Responsible Computing training for the next generation of computer technologists, benefiting society as a whole.

Acknowledgments. This material is based upon work supported by the US National Science Foundation under Grant Nos. 2337132 and 2337133. Any opinions, findings, and conclusions or recommendations expressed in this material are those of the authors and do not necessarily reflect the views of the National Science Foundation.

Disclosure of Interests. The authors have no competing interests to declare that are relevant to the content of this article.

References

1. ACM: ACM code of ethics and professional conduct. https://www.acm.org/code-of-ethics (nd)
2. Andrejevic, M., Selwyn, N.: Facial recognition technology in schools: critical questions and concerns. Learn. Media Technol. **45**(2), 115–128 (2020). https://doi.org/10.1080/17439884.2020.1686014
3. Barab, S., Dede, C.: Games and immersive participatory simulations for science education: an emerging type of curricula. J. Sci. Educ. Technol. **16**(1), 1–3 (2007)
4. Brown, N., Xie, B., Sarder, E., Fiesler, C., Wiese, E.S.: Teaching ethics in computing: a systematic literature review of ACM computer science education publications. ACM Trans. Comput. Educ. **24**(1) (2024). https://doi.org/10.1145/3634685
5. Castro, F., Raipura, S., Conboy, H., Haas, P., Osterweil, L., Arroyo, I.: Piloting an interactive ethics and responsible computing learning environment in undergraduate CS courses. In: Proceeding of the 54th ACM Technical Symposium on Computer Science Education, pp. 659–665. SIGCSE 2023 (2023). https://doi.org/10.1145/3545945.3569753
6. Chernikova, O., Heitzmann, N., Stadler, M., Holzberger, D., Seidel, T., Fischer, F.: Simulation-based learning in higher education: a meta-analysis. Rev. Educ. Res. **90**(4), 499–541 (2020). https://doi.org/10.3102/0034654320933544
7. Cohen, L., Precel, H., Triedman, H., Fisler, K.: A new model for weaving responsible computing into courses across the CS curriculum. In: Proceedings of the 52nd ACM Technical Symposium on Computer Science Education. SIGCSE '21, pp. 858–864 (2021). https://doi.org/10.1145/3408877.3432456
8. Corrêa, N.K., et al.: Worldwide AI ethics: a review of 200 guidelines and recommendations for AI governance. Patterns **4**(10), 100857 (2023). https://doi.org/10.1016/j.patter.2023.100857
9. Cowan, B., Fourquet, E., Kryven, M.: Teaching the societal consequences of computer science: new ideas for increasing student involvement. In: Proceedings of the 23rd Annual ACM Conference on Innovation and Technology in Computer Science Education, pp. 242–247. ITiCSE 2018 (2018). https://doi.org/10.1145/3197091.3197146
10. Feffer, M., Martelaro, N., Heidari, H.: The AI incident database as an educational tool to raise awareness of AI harms: a classroom exploration of efficacy, limitations, & future improvements. In: Proceeding of the 3rd ACM Conference on Equity and Access in Algorithms, Mechanisms, and Optimization. EAAMO '23 (2023). https://doi.org/10.1145/3617694.3623223

11. Fiesler, C., Friske, M., Garrett, N., Muzny, F., Smith, J.J., Zietz, J.: Integrating ethics into introductory programming classes. In: Proceedings of the 52nd ACM Technical Symposium on Computer Science Education. SIGCSE '21, pp. 1027–1033 (2021). https://doi.org/10.1145/3408877.3432510
12. Fiesler, C., Garrett, N., Beard, N.: What do we teach when we teach tech ethics? A syllabi analysis. In: Proceedings of the 51st ACM Technical Symposium on Computer Science Education, pp. 289–295. SIGCSE '20 (2020). https://doi.org/10.1145/3328778.3366825
13. Floridi, L., Cowls, J.: A Unified Framework of Five Principles for AI in Society, pp. 535–545 (2022)
14. de Freitas, A.A., Weingart, T.B.: I'm going to learn what?!? Teaching artificial intelligence to freshmen in an introductory computer science course. In: Proceedings of the 52nd ACM Technical Symposium on Computer Science Education. SIGCSE '21, pp. 198–204 (2021). https://doi.org/10.1145/3408877.3432530
15. Fu, Y., Weng, Z.: Navigating the ethical terrain of AI in education: a systematic review on framing responsible human-centered AI practices. Comput. Educ.: Artif. Intell. **7**, 100306 (2024). https://doi.org/10.1016/j.caeai.2024.100306
16. Garrett, N., Beard, N., Fiesler, C.: More than "if time allows": The role of ethics in AI education. In: Proceedings of the AAAI/ACM Conference on AI, Ethics, and Society. AIES '20, pp. 272–278 (2020). https://doi.org/10.1145/3375627.3375868
17. Hagendorff, T.: The ethics of AI ethics: an evaluation of guidelines. Mind. Mach. **30**(1), 99–120 (2020). https://doi.org/10.1007/s11023-020-09517-8
18. Hedayati-Mehdiabadi, A.: How do computer science students make decisions in ethical situations? Implications for teaching computing ethics based on a grounded theory study. ACM Trans. Comput. Educ. **22**(3) (2022). https://doi.org/10.1145/3483841
19. Holmes, W., et al.: Ethics of AI in education: towards a community-wide framework. Int. J. Artif. Intell. Educ. (1), 1–23 (2021). https://doi.org/10.1007/s40593-021-00239-1
20. Horton, D., McIlraith, S.A., Wang, N., Majedi, M., McClure, E., Wald, B.: Embedding ethics in computer science courses: does it work? In: Proceedings of the 53rd ACM Technical Symposium on Computer Science Education, pp. 481–487. SIGCSE 2022 (2022). https://doi.org/10.1145/3478431.3499407
21. Karan, B., Angadi, G.R.: Potential risks of artificial intelligence integration into school education: a systematic review. Bull. Sci. Technol. Soc. **43**(3–4), 67–85 (2023). https://doi.org/10.1177/02704676231224705
22. Kelly, A.: A tale of two algorithms: the appeal and repeal of calculated grades systems in England and Ireland in 2020. Br. Educ. Res. J. **47**(3), 725–741 (2021). https://doi.org/10.1002/berj.3705
23. Martin, C.D.: The case for integrating ethical and social impact into the computer science curriculum. In: Supplemental Proceedings of the Conference on Integrating Technology into Computer Science Education: Working Group Reports. ITiCSE-WGR '97, pp. 114–120 (1997). https://doi.org/10.1145/266057.266131
24. Petelka, J., Finn, M., Roesner, F., Shilton, K.: Principles matter: integrating an ethics intervention into a computer security course. In: Proceedings of the 53rd ACM Technical Symposium on Computer Science Education, pp. 474–480. SIGCSE 2022 (2022). https://doi.org/10.1145/3478431.3499275
25. Porayska-Pomsta, K., Holmes, W., Nemorin, S.: The ethics of AI in education. In: Handbook of Artificial Intelligence in Education, pp. 571–604. Edward Elgar Publishing (2023). https://doi.org/10.4337/9781800375413.00038

26. Saltz, J., et al.: Integrating ethics within machine learning courses. ACM Trans. Comput. Educ. **19**(4) (2019). https://doi.org/10.1145/3341164
27. Stark, L.: Facial recognition is the plutonium of AI. XRDS **25**(3), 50–55 (2019). https://doi.org/10.1145/3313129

Empower Secondary School Teachers to Create ML-Supported Inquiry-Based Learning Activities

Xiaofei Zhou[1,3](✉), Hanjia Lyu[1], Yuxin Sa[1], Mengfan Li[1], Advait Sarkar[2], Jiebo Luo[1], Michael Daley[1], and Zhen Bai[1]

[1] University of Rochester, Rochester, NY 14627, USA
{xzhou50,zbai7}@ur.rochester.edu, {hlyu5,ysa,mli82}@u.rochester.edu, jluo@cs.rochester.edu, mdaley@warner.rochester.edu

[2] Microsoft Research, Cambridge, UK
advait@microsoft.com

[3] Shanghai Jiao Tong University, Shanghai, China

Abstract. The rapid advancement of Artificial Intelligence (AI) necessitates preparing the next generation to be AI- and data-literate citizens and problem solvers. Despite efforts to integrate AI into K-12 education, many teachers lack the expertise to create meaningful AI learning experiences. We developed ML4Inq, an innovative online authoring tool that enables secondary school teachers to create data-driven inquiry-based learning (IBL) activities with machine learning (ML) technologies such as clustering and classification. Findings of a co-design workshop with 14 secondary school teachers show that teachers successfully created a diverse range of curriculum-aligned activities using ML4Inq, in collaboration with ML experts. We discovered key connections between ML-revealed patterns and IBL behaviors, offering design implications for future tools that support ML practices in secondary schools.

Keywords: Authoring Tool · Inquiry-Based Learning · AI Literacy

1 Introduction

In the era of Big Data and Artificial Intelligence (AI), cultivating data and computational literacy has become critical to prepare the next generation for a data-centric world. Machine learning (ML) techniques like clustering and classification uncover patterns in large datasets, thereby accelerating data-driven scientific inquiry [17]. In K-12 education, inquiry-based learning [29] encourages students to adopt practices akin to professional scientists for knowledge construction [23]. Initiatives like AI4K12 [34], CSTA [8], and AI4ALL [1] have established national guidelines related to applying ML for data analysis in K-12. These range from teaching K-2 students how computers learn from examples to engaging 9th–12th graders to train models using supervised or unsupervised learning algorithms on real-world data and evaluate the results.

A. I. Cristea et al. (Eds.): AIED 2025, LNAI 15877, pp. 150–164, 2025.
https://doi.org/10.1007/978-3-031-98414-3_11

However, effective implementation of ML-supported inquiry-based learning (ML-IBL) in classrooms presents significant challenges, particularly for teachers. The complexity of ML concepts, multidimensional data, and statistical reasoning creates high knowledge barriers, often overwhelming novices before they can effectively use ML to process data, discover patterns, and derive meaningful insights [25]. This complexity, combined with students' lack of ML literacy, highlights the need for pedagogically sound ML practices that captivate students' interests [33]. However, there remains a critical gap in teaching resources that support the integration of customized ML practices into IBL, ensuring alignment with K-12 curriculum standards while addressing teachers' needs and interests [33]. Furthermore, over 60% of pre-service math teachers feel underprepared to teach statistics [24], let alone the integration of ML, which requires additional statistical expertise [25].

Our work presents ML4Inq, a web-based authoring tool [40] with low entry barriers for secondary teachers to create ML-IBL activities. ML4Inq enables teachers to explore data, adjust parameters for K-means clustering and K-nearest neighbors (KNN), interpret ML-revealed patterns, and link with IBL activities for their classrooms without requiring extensive programming or statistics expertise. Our main research question is how secondary school teachers incorporate ML into curriculum-aligned IBL activities using ML4Inq.

We invited 14 secondary school teachers to use datasets of their teaching interests and create ML-IBL activities, by co-designing with ML experts who ensured the validity of ML usage. We collected and analyzed 26 ML-IBL activities with K-12 topics ranging from biology to world history. Teachers applied ML-revealed patterns to promote various desired IBL behaviors for students, such as questioning and hypothesis formation [29]. For example, they first developed hypotheses through cluster analysis, used KNN to retrieve the nearest neighbors as specific data groups, and analyzed patterns within and between these groups to test existing hypotheses. Incorrect predictions were used as opportunities to prompt students to explore potential causes, such as low correlations between the target variable and the selected independent variables. While this study references U.S. educational standards such as NGSS and the Common Core State Standards (CCSS) [15], the findings and tools could be adaptable for integration into other national and regional educational frameworks. In summary, our main contributions include:

1. ML4Inq, a novel authoring tool for teachers to create ML-IBL activities aligned with the curriculum;
2. A key set of connections between ML-revealed patterns and IBL;
3. Design implications of tools for supporting ML practices in secondary school.

2 Data Analysis and IBL in Secondary Education

Recent advancements in statistics education underscore exploring, modeling, and understanding the computational aspects of data [13]. This approach seeks to enhance students' engagement with data and prepare them for more advanced topics, such as inferential statistics and ML. However, complex statistical techniques may be inaccessible to younger students.

To address this challenge, researchers advocate for making computation more accessible through different programming modalities [36], computational notebooks [4], etc. For example, CODAP, an online data analysis platform with embedded binary data visualization, has shown promise in engaging secondary school students in data exploration and analysis [16]. Inq-ITS provides real-time support for inquiry-based science learning [19]. Computational notebooks and block-based programming platforms apply cell grouping and labeling features [7] to improve data sensemaking.

Despite these tool advancements, teachers tend to have low confidence in teaching statistics [24] or ML-related content [33]. Research also highlights the practical need for effective instructional resources to contextualize data practices into STEM and non-STEM curricula [32]. However, a gap exists in supporting teachers to author authentic ML-IBL activities for their classrooms [21]. Studies have identified obstacles in data interpretation resulting from unexpected uses, providing insights to improve educational tools and practices [14].

Research in preparing teachers to teach ML in K-12 settings highlights the scarcity of teaching resources [25]. Professional development (PD) programs have been developed for STEM teachers to integrate computational thinking with science education using Logic Programming [37] or to conceptually create high-level lesson plans integrating basic ML methods [39]. These initiatives relied primarily on direct instruction methods, such as presentations and textbooks, which may not fully connect ML applications with classroom practice.

To address these gaps and obstacles, our design aims to integrate ML-related data practices into the curriculum through data visualization and IBL [29], a pedagogical approach familiar to teachers. We focus on three key IBL phases with direct relevance to data: conceptualization, where students propose research questions or hypotheses, investigation, where students explore, experiment, analyze, and interpret data, and conclusion, where students evaluate whether their research questions or hypotheses have been effectively addressed by their study results. Our design adheres to guidelines for teaching statistics: (1) using large, multivariate datasets, (2) maintaining contextual relevance, and (3) engaging in iterative investigation cycles [6]. Additionally, it incorporates essential capabilities of K-12 data science tools [21]: data manipulation, statistical analysis, data visualization, and dataset availability.

3 Design of ML4Inq

3.1 Design Goals

This section outlines the ML practices and IBL behaviors that ML4Inq aims to support as an authoring tool and explains the rationale behind them.

Selection of ML practices incorporates cluster analysis and predictive analysis through K-means clustering and KNN algorithms, respectively, for three reasons. **First**, with simplicity, transparency, and interpretability [10], K-means

Table 1. Three categories of ML practices.

Exploration	Customization	Evaluation and Analysis
Read attributes: Examine and understand the attributes of the dataset. **Read data**: Browse the raw data that will be used for IBL. **Manual clustering**: Manually sort similar data points together.	**Feature selection**: Identify attributes of interest to build ML algorithms. **Update input**: Modify the dataset fed into the ML algorithm. **Parameter adjustment**: Fine-tune the parameters of ML algorithms.	**Automatic clustering**: Apply K-means clustering algorithm for the k value evaluation and cluster analysis. **Predict with KNN**: Apply the KNN algorithm for performance evaluation and predictive analysis.

clustering groups data into a requested number of clusters, and KNN helps with classification or regression tasks by identifying the nearest neighbors based on distance. Both algorithms require minimal parameter tuning, allowing teachers to get started quickly without extensive knowledge of ML concepts. **Second**, these two similarity-based algorithms are particularly amenable to visualization, which provides immediate feedback that facilitates teachers to gradually adjust parameters and see visual changes in real time. **Third**, they are widely applicable across various science and social study domains [3] and are useful for diverse analysis tasks, such as segmenting data or making predictions.

Based on data science and ML life-cycle (i.e., data exploration, feature engineering, build models, evaluate models) [35], as well as key operations in K-means clustering and KNN, we define a set of ML practices (Table 1). More details are described in Sect. 3.2.

Selection of IBL behaviors is guided by an extensive review of established IBL frameworks [29]: **(1)** questioning (formulate investigable questions for IBL), **(2)** data analysis (analyze the data to identify patterns), **(3)** hypothesis iteration (generate and refine hypotheses based on insights gained in IBL), **(4)** pattern interpretation (make sense of collected patterns in the subject context and synthesize new knowledge), **(5)** conclusion (draw and justify inferences and conclusions).

3.2 Design Features

F1. Modular ML/SI blocks initiate pre-designed ML and IBL components (Fig. 1.a1). When teachers drag and drop them into the main workspace with a side-by-side layout (Fig. 1.a2), the corresponding ML methods or IBL behaviors are added to the learning activity.

ML components (Fig. 1 left) enable the application of ML techniques. For instance, "Build Predictor" and "Make a Prediction" (Fig. 1.b) enable predictive analysis with KNN and the evaluation of prediction accuracy; "Automatic Clustering" applies K-means clustering to analyze input data and visually represent the resulting clusters (Fig. 2); "Manual Clustering" allows users to explore patterns within a subset by manually overlaying data visualizations to compare

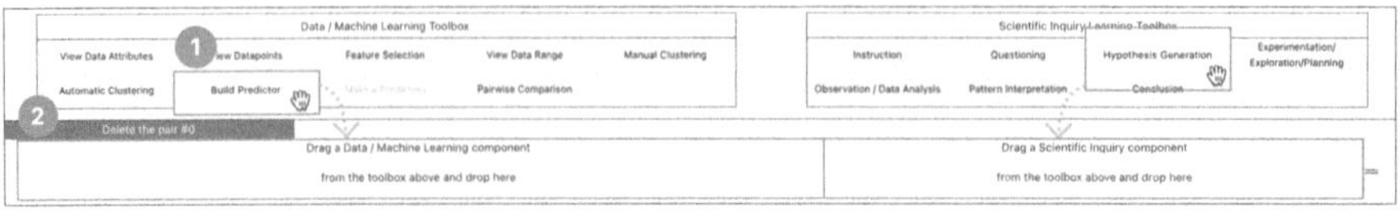

(a)

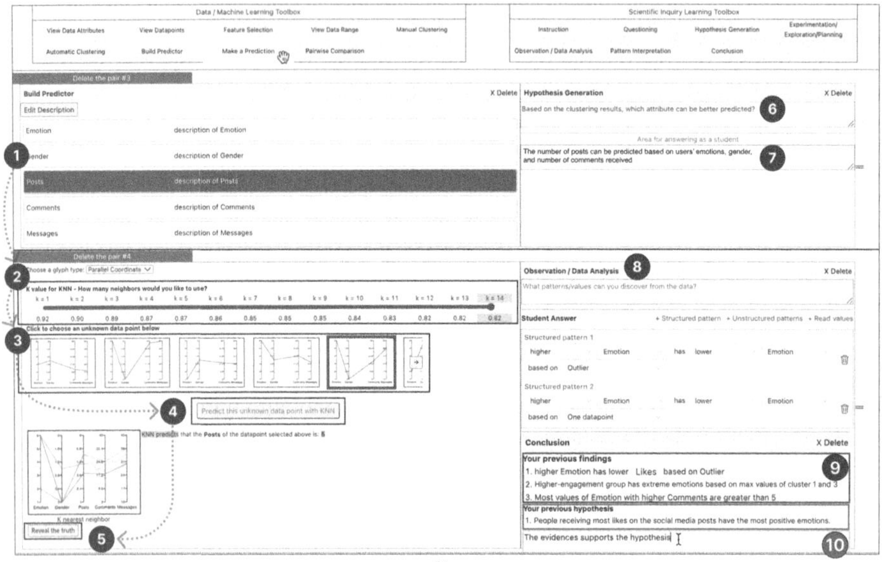

(b)

Fig. 1. (a1) Draggable blocks to initiate ML and IBL components; (a2) side-by-side layout for designing ML (e.g., build predictor) and IBL (e.g., hypothesis generation) steps; (b) a teacher-designed activity: (b1) select an attribute to predict with KNN; (b2) adjust the parameter for the number of neighbors; (b3&b4) select an unknown data point to predict, (b5) evaluate KNN output by comparing with ground truth.

similarities using superposition comparative visualization [18]. This enhances transparency and hands-on manipulation for students to grasp the basics of clustering, helping them understand clustering algorithms when encountered [12].

SI components (Fig. 1 right) support established IBL behaviors [29] (Sect. 3.1). Teachers add "Questioning" or "Hypothesis Generation", customize instructional text, and provide answers from their students' perspective (Fig. 1.b6 & 1.b7) based on the paired ML component (Fig. 1.b left).

With "Data Analysis" (Fig. 1.b8), teachers document the ML-revealed patterns. Based on cluster analysis and predictive analysis in data science [3], seven potential patterns can be identified using K-means clustering and KNN: (1) similarities and differences between two data points, (2) intra-cluster similarities and variations, (3) inter-cluster comparisons, (4) centroid, (5) outlier analysis, (6) data range (minimum and maximum values), (7) prediction results compared to ground truth. The identification and analysis of the aforementioned patterns align with CCSS [15] for Mathematics in the U.S., particularly in reasoning abstractly and quantitatively, constructing viable arguments, and modeling with mathematics. This extends the CCSS as the high school math curriculum in the U.S. typically only covers patterns of association in bivariate data and the shapes of two- and three-dimensional data. With "Conclusion", teachers can view a list of automatically tracked findings from "Data Analysis" (Fig. 1.b9) and compare them to their existing hypothesis (Fig. 1.b10).

F2. Side-by-side ML-IBL layout showcases the final design's visual (Fig. 1.b), which matches common templates for secondary teachers to construct lesson plans. Teachers can add, reorder, and remove individual or pairs of ML and IBL components. They can experiment with various combinations for the learning design, evaluating how to interact with the ML components to best support a specific IBL behavior, or identifying which IBL behaviors students are likely to exhibit when using a particular ML technique.

F3. Customizable ML components enable teachers to input different data, ranging from the entire dataset to a cluster formed by a previous clustering component, or a manually selected subset (Fig. 2). For instance, a teacher might save the clusters generated by K-means clustering (Fig. 2.5) and re-apply K-means clustering on a specific cluster. This supports the incremental construction of ML-related data practices throughout the iterative IBL process.

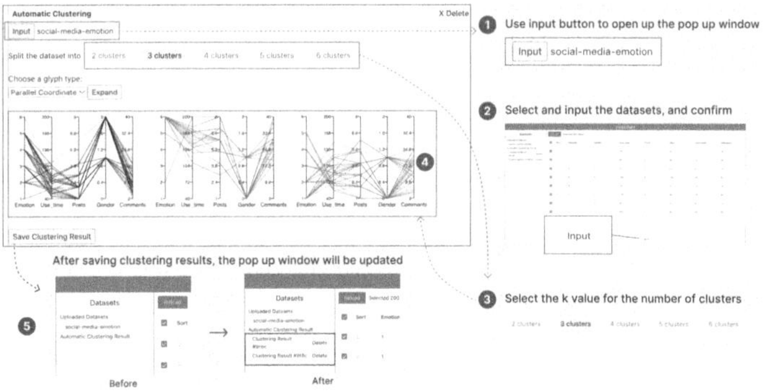

Fig. 2. (1) Update input for K-means clustering; (2) select and view the entire "social media use and emotions" dataset [5] as the input; (3) select K = 3 for the number of clusters; (4) visualize the clustering results with parallel coordinates; (5) click to save the newly-generated clusters; the new clusters saved are added to the available inputs.

4 Research Method

4.1 Participants

Through education-related mailing lists and teacher education program coordinators, we recruited 14 secondary school teachers (Table 2). The study was approved by the Institutional Research Subjects Review Board (Case Number: STUDY00003947).

Table 2. Demographics and teaching backgrounds of teachers.

PID	Gender	Types of Schools	Grade(s)	Subject(s)	Years
P1	Female	Public schools	9–12th	Algebra and AP Statistics	16
P2	Female	Public schools	9–12th	Computer Science, Business Technology	5
P3	Male	Public schools	9–12th	Math, Science	8
P4	Female	Public schools	9–12th	Biology (Science)	7
P5	Female	Public schools	7–9th, 12th	7th grade Life Science. 8th grade Accelerated Living Environment, 9th grade Living Environment, 12 grade AP Biology	5
P6	Female	Public schools	9th	World History, writing	31
P7	Male	Private schools	6–9th	Computer Science, Robotics, Pre-Algebra	27
P8	Female	Public schools	6, 8–12th	Biology, General Science, Earth Science	15
P9	Female	Public schools	K-5th, 9–10th	Science, Computer Science	12
P10	Male	Public, Charter schools	5–8th	Engineering, Computer Science	9
P11	Male	Public schools	9–12th	AP Physics, Physics, Mathematics, Computer Science, Chemistry, Earth Science	28
P12	Female	Public, Private, Charter schools	5–12th	Computer Science, Computational Thinking	23
P13	Male	Public, Private, Charter schools, Outreach programs.	6–12th	Earth Science, Chemistry, Engineering, Computer Science, Data Science	5
P14	Male	Public, Private, Charter schools	K-12th	Science, STEM/Maker Education	20

4.2 Study Procedure and Data Collection

Secondary school teachers use ML4Inq to co-design ML-IBL activities with ML experts. We chose co-design approach [30], for three reasons:

(1) Teachers' expertise is essential due to the lack of pedagogical theories on integrating ML methods into K-12 IBL [33];
(2) Despite specific training and technology enhancement, teachers often limit their instruction designs to surface-level data interpretation [6] and underestimate their ability to teach ML [25];
(3) Co-designing with teachers can promote curriculum innovation, support classroom technology integration, enhance teacher ownership and sustainability of materials, and foster teacher learning [30].

The study consists of three one-hour sessions and is conducted online via Zoom.

Session 1: Teacher-as-Learner. Before this session, teachers filled out the pre-study survey collecting demographic information and teaching backgrounds.

During this session, a researcher guided teachers to go through and get familiar with each component in ML4Inq, including (1) ML components with data visualization, (3) IBL components, and (4) the design flow in ML4Inq. In the end, the teacher and the researcher discussed which datasets the teacher wished to use for the design sessions. A minimum one-day interval is scheduled for the researcher or the teacher to acquire new datasets. The researcher pre-processed data by eliminating data points with missing values and non-numeric features, ensuring compatibility with ML4Inq.

Session 2 and 3: Teacher-as-Designer. In the two design sessions, teachers used ML4Inq to create ML-IBL activities using the datasets of their choice. They first define high-level learning objectives, explore the data using ML components, design the IBL instructions for individual steps, and conduct the specific IBL behaviors from their students' perspective. A researcher and an ML expert provided facilitation when needed. Upon completion, teachers were asked to review their process and contemplate modifications to the learning activity they created. We collected screen recordings and the log of teachers' text input and interaction with ML4Inq.

4.3 Measures and Data Analysis

To investigate how secondary school teachers incorporate ML into curriculum-aligned IBL activities using ML4Inq, we first compared the learning goals with curriculum standards by categorizing the teacher-designed ML-IBL activities based on the disciplines outlined in U.S. K-12 curriculum standards, including Next Generation Science Standards (NGSS) [9] and standards set by the National Council for the Social Studies (NCSS) [27]. We also measured the frequency of dataset subjects.

To analyze how ML and IBL were integrated in teachers' design, we measured the frequency of ML-revealed data patterns applied by teachers and examined the occurrence of the immediate subsequent IBL component that follows various data patterns to gain insights into their specific usage.

5 Results

5.1 Diversity of Curriculum-Aligned Data Topics

14 teachers created 26 learning activities. Among the 21 different datasets used by teachers, two were provided by teachers; 17 were found and retrieved by researchers based on the topics or disciplines requested by teachers; two were chosen by teachers from our example datasets. The disciplines ranged from science (N = 10) to social studies (N = 11) (Table 3). In the science-related datasets, we identified seven out of 13 Disciplinary Core Ideas in NGSS for the U.S. STEM education [9], which encompass four key disciplines: (1) Physical Sciences, (2) Life Sciences, (3) Earth and Space Sciences, and (4) Engineering, Technology, and Applications of Science. In the rest datasets, all five disciplines outlined in the U.S. social study standards [27] are identified: History, Civic and Government, Geography, Economics, and Psychology. Some are interdisciplinary, such as "Social Complexity in Ancient Civilizations," which integrates data attributes from History, Civic and Government, and Geography.

Table 3. Dataset discipline used in teacher-designed ML-IBL activities.

Discipline	Dataset Subject
Environmental Science (N = 6)	Air Composition, Air Quality, Forest Coverage, Water Quality, Climate Change, Weather Pattern
Biology and Ecology (N = 4)	Fishery, Blueberry Yield, Ocean Animals, Alien Rose, Bacteria Growth
Social Studies: History, Geography, Economics, Civics, Psychology (N = 11)	Marvel Movie, Worldwide Country Development, Social Complexity in Ancient Civilization, CS Career, AI Development, Social Media Usage and Emotion, Student Stress, Teen Well-being, Worldwide Cost of Living, Adult Income, Baseball Game Logs

5.2 Distribution and Usage of ML-Revealed Patterns for IBL

Teachers applied ML algorithms to discover a diverse range of patterns (Table 4) and used them to promote students' IBL behaviors (Table 5–7).

Table 4. The distribution of patterns covered by teacher-designed ML-IBL activities.

Pattern	Number of ML-IBL activities
Intra-cluster similarity	26
Inter-cluster comparison	26
Centroid	18
Intra-cluster variation	22
Outlier	7
Comparison of the prediction and the ground truth	18
Inter-cluster comparison of neighboring data points	3

(1) Intra-cluster similarities, inter-cluster differences, and centroids. All of the 26 ML-IBL activities involve interpreting correlations between attributes by analyzing intra-cluster similarities and inter-cluster differences. 18 of them introduced centroids for inter-cluster comparison. Such cluster analysis supported hypothesis iteration in all activities. For instance, P5 identified a counterintuitive pattern through inter-cluster comparison. She found that clone size negatively impacted blueberry yield, searched for a research paper about the underlying causes related to biodiversity, and used this as a learning opportunity for students to discuss the importance of biodiversity. P5 found it very important for students to interact with the real-world dataset and discover the patterns themselves could be more memorable. P13 and P14 utilized intra- and inter-cluster patterns to identify that most data points have higher cs credits and discussed how such data bias influenced the analysis.

(2) Analyzing Variations in Real-World Data. 22 out of the 26 ML-IBL activities guided students in identifying and interpreting variances. Four types of applications of variance analysis in IBL are identified (see details in Table 5).

Table 5. Analyzing variations in real-world data (N = 22).

IBL applications	Example
Use varying features to evaluate and refine hypotheses (N = 9)	*An activity about students' GPAs and course registration*: (1) **Hypothesis**: High CS GPA students have high math GPAs. (2) **Cluster analysis**: High CS GPA students have varying math GPAs. (3) **Conclusion**: The finding "high CS GPA students have varying math GPAs" rejects my hypothesis "high CS GPA students have high math GPAs". *An activity about blueberry yield*: (1) **Cluster analysis**: There are large variations in bumble bee intensity for all the clusters with different levels of blueberry yield. (2) **Hypothesis**: There is little correlation between bumble bee intensity and blueberry yield. (3) **New question**: What are other attributes that could be correlated with blueberry yield? (4) **Hypothesis iteration and feature selection**: Select a few new data attributes based on the updated hypothesis. (5) **Predict with KNN to test hypothesis**: Test the new set of attributes to see if they can accurately predict blueberry yield.
Interpret in real-world contexts (N = 5)	*An activity about CS career*: Identified the same finding, and further interpreted why high school CS GPA seems not to be strongly correlated with math GPA: "HS Math mostly deals with procedure fluency and has little to do with logic and abstraction. CS must do more with logic and abstraction.
Probe further question-asking with large variances (N = 4)	*An activity about Marvel movies*: (1) **Cluster analysis**: There is a large variance in the phases of Marvel movies with higher box office. (2) **New question**: Why do the phases vary for Marvel movies with higher box office? (3) **Update input**: Input a cluster with high box office and varying phases. (4) **New cluster analysis**: Apply K-means clustering on the new input.
Discuss the tolerance for variances (N = 4)	(1) **Variance analysis**: compare the variance in fish stock with the data range. (2) **Cluster analysis**: Tolerate variances to interpret the shared similarity.

(3) Outlier Analysis for Further Inquiry. Seven out of the 26 ML-IBL activities utilized outliers revealed by ML methods to promote IBL, with three types of IBL applications identified (see details in Table 6).

(4) Evaluation and Interpretation of KNN Outputs. Teachers used KNN in 18 activities. Three types of IBL applications are identified (see details in Table 7).

The analysis and interpretation of patterns (Table 5, 6 and 7) align with the U.S. CCSS for Mathematics [15], specifically with reasoning abstractly and quantitatively, constructing viable arguments, and modeling with mathematics. ML-supported data analysis practices extend beyond the typical high school mathematics curriculum, which generally focuses only on patterns of association in bivariate data and the shapes of two- and three-dimensional data. The findings highlight teaching opportunities in science subjects to introduce advanced (1)

Table 6. Outlier analysis for further inquiry (N = 7).

IBL applications	Example
Validate outliers with clustering (N = 4)	**(1)** Conduct clustering multiple times and analyze that the data points don't fit any clusters generated. **(2)** Interpret the potential causes of the outliers. For example, "this is a country with resources significantly higher than the rest countries for AI development, and thus, has an AI index outlier".
Multiple IBL cycles follow up the outlier analysis (N = 3)	*An activity about mental health*: **(1) Cluster analysis**: Some outliers in a high-workload cluster have low stress and low workload. **(2) New questions**: Why do some students in low-stress and high-workload clusters have low workloads? **(3) Hypothesis**: These students with low workloads but high stress may have bad living environments, such as lower safety and lower living condition indexes. **(4) Feature selection**: Add new features "safety" and "living condition" to build ML algorithms. **(5) New cluster analysis**: Apply K-means clustering with the new set of features and analyze the clusters. **(6) Conclusion**: Students with low workloads but high stress have low safety and low living conditions.
Cluster the outlier cluster for further investigation and explanations (N = 3)	*An activity about social media use*: **(1) Hypothesis**: The cluster receiving the most likes has the most positive emotions. **(2) Cluster analysis**: Identify an outlier cluster with both the most positive and the most negative emotions. **(3) Update input**: Input the cluster with the outliers. **(4) New cluster analysis**: Apply K-means clustering on the new input. **(5) Conclusion**: Extreme emotions are related to extreme engagement with social media (i.e., receiving the most likes, posting more frequently, sending the most messages).

Table 7. Evaluation and interpretation of KNN outputs (N = 18).

IBL applications	Example
Predict multiple unknown data points (N = 13)	Analyze the prediction accuracy to determine if the feature predicted is highly correlated with the independent features selected. If the accuracy is low for many trials of unknown data points, students can experiment by updating the feature selection to refine the KNN predictor.
Alternate target features for prediction (N = 5)	**(1) KNN interpretation**: Compare the predicted daily stress with the ground truth. **(2) Feature selection**: Select another set of features to predict well-being scores. **(3) KNN interpretation**.
Interpret group patterns of the k-nearest neighbors (N = 3)	*An activity about ecological field sites*: **(1) Parameter adjustment**: Select k values to predict field sites' livability based on the neighboring data points. **(2) KNN**: Predict an unknown data point with a high canopy height, and then predict a low-canopy data point. **Data analysis**: Compare the two sets of neighboring data points and their livability.

statistical concepts (e.g., outliers, variance, and centroids) and (2) data practices (e.g., data collection and curation, evaluating the statistical power of various types of evidence, and interpreting findings with subject-specific expertise).

6 Discussion and Future Work

Design Implications for Supporting Advanced ML Practices through Novice-Centric Tools. Beyond the K-12 education context, our findings provide broader insights into designing computer-supported experiences for novices to build ML expertise incrementally through hands-on practices.

Customizable ML for incremental sensemaking in ML-IBL. The data analyst's sensemaking process [11], which involves collecting and organizing data to generate knowledge outputs, offers valuable perspectives on how customizable ML practices can support hypothesis iteration across different inquiry phases. The sensemaking process contains four major transitions, two for information foraging: (1) *filter* relevant data, (2) *search* for a larger set of data, and two for sensemaking: (3) *hypothesize* based on the relevant data, (4) *test* hypothesis with the relevant data. By looking into how teachers connected ML-revealed patterns with IBL, we identified that conducting clustering and KNN can be used to filter larger data to relevant subsets and reveal patterns for hypothesizing. ML customization practices, including updating input, parameter adjustment, and feature selection, can support hypothesis testing or enable more efficient searching of a larger dataset. These ML-IBL connections represent incremental constructions of ML and capture ML's finer-grained roles within higher-level IBL phases [29]: filtering, hypothesizing, testing, and searching. With the advances in generative AI, we can extend the sensemaking roles offered by classic ML algorithms to cover more capabilities offered by AI [38].

Modular systems have been recognized in HCI as effective for fostering flexibility and reusability in diverse contexts [26]. For instance, end-user programming environments such as Scratch and Blockly demonstrate how modularity enables users to focus on creativity and problem-solving without requiring advanced technical knowledge [31]. Modular ML components break tasks into smaller, manageable steps, reducing cognitive load and building confidence [36], allowing novices to experiment with ML and interpret the output immediately. However, we did observe an imbalanced usage of different ML components. For example, "Manual Clustering" and "Update Input" rarely appeared, even though they encourage deeper engagement by allowing teachers to group data based on their interpretations and conduct follow-up analyses. This underscores the importance of balancing usability with cognitive demand in tool design. Prior research shows that users often prefer automated over manual features when faced with time constraints or steep learning curves [22,28]. Thus, teachers may have avoided them due to the perceived complexity or lack of immediate utility [20] compared to using the default input and automatic clustering. Future iterations could balance usability with learnability and cognitive demand [2] with contextual hints or example demonstrations.

Limitations and Future Work. While the authoring tool presents a promising approach for integrating ML into K-12 education, several limitations and the corresponding next steps should be acknowledged. First, the tool in its current version relies heavily on pre-designed modular ML components, which may limit flexibility for diverse educational scenarios. Second, the limited time for co-design constrained the coverage of subject topics, ML-IBL design possibilities, and thorough iterations to refine details. Third, there is no comparative study for teachers to design similar activities with existing conventional tools under the guidance of ML experts. We plan to conduct deeper analyses of teachers' decision-making processes and evaluate the ML-IBL activities with students. Insights from existing and future analyses on the interplays between ML practices and IBL behaviors could inform new features to enhance ML4Inq's capabilities, including a broader range of ML techniques and intelligent scaffolding to provide personalized support to users.

7 Conclusion

This work tackles the challenge K-12 teachers face in integrating ML into the curriculum due to limited preparation in statistics and ML. We created ML4Inq for teachers to customize ML and IBL components to design curriculum-aligned ML-supported IBL in their classrooms. Our study reveals how teachers applied ML practices and ML-revealed patterns to foster meaningful IBL in students.

Acknowledgments. We want to acknowledge our anonymous study participants for their time and Minh Nguyen for contributing to the system development. We would like to thank the support from the National Science Foundation (NSF) RETTL program (Award No. 2238675) and the industry fellowship through the NSF NRT project (Award No. 1922591).

References

1. AI4ALL. AI4ALL: Opening Doors to Artificial Intelligence. Website (2024). https://ai-4-all.org/. Accessed 17 Nov 2024
2. Amershi, S., Cakmak, M., Knox, W.B., Kulesza, T.: Power to the people: the role of humans in interactive machine learning. AI Mag. **35**(4), 105–120 (2014)
3. Anderberg, M.R.: Cluster Analysis for Applications: Probability and Mathematical Statistics: A Series of Monographs and Textbooks, vol. 19. Academic Press (2014)
4. Biswas, S., Wardat, M., Rajan, H.: The art and practice of data science pipelines: a comprehensive study of data science pipelines in theory, in-the-small, and in-the-large. In: Proceedings of the 44th International Conference on Software Engineering, pp. 2091–2103 (2022)
5. Emirhan BULUT. Social media usage and emotional well-being (2024). https://www.kaggle.com/dsv/8460631
6. Casey, S., Hudson, R., Harrison, T., Barker, H., Draper, J.: Preservice teachers' design of technology-enhanced statistical tasks. Contemp. Issues Technol. Teacher Educ. **20**(2), 269–292 (2020)

7. Chattopadhyay, S., et al.: Make it make sense! understanding and facilitating sensemaking in computational notebooks (2023)
8. Computer Science Teachers Association. Computer science teachers association (CSTA) (2024). https://csteachers.org/. Accessed 17 Nov 2024
9. National Research Council et al. Next generation science standards: For states, by states (2013)
10. Doshi-Velez, F., Kim, B.: Towards a rigorous science of interpretable machine learning. arXiv preprint arXiv:1702.08608 (2017)
11. Drosos, I., Sarkar, A., Xu, X., Negreanu, C., Rintel, S., Tankelevitch, L.: "it's like a rubber duck that talks back": understanding generative AI-assisted data analysis workflows through a participatory prompting study. In: Proceedings of the 3rd Annual Meeting of the Symposium on Human-Computer Interaction for Work, pp. 1–21 (2024)
12. Erickson, T., Engel, J.: What goes before the cart? Introducing classification trees with arbor and codap. Teach. Stat. **45**, S104–S113 (2023)
13. Erickson, T., Wilkerson, M., Finzer, W., Reichsman, F.: Data moves. Technol. Innov. Stat. Educ. **12**(1) (2019)
14. Fernandez, C., Blikstein, P., De Deus Lopes Lopes, R.: Design failures in data visualization programming activities. In: Proceedings of the 23rd Annual ACM Interaction Design and Children Conference, pp. 574–586 (2024)
15. National Governors Association Center for Best Practices. Common core science standards. national governors association center for best practices, council of chief state school (2010)
16. Frischemeier, D., Biehler, R., Podworny, S., Budde, L.: A first introduction to data science education in secondary schools: Teaching and learning about data exploration with codap using survey data. Teach. Stat. **43**, S182–S189 (2021)
17. Gil, Y., Greaves, M., Hendler, J., Hirsh, H.: Amplify scientific discovery with artificial intelligence. Science **346**(6206), 171–172 (2014)
18. Gleicher, M., Albers, D., Walker, R., Jusufi, I., Hansen, C.D., Roberts, J.C.: Visual comparison for information visualization. Inf. Vis. **10**(4), 289–309 (2011)
19. Gobert, J.D.: Inq-its: creating rigorous assessment and real-time support of science learning. XRDS: Crossroads ACM Mag. Stud. **29**(3), 36–40 (2023)
20. Horvitz, E.: Principles of mixed-initiative user interfaces. In: Proceedings of the SIGCHI Conference on Human Factors in Computing Systems, pp. 159–166 (1999)
21. Israel-Fishelson, R., Moon, P.F., Tabak, R., Weintrop, D.: Preparing students to meet their data: an evaluation of k-12 data science tools. Behav. Inf. Technol. 1–20 (2023)
22. Kaptelinin, V., Nardi, B.A.: Acting with Technology: Activity Theory and Interaction Design. MIT Press (2009)
23. Keselman, A.: Supporting inquiry learning by promoting normative understanding of multivariable causality. J. Res. Sci. Teach. **40**(9), 898–921 (2003)
24. Lovett, J.N., Lee, H.S.: New standards require teaching more statistics: are preservice secondary mathematics teachers ready? J. Teach. Educ. **68**(3), 299–311 (2017)
25. Marques, L.S., von Wangenheim, C.G., Hauck, J.: Teaching machine learning in school: a systematic mapping of the state of the art. Inform. Educ. **19**(2), 283–321 (2020)
26. Myers, B., Hudson, S.E., Pausch, R.: Past, present, and future of user interface software tools. ACM Trans. Comput.-Hum. Interact. (TOCHI) **7**(1), 3–28 (2000)
27. Myers, C.B., et al.: National standards for social studies teachers. Natl. Council Soc. Stud. (2006)

28. Norman, D.: The Design of Everyday Things: Revised and Expanded Edition. Basic Books (2013)
29. Pedaste, M., et al.: Phases of inquiry-based learning: definitions and the inquiry cycle. Educ. Res. Rev. **14**, 47–61 (2015)
30. Penuel, W.R.: Co-design as infrastructuring with attention to power: building collective capacity for equitable teaching and learning through design-based implementation research. In: Collaborative Curriculum Design for Sustainable Innovation and Teacher Learning, pp. 387–401 (2019)
31. Resnick, M., et al.: Scratch: programming for all. Commun. ACM **52**(11), 60–67 (2009)
32. Schwab-McCoy, A., Baker, C.M., Gasper, R.E.: Data science in 2020: computing, curricula, and challenges for the next 10 years. J. Stat. Data Science Educ. **29**(sup1), S40–S50 (2021)
33. Tedre, M., et al.: Teaching machine learning in k-12 classroom: pedagogical and technological trajectories for artificial intelligence education. IEEE Access **9**, 110558–110572 (2021)
34. Touretzky, D., Gardner-McCune, C., Martin, F., Seehorn, D.: Envisioning AI for k-12: What should every child know about AI? In: Proceedings of the AAAI Conference on Artificial Intelligence, vol. 33, pp. 9795–9799 (2019)
35. Wang, D., Andres, J., Weisz, J.D., Oduor, E., Dugan, C.: Autods: towards human-centered automation of data science. In: Proceedings of the 2021 CHI Conference on Human Factors in Computing Systems, pp. 1–12 (2021)
36. Weintrop, D., Wilensky, U.: To block or not to block, that is the question: students' perceptions of blocks-based programming. In: Proceedings of the 14th International Conference on Interaction Design and Children, pp. 199–208 (2015)
37. Zhang, Y., Wang, J., Bolduc, F., Murray, W.G., Staffen, W.: A preliminary report of integrating science and computing teaching using logic programming. In: Proceedings of the AAAI Conference on Artificial Intelligence, vol. 33, pp. 9737–9744 (2019)
38. Zheng, C., et al.: Charting the future of AI in project-based learning: a co-design exploration with students. In: Proceedings of the CHI Conference on Human Factors in Computing Systems, pp. 1–19 (2024)
39. Zhou, X., Tang, J., Daley, M., Ahmad, S., Bai, Z.: "now, i want to teach it for real!": introducing machine learning as a scientific discovery tool for k-12 teachers. In: Artificial Intelligence in Education: 22nd International Conference, AIED 2021, Utrecht, The Netherlands, June 14–18, 2021, Proceedings, Part I 22, pp. 486–499. Springer (2021)
40. Zhou, X., et al.: Creating an authoring tool for k-12 teachers to design ml-supported scientific inquiry learning. In: Extended Abstracts of the CHI Conference on Human Factors in Computing Systems, pp. 1–7 (2024)

Learning Feedback Policy from Historical Data: An Offline Approach Within Pyrates

Badmavasan Kirouchenassamy[1(✉)], Amel Yessad[1], Sébastien Jolivet[1,2], Matthieu Branthôme[3], Sébastien Lallé[1], and Vanda Luengo[1]

[1] Sorbonne Université, CNRS, LIP6, 75005 Paris, France
{badamavsan.kirouchenassamy,amel.yessad,sebastien.lalle, vanda.luengo}@lip6.fr, sebastien.jolivet@unige.ch
[2] IUFE & TECFA, Université de Genève, Geneva, Switzerland
[3] Université de Rennes, IRISA, CNRS, Lannion, France
matthieu.branthome@univ-rennes.fr

Abstract. The expense and logistics of organizing experiments to train and evaluate teaching policies, as well as the potential negative impacts of these policies on the very first students, are significant challenges in the field of education. In this paper, we explore the feasibility of using offline reinforcement learning (RL) to learn an adaptive feedback policy that improves student progress in *Pyrates*, a programming platform. Leveraging an existing dataset of teacher-provided feedback and student interactions and codes, we have developed an offline RL model capable of learning an optimal feedback policy without direct interaction with students. The trained policy is then evaluated to assess its effectiveness in maximizing student progress and its suitability for online deployment in real-world educational settings. Our evaluation yields promising results, demonstrating that offline-trained policies can significantly enhance student progress, highlighting their potential for scalable deployment in programming platforms. However, challenges remain in ensuring robustness and adaptability when transitioning to online use.

Keywords: Feedback Policy · Computer science Education · Programming Platform · Offline Reinforcement Learning

1 Introduction

Feedback is one of the most powerful influences on learning and achievement [10,21]. It is crucial in K-12 programming education as it helps students identify, understand and correct their errors, thereby enhancing their problem-solving skills [5,11,17]. However, a major challenge on platforms designed for young learners is the capacity of teachers to provide personalized feedback across different types of feedback [16,30]. In crowded classrooms, teachers often lack the time and resources to thoroughly review students' codes and offer personalized feedback [3,23,26]. Automating feedback further ensures that students

A. I. Cristea et al. (Eds.): AIED 2025, LNAI 15877, pp. 165–178, 2025.
https://doi.org/10.1007/978-3-031-98414-3_12

receive immediate, consistent, and scalable guidance while reducing the burden on teachers, especially in large-scale online courses [27]. The lack of mechanisms to automate and adapt feedback significantly limits the student's progress, highlighting the need for intelligent systems capable of providing automated adaptive feedback in real time [28].

The process of determining adaptive feedback involves decision-making under uncertainty for two key reasons. First, it's unclear which feedback type is best in a given situation since the system receives noisy, incomplete, and uncertain data about the student and their activity. Second, the impact of feedback on the student is also uncertain. Moreover, feedback policy may vary based on different objectives. For example, a policy designed to minimize the time it takes for a student to solve a problem could differ significantly from a policy that aims to improve the student's understanding of the underlying concepts. Based on these observations, Is it possible to train an AI model to automatically decide an adaptive feedback in such an uncertain context?

Among AI learning paradigms, Reinforcement Learning (RL) models are particularly well-suited for optimizing decisions via a trial-and-error strategy without any supervision from experts, with delayed rewards capturing the cumulative effect of sequential decisions [24,25]. Several research [2,6,7,29] have shown the interest of reinforcement learning (RL) for instructional policies, as RL models can learn complex and latent relationships between instructional tasks, students actions, and knowledge outcomes.

Online reinforcement learning (RL) approaches rely on direct interaction with students to learn an effective feedback decision model. However, conducting such experiments requires significant logistical effort and resources, making it costly and complex to organize. Moreover, during the initial training phase, students may receive suboptimal feedback until the policy converges to an optimal one, potentially impacting their learning experience.

An alternate approach is to use offline RL algorithms that effectively leverage previously collected experiences without requiring online interaction. In theory, these approaches would allow learning an optimal feedback policy from data generated with any other feedback policy. However, offline RL remains a largely underexplored avenue in educational research, particularly regarding the autonomous selection of appropriate feedback across diverse feedback categories.

Therefore, in this paper, we address the following research questions:

- **RQ1**: To what extent can a feedback policy be learned from historical data using offline reinforcement learning to effectively maximize student progress?
- **RQ2**: How does the learned feedback policy compare to the policy used to generate the historical data in terms of effectiveness and decision-making patterns?

To answer these two research questions, we use the logs generated by the programming platform named Pyrates [3] (Cf. Sect. 3). Our approach focuses on leveraging offline RL to learn a feedback policy that aims to maximize students' progress using Pyrates' historical data.

In this article, we begin by reviewing related work, followed by an introduction to the context of Pyrates and our data collection process. We then formalize the feedback decision problem before presenting and discussing the study results.

2 Related Work

2.1 Single vs. Multiple Feedback Types

In the early works, automated feedback systems in educational settings have increasingly leveraged Markov Decision Processes (MDPs) which is also a foundational framework for reinforcement learning. In the context of programming education, a prominent application of MDPs has been in automated hint generation [15,18–20,22]. These approaches typically formulate the feedback decision problem as selecting the most appropriate hint to guide students toward a correct solution. However, these methods often operate within a constrained decision space, limiting choices to the "best" feedback within a predefined type rather than considering fundamentally different feedback types. In contrast, our study aims to develop an system capable of dynamically selecting from multiple feedback types.

2.2 Online vs. Offline Reinforcement Learning

In the context of educational feedback, online reinforcement learning has gained traction, with models deployed directly within learning platforms to learn from real-time student interactions [8,9]. These online methods aim to continuously adapt feedback policies based on immediate student responses. However, as highlighted in [6] and further emphasized by the challenges of real-world educational deployments, online RL faces significant limitations. These include the extensive interaction time required for convergence, the risk of exposing early students to suboptimal policies, and the potential for inconsistent feedback delivery due to continuous model updates.

To address these shortcomings, particularly the issues of suboptimal early feedback and the need for efficient learning, offline reinforcement learning presents a promising alternative [13,14]. [6] discusses the application of offline RL in educational settings, demonstrating its potential to train models offline and deploy them online, mitigating the risks associated with online learning. Offline RL, which learns policies from previously collected datasets without further online interaction, has achieved significant success in other domains, notably robotics [12]. Another benefit of offline RL approaches is the ability to learn different policies that optimize different criteria from the same dataset generated with any policy.

The application offline RL techniques, such as Conservative Q-Learning (CQL) [13], to address the feedback decision in educational settings has not been explored to our knowledge. Therefore, this work is dedicated to bridging this gap, by applying CQL in feedback decision context.

3 Presentation of Pyrates

Pyrates[1] is a serious-game-based programming learning platform, engaging students in writing Python code to control the movement of an avatar [3]. In the context of Pyrates, there are 8 game levels, and each level has 5 types of feedback. For each level, experts have predefined feedback corresponding to the different types of feedback. The feedback types are incremental, offering detailed help: **TR** where the level's goal and relevant control functions are explained, **CO** where the relevant programming concept (e.g., for loop) is revealed, with a reference to the programming memo, **PI** where a guidance on implementing the concept in Python is presented, and **CR** where a sample solution is provided and finally **OTHER** where the teacher provided customized feedback that is different from the other four types of feedback. However, due to the very limited instances of this type of feedback and the lack of data on its specific content, we have chosen to exclude it from our study. Apart from this, all other types of feedback were selected by the teacher through the Pyrates interface in response to student requests. These feedback entries were systematically recorded alongside the students' activity traces, forming the dataset[2] used for our analysis. More details on this dataset and its collection can be found in [4].

As discussed earlier, to avoid deploying online learning models that learn through interaction or rely on random feedback selection, we positioned the teacher as the decision-maker for feedback types. This approach allowed us to collect a reliable dataset without affecting students' learning experience. We gathered data from eight high school teachers, each deciding the type of feedback whenever students requested it. Upon exploring the collected data, we report in Table 2 the amount of feedback delivered per game level. Levels 6 to 8 are not included because too many students ran out of time. Level 2 also required less feedback, as sown in Table 2, most likely because it targets the same concept (loop) as Level 1. Thus in this paper, we focus only on Levels 1, 3, 4 and 5, i.e., the levels where feedback was the most needed and in which a sufficient amount of data was collected to train the RL feedback policy (Table 1).

Table 1. Sample size and distribution of the feedback received per level.

Level	#students	#feedback	Feedback type distribution			
			TR	CO	PI	CR
Level 1	215	176	22 (13%)	91 (52%)	51 (29%)	12 (7%)
Level 2	215	35	10 (29%)	5 (17%)	13 (37%)	7 (20%)
Level 3	215	408	69 (17%)	136 (33%)	134 (33%)	69 (17%)
Level 4	209	338	22 (7%)	97 (29%)	122 (36%)	97 (29%)
Level 5	187	164	18 (11%)	58 (35%)	53 (32%)	35 (21%)

[1] https://py-rates.fr/.

[2] https://github.com/Matthieu-BRANTHOME/PyratesIA/tree/L%40S_2025.

4 Learning Feedback Policy Using Offline RL

In this study, student progress refers to the degree of completion of the current game level relative to predefined objectives, which we assume directly reflects their in-game progression.

Within Pyrates, teachers choose the feedback type provided to students; nevertheless, around 40% of the feedback appears ineffective in producing immediate progress, based on the observed differences in student progress between consecutive submissions. We observe that even feedback type CR, which provides the solution to the student, does not always lead to the student's progress (16.3% of the provided feedback does not induce students' progress). Several reasons may explain this outcome. Teachers may adopt a long-term strategy, using feedback to promote student reflection, establish foundational understanding, or assess comprehension. Another reason is that the selection of feedback may not always align with the student's current stage, potentially limiting its effectiveness.

Thus, we frame feedback selection as a sequential decision process, where each feedback decision affects the student's subsequent state, with the overall impact determined by multiple interdependent choices over time. The 40% of teacher feedback that did not lead to immediate progress may have served as stepping stones for long-term learning. Following prior work on hint decision-making [1,7], we adopt the same sequential decision framework and optimize the sequential decision making via RL approaches.

In RL, the **behavior policy** is the strategy that generates the training data, while the **target policy** is the one learned through optimization to maximize rewards. In our study, the behavior policy refers to the teacher's feedback policy used to generate the data, and the objective is to learn a target policy from the teacher's decisions that better optimizes student progress.

4.1 Problem Formulation

In RL, the model (or agent) interacts with an environment, which is typically modeled as a Markov Decision Process (MDP). In the context of Pyrates, the MDP is defined by the tuple $M = (\mathcal{S}, \mathcal{A}, P, R)$ as follows:

- Each state $s \in \mathcal{S}$ represents the environment at a given time step with which the RL agent interacts. Although various pieces of information are available from the Pyrates student log data, we chose to represent the state using only two attributes—student progress and attempt count (i.e., the number of feedback instances provided). This simplification is driven by the necessity to maintain sufficient data coverage and improve learning performance, considering the limited availability of data, a lower-dimensional state representation leads to better data coverage and improved learning performance. However, it may fail to capture nuanced feedback strategies. Using many features would create a large number of unique states, each with fewer data points, thus limiting the exploration of the state space. Student progress provides insights into the types of errors made, while the attempt count reflects the level of student

struggle; together, they form a concise yet informative state representation. In our implementation, we experimented with state representations based solely on student progress, solely on attempt count, and a combination of both to analyze the impact of state dimensionality on model learning outcomes.
- Each action $a \in \mathcal{A}$ corresponds to a specific type of feedback provided by teachers. The set $\mathcal{A}$ is composed of the 5 types of feedback.
- The dynamics are governed by the probability transition function: $P(s' \mid s, a) = \Pr\{s_{t+1} = s' \mid s_t = s, a_t = a\}$, where s' denotes the subsequent state of the student after receiving feedback a in state s. In our setting, these dynamics are not known a priori; however, we aim to learn them through offline RL agent learning.
- The reward function R plays a crucial role in guiding policy learning and must be carefully designed. In the Pyrates context, feedback types vary in the amount of information they reveal to students. Notably, one feedback type, CR, containing significantly more information than other types. To avoid biasing the learning policy towards this feedback, we introduce a reward framework that normalizes rewards based on the degree of information revealed in each action (noted as *I(a))*. Therefore, the reward for each feedback action a is given by:

$$R(s, a, s') = \begin{cases} \frac{1}{I(a)}, & \text{if the feedback } a \text{ improves the student's} \\ & \text{progress,} \\ 0, & \text{otherwise.} \end{cases}$$

The goal is to iteratively learn the target policy $\pi* : \mathcal{S} \rightarrow \mathcal{A}$ that maximizes students' progress over time. We choose student' progress in the game as the primary metric to track improvement over time.

4.2 Data Collection and Q-Learning for Offline RL

Formally, the offline dataset is given by: $D = \{(s_i, a_i, r_i, s'_i)\}_{i=1}^{N}$, where: $s_i \in \mathcal{S}$ is the state (student's state) at time step i, $a_i \in \mathcal{A}$ is the feedback type provided by the teacher, $r_i = R(s_i, a_i, s'_i)$ is the observed reward, $s'_i \in \mathcal{S}$ is the next state after provision of the feedback. This dataset is generated by a behavior policy $\mu(a \mid s)$ that may differ from the target policy we want to learn.

As illustrated in Fig. 1, the distribution of actions per state is markedly uneven, with certain states being explored much more frequently than others. This imbalance in state exploration poses a challenge for conventional Q-learning, particularly in an offline training context, where many state-action pairs remain under-sampled or unexplored. To address this issue, we adopt a conservative Q-learning approach [13], which incorporates a penalty for actions associated with high uncertainty or sparse data, reducing the overestimation bias in Q-values and stabilizing learning in offline RL.

Essentially, a Q-value estimates the benefit of performing an action in a given state. In standard Q-learning, the Q-value is updated via the Bellman equation

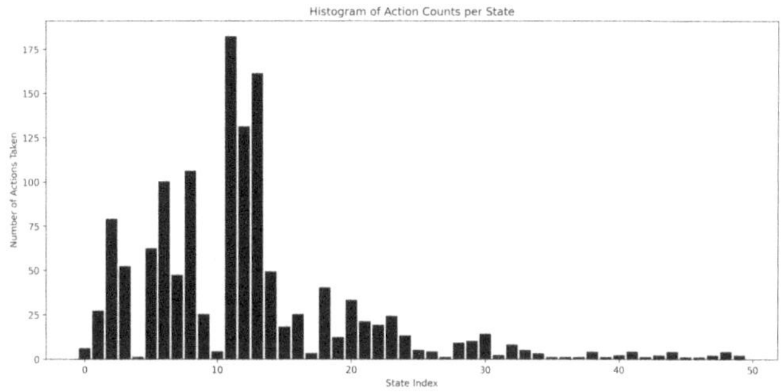

Fig. 1. Distribution of Actions counts across different states

as follows: $Q(s,a) \leftarrow Q(s,a) + \alpha\Big[r + \gamma \max_{a' \in \mathcal{A}} Q(s',a')\,(1-d) - Q(s,a)\Big]$, where r is the immediate reward received when transitioning from s to s' after taking action a, d is 1 if s' is terminal (0 otherwise), γ is the *discount factor* and determines the importance of future rewards compared to immediate reward, and α is the *learning rate* which determines how much new information overrides old information.

In the conservative Q-learning variant, a penalty term is subtracted from the target to discourage overestimation for uncertain or rare state-action pairs: $Q(s,a) \leftarrow Q(s,a) + \alpha\Big[r + \gamma\Big(\max_{a' \in \mathcal{A}} Q(s',a') - \beta\, C(s',a')\Big)(1-d) - Q(s,a)\Big]$, where $C(s',a')$ quantifies the uncertainty or rarity of the state-action pair, and $\beta \geq 0$ is a parameter controlling the strength of the penalty. This modification helps ensure that overestimated Q-values for out-of-distribution actions are effectively suppressed. In essence, conservative Q-learning "plays it safe" by tempering the Q-value estimates for actions that are poorly represented in the dataset, thereby reducing the risk of overestimation. This adjustment is crucial in our scenario, as it ensures that the learned policy remains robust and reliable, even when faced with the uneven distribution of explored states.

In our implementation, we trained the model using mini-batches of size 32 from the offline dataset, repeated over 1,000 iterations, ensuring stable and efficient parameter updates while balancing computational cost. To minimize random variability, we repeated the experiment 10 times. We applied a decaying discount factor, gradually reducing the importance of future rewards over time. This transition shifted the model's focus from long-term rewards (γ close to 1) to more immediate rewards (γ approaching 0), ensuring adaptability and improved decision-making as training progressed.

4.3 Evaluation Metrics

Evaluating policies derived from offline training is a challenge in itself. Unlike online methods, offline training relies on pre-collected datasets, which can introduce biases due to distributional shifts and limited state–action coverage. This setting prevents direct interaction with the environment, making it essential to employ robust evaluation techniques that can accurately assess policy performance without real–time feedback. In our study, we adopt a three–pronged evaluation approach:

1. **Offline Policy Evaluation Metrics**
   - **Importance Sampling (IS)**: We use IS to evaluate a new policy using offline data. It works by reweighting each observed reward according to how likely the new policy would have taken that action compared to the behavior policy. The sum of these weighted rewards estimates the expected return of the new policy. The overall estimate varies between 0 and 1. For example, if the overall IS estimate is 0.5, it means that—on average—the new policy is expected to yield a reward of 0.5 per decision. This helps to gauge how much better (or worse) the new policy might perform compared to the data-generating policy. A low IS estimate does not mean the target policy is performing poorly. It simply means the target policy is already close to the behavior policy, and there may not be much room for improvement.
   - **Fitted Q Evaluation (FQE)**: FQE metric quantifies the expected cumulative reward that a target policy will accumulate over time, starting from a given state. Although individual rewards are bounded between 0 and 1, the FQE value can exceed 1 because it represents the sum of rewards over many time steps. In this context, a higher FQE estimate indicates superior policy performance, as it reflects the policy's ability to accrue a greater total reward in the long run. The exact value of the FQE metric is influenced by factors such as the discount factor(cf. Sect. 4.2) and the length of the decision horizon, providing a comprehensive measure of the policy's long-term efficacy.
2. **Policy Convergence Metrics**: Ensuring Q-value stabilization is key in offline training. We track Q-values during training, and their stabilization indicates that further iterations yield minimal changes. This convergence suggests the policy has captured the dataset's underlying dynamics, increasing confidence in its reliability.
3. **Comparison Analysis Between the Teacher and the RL Policies**: We introduce a novel comparison approach to evaluate whether the target policy outperforms the teachers' policy (which is the behavior policy used to generate the data). First, a teacher-weighted Q-value is calculated for each state by averaging the teacher's action frequencies with the corresponding model Q-values. This is compared to the best Q-value, which is the highest Q-value among the model's actions. A paired statistical test is conducted to determine if there is a significant difference between the teacher-weighted Q-values and the best Q-values, indicating whether the teacher's decisions systematically lead to suboptimal outcomes. Additionally, Cohen's kappa quantifies the agreement between teacher decisions (highest frequency action) and model decisions (highest Q-value). A permutation test generates a null distribution to assess the significance of this agreement.

5 Results

In this section, we present the results of our study. First, in Sects. 5.1 and 5.2, we analyze the convergence and performance of the trained policy to address RQ1. This includes evaluating how effectively the policy learns and adapts over time. Next, in Sect. 5.3, we conduct a comparative analysis between the model's policy and the teacher's policy to answer RQ2, providing insights into their similarities, differences, and potential advantages.

5.1 Policy Convergence Metrics

Figure 2 shows that most models' Q-values converge during training, indicating the policy effectively learns the dataset's underlying dynamics and reward structure. A single feature state (student progress or attempt counts) stabilize faster, as they help the model quickly identify effective actions. In contrast, the combined feature state (student progress + attempt count) converges more slowly due to higher complexity, increased dimensionality, and potential noise. These results highlight that simpler state features promote faster convergence. Therefore, based on the shape of these curves, we can partially answer **RQ1**, concluding that it is possible to learn an optimal policy without knowing the policy used to generate the data.

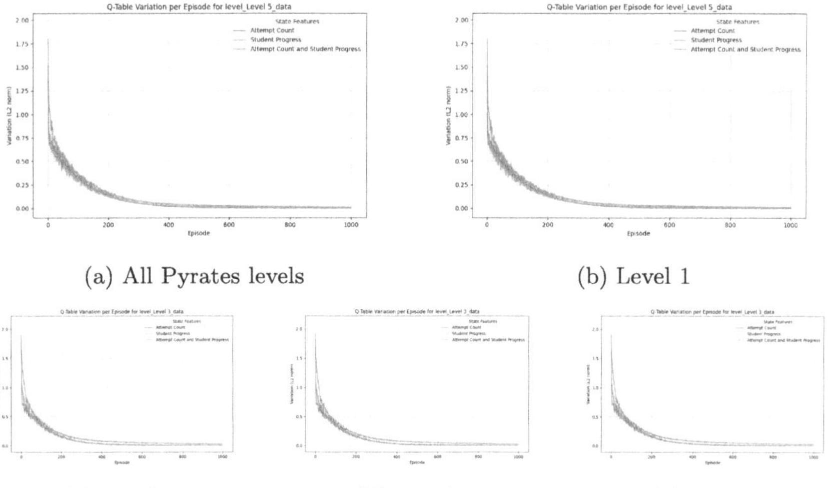

(a) All Pyrates levels (b) Level 1

(c) Level 3 (d) Level 4 (c) Level 5

Fig. 2. Q-value variations across training episodes

Table 2. Offline Policy Evaluation Performance Metrics: Analysis Across State Features and Levels

Level	State Feature	IS estimate	FQE	IS Weighted Sum
All Levels	Student Progress	0.3204	1.5577	1332.0
	Attempt Count	0.2649	1.5725	1332.0
	Student Progress, Attempt Count	0.2607	1.9094	1332.0
Level 1	Student Progress	0.4988	1.7925	212.0
	Attempt Count	0.5532	1.7707	212.0
	Student Progress, Attempt Count	0.4973	2.2579	212.0
Level 3	Student Progress	0.2456	1.6952	476.0
	Attempt Count	0.3132	1.5921	476.0
	Student Progress, Attempt Count	0.2240	2.2735	476.0
Level 4	Student Progress	0.2702	1.5858	404.0
	Attempt Count	0.1382	1.5716	404.0
	Student Progress, Attempt Count	0.1641	1.7941	404.0
Level 5	Student Progress	0.2805	1.2562	196.0
	Attempt Count	0.2236	1.2256	196.0
	Student Progress, Attempt Count	0.2321	1.7656	196.0

5.2 Offline Policy Evaluation Metrics

Across all levels and state representations (cf. Table 2), the IS estimates are positive. This consistent positivity suggests that, on average, the target policy is yielding positive returns when adjusted against the behavior policy. In practical terms, a positive IS estimate indicates that the re–weighted returns are not only non–negative but also potentially signal an improvement over the baseline behavior (i.e. The teachers' policy).

In Level 1, the IS estimates range from 0.4988 to 0.5532, showing that the target policy performs significantly better than the behavior policy once we adjust for each action's likelihood. In contrast, Levels 3, 4, and 5 have lower IS estimates (typically between 0.1382 and 0.3132), meaning the target policy's advantage is not as evident in these levels.

The IS weighted sum reflects the total number of samples used for the estimate. Although Level 1 has a weighted sum of 212.0, the repeated sampling of the same state-action pair results in a high IS estimate. On the other hand, Level 3's weighted sum is larger at 476.0 as its data come from a broader range of state-action pairs. This broader coverage makes the IS estimate more conservative, as it does not rely heavily on a single frequently observed state-action pair.

Several factors may explain why Level 1 shows better metrics. First, Level 1 may be inherently easier or more predictable, allowing the target policy to clearly outperform the behavior policy. Second, even though there are fewer samples, the data in Level 1 might be more representative of optimal behavior, consistently yielding high returns. Third, the target policy may have learned the optimal actions for Level 1 more effectively, as indicated by the higher IS estimates and FQE values (up to 2.2579) that signal strong long-term value.

While Level 3 has the largest dataset, its increased diversity dilutes the performance gains; the behavior policy in Level 3 may also be well-tuned, leaving less room for improvement by the target policy to show significant improvements.

Across all levels, we see that FQE values are generally higher when both student progress and attempt count are combined. For example, at All Levels, FQE is 1.5577 for Student Progress, 1.5725 for Attempt Count, and 1.9094 for the combined state representation. This pattern is echoed at the individual level granularity: at Level 1, while the IS estimate is fairly similar across representations, the combined representation yields the highest FQE (2.2579), and similar trends appear for Levels 3, 4, and 5. This suggests that the long–term q-values of the policy are enhanced when both state features are considered, even if the immediate (IS) estimates do not always show a big difference. But FQE values vary across levels and combinations, highlighting the importance of feature selection and model tuning to improve policy evaluation accuracy.

Inconsistent performance of state features across levels suggests that the relevance and effectiveness of these features are context-dependent. In some levels, one state feature may capture critical aspects of the environment more effectively than in others, leading to better policy performance. In levels with simpler dynamics, the model might rely more on straightforward features like "Student Progress" whereas in levels with complex dynamics, the model might struggle to leverage simple features effectively, requiring more nuanced features like "Attempt Count". This variability could be due to differences in the underlying dynamics, complexity, or structure of each level. Essentially, if one state feature allows the model to outperform another in a given level, it means that the feature is more informative or better aligned with the key decision-making elements in that specific context. Conversely, the lack of consistent superiority across all levels highlights the importance of tailoring state representations or combining features to account for the diversity in environmental challenges.

Our findings support **RQ1**, demonstrating that a feedback policy can be learned from historical data using offline RL to maximize student progress. Higher IS and FQE estimates, particularly with combined state features, indicate that the learned policy outperforms the behavioral policy in both immediate returns and long-term value. This confirms the potential of offline RL for optimizing feedback strategies. However, the approach depends on the quality and coverage of historical data. If key aspects of student behavior are underrepresented, the learned policy may struggle to generalize.

5.3 Teacher Policy vs Model Policy

The results of the paired-t test reveal that, in 12 out of 13 comparisons, the expected rewards of the teachers' policy are significantly different from the expected rewards of the model (with p-values ranging from 0.0000 to 0.0258), indicating that the policy of the teachers can systematically lead to suboptimal results relative to the optimal decisions learned by the model in regard to the objective of improving student progress. In parallel, Cohen's kappa values, which mostly range between 0.8082 and 1.0000 (with significant p-values except for one Level 5 instance), suggest a high degree of agreement between the teacher's most frequent action in each state and the model's highest Q-value action in the same state. This apparent contradiction implies that, while the teacher and model generally concur on the preferred actions, the teacher's approach tends to yield lower expected rewards compared to the model's best feedback choices. These findings indicate that while teacher feedback may be noisy—reflecting variability across multiple teachers and even inconsistent choices by a single teacher—the model reliably captures the underlying decision tendencies by filtering out such noise. As a result, the learned policy generally agrees with the teachers in its actions, yet it identifies subtle improvements in reward outcomes, reinforcing its potential to outperform the teacher's strategy in practice. As for **RQ2**, our findings confirm that the learned policy is statistically significantly different from the teacher's feedback policy in terms of expected rewards and, as a result, students' progress, despite a high overall agreement in action decisions.

6 Conclusion and Future Work

Our results demonstrate that a feedback policy can be effectively learned from historical data, provided there is sufficient coverage of state-action pairs, ensuring diverse contextual representation. This feasibility study confirms that the learned policy aligns better with the current goal of improving student's game progress than the teacher-generated policy, enabling its deployment for automated feedback decision at scale. If certain model actions fail to induce game progress, this may indicate gaps in the current-state representation, emphasizing the need for more comprehensive data and feature enhancements. Ultimately, this iterative approach enables increasingly fine-grained decisions, and with additional metrics such as pre- and post-tests, it could extend beyond the goal of improving students' game progress to improving students' mastery concepts.

Importantly, our findings directly address the research gap regarding the feedback decision-making especially on cold start as the model has proven to be viable to be deployed in the online environment. While prior work has focused extensively on using RL to optimize overall instructional policies, our study shows that an effective feedback policy can still be learned through historical data. This not only confirms the viability of using offline data for policy induction in educational contexts but also suggests that further enhancements—such as richer state representations and additional performance metrics—could lead to even more personalized and adaptive feedback strategies.

Future work should explore deploying the learned feedback policy to provide real-world evidence of whether the policy leads to measurable learning gains compared to traditional teacher feedback. Additionally, future research could consider a richer pool of feedback, where each instance is characterized by multiple features (e.g., tone, format, and content). This raises an open question: can conservative Q-learning handle the complexity and noise of multi-dimensional feedback, or are further changes needed? Exploring this could refine our approach and boost reinforcement learning in education.

Acknowledgments. This study was funded by Generation5 as part of Badmavasan Kirouchenassamy's CIFRE PhD. We thank the students and teachers who participated in the Pyrates experiments and allowed us to collect data.

References

1. Barnes, T., Stamper, J.: Toward automatic hint generation for logic proof tutoring using historical student data. In: International Conference on Intelligent Tutoring Systems, pp. 373–382. Springer (2008)
2. Bassen, J., et al.: Reinforcement learning for the adaptive scheduling of educational activities. In: Proceedings of the 2020 CHI Conference on Human Factors in Computing Systems, pp. 1–12 (2020)
3. Branthome, M.: Apprentissage de la programmation informatique: analyses et ressources pour accompagner la transition collège-lycée. Ph.D. thesis, Université de Bretagne occidentale-Brest (2023)
4. Branthôme, M., Lallé, S.: Learning from teachers: AI-driven feedback for a high school python serious game. In: Proceedings of the 12th ACM Learning @ Scale Conference (L@S '25), Palermo, Italy (2025)
5. Crow, T., Luxton-Reilly, A., Wuensche, B.: Intelligent tutoring systems for programming education: a systematic review. In: Proceedings of the 20th Australasian Computing Education Conference, pp. 53–62 (2018)
6. Doroudi, S., Aleven, V., Brunskill, E.: Where's the reward? Int. J. Artif. Intell. Educ. **29**(4), 568–620 (2019)
7. Efremov, A., Ghosh, A., Singla, A.: Zero-shot learning of hint policy via reinforcement learning and program synthesis. In: International Educational Data Mining Society (2020)
8. Fahid, F.M., Rowe, J., Kim, Y., Srivastava, S., Lester, J.: Online reinforcement learning-based pedagogical planning for narrative-centered learning environments. In: Proceedings of the AAAI Conference on Artificial Intelligence, vol. 38, pp. 23191–23199 (2024)
9. Siyong, F.: A reinforcement learning-based smart educational environment for higher education. Int. J. e-Collaboration (IJeC) **19**(6), 1–17 (2022)
10. Hattie, J., Timperley, H.: The power of feedback. Rev. Educ. Res. **77**(1), 81–112 (2007)
11. Keuning, H., Jeuring, J., Heeren, B.: A systematic literature review of automated feedback generation for programming exercises. ACM Trans. Comput. Educ. **19**(1), 1–43 (2019)
12. Kumar, A., et al.: Pre-training for robots: offline RL enables learning new tasks from a handful of trials (2023)
13. Kumar, A., Zhou, A., Tucker, G., Levine, S.: Conservative q-learning for offline reinforcement learning. Adv. Neural. Inf. Process. Syst. **33**, 1179–1191 (2020)
14. Levine, S., Kumar, A., Tucker, G., Fu, J.: Offline reinforcement learning: tutorial, review, and perspectives on open problems. arXiv preprint arXiv:2005.01643 (2020)

15. Malik, A., et al.: Generative grading: near human-level accuracy for automated feedback on richly structured problems. arXiv preprint arXiv:1905.09916, 2019
16. Masantiah, C., Pasiphol, S., Tangdhanakanond, K.: Student and feedback: which type of feedback is preferable? Kasetsart J. Soc. Sci. **41**(2), 269–274 (2020)
17. Messer, M., Brown, N., Kölling, M., Shi, M.: Automated grading and feedback tools for programming education: a systematic review. ACM Trans. Comput. Educ. **24**(1), 1–43 (2024)
18. Piech, C., Sahami, M., Huang, J., Guibas, L.: Autonomously generating hints by inferring problem solving policies. In: Proceedings of the Second (2015) ACM Conference on Learning@ Scale, pp. 195–204 (2015)
19. Price, T., Zhi, R., Barnes, T.: Evaluation of a data-driven feedback algorithm for open-ended programming. In: International Educational Data Mining Society (2017)
20. Rivers, K., Koedinger, K.R.: Data-driven hint generation in vast solution spaces: a self-improving python programming tutor. Int. J. Artif. Intell. Educ. **27**, 37–64 (2017)
21. Shute, V.J.: Focus on formative feedback. Rev. Educ. Res. **78**(1), 153–189 (2008)
22. Singh, R., Gulwani, S., Solar-Lezama, A.: Automated feedback generation for introductory programming assignments. In: Proceedings of the 34th ACM SIGPLAN Conference on Programming Language Design and Implementation, pp. 15–26, Seattle Washington USA, June 2013. ACM (2013)
23. Sun, L., Guo, Z., Linlin, H.: Educational games promote the development of students' computational thinking: a meta-analytic review. Interact. Learn. Environ. **31**(6), 3476–3490 (2023)
24. Sutton, R.S., Barto, A.G.: Reinforcement learning: An introduction. MIT Press (2018)
25. Tessler, C., Mankowitz, D.J., Mannor, S.: Reward constrained policy optimization. arXiv preprint arXiv:1805.11074 (2018)
26. Tonbuloğlu, B., Tonbuloğlu, I.: The effect of unplugged coding activities on computational thinking skills of middle school students. Inf. Educ. **18**(2), 403–426 (2019)
27. Wang, K., Singh, R., Su, Z.: Data-driven feedback generation for introductory programming exercises (2017)
28. Yaseen, H., et al.: The impact of adaptive learning technologies, personalized feedback, and interactive AI tools on student engagement: The moderating role of digital literacy. Sustainability **17**(3), 1133 (2025)
29. Yessad, A.: Personalizing the sequencing of learning activities by using the q-learning and the Bayesian knowledge tracing. In: European Conference on Technology Enhanced Learning, pp. 638–644. Springer (2022)
30. Zhe Victor Zhang and Ken Hyland: Fostering student engagement with feedback: an integrated approach. Assess. Writ. **51**, 100586 (2022)

AI-Coding Hackathon: Designing an Innovative Learning Space for Building a Better Community

Guangji Yuan[1(✉)], Monica Woei Ling Ong[2], Chew Lee Teo[1], Peter Sen Kee Seow[1], Munirah Binte Shaik Kadir[1], Shu Shing Lee[1], Nanditha Das[3], and Beverly Anne Devakishen[3]

[1] Nanyang Technological University, Singapore, Singapore
{guangji.yuan,chewlee.teo,peter.seow,munirah.kadir, shushing.lee}@nie.edu.sg

[2] Academy of Singapore Teachers, Singapore, Singapore
monica_ong@moe.gov.sg

[3] Singapore Indian Development Association (SINDA), Singapore, Singapore
{nanditha,beverly}@sinda.org.sg

Abstract. The current education system urgently needs innovative learning spaces to help students develop the ability to solve real-world problems and improve their adaptability in the complex era of new technologies such as Artificial Intelligence (AI). This study describes an AI-coding hackathon designed to cultivate an inclusive and innovative learning space where students collaborate to solve real-world community problems. This project is designed according to Knowledge Building (KB) pedagogies, combined with AI-assisted learning support tools and chatbots, to provide students with learning scaffolds to help them develop programming and problem-solving abilities. The three-day program attracted students of different age groups from low socioeconomic backgrounds. The program is structured to guide students through basic machine learning concepts, basic Python programming syntax, and developing projects and solutions using prompt engineering to create an AI-supported application (digital books, chatbots, simple trained Machine Learning datasets) as the final product. The project emphasizes student agency, encouraging students to identify community problems, choose AI tools independently, and continuously revise solutions based on expert and group mentors' feedback. Data collection included focus group interviews, classroom observations, and pretest-posttest questionnaires to measure students' changes in programming skills, design thinking abilities, learning motivation, and knowledge building abilities. This study proposes a new pedagogical application, Knowledge Building, for AI education to promote a more equitable and meaningful AI learning experience.

Keywords: AI-Coding Hackathon · AI Literacy · Knowledge Building

A. I. Cristea et al. (Eds.): AIED 2025, LNAI 15877, pp. 179–192, 2025.
https://doi.org/10.1007/978-3-031-98414-3_13

1 Introduction

In the rapidly evolving education environment, integrating Artificial Intelligence (AI) technology brings unprecedented opportunities and significant challenges. As we move through the industry 4.0 changes led by AI, education systems must evolve to prepare students for a future where AI literacy is not just an advantage but a necessity [1, 2]. AI redefines how we think about learning, teaching, and problem solving through technologies like Generative Pretrained Transformers (GPT), which mimic human reasoning capabilities [3]. Current research mainly explores the application of AI in higher education, where AI serves as a teacher assistant, learning aid, or research tool [4–7]. However, this exploration further reveals critical issues such as potential inaccuracies and the phenomenon of AI hallucinations [2]. These challenges underscore the need for a nuanced approach in educational design focused on improving AI literacy via human-computer interaction and developing critical thinking to verify the authenticity of AI-generated content [8–10]. AI serves as a double-edged sword for education, both a boon and a potential pitfall, which requires a strategic approach in terms of curriculum development. Educators must teach about AI and provide students with practical experience in its application. This includes understanding AI's ethical implications, its technical foundations, and its practical applications in solving real-world problems [1, 5]. This study aims to address these educational needs by proposing an AI-coding hackathon, an innovative learning space aimed at cultivating AI literacy. By fostering collaborative, community-driven projects, the initiative seeks to bridge the digital divide and provide an inclusive platform for students to develop AI programming and problem-solving skills. This approach is consistent with the broader educational goal of developing a generation that uses AI and engages critically to innovate and solve social problems.

2 Literature Review

2.1 AI Literacy

AI is defined as the science and engineering of making intelligent machines [11]. AI has penetrated every aspect of life for decades, changing industry and affecting education. The future job market will increasingly favor those who can leverage rather than those who simply use AI [12]. Literacy has traditionally been understood as the ability to read and write but has now expanded to include domain-specific skills like AI literacy. AI literacy covers technical proficiency in using AI, engaging critically with AI systems, understanding their implications, and applying them ethically. Ng and colleagues [12] proposed a comprehensive AI literacy framework, identifying four key aspects: knowledge and understanding, use and application, evaluation and creation, and ethical issues. This framework is based on Bloom's taxonomy and advocates an educational approach beyond purely technical knowledge. It also encourages learners to develop higher-order skills such as critical thinking and moral reasoning. For example, learning Python programming or participating in prompt engineering requires understanding the theoretical foundations of machine learning and the ethical dilemmas raised by AI. This comprehensive understanding of AI literacy is critical to equip students, especially those from disadvantaged backgrounds, so they will not face more barriers in the future job market. The latest developments in AI education include integrating AI into the early education system and recognizing the importance of cultivating basic knowledge of AI from an early age [13]. However, uneven access to digital resources highlights the need for equity-centered approaches in AI education [14].

2.2 Design Learning Space

In the rapidly evolving field of education, the design of innovative learning spaces has become a key factor in supporting modern teaching methods and improving student learning outcomes [15]. These spaces transcend the constraints of traditional classrooms and foster engagement and creativity by integrating flexibility, advanced technology, and collaborative environments. For the Artificial Intelligence in Education (AIED) community, incorporating AI technology into these spaces is a transformative opportunity to redefine how learning is and is experienced. The hallmark of innovative learning spaces is their adaptability, achieved through physical design elements such as modular furniture and reconfigurable layouts. These characteristics enable the space to support a variety of teaching methods, from lectures to hands-on group activities, accommodating a variety of learning styles and preferences [13, 16]. This flexibility is amplified with AI. AI-driven systems can analyze usage patterns and recommend optimal configurations for specific educational goals or student dynamics. This adaptability ensures that the learning environment is responsive to the changing needs of educators and learners. While the application of generative AI has brought about changes, it has also exacerbated the problem of inequality in accessing learning resources for students from low-income households. Despite these advances, integrating AI into learning spaces poses ethical and practical challenges that must be addressed. Data privacy concerns, algorithmic bias, and transparency in AI decision-making processes require strong frameworks to ensure fair and responsible use [16]. As the field advances, designing innovative learning spaces requires a holistic approach that reconciles technological innovation with educational values and ensures that AI is used as a tool to augment, rather than replace, human interaction and expertise.

Knowledge Building (KB) provides a pedagogical framework that emphasizes the collaborative creation, improvement, and dissemination of knowledge within a learning community [17, 18]. Compared to traditional teaching, KB positions students as active knowledge builders and encourages them to participate in inquiry, criticism, and integration of knowledge [19]. Core concepts of KB, such as epistemic agency, enable students to guide their learning paths, especially in solving open-ended, real-world problems [20] that reflect the complexity of AI applications. KB has shown effectiveness in various educational contexts, including science education, where it promotes inquiry-based learning, experimental design, and evidence-based implementation and teaching strategies [21, 22].

The emergence of large-scale language models (LLMs) such as GPT-4 has changed the educational landscape by automating knowledge retrieval. Still, it has also emphasized the need for human skills beyond mere data processing [5]. KB encourages learners to view AI as an augmentative tool rather than a competitor. Students can use AI to stimulate creative ideas, but these suggestions must be critically evaluated and implemented ethically. This synergy between human creativity and AI capabilities highlights the need for educational strategies to cultivate uniquely human abilities such as creativity, empathy, and moral judgment. Therefore, this study examines the implementation of an AI-focused coding hackathon in an innovative learning space to enhance AI literacy among students from low socioeconomic backgrounds.

Through this initiative, we seek to understand how the pedagogical framework and designs can effectively bridge the gap between theoretical AI literacy and practical applications that address real-world community challenges with the following research questions (RQ). RQ1: How does an AI-coding hackathon program integrate the KB approach to foster AI literacy and coding skills through reflective collaboration? RQ2: In what ways do students collaborate, ideate, and co-create innovative solutions in an AI-coding program to solve community-based real-world problems? RQ3: How do students perceive the impact of an AI coding program on their evolving understanding, confidence, and application of AI coding skills?

3 Methodology

As a design-based research project, the AI-coding hackathon took place from September 2 to 4, 2024 and employed innovative open learning spaces that encourage students of low-income households to collaborate to solve real-world community problems. The event was organized by a local university in partnership with a government-funded self-help group. Grouped by age to ensure personalized instruction, students can freely choose to focus on topics of their interests and apply AI tools creatively (Fig. 1). The activities are mainly guided by KB pedagogies and integrated expert guidance (such as data scientists and education researchers) and peer experience sharing, leveraging the Knowledge Forum (KF) platform for collaboration and reflection and recording progress through the Journey of Thinking reflective notes (Fig. 2). The three-day program includes community issue brainstorming, prototype development and expert feedback, results presentation, and reflection.

3.1 Participants

Participants were 14 volunteer students from diverse school backgrounds, most of whom had a strong interest in AI exploration. They consist of 5 girls and nine boys between the age of 9 to 15 years old. Based on their age range, the participants formed three groups, with the first group made up of participants of younger age between the ages of 9 to 10, the second group consisting of a mixed age group of students of lower and upper elementary students, and the third, consisting of high school students, aged between 13 to 15 years old. This grouping and sample allow for an in-depth exploration of the application of KB principles with students of diverse backgrounds with plans for future expansion.

3.2 Research Design: Learning Space Design and Implementation

The AI-coding hackathon aims to promote authentic community-oriented learning through KB pedagogies, guided by KB key principles, especially *Real ideas authentic problems*, *Epistemic Agency*, and *Idea Improvement*, as the core principles emphasize that students share the responsibility for knowledge building [17]. The program includes both face-to-face learning activities and online discussions. To facilitate students' online discussion and learning activities, the program used a KF as the main platform for students to share their reflections and ideas [19, 20]. A specially designed AI-coding Hackathon Chatbot Facilitator in extending their interests by guiding prompts, generating requested graphs and stories, and answering participants' questions with age-appropriate content. It is created using child-friendly language, inquiry-based guidance, and interest-spiking prompts (e.g., What can you try next to solve the problem?) to avoid direct answers. Its design protects students from inappropriate content and reflects safety protection in response to the recommended usage guidelines of ChatGPT for those over 13 years old.

An important component of the new learning space was the role of the group mentors, designed to support students' collective cognitive responsibility at the AI-coding hackathon. A total of 8 mentors participated in the hackathon over the three days, supporting activities at different times based on their availability, ensuring that each group had at least one mentor. The first group (9–10 years old, n = 5) had two mentors to guide the learning process and answer questions in real-time throughout the entire process to meet the high needs of the younger students in guiding collaboration and engagement. The second and third groups (mixed elementary school and high school, n = 5) each have at least one mentor. Among them, the mentors in the older group (13–15 years old, n = 4) had a stronger computer coding background and provided customized learning experiences for the students based on their interests and needs during the project design process. In addition, they helped address programming and prompt design-related questions from the students.

Fig. 1. Students' concept learning, hands-on designing, and final projects

3.3 Data Collection

Mixed methods were used to collect data to fully capture the learning process and results over three days, with daily activities ranging from 9:00 am to 4:00 pm (7 h per day, 21 h total). (1) The pretest and posttest questionnaires were administered to 14 participants, and 11 valid responses were obtained due to absence or incomplete submission. The questionnaire uses a 5-point Likert scale to assess AI literacy (8 items, such as I can explain the role of machine learning), motivation (6 items, such as I am excited about programming), and collaboration (6 items, such as I contribute ideas to the group). It was verified through pilot testing with Cronbach's $\alpha = 0.83$. (2) Observations covered 21 h, using audio and videos to record classroom interactions, group discussions, chatbot usage, and field notes by five group mentors and two researchers to ensure that participation and collaboration were recorded. After the posttest, three focus group interviews were conducted with 11 participants, totaling 844 lines of transcribed text. The audio of the interviews was carefully transcribed by a research assistant and cross-checked with video to ensure accuracy. The ambiguities were subsequently corrected to provide the basis for analysis. (3) Focus group interviews (844 lines of transcribed text) were thematically coded to analyze collaboration patterns, skill improvement, and problem-solving strategies. (4) KF collected 143 individual notes within three days. The collaborative exchanges (build-on notes) and timestamps were automatically recorded, reflecting the principle of continuous knowledge improvement. Group reflections in the Journey of Thinking [21] were collected from three age groups.

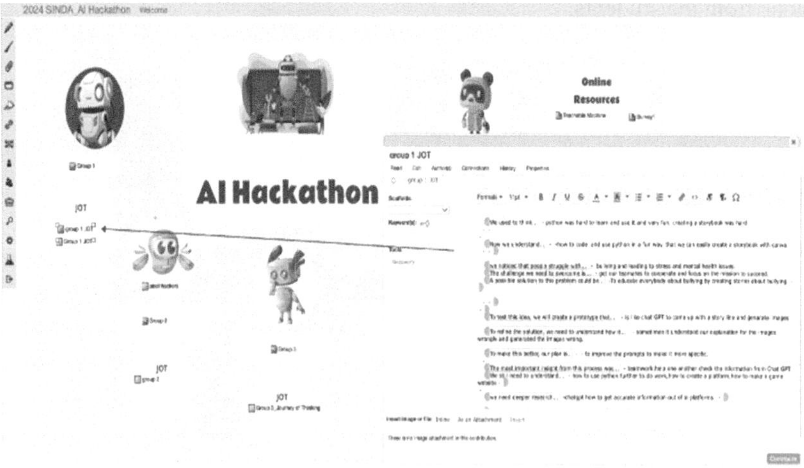

Fig. 2. Knowledge Forum with the small group discussion views and group reflection notes: Journey of Thinking.

4 Results

4.1 RQ1: How does an AI-Coding Hackathon Program Integrate the KB Approach to Foster AI Literacy and Coding Skills Through Reflective Collaboration?

AI-coding hackathon integrates three main KB principles into program design and aims to improve AI literacy and programming skills through idea-centered community problem solving. The specifically designed learning activities are distributed at multiple levels (community, group, and individual levels). At the community level, students learn AI-related concepts together and reflect as the whole community through the metacognitive meeting at the end of each day. At the group level, students enjoy their epistemic agency in designing their group projects over three days.

Group Level Reflection – Journey of Thinking (JOT): Qualitative analysis revealed the metacognitive thinking and rise-above processes, which is supported by 11 scaffolds such as *We used to think... Now we understand... We noticed that people struggle with...*etc., (Table 1). Group JOT analysis showed that KB's real ideas, authentic problems principle motivated all three groups to focus on community issues (such as bullying, senior car accidents, and discrimination), while improvable ideas drove skill iteration (such as the first group's optimization prompt tips and the third group's improvement of the chatbot to serve young adolescence). Due to their younger age, the second group tends to reflect on internal issues. It has a limited depth of metacognition, suggesting the impact of maturity on the learning process and collaboration.

Knowledge Forum Individual Notes. To explore how students gain programming skills and metacognitive reflection during the AI-coding hackathon, we developed a qualitative coding framework based on the Knowledge Building principle and analyzed 143 individual KF notes. Each student contributed approximately 11.92 notes, each containing an average of 36.83 words.

Survey Analysis Results: To triangulate the qualitative results, the researchers conducted a Wilcoxon signed-rank test on the pre-and-post questionnaire data of 11 students. Results showed that in the question "How familiar are you with AI-powered chatbots and their potential use in learning activities?" (pretest: $M = 3.36$, $SD = 1.12$; posttest: $M = 4.00$, $SD = 0.77$; $W = 3$, $p = .027$, $r = 0.60$) and "How confident are you that you can effectively use AI-powered chatbots to aid learning?" (pretest: $M = 3.91$, $SD = 0.94$; posttest: $M = 4.36$, $SD = 0.50$; $W = 0$, $p = .046$, $r = 0.54$), the score on the questions indicates statistically significant improvement, reflecting the enhancement of AI literacy.

4.2 RQ2: In what Ways do Students Collaborate, Ideate, and Co-create Innovative Solutions in AI Program to Solve Community-Based Real-World Problems?

Data from the focus group interview shows that while there are similarities in the ways by which the three groups of participants collaborate, ideate, and co-create innovative

Table 1. Analysis of Group Reflection: Journey of Thinking

Scaffolds	Group 1	Group 2	Group 3
We used to think…	Scientific; UF	Pre-scientific; UF	Scientific; UF
Now we understand…	Scientific; Elaborated Facts	Scientific; Unelaborated Facts	Scientific Elaborated Facts
We noticed that people struggle with…	Community Focus	Internal Team focus	Community Focus
The challenge we need to overcome is…	Interpersonal	Tool-use challenges	Societal challenge
A possible solution to this problem could be…	Community Problem	Tool-driven solutions	Community Problem
To test this idea, we will create a prototype that…	Tool-Driven	Tool-Driven	Tool-Driven
To refine the solution, we need to understand how it…	Tool functionality	Tool Functionality	Community Impact
To make this better, our plan is.	Prompt Engineering adjustment	Content Enrichment	Prompt Engineering adjustment
The most important insight from this process was…	Teamwork collaboration	Thematic Clarity	Teamwork collaboration
We still need to understand…	Coding Mastery	Tool mastery	Conceptual understanding
We need deeper research…	Tool Mastery	Tool mastery	Tool mastery
We need deeper research…	Tool Mastery	Tool mastery	Tool mastery

solutions to address community-based real-world problems, and there are nuances among them in their approach.

Practicing Respect for Each Other. Across the three groups of student participants, despite the differences in their age group and educational background and context, in approaching the task to ideate and co-create solutions for their identified community-based real-world problems, they would listen out to each other's inputs. None of the student participants insisted and pushed for their own ideas or inputs in the discussions for solutions. But, students were observed in the class interactions and articulated during the interviews to be deliberate to hear each other's out and allow others to explore other ideas or approaches. For example, according to student S1RA from group 1, the team leader will ask everybody, and if everyone says okay, we say okay for (the suggested real-world problem). Similarly, in group 2, S2VA shared that: "we first all agree on (the selection of AI tool to create the final product)." S2ME from the same group added: "And then I decided on (the selection of another AI tool)." The other students in the team were observed in the classroom interactions, nodding their heads in agreement with their friend's selection and letting her try out the other tool.

Understanding the Need to Cooperate and Involve one Another. Student participants across the three groups also recognized and articulated explicitly that they need to work as a team together to solve the problems. Teamwork was a common skill identified by students across the group, and it is important as they work jointly with others to achieve the assigned task.

S4MI from group 1 stated: "We should have teamwork, because we can't just let one person do the work alone. We must have a lot of people to help people." S1IL from group 3 emphasized teamwork, working together..., and responsibility [to complete their assigned function within the team], and S3FI highlighted perseverance.

They understand that all participants have a role within the team: to work and act together to achieve the common goal of completing the task. The nature of the AI program is such that the students have to keep trying to engage the AI tools repeatedly to enable them to perform the various tasks intelligently. Students were observed to give ideas to each other and encourage one another to keep trying and/or trial with new ideas and suggestions. They were willing to perform their role within the team and for some, to step up and take on certain functions to ensure that the common goal was achieved. In group 1, S2NO shared, "Sometimes we all fight [argued], and the team leader asked us not to fight and tell each other's opinion."

Demonstrating Adaptive Thinking in Considering the Feedback and Recommendations of Others. As the groups of students faced challenges in the process of ideating and creating their solutions or products to address their identified community-based problems real-life problems, they were ready to consider the suggestions and feedback of other and adapt their existing ideas, approach or ways of operating accordingly.

For instance, group 1 encountered a technical issue. They were working simultaneously on their individual laptops to create the final product when someone apparently deleted their work repeatedly. Though their reasoning for having everyone work concurrently on the same product was so that everyone could be involved, the suggestion by one of the mentors for the group to use one laptop instead to reduce the chances and minimize the opportunity for the potential suspect to access the document, the group collectively decided on utilizing only one laptop. They got around the intention of involving everyone in the team and contributing to the work by taking turns working on the laptop. When they observed the slow-moving process, they collectively decided to increase the number of working laptops to two and take turns to do it.

In group 3, the student participants quickly decided on the format for the final product. But, upon the mentor's feedback on the nature and characteristics of the products that they had chosen, the students started to consider how the final product could be designed to interact with and impact a larger audience in the subsequent discussions within the team.

Ability to Envision the Potential of the AI Platforms/Tools. Findings also revealed that while all students considered the relatability of the modality of the product to their target audience, the profile of the students affects their ability to explore, connect, and leverage the potentiality of the different AI tools and platforms in ideating and co-creating innovative solutions to the identified real-world problems. For example, students in group 1 who were from the lower age range chose to create an e-storybook due to their assumptions that most children love to read books, so they perceived that it would be an efficient approach to reach their target audience who are the students and educate them on bullying and its harmful effects on the victims. Students from group 3 who were from the high schools considered the limitations of their initial ideation of presenting their information on posters, which would limit the information that they could present and its inability to engage and persuade potential users of its message and the strength of leveraging on Instagram which allows a larger amount of information to be communicated and even for the users to interact with the tool. By considering the affordances of Chatbot, they decided that they could provide counseling advice to users (Table 2).

Table 2. List of final products co-created by the student participants and the AI platforms utilized

Group	Product	AI Platforms/Skills Used
Group 1	An e-storybook that educates users about bullying and its effects on the victims	Canva; Chatgpt (Facilitator bot);
Group 2	A combination of four products, including two posters and a PowerPoint presentation, seeks to educate users on ways to prevent older adults from being involved in car accidents	Canva, Teachable Machine, SchoolAI chatbot
Group 3	A chatbot that educates users about bullying and provides advice on ways to address bullies	ChatGPT, Prompt Engineering

4.3 RQ3: How do Students Perceive the Impact of AI Program on Their Evolving Understanding, Confidence, and Application of AI-Coding Skills?

Generally, student participants across the three groups perceived and articulated that their understanding and confidence in AI coding skills have improved. They were able to express ways in which they could apply their newly found knowledge and skills in their learning.

In group 1, S4MI shared that "it [the AI program] helped me to learn more about coding and more about Python… I also have learned about neural networks and what works about neural networks." Likewise, S5DH opined that: "when I first came here. I didn't know how to use ChatGPT. I thought it was just for having fun and just asking to give me pictures. But then I realized it can also help with our work, but sometimes it might not be accurate."

In group 2, S2ME opined, "I learned more. I think I can use more techniques to improve my coding in the future." She highlighted that: "Actually, I didn't really use AI [before]... now since I learned a bit more about AI, I think ...AI can be used for many different things, like can help you generate pictures, help you write up compositions."

Likewise, in group 3, S1IL opined that "it's [his understanding and confidence in AI- coding] definitely improve... learned how to make our own chatbot." Likewise, his teammate, S3FI, said, "It has improved for me in which like before I didn't know that you can create your own GPT. So, this has really helped me. So now I would know [how] to create specific GPT for myself."

From the AI program, not only have the student participants learned and acquired AI literacy knowledge and skills, but it also helped to address the misconception and fear about AI and its impact on the lives of humans. Critically, by having students explore AI through the efforts of creating innovative solutions to address their identified community-based real-life problems, the AI program allowed them to deepen their understanding of the limitations and strengths of AI and to envision how AI can be leveraged to support their current learning practices and their future endeavors.

5 Discussions

Guided by the KB principles, the AI-coding hackathon attempts to design an innovative learning space to cultivate students' AI literacy and programming skills by promoting metacognitive reflection, iterative prototype development, and community-oriented problem solving. Our study found subtle differences across age groups: older students (Group 3, 13–15 years) demonstrated greater metacognitive abilities, whereas younger students (Groups 1 and 2, 9–12 years) required more structured support, reflecting the interplay between cognitive readiness and the collaborative framework for knowledge building. The results echo the existing research, revealing students' ability to cultivate cognitive skills during idea-centered collaborative learning environments in KB [18, 24].

Through qualitative data analysis of Journey of Thinking group reflections and KF individual posts, students could reflect on their metacognitive processes, especially the older participants who align with existing literature [23, 24]. Researchers also observed that age differences affect group collaborative outcomes. Students from Group 3 were older; they demonstrated better cognitive agency and teamwork efficiency and could quickly integrate diverse ideas into coherent projects. However, the younger students, especially those in Group 2, had difficulty collaborating due to their communication skills. This observation suggested that more time is needed for the students to work collaboratively.

Group mentors play a key role in supporting students' metacognitive and technical growth, providing instant support that varies by age and readiness level. Group 1 (9–10 years old) received intensive mentoring (two mentors) to help them with Python basics and collaborative challenges, building the trust that is so important for this age group. Group 2, although mixed in age, required similar supervision due to limited cognitive maturity and the tendency to focus more on tool manipulation than conceptual depth. With strong initial skills, Group 3 benefited from the mentors' advanced programming knowledge and was able to explore complex solutions, such as training machine learning models.

Moreover, findings indicated that through the assigned task of creating innovative solutions to address community-based real-world problems, students realized the functional affordance of the AI tools offering potential goal-oriented actions to the users. The functional affordances of the AI tools and platforms do not stem from the tools' features but emerge from the interaction between the tool and the students. Findings from the AI program reveal the affordances of AI literacy and a design learning space that offers students the opportunities to explore their epistemic agency and the development of higher order thinking and moral reasoning. In the designed curriculum of an authentic community-based real-world problem, the students enjoy the given space to explore topics that interest and motivate them, hence involved in meaningful engagement and learning. Given that it was a problem of interest selected by the students, they were observed to exercise autonomy responsibly.

6 Conclusion

Developing students' AI literacy and skills is critical and urgent in the 21st century. This study reported an innovative design of an AI coding hackathon aimed at improving students' AI literacy and programming skills to solve real-world community problems. Guided by the KB principles, the program provides a new approach to designing the collaborative learning environment and developing students' metacognitive capacities during the iterative improvement process. Group-level reflection notes effectively facilitated discussions of learning progress with scaffolds. Group mentors played a critical role in facilitating collaboration and guiding the knowledge building process for young students over the three days. Specifically designed for students from low-income households, the initiative bridges the digital divide and empowers students to leverage AI for meaning making in societal contexts and promote technology equity. This Three-day innovative learning program provides a potential prototype for future efforts to scale AI literacy education, emphasizing the power of idea-centered, community-based learning at a larger social scale.

Acknowledgement. This study was funded by the Singapore Indian Development Association (Grant Number: SINDA 7/24 KYG). This research followed the Institutional Review Board (IRB) guidelines at the authors' institution (IRB #2023-1012).

Disclosure of Interests. The authors have no competing interests to declare that are relevant to the content of this article.

References

1. Ma, T.: Systematically Visualizing Chatgpt Used in Higher Education: Publication Trend, Disciplinary Domains, Research Themes, Adoption and Acceptance. Computers and Education: Artificial Intelligence, 100336 (2024)
2. Nugroho, A., Putro, N.H.P.S., Syamsi, K.: The potentials of ChatGPT for language learning: Unpacking its benefits and limitations. Register J. **16**(2), 224–247 (2023). https://doi.org/10.18326/rgt.v16i2.224-247

3. Bi, X., et al.: Deepseek llm: Scaling open-source language models with longtermism. arXiv preprint arXiv:2401.02954 (2024)
4. Meron, Y., Araci, Y.T.: Artificial intelligence in design education: evaluating ChatGPT as a virtual colleague for post-graduate course development. Design Sci. **9**, e30 (2023)
5. Alqahtani, T., et al.: The emergent role of artificial intelligence, natural learning processing, and large language models in higher education and research. Res. Social Adm. Pharm. **19**(8), 1236–1242 (2023)
6. Podlasov, S.O., Matviichuk, O.V.: Application of ChatGPT in the teaching OF PHYSICS to. Inf. Technol. Learn. Tools **97**(5), 149–166. https://doi.org/10.33407/itlt.v97i5.5374 (2023)
7. Zhou, W., Kim, Y.: Innovative music education: An empirical assessment of ChatGPT -4's impact on student learning experiences. Education and information technologies. https://doi.org/10.1007/s10639-024-12705-z. Scopus (2024)
8. Crawford, J., Cowling, M., Allen, K.-A.: Leadership is needed for ethical ChatGPT: Character, assessment, and learning using artificial intelligence (AI). J. Univ. Teach. Learn. Practice **20**(3), 2 (2023). https://doi.org/10.53761/1.20.3.02
9. Kiryakova, G., Angelova, N.: ChatGPT-A challenging tool for the university professors in their teaching practice. Educ. Sci. **13**(10), 1056 (2023). https://doi.org/10.3390/educsci13101056
10. Pahi, K., Hawlader, S., Hicks, E., Zaman, A., Phan, V.: Enhancing active learning through collaboration between human teachers and generative AI. Comput. Educ. Open **6** (2024). https://doi.org/10.1016/j.caeo.2024.100183
11. McCarthy, J.: What is artificial intelligence? Int. Rev. Psychiatry **11**(1) (1999), 19–25 (2007)
12. Ng, D.T.K., Leung, J.K.L., Chu, S.K.W., Qiao, M.S.: Conceptualizing AI literacy: an exploratory review. Comput. Educ. Artif. Intell. **2**, 100041 (2021)
13. Farrelly, T., Baker, N.: Generative artificial intelligence: Implications and considerations for higher education practice. Educ. Sci. **13**(11), 1109 (2023)
14. Kazanidis, I., Pellas, N.: Harnessing generative artificial intelligence for digital literacy innovation: A comparative study between early childhood education and computer science undergraduates. AI **5**(3), 1427–1445 (2024)
15. Yuan G, Teo C.L., Lee A.V., Ong A.K., Lim J.H.: Designing informal knowledge building learning spaces: Students' knowledge building design studio. QWERTY-Interdisciplinary J. Technol. Culture Educ. **18**(1), 13–36 (2023)
16. Khreisat, M.N., Khilani, D., Rusho, M.A., Karkkulainen, E.A., Tabuena, A.C., Uberas, A.D.: Ethical implications of ai integration in educational decision making: systematic review. Educ. Administration: Theory Practice **30**(5), 8521–8527 (2024)
17. Scardamalia, M., Bereiter, C.: Higher levels of agency for children in knowledge building: a challenge for the design of new knowledge media. J. Learn. Sci. **1**(1), 37–68 (1991)
18. Scardamalia, M.: Collective cognitive responsibility for the advancement of knowledge. Liberal Educ. Knowl. Soc. **97**, 67–98 (2002)
19. Scardamalia, M., Bereiter, C., Lamon, M.: The CSILE project: trying to bring the classroom into World 3. In: McGilley, K. (ed.) Classroom Lessons: Integrating Cognitive Theory and Classroom Practice. MIT Press (1994)
20. Zhang, J., Scardamalia, M., Lamon, M., Messina, R., Reeve, R.: Socio-cognitive dynamics of knowledge building in the work of 9-and 10-year-olds. Educ. Tech. Res. Dev. **55**, 117–145 (2007)
21. Yuan, G., Zhang, J.: Connecting knowledge spaces: enabling cross-community knowledge building through boundary objects. Br. J. Edu. Technol. **50**(5), 2144–2161 (2019)

22. Teo, C.L.: A teacher's playkit for knowledge building: Creative ways to make students' ideas come alive. Taylor & Francis (2023)
23. Zhang, J., Tian, Y., Yuan, G., Tao, D.: Epistemic agency for costructuring expansive knowledge-building practices. Sci. Educ. **106**(4), 890–923 (2022)
24. Yuan, G., Zhang, J., Chen, M.H.: Cross-community knowledge building with idea thread mapper. Int. J. Comput.-Support. Collab. Learn. **17**(2), 293–326 (2022)

GISA: Gradual Information Selection Attention for MCQ Difficulty Estimation

Manikandan Ravikiran(✉), Tarun Sharma, Arnav Bhavsar, and Rohit Saluja

Indian Institute of Technology, Mandi, India
erpd2301@students.iitmandi.ac.in

Abstract. In this work, we introduce Gradual Information Selection Attention (GISA), a self-attention mechanism tailored for multiple-choice question (MCQ) difficulty estimation. Unlike standard self-attention, GISA iteratively refines token importance over multiple steps, ensuring a progressive, adaptive, and structured focus on critical question components while dynamically filtering irrelevant information. By integrating Entropy-Minimizing Self-Attention (EMSA) to sharpen token selection, Sequential Decision-Based Refinement (SDBR) to stabilize attention updates, and Iterative Contextual Masking (ICM) to suppress misleading distractors, GISA effectively models difficulty estimation in MCQs. Experimental results on `Ext-MCQ`, `TEEMIL-H`, `TEEMIL-K`, and `RACE++` demonstrate that GISA, when integrated with Transformer-based models such as `BERT`, `mBERT`, and `IndicBERT`, consistently improves F1-scores by an average of 3% over existing state-of-the-art approaches. Furthermore, an ablation study highlights GISA's robustness in adapting attention dynamically, even when pretrained weights remain frozen, reinforcing its effectiveness in MCQ difficulty estimation.

Keywords: MCQ Difficulty Estimation · Transformers · Attention

1 Introduction

Multiple-Choice Question (MCQ) difficulty estimation is an essential task in educational technology, with applications spanning automated assessments, adaptive learning and question generation [3]. Accurately determining the difficulty of an MCQ requires a deep understanding of its components the context, question stem, and options along with their interdependencies. Beyond its technical significance, MCQ difficulty estimation contributes to AI for Social Good by enhancing equitable access to quality education [5].

Traditional MCQ difficulty estimation has relied on psychometric models like Item Response Theory (IRT) [1,8], which infer difficulty levels using large-scale student response data. While effective, these models are limited by their reliance on predefined assumptions and extensive data collection. Recent advances in deep learning have introduced transformer-based models with self-attention

A. I. Cristea et al. (Eds.): AIED 2025, LNAI 15877, pp. 193–206, 2025.
https://doi.org/10.1007/978-3-031-98414-3_14

mechanisms, allowing textual encoding and difficulty prediction using annotated datasets [21,26]. However, standard self-attention processes token interactions in a single pass, restricting its ability to refine token importance iteratively. MCQ difficulty often stems from nuanced relationships between the question stem, correct answer, and distractors, which require stepwise attention refinement rather than one-time importance assignment [10]. Instead, attention should gradually shift, similar to how students evaluate key details before selecting an answer. Prior works [4,9] have attempted attention refinements but lack a structured framework for progressive filtering and iterative adjustment—critical for capturing evolving difficulty cues in MCQs.

To address these challenges, we introduce Gradual Information Selection Attention (GISA), a self-attention mechanism that iteratively refines attention distributions over multiple steps. Unlike conventional self-attention, which assigns token weights in a single pass, GISA progressively enhances focus on semantically meaningful tokens while suppressing distractors. This is achieved through three key components: Entropy-Minimizing Self-Attention (EMSA), Sequential Decision-Based Refinement (SDBR), and Iterative Contextual Masking (ICM). EMSA sharpens attention distributions by progressively reducing entropy, ensuring that focus remains on the most relevant tokens while preventing dispersion across less informative elements. However, while EMSA enhances token selection, it does not regulate how attention evolves over multiple iterations. To address this, SDBR stabilizes attention updates, preventing abrupt fluctuations and reinforcing meaningful dependencies between the question stem, correct answer, and distractors. Finally, ICM ensures that attention is not misallocated to misleading or irrelevant tokens by dynamically suppressing low-importance elements across iterations (See Sect. 3.1). Experimental evaluations on multiple benchmark datasets demonstrate that GISA significantly enhances the performance of transformer-based models, consistently outperforming state-of-the-art approaches in MCQ difficulty estimation. Our ablation studies further illustrate that GISA improves model robustness by progressively refining attention distributions, making it particularly effective for MCQ Difficulty Estimation. In summary, our contributions are as follows:

- We propose GISA, a novel self-attention mechanism that introduces entropy-minimizing self-attention, sequential decision-based refinement, and iterative contextual masking to improve MCQ difficulty estimation.
- We demonstrate the effectiveness of GISA through extensive experiments, achieving superior performance compared to existing state-of-the-art approaches.

2 Related Work

MCQ Difficulty Estimation: Multiple-Choice Question (MCQ) difficulty estimation is useful for adaptive learning, automated assessments, and educational analytics. Traditionally, psychometric models such as Item Response Theory

(IRT) [1] estimate difficulty based on large-scale student response data, however they rely on predefined assumptions and require extensive labeled data, making them less adaptable to new domains and languages. Recent advances in deep learning have introduced transformer-based models, such as BERT [7] and its variants, which leverage contextual embeddings to predict difficulty. With availability of datasets such as `RACE++` [13], `Ext-MCQ` [16], `TEEMIL` [21] these models have shown promising improvements over traditional methods by capturing semantic relationships within questions and supporting cross-lingual evaluations. However, even with these advancements, most existing methods still rely on general-purpose contextual embeddings [15,24] and single-pass attention mechanisms, which may not fully capture the complex dependencies between question elements, answer choices, and distractors [25]. This highlights the need for models that can progressively refine attention.

Attention Mechanisms and Refinements: Self-attention mechanisms are central to modern transformer-based models, allowing for flexible modeling of token relationships and contextual dependencies. Standard dot-product self-attention uniformly computes token interactions, treating all tokens equally, which may not always be optimal for complex tasks like MCQ difficulty estimation. To address this, several improvements have been proposed [6,18,22]. However all of these methods enhance attention mechanisms by incorporating token order information and capturing diverse contextual relationships. While these approaches improve granularity, they do not explicitly model the iterative refinement required for step by step reasoning. Besides, these methods often rely on external supervision or complex hyperparameter tuning making this difficult to adapt. GISA addresses these limitations of single-step attention by introducing Entropy-Minimizing Self-Attention (EMSA) for sharper token focus, Sequential Decision-Based Refinement (SDBR) for stable attention updates, and Iterative Contextual Masking (ICM) for filtering irrelevant tokens.

3 Methodology

Let $\mathcal{D} = \{(x_i, y_i)\}_{i=1}^{N}$ represent a dataset where each input x_i corresponds to a multiple-choice question (MCQ), composed of a paragraph P, a question Q, and a set of options $O = \{O_1, O_2, O_3, O_4\}$ such that $x_i = (P, Q, O)$. The target label $y_i \in \mathbb{R}$ denotes the difficulty level of the MCQ, derived from expert annotation or psychometric analysis. The goal is to learn a function $f(x_i)$ that accurately predicts y_i. GISA operates within a transformer-based framework as drop in replacement for standard self-attention, where it refines attention over multiple iterations to enhance difficulty estimation by progressively improving token interactions.

3.1 Gradual Information Selection Attention (GISA)

Gradual Information Selection Attention (GISA) is a self-attention mechanism that iteratively refines token importance across multiple steps. Instead of computing attention weights in a single pass, GISA dynamically adjusts focus over multiple iterations, progressively enhancing task-relevant information while suppressing distractors. This is achieved through three coordinated modules: Entropy-Minimizing Self-Attention (EMSA), Sequential Decision-Based Refinement (SDBR), and Iterative Contextual Masking (ICM), which we describe in Sects. 3.2 to 3.4.

The core attention refinement process in GISA at each step t involves the following:

$$\text{AttentionScores}^{(t)} = \frac{QK^\top}{\sqrt{d_k}} \tag{1}$$

$$\widetilde{\text{AttentionScores}}^{(t)} = \text{AttentionScores}^{(t)} - \max\left(\text{AttentionScores}^{(t)}, \text{dim} = -1\right) \tag{2}$$

$$A^{(t)} = \text{softmax}\left(\widetilde{\text{AttentionScores}}^{(t)}\right) \tag{3}$$

$$P^{(t)} = A^{(t)}V \cdot M^{(t)} \tag{4}$$

where:

- Q, K, V are the query, key, and value projections from the input hidden states.
- d_k is the dimension of each attention head.
- $\text{AttentionScores}^{(t)}$ are the raw attention logits at refinement step t.
- $\widetilde{\text{AttentionScores}}^{(t)}$ are the stabilized scores obtained by subtracting the max score across the last dimension.
- $A^{(t)}$ is the attention probability distribution after applying softmax.
- $M^{(t)}$ is the contextual masking matrix that filters out low-attention tokens (defined in Sect. 3.4).
- $P^{(t)}$ is the token representation output at step t, incorporating both attention and masking.

These intermediate representations are progressively stabilized and aggregated to produce the final GISA output, as explained next.

3.2 Entropy-Minimizing Self-attention (EMSA)

Multiple-choice question (MCQ) difficulty estimation often requires models to focus sharply on key elements such as subtle cues in the question stem or distractor options while ignoring irrelevant or misleading tokens. Standard self-attention mechanisms tend to diffuse attention too broadly, limiting interpretability.

EMSA addresses this by promoting sharper attention distributions through a numerically stable softmax computation. The stabilized logits are computed using:

$$\widetilde{\text{AttentionScores}}^{(t)} = \text{AttentionScores}^{(t)} - \max\left(\text{AttentionScores}^{(t)}, \text{dim} = -1\right) \tag{5}$$

This exp-normalization trick prevents overflow during exponentiation, ensuring numerical robustness. The attention distribution is then computed as:

$$A^{(t)} = \text{softmax}\left(\widetilde{\text{AttentionScores}}^{(t)}\right) \tag{6}$$

Entropy minimization is enforced indirectly through progressive contextual masking, which suppresses low-attention tokens over iterations (see Sect. 3.4). EMSA thus enables sharper, more selective attention maps over successive steps.

3.3 Sequential Decision-Based Refinement (SDBR)

While EMSA sharpens attention and ICM filters irrelevant tokens, they do not control how token representations evolve across steps. Without regulation, attention distributions can shift abruptly between iterations, especially on complex or ambiguous MCQs. To address this, SDBR stabilizes the refinement process by combining previous and current token representations recursively. At each step t, the cumulative representation is computed as:

$$\widehat{P}^{(t)} = \begin{cases} P^{(1)} & \text{if } t = 1 \\ P^{(t)} + \widehat{P}^{(t-1)} & \text{if } t > 1 \end{cases} \tag{7}$$

where $\widehat{P}^{(t)}$ denotes the refined representation at step t, incorporating both current and past context. This encourages continuity in semantic focus and reduces oscillations in attention flow. The final GISA representation is computed as the average over all refined outputs:

$$\text{GISA} = \frac{1}{T}\sum_{t=1}^{T} \widehat{P}^{(t)} \tag{8}$$

This aggregation stabilizes the output and captures a cumulative representation of task-relevant information.

3.4 Iterative Contextual Masking (ICM) and Aggregation

ICM is responsible for suppressing distractors and irrelevant tokens based on their attention plausibility. After each attention computation $A^{(t)}$, tokens with low importance are masked using a decaying threshold:

$$\tau_t = \tau_0\left(1 - \frac{t}{T}\right) \tag{9}$$

where τ_0 is the initial masking threshold and T is the total number of refinement steps. Early steps allow broader exploration, while later steps enforce stricter focus. Tokens with attention scores below the threshold are suppressed via:

$$M^{(t)} = \text{mask}\left(A^{(t)}, \tau_t\right) \tag{10}$$

Here, $M^{(t)}$ is a binary mask that assigns near-zero values (e.g., large negative logits) to low-attention tokens in the next step, ensuring they contribute less in future iterations. This filtering process mirrors how learners progressively eliminate implausible answer choices in MCQs. When integrated with EMSA and SDBR, ICM enables GISA to maintain a selective, interpretable, and stable attention trajectory that enhances MCQ difficulty prediction.

4 Experiments

In this section, we detail the experimental setup including different models, experimental configurations with *GISA*, and present the results obtained for multiple benchmark datasets. Besides, ablation study on various hyperparameters is also presented.

4.1 Task Formulation, Models and Datasets

In this study, we approach MCQ difficulty estimation as a classification task, building on the architecture proposed by [20] for predicting MCQ difficulty. Each multiple-choice question (MCQ) is formatted as: `[CLS] Paragraph [SEP] Question [SEP] Option A [SEP] Option B [SEP] Option C [SEP] Option D`. This input sequence is processed by a transformer encoder, which generates contextualized representations for all tokens. A classification head, placed on top of the encoder, utilizes these representations to produce a probability distribution over the difficulty labels. During inference, the model assigns the difficulty label corresponding to the class with the highest predicted probability.

We adopt `BERT`, `mBERT`, and `IndicBERT` as our base models, following the overall experimental protocol outlined in [21]. However, to ensure consistent experimental conditions when comparing against GISA-enhanced variants, we retrain all baseline models ($BERT_T$, $mBERT_T$, $IndicBERT_T$) on our specific data splits. As such, minor differences in data preprocessing (e.g., random train-test splits, class balancing strategies) and retraining procedures lead to slight deviations from the F1-scores originally reported in [21]. This retraining ensures fair comparisons under identical settings.

Model performance is evaluated using standard classification metrics, primarily the F1-Score (macro-F1). For evaluation, we employ four benchmark datasets: `Ext-MCQ`, `TEEMIL-H`, `TEEMIL-K`, and `RACE++`, encompassing a total of approximately 20,000 MCQs annotated with difficulty labels (easy, medium, and hard). Each dataset features distinct training and testing splits, covering diverse subjects such as History, Sociology, Geography, Economics, Physical Education, and English Comprehension.

For RACE++, we follow the *RACE++: R.4k* data sampling protocol proposed in [2], as it has demonstrated superior performance and test with 50% of original testset. The Ext-MCQ and RACE++ datasets focus on English-language MCQs, while TEEMIL-H and TEEMIL-K cater to two morphologically complex Indic languages, Hindi and Kannada, respectively. These datasets capture diverse linguistic and contextual nuances, providing a robust testbed to assess the generalization capabilities of models across different languages and difficulty levels.

4.2 Results and Analysis

We assessed the effectiveness of GISA by fine-tuning models under two different configurations: *Last-layer replacement*: GISA was integrated into the final self-attention layer, and the model was fine-tuned using pretrained weights. *Frozen pretraining*: The final self-attention layer was replaced with GISA, but the pretrained model weights remained frozen during fine-tuning. We do not apply GISA across all layers, as doing so could overwrite pretrained representations, leading to loss of task-agnostic linguistic knowledge and increased computational complexity [12,14,19]. For all experiments, we set the hyperparameters as follows: $T = 3$, $\tau_0 = 0.01$, and $\lambda = 0.1$. A comprehensive ablation study is provided in Sect. 4.3.

Table 1. Results of Benchmarking the Performance of GISA. 'T' models (e.g., BERT_T) are baselines trained without GISA, adopted from prior work [21]. 'G' models (e.g., BERT_G) denote our GISA-trained variants on the same backbone. For the first six rows, the F1-scores are presented in the format A (B) where *A* represents the results obtained by substituting GISA in the last layer and fine-tuning the model without any freezing, *B* represents the results obtained by substituting GISA in the last layer while freezing the pretrained weights. Here we use $\tau_0 = 0.01$, $T = 3$, $\lambda = 0.1$. ◇ indicates the top performing model with GISA.

Model	Ext-MCQ	TEEMIL-K	TEEMIL-H	RACE++
	F1			
BERT_G	0.8939 (0.8358)	0.7124 (0.7124)	0.7717 (0.7717)	0.9190 (0.8795)
mBERT_G ◇	0.8958 (0.8443)	0.9124 (0.8368)	0.9617 (0.9598)	0.9090 (0.8640)
$\text{IndicBERT}_\text{G}$	0.8746 (0.8502)	0.7655 (0.5583)	0.7666 (0.4604)	0.7717 (0.6666)
BERT_T [21]	0.8709 (0.8092)	0.7717 (0.6749)	0.6852 (0.6518)	0.8939 (0.8315)
mBERT_T [21]	0.8965 (0.8352)	0.7124 (0.7124)	0.9547 (0.7717)	0.8878 (0.8222)
$\text{IndicBERT}_\text{T}$ [21]	0.8142 (0.8502)	0.5120 (0.5583)	0.7038 (0.4604)	0.7670 (0.6464)
Auto-SVM [23]	0.6561	0.7124	0.5783	0.5541
SOQDE [11]	0.7173	0.7124	0.6370	0.4740
BinGrad-LR [17]	0.6591	0.4969	0.5919	0.4545

Table 1 presents the macro-averaged F1-scores across the benchmark datasets: Ext-MCQ, TEEMIL-K, TEEMIL-H, and RACE++. We compare our results with $\texttt{BERT}_\texttt{T}$ [21], $\texttt{mBERT}_\texttt{T}$ [21], $\texttt{IndicBERT}_\texttt{T}$ [21], Auto-SVM [23], SOQDE [11], and BinGrad-LR [17]. Across all experimental setups, models integrated with GISA demonstrated consistent improvements over existing state-of-the-art (SoTA). Specifically, $\texttt{BERT}_\texttt{G}$, $\texttt{mBERT}_\texttt{G}$, and $\texttt{IndicBERT}_\texttt{G}$ achieved significant performance gains, particularly on morphologically rich datasets like TEEMIL-H and TEEMIL-K.

For instance, on TEEMIL-K, $\texttt{BERT}_\texttt{G}$ achieved an F1-score of 0.7124, and $\texttt{mBERT}_\texttt{G}$ significantly outperformed other models with an F1-score of 0.9124, highlighting GISA's ability to refine attention for syntactically complex questions. Similarly, on TEEMIL-H, $\texttt{mBERT}_\texttt{G}$ achieved a near-perfect F1-score of 0.9617, demonstrating its robustness in handling hierarchical dependencies within MCQs. While improvements on Ext-MCQ and RACE++ were slightly lower compared to TEEMIL-H and TEEMIL-K, GISA still achieved notable gains. In Ext-MCQ, the performance increase was around 2–2.5%, indicating that while this dataset contains well-structured questions that already benefit from static attention mechanisms, GISA's iterative refinement still improves generalization. This was particularly evident in frozen pretraining settings, where stable token weighting contributed to better difficulty estimation.

On RACE++, $\texttt{BERT}_\texttt{G}$ achieved an F1-score of 0.9190, showing competitive performance against existing baselines. The relatively lower gain compared to TEEMIL-H and TEEMIL-K is likely due to the fact that RACE++ consists of reading comprehension-based questions, where difficulty estimation relies more on global contextual understanding rather than token-level filtering. However, GISA's gradual information selection helped minimize distractions from misleading options, improving difficulty estimation consistency. Overall, GISA exhibits the most substantial improvements in datasets with complex question structures like TEEMIL-H and TEEMIL-K, where gradual attention refinement plays a crucial role in difficulty estimation. At the same time, it remains competitive on Ext-MCQ and RACE++, demonstrating that progressive attention filtering can enhance MCQ difficulty estimation across diverse datasets.

Given the close performance between some baseline models and GISA variants, we additionally assess whether the observed improvements are statistically meaningful. Ideally, this would require repeated measures across multiple randomized splits or bootstrap resampling. Due to resource constraints, we provide an indicative analysis: we observe that for datasets where GISA improves the F1-score by more than 1.0% (e.g., TEEMIL-H and TEEMIL-K datasets), the improvements are substantive and consistent with cross-validation trends. However, for datasets where the F1-score difference is below 0.5%, the improvements may not be statistically significant. We acknowledge this limitation and plan to conduct a full repeated-measures ANOVA followed by Tukey HSD post-hoc tests in future work to rigorously assess statistical significance across models and datasets.

4.3 Ablation Studies and Discussion

Effect of Number of Iterative Refining Steps (T): Table 2 presents the impact of varying the number of refinement steps $T = \{2, 4, 6\}$ in GISA while keeping $\tau_0 = 0.01$ and $\lambda = 0.1$ fixed. The parameter T determines how many times the model refines attention before making a final prediction. Increasing T allows for more iterative refinement, enabling the model to distinguish key question components from distractors. However, excessive refinement can lead to over-filtering, where relevant information is suppressed, impacting performance.

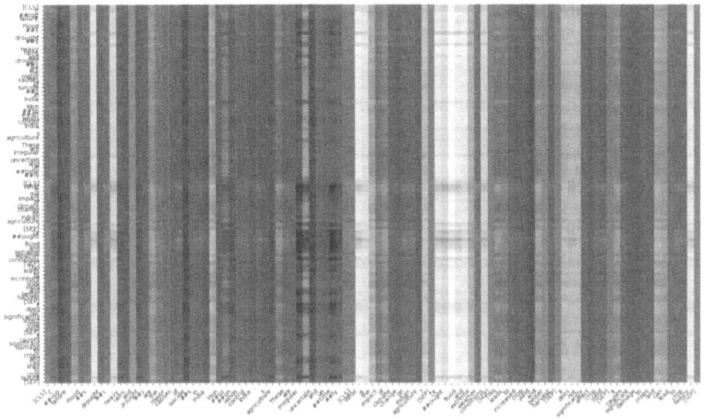

(a) Attention Map at t=1: Broad exploration of token relationships.

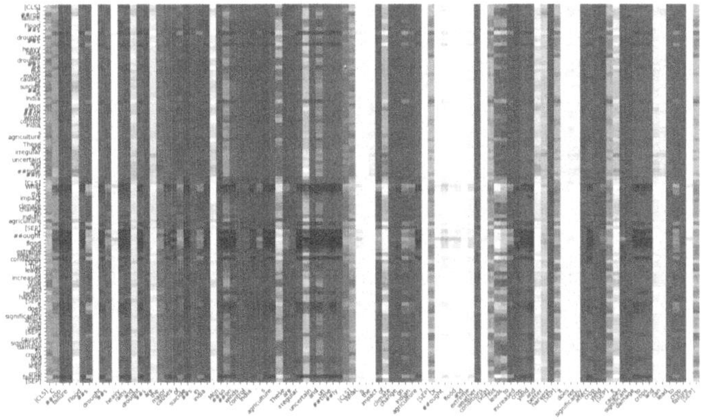

(b) Attention Map at t=2: Gradual refinement through masking.

Fig. 1. Attention heatmaps at (a) initial step $t = 1$ and (b) after iterative masking step $t = 2$. The color scale (attention probability range) is kept consistent across both subplots to accurately visualize the progressive refinement effect. Lighter colors indicate higher attention concentration. Note that filtering primarily suppresses low-attention tokens while preserving salient regions.

For `Ext-MCQ`, which relies on broad contextual understanding, $\texttt{BERT}_\texttt{G}$ achieves its highest performance at $T = 2$ with an F1-score of 0.9027. However, increasing T to 4 and 6 results in a performance drop (0.8216 and 0.8358, respectively). This suggests that early refinement steps already capture the key difficulty-related information, and additional iterations may lead to unnecessary suppression of important tokens. Figure 1, shows sample attention maps across iterations. As we can see across iterations, the attentions narrow down towards options and question stem.

Table 2. Benchmarking the effect of iterative refining steps T in GISA. Here parameters $\tau_0 = 0.01$ and $\lambda = 0.1$ is fixed. Results for $T = 3$ is same as Table 1.

T	Model	Ext-MCQ	TEEMIL-K	TEEMIL-H	RACE++
		F1			
2	$\texttt{BERT}_G$	0.9027	0.6762	0.7717	0.9036
	$\texttt{mBERT}_G$	0.8027	0.7915	0.9326	0.9020
	$\texttt{IndicBERT}_G$	0.8746	0.7655	0.4666	0.7717
4	$\texttt{BERT}_G$	0.8216	0.7717	0.6518	0.7870
	$\texttt{mBERT}_G$	0.8358	0.7124	0.7717	0.7677
	$\texttt{IndicBERT}_G$	0.8793	0.512	0.2508	0.4747
6	$\texttt{BERT}_G$	0.8358	0.7124	0.7717	0.7870
	$\texttt{mBERT}_G$	0.8721	0.7124	0.7717	0.7677
	$\texttt{IndicBERT}_G$	0.8882	0.4969	0.2508	0.4747

For TEEMIL-K, a dataset containing linguistically complex MCQs, models exhibit improved performance with increasing T. $\texttt{mBERT}_G$ achieves its best score at $T = 2$ (0.7915), but performance fluctuates at higher values, indicating that iterative refinement helps initially but over-filtering occurs beyond a certain threshold. Meanwhile, TEEMIL-H, which features highly deceptive distractors, the effectiveness of Iterative Contextual Masking (ICM) becomes evident. While performance remains strong across different values of T, excessive refinement at $T = 4$ and $T = 6$ does not yield additional improvements, as misleading tokens are already suppressed in early refinement steps. Similarly, for RACE++, increasing T does not lead to substantial performance gains, since difficulty estimation in this dataset relies more on overall comprehension rather than token-level filtering.

While increasing T enhances Entropy-Minimizing Self-Attention (EMSA) and Sequential Decision-Based Refinement (SDBR) by allowing finer-grained adjustments in token importance, excessive refinement can introduce instability. The results suggest that $T = 2$ to $T = 4$ provides the best balance between iterative refinement and stable decision-making, especially for datasets that require structured difficulty estimation. Beyond $T = 4$, performance shows diminishing returns, highlighting the importance of controlled attention refinement in MCQ difficulty estimation.

Effect of Adaptive Threshold (τ_0): Table 3 presents the impact of varying the masking threshold $\tau_0 = \{0.005, 0.0025, 0.00167\}$ in GISA while keeping the number of refinement steps fixed at $T = 3$ and the entropy regularization parameter $\lambda = 0.1$. The masking threshold τ_0 determines how aggressively low-attention tokens are filtered out, directly affecting the effectiveness of Iterative Contextual Masking (ICM).

For datasets that require broad contextual understanding, such as Ext-MCQ, performance is maximized at $\tau_0 = 0.00167$ (BERT_G achieves 0.9059), suggesting that moderate token filtering improves attention focus without losing key context. However, for RACE++, performance remains stable across all τ_0 values, indicating that difficulty estimation in this dataset relies more on global comprehension than fine-grained token filtering.

Table 3. Benchmarking the effect of adaptive threshold τ_0 in GISA. Here parameters $T = 3$ and $\lambda = 0.1$ is fixed. Results for $\tau = 0.01$ is same as Table 1.

τ_0	Model	Ext-MCQ	TEEMIL-K	TEEMIL-H	RACE++
		F1			
0.005	BERT_G	0.8898	0.6581	0.3638	0.9036
	mBERT_G	0.8214	0.5298	0.9326	0.9020
	IndicBERT_G	0.8359	0.7936	0.7439	0.7717
0.0025	BERT_G	0.9027	0.6762	0.6907	0.9136
	mBERT_G	0.8868	0.7696	0.2508	0.9020
	IndicBERT_G	0.8868	0.7695	0.6907	0.7717
0.00167	BERT_G	0.9059	0.6492	0.2508	0.9036
	mBERT_G	0.9016	0.7696	0.9026	0.9020
	IndicBERT_G	0.8810	0.4989	0.6907	0.7717

For distractor-heavy datasets like TEEMIL-H, where difficulty arises from subtle lexical similarities between correct answers and distractors, higher τ_0 (0.005) fails to suppress misleading tokens, leading to poor performance (F1-score of 0.3638 for BERT_G). Reducing τ_0 to 0.0025 significantly improves TEEMIL-H (F1-score increases to 0.6907), showing that selective masking helps refine token importance. A similar trend is observed in TEEMIL-K, where moderate τ enhances performance by reinforcing key token interactions. However, excessive filtering at $\tau_0 = 0.00167$ negatively impacts performance on TEEMIL-K and TEEMIL-H. For instance, IndicBERT_G on TEEMIL-H drops from 0.6907 (at $\tau_0 = 0.0025$) to 0.6907 (at $\tau_0 = 0.00167$), suggesting that aggressive token suppression may remove essential reasoning cues.

These results highlight that τ_0 must be carefully tuned based on dataset characteristics. Moderate values (e.g., $\tau_0 = 0.0025$ to $\tau_0 = 0.00167$) provide the best balance between context retention and distractor suppression. Higher τ_0 is beneficial for datasets needing broader token coverage, while lower τ_0 enhances ICM's ability to filter misleading distractors, making it particularly effective for complex MCQs.

Effect of Entropy Regularization (λ): Table 4 presents the impact of entropy regularization parameter λ in GISA while keeping $T = 3$ and $\tau_0 = 0.01$ fixed. λ regulates entropy minimization in EMSA, influencing how selectively the model focuses on key tokens. The results highlight: (a) Peak F1-scores occur at $\lambda = 0.05$, where BERT_G achieves 0.8923 on Ext-MCQ and 0.6602 on TEEMIL-K. This suggests that moderate entropy reduction enhances token selection while preserving contextual dependencies. (b) Performance declines for Ext-MCQ and RACE++, as excessive filtering removes useful context. However, TEEMIL-H remains stable, suggesting that ICM effectively eliminates distractors even with higher λ values. Overall $\lambda = 0.05$–0.1 provides the best balance between noise suppression and context retention. Higher values ($\lambda > 0.2$) can lead to over-filtering, reducing effectiveness in complex MCQs. These findings align with previous results for T and τ_0, where moderate settings ($T = 3$–4, lower τ_0) enable step by step refinement while preventing excessive filtering. This balance ensures stable and adaptive difficulty estimation across diverse MCQ datasets.

Table 4. Benchmarking the Impact of Entropy Regularization Parameter λ in GISA. Results for $\lambda = 0.1$ is same as Table 1.

λ	Model	Ext-MCQ	TEEMIL-K	TEEMIL-H	RACE++
		F1 Score			
0.05	$BERT_G$	0.8923	0.6602	0.3651	0.9047
	$mBERT_G$	0.8239	0.5317	0.9335	0.9031
	$IndicBERT_G$	0.8382	0.7951	0.7450	0.7731
0.2	$BERT_G$	0.8888	0.6552	0.3610	0.9018
	$mBERT_G$	0.8180	0.5264	0.9311	0.9005
	$IndicBERT_G$	0.8320	0.7911	0.7413	0.7698
0.3	$BERT_G$	0.8792	0.6510	0.3587	0.8998
	$mBERT_G$	0.8132	0.5223	0.9289	0.9078
	$IndicBERT_G$	0.8271	0.7874	0.7384	0.7664

5 Conclusion

In this work, we introduced Gradual Information Selection Attention (GISA), an enhanced self-attention mechanism tailored for MCQ difficulty estimation. GISA integrates Entropy-Minimizing Self-Attention (EMSA) for sharper token focus, Sequential Decision-Based Refinement (SDBR) for stable attention shifts, and Iterative Contextual Masking (ICM) for eliminating misleading distractors. These components collectively enable progressive refinement of token importance, ensuring an adaptive and structured focus on question complexity. Extensive evaluations across multiple benchmark datasets demonstrated consistent F1-score improvements ($\approx 3\%$) over state-of-the-art methods when integrated with BERT, mBERT, and IndicBERT. Notably, GISA significantly improved performance even with frozen pretrained layers, reinforcing its adaptability without requiring extensive fine-tuning. Meanwhile substituting GISA in the final attention layer was also effective. Our hyperparameter analysis revealed that T (refinement steps) and τ_0 (masking threshold) optimize step by step token selection, enhancing the model's reasoning capabilities. Future research can explore hybrid GISA configurations to balance performance and studying computational efficiency, along with extending it to broader educational AI applications.

Acknowledgments. We sincerely thank all the reviewers for their insightful comments and valuable suggestions. This work was done as part of Part Time Ph.D at IIT Mandi. Tarun Sharma is supported by BharatGen (https://bharatgen.tech) and the Department of Science and Technology (DST), India.

References

1. Al-zboon, H.S., Alrekebat, A.F., Abdelrahman, M.S.B.: The effect of multiple-choice test items' difficulty degree on the reliability coefficient and the standard error of measurement depending on the item response theory (IRT). Int. J. Higher Educ. **10**, 22 (2021). https://api.semanticscholar.org/CorpusID:236349900
2. Benedetto, L.: A quantitative study of NLP approaches to question difficulty estimation. In: International Conference on Artificial Intelligence in Education (2023). https://api.semanticscholar.org/CorpusID:258741250
3. Benedetto, L., Cappelli, A., Turrin, R., Cremonesi, P.: Introducing a framework to assess newly created questions with natural language processing. Artif. Intell. Educ. **12163**, 43–54 (2020). https://api.semanticscholar.org/CorpusID:216562628
4. Chen, B., Zhang, Y., Tan, H., Yin, B., Liu, X.: PMAN: progressive multi-attention network for human pose transfer. IEEE Trans. Circuits Syst. Video Technol. **32**, 302–314 (2021). https://api.semanticscholar.org/CorpusID:234159688
5. Chen, Y., Granco, G., Hou, Y., Macias, H., Gomez, F.A.: AI for social good education at hispanic serving institutions. In: AAAI Spring Symposia (2024). https://api.semanticscholar.org/CorpusID:269957748
6. De Cao, N., Aziz, W., Titov, I.: Explainable multi-hop verbal reasoning through internal monologue. In: Proceedings of the 2020 Conference on Empirical Methods in Natural Language Processing (EMNLP), pp. 3255–3272 (2020)
7. Devlin, J., Chang, M.W., Lee, K., Toutanova, K.: Bert: pre-training of deep bidirectional transformers for language understanding. In: North American Chapter of the Association for Computational Linguistics (2019). https://api.semanticscholar.org/CorpusID:52967399
8. Fayers, P.M.: Item response theory for psychologists. Qual. Life Res. **13**, 715–716 (2004). https://api.semanticscholar.org/CorpusID:28158396
9. Guo, M.H., et al.: Attention mechanisms in computer vision: a survey. Comput. Visual Media **8**, 331–368 (2021). https://api.semanticscholar.org/CorpusID:244117862
10. Hahn, M.: Theoretical limitations of self-attention in neural sequence models. Trans. Assoc. Comput. Linguist. **8**, 156–171 (2019). https://api.semanticscholar.org/CorpusID:189928186
11. Hassan, S., Das, D., Iqbal, A., Bosu, A., Shahriyar, R., Ahmed, T.: SOQDE: a supervised learning based question difficulty estimation model for stack overflow. In: 2018 25th Asia-Pacific Software Engineering Conference (APSEC), pp. 445–454 (2018)
12. Howard, J., Ruder, S.: Universal language model fine-tuning for text classification. In: Proceedings of the 56th Annual Meeting of the Association for Computational Linguistics, pp. 328–339 (2018)
13. Lai, G., Xie, Q., Liu, H., Yang, Y., Hovy, E.: RACE: large-scale ReAding comprehension dataset from examinations. In: Palmer, M., Hwa, R., Riedel, S. (eds.) Proceedings of the 2017 Conference on Empirical Methods in Natural Language Processing, pp. 785–794. Association for Computational Linguistics, Copenhagen, Denmark (2017). https://doi.org/10.18653/v1/D17-1082, https://aclanthology.org/D17-1082

14. Lee, D.Z.H., Callan, J., Raj, B.: Mixout: effective regularization to finetune large-scale pretrained language models. In: Proceedings of ICLR 2020 (2020)
15. Loukina, A., Yoon, S.Y., Sakano, J., Wei, Y., Sheehan, K.: Textual complexity as a predictor of difficulty of listening items in language proficiency tests. In: Matsumoto, Y., Prasad, R. (eds.) Proceedings of COLING 2016, the 26th International Conference on Computational Linguistics: Technical Papers, pp. 3245–3253. The COLING 2016 Organizing Committee, Osaka, Japan (2016). https://aclanthology.org/C16-1306
16. Manikandan, R., Vohra, S., Verma, R., Saluja, R., Bhavsar, A.: Ext-MCQ: extending educational MCQ difficulty estimation for English via academic textbooks. GitHub Repository (2025). https://github.com/username/repositoryname
17. Padó, U.: Question difficulty – how to estimate without norming, how to use for automated grading. In: Proceedings of BEA@EMNLP (2017)
18. Parikh, A.P., Täckström, O., Das, D., Uszkoreit, J.: A decomposable attention model for natural language inference. In: Proceedings of the 2016 Conference on Empirical Methods in Natural Language Processing (EMNLP), pp. 2249–2255 (2016). https://doi.org/10.18653/v1/D16-1244
19. Peters, M.E., et al.: Dissecting contextual word embeddings: architecture and representation. In: Proceedings of NAACL-HLT 2019, pp. 1499–1509 (2019)
20. Raina, V., Gales, M.J.F.: Multiple-choice question generation: towards an automated assessment framework (2022). https://api.semanticscholar.org/CorpusID:252532175
21. Ravikiran, M., Vohra, S., Verma, R., Saluja, R., Bhavsar, A.: TEEMIL: towards educational MCQ difficulty estimation in Indic languages. In: Rambow, O., Wanner, L., Apidianaki, M., Al-Khalifa, H., Eugenio, B.D., Schockaert, S. (eds.) Proceedings of the 31st International Conference on Computational Linguistics, pp. 2085–2099, Abu Dhabi, UAE. Association for Computational Linguistics (2025). https://aclanthology.org/2025.coling-main.142/
22. Shaw, P., Uszkoreit, J., Vaswani, A.: Self-attention with relative position representations. In: Proceedings of the 2018 Conference of the North American Chapter of the Association for Computational Linguistics: Human Language Technologies, vol. 1, pp. 464–468 (2018). https://doi.org/10.18653/v1/N18-2074
23. Supraja, S., Hartman, K., Tatinati, S., Khong, A.: Toward the automatic labeling of course questions for ensuring their alignment with learning outcomes. In: Proceedings of Educational Data Mining (2017)
24. Veeramani, H., Thapa, S., Shankar, N.B., Alwan, A.: Large language model-based pipeline for item difficulty and response time estimation for educational assessments. In: Workshop on Innovative Use of NLP for Building Educational Applications (2024). https://api.semanticscholar.org/CorpusID:270766172
25. Venktesh, V., Akhtar, M.S., Mohania, M.K., Goyal, V.: Auxiliary task guided interactive attention model for question difficulty prediction. In: International Conference on Artificial Intelligence in Education (2022). https://api.semanticscholar.org/CorpusID:250264337
26. Yaneva, V., et al.: Findings from the first shared task on automated prediction of difficulty and response time for multiple-choice questions. In: Proceedings of the 19th Workshop on Innovative Use of NLP for Building Educational Applications (BEA 2024), Mexico City, Mexico, pp. 470–482. Association for Computational Linguistics (2024). https://aclanthology.org/2024.bea-1.39

Learning Design with an AI Assistant

Blaženka Divjak(✉), Barbi Svetec, Petra Vondra, Josipa Bađari, and Darko Grabar

Faculty of Organization and Informatics, University of Zagreb, Pavlinska 2, Varaždin, Croatia
{blazenka.divjak,barbi.svetec,petra.vondra,josipa.badjari,
darko.grabar}@foi.unizg.hr

Abstract. This paper presents the ongoing experimental work related to the design of an AI assistant using API calls to an LLM to support educators in creating sound learning design (LD): LeDA. LeDA is one of the innovative features of a collaborative LD tool *Balanced Design Planning*, founded on the principles of student-centeredness and constructive alignment, that has so far been used by more than 2000 users in over 40 countries. We explain LeDA's background in research and international projects, outline the software development, and present the results of ongoing validation. LeDA has been validated in 34 higher education courses, helping 22 teachers to generate, customize, and optimize LDs. Data on the use of LeDA has been automatically collected in the tool, user feedback gathered via integrated forms, and through a questionnaire administered among the teachers. In the current total of 664 interactions with LeDA, the rate of accepting AI's suggestions without modification is around 40%, with the majority relating to creating teaching and learning activities (TLAs). User feedback suggests that teachers recognized LeDA's potential in generating learning outcomes, topics, units, and TLAs, while they were less satisfied with the assistance in integrating innovative pedagogies. Generally, it was reported that LeDA is more efficient in generating solutions on a lower conceptual level, especially if it is provided with the user's comprehensive input. The findings showed that LeDA was easy to use, but pointed to possible adjustments, which would contribute to higher usability.

Keywords: Learning Design · AI · AI assistant · Learning Analytics · API · LLM

1 Introduction

In the last couple of years, the rapid advancement of generative artificial intelligence (GenAI) has opened new challenges and possibilities in education. One of the possibilities refers to supporting educators in designing (more) effective learning experiences, including through provision of evidence-base for meaningful decision-making, as well assistance in the design of curricula and teaching and learning activities (TLAs). This means that educators have to learn how to use GenAI constructively, exploiting its benefits, but at the same time being aware of its limitations and their own responsibility to act as critical thinkers and role models in terms of ethics and academic integrity.

A. I. Cristea et al. (Eds.): AIED 2025, LNAI 15877, pp. 207–220, 2025.
https://doi.org/10.1007/978-3-031-98414-3_15

In this paper, we present the ongoing experimental work related to an AI assistant developed to support educators in creating sound learning design (LD): LeDA. LeDA is a part of the innovative, collaborative, free-to-use LD tool *Balanced Design Planning* (BDP) (learning-design.eu), which is based on the principles of student-centeredness and constructive alignment and currently has over 2000 users across 40 countries.

After briefly explaining the overall BDP concept and tool, we outline the development of LeDA and demonstrate its main features. We present the results of the pilot and validation exercise, which included 34 higher education (HE) courses and 22 HE teachers. The pilot identified LeDA's strengths and weaknesses and informed the recommendations for more effective work with and optimization of an AI assistant in LD, which could be of use in the development of other similar tools in the evolving landscape of digital pedagogy and contribute to the overall discourse on AI in education.

2 Background

2.1 Potentials and Challenges of AI in Education

GenAI has a potential to transform education as we know it [7]. On the one hand, it can support teachers in informed decision-making during instructional design, based on learning analytics [20, 22], and help them make teaching and learning more personalized [16]. For example, AI can be used to track and analyze students' learning performance in real-time to develop a student learning profile. Teachers can use this data to suggest personalized LD and methods to meet different needs and interest of students [17]. GenAI can also decrease educators' workload, help them deal with challenges and enhance LD [5, 16]. On the other hand, GenAI causes concerns about ethics, academic integrity, and unfair practices [4]. Some studies [5] have pointed out the weaknesses of using GenAI for course design, in terms of lacking understanding of the course context, generating unfeasible activities and suggesting resources and materials that do not exist.

To make meaningful use of GenAI in education, including in LD, it is necessary to balance its use with critical thinking and creativity, and avoid overreliance on AI tools [5]. In fact, it has been pointed out that the most significant AI effects occur when machines complement humans and collaboration takes place [13, 26]. In this paper, we present an example of an AI assistant supporting such educator-AI collaboration in LD, mindful of the importance of designers' domain knowledge and critical approach to AI's outputs, aiming to support responsible integration of AI in educational practices.

2.2 Learning Design

There are different definitions of learning design (LD), but in most basic terms, it refers to the order of TLAs, with respective resources and student support [19], which teachers and students should do so that students would acquire the intended learning outcomes [18]. LD guides educators, helping them make informed decisions when designing TLAs, in line with a particular pedagogical approach [6], to ensure efficient teaching and learning [2]. LD should be learner-centered and correspond with student needs [2].

As a field of practice and research, LD emerged in the 2000s [19], so it stresses the use of technology [2]. Recently, there has also been an increase in exploring the possibilities for synergies and integration of LD with learning analytics [19, 23]. Different approaches and tools have been developed to support LD (e.g., ABC LD by University College London; OULDI by The Open University UK). In this paper, we present an innovative approach that builds on the previous ones, on contemporary research, and the latest technological developments, to support educators in development of LD that is not only pedagogically sound but also data-informed, innovative and creative.

2.3 Learning Design Concept, Tool, and AI Assistant

Motivated by the needs expressed by HE teachers in several HE institutions around Europe, the University of Zagreb (UNIZG) Faculty of Organization and Informatics' Laboratory for Learning Analytics has developed an innovative LD concept and tool: the BDP (learning-design.eu). The BDP concept and tool have been explained in several publications [10, 11, 12, 8, 24]. The tool has undergone several cycles of development in line with the design cycle methodology [25]. The BDP supports educators in developing student-centered LD, which is strongly based on learning outcomes and constructive alignment between learning outcomes, TLAs and assessment [3], and student workload. It encourages the use of innovative pedagogies and design analytics.

The BDP approach starts with basic course information. It continues with course learning outcomes, their levels [1] and prioritization [8, 10]. In the following steps, LD is developed to the level of topics, units and TLAs, linked to the intended learning outcomes. TLAs are planned in detail, including the corresponding workload, assessment, and learning type (acquisition, discussion, investigation, practice, production, assessment). In every step, users have access to detailed design analytics to ensure the quality of LD. The BDP tool enables direct export of course LDs to the Moodle LMS.

This paper focuses on one of the latest developments of the BDP tool: an AI assistant in LD which uses API calls to an LLM (GPT-4o): LeDA. LeDA follows the BDP theoretical concept [10] and is built around two principles. First, LeDA enables interactivity, cooperating with an educator through written text, providing responses to clearly formulated prompts. Second, LeDA provides assistance, as it depends on educators' input, needs and requests, but does not make decisions autonomously. Similar to the overall development of the BDP tool, the development of LeDA has included the three phases of the design cycle [25] (Fig. 1) and followed human-centered design [15].

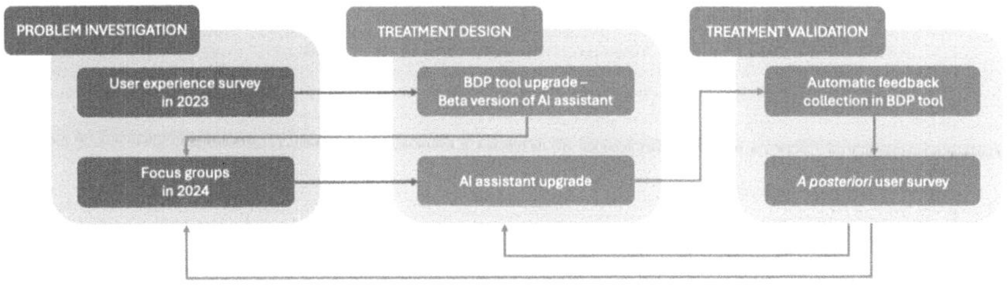

Fig. 1. Development of the AI assistant as part of the LD tool design cycle

In the **problem investigation** phase, the requirements for the AI assistant were determined as part of the process of validation of the BDP LD tool. This phase included:

(1) *A user experience survey* conducted in 2023, as part of the *Innovating Learning Design in HE* (iLed) project, with 53 teachers from HEIs in four European countries [11]. The survey showed that teachers would appreciate the help of a chatbot in the formulation of learning outcomes, support in ensuring constructive alignment, help with design analytics interpretation, and real-time guidance in LD. This motivated the development of the beta-version of LeDA. (2) *Focus groups on AI algorithms to support LD* held in 2024, as part of the *Trustworthy Learning Analytics and Artificial Intelligence for Sound Learning Design* (TRUELA) project, with 18 experts from Europe and Africa. The focus groups (held after the preliminary treatment design) were presented with the beta-version of LeDA and provided preliminary highly positive feedback, but also included ideas for further development, related to AI's help in design analytics interpretation, integration of innovative pedagogies, and content creation.

In the **treatment design** phase, a technical upgrade of the BDP tool was done resulting in the beta version of LeDA (Fig. 2). An important aspect was the preparation of context-based prompts. Each prepared prompt consists of five parts: GPT role (learning designer), Context (course details), Query (desired output), Rules & Constraints (BDP tool related definitions/rules/constraints) and Output Specification (format of output that responds to BDP course format). An example of a prompt is provided below.

````
{
"model": "gpt-4o",
"messages": [

    {"role": "system",
    "content": "You are acting as a learning designer, supporting teachers/educators in designing their courses.\n\nHere are some definitions for key terms:\n\n- **Learning outcomes** are statements of what a learner knows, understands and is able to do on completion of a learning process. Each learning outcome has a corresponding level of Bloom's taxonomy:\n\n 1. **Remembering** – Exhibit memory of previously learned material by recalling facts, terms, basic concepts, and answers. \n   - *Verbs:* Choose, Define, Find, List, Match, Name, Recall, Relate, Select, Describe\n 2. **Understanding** – Demonstrate understanding of facts and ideas by organizing, comparing, translating, interpreting, giving descriptions, and stating main ideas. \n   - *Verbs:* Classify, Compare, Contrast, Demonstrate, Explain, Illustrate, Interpret, Outline, Relate, Rephrase, Summarize\n 3. **Applying** – Solve problems to new situations by applying acquired knowledge, facts, techniques and rules in a different way. \n   - *Verbs:* Apply, Build, Choose, Construct, Develop, Experiment with, Identify, Interview, Make use of, Model, Organize, Plan, Select, Solve\n 4. **Analyzing** – Examine and break information into parts by identifying motives or causes. Make inferences and find evidence to support generalizations. \n   - *Verbs:* Analyze, Assume, Categorize, Classify, Compare, Distinguish, Divide, Examine, Inspect, List, Simplify, Survey, Test for\n 5. **Evaluating** – Present and defend opinions by making judgments about information, validity of ideas, or quality of work based on a set of criteria. \n   - *Verbs:* Assess, Choose, Compare, Conclude, Criticize, Decide, Deduct, Defend, Determine, Estimate, Evaluate, Explain, Interpret, Judge, Justify, Mark, Measure, Prioritize, Prove, Recommend, Select\n 6. **Creating** – Compile information together in a different way by combining elements in a new pattern or proposing alternative solutions. \n   - *Verbs:* Adapt, Build, Choose, Combine, Compose, Construct, Create, Design, Develop, Elaborate, Estimate, Formulate, Improve, Invent, Plan, Predict, Propose, Solve, Test a theory\n\nYou MUST respond in the **Croatian language**, even if existing content is in a different language.\n\nYou will be asked to suggest **units for a topic** based on provided course and topic information, which will be given in JSON format. \n\nThe topic you're working with has **ID 8281**.\n\nYou should:\n- Suggest up to **8 units** within defined topics\n- Specify the **learning outcomes** each unit contributes to\n- Indicate the **percentage of contribution** to those outcomes\n- Define the **level of Bloom's taxonomy** for each\n- Provide a **summary explanation** of why you're suggesting those units\n\n**Units** must include:\n- A **title**\n- A **description**\n\nFormat your response as **JSON** with the following structure:\n\n```json\n{\n \"suggestions\": [\n  {\n   \"unit\": \"Unit title\",\n   \"description\": \"Unit description\"\n },\n  ...\n ],\n \"explanation\": \"Short explanation of why these units were suggested\"\n}\n```\n\n**Constraints:**\n- The topic is the highest level part of a course, consisting of units and TLAs related to one comprehensive learning topic (e.g., one chapter).\n- A unit is a mid-level component of a topic, consisting of TLAs that are content-related and sequenced according to a pedagogical approach.\n- The topic with ID 8281 already has defined units — avoid overlaps when suggesting new ones."
    },
    {
    "role": "user",
     "content": "**Course data (as JSON)**"
    }

    ]
}
````

With this upgrade, LD is supported by an AI assistant able to: 1.1. Generate learning outcome(s), 1. 2. Generate learning outcome(s) according to selected prevailing level of Bloom's taxonomy (Fig. 3), 2.1. Generate topic(s), 2.2. Generate topics and their contribution (%) to learning outcome(s) achievement, 3.1. Generate unit(s) within a selected topic, 3.2. Generate units within a topic according to selected specific teaching and learning approach, 4.1. Generate TLAs within the selected unit (Fig. 4), 4.2. Generate TLAs supporting the prevailing learning type within the selected unit.

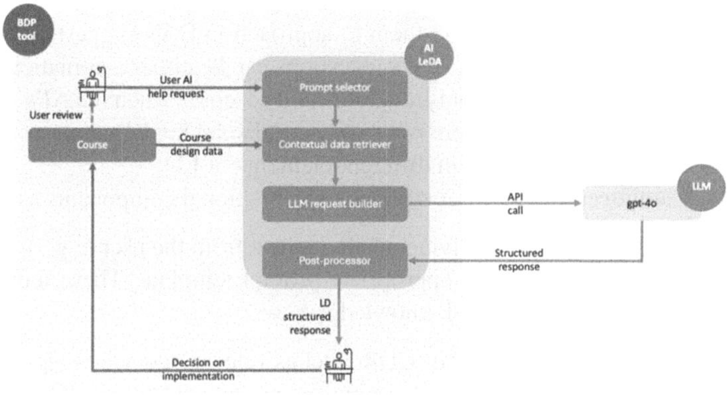

Fig. 2. LeDA's architecture

Importantly, on each level (e.g., topic) proposals are generated considering the content of higher levels of design (e.g., learning outcomes), in line with the principles of LD: (a) Learning outcomes are generated based on course data (description, keywords, target audience, course type, education level, workload in hours, number of course participants, and delivery mode). (b) Topics are generated based on course data and learning outcomes. (c) Units are generated based on course data, learning outcomes, topics and how much (%) the topic contributes to a specific learning outcome. (d) TLAs are generated based on course data, learning outcomes, topics and units.

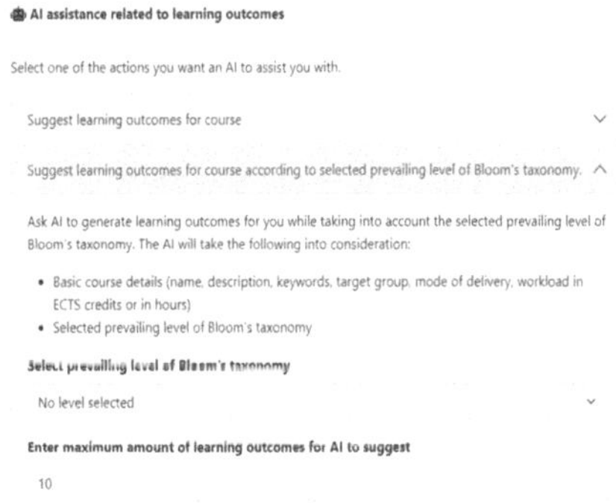

Fig. 3. Query for LeDA: suggest Los

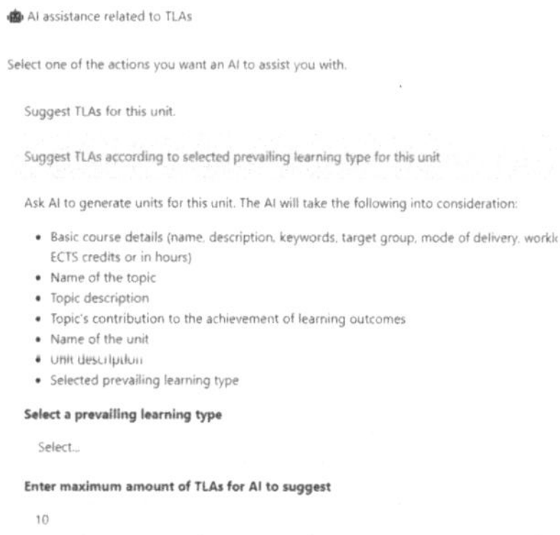

Fig. 4. Query for LeDA: suggest TLA

While the prompts are pre-developed, educators can also direct the AI assistant further. This means they can determine the number and some characteristics of the LD elements they wish to be suggested by LeDA, including the preferred pedagogical approach and required learning types. Furthermore, the AI-assisted LD process is designed to encourage educators' critical thinking and interventions into AI's suggestions. Therefore, besides the suggestion of an LD element (e.g., a TLA), LeDA also provides an educator with a disclaimer reminding them to approach LeDA's suggestions critically. To support human critical thinking, AI's suggestions can be either automatically implemented in course design or a prompt is reiterated and accepted when the AI's suggestion meets a satisfactory LD quality. There is a dashboard displaying LD analyses, including the acceptance of AI's suggestions in different elements of LD.

In terms of architecture, LeDA comprises four functional components as follows:

Prompt Selector (PS): Upon receiving a help request from the user (e.g., for new unit suggestions), the PS identifies the appropriate prompt template. These templates are crafted in advance to align with BDP knowledge base.

Contextual Data Retriever (CDR): CDR fetches relevant course design data from the BDP tool, such as existing units, learning outcomes, and topics. This contextual information is necessary to ground the LLM's response in the current state of the course, thereby avoiding redundancy and ensuring alignment with pedagogical intentions.

LLM Request Builder (RB): RB synthesizes the selected prompt template and contextual data into a unified API request. This includes formatting the input according to the expected structure (e.g. JSON), setting parameters for model behavior, and ensuring that instructions are language-specific.

Post-Processor (PP): Once the LLM returns a structured response, PP validates and adapts the output for the BDP environment. This includes formatting adjustments, semantic validations, and error handling. PP ensures that the final output is pedagogically coherent, correctly structured, and ready for user review within the BDP interface.

In the **treatment validation** phase, users' feedback was collected. The pre-testing was done on several selected courses, followed by a wider pilot and validation. The feedback was collected with two aims: to provide input for the next upgrade of LeDA, and to provide a basis for recommendations for educators and meaningful use of LeDA. We report on the treatment validation, i.e. the pilot, in the following sections.

3 Methodology

In the treatment validation phase (Fig. 5), a pilot was conducted at UNIZG, encompassing a total of 34 courses and 22 HE teachers (users) in the interdisciplinary field, mainly Information Technology (IT). Most of the courses are delivered at undergraduate and graduate study levels (26), but there are also courses from professional studies (2), postgraduate studies (2) and a lifelong learning training (4). For most of the courses, LD had already been developed in the BDP tool without AI assistance. Now, the users were asked to redesign their courses with LeDA's support, so that the LDs created without and with AI assistance could be analyzed. Several users could work on one course, and each user had a possibility to (re)design more than one of the courses they teach. All the users included in the pilot had previous experience with LD in the BDP tool and were motivated for educational innovation.

The users' feedback on the LeDA functionality was collected in two ways: **(a) Automatic collection in the LD tool.** The BDP tool enables collection of user feedback immediately after each interaction with LeDA. This includes a numerical grade (1 - 5) and qualitative written comments. **(b) *A posteriori* user survey.** A questionnaire was distributed among the HE teachers who took part in the pilot. It included 24 questions, divided into four groups: information about users and courses, general usefulness of the AI assistant, usefulness of the AI assistant in LD aspects, and acceptance of AI in education. The questions were either multiple-choice or open-ended (qualitative).

With this pilot, we aimed to respond to the following research questions (RQ):

RQ1: In what aspects does the AI assistant (LeDA) enhance the efficiency and quality of learning design for educators and what aspects present a challenge?

RQ2: What are the recommendations for users and developers that could contribute to the more efficient use of LeDA?

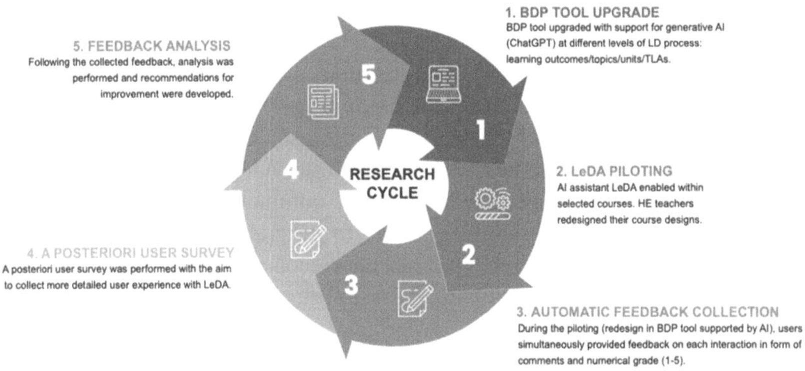

Fig. 5. Research cucle

4 Results

4.1 LeDA System Data

By 5 February 2025, a total number of interactions with LeDA (i.e. users asking for LD suggestions) was 664. According to quantitative data, based on the numerical grades awarded by the users (HE teachers) in real time, the acceptance rate of LeDA's responses without any user modification was 38%. The highest proportion of the accepted responses refers to creating units (48%), followed by TLAs (40%) and topics (34%), while the acceptance of learning outcomes comes last (24%). As for LeDA's usefulness, the mean mark (1 – 5 scale) awarded by the users was 3.

When it comes to the qualitative comments given by HE teachers during design with LeDA, the feedback is categorized based on different LD elements:

Learning Outcomes. In general, users found LeDA's suggestions related to learning outcomes somewhat useful but inconsistent in quality. While some suggestions were rated positively, most were either rejected or required modification. Users preferred learning outcomes that were better contextualized and tailored to course content. The low acceptance rate (24%) indicates that most suggestions were not fully satisfactory. The main groups of users' comments indicated that suggested learning outcomes were either too high or too low on the Bloom's taxonomy scale and required better calibration, did not fully align with the course description or not entirely relevant to the course. Moreover, they thought the proposals were not well-phrased to correspond to the standard learning outcome format or were too general and needed more specificity.

Topics. In general, users indicated that AI-generated topics were moderately relevant but sometimes redundant. Some topics repeated content instead of introducing new ideas and users wanted more diverse and specific topic suggestions. The acceptance rate of 34% indicates that some suggestions were useful, but many required users' interventions. The main groups of users' comments indicated that suggested topics overlapped too much, were not always relevant to the course or lacked practical application, were sometimes repetitive, making it difficult to structure diverse course content, and could be too generic, lacking depth or specificity.

Units. Users generally found the AI-generated units more useful than topics and learning outcomes. They found that in most cases unit suggestions were well-structured and aligned with learning outcomes. However, some suggested units lacked depth or connection to the broader course structure. Nearly half of the AI-generated units (48%) were immediately accepted. The main groups of users' comments indicated that suggested units were appreciated, confirming AI's ability to generate useful ideas, but could be too broad, generic, lack innovation, or cover entire courses instead of specific topics; sometimes they were not sufficiently aligned with learning outcomes or topics.

TLAs. According to users' general perspective, LeDA was partially effective in suggesting appropriate TLAs. The 40% acceptance rate indicates that some activities were useful, but many needed user improvements. The main groups of users' comments indicated that suggested TLAs were useful but needed refinements to fit the course structure; they were sometimes too generic and not well-adapted to specific course needs, not applicable to the learning context or lacked practical implementation strategies.

4.2 *A Posteriori* Survey Data

A total of 22 HE teachers participated in the survey, from different fields: pedagogy (1), mathematics (4), IT (8), economy (6), interdisciplinary (9). We present the highlights of results, with percentages rounded to the nearest integer due to the sample size.

A significant portion were novel HE teachers, with 1 – 5 (36.4%) or 5 - 10 years of teaching experience in HE (5%), and mid-career teachers with 10 - 20 years of experience (36%), followed by highly experienced teachers, with 20 - 30 (14%) or more than 30 years (9%) of teaching experience. In terms of their previous experience with BDP LD, the total range was from 0 to 12 LDs: a majority had created between 1 and 5

LDs (73%); several had no previous experience with the BDP tool (14%). For a majority (64%), this was the first time to work with an educational chatbot.

As presented in Fig. 6, a majority of the users (68%) were (very) satisfied with their LDs prepared previously without AI assistance. Interestingly, a vast majority (86%) felt improvements in LD would be welcome, and a majority (73%) would apply the LD designed with LeDA at least to some extent if they were authorized to do so.

As shown in Fig. 7, all survey participants agreed that LeDA is easy to use (completely or mostly agree). A great majority (82%) recognized LeDA as useful for their work in teaching and research and almost three quarters (73%) plan to use it in future. In qualitative comments, the users pointed out it would be useful if it were possible to partially accept LeDA's suggestions, combine them with pre-existing LD, provide LeDA with additional instructions, and use AI's help to improve the existing LD. Some also asked for more insight into AI's reasoning. They also thought it would be useful to train LeDA on quality assured examples of sound LD.

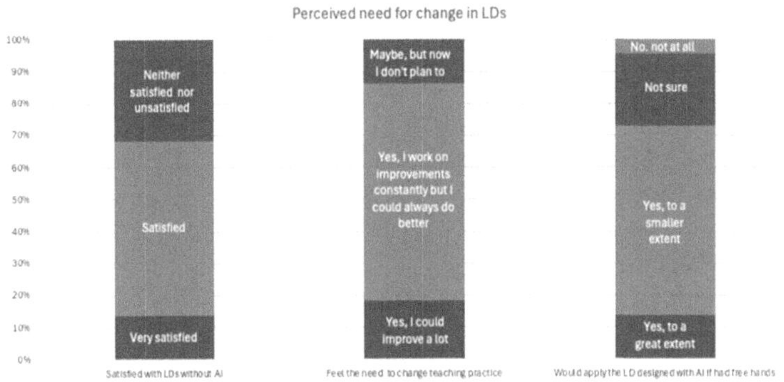

Fig. 6. Perceived need for change in LDs

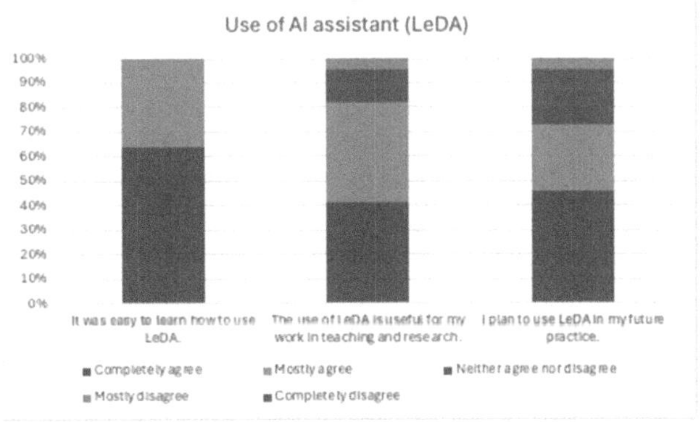

Fig. 7. Use of AI assistant

In terms of the usefulness of LeDA in different aspects of LD (Fig. 8), most of the users (68%) found it very useful or mostly useful in designing TLAs and planning topics related to learning outcomes. A bit smaller portion (64%), but still a majority, evaluated LeDA as very useful or mostly useful in helping them to improve learning outcomes. The lowest usefulness was found in terms of support for integrating innovative pedagogies in LD, which was found very/mostly useful by a half of the teachers (55%). Many users still have reservations about this, as one-third of them (32%) were not sure. In their qualitative comments, users reported that LeDA enticed them to make changes in LD (even if they did not accept its original proposal), especially when it comes to embracing a more creative approach to the design of TLAs. In terms of lessons learnt, several users pointed out that LeDA was a useful tool for improvements and a source of ideas, which should be taken critically and adjusted as needed.

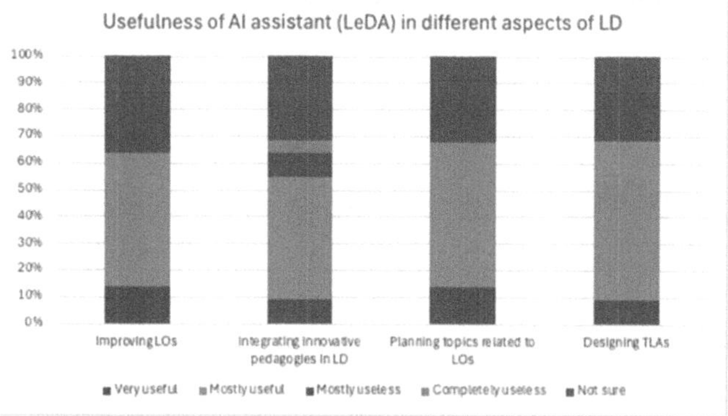

Fig. 8. Usefulness of the AI assistant in different aspects of LD

A vast majority of the users thought AI can have a positive influence on their teaching and research, especially when it comes to improving some aspects of their work or saving time (68%) and helping them be more efficient (27%). A majority (68%) considered themselves (mostly) ready to meaningfully apply AI in practice. However, the most frequent grade they assigned to their current success in integrating AI in teaching (1 – insufficient, 5 – excellent) was 3 (41%), followed by 2 (27%) and 4 (23%), while only a minority chose 5 (9%). As for concerns about AI in education, in qualitative comments, the users stressed the ethical use of AI by users and students, issues with assessment, lack of critical approach to solutions proposed by AI, and the unpreparedness of institutions for fast development of AI. They also pointed out that students could use AI more than teachers and become more skilled users, at the same time not developing critical thinking and possibly developing dependence on AI. One user warned that teachers and students can accept AI tools that are not scientifically grounded.

5 Discussion

5.1 RQ1: Benefits and Challenges of LeDA

Our results from the two data sources were highly aligned; we provide them with a link to recommendations for users (RU) and developers (RD). The results show that the teachers were generally satisfied with the AI assistant, and especially some aspects of

AI assistance. In principle, the users found that LeDA is more effective on lower levels of LD (units, TLAs), which is reflected in the higher acceptance rate of AI's suggestions without any modification (48% and 40% respectively). They were less content with AI assistance on the higher levels of LD (learning outcomes, topics), which are more abstract and overarching, as reflected in the acceptance rate (24% and 34% respectively). The reasons for that might be three-fold. First, LeDA uses input from a specific LLM (GPT-4o), but also from basic descriptions and features of a course as provided by a teacher. If this descriptive part is not informative enough, LeDA infers from the pre-training data of GPT-4o and generates outputs that may lack specificity [21]. Consequently, teachers can be reluctant to use its suggestions without any modification. (RU1 and RD1) Second, higher-level elements of LD are normally parts of study program curricula [14], meaning that teachers have less flexibility to change them outside the regular (often lengthy and complex) QA procedures. Therefore, it would be commendable to start LD from the study program level. (RU2 and RD2) Third, the current possibilities provided by LeDA do not enable teachers to choose some (but not all) of the proposed learning outcomes and topics. This calls for more flexibility in the tool (RD3).

When it came to units and TLAs, teachers were highly satisfied, but also pointed to some aspects for improvement. First, the teachers noted that there is a need for consistent alignment between units, topics and learning outcomes. This implies that teachers need to be experts in pedagogy and LD, which would enable them to meaningfully evaluate the AI results, taking into account the design analytics. It suggests that more coherent results could be achieved if the AI assistant was trained on examples of good LDs. This could be achieved by applying the Retrieval-Augmented Generation (RAG) which includes the development of a structural knowledge base on LD. This could enable higher specificity in unit and TLA descriptions, more context-specific suggestions and avoiding generic or overly broad suggestions. (RU3 and RD4) Moreover, the teachers noted that LeDA could be more innovative in proposing TLAs. While this could be further improved on the technical level, for example by introducing a storyboard and course visualization, it should be stressed that meaningful use of AI means that teachers are still conductors and must approach AI's outputs critically. (RU4, RU5 and RD5) Finally, the teachers were concerned about AI's reasoning in general, and asked for more insight into how LeDA functions and creates suggestions (RU6 and RD6).

5.2 RQ2: Recommendations for Users and Developers

Based on the challenges identified in relation to RQ1, we provide a list of recommendations for users and developers that could contribute to the quality of LeDA's output and its more meaningful use, so as to increase the efficiency of teaching and learning.

Recommendations for users (RU):

RU1. Be detailed, focused and informative in the basic description of the course LD. Enhance AI's understanding of course context to generate more relevant learning outcomes and topics.

RU2. Consider the overarching study program perspective when designing a course.

RU3. Work on your data literacy and skills enabling you to make sense of design analytics and learning analytics.

RU4. Be aware of your conductor / decision-making role in LD and its orchestration.

RU5. Be aware that an AI assistant is not a person but a very capable, although not unmistakable machine.

RU6. Work on your AI literacy as a basis for a critical approach to AI's suggestions.

Recommendations for developers (RD):

RD1.To support better AI's suggestions related to higher levels of LD, the BDP tool has recently been upgraded with additional fields to fill in information about the course, e.g. target groups of learners, level of education, type of the course.

RD2. To support the study program perspective, the BDP tool should enable linking courses to study program learning outcomes and workload.

RD3. It would be useful to enable users to select the preferred learning outcomes among AI-generated suggestions.

RD4. The possibilities to train LeDA on examples of LD with a quality mark should be explored. This is in relation with the application of RAG which includes development of a structural knowledge base on LD.

RD5. It would be valuable to enable course visualization and a storyboard, to start LD from the fundamental idea of the course, and that way support more creativity in LD.

RD6. Additional explanations of AI's reasoning and a help section should be introduced to support users in critical evaluation of the suggestions.

5.3 Limitations

The main limitation of this pilot is that it was conducted with a limited number of users, from a limited number of courses, on one HEI. Examining user experience with more users in different educational contexts might provide additional insights. Moreover, the teachers included in this pilot had previous experience with the BDP concept and tool, and belonged to a HEI which is mainly in the field of IT, both of which might have made them more critical towards the LeDA's suggestions.

6 Conclusion

We presented one of the innovative functionalities of the BDP learning design (LD) concept and tool, namely, the LD AI assistant (LeDA). To validate the usefulness of LeDA, as well as to identify the key challenges and recommendations for more effective use of AI's assistance by educators and for further technical upgrades by developers, we analyzed LeDA system data and user feedback. We found that users generally appreciated the assistance provided by LeDA, especially when it comes to lower levels of LD (units and TLAs), while they were more critical about LeDA's outputs at higher levels (learning outcomes and topics). We recommended that educators should be more concrete in providing course descriptions, aware of their responsibilities as the conductors of LD, work on their data and AI literacies, and consider the broader study program perspective. We should all be aware that the dignity and conductor role of humans should always be preserved, as AI can be a powerful assistant but is still a machine.

Acknowledgements. This study has been conducted with the support of the iLed (Erasmus+, financed by the European Union, 2022–1-HR01-KA220-HED-000085818) and TRUELA (financed by the Croatian Science Foundation, IP-2022–10-2854) project.

References

1. Anderson, L.W., Krathwohl, D.R.: A Taxonomy for Learning, Teaching and Assessing: A Revision of Bloom's Taxonomy of Educational Objectives, Complete Longman, New York (2001)
2. Bennett, S., Agostinho, S., Lockyer, L.: Technology tools to support learning design: Implications derived from an investigation of university teachers' design practices. Comput. Educ. **81**, 211–220 (2015). https://doi.org/10.1016/j.compedu.2014.10.016
3. Biggs, J.: Enhancing teaching through constructive alignment. High. Educ. **32**(3), 347–364 (1996). https://doi.org/10.1007/BF00138871
4. Chang, D.H., Lin, M.P.-C., Hajian, S., Wang, Q.Q.: Educational design principles of using AI Chatbot that supports self-regulated learning in education: goal setting, feedback, and personalization. Sustainability **15**, 12921 (2023). https://doi.org/10.3390/su151712921
5. Choi, G.W., Kim, S.H., Lee, D., et al.: Utilizing generative ai for instructional design: exploring strengths, weaknesses, opportunities, and threats. TechTrends **68**, 832–844 (2024). https://doi.org/10.1007/s11528-024-00967-w
6. Conole, G.: Designing for Learning in an Open World. Springer New York, New York, NY (2013). https://doi.org/10.1007/978-1-4419-8517-0
7. Cooper, G.: Examining science education in ChatGPT: an exploratory study of generative artificial intelligence. J. Sci. Educ. Technol. **32**, 444–452 (2023)
8. Divjak, B., Grabar, D., Svetec, B., Vondra, P.: Automating the comparison of learning design and delivery using course scaffolding in moodle. In: Novitzká, V., Szakál, A. (eds.) INFORMATICS 2024 PROCEEDINGS, pp. 54–59. IEEE, Poprad (2024)
9. Divjak, B., Grabar, D., Svetec, B., Vondra, P.: Balanced Learning Design Planning. J. Inf. Organizational Sci. **46**(2), 361–375 (2022). https://doi.org/10.31341/jios.46.2.6
10. Divjak, B., Kadoic, N., Zugec, B.: The use of decision-making methods to ensure assessment validity. In: 2021 IEEE Technology & Engineering Management Conference - Europe (TEMSCON-EUR). IEEE, May 2021, pp. 1–6. https://doi.org/10.1109/TEMSCON-EUR52034.2021.9488580
11. Divjak, B., Rienties, B., Bađari, J., Grabar, D., Horvat, D., Vondra, P.: Enhancing learning design through user experience research: insights from a survey in four european countries. In: Proceedings of the Central European Conference on Information and Intelligent Systems, Dubrovnik, Croatia, pp. 213–221 (2023)
12. Divjak, B., Svetec, B., Horvat, D., Kadoić, N.: Assessment validity and learning analytics as prerequisites for ensuring student-centred learning design. Br. J. Edu. Technol. **54**(1), 313–334 (2023). https://doi.org/10.1111/bjet.13290
13. Duan, Y., Edwards, J.S., Dwivedi, J.K.: Artificial intelligence for decision making in the era of Big Data – evolution, challenges and research agenda. Int. J. Inf. Manage. **48**, 63–71 (2019). https://doi.org/10.1016/j.ijinfomgt.2019.01.021
14. European Higher Education Area: Rome Ministerial Communiqué 2020 (2020). https://ehea.info/Upload/Rome_Ministerial_Communique_Annex_III.pdf
15. Giacomin, J.: What Is Human Centred Design? Des. J. **17**(4), 606–623 (2014). https://doi.org/10.2752/175630614X14056185480186

16. Giannakos, M., Azevedo, R., Brusilovsky, P., Cukurova, M., Dimitriadis, Y., Hernandez-Leo, D., Rienties, B.: The promise and challenges of generative AI in education. Behav. Inf. Technol., 1–27 (2024). https://doi.org/10.1080/0144929X.2024.2394886
17. Kim, J.: Leading teachers' perspective on teacher-AI collaboration in education. Education and Information Technologies 29 (2023). https://doi.org/10.1007/s10639-023-12109-5
18. Koper, R., Olivier, B.: Representing the learning design of units of learning. Educ. Technol. Soc. **7**(3), 97–111 (2004)
19. Lockyer, L., Heathcote, E., Dawson, S.: Informing pedagogical action. Am. Behav. Sci. **57**(10), 1439–1459 (2013). https://doi.org/10.1177/0002764213479367
20. Mangaroska, K., Giannakos, M.: Learning analytics for learning design: a systematic literature review of analytics-driven design to enhance learning. IEEE Trans. Learn. Technol. **12**(4), 516–534 (2018)
21. Meyer, J.G., Urbanowicz, R.J., Martin, P.C.N., et al.: ChatGPT and large language models in academia: opportunities and challenges. BioData Mining **16**, 20 (2023). https://doi.org/10.1186/s13040-023-00339-9
22. Muljana, P.S., Luo, T.: Utilizing learning analytics in course design: voices from instructional designers in higher education. J. Comput. High. Educ. **33**(1), 206–234 (2021)
23. Pishtari, G., et al.: Learning design and learning analytics in mobile and ubiquitous learning: a systematic review. Br. J. Edu. Technol. **51**(4), 1078–1100 (2020). https://doi.org/10.1111/bjet.12944
24. Rienties, B., Balaban, I., Divjak, B., Grabar, D., Svetec, B., Vondra, P.: Applying and Translating Learning Design and Analytics Approaches Across Borders. In: Springer (2023), pp. 35–53. https://doi.org/10.1007/978-3-031-27646-0_3
25. Wieringa, R.J.: Design Science Methodology for Information Systems and Software Engineering. Springer, Heidelberg (2014). https://doi.org/10.1007/978-3-662-43839-8
26. Wilson, H.J., Daugherty, P.R.: Human + Machine: Reimagining Work in the Age of AI. Harvard Business Review Press, Boston, MA (2018)

Automatic Modeling and Analysis of Students' Problem-Solving Handwriting Trajectories

Zhonghua Sheng[1], Shuyu Shen[2], Leixian Shen[1(✉)], Qiqi Duan[2], Nan Tang[1,2], Pan Hui[1,2], Huamin Qu[1], and Yuyu Luo[1,2]

[1] The Hong Kong University of Science and Technology, Hong Kong, China
lshenaj@connect.ust.hk

[2] The Hong Kong University of Science and Technology (Guangzhou), Guangzhou, China

Abstract. Understanding students' cognitive patterns in problem-solving is crucial for personalized education, yet traditional methods struggle to effectively capture and analyze these patterns. This paper presents CogChain, a novel method that synergistically combines digital pen technology with Multi-modal Large Language Models (MLLMs) to automatically construct students' logic chains during examinations. We collected a comprehensive dataset of 87,679 handwriting trajectories in mathematics, physics, and chemistry from 25 real-world high school students. Based on the constructed logic chains of students, we conduct an in-depth analysis across three dimensions: solution, time, and course, revealing a set of findings about their problem-solving behaviors. (1) Solution Dimension: We identify four distinct solution trajectory patterns, showing that moderate-complexity approaches achieve the highest accuracy. (2) Time Dimension: We uncover three types of time-allocation patterns, showing that students who allocate more time to structured reasoning achieve higher accuracy, whereas those who prioritize writing speed tend to perform worse. (3) Course Dimension: Different subjects require distinct problem-solving and time management strategies, with mathematics benefiting from step-by-step derivation, physics from visual reasoning, and chemistry from quick solutions. These insights provide valuable guidance for developing personalized teaching strategies.

Keywords: Handwriting Trajectory · Multi-modal Large Language Model · Logic Chains · Cognitive Patterns

1 Introduction

Examinations are essential for assessing student learning, with students documenting their problem-solving processes and answers on paper, which educators evaluate for accuracy and completeness [2,24]. These written records contain

Z. Sheng and S. Shen—Contributed equally to this work.

A. I. Cristea et al. (Eds.): AIED 2025, LNAI 15877, pp. 221–235, 2025.
https://doi.org/10.1007/978-3-031-98414-3_16

rich information about students' problem-solving trajectories, offering insights into students' thinking patterns and cognitive modes [18,19]. For example, some students tend to use sketches to draw auxiliary diagrams, visually constructing their solution approaches, while others directly enter the equation phase, focusing on formula derivation and calculations.

However, faced with large numbers of students and complex test questions, it is challenging to analyze each student's entire solution process individually, and students often struggle to accurately recall their thought processes during problem solving [1,5,27]. To tackle this challenge, analyzing handwriting trajectories can reconstruct the sequential steps linking initial understanding to final solutions, forming what we call ***logic chains*** [4,7,8,15]. These chains represent the structured progression of reasoning and actions taken to solve a problem, revealing two key aspects of students' cognitive patterns: solution trajectory patterns that show how students construct their solutions (e.g., through visual aids or direct equation derivation), and time allocation patterns that reflect how students manage their problem-solving process. Understanding these cognitive patterns provides opportunities for more targeted personalized guidance and helps educators optimize teaching strategies [3,14].

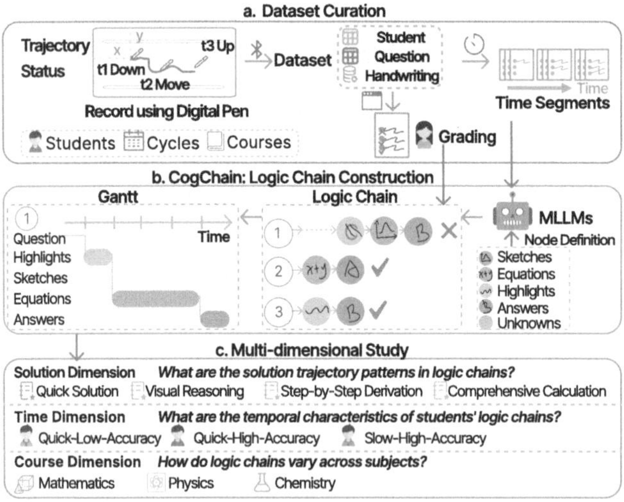

Fig. 1. Overview of three key components: (a) Data collection via digital pens. (b) CogChain: MLLM-based logic chain construction from handwriting trajectories. (c) Multi-dimensional analysis of logic chains across solution, time, and course dimensions.

Capturing Handwriting Trajectories with Digital Pens. Digital pens, as innovative data collection tools, can record real-time trajectory coordinates (x, y) and temporal information (time, status) of pen movements on paper during students' problem-solving processes, as shown in Fig. 1(a) and Fig. 2. These raw data consist merely of spatiotemporal coordinate points that require alignment with answer sheets for meaningful analysis. However, without proper processing, it remains challenging for educators to extract meaningful insights from this rich dataset [28,32].

Logic Chain Modeling. To address the challenge of extracting insights from raw trajectory data, we leverage the recent advances in Multimodal Large Language Models (MLLMs) [12,23]. Their ability to process multimodal inputs, including handwritten notes, makes them a promising tool for analyzing students' problem-solving handwriting trajectories. Building on this, we propose CogChain, an MLLM-based method to automatically analyze students' time-sequential handwritten trajectories with digital pens (see Fig. 1(b)). CogChain extracts spatiotemporal features, visualizing them as logic chains that can be transformed into Gantt charts [9], illustrating different cognitive phases (e.g., sketch drawing and thinking processes).

Based on the extracted logic chains, we further analyze students' cognitive patterns in three dimensions: solution, time, and course (Fig. 1(c)).

- ***Q1:*** What are the solution trajectory patterns in logic chains (Solution Dimension)? We aim to explore the relationships between students' solution trajectory patterns and knowledge topics to reveal trajectory characteristics.
- ***Q2:*** What are the temporal characteristics of students' logic chains (Time Dimension)? We aim to explore the relationships between students' time allocation and solution trajectory patterns to reveal temporal characteristics.
- ***Q3:*** How do logic chains vary across subjects (Course Dimension)? We aim to compare solution trajectory patterns across different courses to identify cognitive differences.

Our contributions are summarized as follows:

- **Dataset Curation.** We developed a handwriting dataset with digital pens, containing two months of records from 25 high school students (see Fig. 1(a)). The dataset comprises test papers in mathematics, physics, and chemistry, with a total of 87,679 handwriting trajectories.
- **CogChain: Automatic Logic Chain Construction.** We propose CogChain, an MLLM-based method to automatically generate logic chains from handwriting trajectories (see Fig. 1(b)). Logic chains display temporal distribution and relationships between trajectories, providing a new method for understanding students' problem-solving behaviors.
- **Multi-Dimensional Study of Logic Chains.** We conducted an in-depth analysis of logic chains in three dimensions: solution, time, and course (see Fig. 1(c)). By analyzing logic chains, we explore the students' solution trajectory patterns and time management patterns across different subjects, providing valuable insights into students' cognitive patterns.

2 Related Work

2.1 Digital Pen for Education

Digitalizing student handwriting can significantly enhance grading efficiency and has the potential to enable intelligent, personalized education [11]. Compared to handwritten word recognition systems [13], digital pens offer several advantages: they capture temporal information [29], facilitate intuitive interaction [28], and allow for fine-grained analysis of raw data [6,10,17,25,31,32]. For instance, Yan [31] demonstrated that smart paper-pen technology improves classroom interactions by making them more efficient. Guo et al. [10] developed a learning platform utilizing digital pens, incorporating an analytical model to assess learners' engagement with assignments based on validated indicators. Similarly, Siddiqui and Muntjir [25] introduced a smart study platform integrating digital pens and paper to support students in reading, writing, and solving classroom exercises. Despite these advantages, there remains a lack of digital pen handwriting trajectory datasets, and a shortage of fine-grained analyses of these trajectories. This paper addresses this by constructing a real-world dataset and leveraging MLLMs to analyze cognitive patterns from handwriting trajectories.

2.2 Student Logic Chain Analysis

Understanding and modeling students' logic chains during problem-solving has attracted significant attention. Wang and Chiew [30] highlighted problem-solving as a core cognitive function intertwined with abstraction, learning, decision-making, inference, and synthesis. They further captured these interactions to study the complexities of student cognition. Recent AI advancements have introduced techniques like chain-of-thought prompting [26], which train models to use step-by-step reasoning to handle complex tasks with greater accuracy. This aligns with the goal of modeling student logic chains, as it emphasizes the decomposition of complex problems into manageable steps. Furthermore, the use of digital tools in education has opened new avenues for capturing and analyzing student problem-solving processes. Digital pens, for instance, can record real-time trajectory coordinates and temporal information during students' problem-solving activities. This data can be analyzed to reconstruct the sequence of cognitive steps taken by students, providing insights into their logic chains [10,25]. Despite these advances, current methods face key limitations of insufficient granularity in capturing transitions between cognitive phases [16,20]. To address these gaps, we propose leveraging MLLMs to reconstruct fine-grained, time-sequential logic chains from digital pen handwriting trajectories.

3 Dataset Curation

We collected data from a secondary school class with 25 students (10 male and 15 female, aged 17–19). The examinations were conducted under standard conditions, following students' training on digital pen usage. Students then completed timed exams using specially designed answer sheets embedded with coordinates, enabling precise tracking of pen movements (see Fig. 2(a)). Their problem-solving experience remained identical to traditional paper-based exams, while we collected handwriting trajectory data via the pen's Bluetooth functionality.

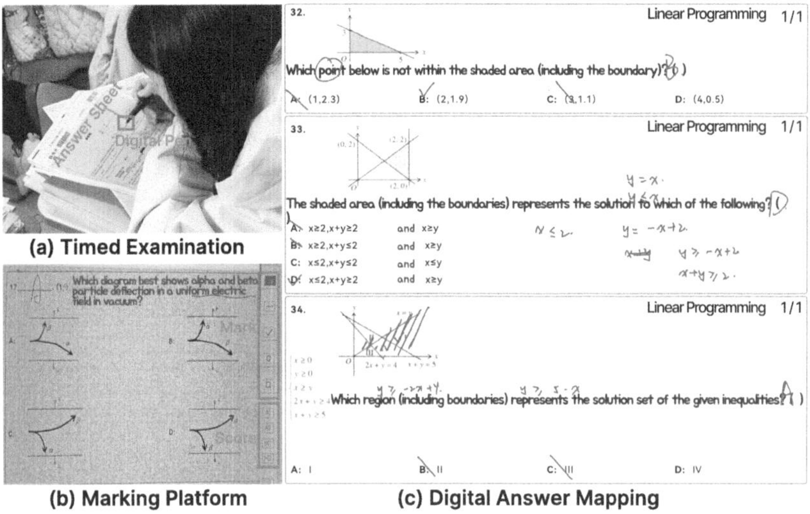

Fig. 2. Example of handwriting samples in the dataset

Over a two-month period, we collected 37 examination papers across mathematics, physics, and chemistry. Each pen stroke was recorded with state information (pen down, movement, and pen up), spatial features (x- and y-coordinates), and timestamps. We define a trajectory as the complete sequence of pen movements from pen-down to pen-up, including all intermediate positions and their spatial coordinates. This process resulted in 87,679 trajectory segments. We further preprocessed these trajectories by mapping the coordinates to standard answer sheets. Figure 2(c) illustrates how a student solved three linear programming problems. For Q32, the student circled the question stem, eliminated incorrect options, and wrote 'B'. For Q33, the student wrote equations, crossed out wrong choices, and selected 'D'. For Q34, the student wrote equations, created graphs, and chose 'A' after eliminating incorrect options. Educators can grade and recorde results through a marking platform (see Fig. 2(b)).

The dataset comprises three main components: student information with unique identifiers, question information including correct answers and knowledge topics, and handwriting data containing these detailed pen stroke records (see Fig. 1(a)). This dataset enables in-depth analysis of problem-solving patterns, cognitive strategies, and personalized learning insights.

4 CogChain: Automatic Logic Chain Construction

A logic chain represents a student's structured problem-solving process, comprising writing phases (e.g., equations, sketches), thinking gaps (pauses indicating reasoning or analysis), and temporal organization (the sequential flow reflecting logic and time allocation). To gain insights into students' cognitive patterns, we propose CogChain, a method that leverages MLLMs to automatically construct and visualize logic chains from students' raw handwritten trajectory data. As shown in Fig. 3, CogChain comprises three modules: time-based trajectory segmentation, trajectory classification, and logic chain visualization.

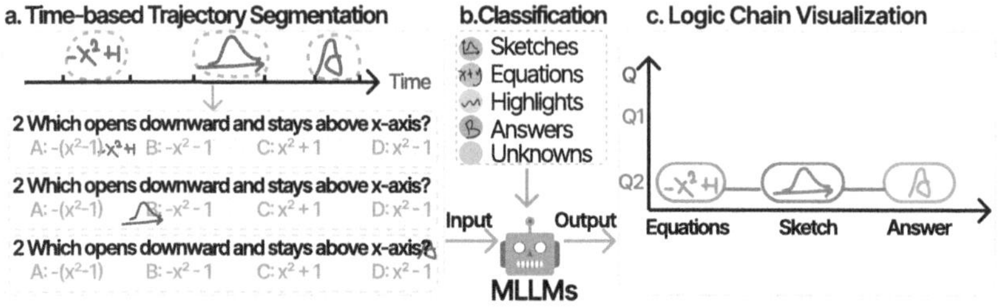

Fig. 3. CogChain: time-sequential handwriting-based logic chain construction.

4.1 Time-Based Trajectory Segmentation

To generate students' logic chains more accurately, we first adopt a time-based trajectory segmentation method to process large amounts of the handwritten trajectories (see Fig. 3(a)). Considering that inputting all trajectories at once would lose temporal sequence information and excessive trajectory might result in a loss of accuracy, we employ a heuristic grouping method by setting a time threshold (2s) to segment students' writing behavior. When the time interval between adjacent trajectories is less than the 2s threshold, we consider it a continuous writing phase. For example, when a student continuously writes a sequence of a 'x' letter within the 2-second threshold, these strokes are grouped as a single writing behavior, preserving the natural flow of writing. During this phase, we group these continuous pen trajectories together and record their writing duration. When the time interval exceeds the 2s threshold, we identify it as a student's thinking pause phase and record this period as a thinking gap.

As shown in Fig. 3(a), this method segments the student's trajectory into three distinct writing groups, each associated with a writing duration, with two thinking gaps in between. To facilitate logic chain construction, we map these groups onto answer sheets in chronological order. Figure 3(a) illustrates how these three writing groups are mapped onto three separate answer sheets.

4.2 Handwritten Trajectory Classification

Based on a comprehensive analysis of our dataset, we categorized handwritten trajectory groups into five distinct types that constitute the writing phases of students' logic chains (see Fig. 3(b)): *Sketches*: Mathematical diagrams and graphical elements (e.g., coordinate axes, numerical lines); *Equations*: Mathematical expressions serving as auxiliary calculations or final answers; *Highlights*: Marking symbols including strikethroughs and underlines; *Multiple-choice answer*: Letter-based responses (e.g., A, B, C, D) enclosed in brackets; and *Unknowns*: Unidentifiable marks or irrelevant content (e.g., doodles, stray marks).

The classification process leverages MLLMs to analyze segmented handwriting. As students often switch between questions, handwriting may inadvertently overlap with neighboring questions. To address this, our MLLMs perform dual classification, identifying both handwriting type and corresponding question. By analyzing spatial distribution and content features of trajectory images mapped to answer sheets, MLLMs ensure accurate categorization.

4.3 Logic Chain Visualization

We represent the logic chain of students' problem-solving processes using Gantt charts (see Fig. 3(c)). These charts integrate three key data components: writing durations and thinking gaps from trajectory segmentation, and handwriting classification results from MLLMs. The Gantt chart's horizontal axis represents the temporal progression, while the vertical axis denotes different questions. Writing phases are color-coded based on their types (e.g., equation, sketch, answer), and thinking gaps appear as grey regions. As an example of how our visualization method captures problem-solving processes, consider a student's solution to the question *"Which opens downward and stays above the x-axis?"* shown in Fig. 3. The Gantt chart reveals a structured sequence: the student began by noting relevant formulas, paused for strategic thinking, constructed function coordinates, and concluded by marking 'A' as the final answer. This visualization approach effectively captures both the sequential nature of students' solution trajectory patterns and their time allocation patterns.

5 Multi-dimensional Study of Logic Chains

Through the automatic logic chain construction method described in Sect. 4, we analyze 87,679 digital pen trajectory segments collected from 37 examination papers, thus identifying 8,304 trajectory groups utilizing CogChain. By associating these trajectory groups with their corresponding questions, we obtain 1,765 complete problem-solving processes, where each process might contain multiple trajectory groups representing different phases of solving a question. We further conduct an analysis of students' cognitive patterns based on these logic chains across three dimensions: solution, time, and course.

5.1 Solution Dimension

Experiment Design. To analyze students' problem-solving trajectory characteristics, we first define solution trajectory patterns as clusters of similar writing phase sequences within logic chains for individual questions. To identify these patterns, we perform cluster analysis on 1,765 problem-solving processes by extracting two features from each logic chain: the total number of trajectory groups and the time-based distribution of different trajectory types defined in Sect. 4.

Using these features, we employ K-means clustering with the elbow method to determine the optimal number of clusters. Through this analysis, we identified four typical solution trajectory patterns:

- *Quick Solution*: A concise problem-solving approach with few trajectory groups (avg. 2.8) where students predominantly use highlighting (49.1%) for multiple-choice questions. The key feature is minimal calculation (avg. 0.6 equations) and highlighting use (avg. 0.8), achieving 71.8% accuracy.
- *Visual Reasoning*: A solution method with moderate trajectory groups (avg. 6.7) dominated by sketches (54.4%). The distinguishing characteristic is the incorporation of graphical elements (avg. 2.8 sketches), such as coordinate systems and function plots, reaching 70.7% accuracy.
- *Step-by-Step Derivation*: A solution process with more trajectory groups (avg. 11.2) combining equations (44.9%) and highlighting (46.9%). It is characterized by equation derivations (avg. 3.8) and highlighting (avg. 3.9), showing systematic problem-solving logic with 74.1% accuracy.
- *Comprehensive Calculation*: An extensive solution approach with numerous trajectory groups (avg. 29.5) characterized by detailed mathematical derivations (51.4% equations). It features equation derivation (avg. 12.3 equations), maintaining 73.6% accuracy.

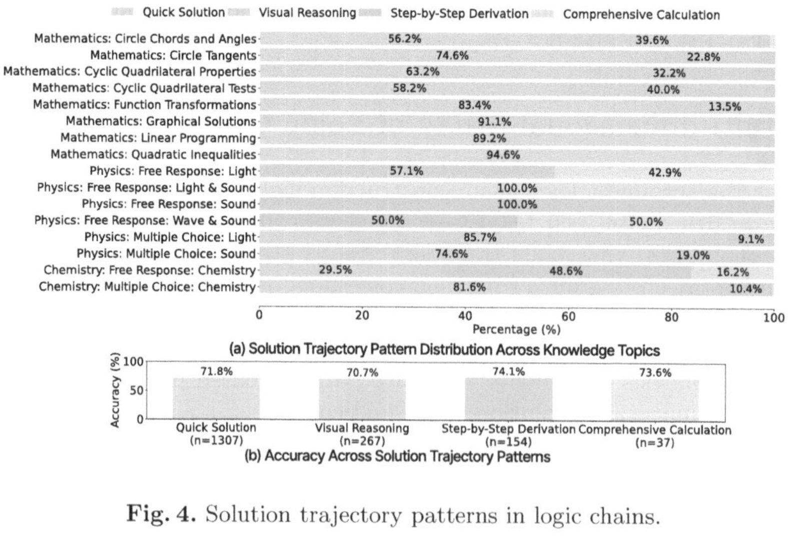

Fig. 4. Solution trajectory patterns in logic chains.

Findings. To evaluate the effectiveness of different solution trajectory patterns, we analyze: (1) knowledge topics and question types derived from the question information, and (2) solution accuracy based on educators' grading in the marking platform. Through a comprehensive analysis of these metrics across different solutions trajectory patterns (see Fig. 4), we identify several key findings:

Trajectory Patterns Correspond to Knowledge Topics and Question Types. Students demonstrate distinct problem-solving preferences across various knowledge topics and question types as shown in Fig. 4(a). In geometry-related content like circle chords and angles and cyclic quadrilateral tests, which are visual and spatial, students tend to use visual reasoning in over 20% of solutions. For algebraic topics such as function transformations and graphical solutions, with numerical and symbolic nature, students predominantly prefer quick solution methods, making up over 80% of solutions. Regarding question types, in free-response questions that demand detailed explanations, students are more inclined to use step-by-step derivation and comprehensive calculation, with the combined proportion of these two methods exceeding 60% across knowledge topics. In contrast, quick solution methods dominate in multiple-choice questions, with each method exceeding 60% of responses. These patterns suggest that students adaptively select solution methods based on both the inherent nature of knowledge topics and the specific requirements of question formats.

Solution Complexity Does Not Guarantee Accuracy. We find that extensive solution patterns do not necessarily lead to higher accuracy (see Fig. 4(b)). While step-by-step derivations (10–15 trajectory groups) show the highest accuracy at 74.1%, this moderate-complexity approach was only chosen in 154 problem-solving processes. In comparison, quick solutions, which involve just 2–4 trajectory groups with minimal calculations, appear in 1,307 processes and achieve a comparable 71.8% accuracy. Visual reasoning with 5–9 trajectory groups (70.7%, n = 267) and comprehensive calculations involving over 15 trajectory groups(73.6%, n = 37) show similar performance levels. This suggests that effective problem-solving depends on finding an appropriate balance between detail and conciseness, rather than simply maximizing or minimizing solution trajectories.

5.2 Time Dimension

Experiment Design. To deeply understand students' time management during examinations, we first define time allocation patterns as clusters of similar temporal organizations within logic chains for individual students throughout an entire exam. Then, we conduct a cluster analysis of examination time distribution data from 37 completed test papers, which includes several temporal features: average time and standard deviation of thinking gaps and writing durations, exam time management allocations (average time spent during the first and final thirds of the examination), and answer sequence characteristics (reverse order answering ratio). Following the same clustering approach described in Sect. 5.1, we categorize students into three typical time allocation patterns:

- *Quick-Low-Accuracy*: Characterized by quick writing speeds (avg. 12.1 s) with long gap times (avg. 95.8 s) and lowest accuracy (45%). Notable for their reverse order answering ratio of 5.3%.

- *Quick-High-Accuracy*: Displaying quick writing speeds (avg. 12.7 s) with shortest gap times (avg. 47.2 s) and good accuracy (65.5%). Most time-efficient among all clusters with the lowest total solution time (avg. 59.8 s).
- *Slow-High-Accuracy*: Showing longer writing times (avg. 42.8 s) with long gap times (avg. 106.6 s) but highest accuracy (70.3%). Characterized by significant deceleration, with late-stage average time (avg. 249.4 s) substantially higher than early stage (avg. 94.3 s).

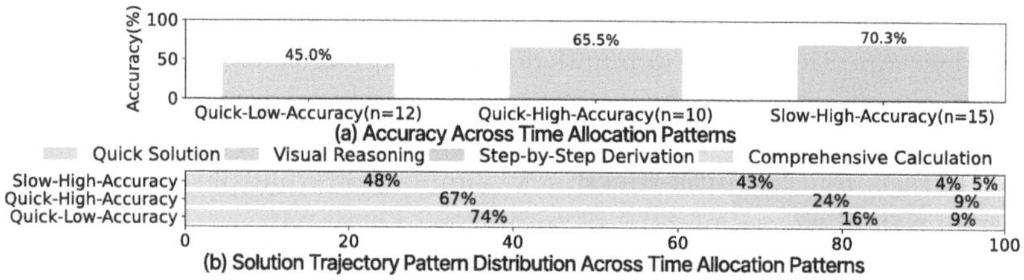

Fig. 5. Time allocation patterns across accuracy and solution trajectory patterns.

Findings. To identify personalized cognitive patterns in time management, we compare time allocation patterns with both answer accuracy and solution trajectory patterns (derived following Sect. 5.1), as illustrated in Fig. 5.

Gap Time Serves Different Cognitive Functions. As shown in Fig. 5 (a), distinct gap time patterns across clusters reveal their different roles: the quick-low-accuracy group's long gaps (95.8 s) coupled with their low accuracy (45%) may indicate difficulty in problem comprehension despite the extended thinking time, while the slow-high-accuracy group's extended gaps (106.6 s) likely reflect deeper analytical processing, contributing to their superior accuracy (70.3%). The quick-high-accuracy group's shorter gaps (47.2 s) combined with good accuracy (65.5%) suggest efficient information processing and decision-making capabilities, demonstrating that longer thinking time does not necessarily translate to better performance.

Guiding Students Toward Structured Reasoning is Essential. As illustrated in Fig. 5(b), there are distinct differences in solution approaches across student groups. The quick-low-accuracy group heavily relies on quick solutions (74%), which may contribute to their lower accuracy (45.0%). In contrast, the quick-high-accuracy and slow-high-accuracy groups employ step-by-step derivations more frequently (24% and 43% respectively), achieving notably better results (65.5% and 70.3% accuracy respectively). These findings suggest that encouraging students to spend time identifying key information through highlighting and formulating equations can be beneficial. Particularly, quick-low-accuracy students should be guided to reduce their over-reliance on quick solutions in favor of more systematic approaches, while quick-high-accuracy students could benefit from increased use of step-by-step derivation strategies.

5.3 Course Dimension

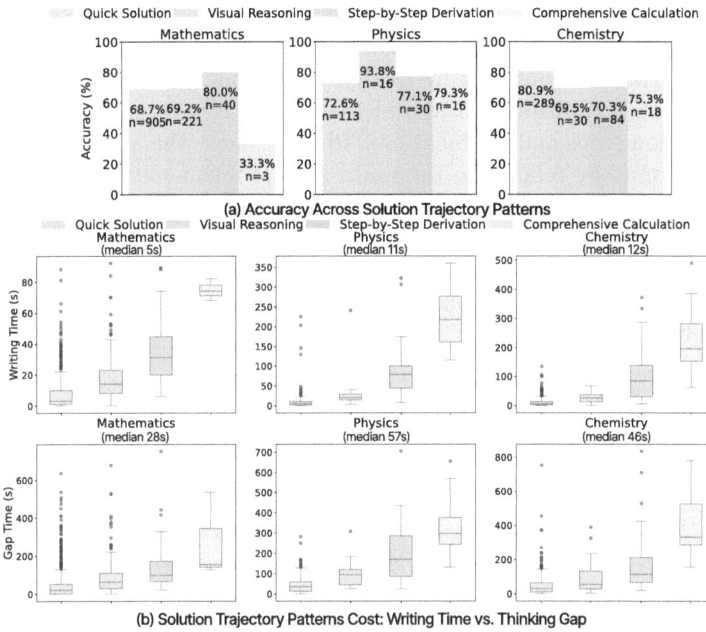

Fig. 6. Solution trajectory patterns across courses: accuracy and time allocation.

Findings. Through a systematic comparison of solution trajectory patterns across different subjects, as shown in Fig. 6, we identify differences in answer accuracy, writing duration, and thinking gap (as defined in Sect. 4.1).

Subject Characteristics Influence Problem-Solving Strategies and Habits. The knowledge structures of different subjects determine their suitable problem-solving strategies (see Fig. 6(a)). Mathematics, with its strict logical nature, is best approached through step-by-step derivation, achieving an average accuracy of 80%. Physics, which involves abstract concepts, benefits from visual reasoning, with this method yielding a high accuracy of 93.8%. Chemistry, characterized by its diverse and complex topics, sees the greatest advantage in quick solution approaches, with an accuracy rate of 80.9%. However, students' actual problem-solving habits do not always align with the optimal strategies. For instance, in mathematics, students tend to favor quick solutions (n = 905), but this approach often results in lower accuracy. Conversely, in physics (n = 113) and chemistry (n = 289), students are more inclined to adopt slower problem-solving strategies. Therefore, students should adjust their problem-solving habits according to the characteristics of each subject to avoid the negative impact of rigid habits on problem-solving effectiveness.

Each Subject Has Its Unique Time Management Pattern. As shown in Fig. 6(b), mathematics typically has a short writing time (median 5 s) and a relatively long thinking time (median 28 s), while physics has a writing time of 11 s and a thinking time of 57 s, and chemistry has a writing time of 12 s and a thinking time of 46 s. Given that all math questions are multiple-choice, answers are relatively concise, contributing to shorter writing times. Physics and chemistry include both multiple-choice and free-response questions, requiring more detailed solution steps and explanations. Physics shows the longest thinking gap (57 s), which may be related to the multi-step problem-solving processes often required in physics problems. Overall, the median of the thinking gap is 4–5 times that of the writing time, indicating a cognitive pattern where analysis and planning dominate the solution process. Notably, quick solutions in all subjects show scattered time distributions, reflecting the inherent instability of rapid problem-solving methods.

6 Discussion

Implication. Our study offers implications across three dimensions:

Cognitive Diagnosis Dimension. Based on our dataset of handwriting trajectories in Sect. 3, we used CogChain to generate logic chain visualizations (Sect. 4). Through this analysis, we identified students' cognitive patterns, including problem-solving strategies and time allocation patterns (Sect. 5). These findings help educators analyze students' problem-solving processes. The cognitive pattern features provide data-driven support for intelligent question bank systems to better assess and adapt to students' learning needs.

Learning Strategy Dimension. Through the analysis of problem-solving data (Sect. 5), we identified significant individual differences in thinking time allocation, solution selection, and solution accuracy. We constructed comprehensive student cognitive profiles by analyzing trajectory patterns across knowledge points (Sect. 5.1), examination time management (Sect. 5.2), and cross-subject strategy adaptations (Sect. 5.3). These profiles provide students and educators with insights to make informed decisions about learning strategies.

Subject-Specific Cognitive Dimension. Our analysis (Sect. 5.3) reveals distinct cognitive patterns across subjects. Mathematics learning requires systematic logical derivation and involves longer reflection times for conceptual understanding. Physics benefits from graphical reasoning approaches combined with logical thinking, while chemistry favors efficient problem-solving strategies with concise solution methods. With data from a larger sample across multiple institutions and regions, these findings could be further validated to inform textbook development for enhanced thinking skill guidance and examination design with better-aligned question types and time allocations.

Limitations and Future Work. Our research also has several limitations, with opportunities for future work.

Dataset. The dataset in Sect. 3 used in this study is limited in both size and diversity, as it focuses only on science subjects (Physics, Chemistry, and Mathematics) from a single class of students. This narrow scope may not fully reflect the diversity of student populations across different academic streams, socioeconomic backgrounds, and learning needs. Future research could expand the analysis to encompass a wider variety of subjects, student demographics, and long-term studies to track individual performance trajectories over time.

MLLMs Integration. While CogChain effectively analyzes students' problem-solving patterns, current MLLMs primarily rely on surface-level pattern matching, which limits their ability to grasp deep reasoning and detect conceptual errors [21,22]. Challenges remain in comprehending complex reasoning and generating adaptive feedback. Future research will focus on enhancing CogChain's capacity to model intricate cognitive processes, integrating more refined learning behavior databases, and advancing personalized AI-driven support [23].

Acknowledgments. This paper is supported by NSF of China (62402409), Guangdong provincial project 2023CX10X008, Guangzhou Municipality Big Data Intelligence Key Lab (2023A03J0012), Guangdong Basic and Applied Basic Research Foundation (2023A1515110545), Guangzhou Basic and Applied Basic Research Foundation (2025A04J3935), and Guangzhou-HKUST(GZ) Joint Funding Program (2025A03J3714).

References

1. Akben, N.: Effects of the Problem-posing approach on students' problem solving skills and metacognitive awareness in science education. Res. Sci. Educ. **50**(3), 1143–1165 (2020)
2. Arnold, I.J.: Do examinations influence student evaluations? Int. J. Educ. Res. **48**(4), 215–224 (2009)
3. Bhutoria, A.: Personalized education and Artificial Intelligence in the United States, China, and India: A systematic review using a Human-In-The-Loop model. Comput. Educ. Artif. Intell. **3**(100068), 1–18 (2022)
4. Bridgwood, M.: Guidelines for communication and engineering problem solving at the basic level. IEEE Trans. Prof. Commun. **42**(3), 156–165 (1999)
5. Chaudhury, R., Chilana, P.K.: Designing visual and interactive self-monitoring interventions to facilitate learning: insights from informal learners and experts. IEEE Trans. Visual Comput. Graphics **31**(2), 1542–1556 (2025)
6. Cho, Y.I., Altayeva, A.B.: Android-based E-board smart education platform using digital pen and dot pattern. Int. J. Fuzzy Logic Intell. Syst. **15**(4), 260–267 (2015)
7. Cirillo, M., Hummer, J.: Competencies and behaviors observed when students solve geometry proof problems: an interview study with smartpen technology. ZDM - Math. Educ. **53**(4), 861–875 (2021)
8. Docktor, J.L., Dornfeld, J., Frodermann, E., Heller, K., Hsu, L., Jackson, K.A., Mason, A., Ryan, Q.X., Yang, J.: Assessing student written problem solutions: a problem-solving rubric with application to introductory physics. Phys. Rev. Phys. Educ. Res. **12**(1), 1–18 (2016)

9. Geraldi, J., Lechter, T.: Gantt charts revisited: a critical analysis of its roots and implications to the management of projects today. Int. J. Manag. Proj. Bus. **5**(4), 578–594 (2012)
10. Guo, P., Shao, J., Ji, J., Pan, L., Pu, H., Pu, R.: Application status and prospect of dot matrix digital pen. In: Yu, Z., Patnaik, S., Wang, J., Dey, N. (eds.) Advancements in Mechatronics and Intelligent Robotics. pp. 545–549. Springer (2021)
11. Guruloo, T.N.M., Osman, K.: Beyond Pen and Paper: Understanding the Landscape of Digital Assessment in Stem Higher Education. In: Lecture Notes in Educational Technology, vol. Part F3676, pp. 177–197. Springer (2024)
12. Han, A., Zhou, X., Cai, Z., Han, S., Ko, R., Corrigan, S., Peppler, K.A.: Teachers, parents, and students' perspectives on integrating generative AI into elementary literacy education. In: Proceedings of the CHI Conference on Human Factors in Computing Systems, pp. 1–17. ACM (2024)
13. Islam, M.S., Doumbouya, M.K.B., Manning, C.D., Piech, C.: Handwritten code recognition for pen-and-paper CS Education. In: Proceedings of the Eleventh ACM Conference on Learning @ Scale, pp. 200–210. ACM (2024)
14. Jovanovic, M., Vukicevic, M., Milovanovic, M., Minovic, M.: Using data mining on student behavior and cognitive style data for improving e-learning systems: a case study. Int. J. Comput. Intell. Syst. **5**(3), 597 (2012)
15. Labahn, G., Lank, E., MacLean, S., Marzouk, M., Tausky, D.: MathBrush: a system for doing math on pen-based devices. In: 2008 The Eighth IAPR International Workshop on Document Analysis Systems, pp. 599–606. IEEE (2008)
16. Li, B., Luo, Y., Chai, C., Li, G., Tang, N.: The dawn of natural language to sql: are we fully ready? Proceedings of the VLDB Endowment **17**(11), 3318–3331 (2024)
17. Li, W., Hilton, E., Hammond, T., Linsey, J.: Persketchtivity: An Intelligent Pen-Based Online Education Platform for Sketching Instruction. In: Electronic Visualisation and the Arts, pp. 1–9 (2016)
18. Liang, Z., Sha, L., Tsai, Y.S., Gašević, D., Chen, G.: Towards the automated generation of readily applicable personalised feedback in education. In: Proceedings of the 25th International Conference on Artificial Intelligence in Education, AIED 2024, pp. 75–88. Springer Nature Switzerland (2024)
19. Liu, J., Huang, Z., Xiao, T., Sha, J., Wu, J., Liu, Q., Wang, S., Chen, E.: SocraticLM: Exploring socratic personalized teaching with large language models. In: The 38th Annual Conference on Neural Information Processing Systems (2024)
20. Liu, X., et al.: A survey of NL2SQL with large language models: Where are we, and where are we going? (2025). https://arxiv.org/abs/2408.05109
21. Liu, X., Shen, S., Li, B., Tang, N., Luo, Y.: Nl2sql-bugs: A benchmark for detecting semantic errors in nl2sql translation. arXiv preprint arXiv:2503.11984 (2025)
22. Luo, T., et al.: nvbench 2.0: A benchmark for natural language to visualization under ambiguity (2025). https://arxiv.org/abs/2503.12880
23. Shen, L., Li, H., Wang, Y., Xie, X., Qu, H.: Prompting Generative AI with Interaction-Augmented Instructions. In: Extended Abstracts of the CHI Conference on Human Factors in Computing Systems, CHI EA '25, pp. 1–9. ACM (2025). https://doi.org/10.1145/3706599.3720080
24. Shen, S., Lu, S., Shen, L., Sheng, Z., Tang, N., Luo, Y.: Ask humans or ai? exploring their roles in visualization troubleshooting. arXiv preprint arXiv:2412.07673 (2024)
25. Siddiqui, A.T., Muntjir, M.: An approach to smart study using pen and paper learning. Int. J. Emerg. Technol. Learn. **12**(05), 117 (2017)
26. Tang, N., Yang, C., Fan, J., Cao, L., Luo, Y., Halevy, A.Y.: Verifai: Verified generative AI. In: CIDR. www.cidrdb.org (2024)

27. Van Mechelen, M., et al.: Emerging Technologies in K-12 Education: A Future HCI Research Agenda. ACM Trans. Comput.-Hum. Interact. **30**(3), 1–40 (2023)
28. Walny, J., Lee, B., Johns, P., Henry Riche, N., Carpendale, S.: Understanding pen and touch interaction for data exploration on interactive whiteboards. IEEE Trans. Visual Comput. Graphics **18**(12), 2779–2788 (2012)
29. Wang, J.S., Chuang, F.C.: An accelerometer-based digital pen with a trajectory recognition algorithm for handwritten digit and gesture recognition. IEEE Trans. Industr. Electron. **59**(7), 2998–3007 (2012)
30. Wang, Y., Chiew, V.: On the cognitive process of human problem solving. Cogn. Syst. Res. **11**(1), 81–92 (2010)
31. Yan, Y.: Analysis of Teachers' and Students' Technology Application Behaviors in a Smart Paper-Pen Environment. In: Proceedings of the 2023 6th International Conference on Educational Technology Management, pp. 42–48. ACM (2023)
32. Yang, Q., Zhan, Z., Du, X.: A Learning Engagement Analysis Model for Assignments based on Dot Matrix Pen Technology. In: Proceedings of International Conference on Education and Multimedia Technology. pp. 90–96. ACM (2022)

Supporting Teachers Through AI-Augmented Web Search for Educational Resource Discovery

Ratan J. Sebastian[1,2(✉)] and Anett Hoppe[1,2,3]

[1] L3S Research Center, Leibniz University Hannover, Hannover, Germany
Ratan.Sebastian@tib.eu
[2] TIB – Leibniz Information Centre for Science and Technology, Hannover, Germany
[3] University of Marburg and Hessian.AI (Hessian Center for Artificial Intelligence), Marburg, Germany

Abstract. While educational repositories offer specialised metadata, teachers prefer general-purpose web search engines due to better results and familiar interfaces. But web search engines do not surface the educationally relevant information required for effective resource evaluation. This creates a key problem: integrating educational information into web search without disrupting existing workflows. Through a design study, we investigated how AI-enhanced interfaces can support teacher-AI collaboration in resource selection. After observing current search practices (N = 9), we identified opportunities for AI assistance and developed a browser extension to augment web search interfaces with adaptive educational summaries. We designed the interface through an iterative refinement stage with four participants, followed by a final evaluation using think-aloud protocols, search logs, questionnaires and semi-structured interviews (N = 8). Our evaluation revealed some guidelines for teacher-AI educational partnerships in search: a.) interfaces should support a two-stage decision process combining quick metadata-based decisions followed by detailed pedagogical assessment b.) pedagogical details must be presented selectively to balance insight with cognitive load, and c.) interfaces must support customisation as teachers have distinct resource evaluation approaches. These findings could inform the design of AI assistance systems that complement teacher expertise and fit into their existing workflows.

Keywords: Educational resource discovery · Search interfaces · Teacher-AI collaboration · Human-AI partnership

1 Introduction

Teachers increasingly rely on web resources for lesson planning and classroom materials, with generic search engines like Google serving as a primary tool for discovering educational content [3,11]. While specialised educational repositories with detailed metadata and filtering options exist, teachers predominantly prefer

A. I. Cristea et al. (Eds.): AIED 2025, LNAI 15877, pp. 236–250, 2025.
https://doi.org/10.1007/978-3-031-98414-3_17

general-purpose search interfaces due to better results [11] and familiarity [3]. However, these interfaces fail to surface critical educational information that teachers need to effectively evaluate resources [16,23].

This challenge represents an opportunity for AI assistance explored in this work: How can generic search interfaces be augmented to provide educationally relevant information within existing processes? Studies have shown that teachers reject advanced technical features that do not align with their established decision-making patterns [4], and resist systems that attempt to replace rather than augment teacher judgement [7]. Bringing together work on general search processes [9] with work on teachers' relevance and quality judgements [16,23], we developed and evaluated a browser extension (LessonLens) to augment web search interfaces with the goal of helping teachers' existing relevance judgement making behaviours rather than replacing them.

First, we conducted an observational study with nine participants to make sure that we design toward actual teachers' needs. Based on these insights, we developed interface elements that summarise entire search engine result pages (SERPs) as well as individual search results in ways that are specifically useful to teachers' relevance judgements. We first remediated initial usability issues in tests with four participants; then performed a more systematic qualitative evaluation using triangulated data from think-aloud protocols, questionnaires, and semi-structured interviews with eight participants.

Our studies revealed three principles for designing AI assistance systems that complement teacher expertise: a.) interfaces should support a two-stage decision process combining quick metadata-based relevance judgements followed by a detailed assessment of pedagogical properties, b.) simple visualisations with confidence indicators increase trust compared to complex displays, and c.) significant variation in feature usage demonstrates the necessity of user control. These findings provide crucial insights for developing AI systems that enhance rather than replace teacher judgement in educational resource selection.

2 Related Work

In this section, we present salient work from three areas related to AI-enhanced search interfaces for teachers. First, we examine teachers' information-seeking behaviours and resource evaluation practices. Then we survey work on teacher-AI partnerships to identify design principles in this field. Finally, we cover work on search interface interaction models and designs for search systems that have been shown to be useful for other kinds of users.

2.1 Teacher Information Seeking and Resource Evaluation

Teachers' search activities occur within broader professional contexts – teachers might be searching for resources to use in the classroom or for professional development [2]. In information retrieval terms, their search tasks are on a spectrum between goal-oriented, "lookup" and open-ended, "exploratory" tasks [22]. When designing a search tool both kinds of tasks need to be examined.

Research shows that teachers predominantly rely on generic web search engines over specialised educational repositories for finding resources [3] for teaching. We have limited information about their behaviour while using these search engines. Little is known about the characteristics of keyword selection and query refinement patterns throughout search sessions.

When it comes to evaluating the results of a search, Zimmerman et al. [25] found that actual content quality was rarely evaluated (13% of 77 pre-service teachers). A potential reason is that actual content quality is a complex multidimensional evaluation that imposes high cognitive load [23]. Supporting AI systems could analyse and surface the most salient content features, allowing teachers to make more informed quality judgements.

Previous approaches have tried displaying educational metadata alongside search results [3], which teachers appreciated. However, such approaches face challenges due to scarce and non-standardised metadata [20].

Other work tries to identify quality and relevance criteria used by teachers. Reitsma et al. [16] identified nine alignment criteria for K-12 teaching, including factors like motivation, concept coverage, and grade-level appropriateness. A meta-analysis [23] determined top quality dimensions for educational web resources. Both these works examined relevance or quality judgements in isolation, outside the context of a search task or interactive search session.

2.2 Human-AI Partnership in Educational Settings

Research shows that successful AI tools in education must work within teachers' existing practices [7] and utilise teachers' feedback in development [4]. Studies have found that teachers reject technically advanced features that do not align with their established decision-making patterns [4]. This resistance extends to automated systems that attempt to replace rather than augment teacher judgement [7].

Van Leeuwen et al. [8] provide a three-layer framework for understanding how teachers interact with educational technology: core use phases (awareness, interpretation, enactment), complex teacher characteristics (pedagogical knowledge, professional routines, data literacy), and general teacher characteristics (demographics, technical skills). We use this framework to examine how teachers interact with our search augmentation (becoming aware of AI features, interpreting additional information, incorporating it into relevance judgements) and how these interactions vary based on teachers' complex characteristics.

2.3 Search Interactions and Interface Design

A framework of information search behaviour guides our exploration of possible interface augmentations: The Complex Searcher Model (CSM) [9] identifies three decision points during the search process: *Search Engine Result Page (SERP) level* (whether to continue examining a result page or try a different query), *Snippet level* (whether to click on a particular result), *Session level* (whether to end the search session). This informs the two kinds of search augmentations that we consider: augmentations that inform SERP-level decisions and ones that inform snippet-level decisions.

At the *SERP level*, users try to understand the information space as a whole and whether they should look deeper into the results. Interfaces like IntentRadar [18] and VisGets [6] have demonstrated how visualisations of multiple filters can help users understand and navigate complex information spaces. This informs our decision to use SERP-level visual summaries.

Previous work on the *presentation of individual search results* [10] found that while users prefer longer result summaries, increased length does not necessarily improve relevance judgements – suggesting a need for adapting the information presented to the current query. Syed et al. [21] have highlighted how abstractive snippets could enable this kind of adaptation of search results. In educational contexts, metadata have shown promise in supporting teacher decision-making [3]. Based on these findings, we focus on two approaches: static metadata-based result summaries, and Q&A style abstractive summaries that can surface fine-grained information based on the query.

3 Interface Design

Based on the reviewed related work, we identified the need to augment general-purpose search engines [3,11] with features that help teachers make decisions at both the SERP and snippet levels [6,9,18]. We implemented this in a browser extension called LessonLens. It includes SERP Overviews to help with SERP-level decisions and both Metadata and Task Summaries for result-level decisions which are detailed below in this section. The latter extends Metadata Summaries by implementing task-adapted summarisation, addressing the issue of varying relevance criteria by task identified in the related work [16,23]. We first conducted an observational study (Sect. 4) to understand what search behaviours could inform this task adaptation. We then iteratively refined the design elements before evaluating the final design with a within-subjects user study (Sect. 5).

SERP Overview. The SERP Overview (Fig. 1b&1c) aims to help teachers make decisions about search result sets and guide query reformulation. Technically, there were two constraints on this component: First, it must process and display information rapidly enough not to disrupt the natural search process [13]. Second, it must contain enough information to decide whether a result set should be further examined. Hence we needed to balance inference speed, and the utility of educational characteristics to be displayed. To implement this component effectively, we investigated: a.) key dimensions of educational content that support rapid decision-making (Sect. 4), and b.) visualisation approaches for quick overview assessment (Sect. 5).

Metadata Summaries. Metadata Snippets (Fig. 1a) augment search results with structured educational metadata extracted from resource content. The interface design is taken from prior work [3] however the content is implemented using a metadata extraction system rather than relying on often non-existent embedded metadata. Extraction was done using *gpt-4o-2024-08-06* with a prompt using the popular "Chain-of-thought prompting" technique [19]. Due to lack of space, a detailed report on this method is elided and curious readers are referred to the extensions' source code[1]. The attributes shown are the five most used LRMI attributes [20]. This aligns with Miller's findings [12] that humans process information most effectively when making simple binary or ternary decisions across multiple dimensions, rather than complex judgements on fewer dimensions.

Task Summaries. Task summaries (Fig. 1c) augment individual search results with abstractive summaries [21] of the resource content in order to highlight content that is useful to the teachers' current information need. Prior work has identified sub-dimensions of resource relevance [16] and shown their importance varies by search task. Further, teachers often only reuse parts of educational resources [5,17]. Hence, to provide effective task summaries, the system must identify the important relevance dimensions to the given search task (as expressed by the search query) and extract the resource information that addresses that dimension. The provided summary must adapt as information needs evolve throughout the search session. We again use *gpt-4o-2024-08-06* for information extraction with "Chain-of-thought" prompting [19]. As a prerequisite, we must understand how teachers express task-dependent information needs in search queries, and how these reveal pertinent relevance dimensions (Sect. 4).

To summarise, we implemented an extension with three types of search augmentations: SERP Overviews for to help teachers with SERP-level decisions and Metadata and Task summaries to help with result-level decisions. To implement SERP Overviews, we needed to gather what dimensions can and need to be visualised. To implement Task Summaries, we needed to understand how search queries can be used to adapt the presented summaries. How this was done is presented in the following section.

4 Study 1: Understanding Teacher Search Behaviour

We conducted an observational study to understand teachers' search strategies and evaluation criteria, which would guide our subsequent interface design.

4.1 Method

The initial study had nine participants (three in-service teachers, three teacher students, and three didactics PhD students) across Physics, Chemistry, and Mathematics. The participants performed six search tasks, including lookup and exploratory tasks. The tasks were designed in collaboration with subject experts to ensure realistic scenarios and constraints encountered by teachers in practice and are available in full here.

[1] https://github.com/rxvl-d/LessonLens.

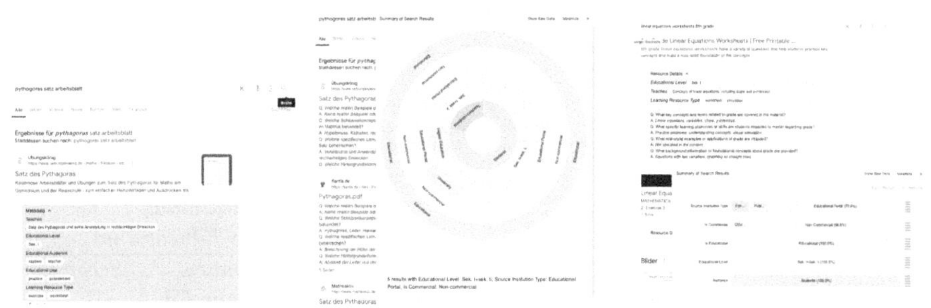

(a) Metadata Summary Design: Top 5 LRMI attributes with 2-3 values for each.

(b) Initial Design: SERP Overview with hierarchical Sunburst visualization, considered too complex by participants.

(c) Final Design: SERP Overview with stacked bar visualisation and Task Summary showing metadata (above) and adaptive Q&A (below).

Fig. 1. Screenshots of various components of LessonLens.

Data Collection : The YASBIL [1] logging framework was used to capture detailed interaction data including search queries and SERP interactions. Post-task questionnaires asked participants about search success and search strategies used. The terms of 97 unique search queries were manually annotated, coding them into class context (e.g., "grade 8", "high school"), publisher (e.g., "university", "government"), subject (e.g., "physics", "chemistry"), topic (e.g., "photosynthesis", "quadratic equations"), and material type terms (e.g., "worksheet", "experiment", "video"). An analysis of the co-occurrence patterns between these term types is shown in Fig. 2. The self-reported search strategies were also manually coded to identify relevance criteria that teachers mentioned.

4.2 Key Findings

Teachers used six key dimensions for rapid evaluation as shown in Fig. 3: Access Type, Educational Focus, Educational Level, Source Type, Target Audience, and Publisher Reputation. These aligned well with similar breakdowns of relevance criteria in other contexts [16,23,24]. We thus used these dimensions to structure the SERP overview.

Participants always included a "Topic" term in their queries which often implied educational level. The term that was most often added to the topic was the "Material Type" (video, worksheet, etc. - 25.31%) followed by "Class Context" (8th grade, etc. - 4.94%). This observed strategy informed our implementation of Task Summaries.

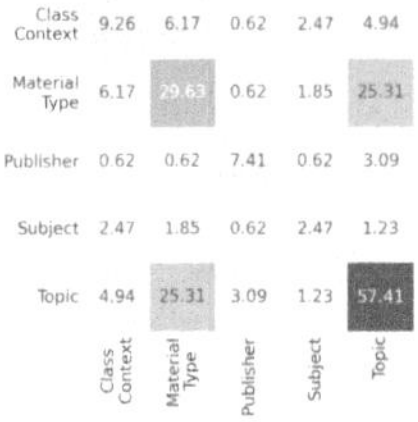

Fig. 2. Co-occurrence of query term types. Values are the percentage of times a query term co-occurs with another.

Dimension	Description/ *Values*
Access Type	Resource accessibility & cost considerations *Free, Commercial*
Educational Focus	Is resource designed for educational use *Educational, Non-Educational*
Educational Level	*Primary, Secondary, Higher Ed*
Source Type	*Government, Academic, Commercial, Individual*
Target Audience	*Teacher, Student, General Public*

Fig. 3. SERP Overview Dimensions

Resulting Implementation

SERP Overviews : To automatically classify search snippets along the dimensions in Fig. 3 we used a knowledge distillation methodology inspired by the FineWeb-Edu dataset [15]. We first used LLaMA (*meta-llama/Llama-3.3-70B-Instruct*) to annotate 500 resources from search results collected during this study. We validated the performance using 100 manual annotations to verify that it achieved F1 scores above 0.8. We then used all 500 LLaMA-annotated resources to train faster models: a BERT classifier for educational level where deeper semantic understanding was required, and SVM classifiers with TF-IDF features for other characteristics, using both word-based TF-IDF on the content and character n-gram TF-IDF on the URLs. This approach allowed us to quickly train light-weight models without expensive data collection.

Task Summary : We trained a Named Entity Recognition (NER) model to identify three types of entities in the query – "Material Types" (e.g., "video", "experiment"), "Class Context" (e.g., "middle school", "grade 8"), and "Topics" (e.g., "photosynthesis", "quadratic equations"). Based on the entities found, a heuristic prioritises dimensions of relevance distilled from the prior work [16,23]. For instance, queries containing "Material Types" prioritise the corresponding resource dimension (e.g., "video" prioritises the "Non-textuals" dimensions) along with "Concepts" and "Grade Level" dimensions. Topic-only queries prioritise "Concepts", "Background", and "Examples" dimensions. Each prioritised dimension is associated with template questions that are filled with the recognised entities (e.g., "How does this *video* demonstrate *photosynthesis*?"). The details of this method are available for inspection in the LessonLens repository.

5 Study 2: Evaluating the Design

Having designed and developed LessonLens based on observed teachers' search behaviour, we proceeded to systematically evaluate its effectiveness and utility in real-world contexts. The overall goal was to see if and how teachers would use LessonLens to help with resource judgement and selection. Particularly, we were interested in a.) whether the interface augmentations supported existing search behaviour, b.) whether our interface design balanced information access with cognitive load and c.) what impact search task context had on the usage of various features.

5.1 Method

We first did a usability test on our extension with four participants in line with Nielsen's recommendations [14]. We made changes to the design based on the feedback. We then proceeded to validate our final design with a within-subjects study with eight participants. Participants included four in-service teachers, three teacher students, and five educational researchers, all with STEM lesson planning experience. Each two-hour session comprised an introduction to the extension's features, a practice task and six experimental tasks (three lookup, three exploratory) under three conditions: (a) baseline (no extension features), (b) SERP Overview with Metadata Summaries, (c) and SERP Overview with Task Summaries. Condition order was randomised to account for learning effects. This study design allowed us to compare the impact of various LessonLens features for the same participant in various search task contexts.

This sample size achieved data saturation for our core observations. By the eighth participant, each interaction pattern or usability concern had been already demonstrated by at least four participants. While a greater sample size might reveal more nuanced patterns, the current participant pool provided sufficient evidence for our primary conclusions.

Data Collection. To mitigate biases in qualitative data collection, we triangulated data from think-aloud protocols (capturing in-moment behaviours), post-task questionnaires (providing structured metrics), and a final semi-structured interview (enabling holistic reflection and validation of findings).

Think-Aloud Protocols. Participants were asked to verbalise their thoughts about the interface elements and their relevance decisions. They were prompted if silent for more than 15 s. Audio recordings were transcribed using notta.ai with human verification.

Post-task Questionnaire. The questionnaire contained six Likert-scale items to evaluate specific interface features. "SERP Overview understanding" measured the utility of SERP Overviews to understanding the kind of results available on the search result page. "Query reformulation aid" measured its utility in query

Table 1. Responses to the Post-Task Questionnaires for usability testing and evaluation phases across conditions (N = 4, N = 8). Values are presented as Median(SD). These should be interpreted as descriptive statistics only. Metadata refers to the Metadata Summary + SERP Overview setting and Task refers to the Task Summary + SERP Overview setting.

Questionnaire Segment	Iterative Design Phase		Evaluation Phase	
	Metadata	Task	Metadata	Task
	M(SD)	M(SD)	M(SD)	M(SD)
SERP Overview Understanding	3.0(0.99)	3.0(0.89)	3.0(0.88)	3.0(1.02)
Query Reformulation Aid	3.0(0.76)	3.0(1.13)	3.0(1.23)	4.0(1.33)
Filtering Irrelevant Results	4.5(1.31)	4.0(0.89)	4.0(1.41)	4.0(0.80)
Finding Relevant Results	3.0(1.28)	3.5(1.51)	4.0(1.52)	4.0(0.89)
Summary Accuracy	4.0(0.52)	4.0(0.64)	5.0(0.64)	4.0(0.70)
Information Amount	2.0(1.55)	3.0(1.55)	3.0(1.21)	3.0(1.25)

reformulation. "Filtering irrelevant results" measured the use of Metadata or Task Summaries to avoid irrelevant results. "Filtering relevant results" measured the use of the same for selecting relevant results. "Summary accuracy" measured the participants' perception of the accuracy of the information presented in all augmentations. "Information Amount" measured how overwhelming the amount of information presented was (1 - too much information, 5 - just the right amount).

Final Interview. The semi-structured interview followed a protocol organised into five sections: i.) general impressions and usability, ii.) specific utility of, iii.) and comparisons between interface augmentations, iv.) integration into everyday workflow and v.) suggested improvements.

Data Analysis. *Think-aloud protocols & Final interview* transcripts were first segmented into logical utterances and given identifiers so that evidencing statements could be traced back to the transcript. A two-dimensional coding framework was developed based on what we were interested in observing. Along the "Statement Type" dimension, we categorised utterances into Search Strategy (ST), Relevance Judgements (RJ) and Interface Commentary (INT). Along the "Interface" dimension, we categorised utterances into those about SERP Overview (SO), Metadata Summary (MS) and Task Summary (TS)

Questionnaire responses were analysed using descriptive statistics, calculating medians and standard deviations for each Likert-scale item across both study phases and interface conditions. Due to small sample sizes, we focused on descriptive comparisons between phases and conditions rather than inferential statistics (Table 1).

5.2 Results

In this section we present our findings for each interface element focusing on how participants integrated these features into their search processes or rejected them in various contexts.

SERP Overview. was designed to provide teachers with a rapid understanding of result set characteristics and to support query reformulation. The initial implementation used a hierarchical sunburst visualisation (Fig. 1b). However, participants found this hierarchical visualisation cognitively demanding, with several noting they would dismiss it as "too complex" or "distracting." While some participants valued specific aspects, particularly for identifying gaps in the available resources on the result page, most engaged with single dimensions rather than performing the intended multi-dimensional analysis.

These findings prompted a shift from the hierarchical visualisation to a simpler stacked bar (Fig. 1c) representation. Participants particularly valued specific dimensions of the overview, with Educational Level and Access Type summaries were cited as aids in reformulation decisions.

The appearance of the SERP Overview on load of the SERP had a negative effect on participants since it recalled annoying popups. Based on this finding, the tool was altered to allow participants to turn it off. We then observed that participants would turn it off by default and only turn it on in search tasks where they were repeatedly getting irrelevant results.

Metadata Summaries. were designed to support rapid assessment of individual results through standardised presentation of LRMI attributes. Participants intuitively integrated them into their scanning patterns. Participants particularly valued these summaries for quick filtering decisions. This observation aligned with questionnaire responses showing stronger utility for filtering out irrelevant results (median=4.5) compared to identifying relevant ones (3.0).

However, participants identified limitations in contexts where results shared similar metadata attributes. For instance, adding a term like "worksheet" to the query made the "Learning Resource Type" attribute largely the same across results and hence useless.

They also identified the coarseness of the presented metadata attributes as a limitation to their utility. For instance, the "Teaches" attribute only presented the topic of the resource at a very high level (e.g. "Pythagorean theorem and its application in right-angled triangles") when the teacher would need specifics like "introduces basic Pythagorean theorem proof", "practices finding missing sides in right triangles", or "applies theorem to real-world distance calculations".

Task Summaries. aimed to provide contextually relevant information through generated questions and answers about each resource. Initial participant feedback highlighted cognitive load concerns, noting dense information and lengthy reading times. However, during longer search tasks, participants began valuing the structured question-answer format as they grew familiar with recurring questions. Participants particularly appreciated the personalised summaries: "I liked the [Task Summary] because it was in a question and answer format and the questions were similar to questions I would ask myself."

To address cognitive load issues, we enhanced the Task Summaries by adding metadata above the Q&As. This allowed participants to use metadata for initial filtering while accessing the more detailed Q&A when needed. The redesigned summaries showed significant utility improvement. In most tasks the metadata was sufficient to make a good relevance judgement however when it proved to be too coarse, participants indicates a strong support for this hybrid approach. One participant explained, "So, I would just scroll through and I see, like, most results are worksheets and then there's this question about what the learning goals are and I could see easily if it aligned for 7th/8th students." This comment exemplifies the two-stage evaluation process: rapid filtering via metadata followed by deeper evaluation through targeted questions.

6 Discussion

Our analysis revealed distinct patterns in how teachers engaged with and valued different aspects of the search interface augmentations, yielding important insights for designing AI-assisted educational resource search.

Supporting Two-Stage Decision Making. Our findings demonstrated teachers' preference for a two-phase evaluation process. Metadata Summaries enabled initial filtering: "When I see it's mostly higher education resources, I know right away I need to change my search." However, these summaries proved less useful for detailed assessment, particularly in homogeneous result sets: "Once I've filtered down to worksheets for my grade level, the metadata all looks the same." For the second stage of detailed pedagogical evaluation, Task Summaries provided more useful information: "The questions about what specific experiments are included really helps me understand if it will work in my classroom." This two-stage approach aligned with teachers' natural workflow.

Balancing Information and Cognitive Load. The challenge of providing sufficient pedagogical detail while managing cognitive load emerged as a critical consideration. While Task Summaries offered valuable detailed insights, their density sometimes deterred engagement: "I found myself just looking at the titles when there was too much to read in the summaries." The Metadata Summaries' structured format enabled rapid scanning, but teachers noted limitations: "Once I've got the keywords right, these [metadata attributes] just tell me what I already know from looking at the results." This tension between detail and usability was particularly evident in the SERP Overview visualisation, where simpler representations proved more actionable than complex ones.

Supporting Customised Evaluation Approaches. Teachers demonstrated distinct preferences in how they evaluated resources, highlighting the importance of customisable interfaces. For some, Task Summaries' specificity was worth the additional cognitive effort: "The specific content questions help me choose between similar worksheets." Others preferred quick metadata-based filtering. Allowing teachers to control information density proved crucial for task-appropriate detail This variation in preferences and strategies highlights the importance of flexible interfaces that can adapt to different evaluation approaches and contexts.

Limitations. This exploratory design study was performed with a limited sample of STEM teachers, constraining the applicability of statistical analysis tools. While the rich qualitative data supports our findings, validation with a larger sample and quantitative criteria would yield more robust results. The 2-hour observation sessions revealed learning effects that warrant longer-term studies w.r.t. long-term adaptation patterns.

7 Conclusion

Our study demonstrates how AI-enhanced search interfaces can effectively support teachers in discovering and evaluating educational resources. We developed and evaluated a browser extension that provided SERP overviews to highlight educational characteristics of search results, and dual-layer Task Summaries to support both rapid filtering and detailed pedagogical assessment.

Our study suggests three guidelines for designing AI-assisted educational resource discovery: First, search augmentations should support teachers' progression from quick filtering to detailed evaluation - providing appropriate information at each stage rather than overwhelming them with details upfront. Second, simple, trustworthy information displays should take precedence over complex visualisations. Third, interfaces must remain flexible to accommodate diverse teaching contexts and preferences.

These insights suggest that effective AI tools should complement rather than reshape existing practices. By providing educationally-relevant information within familiar search interfaces, we can enhance teachers' resource discovery while respecting their professional judgement and established workflows.

Future work should explore these augmentations across a broader range of teaching contexts and longer periods of authentic lesson planning. Longitudinal studies could reveal how teachers integrate tools into their planning routines over full academic years. Additional research is needed to adapt the interface for different pedagogical approaches, i.e. how generated summaries could adapt to different teaching styles.

Acknowledgements. This work has been supported by the PhD training program LernMINT funded by the Ministry of Science and Culture, Lower Saxony, Germany.

References

1. Bhattacharya, N., Gwizdka, J.: YASBIL: yet another search behaviour (and) interaction logger. In: Diaz, F., Shah, C., Suel, T., Castells, P., Jones, R., Sakai, T. (eds.) SIGIR '21: The 44th International ACM SIGIR Conference on Research and Development in Information Retrieval, Virtual Event, Canada, July 11-15, 2021, pp. 2585–2589. ACM, Canada (2021). https://doi.org/10.1145/3404835.3462800
2. Bortoluzzi, M., Marenzi, I.: Web searches for learning. how language teachers search for online resources. Lingue e Linguaggi **23**, 21–36 (2017). https://doi.org/10.1285/i22390359v23p21
3. Cortinovis, R., Mikroyannidis, A., Domingue, J., Mulholland, P., Farrow, R.: Supporting the discoverability of open educational resources. Educ. Inf. Technol. **24**(5), 3129–3161 (2019). https://doi.org/10.1007/S10639-019-09921-3
4. Cukurova, M., Miao, X., Brooker, R.: Adoption of artificial intelligence in schools: Unveiling factors influencing teachers' engagement. In: Wang, N., Rebolledo-Mendez, G., Matsuda, N., Santos, O.C., Dimitrova, V. (eds.) Artificial Intelligence in Education - 24th International Conference, AIED 2023, Tokyo, Japan, July 3-7, 2023, Proceedings. Lecture Notes in Computer Science, vol. 13916, pp. 151–163. Springer (2023). https://doi.org/10.1007/978-3-031-36272-9_13
5. Diekema, A.R., Olsen, M.W.: The notion of relevance in teacher information behavior. Proc. Am. Soc. Inf. Sci. Technol. **49**(1), 1–9 (2012). https://doi.org/10.1002/meet.14504901202
6. Dörk, M., Carpendale, S., Collins, C., Williamson, C.: Visgets: coordinated visualizations for web-based information exploration and discovery. IEEE Trans. Vis. Comput. Graph. **14**(6), 1205–1212 (2008). https://doi.org/10.1109/TVCG.2008.175
7. Holstein, K., Aleven, V.: Designing for human-ai complementarity in K-12 education. AI Mag. **43**(2), 239–248 (2022). https://doi.org/10.1002/AAAI.12058
8. van Leeuwen, A., Campen, C.A.N.K., Molenaar, I., Rummel, N.: How teacher characteristics relate to how teachers use dashboards: Results from two case studies in K-12. J. Learn. Anal. **8**(2), 6–21 (2021). https://doi.org/10.18608/JLA.2021.7325
9. Maxwell, D., Azzopardi, L.: Information scent, searching and stopping - modelling SERP level stopping behaviour. In: Pasi, G., Piwowarski, B., Azzopardi, L., Hanbury, A. (eds.) Advances in Information Retrieval - 40th European Conference on IR Research, ECIR 2018, Grenoble, France, March 26-29, 2018, Proceedings. Lecture Notes in Computer Science, vol. 10772, pp. 210–222. Springer (2018). https://doi.org/10.1007/978-3-319-76941-7_16
10. Maxwell, D., Azzopardi, L., Moshfeghi, Y.: A study of snippet length and informativeness: Behaviour, performance and user experience. In: Kando, N., Sakai, T., Joho, H., Li, H., de Vries, A.P., White, R.W. (eds.) Proceedings of the 40th International ACM SIGIR Conference on Research and Development in Information Retrieval, Shinjuku, Tokyo, Japan, August 7-11, 2017, pp. 135–144. ACM (2017). https://doi.org/10.1145/3077136.3080824

11. Medio, C.D., Limongelli, C., Marani, A., Taibi, D.: Retrieval of educational resources from the web: A comparison between google and online educational repositories. In: Herzog, M.A., Kubincová, Z., Han, P., Temperini, M. (eds.) Advances in Web-Based Learning - ICWL 2019 - 18th International Conference, Magdeburg, Germany, September 23-25, 2019, Proceedings. Lecture Notes in Computer Science, vol. 11841, pp. 28–38. Springer, Magdeburg, Germany (2019). https://doi.org/10.1007/978-3-030-35758-0_3
12. Miller, G.A.: The magical number seven, plus or minus two: Some limits on our capacity for processing information. Psychological review **63**(2), 81 (1956). https://psycnet.apa.org/record/1957-02914-001
13. Nielsen, J.: Usability engineering. In: Tucker, A.B. (ed.) The Computer Science and Engineering Handbook, pp. 1440–1460. CRC Press, Boca Raton, Florida (1997)
14. Nielsen, J., Landauer, T.K.: A mathematical model of the finding of usability problems. In: Arnold, B., van der Veer, G.C., White, T.N. (eds.) Human-Computer Interaction, INTERACT '93, IFIP TC13 International Conference on Human-Computer Interaction, 24-29 April 1993, Amsterdam, The Netherlands, jointly organised with ACM Conference on Human Aspects in Computing Systems CHI'93, pp. 206–213. ACM (1993), https://dl.acm.org/doi/abs/10.5555/2821575
15. Penedo, G., et al.: The fineweb datasets: Decanting the web for the finest text data at scale. In: Globersons, A., Mackey, L., Belgrave, D., Fan, A., Paquet, U., Tomczak, J.M., Zhang, C. (eds.) Advances in Neural Information Processing Systems 38: Annual Conference on Neural Information Processing Systems 2024, NeurIPS 2024, Vancouver, BC, Canada, December 10 - 15, 2024 (2024). http://papers.nips.cc/paper_files/paper/2024/hash/370df50ccfdf8bde18f8f9c2d9151bda-Abstract-Datasets_and_Benchmarks_Track.html
16. Reitsma, R., Marshall, B., Zarske, M.: Aspects of 'relevance' in the alignment of curriculum with educational standards. Inf. Process. Manage. **46**(3), 362–376 (2010). https://doi.org/10.1016/j.ipm.2009.08.006
17. Richter, T., Ehlers, U.D.: Barriers and motivators for using open educational resources in schools. Open ED 2010 Proceedings **1**, 12 (2010)
18. Ruotsalo, T., et al.: Interactive intent modeling for exploratory search. ACM Trans. Inf. Syst. **36**(4), 44:1–44:46 (2018). https://doi.org/10.1145/3231593
19. Schulhoff, S., et al.: The prompt report: A systematic survey of prompting techniques. CoRR abs/2406.06608 (2024). https://doi.org/10.48550/arXiv.2406.06608
20. Sebastian, R., Hoppe, A.: An updated analysis of learning resource metadata usage on the web. In: Antonacopoulos, A., Hinze, A., Piwowarski, B., Coustaty, M., Nunzio, G.M.D., Gelati, F., Vanderschantz, N. (eds.) Linking Theory and Practice of Digital Libraries - 28th International Conference on Theory and Practice of Digital Libraries, TPDL 2024, Ljubljana, Slovenia, September 24-27, 2024, Proceedings, Part II. Lecture Notes in Computer Science, vol. 15178, pp. 85–94. Springer, Ljubljanja, Slovenia (2024). https://doi.org/10.1007/978-3-031-72440-4_8
21. Syed, S., Chen, W., Hagen, M., Stein, B., Wachsmuth, H., Potthast, M.: Task proposal: Abstractive snippet generation for web pages. In: Davis, B., Graham, Y., Kelleher, J.D., Sripada, Y. (eds.) Proceedings of the 13th International Conference on Natural Language Generation, INLG 2020. pp. 237–241. Association for Computational Linguistics, Dublin, Ireland (2020). https://doi.org/10.18653/V1/2020.INLG-1.30
22. Tanni, M.: Teacher trainees' information acquisition in lesson planning. Inf. Res. **17**(3), 10 (2012). http://www.informationr.net/ir/17-3/paper530.html

23. Wetzler, P.G.: Characterizing the quality of resources in educational digital libraries with natural language processing and machine learning. Bull. IEEE Tech. Comm. Digit. Libr. **5**(3) (2009). https://bulletin.jcdl.org/Bulletin/v5n3/Wetzler/wetzler.html
24. Yalcinalp, S., Emiroglu, B.G.: Through efficient use of lors: prospective teachers' views on operational aspects of learning object repositories. Br. J. Educ. Technol. **43**(3), 474–488 (2012). https://doi.org/10.1111/J.1467-8535.2011.01212.X
25. Zimmermann, M., Engel, O., Mayweg-Paus, E.: Pre-service teachers' search strategies when sourcing educational information on the internet. Front. Educ. **7**, 976346 (2022). https://doi.org/10.3389/feduc.2022.976346

Training LLM-Based Tutors to Improve Student Learning Outcomes in Dialogues

Alexander Scarlatos[1(✉)], Naiming Liu[2], Jaewook Lee[1], Richard Baraniuk[2], and Andrew Lan[1]

[1] University of Massachusetts Amherst, Amherst, USA
{ajscarlatos,jaewooklee,andrewlan}@cs.umass.edu
[2] Rice University, Houston, USA
{nl35,richb}@rice.edu

Abstract. Generative artificial intelligence (AI) has the potential to scale up personalized tutoring through large language models (LLMs), with recent works focusing on training or prompting LLMs to follow effective pedagogical principles. However, these models are not trained to maximize student learning throughout the course of a dialogue, so may engage with students in a suboptimal way. We address this limitation by introducing an approach to train LLMs to generate tutor utterances that maximize the likelihood of student correctness, while still encouraging the model to follow good pedagogical practice. Specifically, we generate a set of candidate tutor utterances and score them using (1) an LLM-based student model to predict the chance of correct student responses and (2) a pedagogical rubric evaluated by GPT-4o. We then use the resulting data to train an open-source LLM, Llama 3.1 8B, using direct preference optimization (DPO). We show that tutor utterances generated by our model lead to significantly higher chances of correct student responses while maintaining the pedagogical quality of GPT-4o. We also conduct qualitative analyses and a human evaluation to demonstrate that our model generates high quality tutor utterances. (This work is partially supported by Renaissance Philanthropy via the learning engineering virtual institute (LEVI) and NSF grants 2118706, 2237676, and 2341948.) (Our code is available at https://github.com/umass-ml4ed/tutorbot-dpo.)

Keywords: Large Language Models · Math Education · Reinforcement Learning · Tutor-Student Dialogues

1 Introduction

Recent advances in generative artificial intelligence (AI), including large language models (LLMs), have opened new possibilities in education and in particular on scaling up personalization. One form of personalization that generative AI powers is interactive learning via *tutoring dialogues* between AI-powered tutors and students. These interactions have the potential to tailor instruction

A. I. Cristea et al. (Eds.): AIED 2025, LNAI 15877, pp. 251–266, 2025.
https://doi.org/10.1007/978-3-031-98414-3_18

to each student's needs and progress, while offering personalized feedback, all in real time, in a scalable way. Given the widespread success of human tutors for improving student outcomes [29], many recent works have developed LLM-based tutors, showing promise across various educational domains [25,31,32,38,41,47]. Many LLM-based tutors are even deployed in practice, such as Khan Academy's Khanmigo [21] and Carnegie Learning's LiveHint [4]. Several preliminary studies have shown that interacting with LLMs can increase student learning [49], although some have shown that students can develop an over-reliance on LLMs which negatively impacts their learning [23].

Many prior works have focused on improving LLMs' ability to follow effective tutoring principles, adapting them for the tutoring task that they are not pre-trained for. One approach, explored in [45], analyzes the decision-making process underlying human tutor utterances, showing that integrating expert decisions enhances LLM-based tutoring. Another study, [28], examines tutor moves in interactions with an LLM-powered simulated student agent, demonstrating that move annotation data contributes to better tutoring performance. Similarly, [43] investigates the role of AI roleplay in generating synthetic tutoring data and finds that fine-tuning LLMs on this data, along with human tutor-student interactions, significantly improves their pedagogical effectiveness. Moreover, [9] introduces the concept of tutor uptake—acknowledging student responses—as a valuable strategy for LLMs to adopt.

While these efforts offer valuable insights into how LLMs can emulate effective human tutoring strategies, the question remains whether such approaches truly maximize student learning outcomes. Rather, a data-driven approach, where student outcomes form a reward signal, could potentially lead to AI tutors that are more aligned with educational goals. Additionally, current approaches often rely on large proprietary LLMs, coming with many downsides; they are not fully controllable and cannot be easily customized, can be costly to use, and relinquish control of private student data. Therefore, developing effective AI tutors with smaller, open-source LLMs remains an important goal.

1.1 Contributions

In this paper, we propose a novel approach to train a small, open-source LLM to not only follow effective pedagogical principles, but directly optimize for student learning outcomes. Our method performs three key steps. First, at each dialogue turn, we gather multiple candidate tutor utterances from a variety of sources, including human tutors and LLMs with varying styles and sizes. Second, we evaluate each candidate utterance on two aspects: (1) whether it elicits a correct response in the next student turn, using a trained student model for dialogues to predict student behavior, and (2) whether it adheres to a set of effective pedagogical principles, using GPT-4o in a LLM-as-a-judge evaluation setup. Third, we contrast good candidate utterances with poor ones, and fine-tune Llama 3.1 8B [10] with offline Reinforcement Learning (RL), specifically Direct Preference Optimization (DPO) [34]. We demonstrate that our optimized LLM tutor significantly increases the likelihood of next turn student response correctness, while reaching comparable pedagogical quality to that of a much larger, proprietary LLM, GPT-4o [30]. Through qualitative analysis and human evaluation, we confirm that our approach produces high-quality tutor utterances and reveal emergent tutoring strategies that arise from our training approach.

We acknowledge up front that the most significant limitation of our work is that we do not experiment with real students. Since access to students at the scale necessary for our work is beyond our capability, we use a simulated student model instead. While we believe that our work is a reasonable starting point to train LLM-based tutors to maximize student outcomes, future work with real students in the loop is highly important. Therefore, to facilitate further research, we will publicly release our code and encourage researchers and practitioners with access to real-world tutoring dialogue settings to build on our work.

2 Related Work

AI Tutors in Dialogues. There is a long history of AI-based tutors in education that interact with students through dialogues. Early systems, such as Cognitive Tutors, construct cognitive models of students to provide targeted feedback [1]. AutoTutor engages students by asking targeted questions, and assesses student correctness using latent semantic analysis [14]. Why2-Atlas converts a student response to a proof, which it uses to identify misconceptions and guide a dialogue [44]. While these systems were often effective for improving student learning, they required significant engineering and had limited flexibility. In contrast, recent LLM tutors can more easily adapt to new contexts, interpret student responses, and cater personalized content towards the student. Several LLM tutors are implemented through refined prompt engineering [21], with some taking on specialized roles such as teachable agents [38] or "co-pilots" for human tutors [46]. Other works fine-tune LLM tutors to enhance the pedagogical capabilities over the base models. A common approach is to generate simulated dialogues, where the tutor utterances are constructed to follow good pedagogical practice, and fine-tune on those [39,43]. Several works also generate examples of low quality tutor utterances and use them as negative samples in DPO training to improve over fine-tuning [2,40].

Student Outcome Modeling. While there are many ways of measuring student outcomes, in this work we focus on the well-studied setting of *next item correctness*. Student modeling in this setting is typically handled by knowledge tracing (KT), where a binary correctness is predicted for the next item a student attempts based on the student's history so far [7]. KT models have used recurrent neural networks [33], self-attention networks [13], and, more recently, LLMs [8,27]. A recent work introduces LLMKT [36], an LLM-based model that predicts *next turn* student correctness in dialogues. Therefore, we leverage LLMKT to predict student outcomes in this work. Similar to our work, prior works have used RL to discover teaching policies with rewards derived from student models [3,16,35]. Another recent work used LLM estimates of student post-test scores to refine math worksheets [15]. To the best of our knowledge, our work is the first to use student performance estimates to improve tutoring in dialogues.

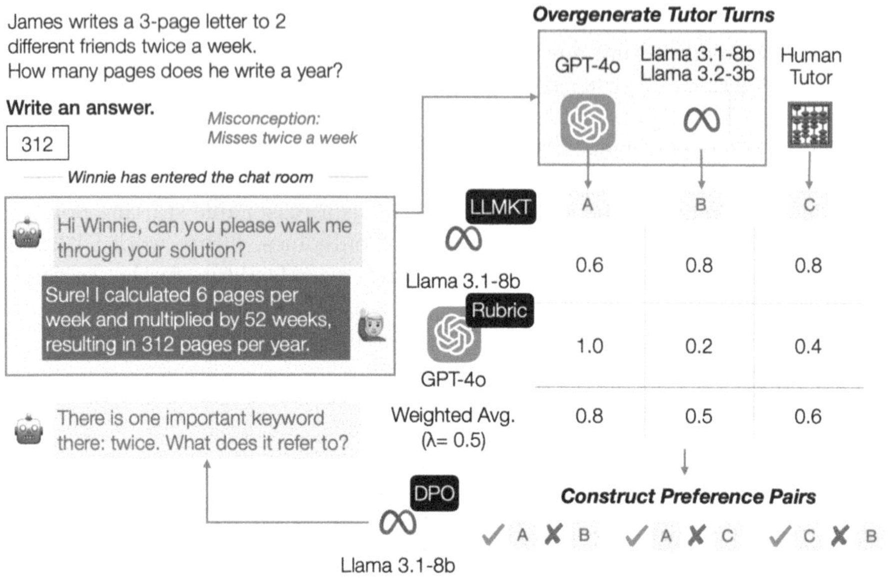

Fig. 1. An overview of our methodology for training LLMs to generate tutor utterances with the joint objective of maximizing student learning outcomes and following good pedagogical principles. *Human tutor* refers to tutor utterances in MathDial.

Evaluating Pedagogical Quality of LLMs. To validate LLM tutors, we need to be able to evaluate them along pedagogical measures. Typically, researchers construct a pedagogical *rubric*, which defines multiple properties that tutor utterances should follow. Rubric-based evaluation of generated utterances is then performed by human experts [18,43,45] or by LLMs [19,37]. In this work, we design a pedagogical rubric and primarily use LLMs to evaluate tutor utterances, but also humans at a smaller scale to ensure our results are reliable. Similar to [37], we also use LLM-assigned rubric scores to form DPO preference pairs.

3 Methodology

We now detail our methodology to generate tutor dialogue utterances to maximize student learning outcomes. Figure 1 shows an overview of our approach with an example, where the problem is from the MathDial [28] dataset. Before detailing each component, we define some key notations: a dialogue d consists of an alternating sequence of tutor and student turns, $d = (t_1, s_1, \ldots, t_M, s_M)$, where M is the number of turn pairs, indexed by m, and the textual content of each turn is the "utterance".

3.1 Student Outcome Prediction

We now detail the model we use for predicting student outcomes in dialogues. We leverage recent work on knowledge tracing (KT) in dialogues, LLMKT [36],

Table 1. Pedagogical evaluation criteria for tutor utterances in dialogues.

Criteria	Explanation
Accuracy	Ensuring the response does not contain false or misleading statements.
Progress	Determining whether the response helps the student move forward.
Guidance	1. Error identification: Correctly pinpoints the student's mistake.
	2. Strategic Hinting: New information or guidance for help.
	3. Withholding: Refrains from directly providing the final answer.
	4. Encouraging: Motivates the student to persist in their attempt.

an LLM-based model that predicts if a student will respond correctly to a tutor-posed task in their next turn, given dialogue history and the knowledge components (KCs) [6] embedded in a tutor turn. The model is highly accurate at predicting student correctness, achieving 0.76 AUC on the MathDial test set, making it a reliable automated source for estimating student outcomes.

In LLMKT, at the m-th dialogue turn for the student, the model analyzes the conversation history $t_{\leq m}, s_{<m}, \mathcal{C}_m$, which denote the tutor utterances up to and including this current turn, prior student turns, and the set of KCs involved in the tutor-posed task in the current turn, respectively. It estimates student knowledge levels on each KC, and combines these estimates to predict whether the student will respond to the tutor-posed task in the current turn correctly. Therefore, we leverage LLMKT as a *student simulator* and use it to evaluate whether a generated tutor utterance at a dialogue turn will elicit a correct response from the student.

3.2 Following Pedagogical Principles

In addition to promoting correct student responses, we also hand-craft a set of rubric items for effective pedagogical principles, listed Table 1. We then employ GPT-4o to assess how well the generated tutor utterances align with the rubric. By incorporating pedagogical evaluation aspects rather than focusing solely on correctness prediction, our approach discourages oversimplification of tutor utterances and instead encourages utterances that provide meaningful guidance.

Our evaluation draws inspiration from feedback assessment studies [18,19,42] and focuses on common errors made by LLMs when generating feedback for math problems [37]. The rubric evaluates generated tutor utterances on six granular items, each assigned a binary label, across three core aspects: *Accuracy*, *Progress*, and *Guidance*. Considering all aspects, we also have GPT-4o provide an *overall score* for the utterance on a 1–10 scale. Our prompt leverages chain-of-thought so that GPT-4o provides reasoning about the utterance before assigning its scores.

We include the human tutor utterance from MathDial in our prompt as a point of comparison, mainly to assist with evaluating *Accuracy*, which can be challenging [37]. We find the 1–10 scale works slightly better than simply averaging all the binary rubric items, possibly because it enables GPT-4o to decide which rubric items are more relevant given the context of the dialogue.

3.3 Preference Pair Construction

To create a dataset of preference pairs for DPO training, we collect candidate tutor utterances from four sources: (1) the human tutor utterances from the MathDial dataset, (2) utterances generated by GPT-4o, where the evaluation criteria (rubric and intending to elicit correct student responses) are included in the prompt, (3) utterances generated by Llama 3.1 8B using a generic prompt about behaving like a math tutor (without the rubric), and (4) utterances generated by Llama 3.2 3B using the same generic prompt. In general, method (2) contains high-quality tutor utterances that serve as positive examples that score high under our rubric. However, we found that in many cases (1) performs better for eliciting correct student responses due to the concise nature of the utterances. Utterances generated by (3) are a mix of high and low quality, while utterances generated by (4) are typically lower quality and serve as a source of negative examples for preference optimization. Prior work has shown diverse candidate quality, particularly negative examples, to improve DPO performance [37].

After evaluating each candidate using LLMKT and the rubric, we create a combined weighted score for a candidate tutor utterance at turn m:

$$s_m = \lambda \cdot y_m + (1 - \lambda) \cdot r_m,$$

where y_m is the probability of a correct student response predicted by LLMKT at this turn, and r_m is the overall rubric score at this turn normalized in $[0, 1]$. We adjust λ to balance the tradeoff between how much the generated utterances elicit correct student responses compared to how much they follow pedagogical practice. By default, we set $\lambda = 0.5$ to achieve a balance between these objectives; in our experiments, we show how varying λ affects the balance between both.

We then use the score s_m to construct preference pairs between candidate tutor utterances. We consider a candidate with score s_m^1 to be preferred over a candidate with score s_m^2 if the former is greater by some threshold, i.e., $s_m^1 - s_m^2 > \epsilon$. If the scores are within ϵ, we do not form a preference pair. In practice, we set $\epsilon = 0.1$ to achieve a balance where noisy preference pairs are excluded, but we retain enough data to sufficiently train the model, both of which have been shown to be important considerations for DPO [22].

3.4 Model Training

We train our model in a two-stage process: (1) distillation and (2) DPO. Distillation is a common way to enhance the capabilities of small LLMs by mimicking the behavior of much larger LLMs [48]. In our case, we fine-tune Llama 3.1 8B on candidate tutor utterances generated by GPT-4o. Through this distillation stage, we gain access to a *local* model that scores well on our pedagogical rubric.

We then use DPO and our preference pairs to further steer the distilled model towards effective tutoring. DPO trains an LLM by contrasting outputs in a preference pair given the same input prompt, using the following objective:

$$\mathcal{L}_{\text{DPO}}(\theta) = -\mathbb{E}_{(x,t_m^w,t_m^l)\sim\mathcal{D}}\left[\log\sigma\left(\beta\log\frac{\pi_\theta(t_m^w|x)}{\pi_{\text{ref}}(t_m^w|x)} - \beta\log\frac{\pi_\theta(t_m^l|x)}{\pi_{\text{ref}}(t_m^l|x)}\right)\right],$$

where t_m^w and t_m^l represent the preferred and unpreferred tutor utterances, respectively. x represents the input prompt, comprising an instruction, the context of the dialogue, and the dialogue history $t_{<m}, s_{<m}$. π_θ denotes the model being trained, π_{ref} represents a frozen reference model, and β is a hyperparameter that controls the divergence between the learned and reference policies.

In this work, we use the distilled model as the reference model π_{ref} and for initializing the weights of π_θ. We find the distilled model works much better than using the base Llama model, since the distilled model already performs better on the rubric. Additionally, we set $\beta = 0.1$, a relatively low value for DPO compared to a common value of $\beta = 0.5$. The low β value allows π_θ to diverge more from π_{ref}, which we find necessary to increase LLMKT's predictions of eliciting correct student responses in the next dialogue turn.

4 Experimental Settings

4.1 Dataset

We evaluate our framework using the MathDial dataset [28], which consists of tutoring dialogues focused on mathematics problems from GSM8K [5]. Each dialogue is centered around an incorrect student solution to the math problem, and the goal of the dialogue is for the tutor to guide the student to the correct solution by addressing their misconceptions. Tutors are role-played by crowd workers, while students are simulated by GPT-3.5. Despite only being half-authentic, MathDial is the largest publicly available one-on-one tutor-student math dialogue dataset to the best of our knowledge. To estimate correctness with LLMKT, which requires knowledge component labels at the current turn, we use the annotated knowledge components from the Dialogue KT version of the dataset [36] and filter out unlabeled turns.

We follow the original MathDial train/test split. After filtering, our test set has 588 dialogues with 3,101 tutor turns. We split the train set into a 80/20 train/validation split at the dialogue-level, resulting in 1,809/453 dialogues with 11,058/2,811 tutor turns. When creating our overgenerated tutor turn dataset for distillation and DPO training, we take a subset of the train/validation split to reduce labeling costs, resulting in 483/135 dialogues with 3,080/920 GPT-4o-generated tutor utterances for distillation and 9,662/3,095 preference pairs, with our default parameters of $\lambda = 0.5$ and $\epsilon = 0.1$, for DPO.

4.2 Baselines

We compare our preference-optimized LLM, which we refer to as **DPO**, with Llama 3.1 8B as the base model, against the following baselines: the **Base model** of Llama 3.1 8B prompted with our evaluation criteria (rubric and intending to elicit correct student responses); its supervised fine-tuned version on human tutor utterances in the original dataset, **SFT**; a fine-tuned version distilled from GPT-4o-generated utterances detailed above in Sect. 3.4, **Distill**; **GPT-4o**, the large, proprietary LLM, which is prompted with our evaluation criteria; and finally, the **Human Tutor** utterances from the original MathDial dataset.

4.3 Automated Metrics

We evaluate tutor utterances on both **student outcomes** and **pedagogical principles**. Student outcome prediction uses LLMKT to estimate the probability of a correct student response, averaged across turns. Evaluating how well the utterance follows the pedagogical principles will be reported in the same order as in Table 1, reporting scores for **Acc.** (Accuracy), **Prog.** (Progress), **Err.** (Error Identification), **Hint** (Strategic Hinting), **Wth.** (Withholding), and **Enc.** (Encouraging), along with an **Overall** score.

4.4 Model Parameters

We use the `meta-llama/Meta-Llama-3.1-8B-Instruct` model from Hugging Face [11] for all local experiments. To adapt the model, we use Low-Rank Adaptation (LoRA) [17] with a rank parameter of $r = 64$, scaling factor $\alpha = 32$, and a dropout rate of 0.05. We train using the AdamW optimizer, with a learning rate of 1×10^{-4} for distillation and 3×10^{-5} for DPO, with a linear warmup phase for the first 10% of training steps. We use an effective batch size of 64 with gradient accumulation, set weight decay to 1×10^{-2}, and set a gradient clipping maximum norm of 1.0. We evaluate the loss on the validation set after each epoch, and achieve the minimum validation loss after three epochs for distillation and after one epoch for DPO. At test time, we generate tutor utterances using greedy decoding. We conduct all experiments on NVIDIA RTX A6000 GPUs.

5 Experimental Results

5.1 Quantitative Results

Table 2 shows the results of tutor utterance generation on the MathDial test set, across all methods on the automated metrics. We observe that DPO significantly outperforms all other methods on student correctness prediction, improving over the next best method, GPT-4o, by 33%. This result shows that DPO training is necessary to generate tutor utterances that are more likely to achieve correct student responses, which cannot be achieved simply through prompting. Additionally, DPO achieves similar scores to GPT-4o on the pedagogical rubric, with both methods scoring very high on all rubric items and the overall score. This result shows that our DPO training pipeline can effectively bring the pedagogical ability of small, open-source LLMs with only 8B parameters to the level of very

Table 2. Tutor utterance evaluations for each method on the test set. The best result for each metric is in **bold** while the second best is underlined. DPO significantly outperforms all methods on improving student correctness predictions, and closely matches the performance of GPT-4o on the pedagogical rubric.

	Student Outcomes	Pedagogical Principles						
Method		**Acc.**	**Prog.**	**Err.**	**Hint**	**Wth.**	**Enc.**	**Overall**
Human Tutor	0.45	**0.99**	0.66	0.58	0.49	0.97	0.53	6.97
GPT-4o - Proprietary LLM								
Base Model	0.49	**0.99**	**0.97**	**0.92**	**0.96**	**0.99**	0.89	**9.40**
Llama 3.1 8B Instruct - Open-source LLM								
Base Model	0.43	0.82	0.69	0.70	0.64	0.94	0.62	7.20
SFT	0.47	0.86	0.32	0.23	0.21	0.90	0.31	4.73
Distill	0.47	0.95	0.92	0.90	0.91	**0.99**	0.82	8.93
DPO ($\lambda = 0.5$)	**0.65**	0.97	0.96	**0.92**	**0.96**	**0.99**	**0.92**	9.37

large, proprietary LLMs. Moreover, we see that DPO improves over distillation on almost all metrics, showing that DPO is necessary to achieve both objectives.

A notable observation is that human-written tutor utterances, while almost always accurate, score relatively low on most other rubric items. This result is not surprising since human tutors do not act according to our evaluation rubric; many of the human utterances are relatively short and simply ask the student to retry without giving guidance, and occasionally feature the tutor getting frustrated with the student. As a result, the SFT model, trained on human tutor utterances, does not score high on our rubric; the distilled model and even the base Llama model significantly outperform it on the rubric items.

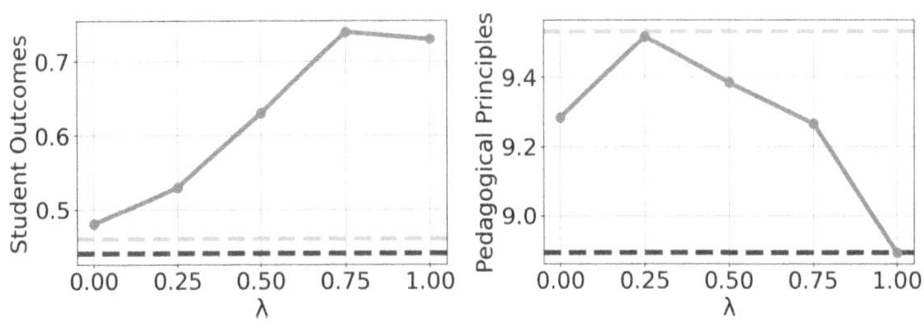

Fig. 2. Results of our experiment adjusting the value of λ in DPO training. Left: student correctness prediction changing with λ. Right: pedagogical rubric score changing with λ. We also show values for GPT-4o and the Distill model for comparison.

Student Outcomes vs. Pedagogical Principles We investigate how adjusting the value of λ can balance the two goals of maximizing student outcomes under LLMKT and following pedagogical principles. We vary the value of $\lambda \in \{0.00, 0.25, 0.50, 0.75, 1.00\}$, where larger values attribute more weight to the student correctness prediction objective, and evaluate on a subset of the data with 500 turn pairs. Figure 2 shows the result of this experiment. We see that, as expected, increasing λ from 0 to 1 generally increases student correctness prediction performance while generally decreasing the rubric score. Practitioners can get their desired balance by changing λ; for example, a value of around 0.5 to 0.75 can maintain a relatively high score on the pedagogical rubric while significantly improving performance on soliciting correct responses from students. Perhaps surprisingly, changing λ from 0.75 to 1.0 does not increase student outcome performance, while decreasing λ from 0.25 to 0.0 *decreases* pedagogical performance. This result implies that a small reward signal from correctness prediction may implicitly help pedagogical effectiveness, and vice versa.

Table 3. Comparing human tutor, GPT-4o, and DPO tutor utterances, on student outcomes (SO) and pedagogical principles (PP). Brown highlights the tutor-posed task. Some irrelevant text in the dialogue context has been removed for brevity.

	Problem		
Chloe bought chocolate-dipped strawberries at \$50 a dozen. She then sold them for \$30 for half a dozen. How much is Chloe's profit if she sold 50 dozens?			
	Dialogue History		
t_1	Hey Alejandra. If Chloe buys the strawberries at \$50 for 12 and sells them for \$30 for 6, how much profit would that be for one dozen?		
s_1	For one dozen, Chloe would make a profit of \$20, which is \$50 - \$30 = \$20.		
t_2	Remember that she's selling half a dozen for \$30. How many half dozen can she sell from each \$50 dozen she buys?		
s_2	She can sell two half dozen for each \$50 dozen she buys, so she can make a profit of \$60 from each \$50 dozen.		
	Next Tutor Turn (t_3) Candidates		
Method	**Tutor Utterance**	**SO**	**PP**
Human Tutor	Remember it's not \$60 profit, because they cost her to buy them. Try again.	0.33	4
GPT-4o	It looks like there's a misunderstanding in your calculations. Remember, Chloe's cost for half a dozen is \$25 (since \$50 per dozen divided by 2). She sells half a dozen for \$30, so her profit per half dozen is \$30 - \$25 = \$5. Try recalculating her total profit using this correct profit per half dozen.	0.59	**10**
DPO	It looks like there's a misunderstanding. If Chloe buys a dozen for \$50 and sells half a dozen for \$30, let's first find out how much she paid for half a dozen. If \$50 is for 12, how much is \$50 divided by 2?	**0.84**	**10**

5.2 Qualitative Analysis

We conduct a qualitative analysis of generated tutor utterances to investigate the strengths and weaknesses of our method, how it compares to baselines, and what types of patterns emerge in the model-generated text.

Table 3 shows an example dialogue context and tutor utterances from the human tutor, GPT-4o, and DPO. We see that the human tutor states that the student is not correct and prompts the student to try again, providing a subtle hint to focus on the cost of the dozen. However, this utterance neither gives LLMKT, the student model, any confidence in the student being able to answer correctly, nor follows strong pedagogical principles. GPT-4o guides the student toward correctly calculating the profit, but directly provides half of the solution in its hint, limiting deep student engagement. It also poses the challenging task of computing the total profit, which requires multiple calculation steps. Since the student is still struggling with unit conversion, LLMKT is not confident that the student will respond correctly. In contrast, our DPO-trained model provides an actionable hint for the student, following the rubric. It also poses the simpler task of asking the student to first find the cost of a half dozen, which is necessary for later steps. As a result, LLMKT is confident the student can respond correctly.

Overall, we find that our DPO-trained model excels at posing *concrete* tasks that are nontrivial, but more feasible for students compared to GPT-4o. We observe that the behavior of posing tasks this way is the primary way of achieving higher predictions for student correctness, and appears to be an emergent behavior of training on the LLMKT-derived scores. While the tasks sometimes only ask the student to perform simple arithmetic, they are typically more involved. For example, in another dialogue, the model asks "How long does it take to download 200 GB at a rate of 2 GB/minute?" This task requires the student to set up a single variable equation and understand the roles of the given values. We also find that the DPO-trained model is more likely to ask questions, whereas other methods often directly tell the student to perform a task.

However, both LLMs still have some limitations, particularly when students give partially correct responses. In these cases, the models may ignore the progress the student has made and focus on errors that are irrelevant to the recent student response. Correctly identifying errors in math with LLMs has been shown to be challenging in prior work as well [12,26], indicating additional techniques may be needed to fix this behavior.

5.3 Human Evaluation

We also conduct a human evaluation to further assess different tutor models and how our automated metrics align with human judgment.

We recruit two independent volunteer university students to annotate tutor utterances according to our evaluation metrics. We randomly sample 10 dialogues from the test set after filtering based on toxicity and low quality ground-truth tutor utterances. The annotators evaluate 5 consecutive tutor turns from each dialogue, resulting in a total of 50 evaluation instances. At each instance, we show participants the dialogue so far and next tutor utterance candidates generated by (1) human tutors, (2) GPT-4o, and (3) our DPO-trained model, in random order without revealing the method.

For student outcome prediction, annotators rank the three candidate utterances based on how likely they think each one will lead to a correct student response. We ask annotators to take into account both the task posed in the turn and the student's knowledge demonstrated in prior turns. We use rankings instead of absolute values since the latter may be harder for humans to calibrate. For pedagogical principles, we simply ask annotators to follow the same evaluation rubric outlined in Table 1 and provide an overall score on a 1–10 scale.

Table 4. Human evaluation shows that DPO outperforms human tutors and GPT-4o.

Method	Correctness Rank$^{\downarrow}$	Rubric Score$^{\uparrow}$
Human Tutor	2.12	7.36
GPT-4o	2.13	8.07
DPO	**1.75**	**8.55**

Results. Table 4 shows average student correctness ranks (rank 1 means top-ranked) and rubric scores from human annotators. We see that DPO outperforms both human tutors and GPT-4o on both metrics, with all differences statistically significant ($p < 0.05$) according to a paired t-test. Higher correctness ranks show that DPO learns how to pose tasks that are manageable to students, while the higher rubric score shows that it does so while maintaining pedagogical principles. Additionally, the higher rubric score may imply that the correctness objective also indirectly improves pedagogical quality. While DPO outperforming GPT-4o on the rubric is contrary to the automated results in Table 2, the automated results may reflect self-bias from GPT-4o as the evaluator.

Since these evaluation tasks can be highly subjective, we also investigate the inter-rater agreement between the two human annotators and the automated metrics. We use Kendall's τ [20] for correctness ranks and Pearson's correlation coefficient ρ [24] for rubric scores. For correctness ranks, Kendall's τ is only 0.06 between the two annotators and averages 0.08 between LLMKT and both annotators. This low agreement is not surprising due to the subjective nature of the task; we find that there are many near-ties between different candidate utterances according to LLMKT's output probabilities. For rubric scores, the inter-rater agreement is notably higher: Pearson's ρ is 0.15 between the two annotators and averages 0.27 between GPT-4o and both annotators, the latter being statistically significant. This result suggests that evaluating pedagogical principles is much easier than predicting student correctness, though the former is still subjective, since annotators may value certain rubric items differently.

Overall, despite showing some promise through preliminary evaluation, it is important to deploy our trained tutor LLMs to real students and test whether they actually lead to good student learning outcomes.

6 Conclusions and Future Work

In this paper, we introduced a methodology to train LLM tutors to maximize student outcomes in dialogues while maintaining high pedagogical quality. We use student simulation to predict how likely a tutor utterance will yield a correct student response, and use GPT-4o to evaluate the pedagogical quality of tutor utterances using a rubric. We use both sets of predictions to score over-generated tutor utterances and fine-tune Llama 3.1 8B with direct preference optimization. Our resulting model significantly outperforms other methods for increasing predicted student outcomes, and matches the performance of GPT-4o, a much larger closed model, on pedagogical aspects. There are many avenues for future work. First, an evaluation with real students should be carried out to determine if our methods are still effective in real-world scenarios. Second, future work should investigate how to optimize for longer-term learning outcomes, such as concept mastery or performance on post-dialogue assessments. Third, future work should optimize for student affect and engagement, rather than just correctness. Finally, future work should apply our method to dialogues in non-math domains, such as language learning or computer science.

References

1. Anderson, J.R., Corbett, A.T., Koedinger, K.R., Pelletier, R.: Cognitive tutors: lessons learned. J. Learn. Sci. **4**(2), 167–207 (1995)
2. Ashok Kumar, N., Lan, A.: Improving socratic question generation using data augmentation and preference optimization. In: Proceedings of the 19th Workshop on Innovative Use of NLP for Building Educational Applications (BEA 2024), pp. 108–118. Association for Computational Linguistics, Mexico City, Mexico, June 2024
3. Cai, D., Zhang, Y., Dai, B.: Learning path recommendation based on knowledge tracing model and reinforcement learning. In: 2019 IEEE 5th International Conference on Computer and Communications (ICCC), pp. 1881–1885. IEEE (2019)
4. Carnegie Learning: Livehint overview (2024). https://support.carnegielearning.com/help-center/math/livehint/article/livehint-overview/
5. Cobbe, K., etal.: Training verifiers to solve math word problems. arXiv preprint arXiv:2110.14168 (2021)
6. Common Core State Standards Initiative: Mathematics standards (2024). https://www.thecorestandards.org/Math/
7. Corbett, A., Anderson, J.: Knowledge tracing: modeling the acquisition of procedural knowledge. User Model. User-adapted Interact. **4**(4), 253–278 (1994)
8. Cui, P., Sachan, M.: Adaptive and personalized exercise generation for online language learning. In: Proceedings of the 61st Annual Meeting of the Association for Computational Linguistics (Volume 1: Long Papers), pp. 10184–10198 (2023)
9. Demszky, D., et al.: Measuring conversational uptake: A case study on student-teacher interactions. In: Proceedings of the 59th Annual Meeting of the Association for Computational Linguistics and the 11th International Joint Conference on Natural Language Processing (Volume 1: Long Papers), pp. 1638–1653 (2021)

10. Dubey, A., et al.: The llama 3 herd of models. arXiv preprint arXiv:2407.21783 (2024)
11. Face, H.: Hugging face - the ai community building the future. https://huggingface.co/ (2025). Accessed 18 Feb 2025
12. Fernandez, N., Scarlatos, A., Feng, W., Woodhead, S., Lan, A.: DiVERT: distractor generation with variational errors represented as text for math multiple-choice questions. In: Proceedings of the 2024 Conference on Empirical Methods in Natural Language Processing, pp. 9063–9081. Association for Computational Linguistics, Miami, Florida, USA, November 2024
13. Ghosh, A., Heffernan, N., Lan, A.S.: Context-aware attentive knowledge tracing. In: Proc. ACM SIGKDD, pp. 2330–2339 (2020)
14. Graesser, A.C., VanLehn, K., Rosé, C.P., Jordan, P.W., Harter, D.: Intelligent tutoring systems with conversational dialogue. AI Mag. **22**(4), 39–39 (2001)
15. He-Yueya, J., Goodman, N.D., Brunskill, E.: Evaluating and optimizing educational content with large language model judgments. In: Proceedings of the 17th International Conference on Educational Data Mining, pp. 68–82 (2024)
16. He-Yueya, J., Singla, A.: Quizzing policy using reinforcement learning for inferring the student knowledge state. International Educational Data Mining Society (2021)
17. Hu, E.J., Shen, Y., Wallis, P., Allen-Zhu, Z., Li, Y., Wang, S., Wang, L., Chen, W.: Lora: Low-rank adaptation of large language models. arXiv preprint arXiv:2106.09685 (2021)
18. Jia, Q., Young, M., Xiao, Y., Cui, J., Liu, C., Rashid, P., Gehringer, E.: Insta-reviewer: a data-driven approach for generating instant feedback on students' project reports. International Educational Data Mining Society (2022)
19. Kakarla, S., Thomas, D., Lin, J., Gupta, S., Koedinger, K.: Using large language models to assess tutors' performance in reacting to students making math errors. In: AI for Education: Bridging Innovation and Responsibility at the 38th AAAI Annual Conference on AI (2024)
20. Kendall, M.G.: Rank correlation methods (1948)
21. Khan Academy: Supercharge your teaching experience with khanmigo (2023). https://www.khanmigo.ai/
22. Kim, K., Seo, A.J., Liu, H., Shin, J., Lee, K.: Margin matching preference optimization: Enhanced model alignment with granular feedback. In: Findings of the Association for Computational Linguistics: EMNLP 2024, pp. 13554–13570. Association for Computational Linguistics, Miami, Florida, USA, November 2024
23. Krupp, L., etal.: Challenges and opportunities of moderating usage of large language models in education. In: Proceedings of the International Conference on Mobile and Ubiquitous Multimedia, pp. 249–254 (2024)
24. Lee Rodgers, J., Nicewander, W.A.: Thirteen ways to look at the correlation coefficient. Am. Stat. **42**(1), 59–66 (1988)
25. Lieb, A., Goel, T.: Student interaction with newtbot: An llm-as-tutor chatbot for secondary physics education. In: Extended Abstracts of the CHI Conference on Human Factors in Computing Systems, pp. 1–8 (2024)
26. Liu, N., Sonkar, S., Wang, Z., Woodhead, S., Baraniuk, R.G.: Novice learner and expert tutor: Evaluating math reasoning abilities of large language models with misconceptions. arXiv preprint arXiv:2310.02439 (2023)
27. Liu, N., Wang, Z., Baraniuk, R., Lan, A.: Open-ended knowledge tracing for computer science education. In: Proceedings of the 2022 Conference on Empirical Methods in Natural Language Processing (2022)

28. Macina, J., et al.: MathDial: a dialogue tutoring dataset with rich pedagogical properties grounded in math reasoning problems. In: Findings of the Association for Computational Linguistics: EMNLP 2023, pp. 5602–5621. Association for Computational Linguistics, Singapore (Dec 2023)
29. Nickow, A., Oreopoulos, P., Quan, V.: The impressive effects of tutoring on prek-12 learning: A systematic review and meta-analysis of the experimental evidence. Working Paper 27476, National Bureau of Economic Research, July 2020
30. OpenAI: Hello gpt-4o, May 2024. https://openai.com/index/hello-gpt-4o/. Accessed 19 Feb 2025
31. Pal Chowdhury, S., Zouhar, V., Sachan, M.: Autotutor meets large language models: a language model tutor with rich pedagogy and guardrails. In: Proceedings of the Eleventh ACM Conference on Learning@ Scale, pp. 5–15 (2024)
32. Park, M., Kim, S., Lee, S., Kwon, S., Kim, K.: Empowering personalized learning through a conversation-based tutoring system with student modeling. In: Extended Abstracts of the CHI Conference on Human Factors in Computing Systems, pp. 1–10 (2024)
33. Piech, C., Bassen, J., Huang, J., Ganguli, S., Sahami, M., Guibas, L.J., Sohl-Dickstein, J.: Deep knowledge tracing. In: Proc. NeurIPS, pp. 505–513 (2015)
34. Rafailov, R., Sharma, A., Mitchell, E., Manning, C.D., Ermon, S., Finn, C.: Direct preference optimization: Your language model is secretly a reward model. Advances in Neural Information Processing Systems **36** (2024)
35. Rafferty, A.N., Brunskill, E., Griffiths, T.L., Shafto, P.: Faster teaching via pomdp planning. Cogn. Sci. **40**(6), 1290–1332 (2016)
36. Scarlatos, A., Baker, R.S., Lan, A.: Exploring knowledge tracing in tutor-student dialogues using llms. In: Proceedings of the 15th Learning Analytics and Knowledge Conference, LAK 2025, Dublin, Ireland, March 3-7, 2025. ACM (2025)
37. Scarlatos, A., Smith, D., Woodhead, S., Lan, A.: Improving the validity of automatically generated feedback via reinforcement learning. In: International Conference on Artificial Intelligence in Education, pp. 280–294. Springer (2024)
38. Schmucker, R., Xia, M., Azaria, A., Mitchell, T.: Ruffle&riley: Insights from designing and evaluating a large language model-based conversational tutoring system. In: International Conference on Artificial Intelligence in Education, pp. 75–90. Springer (2024)
39. Sonkar, S., Liu, N., Mallick, D., Baraniuk, R.: CLASS: a design framework for building intelligent tutoring systems based on learning science principles. In: Findings of the Association for Computational Linguistics: EMNLP 2023, pp. 1941–1961. Association for Computational Linguistics, Singapore, December 2023
40. Sonkar, S., Ni, K., Chaudhary, S., Baraniuk, R.: Pedagogical alignment of large language models. In: Findings of the Association for Computational Linguistics: EMNLP 2024, pp. 13641–13650. Association for Computational Linguistics, Miami, Florida, USA, November 2024
41. Stamper, J., Xiao, R., Hou, X.: Enhancing llm-based feedback: Insights from intelligent tutoring systems and the learning sciences. In: International Conference on Artificial Intelligence in Education, pp. 32–43. Springer (2024)
42. Steiss, J., et al.: Comparing the quality of human and chatgpt feedback of students' writing. Learn. Instr. **91**, 101894 (2024)
43. Team, L.: Learnlm: Improving gemini for learning (2024)
44. VanLehn, K., et al.: The architecture of why2-Atlas: a coach for qualitative physics essay writing. In: Cerri, S.A., Gouardères, G., Paraguaçu, F. (eds.) ITS 2002. LNCS, vol. 2363, pp. 158–167. Springer, Heidelberg (2002). https://doi.org/10.1007/3-540-47987-2_20

45. Wang, R., Zhang, Q., Robinson, C., Loeb, S., Demszky, D.: Bridging the novice-expert gap via models of decision-making: A case study on remediating math mistakes. In: Proceedings of the 2024 Conference of the North American Chapter of the Association for Computational Linguistics: Human Language Technologies (Volume 1: Long Papers), pp. 2174–2199 (2024)
46. Wang, R.E., Ribeiro, A.T., Robinson, C.D., Loeb, S., Demszky, D.: Tutor copilot: A human-ai approach for scaling real-time expertise. arXiv preprint arXiv:2410.03017 (2024)
47. Yang, B., et al.: Cref: an llm-based conversational software repair framework for programming tutors. In: Proceedings of the 33rd ACM SIGSOFT International Symposium on Software Testing and Analysis, pp. 882–894 (2024)
48. Yang, C., et al.: Survey on knowledge distillation for large language models: Methods, evaluation, and application. ACM Trans. Intell. Syst, Technol (2024)
49. Zhang, H., Xie, J., Wu, C., Cai, J., Kim, C., Carroll, J.M.: The future of learning: Large language models through the lens of students. In: Proceedings of the 25th Annual Conference on Information Technology Education, pp. 12–18 (2024)

Prompts Eliciting Active and Constructive Engagement Improve Learning Across ChatGPT and Traditional Resource Contexts

Olga Manakina and Kasia Muldner(✉)

Department of Cognitive Science, Carleton University, Ottawa, Canada
{Olga.Manakina,Kasia.Muldner}@carleton.ca

Abstract. Large language models (LLMs) are artificial intelligence (AI) tools that can generate answers to a variety of student questions. While these tools have the potential to provide personalized instruction, there are also concerns that students will over-rely on them to obtain answers without trying to learn the target concepts. Since LLMs are relatively new, research is needed on their impact on student learning and ways to scaffold learning. We conducted an experimental study ($N = 101$) in which students solved code-tracing problems. We manipulated (1) the presence of prompts encouraging active and constructive engagement, and (2) the type of instructional resource available, either ChatGPT or traditional materials. The prompts significantly increased learning across both instructional resource contexts; there was no significant difference between the ChatGPT and traditional-materials groups. To gain insight into how students used ChatGPT, we used qualitative methods to analyze their interactions with the tool.

Keywords: ChatGPT · active-constructive engagement prompts

1 Introduction

Large language models (LLMs) predict and generate the most likely sequence of words [6]. This functionality makes LLM-powered chatbots, like ChatGPT, potentially useful tools in educational contexts. For instance, LLMs can expand the functionalities of tutoring systems [5,12,14,18,24]. On the instructor side, LLMs can grade and/or assess content [16,17,26], as well as generate content [10,11,13,23,27]. While promising, LLMs also raise concerns [8]. These tools can generate solutions to tests and assignments [20–22], so if students over-rely on them, they will miss learning opportunities. However, findings about the impact of LLMs have been mixed.

Some studies found LLMs to be beneficial (albeit with caveats). Wu et al. [29] developed an educational technology that used LLM functionalities to answer student questions, posed as they solved math problems. Students given this tool had significantly higher learning and self-reported motivation than a control

A. I. Cristea et al. (Eds.): AIED 2025, LNAI 15877, pp. 267–280, 2025.
https://doi.org/10.1007/978-3-031-98414-3_19

group that used a search engine. Kazemitabaar et al. [9] recruited participants from a programming camp. The experimental group was given access to a ‘code generator’ powered by OpenAI’s Codex, which was capable of providing solutions to programs; the control group did not have access to the code generator. The experimental group had higher correctness scores on their programs. While overall there was no difference in posttest scores, the experimental group did score higher on the challenging questions in the delayed posttest. Brender et al. [2] evaluated the utility of ChatGPT in the context of program generation. Students with higher pretest scores performed better on the posttest if they had access to ChatGPT, while students with lower posttest scores performed better if they did not have access to ChatGPT. Clustering was used to analyze the prompts students gave to ChatGPT in the experimental condition. Prompts included asking ChatGPT: (1) for an answer (i.e., partial or final program); (2) for an explanation; (3) for help identifying errors in code. The first category potentially signals over-reliance on ChatGPT - this category was common, accounting for 55% and up to 95% of ChatGPT prompts for about a third of the students. In contrast to these studies, Fan et al. [7] did not find a reliable difference between a group supported by ChatGPT and other forms of support (e.g., a human tutor, a checklist).

The next two studies involved programming activities with a single condition design and qualitative analysis of the data. Prather et al. [19] asked students to write programs and gave them access to Co-Pilot and ChatGPT. Novices used LLMs ineffectively (e.g., accepted the Co-Pilot suggestions regardless of their correctness). Yang et al. [31] analyzed how students prompted LLMs in the context of three debugging tasks. Several prompt categories emerged, including debugging help (asking the LLM to identify the error), implementing a solution (asking the LLM to fix a bug), ideas for hypothesis testing, and error and code comprehension categories. The first two categories correspond to students offloading the debugging task to the LLM; these were relatively common.

Given evidence that some students do not use LLMs effectively, researchers have begun examining ways to encourage effective behaviors in LLM contexts [14,18,24]. To illustrate, Naik et al. [18], developed an LLM-based chatbot that provided adaptive reflection triggers as students worked in groups on data base design. The reflection triggers encouraged students to compare key constructs and engage in discussion. The evaluation showed the chatbot was able to provide contextualized feedback but there was no overall effect on learning. Darvishi et al. [5] evaluated LLM-based prompts reminding students to improve their reviews of learning resources. These prompts significantly improved the review quality, compared to students who were not given prompts or students only given a static checklist. In contrast to these studies, we test the effect of basic prompts embedded in instructional materials that aimed to elicit effective learning.

2 Present Study

We conducted an experimental study in which students were asked to code trace Python programs to predict their output. Code tracing involves simulating the actions a computer takes when it executes a computer program and is a fundamental programming skill [30]. We manipulated two independent variables in our study.

The first independent variable corresponded to whether engagement prompts were present or not. When present, three prompts were embedded in the instructional materials, designed to elicit active and constructive levels of cognitive engagement, per the ICAP theory [3]. To encourage active engagement, the first prompt asked students to show their work while code tracing, inspired by research showing that students often skip steps and so make errors [4]. Constructive engagement was elicited through self-explanation prompts, an established strategy that improves learning [1]. Two such prompts were present: (1) a basic reminder to self-explain instructional materials; (2) after students submitted a solution, a prompt asking them to compare their answer to the canonical solution. Figure 1 shows an example of the prompts.

The second independent variable corresponded to the instructional resources. Specifically, to evaluate the effect of an LLMs on learning, some participants had access to ChatGPT, while others were instead given online instructional materials (referred to as 'traditional materials' below).

We had the following three research questions:

1. Do prompts eliciting active and constructive engagement improve learning?
2. Does the type of instructional resource available to students during problem solving (ChatGPT vs. traditional materials) affect learning?
3. Did participants use ChatGPT and how did their strategies relate to learning outcomes?

2.1 Participants

The participants were 101 individuals (78 female, 20 male, 2 non-binary, 1 did not disclose; $M_{age} = 24.99$, $SD_{age} = 10.53$). To avoid ceiling effects, participants were not eligible to participate if they had taken university-level programming classes, with one exception (a first-year programming class offered to non-computer science (CS) majors). Of the 101 participants, 73 reported no prior programming experience and 28 declared minor programming experience (11 took one university programming class offered to non-CS majors, 17 took a programming class in high school). Participants either received 2% bonus credit for a first-year course that presented an overview of Cognitive Science or $30.

2.2 Materials

Introductory Lesson: A 20-minute video was created providing an introduction to programming. The lesson was based on an animated PowerPoint presentation with a voiceover explaining each slide. The video was designed for programming novices, and covered three key topics: variables, if statements, and loops.

Traditional Materials: We created online materials that provided a review of the lesson topics, organized into three sections (variables, if statements, loops). Each section was presented on a separate screen, using text and visual explanations; each section could be accessed in several ways (e.g., using a menu in the top right corner, via a search bar). We refer to these materials as 'traditional' as this format is common in various educational settings.

Pretest, Posttest, Python Exercises: Several questionnaires were created using the online Jotform survey tool. The pretest and posttest each had eight code-tracing problems (each showed a Python program, and asked what the program printed). The first four problems involved basic programs without loops; the last four had programs with loops (for these, an optional scrap area was provided that participants could use to track the code trace if they wished). The problems were distributed among several screens and participants could only move on to a new screen if they provided an answer for all problems on the current screen (feedback for correctness was not provided). The problems in the two tests were isomorphic except that the variable names and values were varied; the pretest additionally included demographic questions.

The Python exercises questionnaire included an initial introduction to the activity, followed by four code-tracing problems, each shown on a separate screen. Each problem screen had (1) instructions asking participants to code trace a Python program (top, Fig. 1); (2) the Python program to be traced (left, Fig. 1), and a *'work area'* for the intermediate code-tracing steps (right, Fig. 1); (3) a *'Your answer'* text box for the final answer with a corresponding *'See correct answer'* button (bottom, Fig. 1). This button was disabled until an answer was provided; once one was, clicking the button showed the correct answer. Four versions of this questionnaire were created. All versions had the same problems but the two ChatGPT versions had a screen at the start describing how to use it and asking participants to interact with ChatGPT as a warm up exercise. The four versions also varied in (1) the instructions at the top of the problem screens (e.g., whether ChatGPT vs. traditional materials were referenced); (2) if the three engagement prompts described in Sect. 2 were present or not. More details on each version are provided in Sect. 2.4.

2.3 Design

We used a between-subjects design with two independent variables: (1) cognitive engagement prompts (present vs. absent) and (2) instructional resource (ChatGPT vs. traditional materials). Thus, there were four conditions: (1) prompts + ChatGPT; (2) no prompts + ChatGPT; (3) prompts + traditional materials; (4) no prompts + traditional materials.

2.4 Procedure

The study was approved by the university Ethics board. Each study session was conducted by a researcher online using Zoom and lasted no more than two hours. For consistency, each researcher followed a study script; each conducted approximately the same amount of sessions in all four conditions. Participants

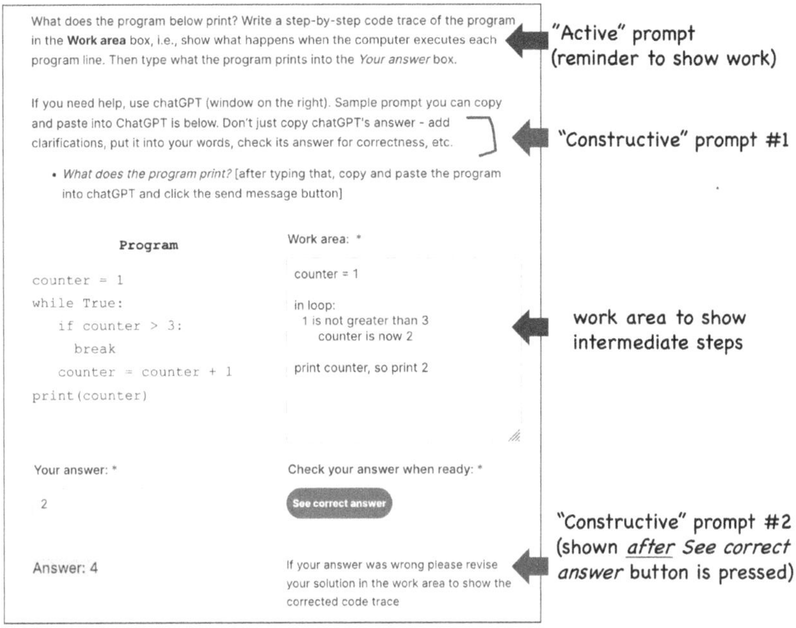

Fig. 1. Screenshot of a problem screen in the *prompts + ChatGPT* condition with a hypothetical incorrect code trace (see work area and final solution boxes - the code trace is incorrect because it only covers one loop iteration). The correct answer (highlighted, bottom left) and the second constructive prompt were only shown after the *'See correct answer'* button is pressed.

were given the link to an online consent form and after they signed it, cameras were turned off (to avoid participants feeling watched). The remainder of the study activities were done via screen sharing, i.e., the researcher gave participants remote access to their screen with the target activity.

Participants first watched the introductory lesson video and then completed the pretest (20 min). The pretest came after the lesson to isolate the effects of the experimental manipulations in the problem-solving phase. Next, participants were assigned to one of the four conditions in a round-robin fashion and given the Python exercises questionnaire. As noted above, the problems in the questionnaire were the same in all four conditions and what was varied was whether prompts were included in the materials and the resource participants had access to while problem solving (ChatGPT or traditional materials). The Python exercises window was shown on the right half of the screen, and ChatGPT or the traditional materials on the left side (this was set up by the researcher, who subsequently provided participants with access to their screen).

Each problem screen included a timer, set to 5 min to solve the problem. In the two prompted conditions, participants were reminded to avoid copying from the instructional resource (see 'Constructive prompt #1', Fig. 1, top right) and that they had to use the 'work area' to show the intermediate steps of their code trace (see 'Active prompt', Fig. 1, top right). Correctness of intermediate code-tracing work was not checked but they could not move on to the next problem until something was entered in this textbox. In the two no-prompts conditions, the prompt was not present and using the work area was optional. In all conditions, after entering the answer in the corresponding field or when the time was up, the *'See correct answer'* button activated and pressing it showed the correct answer (participants had to click this button before moving on to the next problem). Participants were not required to revise their answer and could move on even if it was incorrect. However, in the two prompted conditions, when the correct answer was shown, the instructions encouraged participants to work on their solution if their answer did not match the answer shown (see 'Constructive prompt #2', Fig. 1, bottom right). In the two no-prompts conditions, this prompt was not shown. When all four problems were completed (or 20 min had passed), the researcher stopped the recording, provided a 3-minute break, and proceeded with the posttest (20 min.)

3 Results

3.1 Do Cognitive Engagement Prompts and Instructional Resource (ChatGPT, Traditional) Impact Learning?

To measure the effect of the experimental manipulations on learning, we relied on the pretest and posttest scores. The tests were graded by a single researcher; each test had a maximum score of 16 points (part points were possible). Prior to running this analysis, we removed participants who scored 100% on the pretest (n = 13). The results are based on the remaining 88 participants.

The descriptives are in Table 1. The pretest scores were low, despite the fact that the pretest came after the lesson. By chance, the pretest scores were lower in the prompts + ChatGPT condition (and the effect of prompts was marginally significant, p = .057). Overall, collapsing across conditions, participants learned from study as indicated by a significant pretest to posttest gain, $t(87) = 4.9$, $p < .001$, $d = .5$.

To answer our first two research questions about the effects of engagement prompts (present, absent; RQ1) and instructional resource (ChatGPT, traditional; RQ2) on learning, a two-way ANOVA was conducted with learning as the dependent variable. Learning was operationalized by the change from pretest to posttest, i.e., gain scores (posttest - pretest). The gain scores, shown in Table 1, were within normal range (skew and kurtosis: $[-1, 1]$) and the assumption of homogeneity was not violated.

The main effect of engagement prompts was significant, $F(1, 84) = 4.3$, $p = .040$, $\eta_p^2 = .05$, indicating that participants learned more when the prompts were present (M = 26.1%, SD = 37.1) than if they were absent (M = 10.6%, SD = 33.6). The main effect of instructional resource was not significant, $F(1, 84) = 1.0$, $p = .31$, $\eta_p^2 = .01$, although descriptively, participants had higher gain scores in the ChatGPT conditions (M = 23.2%, SD = 34.9) compared to the

Table 1. Mean and standard deviation for each condition.

		ChatGPT	Traditional Materials
Prompts	Pretest%	37.9 (22.9)	53.4 (30.2)
	Posttest%	71.3 (30.0)	73.0 (27.0)
	Gain %	33.4 (31.6)	19.6 (40.1)
	Normalized Gain	0.54 (.45)	0.39 (.58)
No prompts	Pretest %	57.6 (26.5)	56.5 (29.5)
	Posttest %	69.0 (21.9)	66.3 (28.9)
	Gain %	11.5 (35.6)	9.8 (32.6)
	Normalized Gain	0.25 (.51)	0.28 (.57)

traditional materials ($M = 15.0\%$, $SD = 37.2$). This effect was primarily driven by the *prompts + ChatGPT* condition. This condition had the highest gain score (33.4), substantially higher than the *prompts + Traditional Materials* condition (19.6). When prompts were not present, the gains in the ChatGPT and traditional materials conditions were similar, implying that the effect of prompts may depend on the type of instructional resource. However, the interaction between engagement prompts and instructional resource was not significant, $F(1, 84) = .63$, $p = .43$, $\eta_p^2 = .01$.

The above analysis indicates the engagement prompts increased learning. We conducted a follow up analysis to check for any potential bias related to the fact that the pretest scores were lower in the two prompted conditions. A way to account for this is through normalized gain scores, where the difference from pretest to posttest is normalized by pretest scores [15], as follows:

$$NormalizedGain = \begin{cases} \frac{posttest - pretest}{100 - pretest} & \text{if } posttest > pretest \\ 0 & \text{if } posttest = pretest \\ \frac{posttest - pretest}{pretest} & \text{if } posttest < pretest \end{cases}$$

The descriptives for normalized gain are in Table 1. The assumptions of the ANOVA were met. The overall pattern of results held when normalized gain was used as the dependent variable (the prompted group had marginally higher normalized gains, $F(1, 84) = 3.0$, $p = .086$; the effect of instructional resource was not significant $F(1, 84) = .27$, $p = .61$ and neither was the interaction between prompts and instructional resource, $F(1, 84) = .72$, $p = .40$).

3.2 Did Participants Use ChatGPT and how did their Strategies Relate to Learning Outcomes?

To answer RQ3 about how participants used ChatGPT, we used a qualitative approach to analyze the screen recordings from the two ChatGPT conditions. Six recordings were lost and so the analysis corresponds to 43 participants. The analysis is exploratory and so focused on descriptive statistics. We included all participants, even those who got ceiling on pretest (100%) because we wanted to explore how prior knowledge (either from the lesson or before) influenced ChatGPT usage. Of note, none of these participants had a perfect score on the posttest.

For the analysis, the first author watched the Zoom screen recordings and for each participant and each problem they solved, identified (1) if ChatGPT was used (yes or no), based on whether the participant prompted ChatGPT[1], and (2) if ChatGPT was used, whether it was used before *anything* was first produced in the problem interface (code traces in the working area or the final answer). This coding was objective and straightforward and so inter-rater was not applied as it was not needed.

Based on this analysis, we categorized participants into three groups based on their ChatGPT usage:

- *No ChatGPT use*: 19 participants did not use ChatGPT at all while solving the 4 problems.
- *Problem-solving (PS) attempt first*: 11 participants first produced an answer or partial answer on their own and only after doing so used ChatGPT (for various reasons, details are below). All of the 11 participants in this group used this strategy for at least 1 of the 4 problems; on average, they used it for 2.18 problems out of the 4 total problems; for the remaining problems they did not use ChatGPT at all.
- *ChatGPT first*: 13 participants did not first attempt to solve the problem on their own, instead asking ChatGPT for an answer. On average, they did this for 3.25 problems of the 4 problems; for the remaining problem(s) they did not use ChatGPT.

This analysis shows that about half of the participants did not use ChatGPT at all, while the remaining participants differed in when they used it (before attempting a solution or after). We next investigated relations between ChatGPT strategies and learning. Table 2 shows the normalized gain and pretest scores for each usage category (we focused on normalized gain to account for pretest performance). The pretest scores ranged from 47.7% to 55.8%, with the *no ChatGPT usage* group in the middle. This suggests that prior knowledge alone did not explain differences in ChatGPT usage. The normalized gain scores were on average very similar for the *no ChatGPT usage* and *ChatGPT first* groups, and higher for the *PS first* group, suggesting an advantage of this strategy.

To further analyze the effect of pretest performance, we divided each group into low and high pretest outcomes (low: $< 75\%$; high $>= 75\%$). The results are in Fig. 2. For all three groups, on average the high-pretest participants had a negative normalized gain (meaning the average posttest score was lower than the pretest score). In contrast, the low-pretest participants did gain from pretest to posttest. Descriptively, these gains were similar for the *no ChatGPT* usage and *ChatGPT first* groups (.53 and .47, respectively) and higher for the *PS*

[1] Recall that the ChatGPT window was next to the problem window, and so ChatGPT usage was easy to identify.

Table 2. Average pretest and normalized gain for the three ChatGPT sub-groups (standard deviation in brackets). *Note*: PS = problem solving.

	No ChatGPT use	PS attempt first	ChatGPT first
Pretest %	53.8 (32.5)	47.7 (31.9)	55.8 (29.9)
Normalized Gain	0.27 (.55)	0.42 (.54)	0.26 (.43)

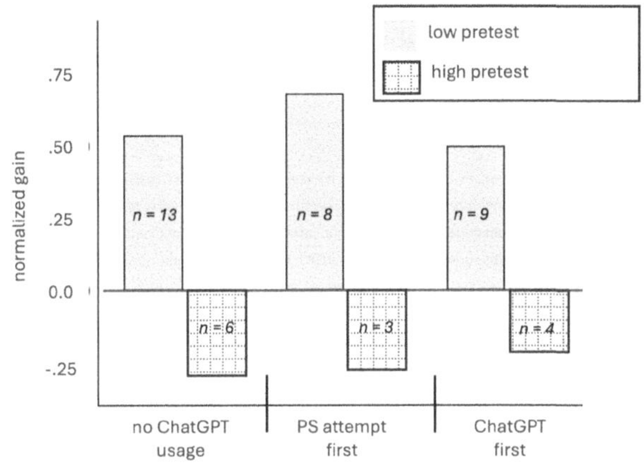

Fig. 2. Average normalized gain for the three ChatGPT sub-groups, divided by low and high pretest scores.

first group (.68), mirroring the results from above when participants were not subdivided by pretest performance. These results are not an artifact of the fact that the low-prior knowledge group had more room to gain as we used normalized gain (so those with higher pretest scores are assigned a higher gain by the formula, compared to those with lower pretest scores given equal gains).

We next provide more information about the strategies used in the *PS first* and *ChatGPT first* groups (we provided key descriptives for the *no-ChatGPT* group above; for space reasons we do not provide data for each participant like we do for the groups who used ChatGPT). Details are in Fig. 3, which shows the data for the *PS first* group on the left (Fig. 3a) and data for the *ChatGPT first* group on the right (Fig. 3b). For both groups, the figure shows the condition (1: prompts present; 0: prompts absent), the pretest score, the normalized gain (NG) (first three columns) and the strategy for each problem (next four columns); the participants in the low knowledge group are shown in the top part of the figure and those with high pretest score are in the bottom; the rows for each subgroup are ordered by the normalized gain. Negative gain scores are shown in red - notably in all cases but one these corresponded to the high-pretest group.

As far as the *PS first* group (Fig. 3a, left), some participants prompted ChatGPT for a code trace after they generated their own answer and did not transfer any content from ChatGPT (blue cells in Fig. 3a). These participants may have

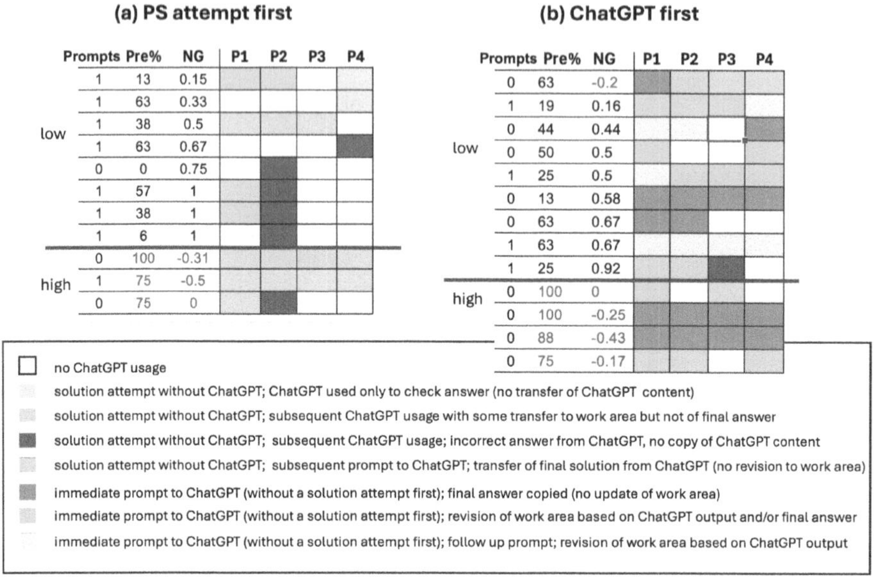

Fig. 3. Details on strategies used for each of the four problems for the *Problem Solving (PS) first* (left) and *ChatGPT first* (right) groups. Each row represents a single participant. The leftmost column shows if the engagement prompts were present (indicated by a 1), or absent (indicated by a 0); the next two columns show the pretest % (Pre%) and normalized gain (NG); the last four columns show the strategy used for solving the corresponding problem - see legend at the bottom of the figure. (Color figure online)

been checking their answer and/or seeking information about the solution process used by ChatGPT. Six participants got an incorrect answer from ChatGPT (red cells, Fig. 3a) - they did not use the incorrect answer and they did not use ChatGPT after that. For the remaining instances of ChatGPT usage in the *PS first* group, participants prompted ChatGPT after attempting a solution, and in three instances they copied ChatGPT's answer with no changes to their working area (see pink cells in Fig. 3a). For the remaining instances (see green cells in Fig. 3a), participants prompted ChatGPT and modified their working area (possibly using ChatGPT output) but none used the final answer provided by ChatGPT (this was clear because the final answer was not visible on the screen when participants entered one into their problem-solving screen).

As far as the *ChatGPT first* group (Fig. 3b, right), 9 of the 13 participants in this group were in the no-prompts condition. Twelve of the 13 participants copied content from ChatGPT over to their problem (see dark and light orange cells in Fig. 3b); six of these participants copied the final answer only without any work in the 'work area' (all were in the no-prompts condition that did not require update of the work area text box). Some participants asked follow-up prompts (see yellow cells in Fig. 3b). In general, however, there was little independent problem solving in this group, compared to the *PS first* group.

4 Discussion, Limitations, and Future Work

We conducted an experimental study that manipulated (1) presence of prompts eliciting active and constructive engagement and (2) instructional resource (ChatGPT, traditional materials). The prompts had a significant positive effect on learning. This is encouraging given that this intervention was basic and easy to implement, asking students to avoid copying, show intermediate code-tracing steps, and to reflect on incorrect answers. This manipulation may have encouraged constructive problem solving for individuals who used ChatGPT at least once. In particular, our qualitative analysis showed that of the participants who tried to solve the problem on their own first and only after used ChatGPT (i.e., the *PS-first* group), 73% were in the condition with prompts. Independent problem solving is a constructive activity that has potential to strengthen and expand knowledge as well as help students to identify their knowledge gaps [3,28]. In contrast, of the participants who immediately used ChatGPT (i.e., the *ChatGPT first* group), only 31% were in the condition with prompts and the others were in the condition without prompts. In this latter group, a substantial proportion of the participants copied the final answer (see dark orange cells, Fig. 3b). In contrast, none of the participants in the *PS first* group did this.

The current qualitative analysis focused on strategies used in the two ChatGPT conditions. As noted above, this analysis provided indirect indications that the prompt intervention reduced shallow strategies, but we did not analyze the effect of the prompts on student behaviors. This is an avenue for future work. The video recordings provide information on how diligently students followed the prompt to show their work in the intermediate 'work area'. The recordings provide less information on whether students followed the other prompts to study the available instructional resource and revise incorrect solutions, as think aloud data was not collected, but they would provide data on time. In particular, we could compare the amount of time spent on incorrect answers in the prompted and unprompted conditions. Another avenue for future work is to examine the individual effects of each prompt.

Like some prior work [7], there was no difference in learning between participants who had access to ChatGPT vs. traditional materials. To investigate why, we extended prior work by analyzing ChatGPT usage. About half of the participants given access to ChatGPT did not use it at all, which would diminish its effect and may explain the null result. It's interesting that this many participants chose not to use ChatGPT, given concerns that students will over-rely on this tool to obtain answers.

Why did some participants choose not to use ChatGPT? Although we did not conduct post-study interviews, we can speculate on several possible reasons. One is that they did not need to, because they already knew how to solve the problems on their own. However, this is unlikely given their low pretest scores. Another possibility is that some participants were not familiar with ChatGPT. We aimed to mitigate this with instructions for the ChatGPT conditions and the warm-up exercise (see Method section). Yet another possibility is that using ChatGPT requires a context switch from the problem over to ChatGPT, as well as effort to understand ChatGPT output. Some participants may have preferred to avoid this as it has potential to increase cognitive load. Other possibilities include the desire to solve problems without help and mistrust of AI technologies [25]. As far as the latter, some participants received an incorrect answer from ChatGPT and stopped using ChatGPT after this point. Finally, the instructional materials did ask participants to treat the problem-solving phase as a learning opportunity, and some may have followed this suggestion.

How did participants who did not use ChatGPT overcome impasses during problem solving? While we do not have direct data on this, prior work provides some insight. VanLehn **(author?)** [28] reported that students learned new rules while solving physics problems without referring to the instructional materials. One mechanism to do so is a form of self-explanation that requires using common sense and overly general knowledge to create new knowledge when an impasse is encountered.

Some results from analysis of the strategies participants used while problem solving aligned with prior work. For instance, some participants transferred the answer from ChatGPT without any revision, which was previously reported [2]. Because our analysis was fine grained, we shed light on whether participants tried solving the problem on their own first vs. whether they turned to ChatGPT first. The former is a more constructive strategy [28] and we did see various instances of it in our data. Of note is that participants with the highest pretest scores ended up with negative normalized gains (see Fig. 2). It is possible that these participants in particular felt the posttest was redundant and so did not seriously attempt to complete it to the best of their ability.

Some limitations were described above. Another is that our study involved a specific problem-solving activity, namely code tracing, which limits generalizability. Thus, future work should investigate whether related activities, like program generation, produce similar results. Another limitation is that the study activities were done outside of a classroom setting, which may influence motivation and reduces ecological validity. Thus, future work could conduct the study in the context of a beginning programming class.

Acknowledgments. This work was supported by an NSERC Discovery Grant. We thank Marie Blais, Tracy Chisholm, Kolene Lamizana and Hannah Stanley for help with data collection and Tracy Chisholm for recommending the survey software (JotForms).

References

1. Bisra, K., Liu, Q., Nesbit, J.C., Salimi, F., Winne, P.H.: Inducing self-explanation: a meta-analysis. Educ. Psychol. Rev. **30**(3), 703–725 (2018)
2. Brender, J., El-Hamamsy, L., Mondada, F., Bumbacher, E.: Who's helping who? When students use ChatGPT to engage in practice lab sessions. In: Conference on Artificial Intelligence in Education, pp. 235–249 (2024)
3. Chi, M., Wylie, R.: The ICAP framework: linking cognitive engagement to active learning outcomes. Educ. Psychol. **49**(4), 219–243 (2014)
4. Cunningham, K., Blanchard, S., Ericson, B., Guzdial, M.: Using tracing and sketching to solve programming problems: replicating and extending an analysis of what students draw. In: Conference on International Computing Education Research, pp. 164–172 (2017)
5. Darvishi, A., Khosravi, H., Sadiq, S., Gašević, D., Siemens, G.: Impact of AI assistance on student agency. Comput. Educ. **210**, 1–18 (2024)
6. Yogesh, K., et al.: Dwivedi. "So what if ChatGPT wrote it?" Multidisciplinary perspectives on opportunities, challenges and implications of generative conversational AI for research, practice and policy. Int. J. Inf. Manage. **71** (2023)
7. Fan, Y., et al.: Beware of metacognitive laziness: effects of generative artificial intelligence on learning motivation, processes, and performance. Br. J. Edu. Technol. **56**, 489–530 (2025)
8. Marc Alier Forment, Francisco José García-Peñalvo, and Jorge Dorribo Camba. Generative artificial intelligence in education: From deceptive to disruptive. *Int. J. Interact. Multim. Artif. Intell.*, 8:5, 2024
9. Kazemitabaar, M., Chow, J., Ma, C., Ericson, B.J., Weintrop, D.,T. Grossman. Studying the effect of AI code generators on supporting novice learners in introductory programming. In: Human Factors in Computing Systems (CHI), pp. 1–23 (2023)
10. Lamsiyah, S., El Mahdaouy, A., Nourbakhsh, A., Schommer, C.: Fine-tuning a large language model with reinforcement learning for educational question generation. In: Conference on Artificial Intelligence in Education, pp. 424–438 (2024)
11. Li, X., Henriksson, A., Duneld, M., Nouri, J., Wu, Y.: Supporting teaching-to-the-curriculum by linking diagnostic tests to curriculum goals: using textbook content as context for retrieval-augmented generation with large language models. In: Conference on Artificial Intelligence in Education, pp. 118–132 (2024)
12. Lin, J., et al.: How can I Get It Right? Using GPT to Rephrase Incorrect Trainee Responses. Int. J. Artif. Intell, Educ (2024)
13. Logacheva, E., Hellas, A., Prather, J., Sarsa, A., Leinonen, J.: Evaluating contextually personalized programming exercises created with generative AI. In: Conference on International Computing Education Research, pp. 95–113 (2024)
14. Ma, Q., Shen, H., Koedinger, K., Wu, T.: How to teach programming in the AI era? Using LLMs as a teachable agent for debugging. In: Conference on Artificial Intelligence in Education, pp. 265–279 (2024)
15. Marx, J., Cummings, K.: Normalized change. Am. J. Phys. **75**, 87–91 (2007)
16. Messer, M., Shi, M., Brown, N.C.C., Kölling, M.: Grading documentation with machine learning. In: Conference on Artificial Intelligence in Education, pp. 105–117 (2024)
17. Moore, S., Costello, E., Nguyen, H., Stamper, J.: An automatic question usability evaluation toolkit. In: Conference on Artificial Intelligence in Education, pp. 31–46 (2024)

18. Naik, A., et al.: Generating situated reflection triggers about alternative solution paths: a case study of generative AI for computer-supported collaborative learning. In: Conference on Artificial Intelligence and Education, pp. 46–59 (2024)
19. Prather, J., et al.: The widening gap: the benefits and harms of generative AI for novice programmers. In: Conference on International Computing Education Research, pp. 469–486 (2024)
20. Richards, M., Waugh, K., Slaymaker, M., Petre, M., Woodthorpe, J., Gooch, D.: Bob or Bot: exploring ChatGPT's answers to university computer science assessment. ACM Trans. Comput. Educ. 24(1) (2024)
21. Rodrigues, L., Pereira, F., Cabral, L., Ramalho, G., Gasevic, D., Mello, R.: Can GPT4 answer educational tests? Empirical analysis of answer quality based on question complexity and difficulty. In: Conference on Artificial Intelligence in Education, pp. 192–205 (2024)
22. Savelka, J., Agarwal, A., An, M., Bogart, C., Sakr, M.: Thrilled by your progress! Large Language Models (GPT-4) no longer struggle to pass assessments in higher education programming courses. In: Conference on International Computing Education Research, pp. 78 – 92 (2023)
23. Scaria, N., Chenna, S., Subramani, D.: Automated educational question generation at different Bloom's skill levels using large language models: Strategies and evaluation. In: Conference on Artificial Intelligence in Education, pp. 165–179 (2024)
24. Schmucker, R., Xia, M., Azaria, A., Mitchell, T.: Ruffle &Riley: insights from designing and evaluating a large language model-based conversational tutoring system. In: Conference on Artificial Intelligence in Education, pp. 75–90 (2024)
25. Sedlbauer, J., Činčera, J., M. Slavík, and A. Hartlová. Students' reflections on their experience with ChatGPT. J. Comput. Assisted Learn. **40**(4), 1526–1534 (2024)
26. Sonkar, S., Ni, K., Lu, L., Kincaid, K., Hutchinson, J., Baraniuk, R.: Automated long answer grading with RiceChem dataset. In: Conference on Artificial Intelligence in Education, pp. 163 – 176 (2024)
27. Steiss, J., et al.: Comparing the quality of human and ChatGPT feedback of students' writing. Learn. Instruction **91** (2024)
28. VanLehn, K.: Rule-learning events in the acquisition of a complex skill: an evaluation of cascade. J. Learn. Sci. **8**(1), 71–125 (1999)
29. Wu, T., Lee, H., Li, P., Huang, C., Huang, Y.: Promoting self-regulation progress and knowledge construction in blended learning via ChatGPT-based learning aid. J. Educ. Comput. Res. **61**(8), 3–31 (2024)
30. Xie, B., et al.: A theory of instruction for introductory programming skills. Comput. Sci. Educ. **29**(2), 205–253 (2019)
31. Yang, S., Zhao, H., Xu, Y., Brennan, K., Schneider, B.: Debugging with an AI tutor: Investigating novice help-seeking behaviors and perceived learning. In: Conference on International Computing Education Research, pp. 84–94 (2024)

Understanding University Students' Use of Generative AI: The Roles of Demographics and Personality Traits

Newnew Deng[1], Edward Jiusi Liu[1], and Xiaoming Zhai[2](✉)

[1] West Lafayette Junior/Senior High School, West Lafayette, IN 47906, USA
[2] University of Georgia, Athens, GA 30666, USA
xiaoming.zhai@uga.edu

Abstract. The use of generative AI (GAI) among university students is rapidly increasing, yet empirical research on students' GAI use and the factors influencing it remains limited. To address this gap, we surveyed 363 undergraduate and graduate students in the United States, examining their GAI usage and how it relates to demographic variables and personality traits based on the Big Five model (i.e., extraversion, agreeableness, Consciousness, and emotional stability, and intellect/imagination). Our findings reveal: (a) Students in higher academic years are more inclined to use GAI and prefer it over traditional resources. (b) Non-native English speakers use and adopt GAI more readily than native speakers. (c) Compared to White, Asian students report higher GAI usage, perceive greater academic benefits, and express a stronger preference for it. Similarly, Black students report a more positive impact of GAI on their academic performance. Personality traits also play a significant role in shaping perceptions and usage of GAI. After controlling for demographic factors, we found that personality still significantly predicts GAI use and attitudes: (a) Students with higher conscientiousness use GAI less. (b) Students who are higher in agreeableness perceive a less positive impact of GAI on academic performance and express more ethical concerns about using it for academic work. (c) Students with higher emotional stability report a more positive impact of GAI on learning and fewer concerns about its academic use. (d) Students with higher extraversion show a stronger preference for GAI over traditional resources. (e) Students with higher intellect/imagination tend to prefer traditional resources. These insights highlight the need for universities to provide personalized guidance to ensure students use GAI effectively, ethically, and equitably in their academic pursuits.

Keywords: Generative AI (GAI) · University Students · Personality Trait · Academic

N. Deng and E. J. Liu—Co-first Author.

A. I. Cristea et al. (Eds.): AIED 2025, LNAI 15877, pp. 281–293, 2025.
https://doi.org/10.1007/978-3-031-98414-3_20

1 Introduction

University students utilize generative AI (GAI) for various academic purposes, such as learning, assignments, essays, programming, and examinations, with differing levels of engagement and embracement [18, 20]. However, empirical evidence is needed to examine the uses and perceptions of GAI in academic work, as well as the influencing factors. In this study, we surveyed university students to understand not only how they integrate GAI into their academic work but also how their use of GAI is associated with student demographics and personality traits. We aim to gain a comprehensive understanding of the factors that drive or hinder GAI adoption in academia so that policymakers, educators, and technology developers can make informed decisions when developing guidelines, interventions, and tools to better support students' learning.

2 Use of GAI and Influencing Factors

University students are increasingly reported to use GAI for various academic work. Research has examined students' use of ChatGPT and its effectiveness in various learning tasks. Some studies have shown that GAI improves students' learning and achievements, such as programming [7], math learning [4], writing [11], English learning [8], and lab tasks [2]. For example, Guhan et al. surveyed Engineering English as a Second Language students regarding their experiences and perceptions of employing ChatGPT in the English language classroom. Overall, the students reported that ChatGPT has greatly enhanced learners' vocabulary, listening, speaking, writing, and reading skills [7]. On the other hand, concerns have been raised about the use of GAI in academic work (e.g., the accuracy of the content), as over-reliance might have a negative impact on students' critical thinking and problem-solving abilities, posing a threat to academic ethics [9].

2.1 Student Demographics and GAI Use

Researchers have explored how GAI use is associated with various factors. A five-country study on the factors influencing university students' attitudes and use of ChatGPT found that students' use of ChatGPT is positively associated with their perceived ease of use, perceived usefulness, positive attitude towards technology, social influence, behavioral and cognitive elements, low anxiety, and minimal perceived risks [1]. They suggested that policies for ChatGPT adoption in higher education should be tailored to individual contexts, considering the variations in student attitudes.

Zhang et al. (2024) investigated the association between socioeconomic status (SES) and digital and AI literacy with the types of Chat GPT use among college students. [21]. They measured students' SES using seven questions that inquired about first-generation university student status, percentage of student loans, parental education, estimated family income, perceived family social class, and socioeconomic status. They found that university students from higher socioeconomic status (SES) families tend to use ChatGPT more frequently. They suggested that future studies should investigate the gender and racial/ethnic divides in ChatGPT use.

Students' academic standing may also influence the use of GAI, with senior students engaging with it more frequently. Surveys found that approximately 46% of high school students use AI tools, while more than half of university students use AI tools, surpassing the proportion of faculty members in higher education [14].

2.2 The Influence of Personality Traits on GAI Use

In addition to demographic information, research has examined the impact of personality on GAI use, as personality is considered one of the most fundamental psychological characteristics that influence the cognitive, affective, and behavioral actions of individuals [16]. The Big Five Personality traits are widely recognized in psychology as a framework for describing human personality and understanding human behavior, encompassing five broad domains (e.g., [3, 15, 17]): (a) Extraversion—Being outgoing, energetic, and sociable. (b) Agreeableness—Being compassionate, cooperative, helpful, empathetic, and trusting. (c) Conscientiousness—being organized, responsible, disciplined, and goal-oriented., (d) Emotional Stability—Being calm, secure, and free from persistent negative feelings, distress, and mood swings. And (e) Intellect/Imagination—being imaginative, creative, curious, and open to unconventional ideas and values.

Faruk et al. (2023) employed the Big Five Personality traits to study the relationship between students' use of AI and their personalities [5]. They found that individuals who were open to learning had a high correlation with the use of ChatGPT. In contrast, traits such as neuroticism and agreeableness have a negative influence on students' perception of GAI usefulness. In contrast, Filippi (2024) found that agreeableness has a positive influence on students' perception of GAI, which in turn impacts students' acceptance of AI [6].

Researchers also examined the combined influence of demographic information and personality on GAI. For example, Kaya et al. (2024) analyzed the relationships between demographic information, personality, and attitudes toward AI among adults recruited online. After controlling for demographic information (age, gender, educational level), they found that higher computer use and greater knowledge of AI are significant positive predictors of positive general attitudes toward AI, as AI learning anxiety is also a significant negative predictor of positive attitudes. Agreeableness significantly predicted negative attitudes toward AI [13].

We further the research on GAI use and influencing factors in the following ways: First, we further explore the conflicting influence of personality on GAI use, given that personality has shown inconsistent effects on students' GAI use in the existing literature, such as the influence of agreeableness. Second, we recruited participants from a diverse range of university students, including GAI users and non-users, as well as undergraduate and graduate students. In contrast, Faruk et al. (2023) only recruited ChatGPT users, excluding those who do not use the platform [5]. Kaya recruited adult participants online. Third, we examine how GAI use, and perception are associated with a range of demographic characteristics specific to college students, such as grade levels, majors, and language status—an under-investigated area—and the Big Five personality traits. This study aims to answer the following research questions:

1. How do university students use generative AI?

2. How is their demographic information—specifically gender, ethnicity, language status, and grade level—associated with GAI use?
3. How are students' personality traits related to their use and perceptions of GAI after controlling for significant demographic factors?

By answering these questions, the study provides valuable insights into the role of individual differences in GAI use and perception, enabling educators to better guide students in using GAI effectively and appropriately in higher education.

3 Methods

3.1 Participants

A total of 363 students from a public university in the USA participated in the study across three days in a university computer lab. After each student had signed the IRB consent form, they completed three surveys via Qualtrics in the lab and received $20 each as compensation for their time. The participants represented a diverse range of gender, ethnicity, academic major, grade level, and native English speaker status (Appendix A[1]).

3.2 Instruments

We developed five items to examine students' demographic information (Appendix A[1]) and 15 items to measure students' GAI use and perceptions (Appendix B[1]). To measure the Big Five Personality, we adopted the 50-item International Personality Item Pool (IPIP) [10, 12], with 10 items measuring each trait. This instrument has been considered the most reliable for measuring the Big Five Personality traits, and its validity has also been examined and supported [19]. After reversing the scores for any reversed statements, we calculated the alpha coefficient for the items measuring each trait based on our data. The results show that all the alpha coefficients are higher than .70 (Table 1). We further created five composite scores for the Big Five traits by averaging all the items measuring each construct and used the composite scores for the analysis.

Table 1. Descriptive Statistics of the Big Five Traits

Traits	Mean	SD	Alpha Coefficient
Extraversion	3.27	.86	.89
Agreeableness	4.00	.60	.76
Emotional Stability	2.82	.73	.80
Conscientiousness	3.58	.70	.81
Intellect/Imagination	3.76	.60	.76

[1] https://github.com/AI4STEM-Education-Center/UnderstandingUniversity-Students-Use-of-Generative-AI.

4 Analysis and Results

4.1 GAI Tool Use

Results suggest that totally 86% of students occasionally, frequently, or very frequently use GAI; about 70% of the students used GAI more than an hour per week; students used GAI for various purposes; About 35% of the students found GAI most useful for problem-solving; the most common concern is over-reliance on AI (44%), the next is the accuracy of the information generated (28%), and the third major concern is ethical concerns (17%); about 53% Students' preferred to use GAI tools over traditional resources for academic help, while 31% of students preferred the traditional resources. Approximately 49% of students learned about GAI from their friends or classmates, while only 12% learned about it from teachers or academic resources. While 53% of students received guidance from teachers/mentors on how to use GAI tools effectively, 39% did not report receiving guidance. Detailed statistics are presented in Appendices A[1] and B[1].

Principal component analysis with Promax rotation revealed three dimensions of the GAI uses: (a) GAI use for academic use, including frequency, duration, group use, peer influence on GAI use, and likelihood of future use; (b) Impact on learning and performance; (c) Ethical Concerns on using GAI. The three dimensions explained 75% of the original variance. Finally, the degree to which students prefer GAI over traditional resources for academic help is shown to be an independent construct. The five items measuring students' use of GAI for academic use have high internal consistency, Cronbach's alpha = .89. Therefore, we calculated the composite score, GAI Use, and used it in further analyses. However, the internal consistency of impact on learning and performance is rather low (alpha coefficient = .57). Therefore, we kept the two variables separate in the following analyses.

Based on the psychometrics validation, we focus on five GAI variables in the following analyses: *GAI Use, Impact on Performance, Impact on Learning, GAI Preference, and Ethical Concerns.* Table 2 reports the means of the five GAI variables. Appendix C includes more details, including the standard deviation of each variable.

Overall, students reported significantly higher GAI Use scores than their ethical concerns about it, t (362) = 2.70, $p < .007$, Cohen's d = .14; students felt that GAI has a more positive impact on their academic performance than their learning, t (362) = 14.26, p < .001, Cohen's d = .75.

4.2 Demographic Factors

To examine whether different student groups differ in their use and attitudes toward GAI, we conducted MANOVA. Results suggest that overall, (a) Male and female students did not differ in the five dimensions. (b) Students with different majors did not significantly differ either. (c) Students in different grades significantly differ in their responses (Fig. 1), Wilk's Lambda = .74, F (25, 1305) = 4.46, $p < .001$. Univariate ANOVA reveals that overall students in higher grades tend to use GAI more than those in lower grades, perceive the positive impact of GAI on their learning and academic performance, and prefer to utilize GAI more frequently. However, students in different grades do not

Table 2. Means of the GAI Variables for Different Groups1

Variable	Value	N	%	GAI Use	Impact on Performance	Impact on Learning	GAI Preference	Ethical Concern
Gender	Male	181	49.9	3.08	3.94	3.14	3.28	2.76
	Female	180	49.6	3.03	3.78	2.78	3.26	2.88
Ethnicity	Asian/PI	175	48.2	3.34	4.04	3.07	3.48	2.79
	Hispanic	45	12.4	2.97	3.76	2.89	3.33	2.73
	Black	23	6.3	2.71	4.17	3.09	3.17	2.65
	White	95	26.2	2.69	3.58	2.94	2.99	2.93
	Multi	22	6.1	2.88	3.76	2.41	2.82	2.94
Major	Agriculture	10	2.8	3.34	3.70	3.20	3.10	3.50
	Business	194	53.4	3.07	3.89	2.99	2.76	3.35
	Engineering	66	18.2	3.19	4.06	3.17	2.82	3.35
	Health	26	7.2	2.57	3.81	2.77	2.85	2.65
	Science	23	6.3	3.01	3.87	2.83	3.04	3.35
	Others	34	9.4	3.85	3.76	2.59	2.94	3.18
Grade	Fresh	112	30.9	2.65	3.65	2.84	3.00	2.85
	Soph	55	15.2	2.77	4.00	2.85	3.15	2.62
	Junior	48	13.2	3.23	4.00	2.98	3.40	2.65
	Senior	40	11.0	2.85	3.30	2.57	3.07	2.97
	Master	85	23.4	3.62	4.20	3.16	3.74	2.91
	PhD	21	5.8	3.51	4.43	3.81	3.19	3.10
Native	Yes	198	54.5	2.73	3.73	2.86	3.12	2.80
Speaker	No	165	45.5	3.43	4.01	3.07	3.44	2.87
Total		363		3.05	3.86	2.96	3.26	2.83

Note: Small groups with sample sizes of fewer than 10 are not included in this table as the results are less stable.

differ in their ethical concerns. (d) Students in different ethnic groups also differ in their responses on all the dimensions except for ethical concerns, Wilk's Lambda = .87, F (20, 1148) = 2.55, $p < .001$. Univariate ANOVA shows that Asian students used GAI significantly more than White and Black students, felt that GAI had a more positive impact on their academic performance than White students, and preferred GAI more than traditional learning resources than White students. (e) Non-native English speakers differ significantly from native English speakers (Fig. 2), Wilk's Lambda = .86, F (5, 357) = 11.74, $p < .001$. Univariate ANOVA shows that non-native English speakers significantly used GAI more than native English speakers (F (1, 361) = 50.43, $p <$ .001), perceived its positive impact on their academic performance more (F(1, 361) =

6.51, $p < .001$), and preferred GAI more than the traditional resources for help (F (1, 361) = 5.55, $p = .019$).

We conducted multiple regressions with various GAI responses as dependent variables, grades, language status (dummy variable), and ethnicity (dummy variables with White as the reference group) as predictors so that we could further examine the association between students' GAI responses and their demographic information after controlling for other demographic information. The results showed similar patterns to what MANOVA showed: (a) GAI Use: The model significantly predicted GAI Use, $R^2 = .23$, F (6, 356) = 17.94, p < .001. The higher the grade level (β = .273, $t = 5.54$, $p < .001$), non-native English speakers (β = .249, $t = 4.77$, $p < .001$), and Asian students (β = .14, $t = 2.39$, $p = .017$) use GAI more. (b) Impact on academic performance: The model significantly predicted a positive impact on academic performance: The model significantly predicted GAI impact on academic performance, $R^2 = .07$, F (6, 356) = 4.23, p < .001. The higher the grade level (β = .13, $t = 2.29$, $p = .023$), Asian students (β = .18, $t = 2.66$, $p = .008$) and Black students (β = .12, $t = 2.16$, $p = .031$) reported more positive impact on their academic performance. (c) Preference of GAI over Traditional Resources: The model significantly predicted to what degree students prefer to use GAI over traditional resources for academic help, $R^2 = .05$, F (6, 362) = 3.13, $p = .005$. The higher the grade level (β = .11, $t = 2.07$, $p = .04$) and Asian students (β = .154, $t = 2.32$, $p = .021$) prefer GAI more. (d) The model does not significantly predict the impact on learning and ethical concerns.

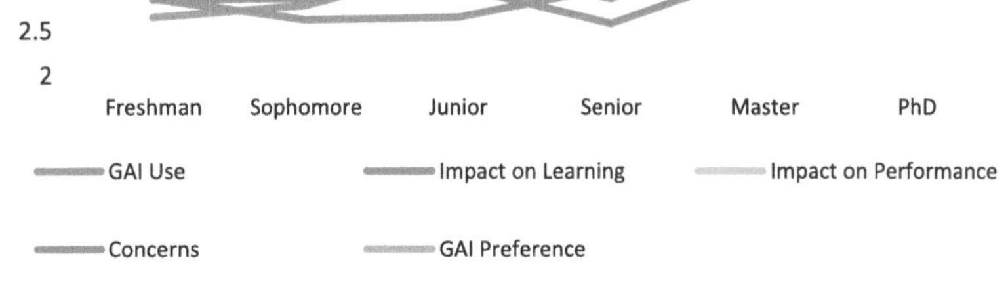

Fig. 1. Students' GAI responses vs. their grade levels

4.3 Personality

Correlation coefficient analyses (Table 3) show that emotional stability is positively correlated with a positive impact of GAI on performance, learning, and GAI preference, and

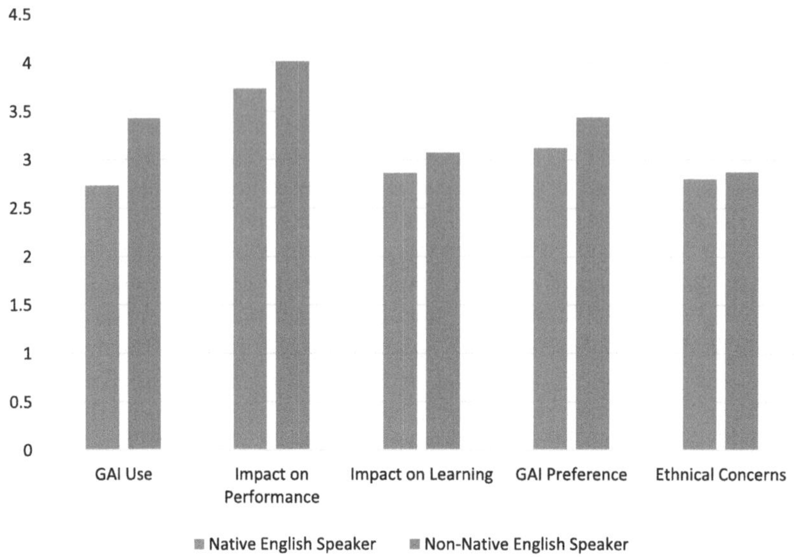

Fig. 2. Students' GAI responses vs. whether they are native English speakers.

is negatively correlated with ethical concerns. Extraversion is also positively correlated with GAI preference. In contrast, conscientiousness and intellect/imagination are negatively correlated with GAI use, and agreeableness is positively correlated with ethical concerns.

We further ran sequential regression to examine how GAI variables are associated with personality after students' demographic information is controlled for, specifically students' grade level and whether they are native English speakers. We did not include ethnicity in the sequential regression model because they are significantly correlated with language status and multiple personality traits. The regression results show (a) the Big Five traits significantly contributed to the prediction of GAI variables after controlling for the demographic information: the GAI Use ($\Delta R^2 = .032$, $F\,(5, 355) = 2.99, p = .012$), impact on performance ($\Delta R^2 = .032$, $F(5, 355) = 2.42$, $p = .035$), impact on learning ($\Delta R^2 = .045$, $F(5, 355) = 3.41, p = .005$), preference for GAI ($\Delta R^2 = .040$, $F(5, 355) = 3.04$, $p = .011$), and ethical concerns ($\Delta R^2 = .052$, $F(5, 355) = 3.93$, $p = .002$), b) GAI Use: individually, those who have higher conscientiousness reported lower GAI use, $\beta = -.122, t = -2.45, p = .015$. (b) Impact on academic performance: Those with higher extraversion reported a higher positive impact of GAI on their academic performance, $\beta = .11, t = 2.01, p = .046$, while those with higher agreeableness reported a lower positive impact of GAI on their academic performance, $\beta = -.12, t = -2.22, p = .027$. (c) Impact on learning experience: Those with higher emotional stability reported a higher positive impact on the learning experience, $\beta = .16, t = 3.16, p = .002$. (e) GAI Preference: Those with higher extraversion prefer GAI over the traditional resources more for academic help, $\beta = .12$, $t = 2.13$, $p = .034$; while those with high intellect/imagination prefer less GAI over the traditional resources, $\beta = -.11, t = -2.00, p = .047$. (d) Ethical concerns:

Table 3. Correlation Coefficients Between GAI Use and Personality

	GAI Use	Impact on Performance	Impact on Learning	GAI Preference	Ethical Concern
Impact on Performance	.270**				
Impact on Learning	.160**	.403**			
GAI Preference	.581**	.294**	.117*		
Ethical Concern	−.153**	−.180**	−.166**	−.304**	
Extraversion	**0.076**	**0.085**	**0.047**	**.125***	**−0.078**
Agreeableness	**−0.046**	**−0.08**	**−0.024**	**0.03**	**.112***
Emotional Stability	**0.002**	**.108***	**.183****	**.104***	**−.157****
Conscientiousness	**−.125***	**−0.013**	**0.065**	**−0.097**	**0.03**
Intellect Imagination	**−.111***	**−0.055**	**0.099**	**−0.094**	**0.046**

**. Correlation is significant at the 0.01 level (2-tailed).
*. Correlation is significant at the 0.05 level (2-tailed).
The correlation coefficients of the Big Five traits and GAI variables are bolded.

Those with high agreeableness tend to have more ethical concerns about GAI, $\beta = .13$, $t = 2.43$, $p = .016$, while those with high extraversion ($\beta = -.11$, $t = -1.99$, $p = .047$) and emotional stability (β = -.17, $t = -3.17$, $p = .002$) fewer ethical concerns about GAI use.

5 Discussion

The survey analysis results indicate that university students utilize GAI extensively for various purposes. However, they also express concerns, primarily regarding the accuracy of information and the potential for over-reliance on GAI. Despite these concerns, students' overall GAI use outweighs their concerns about its use. Additionally, students perceive GAI as having a more positive impact on their academic performance than on their learning, which aligns with their concerns about becoming overly dependent on the tool.

We compared the GAI use of different student subgroups. Students did not show significant differences in GAI use based on gender or academic major. However, students in higher grade levels were more likely to embrace GAI than those in lower grade levels. This trend may be attributed to multiple factors: (a) GAI tools, such as ChatGPT, are often discouraged in K-12 settings, whereas they are less restricted in higher education, particularly for graduate students. (b) Students in higher grade levels have more content knowledge and are therefore more proficient at utilizing GAI; for example, they can provide prompts that align with their desired outcomes. In contrast, younger students may lack the necessary understanding to formulate useful prompts that guide GAI in generating helpful information. For example, individuals who have sufficiently learned a programming language are more likely to utilize and benefit from GAI in coding than those with limited programming knowledge.

A comparison between native and non-native English speakers revealed that non-native English speakers used GAI significantly more than native English speakers. This trend may stem from the language barriers non-native speakers often encounter in academic settings where English is the dominant language, which likely drives them to rely more on GAI. For example, non-native English speakers may use GAI to proofread their essays or generate drafts more often than native English speakers. Interestingly, Asian students demonstrated the highest levels of GAI adoption, and both Asian and Black students reported a more positive impact of GAI on their academic performance compared to their White peers. Although a larger proportion of Asian students are non-native English speaker less than White students, the disparity in GAI use between Asian and White students remains significant even after accounting for language proficiency.

The examination of personality measured by Big Five traits suggests that students' personality traits significantly predict their GAI use and perceptions, even after demographic information is controlled for. Students with higher extraversion reported a more positive impact on performance, more GAI preference, and fewer ethical concerns for GAI use academic assistance, which may be due to their tendency to seek external engagement and collaborative learning.

Students who are highly conscientious are less likely to use GAI. We suspect that their heightened sense of social responsibility and desire to avoid plagiarism or overreliance on GAI could make them more cautious about using GAI for coursework.

Students who have higher agreeableness did not perceive GAI as beneficial for their academic performance. Instead, they expressed greater concerns about the ethical implications of using GAI for academic work. Previous research has reported mixed findings on the relationship between agreeableness and GAI use, with both positive [5] and negative [6] effects observed. We suspect that the discrepancy in the agreeableness measure is due to the information to which the students are most exposed. If students receive more information that discourages them from using GAI and emphasizes the concerns associated with its use, students with high agreeableness may use GAI less and develop negative attitudes. On the other hand, if students are encouraged to use GAI, those with high agreeableness are more likely to adopt it. Given that different universities have varying policies on GAI use and instructors have differing attitudes toward GAI use, students with high agreeableness may be impacted differently in various contexts. Additionally, the outputs from GAI are prone to errors and often require multiple prompts and iterations. Highly agreeable students may be more likely to accept and use false information generated by GAI, only to later realize it is inaccurate, which can lead to mistrust in GAI.

Finally, students who have high extraversion and emotional stability show less ethical concerns about using GAI for academic work. Those with higher extraversion prefer GAI more than traditional resources, while students who have higher intellect/imagination prefer GAI less than traditional resources for academic help.

Overall, university students differ in their GAI use and attitudes. Both demographic information and personality account for these differences. GAI has great potential to improve not only academic performance but also learning. Students seemed to underestimate the benefit of GAI on learning compared to the reported benefit of GAI on academic performance.

It is noted that a large percentage of students reported not receiving guidance on GAI use from mentors or institutional figures. This gap highlights the need to guide students to effectively and appropriately use GAI so that GAI can essentially improve their learning.

The lack of guidance and regulation may also lead to fairness issues due to the differences in students' perceptions of GAI benefits and concerns, and consequently, their use of GAI. Institutional guidance should foster the ethical use of AI, ensuring that students can utilize GAI to effectively enhance their learning rather than avoiding it due to uncertainty or ethical concerns due to their demographic and personality differences.

6 Conclusion

Our study aligns with previous research, highlighting the various ways students integrate GAI into their academic practices, with note summarization, topic revision, and creative brainstorming being the most common uses. The findings suggest that GAI serves as a valuable tool for enhancing students' learning experiences, particularly in areas like problem-solving, coding, and technical writing. However, AI adoption is not uniform across all students; individual demographic information and personality traits influence how students use or perceive GAI tools.

Demographic factors, such as grade level and ethnicity, are also associated with the use of AI among university students. The higher the grade level, the more likely students are to use and prefer GAI. Non-native English speakers used GAI more than native English speakers, probably due to the strength of GAI in English writing. Asian and Black students were more likely to report positive impacts from GAI use on their academic performance.

The results also highlight that students' personalities play a crucial role in shaping their AI use patterns. Students who have high extraversion and emotional stability are more likely to adopt ChatGPT as a source of academic support. In contrast, students who have high z use GAI less, possibly viewing AI as less compatible with their disciplined study habits or moral standards. Similarly, agreeable students exhibit heightened ethical apprehensions about AI's role in academia, possibly reflecting the overall discouragement from instructors of using GAI and their strong social desirability.

This study can be expanded in multiple directions: First, this study is limited to one-time cross-sectional survey data. Future research can collect longitudinal data on students' experiences and attitudes with GAI in their academic work. Investigating whether students' skepticism or acceptance of GAI evolves over time and responds to instructors' guidance, and how this process interacts with their personality traits would provide deeper insights into the dynamics of student engagement with GAI. Moreover, future research should interview students to discover the mechanism underneath the statistical relationship between GAI use and the influencing factors. Finally, empirical data are needed to study how to help students to use GAI to improve their learning, not just academic performance.

References

1. Abdaljaleel, M., et al.: A multinational study on the factors influencing university students' attitudes and usage of chatgpt. Sci. Rep. **14** (2024)
2. Brender, J., El-Hamamsy, L., Mondada, F., Engin Bumbacher: who's helping who? When students use ChatGPT to engage in practice lab sessions. In: Lecture Notes in Computer Science, vol. 14829, pp. 235–249 (2024)
3. Camps, J., Stouten, J., Euwema, M.: The relation between supervisors' big five personality traits and employees' experiences of abusive supervision. Front. Psychol. **7** (2016)
4. Fardian, D., Suryadi, D., Prabawanto, S., Jupri, A.: Integrating Chat-GPT in the classroom: a study on linear algebra learning in higher education. Int. J. Inf. Educ. Technol. **15**, 732–751 (2025)
5. Faruk, L., Rohan, R., Ninrutsirikun, U., Pal, D.: University students' acceptance and usage of generative AI (ChatGPT) from a psycho-technical perspective. In: 13th International Conference on Advances in Information, pp. 1–8 (2023)
6. Filippi, S., Motyl, B.: Development of a tool for evaluating the influence of engineering students' perception of generative AI on university courses based on personality, perceived roles in design teams, and course engagement. Multimodal Technol. Interact. **8**, 84 (2024)
7. Ghimire, A., Edwards, J.: Coding with AI: how are tools like ChatGPT being used by students in foundational programming courses. In: Lecture Notes in Computer Science, vol. 14830, pp. 259–267 (2024)
8. Guhan, M., Suganthan, C.: A study on analyzing the role of ChatGPT in English acquisition among ESL learners during English language classroom. Bodhi Int. J. Res. Hum. Arts Sci. **8**, 75–84 (2023). https://doi.org/10.13140/RG.2.2.28252.56961
9. Hasanein, A.M., Sobaih, A.E.E.: Drivers and consequences of ChatGPT use in higher education: key stakeholder perspectives. Eur. J. Invest. Health Psychol. Educ. **13**, 2599–2614 (2023)
10. IPIP collaboratory: Administering IPIP Measures, with a 50-item Sample Questionnaire. https://ipip.ori.org/new_ipip-50-item-scale.htm
11. Jelson, A., Manesh, D., Jang, A., Dunlap, D., Lee, S.W.: An empirical study to understand how students use ChatGPT for writing essays. arXiv preprint arXiv:2501.10551 (2025)
12. Johnson, J.A.: Measuring thirty facets of the Five Factor Model with a 120-item public domain inventory: development of the IPIP-NEO-120. J. Res. Pers. **51**, 78–89 (2014)
13. Kaya, F., Aydin, F., Schepman, A., Rodway, P., Yetişensoy, O., Kaya, M.: The roles of personality traits, AI anxiety, and demographic factors in attitudes toward artificial intelligence. Int. J. Hum.-Comput. Interact. **40**(2), 497–514 (2022)
14. KTVZ homepage: How many high school and college students are using AI tools? https://ktvz.com/stacker-money/2024/02/29/how-many-high-school-and-college-students-are-using-ai-tools
15. McCrae, R.R., John, O.P.: An introduction to the five-factor model and its applications. J. Pers. **60**(2), 175–215 (1992)
16. McCrae, R.R., Costa, P.T.: The five-factor theory of personality. In: John, O.P., Robins, R.W., Pervin, L.A. (eds.) Handbook of Personality: Theory and Research (3rd ed.), pp. 159–181. The Guilford Press, New York (2008)
17. Mount, M.K., Barrick, M.R., Stewart, G.L.: Five-factor model of personality and performance in jobs involving interpersonal interactions. Hum. Perform. **11**(2–3), 145–165 (2011)
18. Weng, X., Xia, Q., Ahmad, Z., Chiu, T.K.F.: Assessment and learning outcomes for generative AI in higher education: a scoping review on current research status and trends. Australas. J. Educ. Technol. **40**(6), 37–55 (2024)

19. Ypofanti, M., et al.: Psychometric properties of the International Personality Item Pool Big-Five personality questionnaire for the Greek population. Health Psychol. Res. **3**(2), 2206 (2015)
20. Zhai, X.: ChatGPT user experience: implications for education (2022)
21. Zhang, C. (Xinyi), Rice, R.E., Wang, L.H.: College students' literacy, ChatGPT activities, educational outcomes, and trust from a digital divide perspective. New Media Soc. (2024)

Scaling Curriculum Mapping in Higher Education: Evaluating Generative AI's Role in Curriculum Analytics

Vimukthini Jayalath(✉), Abhinava Barthakur, Shane Dawson, Joanne Tingey, Lin Crase, and Vitomir Kovanović

University of South Australia, Adelaide, SA 5000, Australia
balage.jayalath@mymail.unisa.edu.au, {abhinava.barthakur, shane.dawson, joanne.tingey, lin.crase, vitomir.kovanovic}@unisa.edu.au

Abstract. Curriculum mapping plays a critical role in education to ensure alignment between outcomes, content, graduate skills and assessment. Program requirements are typically informed by industry needs and embedded within the curricula and assessment tasks. Curriculum Analytics (CA) has introduced a level of automation to the process of curriculum mapping primarily through machine learning (ML) models. While such CA approaches have served to reduce workload pressures, they continue to face challenges in capturing the nuanced extent to which graduate skills are developed across a program. This study introduces a novel approach using Large Language Models (LLMs) to act as *co-curriculum reviewers*. Using data from an undergraduate program, we evaluate the effectiveness of LLMs in generating weighted mappings of graduate skills across assessments and compare them to those produced by ML based CA methods. The findings suggest that LLM-generated mappings more closely align with expert judgements (Krippendorff's alpha of 0.76) than those produced by ML based CA models (0.65). The results demonstrate the potential for LLM-driven approaches to curriculum mapping to enhance quality assurance processes linked to curricular alignment, accreditation, and personalized learning pathways.

Keywords: Curriculum Analytics · Curriculum Mapping · Skills · Generative AI · Higher Education

1 Introduction

Within higher education, a well-designed curriculum is essential for an effective learning experience. The stated curriculum outlines the knowledge, skills, and competencies students are required to achieve. The articulation and documenting of curriculum is commonly referred to as *curriculum mapping*. Curriculum mapping systematically identifies where and how specific knowledge, skills, and competencies are embedded within course and program curricula [1]. Curriculum mapping is also an important part of the academic

A. I. Cristea et al. (Eds.): AIED 2025, LNAI 15877, pp. 294–308, 2025.
https://doi.org/10.1007/978-3-031-98414-3_21

accreditation process, where the alignment of learning outcomes, activities and assessment across a program is essential. As an initial step in program design, curriculum mapping ensures that courses and modules are aligned, implementing a progressive and scaffolded learning journey for students [2].

Traditionally, the curriculum mapping process has relied on manual methods that are time-consuming and susceptible to inconsistencies [3]. As a result, curriculum mapping is often limited to a small number of courses, leading to inconsistencies, misalignments and fragmented skill development across the study program [4]. These challenges have prompted the development of Curriculum Analytics (CA) [5], that applies data-driven methods to improve curriculum design, program quality, and student outcomes. CA applications extend to serve quality assurance processes, allowing universities to align their curricula with the relevant accreditation standards, where a key component is the mapping of professional skills. CA enhances the mapping process by mitigating the limitations associated with more traditional, manual, time-intensive methods that affect mapping quality [3]. A wide range of Machine Learning (ML) approaches have demonstrated their potential in CA [6, 7], ranging from rule-based methods [8] to transformer-based models like BERT [9].

While the use of ML methods in CA has many benefits, significant issues remain. One of the key issues concerns the use of binary relationships in curriculum mapping that only allows for documenting the presence or absence of knowledge and skills within a particular part of the curriculum. Such relationships do not realistically model the actual skill and knowledge development, neglecting the varying levels of associations and contextual nuances within curricula. With the recent advent of Large Language Models (LLMs), there is a significant opportunity to utilize these models for curriculum mapping to extend the scope of CA and enhance the quality of curriculum mapping that is being produced. LLMs, such as the GPT family of models, have shown promise to be used as a tool for *reviewing the curriculum mapping* process within higher education [10, 11]. Researchers have also used LLMs to align the curricula with learning objectives [12]. However, their ability to establish weighted mappings between the skills and curricula and examine the quality of the mappings remains unexplored.

This paper builds on the earlier work of Zamecnik and colleagues [11] to investigate the potential of LLMs as a *co-curriculum reviewer*. The study aims to explore the use of LLMs to create weighted curriculum mappings that capture the complexity of skill acquisition across an entire program of study. Unlike binary mappings, weighted mappings allow for more nuanced insights into how multiple skills are embedded. For example, an assessment item involving a team-presentation might assign weights for grading. In this instance, Teamwork as 30% and Oral Communication as 70% of the final grade. Binary labels are not able to capture this level of granularity. More fine-grained insights can help curriculum designers to identify where students may receive repeated or balanced exposure to critical skills across their academic journey and whether any skills are disproportionately emphasized or neglected. Using the data from a three-year undergraduate study program in accounting, this research explores its potential to improve curriculum mapping practices within higher education by comparing LLM's performance to traditional ML methods. Furthermore, it investigates how LLMs perform when mapping different skills across varying academic year levels. By enabling more granular mappings of skills across the curricula, we propose that LLMs can support the personalization of the curriculum by catering to the diverse academic needs and backgrounds of students.

2 Background

2.1 Curriculum Analytics and Curriculum Mapping

Curriculum Mapping seeks to systematically align learning objectives, assessments, and instructional activities, ensuring coherence and effectiveness in skill development [13, 14] while also helping educators identify gaps and misalignments in the curriculum. A common application of Curriculum Mapping is to link curricula to specific skill sets, often referred to as Graduate Attributes, Enterprise Skills, or Professional Standards, that students are expected to demonstrate upon graduation [3]. In professional degree programs such as business education, and particularly accounting degrees, skill mapping has gained attention as a key approach for strengthening the employability skills of future professionals while ensuring compliance with accreditation standards [15].

Despite its benefits, institutions often struggle with programmatic oversight of curriculum mapping due to siloed course design, where courses are developed independently by different instructors, leading to misalignment in program-level learning outcomes [4]. Over time, this can result in curriculum drift, where minor, uncoordinated changes in individual courses accumulate, resulting in misalignment with program-level objectives [16]. While course and program objectives, along with assessment practices, are routinely reviewed for accreditation [17], it can be a time-consuming and labor-intensive process and might also lack the broader perspective to provide insights into program-level skill mapping. By addressing these issues, institutions can improve the quality of courses and programs, ensuring students acquire the requisite knowledge and skills.

Curriculum Analytics [5] has emerged as a subfield of Learning Analytics (LA)[18] that leverages computational techniques to enable educators and other stakeholders to make informed, evidence-based decisions regarding curriculum improvements. CA has gained prominence within higher education contexts as it uses advanced data-driven methods to improve curriculum decisions and the overall quality of degree programs [3]. Some of the earliest CA studies employed social network analyses to aid sensemaking of complex curriculum structures [5]. CA integrated with curriculum mapping can bring together the necessary evidence to demonstrate that educational programs have met the required standards and learning outcomes for professional accreditation [3].

2.2 ML and NLP for Curriculum Analytics and Curriculum Mapping

Initial approaches to structured curriculum mapping relied on simple rule-based methods [8], which were limited in their ability to adapt to diverse learning contexts. With the advancement of NLP techniques, transformer-based models, such as BERT [19] and RoBERTa [7], that use contextual embeddings have shown reasonable accuracy in curriculum mapping. Similarly, domain-specific embeddings such as BioBERT [6], JobBERT [20] and NER models [21] provided specialized use cases such as curriculum mapping for medical education, skill extraction for jobs and skill extraction in non-English contexts. Although NLP methods can be optimized for specific fields, they are often limited in their ability to scale for broader applications, such as curriculum mapping across diverse academic disciplines and skill levels. Frameworks like SkillNER and TF-IDF have also been employed to align curriculum content with occupational demands, offering robust solutions for skill extraction [9]. While sentence embedding models such as BERT and its variations and skill extraction methods as SkillNER continue to demonstrate potential in text mapping processes [7, 22], they rely heavily on keyword matching and can miss contextual nuances in course content.

These CA studies have mitigated some of the limitations related to the traditional mapping process that requires different stakeholders to manually review program and course documentation to identify where accredited standards are taught and assessed. This was known to be a time-intensive process [23], prone to human error and bias and lack of scalability [3]. While these CA methods have streamlined the implementation of such mappings, concerns have been raised about the granularity and depth of these connections [24]. A primary limitation of the mapping process is that it only indicates the *presence or absence of skills* in a course/module. As such, this does not capture the varying degrees of association between the skills evaluated and the specific assessments. This limitation is particularly pertinent for business education, where detailed articulation of graduate skills and outcomes is required for compliance with professional accreditation standards [15]. The integration of advanced ML techniques into curriculum mapping to quantify skill development in graduates, presents a foundation for using AI to address the complex process of curriculum mapping [25].

2.3 AI and GenAI for Curriculum Analytics and Mapping.

Integrating AI into curriculum mapping has emerged as a transformative approach to align educational content with skills according to workforce demands. Lai[26] and Ketamo [27] have utilized AI to analyze course descriptions, job advertisements, and industry reports, ensuring curricula remain relevant to external demands using external resources. Whereas McLaren and colleagues [10] have extended this line of work by focusing on the course documentation, aligning content with learning objectives, and addressing the complexity of high-quality curricula. A study on skill extraction for recruitment purposes that compares ML methods and fine-tuned LLMs with tagged data [28] also demonstrates promising results for the use of AI for curriculum mapping.

ChatGPT has been explored for its potential in educational contexts. GPT-4 has been used to generate high-quality learning objectives for courses, with findings indicating that these AI-generated learning objectives align with best practices and cover the cognitive levels required [12]. Another study explored ChatGPT as a *virtual colleague* in course design, highlighting its efficiency in structuring content and brainstorming while noting its limitations, such as generic outputs and the need for human intervention [29]. Zamecnik and colleagues [11] achieved 71% accuracy in mapping skills to 26 higher education courses that only focused on mapping the presence or absence of skills. These studies suggest that integrating GenAI into the curriculum mapping process, using a

Human-AI collaboration, and using the university-provided course outline documentation and expert labelling could improve the alignment between educational outcomes and actual teaching practices.

However, this approach does not account for the significance of each skill in relation to the assessments. For example, some skills may be more central to a given task while others play only a minor role. By incorporating skill weights, a more granular understanding of how each assessment is mapped to the skills could be achieved by allowing for a clear understanding of which assessments strongly develop specific skills and which only provide minimal skill development. Addressing this gap is the main objective of the study, with the aim to refine the skill mapping methodologies to capture the depth and relevance of each skill targeted by assessments.

3 Research Questions

The literature review emphasizes the need to move from binary skill-assessment mappings to weighted mappings to better understand skill development. Additionally, it highlighted the need for empirical studies to assess how AI successfully matches academic curricula with the needs of the digital economy to improve curricular alignment [30]. To address this gap, we aim to build a GenAI model that derives weighted mappings from assessments to skills using course outlines available on the university portal and compare the performance with the traditional ML models for curriculum mapping purposes. More specifically, this study addresses the following two research questions (RQs):

RQ1: How effectively can GenAI assign skill weights to assessments based on course outline documents? How does its performance compare to traditional ML methods in mapping skills to course content?

The first research question explores using GenAI to develop weighted skill-assessment mappings, comparing its outputs to expert weightings and traditional ML methods to determine the possibility of scaling the mapping process.

RQ2: Are there performance differences in mapping various Skills using GenAI, and how does its performance vary across different academic year levels?

The second research question examines whether GenAI's performance in skill-assessment mapping varies by skill type and academic year level, assessing potential biases and its suitability for scalable curriculum mapping. The rationale behind this question is the assumption that different skills have varying levels of complexity within the curriculum [31], and assessment complexity also differs across year levels in a degree program.

4 Methodology

4.1 Study Design

The study was conducted at a large public Australian university, focusing on the Bachelor of Commerce (Accounting) program and its associated courses. The analysis focused on identifying the integration of Enterprise Skills in the Business School, which are high-level skills as follows: 1) Self-management, 2) Problem-solving, 3) Teamwork, 4) Ethical awareness, 5) Written Communication, 6) Oral Communication, 7) International perspective.

To address the RQs, we analyzed all curriculum data from 19 courses in the program, spanning its full three-year duration. For each course, the collected data included the course description, objectives, details of the assignments and binary information about the assessment of enterprise skills in each assignment. We did not include assessment rubrics as these varied between course offerings over the three years.

4.2 Study Methods

Upon initial evaluation of the mapping data within the university course management system, we identified significant data quality issues, with many of the enterprise skills being incorrectly mapped to the curriculum. As a result, our first step in the analysis was to create a gold standard of skill mapping across the curriculum.

- **Step 1: Expert skill mapping evaluation**

To create a gold-standard dataset concerning the assessment of enterprise skills, two domain experts with extensive teaching experience in this program were tasked to identify where and to what extent each of the seven enterprise skills was assessed. The experts were given the definitions of all enterprise skills and were required to assign weights for each skill, for each course assessment, cross-referencing the initial binary mappings from the course management system. These weights were compared using Krippendorff's alpha [32] as the inter-rater reliability measure. Krippendorff's alpha was chosen over other measures such as Cohen's kappa because it accommodates multiple raters, handles missing data, and supports interval-scaled or continuous variables making it more appropriate for comparing the skill weightings in this study. Krippendorff's alpha has values ranging from -1 to + 1 where $\alpha = 1$ indicating perfect agreement, $\alpha = 0$ reflecting random agreement, and $\alpha < 0$ signaling systematic disagreement among raters [33]. The overall Krippendorff's alpha value for the reviewers' labelling was 0.70, reflecting a strong consensus among the two reviewers. The detailed skill level agreements are presented in Table 2, with the interpretation of these agreements following the benchmark values outlined by [34] (Table 1).

After the independent reviewing, the expert annotators compared their results resolve discrepancies to establish a unified ground truth. This collaboratively developed benchmark minimises individual biases improving the reliability and validity of the benchmark dataset for evaluating the performance of mappings generated by GenAI and NLP-based ML models.

- **Step 2: Skill mapping using BERT-based NLP model (Baseline)**

The study's second phase focused on analysing assessment descriptions based on their semantic similarity and mapping them to predefined skill categories to provide weights. The consensus-based seed phrases/words representing specific skills were developed by the reviewers to ensure consistency with the terminology used in the course outline documents (e.g., "Teamwork": "Group Presentation", "Group Report", "Progress Report

Table 1. Comparison of Krippendorff's alpha between two expert reviewers

Skill	KA	Interpretation of KA
Problem-Solving	0.47	Moderate Agreement
Teamwork	0.79	Substantial Agreement
Written Communication	0.29	Fair Agreement
Self-Management	0.73	Moderate Agreement
Ethical Awareness	0.50	Moderate Agreement
Int Perspective	0.68	Moderate Agreement
Oral Communication	0.75	Moderate Agreement

(Group)"). These seed phrases were used as references to match against descriptions in the dataset.

This study utilizes a pre-trained extension of BERT [35], The "RoBERTa" model from Hugging Face's transformers library to generate sentence-level embeddings for skill phrases and assessment descriptions [7], that transformed the text into high-dimensional numerical vectors (embeddings) to be used in this context. This model tokenizes the text, averages the token embeddings, and returns a single vector for the text. It was stored in a dictionary that maps each skill name to its corresponding embedding vector(s).

The assessment descriptions' preprocessing phase involves two main steps: data extraction and stop word removal. The descriptions were extracted from the course outline documents manually. The text was cleaned manually by checking if the description was available for the provided assessment name; if not, it was indicated as NA. This study utilised the Python 'nltk' library to remove stop words that do not carry significant meaning from the assessment descriptions. Finally, the descriptions were transformed into numerical embeddings by iteration using the same model mentioned above. The assessment embeddings were compared to each skill embedding using cosine similarity for each description [9, 22]. If the similarity is below a threshold (0.1), it sets it to 0, to filter out weak matches. A similarity threshold of 0.1 was applied to suppress weak matches. After calculating the similarities for all skills, the similarity scores were normalized to sum to 1, reflecting the relative weight of each skill in the description. These scores were taken as the weights of each skill for comparison.

- **Step 3: Skill mapping using GenAI**

In the third phase of the study, weighted mappings between skills and assessments were generated using GenAI (ChatGPT 4.0). While we focused on improving the reproducibility of the study by utilizing deterministic settings, there were challenges with varying model outputs between model runs due to the complex nature in which LLM responses are generated. The prompting used in this study (Appendix) was iteratively refined, to improve its ability to identify skills based on their definitions and present the results in a clear, user-friendly data table format.

The zero-shot prompt initially assigns the role of a *co-curriculum reviewer* and then guides the model to review each course outline document and analyze the assessments to estimate the percentage weight for each skill, with non-applicable skills receiving a zero, along with the criteria for the sum of the total weight to 100%. It included detailed definitions for each skill. This approach aims to enhance the accuracy of skill mapping and ensure consistency in comparing the derived weights with manual and machine learning-based estimates.

5 Results

5.1 RQ 1: Comparing the NLP and GenAI Skill Mapping Accuracy

To answer the first RQ, the analysis compared the developed expert weightings with those provided by GenAI and NLP. The skill weight tables generated by GenAI closely aligned with the expert-annotated ground truth, achieving an overall Krippendorff's alpha of 0.76, compared to the overall Krippendorff's alpha value of the ML model achieving 0.65, reflecting a moderate level of consensus with the review ratings.

Table 2. Comparison of Krippendorff's alpha from GenAI and ML methods for each Skill

Skill	Krippendorff's alpha and Interpretation			
	GenAI model		BERT-based NLP model	
Problem-Solving	0.59	Moderate Agreement	0.24	Fair Agreement
Teamwork	0.63	Substantial Agreement	−0.05	Systematic Disagreement
Written Comm	0.37	Fair Agreement	0.04	Slight Agreement
Self-Management	0.50	Moderate Agreement	−0.31	Systematic Disagreement
Ethical Awareness	0.47	Moderate Agreement	−0.12	Systematic Disagreement
Int Perspective	0.26	Fair Agreement	0.10	Slight Agreement
Oral Communication	0.86	Near-Perfect Agreement	−0.07	Systematic Disagreement

The results reveal that GenAI consistently outperformed the ML model in agreement levels for Krippendorff's alpha value, considering the interpretation of each across skills. The alpha value was below 0 for most of the skill mappings using the NLP model compared to the GenAI mapping, which consistently had alpha values higher than 0. Some skill (International Perspective) mapping had some alignment between the models with alpha values of 0.26 and 0.10, respectively, while other skills (Self-management, Teamwork) had discrepancies between the two models, with GenAI consistently outperforming the ML model.

5.2 RQ 2: Examining GenAI Mapping Performance Across Different Skills and Academic years

To explore RQ2, we examined the varying ability of the GenAI model to map the seven skills. According to Table 2, Oral Communication stands out with near-perfect agreement (k = 0.86), showcasing exceptional consistency and Teamwork, which achieves substantial agreement (k = 0.63) in AI's interpretation. Problem-solving, self-management, and ethical awareness fall within the moderate range, reflecting a strong overall alignment. However, Written Communication and International Perspectives had lower alpha values than other skills and were observed with fair agreement.

To address the second part of the RQ2, we investigated how the model performed in mapping the skills across the three academic years. The results (Table 3) show a notable variability in Krippendorff's alpha across academic year levels. Year 1 generally exhibits lower agreement, with some very high alpha values (e.g., Teamwork and Oral Communication). Year 2 shows mixed results, with some negative values (e.g., Teamwork, Written Communication and Self-Management) suggesting inconsistencies in AI-based mapping. Year 3 demonstrates the highest agreement across all three years, with just International Perspective indicating an inconsistency.

Table 3. Comparison of Krippendorff's alpha of AI-based method for each Year

Skill	Y1	Y2	Y3
Problem-Solving	0.57	0.44	0.72
Teamwork	0.84	−0.13	0.99
Written Comm	0.41	−0.18	0.74
Self-Management	0.41	−0.11	0.72
Ethical Awareness	0.17	0.80	0.23
Int Perspective	0.38	0.50	−0.08
Oral Communication	0.80	0.77	0.98

6 Discussion

6.1 Addressing the Challenges of Skill Mapping: GenAI's Potential in Improving Efficiency and Alignment with Industry Standards

This study explored the potential of GenAI for curriculum mapping in higher education degree programs. Traditional curriculum mapping is a manual, labor-intensive process that, if not frequently updated, can result in misalignment with industry standards. Any updates to this mapping require a serious undertaking from educational stakeholders. As such, this paper proposes GenAI as a *co-curriculum reviewer* to map several Enterprise skills to assessments across an entire degree program.

Compared to traditional ML methods, GenAI demonstrated stronger performance in agreement with expert annotations. GenAI achieved an overall Krippendorff alpha of 0.76, indicating substantial agreement with the expert-annotated ground truth. In fact, this agreement is higher than the agreement we observed between the two human annotators (0.70). While this may seem counterintuitive, it is important to note that the baseline in this study was developed collaboratively by domain experts through discussion. Further analysis is needed to explore whether the LLM's performance generalizes across domains and how it complements human judgment in practice.

In contrast, the ML model achieved a lower alpha of 0.65, reflecting moderate agreement with the expert ratings. This difference echoes the findings of Herandi and colleagues [28] GenAI can capture contextual nuances compared to traditional ML methods, which may struggle to incorporate the full context provided by course outline documents. This can be due to the limitation of the ML models, which are dependent on its seed phrases to identify and provide weights, as opposed to GenAI, which can go through the document text and get the contextual understanding of most phrases with the help of the provided definition [20]. Prior studies have discussed how LLMs underperform [20, 21] compared to supervised methods, which showcase the difficulty in identifying skills without training data. While the specific context differs (to the curriculum mapping compared with Herandi et al.'s., [28] study on job descriptions), we show that GenAI outperforms traditional ML models in skill identification.

Assessment plays an important role in the curriculum. Assessment acts as a bridge between course-level outcomes and student learning progression. As such, there is a heavy emphasis on ensuring that assessment activities provide appropriate opportunities for students to demonstrate their learning (skills, knowledge, and attributes). However, individual instructors often have the autonomy to shift or change assessment practices or emphasize alternate content or skills. While the flexibility to revise curriculum documents can be argued as a means for updating and maintaining relevance and authenticity, the changes can also dramatically alter how a student is scaffolded through a program of study. As assessment practices at the course level are frequently designed in isolation from broader programmatic goals [17], a shift in a course can significantly change how a student develops and demonstrates professional standards and university graduate qualities. This present study demonstrates how LLMs can be used to provide proactive support and recommendations as individual courses are developed and revised, as well as the potential impact this may have on program-level outcomes.

6.2 Variations Across Skill Categories and Academic Year Levels

The results highlight that GenAI's performance in mapping skills to assessments varies across different skills and academic year levels, indicating potential challenges and strengths in its application for skill-weighting in higher education. Our findings align with Zamecnik and colleagues [11], who reported variability in agreement while mapping different professional skills.

As illustrated in Table 2, skills such Oral Communication achieved a near-perfect agreement, likely due to the clarity and specificity of course activities related to speaking, presenting, and verbal interaction. This clarity aids the model in accurately associating assessments with the correct skill, as shown by the consistent findings in accounting and business education, where oral presentation rubrics are well-defined [36]. Similarly, Teamwork showed substantial agreement, while Problem Solving, Self-Management and Ethical Awareness had moderate agreement. Problem-solving tasks, such as case studies and financial calculations, emphasize analytical thinking but may not always be explicitly labelled in the course materials. Self-management and Ethical Awareness assessments benefit from explicit references, therefore, tasks embedded within rubrics or less directly stated in the course documentation pose a challenge for GenAI's identification capabilities [37].

GenAI's performance was weaker for Written Communication and International Perspective, as these skills are often inferred from contextual cues rather than explicitly stated in course descriptions. This lack of clarity and contextual labeling in course documentation made mapping difficult for GenAI. The low agreement may also be due to limited training data for these skills [11]. The findings suggest that some skills require deeper contextual interpretation, which can challenge AI models without further fine-tuning or domain-specific training. More detailed rubrics, particularly in accounting courses [38], could improve the AI's ability to map skills accurately.

GenAI's performance varied across academic year levels, with the highest agreement in Year 3 assessments, suggesting more structured skill expectations in later years. This is traditionally the level where there is an uptick in career-ready skill development in accounting courses [38]. Year 1 showed mixed results, and Year 2 had the most inconsistency, particularly in skills like Teamwork, Written Communication, and Self-Management. These inconsistencies may stem from a transitional phase in curriculum design, without clear articulation of skill expectations. This can lead to vague or implicit cues that GenAI struggles to interpret. The improved performance in Year 3 courses indicates the stronger articulation and mapping of skill expectations in these later years of the program.

Educators often design the curricula, including assessments, assuming that students have a clear understanding of what is required of them and what skills they need to demonstrate without explicitly stating them [3]. Furthermore, as demonstrated in our findings, the descriptions used at different academic levels vary, making it more challenging for students to comprehend instructors' expectations. Our study demonstrates the capabilities of LLMs in highlighting the discrepancies and the lack of contextual information in course and assessment descriptions. We also observe that the complexity of these assessments evolves, further advocating for making program-level considerations while designing assessments and the curriculum more broadly. LLMs can be trained to make programmatic considerations to improve curriculum design and, thereby, enhance accreditation processes and support personalized learning.

6.3 Implications

Our findings provide a data-driven approach that supports educators to refine their teaching so that students can better understand the connection between coursework and employability. This approach also reduces the manual effort of curriculum mapping, allowing educators to focus more on instructional design. It can also improve decision-making by clearly representing skill distributions across courses and academic levels. Most importantly, it will address the issue of siloed course design, providing a comprehensive view of the entire program. This will improve transparency and help identify gaps or redundancies, ultimately leading to more informed decisions for program improvement. This approach also promotes scalability and efficiency, addressing the issue of curriculum drift if a course undergoes changes, it can be quickly updated, allowing for quick adjustments to ensure it remains relevant and up-to-date with both academic standards and industry demands.

6.4 Limitations and Future Work

Several limitations of this study must be acknowledged. First, the study primarily relies on a single LLM, the current version, and a single program for deriving weighted mappings between assessments and skills that may limit the generalisability of the findings. Second, the course outlines available on the university platforms might not provide sufficient information to understand the underlying skill development and the integration of specific skills in assessments. Third, the study does not extensively explore prompt engineering strategies, and variations of LLM models, which could significantly influence the quality of responses. In future work, we aim to enhance our study findings by exploring multiple LLMs for a better analysis. Additionally, we plan to extend our approach to multiple programs to improve the quality and generalizability of our findings. Future work could explore structured prompt engineering techniques, like Chain of Thought prompting, and models such as GPT o3-mini to understand the reasoning behind assigned weights. Additionally, integrating a human-in-the-loop process would refine and rank the usefulness of justifications, improving the quality of curriculum mappings by combining the strengths of LLM answers with human expertise for more reliable outcomes.

7 Conclusion

This study shows the potential of GenAI in improving curriculum mapping by aligning assessments with skills, particularly Enterprise skills, surpassing traditional ML models in terms of agreement with expert annotations. While GenAI shows strong performance for certain skills, challenges persist, especially with skills that require deeper contextual interpretation or are less explicitly defined in course documents. The variability across different academic years highlights the need for more consistent skill labelling and programmatic considerations when designing the curriculum. Furthermore, the findings suggest that GenAI can play a key role in improving the efficiency and scalability of curriculum mapping, helping educators to refine curriculum alignment with the evolving industry needs. By generating more granular, skill-level insights across multiple assessments and courses, it lays the groundwork for personalized learning pathways where students can be guided toward assessments or modules that target skills they need to strengthen, based on their individual progress. Future work will focus on addressing the limitations of this study, exploring multiple models, and incorporating human-centered analytics to further improve the effectiveness of AI-driven curriculum mapping.

Disclosure of Interests. The authors have no competing interests to declare relevant to this article's content.

Appendix

The prompt used: Link.

References

1. Jacobs, H.H.: Mapping the Big Picture. Integrating Curriculum & Assessment K-12. Association for Supervision and Curriculum Development, 1250 N (1997)
2. Harden, R.M.: AMEE Guide No. 21: curriculum mapping: a tool for transparent and authentic teaching and learning. Medical Teacher. **23**, 123–137 (2001). https://doi.org/10.1080/01421590120036547
3. Barthakur, A., Kovanović, V., Dawson, S., Deneen, C.C.: The application of curriculum analytics for improving assessments and quality assurance in higher education. Australasian J. Educ. Technol. (2024). https://doi.org/10.14742/ajet.9383
4. Rawle, F., Bowen, T., Murck, B., Hong, R.: Curriculum mapping across the disciplines: differences, approaches, and strategies. CELT. **10**, 75–88 (2017). https://doi.org/10.22329/celt.v10i0.4765
5. Dawson, S., Hubball, H.: Curriculum analytics: application of social network analysis for improving strategic curriculum decision-making in a research-intensive university. Teach. Learn. Inq. **2**, 59–74 (2014). https://doi.org/10.20343/teachlearninqu.2.2.59
6. Cher, P.H., Lee, J.W.Y., Bello, F.: Machine learning techniques to evaluate lesson objectives. In: Rodrigo, M.M., Matsuda, N., Cristea, A.I., Dimitrova, V. (eds.) Artificial Intelligence in Education, pp. 193–205. Springer, Cham (2022). https://doi.org/10.1007/978-3-031-11644-5_16
7. Sengupta, S., Das, A.K.: Automated mapping of course outcomes to program outcomes using natural language processing and machine learning. In: 2023 IEEE 3rd Applied Signal Processing Conference (ASPCON), pp. 44–48 (2023). https://doi.org/10.1109/ASPCON59071.2023.10396272
8. Alshanqiti, A., Alam, T., Benaida, M., Namoun, A., Taleb, A.: A rule-based approach toward automating the assessments of academic curriculum mapping. IJACSA **11** (2020). https://doi.org/10.14569/IJACSA.2020.0111285
9. Russell E., W.: Mapping curricula to skills and occupations using course descriptions. In: 2024 IEEE World Engineering Education Conference (EDUNINE), pp. 1–6 (2024). https://doi.org/10.1109/EDUNINE60625.2024.10500452
10. McLaren, B.M., et al.: Community college information technology education: curriculum mapping, a learning science framework, and AI learning technologies (2024)
11. Zamecnik, A., Barthakur, A., Wang, H., Dawson, S.: Mapping employable skills in higher education curriculum using LLMs. In: Ferreira Mello, R., Rummel, N., Jivet, I., Pishtari, G., Ruipérez Valiente, J.A. (eds.) Technology Enhanced Learning for Inclusive and Equitable Quality Education. pp. 18–32. Springer, Cham (2024). https://doi.org/10.1007/978-3-031-72312-4_2
12. Sridhar, P., Doyle, A., Agarwal, A., Bogart, C., Savelka, J., Sakr, M.: Harnessing LLMs in curricular design: using GPT-4 to support authoring of learning objectives (2023). http://arxiv.org/abs/2306.17459. https://doi.org/10.48550/arXiv.2306.17459
13. Oliver, B.: Assuring graduate outcomes. In: The Australian Learning and Teaching Council (2011)
14. Stewart, J., Shanmugam, S., Seenan, C.: Developing 21st century graduate attributes: incorporating novel teaching strategies in a physiotherapy curriculum. Eur. J. Physiotherapy. **18**, 194–199 (2016). https://doi.org/10.1080/21679169.2016.1181205
15. Treleaven, L., Voola, R.: Integrating the development of graduate attributes through constructive alignment. J. Mark. Educ. **30**, 160–173 (2008). https://doi.org/10.1177/0273475308319352
16. Johns-Boast, L.: Curriculum drift: a multi-dimensional perspective (2014)

17. Dawson, S., Pardo, A., Salehian Kia, F., Panadero, E.: An integrated model of feedback and assessment: from fine grained to holistic programmatic review. In: LAK23: 13th International Learning Analytics and Knowledge Conference, pp. 579–584. ACM, Arlington TX USA (2023). https://doi.org/10.1145/3576050.3576074
18. Siemens, G., Long, P.: Penetrating the fog: analytics in learning and education. EDUCAUSE Rev. **46**, 30–32+ (2011)
19. Yang, A.C.M., Chen, I.Y.L., Flanagan, B., Ogata, H.: From Human Grading to Machine Grading (2021)
20. Nguyen, K.C., Zhang, M., Montariol, S., Bosselut, A.: Rethinking skill extraction in the job market domain using large language models (2024). http://arxiv.org/abs/2402.03832. https://doi.org/10.48550/arXiv.2402.03832
21. Matkin, N., et al.: Comparative analysis of encoder-based NER and large language models for skill extraction from Russian job vacancies (2024). http://arxiv.org/abs/2407.19816. https://doi.org/10.48550/arXiv.2407.19816
22. Zaki, N., Turaev, S., Shuaib, K., Krishnan, A., Mohamed, E.: Automating the mapping of course learning outcomes to program learning outcomes using natural language processing for accurate educational program evaluation. Educ. Inf. Technol. **28**, 16723–16742 (2023). https://doi.org/10.1007/s10639-023-11877-4
23. Harvey, A., Kamvounias, P.: Bridging the implementation gap: a teacher-as-learner approach to teaching and learning policy. High. Educ. Res. Dev. **27**, 31–41 (2008). https://doi.org/10.1080/07294360701658716
24. Hughes, C., Barrie, S.: Influences on the assessment of graduate attributes in higher education. Assess. Eval. High. Educ.Eval. High. Educ. **35**, 325–334 (2010). https://doi.org/10.1080/02602930903221485
25. Jiang, Y., Xiao, F.: Intelligent optimization of curriculum system based on Washington accord graduate attribute. In: 2020 IEEE 9th Joint International Information Technology and Artificial Intelligence Conference (ITAIC), pp. 1815–1821 (2020). https://doi.org/10.1109/ITAIC49862.2020.9339107
26. Lai, J.W., Zhang, L., Chan, Y.S., Sze, C.C., Lim, F.S.: Compelling educational offerings: a study on the efficacy of skills identification platforms with course descriptions. In: INTED2024 Proceedings, pp. 2553–2561 (2024). https://doi.org/10.21125/inted.2024.0709
27. Ketamo, H., Moisio, A., Passi-Rauste, A., Alamäki, A.: Mapping the future curriculum: adopting artificial intelligence and analytics in forecasting competence needs. http://www.theseus.fi/handle/10024/172083. Accessed 10 Jun 2024
28. Herandi, A., Li, Y., Liu, Z., Hu, X., Cai, X.: Skill-LLM: repurposing general-purpose LLMs for skill extraction (2024). http://arxiv.org/abs/2410.12052. https://doi.org/10.48550/arXiv.2410.12052
29. Meron, Y., Tekmen Araci, Y.: Artificial intelligence in design education: evaluating ChatGPT as a virtual colleague for post-graduate course development. Des. Sci. **9**, e30 (2023). https://doi.org/10.1017/dsj.2023.28
30. Nyale, D., Karume, S., Kipkebut, A.: A comprehensive analysis of the role of artificial intelligence in aligning tertiary institutions academic programs to the emerging digital enterprise. Educ. Inf. Technol. (2024). https://doi.org/10.1007/s10639-024-12743-7
31. Singh, D., Morkel, J.D.: Holistic student development powering the student journey: a model for graduate attributes, curriculum, and the second transcript. CE **15**, 1784–1795 (2024). https://doi.org/10.4236/ce.2024.159109
32. Krippendorff, K.: Computing Krippendorff's Alpha-Reliability (2011)
33. Marzi, G., Balzano, M., Marchiori, D.: K-Alpha calculator–Krippendorff's alpha calculator: a user-friendly tool for computing Krippendorff's Alpha inter-rater reliability coefficient. MethodsX. **12**, 102545 (2024). https://doi.org/10.1016/j.mex.2023.102545

34. Hughes, J.: krippendorffsalpha: An R Package for Measuring Agreement Using Krippendorff's Alpha Coefficient (2021). http://arxiv.org/abs/2103.12170. https://doi.org/10.48550/arXiv.2103.12170
35. Devlin, J., Chang, M.-W., Lee, K., Toutanova, K.: BERT: pre-training of deep bidirectional transformers for language understanding (2019). http://arxiv.org/abs/1810.04805. https://doi.org/10.48550/arXiv.1810.04805
36. Kerby, D., Romine, J.: Develop oral presentation skills through accounting curriculum design and course-embedded assessment. J. Educ. Bus. **85**, 172–179 (2009). https://doi.org/10.1080/08832320903252389
37. Apostolou, B., Dull, R.B., Schleifer, L.L.F.: A framework for the pedagogy of accounting ethics. Acc. Educ. **22**, 1–17 (2013). https://doi.org/10.1080/09639284.2012.698477
38. Riebe, L., Jackson, D.: The use of rubrics in benchmarking and assessing employability skills. J. Manag. Educ.Manag. Educ. **38**, 319–344 (2014). https://doi.org/10.1177/1052562913511437

DrawAA-Net: An AI-Supported Evaluation Tool for Children's Drawings

Sinuo Wang[1], Wei Liu[1], Jixuan Wang[1], Yingying Yi[2], and Jing Xu[1(✉)]

[1] The Hubei Key Laboratory of Internet of Intelligence, School of Electronics Information and Communications, Huazhong University of Science and Technology, Wuhan 430074, China
{sinuo,liuwei,xujing}@hust.edu.cn

[2] Technological and Higher Education Institute of Hong Kong, Chai Wan, Hong Kong
yiyingying@thei.edu.hk

Abstract. Children's drawings serve as a vital window into their cognitive and emotional development, offering profound insights into their perspectives, creativity, and psychological states. However, traditional evaluation methods, reliant on subjective expert judgment, are often inconsistent, time-consuming, and impractical for large-scale educational applications. These limitations hinder the ability to provide timely, objective feedback, creating a critical gap in leveraging children's artistic expressions for educational and developmental purposes. To address these challenges, we introduce DrawAA-Net, an AI-supported framework designed to automate the evaluation of children's drawings. By integrating advanced deep learning and computer vision techniques, DrawAA-Net assesses multiple dimensions of artistic expression, including technical skills and aesthetic quality. Through extensive experimentation, we demonstrate that DrawAA-Net provides consistent, real-time feedback while balancing scientific rigor with human aesthetic preferences. This innovative tool not only enhances the efficiency and objectivity of drawing evaluations but also supports educators in fostering children's cognitive and emotional growth. Furthermore, by automating the assessment process, DrawAA-Net empowers educators to unlock the full potential of children's artistic expressions, offering a scalable solution for educational practice and developmental research. Project page: https://github.com/Nancywsn/DrawAA.

Keywords: Image Aesthetic Assessment · Aesthetic Evaluation Framework · Multitasking · Feature Fusion

1 Introduction

Children's drawings serve as a powerful medium for understanding their cognitive, emotional, and creative development. Through drawings, children express their perceptions, emotions, and imaginations, offering educators and psychologists unique insights into their psychological states and developmental stages

A. I. Cristea et al. (Eds.): AIED 2025, LNAI 15877, pp. 309–322, 2025.
https://doi.org/10.1007/978-3-031-98414-3_22

[1,2]. Research has shown that analyzing children's drawings can reveal critical information about their problem-solving abilities, emotional well-being, and creative potential [3]. As such, the evaluation of children's drawings is not merely an artistic exercise but a vital tool for fostering holistic development and tailoring educational strategies to individual needs.

However, traditional methods used by educators for evaluating children's drawings face significant limitations. These methods typically rely on subjective expert judgments, where assessors evaluate drawings based on multidimensional criteria such as technical skill, creativity, and emotional expression [4,5]. While these approaches are theoretically grounded in developmental psychology and art education, they are inherently inconsistent due to the subjective nature of human judgment. Different evaluators may interpret the same drawing in diverse ways, leading to unreliable assessments [6]. Moreover, traditional evaluations are time-consuming and labor-intensive, making them impractical for large-scale educational applications where timely feedback is essential [7]. These limitations highlight the urgent need for a more objective, efficient, and scalable approach to evaluating children's drawings.

The rapid advancement of artificial intelligence (AI) offers a promising solution to these challenges. In recent years, AI has been successfully applied to various domains of education, including automated grading, personalized learning, and sentiment analysis [8]. In the field of image aesthetic assessment (IAA), AI models such as NIMA [9] and SAAN [10] have demonstrated remarkable capabilities in evaluating the aesthetic quality of photographs and digital art. However, applying AI to the evaluation of children's drawings presents unique challenges. Unlike photographs or adult-centric art, children's drawings are often characterized by simplicity, developmental variability, and highly subjective expressiveness. Existing AI models [7,10], which prioritize technical perfection and adult aesthetic preferences, are ill-suited to capture the nuanced and developmental aspects of children's art. This gap underscores the need for a specialized AI framework tailored to the unique demands of children's drawings.

To address these challenges, we propose DrawAA-Net, an AI-supported evaluation tool specifically designed for children's drawings. Our work is motivated by the dual goals of enhancing the objectivity and scalability of drawing assessments while preserving the developmental and expressive richness of children's art. The key contributions of this paper are as follows:

- *A unified evaluation framework* that integrates multiple aesthetic dimensions—technical skill, aesthetic expressiveness, and creativity—into a cohesive assessment model. This framework bridges the gap between scientific rigor and human aesthetic preferences, enabling a more holistic evaluation of children's drawings.
- *A multi-task neural architecture* that combines deep learning with hand-crafted features (e.g., line quality, structural analysis) to capture both broad visual attributes and fine artistic details. This modular design ensures scalability and adaptability, allowing for the seamless integration of additional aesthetic dimensions in the future.

- *Empirical validation* through extensive experiments and expert reviews, demonstrating the precision and alignment of the tool with human evaluations. The results highlight the potential of DrawAA-Net to provide real-time data-driven feedback to educators, support personalized teaching strategies, and foster children's creative growth.

By automating the evaluation process, DrawAA-Net not only addresses the limitations of traditional methods but also opens new avenues for AI-driven developmental assessment. This work represents a significant step forward in the integration of AI technologies into art education, offering a transformative tool for understanding and nurturing children's cognitive and emotional development through their artistic expressions.

2 Related Work

2.1 Theories of Children's Drawings Evaluation

Evaluating children's drawings is inherently interdisciplinary, involving developmental psychology, cognitive science, and cultural studies [1]. Cultural differences among evaluators lead to varied perspectives, criteria, and theoretical frameworks. Theories such as Developmental Stage Theory [11], Multiple Intelligences Theory [12], Visual and Aesthetic Perception Theory [13], and Sociocultural Theory [14] provide diverse lenses through which to understand children's drawings. However, the challenge lies in quantifying these aspects and integrating them into a cohesive assessment framework.

Lowenfeld proposed subjective and objective evaluation scales for the evaluation of artworks, and the objective evaluation dimensions included stages of development, skill and technique, and organization of the work [4]. According to Eisner, artwork evaluation included technique, aesthetics, and creativity [5]. Kong et al. classified the evaluation of art works into the shape of lines, the use of colors, as well as the composition and ideas [15]. Zhu et al. [16] suggested that the grading standard of young children's artworks should be separated into composition, modeling, coloring, and creativity. Traditional frameworks are comprehensive but fragmented and subjective, making them less compatible with AI models. Therefore, there is a need to propose a unified evaluation framework to better meet the requirements of AI models.

2.2 Methods of Image Aesthetic Assessment

Beyond established AI applications in education—such as classroom monitoring and sentiment analysis [8]—we are exploring its integration with art education, particularly in evaluating children's drawings. Image Aesthetic Assessment (IAA) [17] aims to replicate human aesthetic judgment by analyzing visual features like color and composition. Traditional IAA methods relied on handcrafted feature extraction [18], but deep learning has now enabled AI systems to learn aesthetic features directly from large datasets, eliminating the need for manual feature engineering.

Currently, much of the work in IAA has focused on the aesthetic evaluation of photographic images. Li et al. proposed a two-level inference model, Theme-aware Visual Attribute Reasoning (TAVAR), which uses an attribute analysis network and a theme understanding network to extract aesthetic and thematic features [19]. Talebi et al.'s deep convolutional neural network model, Neural Image Assessment (NIMA), which evaluates photographic images by predicting a distribution of aesthetic scores [9]. Yang et al. introduced the multi-level transitional contrastive learning framework (MTCL), which improves aesthetic assessment by transitioning shared aesthetic features into personalized ones through contrastive learning [20]. Xin Jin et al. created a new image aesthetic mixed-attribute dataset (AMD-A) and proposed an effective multi-attribute data-driven method (AAAM) for aesthetic evaluation [21].

While IAA methods significantly improve the assessment of the aesthetic quality of photographic images, their application to art images is more challenging due to the unique nature of visual perception and the inherently subjective qualities of children's art. In response, recent studies have begun adapting IAA models for art-specific evaluation [7,22–24]. Yi et al. proposed a Style-Aware Network Architecture (SAAN), which effectively extracts both style-specific and general aesthetic features to evaluate art images [10]. This approach represents a step forward in adapting AI for the unique demands of art evaluation. However, despite progress in art-specific AI models, these approaches are still in the early stages of development, and further refinement is needed to more accurately assess children's drawings.

3 AI-Supported Evaluation Tool for Children's Drawings

To evaluate the aesthetic quality of children's drawings, we developed a specialized assessment tool through a four-stage process. First, we conducted a comprehensive review of existing evaluation standards to construct a unified theoretical framework for aesthetic evaluation that is compatible with AI. Next, we built a dataset of children's drawings based on this theoretical framework. We then developed a multi-aesthetic-attribute image evaluation network model and created the assessment tool. Finally, we evaluated the tool using network performance metrics and case studies, which are detailed in Sect. 4.

3.1 Theoretical Assessment Framework

Reviewing existing aesthetic evaluation frameworks for children's drawings, we developed a concise model centered on three key dimensions: technical skill, aesthetic value and expressiveness, and creativity and imagination. These dimensions collectively encompass the essential aspects of children's drawings, enabling a comprehensive and balanced assessment.

1. **Technical Skill:** This dimension focuses on the technical execution of the drawings, reflecting the creator's mastery of fundamental artistic techniques.

It is relatively objective, as it can be assessed through standardized criteria and quantitative methods, minimizing subjective bias. Key sub-dimensions include:
  - Line Quality: Evaluates the thickness, curvature, and smoothness of lines, which are critical for understanding the child's control and precision.
  - Color Usage: Assesses the accuracy, contrast, and harmony of color choices, providing insights into the child's understanding of color theory and application.
  - Composition: Analyzes the organization of elements within the drawing, focusing on visual balance and spatial distribution.
  - Structure and Space: Examines the internal organization of objects, perspective, and light/shadow effects, reflecting the child's ability to represent three-dimensional space.
2. **Aesthetic Value and Expressiveness:** This dimension emphasizes the artistic impact of the drawings, evaluating their ability to evoke emotional and aesthetic responses. It is more subjective, often requiring personal aesthetic experience and emotional resonance. Key sub-dimensions include:
  - Visual Appeal: Assesses the overall visual attractiveness and artistic presence of the drawing.
  - Emotional Expression: Evaluates the emotions conveyed and the viewer's emotional resonance, reflecting the depth and power of the child's expressive capabilities.
  - Theme Expression: Examines the clarity and depth of the theme or concept, as well as how effectively the child communicates their ideas and perspectives.
3. **Creativity and Imagination:** This dimension evaluates the uniqueness and originality of the drawings, reflecting the child's artistic vision and individual style. It is inherently subjective, as it involves assessing the child's ability to think outside conventional boundaries. Key sub-dimensions include:
  - Innovation: Measures the demonstration of new and unique creative thinking.
  - Imagination: Assesses the presentation of surreal, fantastical, or unconventional scenes and figures.
  - Originality: Evaluates the distinctiveness of the child's approach or concept, highlighting their ability to create something truly unique.

While AI excels at handling quantifiable, objective features such as line smoothness [25], color complexity [26], and emotion-related color usage [27], it struggles with subjective dimensions that require deeper human understanding. For example, assessing emotional expression or originality often involves interpreting subtle nuances that are deeply rooted in personal experience and cultural context. This underscores the complementary roles of AI and human evaluators: AI can efficiently process objective features and provide scalable, consistent assessments, while human evaluators bring the necessary empathy, cultural awareness, and interpretive depth to evaluate subjective dimensions.

Thus, AI serves as a powerful tool to support rather than replace human assessors, particularly in interpreting the subjective elements of children's drawings. By combining the strengths of AI-driven objectivity with human expertise, our framework aims to provide a more holistic and balanced evaluation of children's artistic expressions.

3.2 Dataset Construction

In our pursuit of enhancing the objective evaluation of children's drawing skills, we have developed a specialized dataset known as the Children's Drawings Dataset (CDData). This dataset was sourced from the Student Evaluation Enhancing Development Platform (SEED)[1] and comprises pencil drawings themed around pencil boxes. These drawings were contributed by over 1,500 students across primary (grades 2–6, ages 7–12) and junior high (grades 7–8, ages 12–14) levels within the Chinese education system. Following a rigorous preprocessing phase, which involved cropping distracting backgrounds and eliminating drawings with significant shadows or those that deviated from the pencil box theme, we meticulously selected 1,240 high-quality images for inclusion in the dataset. The intrinsic characteristics of pencil drawings, such as the extensive use of lines, distinct shapes, and absence of color, render them particularly well-suited for evaluating foundational drawing skills.

To facilitate the evaluation process, we developed a web-based scoring system that invited six evaluators to assess the preprocessed images across various aesthetic attributes, including Aesthetic Value and Expressiveness, Line Quality, and Structure and Space. Drawing on established methods from datasets such as AVA [28] and BAID [10], we normalized the raw scores (originally ranging from 1 to 10) to a 0–1 scale. For each image, we aggregated the scores from all six evaluators, excluding any zero values, and computed the final score as the average of the remaining ratings. This average score served as the "ground truth" label for each image.

3.3 Multi-attribute Network for Drawing Aesthetics

This section outlines the development of DrawAA-Net, an AI-supported evaluation tool for children's drawings. It is essential to emphasize that while this tool primarily focuses on assessing Technical Skill, it is designed to enhance, rather than replace, subjective components such as emotional expression and thematic depth.

Multi-attribute Network Architecture. We propose DrawAA-Net, a Multi-Attribute Network for Drawing Aesthetics, designed with a modular architecture comprising a backbone network and multiple attribute-specific subnetworks. The backbone network extracts general visual features, while the subnetworks analyze

[1] https://seed.bnu.edu.cn/.

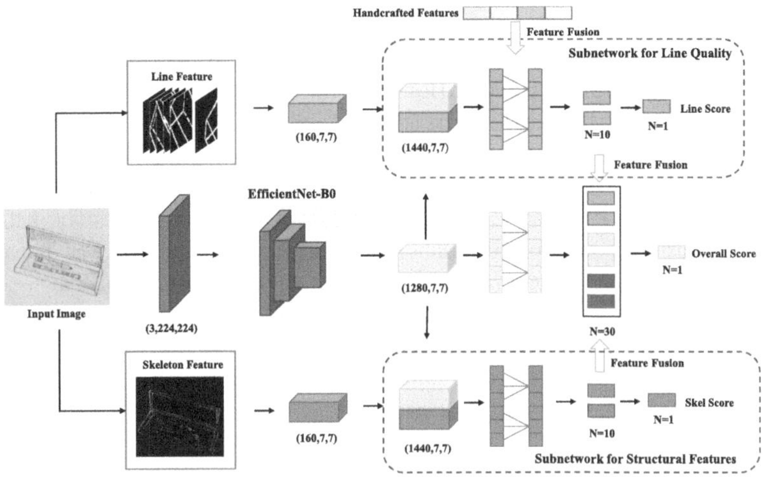

Fig. 1. Multi-tasking network architecture, which consists of a backbone network and three sub-networks.

and evaluate distinct aesthetic dimensions. The overall architecture is illustrated in Fig. 1. The backbone network uses EfficientNet-B0 [29]. The subnetworks are designed to evaluate line quality, structure features (structure and space), and overall aesthetic scoring. Before entering the subnetworks, line and skeleton feature extractors output feature maps, which are merged with the backbone's general features. These combined features are reweighted and processed through each subnetwork's layers, reducing them into 10 attributes that are regressed to yield individual scores. The overall aesthetic scoring subnetwork aggregates outputs from the general aesthetic layer and attribute subnetworks through a fully connected layer to generate the final score.

The multi-task network design of DrawAA-Net enables it to perform both overall aesthetic score regression and individual attribute score regression, providing a comprehensive evaluation of children's drawings. The architecture is inherently extendable, allowing seamless integration of new subnetworks for attributes such as color usage, composition, and emotional expression. Adding a new attribute involves introducing a parallel subnetwork with a tailored feature extractor. For example, to assess color usage, DrawAA-Net can incorporate a dedicated subnetwork using methods for extracting color richness from paintings [26]. This modular approach ensures that DrawAA-Net can evolve into a comprehensive framework for multi-attribute evaluation while maintaining computational efficiency and logical consistency.

Feature Extractors. Given the mixture of image-based low-level and high-level features can account for human preferences for visual artworks [30,31], we designed specialized skeleton feature extractors for structural space analysis and line feature extractors for evaluating line quality, in addition to a backbone network for extracting globally generalized aesthetic features. The skeleton feature extractor generates a comprehensive representation of the overall structure of the image, thereby enabling the evaluation of organizational consistency and spatial relationships within the drawing. In contrast, the line feature extractor focuses on line details by disrupting the overall structure, thus highlighting localized characteristics.

General Feature Extractor: The general feature extractor uses the EfficientNet architecture, known for its efficient feature extraction and low parameter requirements. It enables accurate extraction of generic aesthetic features from painting images, providing a foundation for downstream attribute-specific evaluations.

Skeleton Feature Extractor: To analyze structural space, the skeleton feature extractor employs a multi-step process [32]:

- Edge Detection and Gradient Mapping: initial processing identifies prominent edges and gradients in the image.
- Skeletonization: skeleton anchor points are identified based on refined edge detection.
- Pixel Chain Formation: using a heuristic routing algorithm, these anchor points are connected to form skeletal pixel chains that represent the structural framework of the drawings.

Line Feature Extractor: First, the image skeleton is derived using edge detection techniques similar to those in the skeleton feature extractor. Next, random block extraction isolates specific sections of the skeleton, focusing on line details while disrupting the overall structure to highlight localized characteristics. Finally, additional handcrafted statistical features (F1, F2, F3, and F4) are computed from the skeleton pixel chain, capturing critical aspects of line structure.

- F1 (Global Gradient Mean): Measures the overall mean gradient of the image, reflecting grayscale variation. Higher values indicate intricate details and textures, while lower values suggest a smoother, simpler image.
- F2 (Edge Segment Count): The ratio of edge segments to image shape, indicating line density and distribution. A higher value reflects more intricate linework and finer details.
- F3 (Average Edge Length): The average length of edge segments, indicating the continuity and distribution of lines in the drawings.
- F4 (Median/Maximum Ratio of the Edge Segment): The ratio of the median edge segment length to the maximum edge segment length indicates line continuity and variability. A higher ratio suggests longer, more connected lines.

In summary, DrawAA-Net is an efficient and flexible multi-task network designed for the comprehensive evaluation of children's drawings across multiple aesthetic dimensions. By combining the backbone network general feature extraction with modular subnetworks and handcrafted features for attribute analysis, DrawAA-Net captures both broad visual attributes and fine artistic details. Its scalable architecture allows for the seamless integration of additional aesthetic dimensions, ensuring adaptability while maintaining high performance and computational efficiency.

4 Experiment

4.1 Experiment Setup

To evaluate the proposed AI-driven assessment tool for children's drawings, an experimental study was conducted to measure its effectiveness in assessing objective, measurable aspects of drawings, particularly Technical Skill. DrawAA-Net was trained on CDData and compared with classical network models to benchmark its performance. Ablation experiments were conducted to isolate and analyze the contributions of feature extraction modules and subattributes to the overall performance of the aesthetic quality evaluation network. Expert interviews were conducted with art educators to collect qualitative feedback on the AI-assessed drawings. This combined approach of quantitative assessment and expert feedback offered a comprehensive evaluation of DrawAA-Net performance and its potential applicability in educational settings.

Our networks are designed as end-to-end models, implemented on MindSpore 1.6.0 and run on Nvidia RTX3090 GPUs. The dataset was randomly partitioned into training and validation sets in an 8:2 ratio. We employed the Momentum optimizer with a Dynamic Polynomial Decay Learning Rate (PolynomialDecayLR) strategy, using a batch size of 64. The PolynomialDecayLR schedule featured key hyperparameters: an initial learning rate of 0.1 and an end learning rate of 0.001. For overall aesthetic quality, Score Mse was defined to measure the mean square error of overall scores. Line Mse and Structure Mse (Skel Mse) were introduced to assess line quality and structural features, respectively, for individual subtasks. Acc measured the binary classification accuracy in aesthetic evaluations, classifying images as high or low quality based on a 0.5 threshold in the normalized score range of 0–1. These metrics enabled a detailed analysis of the network's effectiveness across different aesthetic dimensions.

4.2 Results

Comparative experiments on CDData demonstrated that DrawAA-Net outperformed ResNet-50 and SAAN across all metrics listed in Table 1. It is worth noting that ResNet-50 and SAAN are single-task network structures, which are not suitable for simultaneously testing the overall score and two sub-item scores. Therefore, in the comparative experiments, only the performance metrics of ResNet-50 and SAAN in terms of overall aesthetic quality were listed. For a fair comparison, the training parameters and conditions for SAAN were set according to the configurations reported in [10], while ResNet-50 was configured using commonly accepted settings. This highlights the significance of incorporating line and structural features to accurately assess the aesthetic quality of pencil drawings.

Table 1. Comparison experiments with other methods

Methods	Score Mse	Line Mse	Skel Mse	Classify Acc
SAAN	0.01388	-	-	0.734375
Resnet-50	0.01607	-	-	0.759375
DrawAA-Net	**0.01228**	**0.01310**	**0.01425**	**0.7875**

Ablation experiments were conducted using EfficientNet-B0 as the backbone to evaluate the effectiveness of handcrafted features and skeleton feature extractors. As shown in Table 2, adding handcrafted features reduced the Score Mse to 0.01309, while adding Skeleton and Line feature extractors reduced it to 0.01328. Combining both feature sets further reduced the Score Mse to 0.01228. These results demonstrate that handcrafted features provide critical supplementary information, significantly enhancing the model's accuracy and nuance in evaluating children's drawings.

Adding both line and structure evaluation networks reduced the Score Mse from 0.01430 to 0.01228, with other indicators also improving as shown in Table 3. The results demonstrate that incorporating both sub-attribute features is crucial for accurately evaluating the aesthetic quality of pencil drawings, especially those with fixed subjects (e.g., a pencil box).

Table 2. Ablation study on different feature extractors

Network Structure	Score Mse	Line Mse	Skel Mse	Classify Acc
Basebone	0.01365	0.01559	0.01749	0.72687
Basebone+Handcrafted Features	0.01309	0.01521	0.01751	0.74625
Basebone+Skeleton&Line Feature	0.01328	0.01347	0.01575	0.75125
Basebone +Handcrafted Features +Skeleton&Line Feature	**0.01228**	**0.01310**	**0.01425**	**0.7875**

Table 3. Ablation study in different dimensions

Network Structure	Score Mse	Line Mse	Skel Mse	Classify Acc
Overall Score Network	0.01430	-	-	0.7344
Overall+Line Evaluation	0.01365	0.01635	-	0.7750
Overall+Structure Evaluation	0.01378	-	0.01652	0.7813
Overall+Line&Structure Evaluation	**0.01228**	**0.01310**	**0.01425**	**0.7875**

4.3 Case Study

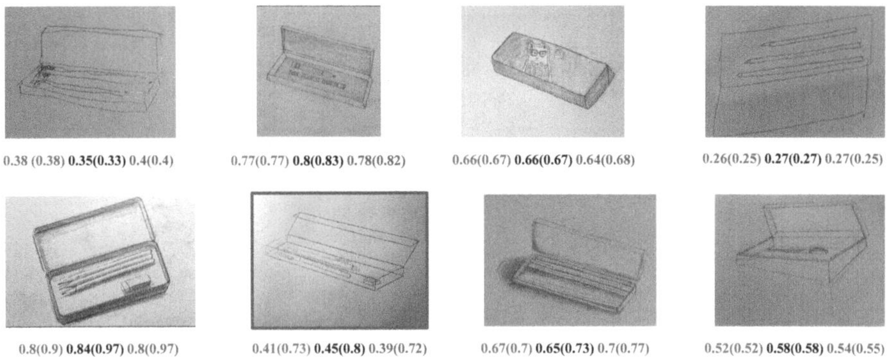

Fig. 2. The test results for a series of representative images are shown. The model's overall aesthetic score is displayed in red, line quality score in black, and structural feature score in blue. Numbers in parentheses are the true dataset scores, while those outside the parentheses are the model's inferred results. (Color figure online)

To further evaluate the efficacy of our proposed method, a selection of representative samples from the validation set of CDData was utilized for inference testing, with the results depicted in Fig. 2. For instance, the top-left drawing scored 0.38 overall, with line quality at 0.35 and structural feature at 0.4. The adjacent drawing scored much higher at 0.77 overall, with line quality at 0.8 and structural feature at 0.78. The disparity in scores can be attributed to the distinct characteristics of the two drawings. The top-left drawing features lines that are irregular, uneven, and discontinuous, which do not effectively convey the three-dimensional structural features of the pencil box. In contrast, the adjacent drawing exhibits smooth, even, and continuous lines that adeptly capture the structural nuances of the pencil box. This superior line usage and structural representation account for the higher scores. This comparison demonstrates our method's ability to accurately assess aesthetic quality based on key attributes like line usage and structural representation.

Notably, images highlighted with red boxes exhibit inference anomalies, where significant deviations occur between predicted scores and ground truth values. These anomalies are primarily due to external factors such as inconsistent lighting and image imperfections, which interfere with key visual features and impair the model's feature extraction process. In the majority of instances, the inference scores are in close alignment with the ground truth values, exhibiting deviations no greater than 0.05, as evidenced by the figure.

We also calculated Pearson correlation coefficients across true and predicted scores for three dimensions. Additionally, we found a high correlation between the scores of two sub-attributes and the overall score, indicating that the sub-attribute features have a significant impact on the overall aesthetic quality. The

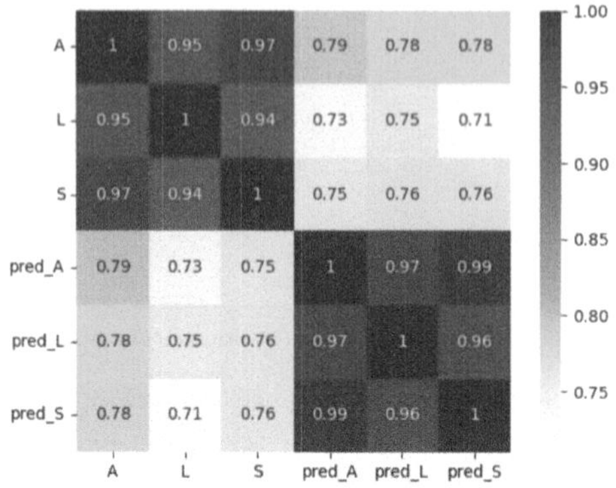

Fig. 3. Heat map of Pearson's correlation coefficient. A, L, and S represent true scores for overall aesthetic quality, line quality, and structural features, respectively. pred_A, pred_L, and pred_S denote the predicted scores for these attributes by the tool.

results, presented as a heat map in Fig. 3, show a high correlation between model predictions and human scores. This validates the model's consistency and reliability in aligning with human evaluations, supporting its effectiveness in aesthetic scoring tasks.

5 Conclusion

In this study, we address the longstanding challenges of subjectivity and inefficiency in evaluating children's drawings by integrating artificial intelligence (AI) into aesthetic assessment. Through a comprehensive review of traditional aesthetic evaluation models, we identified key limitations and defined the unique roles AI can play in this domain. The proposed framework, DrawAA-Net, effectively evaluates drawings across multiple dimensions, including technical skill, aesthetic expressiveness, and creativity. Leveraging advanced deep learning techniques and handcrafted features, DrawAA-Net achieves superior accuracy, scalability, and consistency compared to traditional methods, as validated through experimental results. The results underscore the potential of DrawAA-Net to serve as a transformative educational tool, providing educators with data-driven insights and fostering children's creative growth.

Future work will focus on expanding the capabilities and applications of the proposed framework. The integration of large pre-trained models, such as generative and multimodal architectures, offers opportunities to enhance the interpretive depth of assessments, including nuanced emotional and thematic analyses. Finally, incorporating longitudinal tracking features could allow the system to monitor students' artistic development over time, providing tailored feedback to foster continuous growth.

Acknowledgements. This work is supported by National Key R&D Program of China No. 2021YFC3340802.

References

1. Farokhi, M., Hashemi, M.: The analysis of children's drawings: social, emotional, physical, and psychological aspects. Procedia. Soc. Behav. Sci. **30**, 2219–2224 (2011)
2. Papandreou, M.: Communicating and thinking through drawing activity in early childhood. J. Res. Child. Educ. **28**(1), 85–100 (2014)
3. Michalopoulou, A.: Creativity expressed through drawings in early childhood education. Int. J. Educ. **6**(2), 69 (2014)
4. Lowenfeld, V.: Creative and Mental Growth, 3rd edn. Macmillan (1957)
5. Eisner, E.W.: The contribution of painting to children's cognitive development. J. Curric. Stud. **11**(2), 109–116 (1979)
6. Eisner, E.W.: The arts and the creation of mind. Lang. Arts **80**(5), 340–344 (2003)
7. Zhang, Y., et al.: AestheNet: revolutionizing aesthetic perception diagnosis in education with hybrid deep nets. IEEE Trans. Learn. Technol. (2024)
8. Ahmad, K., et al.: Data-driven artificial intelligence in education: a comprehensive review. IEEE Trans. Learn. Technol. (2023)
9. Talebi, H., Milanfar, P.: NIMA: neural image assessment. IEEE Trans. Image Process. **27**(8), 3998–4011 (2018)
10. Yi, R., Tian, H., Gu, Z., Lai, Y.K., Rosin, P.L.: Towards artistic image aesthetics assessment: a large-scale dataset and a new method. In: Proceedings of the IEEE/CVF Conference on Computer Vision and Pattern Recognition, pp. 22388–22397 (2023)
11. Homer, B.D., Hayward, E.O.: Cognitive and representational development in children. In: Cartwright, K.B. (ed.) Literacy Processes: Cognitive Flexibility in Learning and Teaching, pp. 19–41. The Guilford Press (2008)
12. Davis, K., Christodoulou, J., Seider, S., Gardner, H.E.: The theory of multiple intelligences. In: Sternberg, R.J., Kaufman, S.B. (eds.) The Theory of Multiple Intelligences. Cambridge Handbook of Intelligence, pp. 485–503 (2011)
13. Arnheim, R.: Visual Thinking. University of California Press (2023)
14. Probine, S.: How young children come to value and engage in the visual arts: examining the impact of bi-directional interactions on children as imaginative visual researchers. Early Childhood Educ. J. **50**(5), 795–809 (2022)
15. Qiyin, K.: Preschool Children's Art Education (in Chinese). Nanjing Normal University Press (1998)
16. Lin Lin, Z.J.: Preschool Children's Art Education (in Chinese). East China Normal University Press (2006)
17. Deng, Y., Loy, C.C., Tang, X.: Image aesthetic assessment: an experimental survey. IEEE Signal Process. Mag. **34**(4), 80–106 (2017)
18. Ke, Y., Tang, X., Jing, F.: The design of high-level features for photo quality assessment. In: 2006 IEEE Computer Society Conference on Computer Vision and Pattern Recognition (CVPR 2006), vol. 1, pp. 419–426. IEEE (2006)
19. Li, L., et al.: Theme-aware visual attribute reasoning for image aesthetics assessment. IEEE Trans. Circuits Syst. Video Technol. **33**(9), 4798–4811 (2023)
20. Yang, Z., Li, L., Yang, Y., Li, Y., Lin, W.: Multi-level transitional contrast learning for personalized image aesthetics assessment. IEEE Trans. Multimedia (2023)
21. Jin, X., et al.: Aesthetic attribute assessment of images numerically on mixed multi-attribute datasets. ACM Trans. Multimed. Comput. Commun. Appl. **18**(3s), 1–16 (2023)

22. Yang, B., Xu, D.: Color boosted visual saliency detection and its application to image classification. Multimedia Tools Appl. **69**, 877–896 (2014)
23. Amirshahi, S.A., Denzler, J.: Judging aesthetic quality in paintings based on artistic inspired color features. In: 2017 International Conference on Digital Image Computing: Techniques and Applications (DICTA), pp. 1–8. IEEE (2017)
24. Li, C., Chen, T.: Aesthetic visual quality assessment of paintings. IEEE J. Sel. Top. Sig. Process. **3**(2), 236–252 (2009)
25. Li, J., Yao, L., Hendriks, E., Wang, J.Z.: Rhythmic brushstrokes distinguish van Gogh from his contemporaries: findings via automated brushstroke extraction. IEEE Trans. Pattern Anal. Mach. Intell. **34**(6), 1159–1176 (2011)
26. Fan, Z.B., Li, Y.N., Yu, J., Zhang, K.: Visual complexity of in Chinese ink paintings. In: Proceedings of the ACM Symposium on Applied Perception, pp. 1–8 (2017)
27. Weng, H.C., et al.: Drawing as a window to emotion with insights from tech-transformed participant images. Sci. Rep. **14**(1), 11571 (2024)
28. Murray, N., Marchesotti, L., Perronnin, F.: AVA: a large-scale database for aesthetic visual analysis. In: 2012 IEEE Conference on Computer Vision and Pattern Recognition, pp. 2408–2415. IEEE (2012)
29. Tan, M., Le, Q.: EfficientNet: rethinking model scaling for convolutional neural networks. In: International Conference on Machine Learning, pp. 6105–6114. PMLR (2019)
30. Iigaya, K., Yi, S., Wahle, I.A., Tanwisuth, K., O'Doherty, J.P.: Aesthetic preference for art can be predicted from a mixture of low-and high-level visual features. Nat. Hum. Behav. **5**(6), 743–755 (2021)
31. Zhang, M., Kreiman, G.: Beauty is in the eye of the machine. Nat. Hum. Behav. **5**(6), 675–676 (2021)
32. Topal, C., Akinlar, C.: Edge drawing: a combined real-time edge and segment detector. J. Vis. Commun. Image Represent. **23**(6), 862–872 (2012)

Beyond Final Answers: Evaluating Large Language Models for Math Tutoring

Adit Gupta[1(✉)], Jennifer Reddig[2], Tommaso Calò[3], Daniel Weitekamp[2], and Christopher J. MacLellan[2]

[1] Drexel University, 3230 Market Street, Philadelphia, PA, USA
adit.gupta@drexel.edu
[2] Georgia Institute of Technology, North Avenue, Atlanta, GA, USA
{jreddig,dweitekamp,cmaclellan}@gatech.edu
[3] Politecnico di Torino, Torino, Italy
tommaso.calo@polito.it

Abstract. Researchers have made notable progress in applying large language models (LLMs) to solve math problems, as demonstrated through efforts like GSM8k, ProofNet, AlphaGeometry, and Math-Odyssey. This progress has sparked interest in their potential use for tutoring students in mathematics. However, the reliability of LLMs in tutoring contexts—where correctness and instructional quality are crucial—remains underexplored. Moreover, LLM problem-solving capabilities may not necessarily translate into effective tutoring support for students. In this work, we present two novel approaches to evaluate the correctness and quality of LLMs in math tutoring contexts. The first approach uses an intelligent tutoring system for college algebra as a testbed to assess LLM problem-solving capabilities. We generate benchmark problems using the tutor, prompt multiple LLMs to solve them, and compare the solutions to those generated by the tutor. The second approach evaluates LLM as tutors rather than problem solvers. We employ human evaluators, who act as students seeking tutoring support from each LLM. We then assess the quality and correctness of the support provided by the LLMs via a qualitative coding process. We applied these methods to evaluate several ChatGPT models, including 3.5 Turbo, 4, 4o, o1-mini, and o1-preview. Our findings show that when used as problem solvers, LLMs generate correct final answers for 85.5% of the college algebra problems tested. When employed interactively as tutors, 90% of LLM dialogues show high-quality instructional support; however, many contain errors—only 56.6% are entirely correct. We conclude that, despite their potential, LLMs are not yet suitable as intelligent tutors for math without human oversight or additional mechanisms to ensure correctness and quality.

Keywords: Intelligent Tutors · Large Language Models · Generative AI · Math Education

A. I. Cristea et al. (Eds.): AIED 2025, LNAI 15877, pp. 323–337, 2025.
https://doi.org/10.1007/978-3-031-98414-3_23

1 Introduction

Large language models (LLMs) have started to exhibit moderate proficiency at mathematical problem solving. For example, GPT-4 correctly solves over 90% of the problems in the GSM8K benchmark [5] and approximately 80% of the problems in the MATH benchmark [7] using advanced prompting techniques [22]. Although these results indicate progress, there are still many limitations. Findings from the GSM-Symbolic benchmark [20] suggest that LLMs struggle with perturbed or novel problem formulations that are easily solved by humans, indicating that their relatively high performance on standard benchmarks is partially due to memorization. Furthermore, LLM performance remains inconsistent across different problem classes, in contrast to traditional intelligent tutors, which provide 100% accurate support. These inconsistencies warrant a deeper investigation into the capabilities, limitations, and implications of LLMs for education.

Companies such as Duolingo and Khan Academy have started to leverage LLMs to offer personalized learning experiences, facilitate interactive problem-solving, and provide real-time feedback to learners. However, significant challenges remain to ensure the accuracy, reliability, and adaptability of LLMs in tutoring settings. Despite their remarkable capabilities, studies have shown that LLMs frequently produce plausible yet incorrect solutions to complex mathematical problems, especially in areas that require precise calculations and multi-step reasoning [11,20]. In mathematics, not only is the correctness of the final answer crucial, but also the quality of stepwise guidance that fosters effective learning. One recent classroom study comparing LLM-tutoring to traditional classroom instruction showed positive results [13], but another showed a negative result [4]. Considering that LLMs likely produce errors in around 10% of responses—using the best GSM8k performance as an optimistic measure—there is a possibility that they may do more harm than good. The manner in which LLMs confidently "hallucinate" incorrect yet seemly plausible information is a recipe for several possible negative effects [12]. In the best case, students' trust in LLM tutors may be eroded upon recognizing mistakes. At worst, LLM hallucinations may lead students to form misconceptions that compromise future learning.

LLM tutors mark an unusual inflection in the history of intelligent tutoring systems. It has been known for decades that automated computer-delivered tutors produce learning gains comparable to or greater than those of human tutors [17,26], who famously provide learning gains up to two standard deviations higher than those from traditional classroom instruction [2]. The original artificial intelligence (AI) tutors—hard-coded intelligent tutoring systems—found success through a cognitivist approach to tutoring: tracking and quantifying student knowledge by comparison to an expert model [6], and adapting instruction accordingly [21,25]. As compelling as LLMs' generative capabilities are, when used as standalone tutors, they arguably mark a regression in actual AI tutoring capabilities compared to traditional ITSs since they are consistently inaccurate and lack the cognition-oriented adaptivity of prior approaches.

This study evaluates the potential of LLMs in educational contexts by systematically assessing their performance on structured algebra tasks. We selected algebra for this study, given its long-standing use in previous research on ITSs [1,9,16]. This study aims to investigate the following research questions:

- **RQ1**: How accurately can LLMs generate solutions to the kinds of algebra problems currently supported by intelligent tutoring systems?
- **RQ2**: What is the accuracy and quality of the tutoring support provided by LLMs (e.g., scaffolding, hints, and feedback) on these algebra problems?

We employ two techniques to explore these questions: (1) an automated approach that uses an existing algebra tutor as a testbed for evaluating LLM problem solving and (2) a qualitative approach to assess the quality and correctness of LLM dialogues generated by having evaluators interactively prompt an LLM for tutor support. For the second method, we also conducted a thematic analysis [3] to identify and categorize observations about LLM tutoring behaviors.

The findings of this study contribute to research on ITS by providing empirical evidence on the strengths and limitations of LLMs in math tutoring contexts, thus enriching the ongoing discourse on the role of AI in supporting learning. Specifically, our study makes the following contributions:

- We introduce a novel method that uses intelligent tutors as testbeds for evaluating LLM problem solving.
- We introduce a second method for interactively evaluating LLM tutoring correctness and quality.
- We show that while LLMs largely generate responses aligned with pedagogical best practices, they frequently contain mistakes and inaccuracies, suggesting they are not yet ready for direct in-class deployment.
- We offer actionable guidelines for developers, emphasizing how LLMs can support aspects of tutoring, such as question generation and hint production, rather than serving as comprehensive, standalone tutoring solutions.

2 Related Works

Researchers have begun exploring the use of LLMs in educational applications. The existing literature shows that LLMs can generate worked examples and guide structured problem solving. For example, WorkedGen [28] uses prompt chaining and one-shot learning to produce interactive programming examples. Although user studies indicate that 77% of students found WorkedGen helpful, such self-reported feedback does not necessarily confirm improved learning outcomes. Similarly, Jamplate [15] harnesses AI-powered templates for idea generation, providing reflection-based scaffolding, but noting a tendency toward reduced critical thinking among students.

Although these studies highlight the potential of LLMs to create structured examples and facilitate reflective engagement, researchers must develop a consistent, stepwise evaluation framework for algebraic or multi-step reasoning tasks.

Existing benchmarks, such as GSM8K [5], evaluate only the final answer's accuracy, overlooking the intermediate steps and iterative feedback typical of most tutoring experiences [10]. As a result, there is still a need for a more systematic methodology that tests how effectively LLMs handle multi-step problems and adapt to the pedagogical requirements of a tutoring environment.

Another expanding line of work examines how LLMs function as tutors, focusing on the trade-off between personalized support and instructional accuracy for non-fluent English speakers. For example, a comparative study of models such as GPT-4, Llama-2-ko-DPO-13B, and eT5-chat reveals trade-offs between individualization and correctness [23]. Smaller models provided more personalized interactions, while GPT-4 exhibited greater correctness but less personalized assistance. Tutoring is an immensely personal activity, and both correctness and individualization are needed. These studies demonstrate the need for more investigation into LLMs' shortcomings in stepwise instruction and how to better integrate them into existing intelligent tutoring platforms. Current studies often prioritize correctness of the final answer, overlooking the quality of intermediate steps that are crucial for meaningful learning [27]. For example, in mathematics education, breaking problems down into their steps ensures that students grasp foundational concepts rather than simply arriving at the correct solution.

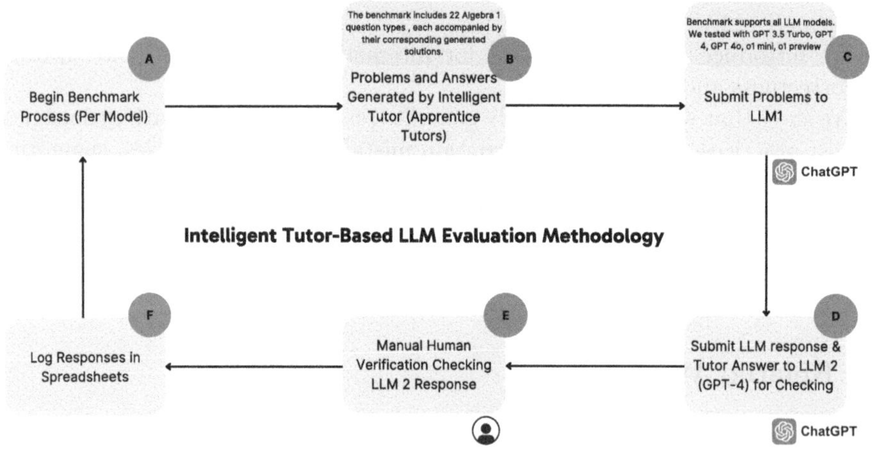

Fig. 1. Our proposed intelligent tutor-based LLM evaluation process. The process begins with the testbed setup - hosted on Google Colab (**A**), followed by generating problems and solutions using the intelligent tutor (Apprentice Tutors, in our case) (**B**). For our evaluation, 22 types of problems are then submitted to LLM models such as GPT-3.5 Turbo and GPT-4 (**C**). Responses from each LLM are checked by submitting them along with the tutor answers to a second LLM (**D**). We then performed manual human verification to validate the accuracy of the second model's responses. Finally, all results are logged into a performance tracker spreadsheet (**F**).

The work in this paper aims to fill this gap by introducing a novel method that evaluates LLM performance on a wide range of math questions from college algebra, generated from the Apprentice Tutors platform [8]. This platform was designed as a web-based intelligent tutoring platform to support personalized learning in mathematics. The platform supports more than ten tutors covering topics like radicals, factoring polynomials, and solving logarithmic equations.

3 Methodology

We employ two complementary approaches to evaluate LLMs. First, we developed an automated approach that uses an existing intelligent tutoring system to assess LLM problem-solving accuracy. We generate problems from the tutor and submit them to multiple LLMs. We then use the tutor expert model to generate correct answers, which were then compared to the LLM answers using a second LLM (to account for minor variations in the math formatting). Second, to evaluate LLMs as tutors, we had evaluators interactively engage with the LLMs to request tutoring guidance as if they were students. We then qualitatively evaluated the tutor support generated by the LLMs.

We collected and analyzed data from both approaches to analyze the strengths and limitations of LLMs in structured problem-solving tasks. Figures 1 and 2 illustrate the workflows for these methodologies, which we describe below.

3.1 Evaluating LLM Using Intelligent Tutors as Testbeds

We developed our evaluation system in Python to automate tutor problem generation, LLM interaction, and response evaluation. This allowed us to systematically test multiple LLMs on a variety of educational tasks. For this study, we evaluated GPT-3.5 Turbo, GPT-4, GPT-4o, o1 Mini, and o1 Preview[1]. Although these models were the focus of this analysis, the benchmarking tool is designed to be extensible to other tutor content and can be easily adapted to test other models, such as Google's Gemini, Anthropic's Claude series, or Deepseek's open models.

The workflow for the tutor-based evaluation process is outlined in Fig. 1. The process begins with the testbed setup (**A**), where we define parameters for the evaluation, including the number and type of algebra problems to be tested. For this study, we identified 22 problem types from the Apprentice Tutors platform and generated five problems of each type. The problems and their corresponding step-by-step solutions were generated directly from the Apprentice Tutors software (**B**). The generated problems were then submitted to each LLM (**C**), which was prompted to produce a solution. The exact prompt provided to each LLM was:

[1] Model snapshots evaluated: `gpt-3.5-turbo-0125`, `gpt-4-0125-preview`, `gpt-4o-2024-05-13`, `o1-mini-2024-09-12`, and `o1-preview-2024-09-12`.

Math Problem Solving Prompt

You will be solving the math questions that are provided as strings. Your task is to parse each question, solve it step-by-step, and provide the final answer in LaTeX format.
Here are the math questions and their answers for verification: <question_answer_text>
Now, here are some new math questions that need answers: <next_question_text>
For each question, think through the <problem_type> problem step-by-step in ⟨scratchpad⟩ tags. Break down the problem into smaller sub-problems if necessary, and solve each one in a logical order. Show your work and reasoning at each step.
After you have thought through each problem and arrived at a final answer, confirm that it matches the provided answer in LaTeX format inside the corresponding ⟨answer⟩ tag.

The benchmarking system processed the responses from the initial LLM prompt and extracted the outputs, generating a structured list of questions paired with their corresponding answers produced by the LLM. The LLM responses were then evaluated by submitting the correct solution (from the tutor) and the generated LLM solution to a second LLM (**D**) to verify accuracy and logical consistency. We used GPT-4 as the evaluation model in all tests. Each LLM was evaluated sequentially and the results were recorded and analyzed before proceeding to the next model. The exact prompt used by the second LLM to evaluate each answer was:

LLM Evaluation Prompt

Just say True or False (nothing else): does <LLM_generated_response> equal the same as <ground_truth_response_from_tutor>?

To further validate the quality of the LLM evaluation, we performed manual human verification (**E**). During this process, reviewers compared the ground-truth responses generated by the Apprentice Tutors platform with the responses produced by the LLM and the correctness assessments provided by the second LLM. In certain cases, discrepancies arose due to differences in interpretation, such as when the second LLM marked an expression like $\sqrt{4}$ as incorrect because it expected the simplified answer of 2. These instances were noted and the human reviewer marked the answer as correct if it was mathematically accurate in its final form. However, stepwise solutions were also considered, ensuring that intermediate simplifications (e.g., distinguishing between $\sqrt{4}$ and 2 when necessary) aligned with expected problem-solving conventions.

Finally, all data collected, including LLM responses, human evaluations, and any discrepancies identified during the validation process, were systematically recorded in a performance tracker spreadsheet (**F**). This structured logging approach facilitated detailed analysis and allowed for a robust comparison between different LLM models and problem types. The goal was to gain insights into their performance and limitations.

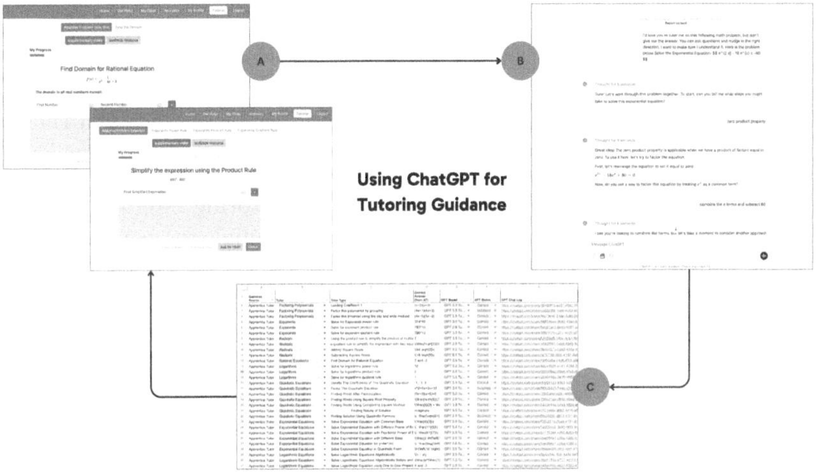

Fig. 2. Our process for evaluating an LLM via interactive prompting. This diagram illustrates the process using ChatGPT's chat interface. The workflow begins by having evaluators prompt ChatGPT to provide tutor guidance on tutor problems as if they were students (**A**). Evaluators interactively submit queries and receive step-by-step guidance from ChatGPT (**B**). The evaluators systematically log each chat dialogue in a spreadsheet tracker for analysis (**C**).

3.2 Evaluating LLMs via Interactive Prompting

We conducted a second study to assess how the LLMs perform when interacting with learners as tutors (see Fig. 2). This study was designed to provide a qualitative perspective on the educational capabilities of the models, in contrast to the previous automated evaluation of their problem-solving capabilities. We performed manual evaluation of the LLMs using a standardized variation of the prompt from Salman Khan's widely cited ChatGPT interview [14] to ensure consistency between sessions. By comparing these human-guided interactions with the outputs of the intelligent tutor, we investigated how well the step-by-step guidance of LLMs align with real user queries and misconceptions in a math tutoring context. Here is the prompt that was used:

Interactive Tutoring Prompt

I'd love you to tutor me on this following math problem, but don't give me the answer. You can ask questions and nudge me in the right direction. I want to make sure I understand it. Here is the problem below. <Problem>

The problems were taken directly from the Apprentice Tutors and entered into ChatGPT. Three evaluators interacted with the model as it guided them through problem-solving, responding to ChatGPT's hints and prompts as they progressed. After each session, they logged a link to the chat history, the final answers provided by ChatGPT, and whether the responses matched the correct answers generated by the Apprentice Tutors. An example of this recording is shown in part B of Fig. 2.

After collecting all responses, two independent reviewers assessed the interactions to answer the following questions about each tutoring dialogue:

- **Quality:** Do the steps represent a high-quality tutoring interaction?
- **Correctness:** Were all the LLM responses in the dialogue correct?

To answer the first question and classify response **quality**, each dialogue was evaluated with respect to a structured rubric that scored clarity of explanation, feedback, scaffold support, problem-solving strategy, and encouragement and reinforcement.[2] Each criterion was scored on a scale from 1 to 4. The rubric was designed to measure several key aspects of tutoring quality. This structured approach aimed to reflect established learning science principles. We summed the scores across all criteria. If the total score was 10 or below, the response was categorized as "No" (not good quality); if the score was above 10, it was categorized as "Yes" (good quality). Once the scores were converted into Yes/No labels, we measured inter-rater reliability using Cohen's Kappa [19] to assess agreement between reviewers and confirm the robustness of our classifications.

To answer the second question and assess response **correctness**, each reviewer also independently assessed whether all the LLM-generated content was correct. These evaluations consisted of considering each LLM response from the dialogue, and noting any mistakes or errors. If there were any errors, then the dialogue was coded as incorrect, otherwise it was recorded as correct. Similar to question 1, we measured inter-rater reliability of the two evaluations using Cohen's Kappa. We also conducted a thematic analysis [3] of the LLM responses to identify recurring patterns in tutoring interactions. The goal was to identify and categorize common patterns, counting their frequency and noting whether they corresponded to positive or negative tutoring behaviors.

4 Results and Analysis

We present the results of the two evaluation methods used to assess the performance of LLMs in math tutoring contexts. We first present the results from our tutor-based evaluation method and then the results from evaluators interactively prompting the LLMs as if they were students.

[2] The rubric is available here: https://osf.io/k4wqc.

4.1 Tutor-Based LLM Evaluation Results

Table 1 summarizes the results from the tutor-based evaluation. The apprentice tutors had 22 problem types and we sampled 5 problems of each type to produce a test set that contained 110 problem and answer pairs.

Table 1. The tutor-based LLM evaluation results, which only assessed the final answer.

Model	# Problem Types	# Problems	# Correct	Accuracy
GPT-3.5 Turbo	22	110	85	77.3%
GPT-4	22	110	83	74.5%
GPT-4o	22	110	107	97.3%
o1-mini	22	110	101	91.8%
o1-preview	22	110	94	85.5%
Overall Avg.	22	110	94	85.5%

Table 2. Assessments of LLM tutoring interaction quality and accuracy across 30 problems. The columns show final answer accuracy as well as the percentage of LLM dialogues that were classified as high quality and fully correct, as indicated by reviewers R1 and R2. The number of problems in each case is noted in parentheses.

Model	Final Accuracy	% High Quality		% Fully Correct	
		R1	R2	R1	R2
GPT 3.5 Turbo	90.0% (27)	90.0% (27)	90.0% (27)	46.7% (14)	53.3% (16)
GPT 4	83.3% (25)	93.3% (28)	93.3% (28)	43.3% (13)	50.0% (15)
GPT 4o	93.3% (28)	90.0% (27)	90.0% (27)	70.0% (21)	80.0% (24)
o1 mini	86.7% (26)	86.7% (26)	80.0% (24)	56.7% (17)	43.3% (13)
o1 preview	90.0% (27)	90.0% (27)	96.7% (29)	73.3% (22)	50.0% (15)
Overall Avg.	88.6%	90.0%		56.6%	

We identified twenty-five instances (6.3% of total responses) where the second LLM marked answers incorrectly. From our observations, the second LLM would incorrectly mark the answer when comparing the tutor-generated response to the LLM-generated response for the following reasons: **(1)** a mismatch in the operational order (e.g., $(3+6)\times 2$ vs. $3+(6\times 2)$), **(2)** differences in simplification (e.g., $\frac{2}{4}$ vs. 0.5), and **(3)** differences in operator context (e.g., multiplication represented by "x" vs. "*").

4.2 Interactive Prompting-Based LLM Evaluation

The evaluators prompted each of the five models to provide tutoring support on the same set of 30 problems, resulting in a total of 150 LLM dialogues. The two reviewers independently analyzed each dialogue to classify whether it was high quality (according to the rubric) and fully correct. We also evaluated the final answer accuracy from each dialogue by comparing it to the tutor solution. Table 2 shows the results of these assessments, breaking out the accuracy of final LLM answers alongside reviewer assessments of the quality and correctness of the LLM dialogues. We calculated Cohen's Kappa (κ) to evaluate the reviewer agreement for both the quality and correctness ratings. This score, which ranges from 0 to 1, represents agreement after correcting for chance. A score greater than 0.7 is typically viewed as strong agreement. For the quality ratings, Cohen's $\kappa_{Quality} \approx 0.85$, and for the assessment of whether the LLM dialogues were entirely correct, Cohen's $\kappa_{Correctness} \approx 0.82$. These scores indicate very strong agreement between the independent reviewers.

Finally, the reviewers evaluated each model's performance, documenting key behavioral patterns and noting any common issues. Table 3 summarizes these findings, classifying observations as positive or negative based on their potential impact on learners. This analysis highlights the strengths and weaknesses of each model's tutoring approach, offering insight into their effectiveness in guiding students through problem-solving.

5 Discussion

Both of our evaluation methods suggest that the LLMs show reasonable final answer accuracy. Our tutor-based evaluation showed that GPT-4o had the highest final-answer accuracy at 97.3%. In the interactive prompting-based evaluation, we found that GPT-4o also got the highest accuracy at 93.3%. Although these accuracies seem reasonable, it still means that these models will generate incorrect final answers for about 1 in 18 problems. Surprisingly, GPT-4 ranked last, and the model ranking changed based on the evaluation.

Newer models (o1-mini) often performed worse than older ones (GPT-4o), despite expected improvements. This suggests that LLM performance can no longer be expected to improve with each new model release. Also, there are still gaps in how LLMs process multi-step math questions, even with chain-of-though models. In terms of final answer accuracy, we observed that the interactive prompt-based evaluation results were higher than those from the tutor-based evaluation, probably because human testers engaged in multi-turn interactions, allowing LLMs to refine responses. In contrast, the tutor-based evaluation provided only a single prompt, requiring the model to solve problems correctly in one step.

During our interactive prompting-based evaluation, we found that LLMs generate high-quality tutoring support most of the time. Although GPT-4 had the lowest final answer accuracy, it scored near the top in terms of quality, with 93.3% of its chat dialogues being classified as having high pedagogical quality.

Table 3. Summary of key observations from the interactive tutoring evaluation.

Observation	Occurrences	Sentiment
The final answer was correct, even though there were Inconsistencies in the sub-steps	6	Negative
Even though the prompt was not to share an answer, it was possible to obtain the answer by manipulating responses (via yes/no questions)	4	Negative
For topics like factoring, there was an overemphasis on teaching basics (e.g., multiplying) instead of demonstrating specific methods (e.g., "slip and slide")	4	Negative
LLM over-indexes on ensuring the final answer is correct rather than emphasizing the student's step-by-step skill acquisition	3	Negative
LLM occasionally produces an incorrect conclusion and refuses to accept a correct student answer	4	Negative
Sub-steps are sometimes flagged as incorrect even though they are actually correct	3	Negative
Difficult math notation (e.g., quadratic expressions) can be challenging to input from a standard keyboard	2	Negative
LLM is flexible about answer formats, accepting multiple notational styles	3	Positive
LLM excels at generating hints and extra worked examples to support instruction	2	Positive
LLM provides encouraging feedback and positive reinforcement, which could benefit student well-being	7	Positive
LLM nudges students to answer queries in sequence when they attempt to skip ahead	2	Positive

Although the LLMs achieved reasonable final answer accuracies, we found that their full tutor dialogues often contained mistakes. Along this dimension, GPT-4o achieved the best performance, with 75% of its dialogues being classified as fully correct (averaging across the two reviewers). Across all five of the LLMs, only 56.6% of the tutor dialogues were entirely correct. This suggests that in almost half of interactive LLM tutoring sessions, students will receive partially incorrect instruction. These results suggest that LLM error rates at tutoring tasks are likely much higher than final answer-based benchmarks suggest. This raises concerns about their use as standalone tutors, as less-than-perfect accuracy can harm learners. If one in two dialogues contains errors, students may lose trust in the tutor and, worse, develop misconceptions that hinder future learning. Our results also suggest that future evaluations must consider the correctness of the entire tutoring dialogue, not just the final answer accuracy.

Traditional intelligent tutoring systems employ explicit scaffolding, guiding students through sequenced substeps that stem from research-based design methods such as cognitive task analysis [18]. In contrast, large language models often provide a complete solution or a fixed step-by-step explanation, offering limited adaptive support for the intermediate reasoning of learners. For example, in factoring problems, LLMs often provide overly general guidance, e.g. generic multiplication rules, instead of the specific "slip and slide" strategy explicitly requested in the task. Although such responses may earn full credit in automated evaluations, omitting the specified method diminishes the tutoring quality.

Table 3 summarizes reviewer observations of tutoring interactions. Reviewers noted that the LLMs sometimes refused to accept correct answers, miscalculated sub-steps, or overemphasized fundamentals at the expense of specialized techniques. However, the LLMs also provided flexible response formats, detailed hints, and encouraging feedback. Manual review of chat logs revealed inconsistencies in how LLMs handled intermediate steps. While they often produced correct final answers, sub-steps were occasionally miscalculated or erroneously flagged as incorrect (8 instances, as shown in Table 3). These errors fell into three categories: (1) simplified vs. unsimplified answers (e.g., 2 vs. $\sqrt{4}$), (2) differences in term order (e.g., $\sqrt{3} + \sqrt{4}$ vs. $\sqrt{4} + \sqrt{3}$), and (3) formatting mismatches (e.g., missing required LaTeX tags). These issues highlight inconsistencies in how LLMs evaluate semantic equivalence.

Although LLMs may be incorrect and pedagogically misaligned compared to ITS when tutoring, recent work demonstrates how LLMs could support ITS in hint generation [24]. By leveraging the expert model of ITS, LLMs can generate correctness feedback personalized to student responses without needing the LLM to perform any mathematical calculations [24]. If integrated with other educational technologies, they could offer several potential benefits. Their ability to generate hints, provide alternative explanations, and accommodate various answer formats makes them flexible and adaptive. However, our finding that LLMs sometimes mark correct answers as incorrect—even when provided with the solutions—suggest that LLMs integrations will need to be carefully evaluated before deployment.

Additionally, their use of positive reinforcement—such as motivational nudges and encouraging feedback—could help foster an engaging learning environment, provided that motivational support is offered equitably to all learners. For example, several chat logs included statements like, "Way to go, you are close to the answer!" or "That's not right, but let's keep trying." These reinforcements might help motivate learners to persist and promote sustained engagement with educational tools. This approach aligns with many learners' needs for constructive feedback and encouragement [8]. Future research should systematically evaluate the motivational potential of LLMs' interactions and whether they translate into improved learning outcomes.

6 Limitations and Future Work

One limitation of our LLM evaluation methods is that they were conducted as an offline evaluation instead of with students. We chose our approach because we knew that LLMs have reliability issues and we did not want to cause harm to students by giving them incorrect tutoring guidance during our experiments. Although our approach provides a means of safe, controlled evaluation, it may not fully capture the unique ways in which real students would engage with LLM tutors. A future iteration of this work could involve deploying the system in real-world educational settings and analyzing chat logs generated from authentic student interactions to gain a more comprehensive understanding of LLM performance. However, since our work suggests that LLMs make mistakes in just over half of their student tutoring dialogues, future research should try to mitigate the risks that LLMs pose to students.

Furthermore, this study was conducted using an earlier version of the Apprentice Tutors platform, which focused exclusively on math-related questions. The Apprentice Tutors platform has since been expanded to include other types of questions, such as those related to nursing education. Future research could explore how LLMs perform in this and other domains, extending the scope of evaluation to understand their domain-specific adaptability and effectiveness.

Finally, another limitation is that the analysis presented was restricted to a set of LLMs within the ChatGPT family. With the rapid development of new LLMs, such as Google's Gemini, Anthropic's Claude and several open-source LLMs, there is an opportunity to expand this study to evaluate these emerging models too. Comparing performance across a broader range of LLMs would provide a more holistic view of their strengths and weaknesses in educational contexts. In addition, this work does not thoroughly address potential biases and limitations in LLM-generated tutoring content—a critical issue for ensuring safe and effective educational use. Lastly, this study used the publicly accessible versions of the ChatGPT models. In practice, commercial production environments often deploy models that are fine-tuned to specific domains or tasks. Evaluating a custom-tuned LLM tailored to specific educational needs could offer a more accurate view of how these tools would perform in real-world applications.

7 Conclusion

In this study, we evaluated the ability of various LLMs to solve college algebra problems and to interactively provide step-by-step tutor guidance. We evaluated multiple models, including GPT-3.5 Turbo, GPT-4, GPT-4o, o1 Mini and o1 Preview, identifying both their strengths and limitations. The results presented in this study, though commendable, are significantly lower than the 100% accuracy achieved by traditional intelligent tutors on the same set of problems. While we saw an overall final accuracy of 85.5% with the automated tutor-based evaluation and 88.6% with our interactive prompting-based evaluation, our analysis of the entire LLM tutoring dialogues showed that only 56.6% were entirely correct. This discrepancy suggests a core limitation of using LLMs as tutors: while they often generate correct final answers, ensuring the pedagogical soundness and accuracy of intermediate steps remains challenging.

Despite these limitations, LLMs exhibit several capabilities that have the potential to improve learning outcomes. Their flexibility in accepting diverse answer formats, the ability to generate hints and alternative problem explanations, and the use of positive reinforcement, such as motivational nudges, could help foster a more supportive and engaging learning environment. However, there are risks associated with the deployment of LLMs in educational settings. For example, biases within the models may lead to inflexibility in pedagogical approaches, such as internal biases that favor some methods of solving problems over others. Furthermore, inaccuracies in responses—with around one in two dialogues containing errors—can undermine the trust of students in the guidance of the tutor and reduce their confidence in the system. To address these challenges, future work might explore how to leverage their independent capabilities, such as problem generation, hint generation, and positive reinforcement. By balancing these strengths with strategies to manage and mitigate their limitations, LLMs could effectively supplement other educational technologies, such as intelligent tutoring systems.

Acknowledgments. Funded in part by NSF AI Institutes program (#2247790 and #2112532). Views are the author's and do not reflect those of the U.S. Govt. We also thanks Kaitlyn Crutcher and Momin Siddiqui for their feedback and suggestions.

References

1. Aleven, V., McLaren, B.M., Sewall, J., Koedinger, K.R.: The cognitive tutor authoring tools (CTAT): preliminary evaluation of efficiency gains. In: Ikeda, M., Ashley, K.D., Chan, T.-W. (eds.) ITS 2006. LNCS, vol. 4053, pp. 61–70. Springer, Heidelberg (2006). https://doi.org/10.1007/11774303_7
2. Bloom, B.S.: The 2 sigma problem: the search for methods of group instruction as effective as one-to-one tutoring. Educ. Res. **13**(6), 4–16 (1984)
3. Braun, V., Clarke, V.: Using thematic analysis in psychology. Qual. Res. Psychol. **3**(2), 77–101 (2006)
4. Cicchetti, C.C.: AI in higher education: does not help, might hurt. J. Educ. Bus. **99**(7–8), 438–443 (2024)
5. Cobbe, K., Kosaraju, V., Bavarian, M., Chen, J.H., Raffel, C., Schulman, J.: Training verifiers to solve math word problems. arXiv:2110.14168 (2021)
6. Corbett, A.T., Anderson, J.R.: Knowledge tracing: modeling the acquisition of procedural knowledge. User Model. User-Adapted Interact. (1994)
7. Fang, M., Wan, X., Lu, F., Xing, F., Zou, K.: MathOdyssey: benchmarking mathematical problem-solving skills in large language models using odyssey math data. arXiv:2406.18321 (2024)
8. Gupta, A., Siddiqui, M., Smith, G., Reddig, J., MacLellan, C.: Intelligent tutors for adult learners: an analysis of needs and challenges. arXiv:2412.04477 (2025)
9. Heffernan, N., Heffernan, C.: The ASSISTments ecosystem: building a platform that brings scientists and teachers together for minimally invasive research on human learning and teaching. Int. J. Artif. Intell. Educ. **24**, 470–497 (2014)
10. Heffernan, N.T., Koedinger, K.R., Razzaq, L.: Expanding the model-tracing architecture: a 3rd generation intelligent tutor for algebra symbolization. Int. J. Artif. Intell. Educ. **18**(2), 153–178 (2008)

11. Hendrycks, D., et al.: Measuring mathematical problem solving with the MATH dataset. arXiv:2103.03874 (2021)
12. Huang, L., et al.: A survey on hallucination in large language models: principles, taxonomy, challenges, and open questions. arXiv:2311.05232 (2023)
13. Kestin, G., Miller, K., Klales, A., et al.: AI tutoring outperforms active learning. Res. Square (2024). https://doi.org/10.21203/rs.3.rs-4243877/v1
14. Khan, S.: Sal Khan explores ChatGPT in education. YouTube video. Published on Khan Academy's Official Channel, March 2023
15. Kim, J.S.: Jamplate: exploring LLM-enhanced templates for idea reflection. In: Proceedings of the 2023 CHI Conference on Human Factors in Computing Systems, New York, NY, USA, pp. 1–14 (2023)
16. Koedinger, K.R., Anderson, J.R., Hadley, W.H., Mark, M.A.: Intelligent tutoring goes to school in the big city. Int. J. Artif. Intell. Educ. **8**, 30–43 (1997). ffhal-00197383
17. Kulik, J.A., Fletcher, J.: Effectiveness of intelligent tutoring systems: a meta-analytic review. Rev. Educ. Res. **86**(1), 42–78 (2016)
18. Lovett, M.C.: Cognitive task analysis in service of intelligent tutoring systems design: a case study in statistics. In: Goettl, B.P., Halff, H.M., Redfield, C.L., Shute, V.J. (eds.) Intelligent Tutoring Systems. LNCS, vol. 1452, pp. 234–243. Springer, New York (1998)
19. McHugh, M.L.: Interrater reliability: the Kappa statistic. Biochemia Medica **22**(3), 276–282 (2012)
20. Mirzadeh, I., Alizadeh, K., Shahrokhi, H., Tuzel, O., Bengio, S., Farajtabar, M.: GSM-symbolic: understanding the limitations of mathematical reasoning in large language models. arXiv:2410.05229 (2024)
21. Nwana, H.S.: Intelligent tutoring systems: an overview. Artif. Intell. Rev. **4**(4), 251–277 (1990)
22. OpenAI. GPT-4 technical report. arXiv:2303.08774 (2023)
23. Park, J.W., Kim, M.J., Lee, S.W.: Developing conversational intelligent tutoring for speaking skills in foreign language education. In: Koch, F., Zhang, L., Chen, F., Dillenbourg, P. (eds.) Artificial Intelligence in Education, pp. 123–134. Springer International Publishing, Cham (2023). https://doi.org/10.1007/978-3-031-63028-6_11
24. Reddig, J.M., Arora, A., MacLellan, C.: Generating in-context, personalized feedback for intelligent tutors with large language models (2024)
25. VanLehn, K.: The behavior of tutoring systems. Int. J. Artif. Intell. Educ., 227–265 (2006)
26. VanLehn, K.: The relative effectiveness of human tutoring, intelligent tutoring systems, and other tutoring systems. Educ. Psychol. (2011)
27. Xia, S., et al.: Evaluating mathematical reasoning beyond accuracy. arXiv:2404.05692 (2024)
28. Zhang, Y., et al.: Workedgen: using LLMs to generate interactive worked programming examples. In: Proceedings of the 2023 Conference on Learning at Scale, pp. 123–134 (2023)

Towards Smarter Decision-Making in Collaborative Problem Solving with Optimized Communication Networks

Percy Jardine(✉)

Monash University, Melbourne, Australia
zheng.fang@monash.edu

Abstract. Effective communication is critical for naval teams operating under high-stress conditions, particularly in tactical decision-making scenarios such as those in the Tactical Decision Making Under Stress (TADMUS) program of the U.S. Navy. This research focuses on optimizing communication patterns in collaborative problem-solving (CPS) environments. Using Epistemic Network Analysis (ENA) as a reference framework, we identify key communication structures that correlate with team performance. We employ ENA to establish optimization objectives, and the optimization process utilizes reward functions based on the spatial positioning of individual communication patterns within the ENA network and the desired sequence of thematic codes corresponding to utterances and turn-taking. Specifically, our approach incorporates the order of thematic codes relative to the number of communication turns, ensuring alignment with the tactical context of hostile and friendly air track classifications in naval decision-making scenarios. A genetic algorithm is employed to iteratively optimize communication strategies, providing a machine learning-driven approach for enhancing team effectiveness. This research offers a data-driven framework for optimizing CPS communication in high-stakes military contexts, with implications for training, operational efficiency, and decision-making under pressure.

Keywords: Optimization · Epistemic Network Analysis · Collaborative Problem Solving

1 Introduction

Collaborative Problem-Solving (CPS) involves team members jointly identifying, analyzing, and responding to complex issues through cognitive, communicative, and interpersonal skills [1,2]. Increasingly critical across fields like healthcare, education, and defense [3], CPS is central to the "21st-century skills" movement, equipping students with essential teamwork, adaptability, critical thinking, and social-emotional competencies, while also enhancing learner engagement and deepening conceptual understanding [1,2,4,5].

In military contexts, effective Collaborative Problem-Solving (CPS) is vital for high-stakes, time-sensitive decision-making, especially in naval command-and-control environments where uncertainty and stress prevail [6]. Structured

A. I. Cristea et al. (Eds.): AIED 2025, LNAI 15877, pp. 338–351, 2025.
https://doi.org/10.1007/978-3-031-98414-3_24

protocols like the U.S. Navy's Tactical Decision Making Under Stress (TADMUS) emphasize clear roles, rapid information exchange, and feedback loops to enhance situational awareness and reduce errors [7–10]. Realistic simulations and deliberate practice further reinforce CPS skills, demonstrating valuable reciprocal insights between military training and educational practices [9–12].

This study focuses on refining communication structures in naval CPS scenarios by integrating Epistemic Network Analysis (ENA) and genetic algorithms to model and optimize team communication [13–17]. Using ENA, the study differentiates between high- and low-performance teams based on their communication structures and thematic code sequences. The optimization process is guided by a reward function that accounts for the location of individual communication patterns within the ENA network, the sequential order of thematic codes in team interactions, and the required response patterns to hostile and friendly air tracks. By applying a genetic algorithm, the study iteratively optimizes these communication sequences to enhance decision-making efficiency [18,19]. The final outcome provides an adaptive framework that generalizes across different naval decision-making contexts, offering insights into improving training and operational effectiveness.

2 Background

The U.S. Navy's Tactical Decision Making Under Stress (TADMUS) program enhances naval team decision-making under cognitive overload by emphasizing effective communication, real-time information exchange, and shared situational understanding [6,9,20,21]. In dynamic combat situations, synchronized communication and role interdependency critically influence teams' situational awareness and adaptation [18,22–24], though variability in communication persists despite rigorous training [9]. ENA, initially used in learning analytics, visualizes how teams connect concepts over time, distinguishing coherent, expert-like reasoning patterns from fragmented discourse, thus highlighting areas for communication and decision-making improvement [25–27].

Beyond these fields, ENA has also informed military and tactical decision-making research by illuminating how teams coordinate, maintain situational awareness, and respond to incoming data. In the context of naval Air Defense Warfare (ADW), high-performing teams have been found to establish stronger conceptual connections between threat assessment [11], situational updates, and tactical actions, while low-performing teams show disorganized or redundant communication patterns. These findings underscore how communication structure directly influences overall mission effectiveness [28].

Previous work analyzing ADW teams with ENA has shown that introducing decision support systems can significantly alter communication patterns. In some studies, commanders using advanced technological tools issued fewer requests for information and focused more intensively on tactical decisions, whereas teams relying on standard procedures spent additional time seeking clarification and interpreting sensor data. Such outcomes point to the importance of optimizing team communication to reduce redundancy and increase task-relevant exchanges [11]. However, most ENA-based analyses to date have been descriptive rather than prescriptive, lacking an integrated approach for real-time optimization of communication patterns. While ENA can successfully identify the differences between high- and low-performing teams, it does not itself offer guidance on how to refine or restructure communication in the moment. To address this limitation, the present research extends ENA through the integration of genetic algorithms, aiming to provide data-driven optimization strategies that enhance collaborative decision-making under stress in naval operations.

To address these limitations, this study aims to go beyond traditional ENA analysis by incorporating genetic algorithms to optimize sequential communication structures in naval CPS scenarios. Optimizing communication patterns in collaborative problem-solving (CPS) scenarios often involves searching for structures that balance the need for robust information exchange with time-sensitive adaptability. A range of optimization techniques—such as gradient-based methods, integer programming, and heuristic search algorithms—has been employed across domains like multi-agent coordination, emergency response, and supply chain management [29]. However, these methods can be constrained by the complexity of the solution space and the combinatorial nature of communication pathways, especially when real-time adaptation is required. Gradient-based approaches, for instance, rely on smooth cost functions and may struggle with discrete or discontinuous decision variables, while linear or mixed-integer programming formulations require precise mathematical models that may not fully capture the subtleties of team discourse [30]. When it comes to refining communication structures in dynamically evolving military environments, evolutionary computation offers distinct advantages by enabling an iterative, population-based search through complex and high-dimensional spaces.

Genetic algorithms (GAs) are effective evolutionary methods for optimizing communication strategies in CPS contexts, iteratively refining solutions by simulating biological evolution—selection, crossover, and mutation—to enhance team communication configurations [31–33]. Their robustness to local optima, maintenance of solution diversity, and capability to handle multiple objectives, such as minimizing redundancy, optimizing response speed, and reducing cognitive load, make them particularly suitable for military scenarios with uncertain or varying conditions [34,35]. Additionally, GAs efficiently tackle discrete optimization problems and combinatorial complexities inherent in tactical communications [36].

2.1 Research Questions

This study is guided by the following research questions:

1. How can ENA be leveraged to quantify and optimize communication patterns in naval CPS scenarios?
2. How can genetic algorithms be applied to optimize the sequence and structure of thematic codes to enhance decision-making effectiveness?

3 Method

3.1 Communication Pattern Generation in Tactical Decision-Making

To model and optimize communication patterns in collaborative problem-solving (CPS) within naval decision-making scenarios, we developed a synthetic communication dataset based on predefined roles, thematic codes, and scenario constraints. The goal was to simulate realistic communication structures using Epistemic Network Analysis (ENA) principles while integrating an optimization framework to refine team coordination strategies.

Communication sequences were generated based on predefined speaker roles in naval air defense warfare teams, including the Commanding Officer (CO), Tactical Action Officer (TAO), Identification Supervisor (IDS), Air Warfare Coordinator (ADWC), Tactical Information Coordinator (TIC), and Electronic Warfare Supervisor (EWS). Each utterance in a conversation was assigned thematic codes that categorize its function within the CPS process. These thematic codes Table 1 included seeking information, detecting and identifying tracks, assessing threat levels, issuing deterrent or defensive orders, providing status updates, and making tactical recommendations.

Table 1. Qualitative codes, definitions, and examples.

Code	Definition	Examples
Detect/Identify	Talk about radar detection of a track or the identification of a track (e.g., vessel type)	1) IR/EW NEW BEARING, BEARING 078 APQ120 CORRELATES TRACK 7036 POSSIBLE F-4 2) TIC/IDC TRACK 7023 NO MODES NO CODES
Track Behavior	Talk about kinematic data about a track or a track's location	1) AIR/IDS TRACK NUMBER 7021 DROP IN ALTITUDE TO 18 THOUSAND FEET 2) TAC/AIR TRACK 7031 THE HELO THAT WAS TAKING OFF THE OIL PLATFORM IS TURNED EAST
Assessment/Prioritization	Talk about whether a track is friendly or hostile, the threat level of a track, or indicating tracks of interest	1) TRACKS OF INTEREST 7013 LEVEL 5 7037 LEVEL 5 7007 LEVEL 4 TRACK 7020 LEVEL 5 AND 7036 LEVEL 5 2) CO, AYE. LET'S UPGRADE OUR THREAT LEVEL TO 6
Status Updates	Talk about procedural information, e.g., track responses to tactical actions, or talk about tactical actions taken by the team	1) TAO ID, STILL NO RESPONSE FROM TRACK 37, POSSIBLE PUMA HELO 2) GOT HIM COVERED
Seeking Information	Asking questions regarding track behavior, identification, or status	1) TAO CO, WE'VE UPGRADED THEM TO LEVEL 7 RIGHT? 2) WHERE IS 23?
Recommendations	Recommending or requesting tactical actions	1) AIR/TIC RECOMMEND LEVEL THREE ON TRACK 7016 7022 2) GB, THIS IS GW, REQUEST PERMISSION TO TAKE TRACK 7022 WITH BIRDS HOSTILE AIR. THREAT LEVEL HIGH. RANGE 7NM
Deterrent Orders	Giving orders meant to warn or deter tracks	1) TIC AIR, CONDUCT LEVEL 2 WARNING ON 7037 2) AIR THIS IS TAC CONDUCT LEVEL ONE QUERY TRACK 7036
Defensive Orders	Giving orders to prepare ship defenses or engage hostile tracks	1) TAO/CO COVER 7016 WITH BIRDS 2) AIR KILL TRACK 7022 WITH BIRDS

3.2 Scenario-Based Event Simulation

Simulation is necessary before optimization because real-world communication data is often limited in scope, highly variable, and lacks structured patterns that can be directly used for optimization. Additionally, real naval operations involve unpredictable interactions, making it difficult to isolate key variables that contribute to effective decision-making under stress. By generating synthetic communication sequences that follow structured yet probabilistic event-driven models, we can systematically control the inputs, constraints, and conditions under which team interactions occur. This allows us to test various communication strategies before applying optimization techniques, ensuring that the model aligns with realistic decision-making dynamics.

To match with the original dataset requirement, communication patterns were generated for three distinct events, each designed to reflect different tactical decision-making phases:

1. Event 1 (Target Identification and Threat Assessment): Prioritizes codes such as "DetectIdentify," "TrackBehavior," and "AssessmentPrioritization", simulating information exchange during target identification.
2. Event 2 (Information Sharing and Coordination): Emphasizes "SeekingInformation," "StatusUpdate," and "Recommendation", representing the discussion and evaluation phase before issuing tactical decisions.
3. Event 3 (Tactical Action Execution): Focuses on "DeterrentOrders" and "DefensiveOrders", simulating engagement or deterrent actions against identified threats.

3.3 Speaker-Turn Structure and Target Assignment

Each turn of communication consisted of a randomly assigned speaker, one or more thematic codes, and an associated target identifier (representing a hostile or friendly air track). The simulation incorporated:

- Randomized conversation lengths, ensuring variability in interactions while maintaining coherence within each event type.
- Probabilistic code assignment, favoring event-relevant thematic codes while allowing variability to introduce realistic communication behaviors.
- Target sequencing mechanisms, where utterances were dynamically assigned to different air tracks based on predefined engagement scenarios.

A structured target-switching mechanism was implemented to ensure that teams sequentially addressed multiple air tracks, with adjustments made based on real-time decision changes. Additionally, a crossover probability was introduced to allow communication strategies to evolve, facilitating the emergence of more efficient information exchange patterns over multiple iterations.

3.4 Epistemic Network Analysis Space

The network space and location calculation in this research is based on ENA, which models the co-occurrence of thematic codes within a given window of discourse. The calculation begins by constructing a co-occurrence matrix, where each entry represents the frequency with which two codes appear together within a specific temporal window of conversation. To ensure that the matrix remains balanced and interpretable, the data undergoes a normalization and centering process. Normalization prevents the influence of magnitude differences, ensuring that high-frequency codes do not dominate the network, while demeaning the data ensures that the vectors are aligned with a centered mean, facilitating accurate spatial projections in the ENA space. The co-occurrence matrix is then transformed into a vector representation, which serves as the basis for analyzing communication patterns and their structural relationships in the interaction network.

The co-occurrence generation process dynamically adjusts the window size, allowing it to capture both immediate and contextually relevant interactions. Within each turn of talk, thematic codes are identified, and co-occurrences are calculated both within the same turn and between turns in the window. By incorporating both current and past interactions, this method reflects the temporal dependencies in CPS communication. To refine the analysis, the co-occurrence vector is extracted from the upper triangular part of the co-occurrence matrix, ensuring that redundant self-connections are removed. This processed vector serves as the input for further dimensional reduction techniques, enabling the identification of distinct communication structures and performance patterns within the ENA network space.

3.5 Reward Functions

Epistemic Network Analysis Network. The primary network-based reward function calculates Manhattan distances between a team's communication structure and pre-defined low- and high-performance team profiles in ENA space. The objective is to minimize the distance from high-performance teams while maximizing the distance from low-performance teams, ensuring that optimized communication sequences exhibit characteristics aligned with effective team interactions. This is achieved by measuring an individual's placement relative to a hyperplane that separates high- and low-performance team structures, rewarding individuals positioned closer to high-performance profiles. The dot product between vector projections determines whether an individual's communication strategy aligns with efficient, structured decision-making processes, thereby guiding the optimization algorithm toward improved solutions.

Constraints Optimization. The reward function incorporates a set of constraints designed to ensure that the simulated communication sequences follow logical and effective structures based on real-world tactical decision-making processes. These constraints enforce temporal dependencies, sequential logic, and strategic coordination in collaborative problem-solving (CPS) scenarios. The constraints are structured to reward effective communication behaviors while penalizing disruptions or inefficient sequences. Each constraint contributes to the overall evaluation score, which is used to optimize communication structures through a genetic algorithm framework.

1. DetectIdentify to TrackBehavior Sequence (Constraint 1): A reward is given if "TrackBehavior" follows "DetectIdentify" within five turns for the same target. This ensures that once a target is detected, its behavior is promptly assessed to improve situational awareness.
2. Proper Sequencing of Tactical Actions (Constraint 2): If a "DeterrentOrder" or "DefensiveOrder" is issued to a friendly target, a penalty is applied. If the order is directed at a hostile target, a reward is given only if the sequence "DetectIdentify → TrackBehavior → Recommendation → Order" is maintained, reinforcing structured engagement decisions.
3. TrackBehavior to AssessmentPrioritization (Constraint 3): "AssessmentPrioritization" should follow "TrackBehavior" within five turns for the same target. This ensures that once a target's behavior is logged, its threat level is assessed promptly, preventing delays in decision-making.
4. AssessmentPrioritization to Engagement (Constraint 4): If no engagement-related action (e.g., "StatusUpdate," "Recommendation," "DeterrentOrder," "DefensiveOrder") follows "AssessmentPrioritization" within five turns, a penalty is applied. This prevents unnecessary delays in responding to threats after assessment.
5. Preventing Premature TrackBehavior (Constraint 5): "TrackBehavior" should not occur before "DetectIdentify." If this happens, a penalty is applied, ensuring that a target is first identified before its behavior is evaluated.
6. Ensuring Preliminary Actions Before Orders (Constraint 6): If "DeterrentOrders" or "DefensiveOrders" are issued before any preliminary actions (such as "SeekingInformation," "DetectIdentify," "TrackBehavior," "StatusUpdate," or "AssessmentPrioritization"), a penalty is applied. This enforces a structured escalation of decision-making.
7. Continuous Threat Assessment for Multiple Targets (Constraint 7): If "DetectIdentify" occurs for multiple targets, but fewer corresponding "AssessmentPrioritization" actions are recorded within the next ten turns, a penalty is applied. This ensures that all detected targets are evaluated before engagement.
8. Coordinated Engagement for Multiple Targets (Constraint 8): If "Recommendation" is issued for multiple targets, but fewer corresponding "DeterrentOrders" or "DefensiveOrders" are observed within the next ten turns, a penalty is applied. This ensures synchronized engagement decisions across multiple threats.

Each of these constraints contributes to the overall evaluation score, reinforcing both thematic correctness and temporal efficiency in team communication. By combining these structured constraints with ENA-based network optimization, the model ensures that high-performance communication behaviors are rewarded while penalizing disruptions and inefficiencies in decision-making.

4 Results

4.1 Optimized and Deoptimized Communication Patterns in ENA Space

The Fig. 1 presents the projected ENA network locations for both the real dataset teams and the optimized and deoptimized results. The real dataset is categorized into three performance groups: high-performance teams (red), middle-performance teams (orange), and low-performance teams (light blue). The optimization algorithm was trained to improve communication efficiency based on high-performance team parameters, including ENA network structure, turn sequences, and thematic code distributions. The results show distinct patterns emerging from the optimization and deoptimization processes, confirming the effectiveness and interpretability of the algorithm.

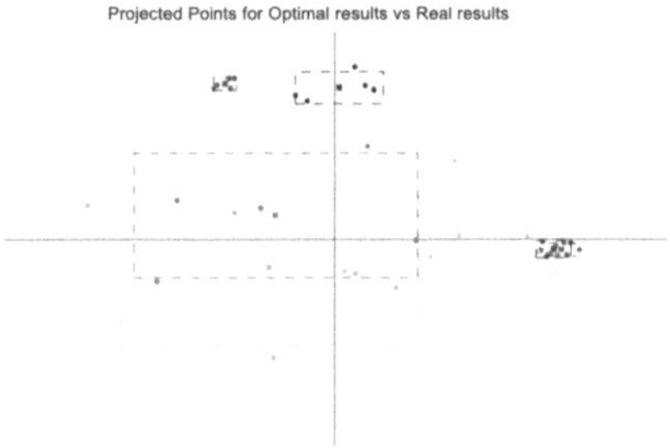

Fig. 1. Projected ENA network locations for real dataset teams and optimized/deoptimized results. Red points represent high-performance teams, orange points represent middle-performance teams, and light blue points represent low-performance teams. The black points indicate optimized results based on high-performance team parameters, while the purple points represent optimization based on low-performance team parameters. Dark blue and dark green points show deoptimized results, illustrating the algorithm's ability to degrade communication performance systematically. (Color figure online)

The optimized communication patterns (black points) are clearly positioned outside the confidence interval of high-performance teams, indicating that the algorithm not only replicated the characteristics of high-performing teams but also uncovered new communication structures that were not observed in the original dataset. This suggests that the optimized strategies offer alternative but functionally superior approaches to structuring communication in tactical decision-making. Conversely, the low-performance team optimization (purple points) shows a shift in the opposite direction of high-performance teams, meaning that the algorithm effectively pushed low-performance teams closer to high-performance behaviors. This confirms that the optimization process is meaningful and improves communication efficiency by reconfiguring low-performing structures to better align with high-performance strategies.

4.2 Validation of Deoptimization Mechanism

To further validate the robustness of the optimization framework, a reverse optimization process was conducted. The deoptimized results (dark blue and dark green points) demonstrate that high-performance team structures can be systematically degraded, with the resulting communication patterns clustering closer to the confidence interval of low-performance teams. This confirms that the algorithm effectively manipulates communication structures, proving that the model is capable of both enhancing and degrading performance-based communication behaviors. The successful degradation of high-performing teams into low-performance structures further supports the conclusion that the optimization algorithm correctly identifies and manipulates the key features that define high-performance communication in collaborative problem-solving scenarios.

4.3 Network Comparison

Event 1. In Event 1 based on Fig. 2, the real network for high-performance teams primarily focuses on DetectIdentify, TrackBehavior, and SeekingInformation, reflecting a structured approach to target identification and situational awareness. These communication patterns indicate that high-performing teams emphasize gathering information, tracking target behaviors, and confirming identifications before making tactical decisions.

However, the optimized network suggests a stronger emphasis on AssessmentPrioritization, which aligns with effective decision-making strategies. By increasing the frequency of AssessmentPrioritization, the optimized network encourages teams to evaluate threats and prioritize responses rather than solely relying on detection and tracking. This adjustment makes sense as it enhances the decision-making process by ensuring that threats are assessed before action is taken, leading to more informed and strategic engagements.

Conversely, the deoptimized network demonstrates a flawed communication structure by prioritizing DeterrentOrders early in the process, bypassing essential information-gathering and assessment steps. Issuing DeterrentOrders prematurely in Event 1 lacks strategic validity, as it results in hasty and uninformed decision-making without the necessary confirmation of threats. This pattern highlights the risks of skipping critical assessment phases, reinforcing the importance of a structured sequence of DetectIdentify, TrackBehavior, and AssessmentPrioritization before engaging in tactical responses.

Event 2. In Event 2, the real network for high-performance teams maintains a structure similar to Event 1 but with more connections across thematic codes, reflecting the increased need for information sharing at this stage. This pattern indicates that high-performing teams focus on collaborative communication, ensuring that relevant information is distributed among team members before advancing toward decision-making. The expanded connections suggest that coordination and verification processes are emphasized, reinforcing the importance of situational awareness before issuing tactical responses.

(a) Real Network - Event 1

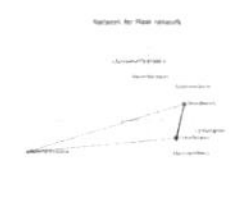

(b) Real Network - Event 2

(c) Real Network - Event 3

(d) Optimal Network - Event 1

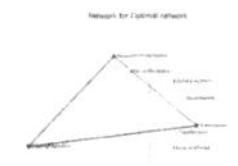

(e) Optimal Network - Event 2

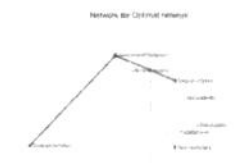

(f) Optimal Network - Event 3

(g) Deoptimal Network - Event 1

(h) Deoptimal Network - Event 2

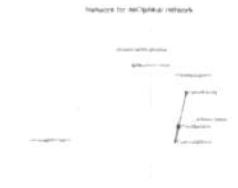

(i) Deoptimal Network - Event 3

Fig. 2. Comparison of Real, Optimized, and Deoptimized Networks across different events. The first row represents the real communication network extracted from the dataset. The second row shows the optimized communication structures based on high-performance teams. The third row presents the deoptimized networks, demonstrating how the algorithm systematically degrades communication performance.

The optimized network refines this structure by recommending a stronger emphasis on StatusUpdate and SeekingInformation, ensuring that team members continuously exchange real-time updates on identified targets and operational changes. Additionally, the optimization maintains a clear assessment phase, reinforcing the necessity of AssessmentPrioritization before issuing any orders. However, if an immediate decision is required, the optimized network still preserves a structured connection between StatusUpdate, AssessmentPrioritization, and DefensiveOrders, ensuring that tactical responses are executed only when justified by the preceding communication sequence. This structured decision-making approach enhances efficiency and risk management, ensuring that teams act based on validated information rather than premature or fragmented exchanges.

Event 3. In Event 3, the real network for high-performance teams shifts back to a structure primarily centered around DetectIdentify and TrackBehavior, without making immediate decisions regarding DefensiveOrders or DeterrentOrders. This suggests that, in this phase, high-performing teams prioritize continued monitoring and tracking rather than prematurely engaging in defensive actions. The absence of direct engagement orders in the real high-performance network indicates a cautious, information-driven approach, ensuring that teams maintain situational awareness before making final tactical decisions.

The optimized network, however, recommends a more proactive structure, integrating DefensiveOrders with AssessmentPrioritization and SeekingInformation to ensure that defensive responses are justified and well-informed. Additionally, the optimized model establishes direct connections between StatusUpdate and DeterrentOrders, meaning that if the track status changes, teams can initiate deterrent actions when necessary. This approach enhances decision-making by ensuring that engagement decisions are data-driven, reducing the risk of delayed defensive actions while still maintaining an assessment process before issuing commands.

Across all three events, the deoptimized networks remain highly similar, showing a rigid focus on DetectIdentify, TrackBehavior, and DeterrentOrders. This pattern indicates a rushed, reactive decision-making process, where teams engage threats too early without gathering sufficient information or conducting assessments. The lack of structured information-sharing and prioritization in the deoptimized networks highlights the risks of premature engagement, reinforcing the importance of structured assessment phases and decision validation in effective communication strategies.

5 Discussion and Conclusion

Overall, these results validate the optimization framework by demonstrating that the algorithm can:

1. Improve low-performance teams by pushing them toward high-performance team structures.
2. Enhance communication efficiency beyond what was observed in the original dataset.
3. Degrade communication effectiveness, reinforcing that the optimization model correctly identifies and manipulates key performance-driving features in ENA network space.

This analysis confirms that machine-learning-driven optimization of communication patterns can systematically refine CPS strategies and generate novel high-performance team structures, offering valuable insights beyond those found in real-world naval team interactions.

A key advantage of this optimization framework is that it is directly built upon the ENA network structure, making it both easy to implement and highly reliable within the existing ENA analytical framework. The validation of optimized communication strategies is supported by the spatial placement of projected points in the ENA network, demonstrating that the optimization model effectively restructures communication behaviors while preserving key performance characteristics. The deoptimized results, on the other hand, consistently degrade team communication by reinforcing inefficient and rushed decision-making processes, aligning with expected low-performance team behaviors. The ability to both optimize and degrade communication structures further validates the robustness of the algorithm, confirming that it correctly manipulates the structural elements that define high-performance and low-performance teams.

Across all three events, the results confirm that high-performance teams rely on structured, information-driven decision-making, while poor communication strategies result in rushed and poorly timed actions. The optimization framework successfully improved low-performance teams by shifting their communication patterns toward high-performance structures, while the deoptimization validated the algorithm's ability to systematically degrade communication efficiency. These findings highlight the importance of structured communication strategies in CPS and tactical decision-making, reinforcing that effective team coordination requires a balance between information gathering, assessment, and execution.

The results also demonstrate that optimizing communication patterns using high-performance team structures leads to improved decision-making strategies, while deoptimization results in rushed and inefficient communication sequences. Across all three events, the optimized networks exhibit a well-structured balance between information gathering, assessment, and tactical execution, whereas the deoptimized networks prioritize early engagement without adequate evaluation, leading to ineffective decision-making.

Beyond validating the optimization model, the findings also hold significant promise for the educational setting, where teachers and students alike stand to benefit from data-driven insights into effective collaboration. By revealing communication strategies that go beyond the best practices currently observed in classrooms, this machine-learning-driven approach can help educators design activities and group structures that cultivate deeper student engagement and stronger CPS skills. The discovery of previously unobserved high-performance patterns suggests that educators might harness these optimized networks to guide classroom discussions, team projects, and peer-led learning in ways that enhance both academic outcomes and social-emotional learning.

Looking ahead, future research should focus on applying this optimization framework in real educational environments. By integrating adaptive learning models that respond to student and teacher inputs in real time, researchers can refine CPS efficiency in dynamic, evolving classrooms. Implementing these insights in live educational scenarios—such as teacher–student teamwork or small-group projects—will help validate the applicability of optimized communication patterns under authentic classroom constraints.

References

1. Hesse, F., Care, E., Buder, J., Sassenberg, K., Griffin, P.: A framework for teachable collaborative problem solving skills. In: Griffin, P., Care, E. (eds.) Assessment and Teaching of 21st Century Skills. EAIA, pp. 37–56. Springer, Dordrecht (2015). https://doi.org/10.1007/978-94-017-9395-7_2
2. Care, E., Griffin, P., Wilson, M. (eds.): Assessment and Teaching of 21st Century Skills. EAIA, Springer, Cham (2018). https://doi.org/10.1007/978-3-319-65368-6
3. PISA OECD: Results (Volume v): Collaborative Problem Solving (2017, 2015)

4. Dillenbourg, P.: Collaborative Learning: Cognitive and Computational Approaches. Advances in Learning and Instruction Series. ERIC (1999)
5. VanLehn, K.: The relative effectiveness of human tutoring, intelligent tutoring systems, and other tutoring systems. Educ. Psychol. **46**(4), 197–221 (2011)
6. Morrison, J.G., Kelly, R.T., Moore, R.A., Hutchins, S.G.: Tactical decision making under stress (TADMUS) decision support system (1996)
7. Cannon-Bowers, J.A., Salas, E., Converse, S.: Shared mental models in expert team decision making. In: Individual and Group Decision Making: Current Issues, vol. 221, pp. 221–246 (1993)
8. Cannon-Bowers, J.A., Salas, E.: Team performance and training in complex environments: recent findings from applied research. Current Directions Psychol. Sci. **7**(3), 83–87 (1998)
9. Salas, E.E., Fiore, S.M.: Team Cognition: Understanding the Factors that Drive Process and Performance. American Psychological Association (2004)
10. Orasanu, J., Connolly, T.: The reinvention of decision making. In: Decision Making in Action: Models and Methods, vol. 1, pp. 3–20 (1993)
11. Swiecki, Z., Ruis, A.R., Farrell, C., Shaffer, D.W.: Assessing individual contributions to collaborative problem solving: a network analysis approach. Comput. Hum. Behav. **104**, 105876 (2020)
12. Shawn Burke, C., Priest, H.A., Salas, E., Sims, D., Mayer, K.: Stress and teams: how stress affects decision making at the team level. In: Performance Under Stress, pp. 197–224. CRC Press (2018)
13. Arastoopour, G., Chesler, N.C., Shaffer, D.W., Swiecki, Z.: Epistemic network analysis as a tool for engineering design assessment. In: 2015 ASEE Annual Conference & Exposition, pp. 26–679 (2015)
14. Zhang, S., et al.: Understanding student teachers' collaborative problem solving: insights from an epistemic network analysis (ENA). Comput. Educ. **183**, 104485 (2022)
15. Fang, Z., Xie, J., Peng, R., Wang, S.: Climate finance: mapping air pollution and finance market in time series. Econometrics **9**(4), 43 (2021)
16. Fang, Z., Yang, Y., Swiecki, Z.: Automated code discovery via graph neural networks and generative AI. In: Arastoopour Irgens, G., Knight, S. (eds.) ICQE 2023. CCIS, vol. 1895, pp. 438–454. Springer, Cham (2023). https://doi.org/10.1007/978-3-031-47014-1_30
17. Swiecki, Z., Ruis, A.R., Shaffer, D.W.: Modeling and visualizing team performance using epistemic net-work analysis. In: Proceedings of the 7th Annual GIFT Users Symposium, pp. 148–156 (2019)
18. Fang, Z., Han, J.Y., Aldino, A.A., Feng, Z., Cai, T.: Decoding the naturally arisen leadership in collaborative learning: a Bayesian simulation and human network study. In: Proceedings of the 39th ACM/SIGAPP Symposium on Applied Computing, pp. 21–28 (2024)
19. Jardine, P., Andrews, B.: Bayesian graph neural networks modeling for naturally arisen leadership. In: Kim, Y.J., Swiecki, Z. (eds.) ICQE 2024. CCIS, vol. 2278, pp. 31–39. Springer, Cham (2024). https://doi.org/10.1007/978-3-031-76335-9_3
20. Johnston, J.H., Cannon-Bowers, J.A., Salas, E.: Tactical decision making under stress (TADMUS): mapping a program of research to a real world incident—the USS Vincennes. In: RTO HFM Symposium on Collaborative Crew Performance in Complex Operational Systems, pp. 20–22. Citeseer (1998)
21. Hutcheon, D., Bevilacua, M.: TADMUS: pairing CBT strategies with job responsibilities to reduce stress and increase return to work potential for affect disordered clientele. Ann. Am. Psychother. Assoc. **13**(2), 32–43 (2010)

22. Fiore, S.M., Ross, K.G., Jentsch, F.: A team cognitive readiness framework for small-unit training. J. Cogn. Eng. Decision Making **6**(3), 325–349 (2012)
23. Smith, C.A.P., Johnston, J., Paris, C.: Decision support for air warfare: detection of deceptive threats. Group Decision Negot. **13**(2), 129–148 (2004)
24. Fang, Z., Wang, W., Chen, G., Swiecki, Z.: Neural epistemic network analysis: combining graph neural networks and epistemic network analysis to model collaborative processes. In: Proceedings of the 14th Learning Analytics and Knowledge Conference, pp. 157–166 (2024)
25. Shaffer, D.W., Collier, W., Ruis, A.R.: A tutorial on epistemic network analysis: analyzing the structure of connections in cognitive, social, and interaction data. J. Learn. Anal. **3**(3), 9–45 (2016)
26. Shaffer, D.W.: Epistemic network analysis: understanding learning by using big data for thick description. In: International Handbook of the Learning Sciences, pp. 520–531. Routledge (2018)
27. Zörgő, S., Peters, G.J.Y., Csajbók-Veres, K., Geröly, A., Jeney, A., Ruis, A.R.: An epistemic network analysis of patient decision-making regarding choice of therapy. Qual. Quan. **57**(4), 3105–3132 (2023)
28. Wang, Y., Swiecki, Z., Ruis, A.R., Shaffer, D.W.: Simplification of epistemic networks using parsimonious removal with interpretive alignment. In: Ruis, A.R., Lee, S.B. (eds.) ICQE 2021. CCIS, vol. 1312, pp. 137–151. Springer, Cham (2021). https://doi.org/10.1007/978-3-030-67788-6_10
29. Michalewicz, Z.: How to Solve it: Modern Heuristics. Springer, Heidelberg (2013). https://doi.org/10.1007/978-3-662-07807-5
30. Panait, L., Luke, S.: Cooperative multi-agent learning: the state of the art. Auton. Agent. Multi-Agent Syst. **11**, 387–434 (2005)
31. Holland, J.H.: Adaptation in Natural and Artificial Systems: An Introductory Analysis with Applications to Biology, Control, and Artificial Intelligence. MIT Press (1992)
32. Goldberg, D.E.: Genetic Algorithm in Search, Optimization and Machine Learning, vol. 1, no. 98, p. 9. Addison Wesley Publishing Company, Reading, MA (1989)
33. Mitchell, M.: An Introduction to Genetic Algorithms. MIT Press (1998)
34. Eiben, A.E., Smith, J.E.: Introduction to Evolutionary Computing. Springer (2015)
35. Deb, K., Pratap, A., Agarwal, S., Meyarivan, T.A.M.T.: A fast and elitist multiobjective genetic algorithm: NSGA-II. IEEE Trans. Evol. Comput. **6**(2), 182–197 (2002)
36. Blum, C., Roli, A.: Metaheuristics in combinatorial optimization: overview and conceptual comparison. ACM Comput. Surv. (CSUR) **35**(3), 268–308 (2003)

From Test Scores to Neural Spikes: Predicting Students' Abstract Reasoning Ability Using EEG with Attention-Based Models

Stefano D'Urso[1(✉)], Ziqi Pan[2], Alexandra I. Cristea[2], and Filippo Sciarrone[1]

[1] Faculty of Technological and Innovation Sciences, Universitas Mercatorum, Piazza Mattei 10, 00189 Rome, Italy
stefano.durso@studenti.unimercatorum.it

[2] Department of Computer Science, Durham University, Stockton Road, Durham DH1 3LE, UK
ziqi.pan2@durham.ac.uk

Abstract. Abstract reasoning is a key ability for students' cognitive development, yet traditional methods often fail to provide an accurate and objective assessment. We propose a novel machine learning approach that utilises EEG data from low-cost headsets to predict response correctness in abstract reasoning tasks. This paper presents an *adaptive LSTM model incorporating multi-head attention* for analysing EEG data acquired during both the reasoning (pre-response) and feedback (post-response) phases of abstract reasoning questions. Results demonstrate the model's ability to predict answer correctness with promising performance across multiple evaluation metrics. Additionally, we investigate the influence of self-reported confidence on EEG-based correctness prediction, yielding valuable insights. Our model demonstrates scalability and robustness when applied to larger datasets. This research paves a way for prospective applications of innovative tools in personalised feedback and adaptive learning systems, and advances methods for assessing and supporting cognitive growth.

Keywords: EEG · Cognitive Assessment · Abstract Reasoning

1 Introduction

Abstract reasoning is the cognitive ability to analyse information, recognise patterns, and solve problems through logical thinking [15]. Developing strong abstract reasoning skills is a key objective of education, as it serves as a cornerstone for effective problem-solving [46], decision-making [7], and overall cognitive growth [24]. Effective cultivation of abstract reasoning necessitates accurate and reliable assessment. Traditionally, abstract reasoning is measured through various standardised tests (e.g., Wechsler Adult Intelligence Scale [44], Raven's Progressive Matrices [30]). However, solely judging based on the final test score

A. I. Cristea et al. (Eds.): AIED 2025, LNAI 15877, pp. 352–367, 2025.
https://doi.org/10.1007/978-3-031-98414-3_25

may not provide an accurate reflection of a student's true abstract reasoning abilities, due to false positive (e.g., correct answers by random guessing) or false negative (e.g., errors due to carelessness or mind-wandering) responses. One solution is to include self-assessment of performance. However, the reliability of the self-assessment may be affected by various individual factors, such as gender [40], personality [37], social and cultural norms [19], and overall self-confidence or self-esteem [39]. Therefore, an ideal assessment method should account for factors such as random guessing and individual differences. One promising and increasingly applied approach involves leveraging techniques that monitor brain activity [29]. Among these techniques, electroencephalography (EEG) stands out, due to its high temporal resolution, portability, and non-invasiveness [26]. While existing research has primarily focused on passively observing brain activity and identifying brain regions and frequency bands associated with reasoning (e.g., [5]), we propose integrate EEG data as an active input to assist in enhancing assessment accuracy. Motivated by this insight, in this study we pose the following Research Questions (RQs):

- ***RQ1: Can an AI-driven analysis of EEG signals, encompassing both reasoning (pre-response) and feedback (post-response) phases predict response correctness?***
- ***RQ2: Does incorporating self-reported confidence levels improve the predictive accuracy of the model?***

The study contributes to the field by providing a novel way to assess the actual reasoning ability of the student. To the best of our knowledge, this is the first research that uses EEG data in both the reasoning and feedback phases to calibrate false positives and negatives in predicting abstract reasoning performance. It introduces the first integrated model combining subjective self-reported confidence levels and objective EEG data for this task, leveraging a novel Long Short-Term Memory (LSTM) architecture with multi-head attention, to capture temporal dependencies and interpret complex relationships between neural activity and reasoning accuracy. The potential applications of this research extend beyond theoretical advancements, offering practical benefits for both educators and students in assessing and developing reasoning ability and various other cognitive abilities.

2 Literature Review

As a non-invasive technique for measuring brain activity, electroencephalography (EEG) has proven valuable for analysing neural processes related to various cognitive activities, such as attention [20], decision making [36], and reasoning [5]. For instance, Amin et al. [5] revealed dominant prefrontal and parietal lobe activation during an abstract reasoning task, with elevated frontal theta band activity (3.5–7.5 Hz). Despite the advantages of EEG in cognitive research, traditional EEG devices used in clinical settings are costly and cumbersome, requiring trained professionals for operation and extensive setup time. Their complexity and size limit their accessibility and practicality for everyday use.

Recent advances in EEG technology have expanded its use to consumer-grade devices, enabling applications in fields such as gaming [43], cybersecurity [34], and education [14,27]. These devices, while cost-effective and portable, reliably capture key neural signatures, such as frontal theta oscillations, and have been used in various cognitive analyses, such as reasoning and working memory [41]. In education, EEG has been used in personalised learning, by monitoring cognitive and emotional engagement [6], as well as detecting and predicting attention [2,42]. Recent work, such as Fuentes et al. [17], demonstrated that consumer-grade EEG headsets could reliably assess student attention and correlate beta-band power with academic performance, underscoring the potential applicability of EEG in real-world educational settings.

The integration of machine learning has further enhanced EEG's capabilities. Techniques like Support Vector Machines (SVMs), Random Forest (RF), and neural networks are widely used to classify cognitive states [32,33]. In the field of education, studies like Apicella et al. [6] combined wearable EEG systems with SVM, to monitor cognitive and emotional engagement, while RF has shown superior accuracy in detecting nuanced cognitive states [2]. Miasnikova et al. [25] explored EEG biomarkers for reasoning, achieving 62.5% accuracy on independent samples using phase-locking values (PLVs) as SVM features. However, their results relied on non-standard tasks and failed to consider subjective measurements. Among all machine learning architectures, outside of educational applications, Recurrent Neural Networks (RNNs) and Long Short-Term Memory (LSTM) networks have demonstrated success in processing EEG time-series data; Alhagry et al. [3] and Chowdary et al. [10] showed that LSTMs effectively capture temporal dependencies, while Naderi et al. [28] combined spectral analysis with RNNs to classify EEG signals. Recent research have demonstrated the effectiveness of multi-head attention in improving model performance, by enabling the network to focus on different parts of the input sequence, simultaneously. Multi-head attention mechanisms have been successfully applied in various domains, such as sentiment analysis [35], neural machine translation [47], anomaly detection [8], and time-series forecasting [1]. These studies illustrate how multi-head attention enhances traditional deep learning architectures, such as LSTM and CNN-RNN models, by capturing richer dependencies across time steps. In particular, the integration of multi-head attention with LSTMs has shown promising results in improving interpretability and performance across sequence-based tasks. For example, Long et al. [23] demonstrated that combining bidirectional LSTMs with multi-head attention significantly improved sentiment classification accuracy. Similarly, Abbasimehr et al. [1] highlighted the role of attention models in refining time-series predictions.

To the best of our knowledge, most studies focus on passively monitoring brain activities during different cognitive states. Our research is the first to address this gap, by actively predicting reasoning performance using EEG, and incorporating confidence as a biasing factor. Rather than treating confidence as an additional input variable, we consider it as an intrinsic influence that modulates the relationship between neural activity and reasoning performance. This approach acknowledges that confidence is not merely a self-reported measure but an integral part of cognitive processing, potentially affecting neural correlates of decision-making and performance. By integrating both neural and subjective measures, our study bridges cognitive neuroscience with educational assessment, offering a novel perspective on how internal cognitive states shape reasoning outcomes and paving the way for future practical applications.

3 Methodology

To investigate these questions, we first established a methodological framework that integrates neural data collection with computational analysis. To this end, we developed an integrated system comprising data collection via EEG hardware devices and a front-end application for human-computer interaction in experiments, followed by data preprocessing and model training in a back-end off-line machine learning environment.

3.1 LSTM with Multi-head Attention ML Models Design

The back-end environment utilises an AI system that operates offline during the training phase. The system is based on Long Short-Term Memory (LSTM) networks, a specialised class of neural networks designed for processing sequential data [12]. The LSTM network has been shown in non-educational applications to be particularly suited for handling EEG data, as it captures temporal dependencies and patterns in brain activity over time [13]. However, standard LSTMs have limitations in capturing long-range dependencies effectively. To address this, we incorporated an attention mechanism, as suggested in [22,45], leading to an ***Adaptive LSTM Model with Multi-Head Attention*** as depicted in Fig. 1. The architecture consists of three LSTM layers, followed by multi-head attention, with L2 regularisation and dropout layers to improve generalisation. Through comparative testing, this configuration provided the best fit for our research questions, effectively capturing both pre-response and post-response EEG activity. We propose two model variants to evaluate EEG-based predictions:

- **Standard Model**: The EEG sequence is processed through masking to ignore padded timesteps. The LSTM layers capture temporal dependencies, while multi-head attention enhances long-range feature extraction. The output is pooled and passed to a sigmoid layer for binary classification.
- **Confidence-Enhanced Model**: This variant integrates a self-reported confidence score h_{conf} as a bias. The confidence value is projected to match the dimensionality of the LSTM output and combined via element-wise addition:

$$h_{\text{combined}} = h_{\text{LSTM}} + h_{\text{conf}}$$

  This allows the model to adjust predictions based on both EEG patterns and subjective confidence, aiming at enhanced robustness and interpretability.

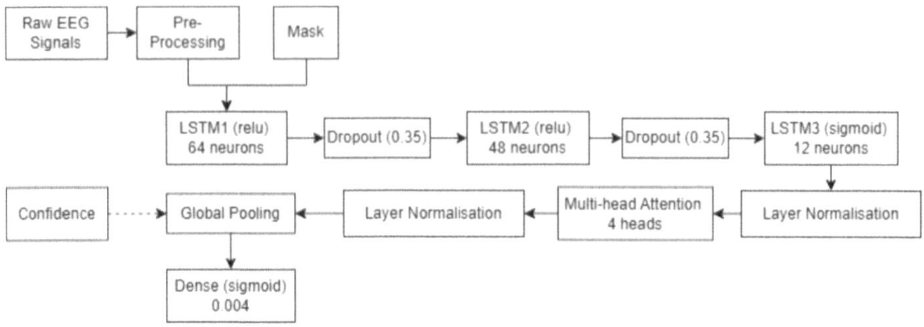

Fig. 1. Proposed LSTM with Multi-Head Attention Machine Learning Model: standard and confidence-enhanced

Several standard preprocessing steps were applied, to ensure EEG data quality and suitability for machine learning models:

- **Outlier Handling:** A quantile-based method (e.g., 5th and 95th percentiles) clipped extreme values, preserving signal variability while minimising distortions. This approach proved more robust than standard deviation thresholds for EEG's non-Gaussian distribution.
- **Normalisation:** Channel-wave combinations were standardised ($M = 0$, $SD = 1$) to ensure consistent scaling while preserving signal characteristics and preventing large amplitude dominance.
- **Zero-Padding:** Shorter EEG segments were padded with zeros at the end to standardise lengths for batch training and maintain temporal alignment.

Input and Masking Layers. The model input is a sequence with the shape (*batch size*, *sample_length*, *num_features*), where *sample_length* (94 timesteps) represents up to 90 s for answering each question plus 4 s for feedback, and *num_features* (33 features) is derived from 4 EEG channels and noise-related data. Sequences are padded with zeros if questions are answered early, ensuring uniform length for batch training. A **Masking layer** automatically ignores these zero-valued timesteps during computation, allowing the model to focus on meaningful data.

LSTM Layers. The **Long Short-Term Memory (LSTM) layers** form the core of the architecture, capturing temporal patterns in EEG data. The model employs a stack of three LSTM layers, each refining the learned representations of EEG sequences at different levels of abstraction. These layers process the sequence output from the masking layer and encode temporal dynamics into progressively richer feature representations. Key parameters include:

- **Number of units**: Defines the dimensionality of learned temporal features.

- **Dropout and recurrent dropout**: Regularisation techniques to prevent overfitting by randomly dropping connections during training. Applied after each LSTM layer.
- L_2 **regularisation**: Applied to LSTM kernel weights to mitigate overfitting, with adjustable strength to balance underfitting and overfitting (lambda = 2e−4)

Each LSTM layer refines the representation of EEG signals, allowing the model to capture short-term dependencies in the early layers and long-term patterns in the deeper layers. The final LSTM output is then passed to the attention mechanism for further refinement.

To enhance the model's ability to selectively focus on important temporal patterns, we incorporate *multi-head attention* after the LSTM layers. This mechanism enables the model to dynamically assign different levels of importance to various time steps, improving the extraction of relevant EEG features. The *multi-head attention* layer operates on the normalised output of the third LSTM layer, refining the learned representations by attending to multiple aspects of the data simultaneously. The number of attention heads is a configurable hyperparameter, while the key dimensionality is determined by the number of units in the third LSTM layer. This attention mechanism enhances the model's ability to capture long-range dependencies in EEG signals, complementing the hierarchical feature extraction performed by the LSTM layers. By integrating attention, the network dynamically reweighs time steps, improving feature selection and predictive performance. To condense the extracted features and prevent overfitting, the model applies Global Average Pooling, reducing the sequence dimension while preserving key information. The pooled features are then passed to a single dense output layer (sigmoid activation) for binary classification.

3.2 Experimental Design

Participants. A total of 23 participants were included in this study via opportunity sampling, 14 females and 9 males, ages ranging from 18 to 32 ($M = 25.5$, **SD** = 4.224). All participants were students or recent graduates.

Instruments. *Muse 2*[1] was selected for this study due to its reliability, portability, and suitability for cognitive research [21]. It features four EEG channels (AF7, AF8, TP9, TP10 according to 10–20 electrode positioning system) and two auxiliary channels, with a sample rate of 256 Hz and 12-bit resolution. The reference electrode is positioned at FPz (CMS/DRL). Studies have validated the Muse 2's reliability and effectiveness in diverse applications, such as monitoring cognitive workload [48], mental workload classification in simulated flight tasks [11], and attention detection [4]. Its utility for abstract reasoning tasks is further supported by its prefrontal electrodes (AF7, AF8), which target executive functions related to abstract reasoning ability.

[1] https://choosemuse.com/products/muse-2.

Standard Raven's Progressive Matrices (SRPM) [30] and *Raven's Advanced Progressive Matrices Practice Book* [9] were used in this study. *SRPM* is one of the most widely used non-verbal assessment tools for measuring abstract reasoning ability. It consists of 60 visual puzzles where participants identify the missing piece in a series of patterns. The *Raven's Advanced Progressive Matrices Practice Book* is a supplementary resource designed to prepare individuals for the advanced version of the test. It includes 60 more complex patterns and tasks. Consequently, this study's database contains a total of 120 questions, each with 6–8 answer options (see Fig. 3 for an example question).

A *Human-computer Interaction Interface* was designed for both participant interaction and concurrent EEG data acquisition. This system presents abstract reasoning questions to participants in a controlled and randomised manner, allows participants to indicate their confidence level, and provides immediate feedback (see Fig. 3). Furthermore, it maintains a stable connection with the EEG headset, acquires and processes data for feature extraction, and ensures precise temporal alignment of EEG data with participant responses for subsequent analysis (Fig. 2).

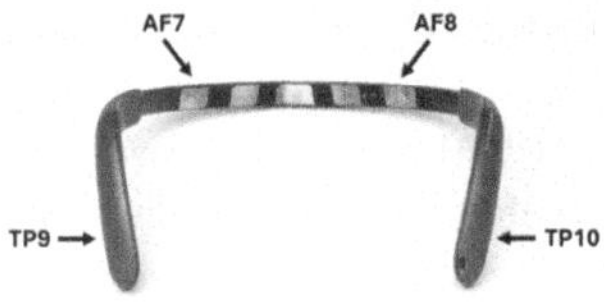

Fig. 2. The Muse 2 Device with Sensors Overview

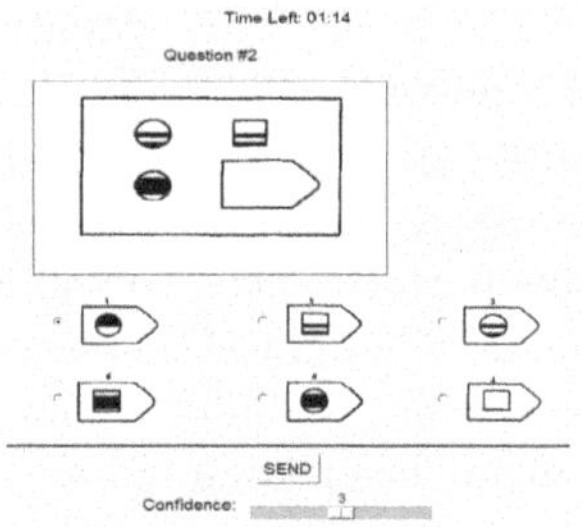

Fig. 3. Human-computer Interaction Interface

Experimental Procedure. This experiment adhered to the ethical guidelines outlined by the Durham University. Participants were allowed to withdraw from the experiment at any time. If they chose to do so, all their data would be immediately deleted. Participants first received an information sheet explaining the study's purpose, data handling, and procedures, followed by a consent form and a demographic questionnaire. The task was explained with an example question, as well as the meaning of confidence scores (0: Not confident at all, 1: Not confident, 2: Somewhat not confident, 3: Neither confident nor not confident, 4: Somewhat confident, 5: Confident, 6: Extremely confident). Participants could ask questions before the EEG device (Muse 2) was fitted. 18 participants were instructed to complete five rounds of tests, each test contained 10 randomly selected questions. 5 participants were instructed to complete as many rounds of tests as they could, aiming to generate the largest possible dataset given the participant count for model evaluation. Participants were instructed to remain still during rounds to reduce EEG noise but could take breaks between rounds. For each question, participants selected an answer, indicated their confidence level using a scroll bar (0 to 6), and then submitted their responses. Feedback was provided immediately: "Correct! Good!" for correct answers and "Wrong! Bad!" for incorrect ones. Each question had a 90-s time limit, unanswered questions would lead to negative feedback. Feedback lasted 2 s before the next question automatically appeared. A debriefing sheet was provided at the end of the experiment.

3.3 Preprocessing and Evaluation Methodology

Feature Selection. The dataset includes 32 features, representing 8 brainwave frequency bands (*Delta, Theta, Low Alpha, High Alpha, Low Beta, High Beta, Low Gamma, Mid Gamma*) across 4 EEG channels: **AF7, AF8, TP9, TP10**. These features capture cognitive processes such as reasoning and problem-solving, though not all features may equally impact model performance. A Random Forest classifier was used to identify the most impactful features, leveraging its ability to model non-linear relationships and rank features based on their importance in reducing prediction uncertainty. This method is known to be robust, interpretable [31,38], and well-suited for high-dimensional EEG data. The analysis highlighted AF7 and AF8 channels (Channel 1 and Channel 2) as the most significant for capturing reasoning-related brain activity. This finding aligns with several previous neuroscientific literature on prefrontal cortex, which have shown that interactions between alpha (8–12 Hz) and theta (4–8 Hz) band oscillations in frontal cortical areas play a crucial role in abilities related to abstract reasoning, such as working memory, attentional processes, and memory integration [18]. Focusing on these key features reduces input dimensionality, potentially enhancing model efficiency and performance. Interestingly, instead of theta or alpha, we found delta as the most important frequency.

Data Augmentation and Cross-Validation Strategy. To enhance model performance and improve generalisation, we introduced data augmentation techniques [16]. Given the sequential nature of EEG signals, we avoided augmentation methods that could alter temporal dependencies, such as time warping or shifting, as preserving the original timing structure was essential for capturing meaningful brain activity patterns. Among the tested techniques, we applied scaling, where the signal was multiplied by a random factor to introduce variability in amplitude, and jittering, which involved adding small random Gaussian noise to simulate natural EEG fluctuations. Experimental results showed that jittering provided the best improvement in model performance, enhancing robustness without distorting key signal characteristics. Additionally, incorporating augmentation allowed for better differentiation between train, validation, and test sets, ensuring a more reliable evaluation of the model's generalisation capabilities.

The analysis uses a 5-fold Stratified K-Fold cross-validation approach to evaluate the model's performance while preserving class distribution and minimising class imbalance. Each student dataset was divided into five folds, with four folds used for training and one for validation in each iteration. This process ensured each fold served as the validation set once, providing robust evaluation. The model was trained on padded EEG sequences prepared via a custom preprocessing pipeline. Training and validation accuracies were averaged across folds to assess generalisation. Validation predictions were further analysed using classification metrics like precision, recall, and F1-score, both for individual classes and macro averages. This comprehensive setup is to ensure reliable evaluation across varying data splits and reduced the impact of dataset variance.

4 Results

Results were generated for the 2 proposed models (standard & confidence-enhanced; see Fig. 1), with 2 different datasets (original and extensive), as follows.

4.1 Adaptive LSTM Model with Multi-head Attention

Initial Testing with Original Dataset (OS). To predict response correctness, for the original dataset, 5 tests of each participant were included. The OS dataset is the one with the largest number of different participants. If the participant completed the test more than 5 times, 5 tests of this participant were randomly selected to include in this dataset. We tested the model with different configurations, and the best configuration employs four attention heads and consists of three LSTM layers, with 64, 48, and 12 units in the first, second, and third layers, respectively. The learning rate is set to 0.0006, ensuring a balanced trade-off between convergence speed and stability. To prevent overfitting, a dropout rate of 0.35 is applied, and L2 regularisation with a lambda value of 0.0002 is incorporated. These hyperparameter choices are designed to enhance model generalisation and performance. This initial test included approximately 1.1 million data points, derived from 23 participants completing 5 tests of 15 min each, with the original data expanded through augmentation by a factor of 4. The results of the standard model's performance with original dataset (OS) are summarised in the Table 1.

The validation metrics suggest that the model effectively learns patterns from the training data, achieving a validation accuracy of 76.45%. With a balanced precision (77.11%) and recall (75.66%), the model avoids overly conservative or lenient classifications. An AUC score of 80.34% confirms strong class differentiation, indicating reliable performance on validation data. On unseen test data, the model achieves 60.23% accuracy, showing some generalisation, but also a drop from validation, suggesting possible overfitting. The test precision (60.87%) and recall (67.12%) indicate a slight preference for recall, meaning the model captures more positive cases at the cost of increased false positives. The F1 score

Table 1. Performance comparison across different datasets and models: *Original dataset with Standard model (OS), Extensive dataset with Standard model (ES), Original dataset with Confidence-enhanced model (OC).*

Metric	OS	ES	OC
Validation Accuracy	76.45%	70.89%	74.52%
Validation Loss	53.76%	61.78%	51.31%
Validation F1 Score	74.23%	75.11%	71.89%
Validation Precision	77.11%	68.12%	72.31%
Validation Recall	75.66%	85.34%	75.40%
Validation AUC	80.34%	76.22%	74.55%
Test Accuracy	60.23%	73.23%	61.39%
Test Loss	80.24%	58.30%	84.81%
Test F1 Score	63.12%	77.78%	58.84%
Test Precision	60.87%	71.56%	59.44%
Test Recall	67.12%	85.90%	63.98%
Test AUC	62.08%	79.87%	62.33%

(63.12%) reflects a reasonable balance, though improvements are possible. With a test AUC of 62.08%, the model differentiates between classes better than random guessing but lacks strong discrimination. Enhancing regularisation, hyperparameter tuning, or data augmentation could improve generalisation further.

Extended Testing with Extensive Dataset (ES). The objective of these additional tests was to explore whether increasing the dataset size could improve model performance and generalisation, particularly for metrics like validation accuracy and macro-averaged F1-scores. We extended the previous dataset with 50 questions (5 tests × 10 questions/test) per student, by using data from the five students who performed more tests, ranging from 110 to 200 questions per participant. Table 1 summarises the key performance metrics of the extensive datasets.

The results show indeed a notable improvement across test accuracy (from 60.23% to 73.23%), F1 score (from 63.12% to 77.78%), and recall (from 67.12% to 85.90%), indicating the model generalises better with more data. However, smaller increments may not immediately translate to performance gains, particularly in the presence of class imbalances. While validation metrics remain similar between datasets, the test metrics demonstrate the advantage of a larger dataset, reinforcing the necessity of training on a comprehensive and representative dataset. The substantial improvements observed with the *Extensive Dataset* underscore the critical importance of investing in larger and more diverse datasets for robust model training and development.

4.2 Confidence-Enhanced Model (OC)

The evaluation of the confidence-enhanced model was conducted on the original dataset, and the results are presented in Table 1. Contrary to our initial expectations, the inclusion of confidence as a bias did not lead to consistent improvements across key performance metrics. In fact, the standard model trained on the original dataset (OS) achieved slightly better validation accuracy (76.45% vs. 74.52%) and precision (77.11% vs. 72.31%) compared to the confidence-enhanced model (OC). However, we can see a slight improvement in test accuracy (60.23% vs. 61.39%) and test AUC (62.08% vs. 62.33%). This suggests that the confidence information, as incorporated in this approach, did not provide significant additional predictive value at the overall level.

Cluster Analysis by Student Response Profile. While confidence did not uniformly improve prediction, its impact may vary between students. Therefore, we performed a cluster analysis, to investigate whether specific student subgroups benefit differentially from confidence-based modelling. We clustered participants into three sets, based on the balance between correct and incorrect responses. Cluster 1 (**Balanced Students**) consists of participants with a relatively even mix of correct and incorrect responses, making them the most neutral group in terms of classification. Cluster 2 (**Correct-Heavy Students**) includes students who predominantly answered correctly, while Cluster 3 (**Incorrect-Heavy Students**) represents those with a higher proportion of incorrect answers (Table 2).

Table 2. Performance metrics for different student clusters

Metric	Balanced Students	Correct-Heavy Students	Incorrect-Heavy Students
Test Accuracy	55.29%	68.75%	45.78%
Test Precision	53.42%	72.34%	40.89%
Test Recall	55.87%	70.21%	42.11%
Test F1 Score	52.89%	71.05%	39.45%
Test Avg Precision	52.13%	70.89%	41.23%
Test Avg Recall	54.11%	71.67%	43.02%
Test Avg F1	51.76%	70.43%	40.19%
Test AUC	60.45%	75.12%	50.89%

The results highlight a clear relationship between correctness patterns and model performance. Cluster 2, consisting of correct-heavy students, achieved the highest test accuracy (68.75%) and AUC (75.12%), showing that the model generalises well when trained on consistent correctness patterns. Cluster 1 had moderate results, with a test accuracy of 55.29%. Their mix of correct and incorrect responses led to reasonable but less confident classification. Cluster

3 performed the worst, with test accuracy at 45.78% and an AUC of 50.89%, suggesting near-random guessing. The model struggled to distinguish patterns in their responses, likely due to class imbalance and variability in incorrect answers. These findings highlight how correctness distributions influence model predictions. Stronger performance for correct-heavy students suggests a bias toward recognising correct responses, potentially explaining weaker results for incorrect-heavy students. Further per-class analysis is needed to assess this bias. A more balanced dataset and refined feature selection could improve the model's ability to distinguish incorrect responses, enhancing robustness and classification accuracy.

5 Discussion and Limitations

This study explored the feasibility of predicting students' answer correctness in abstract reasoning tasks using EEG data from a low-cost headset, considering both the reasoning (pre-response) and feedback (post-response) phases. Additionally, it examined the impact of incorporating self-reported confidence levels as a bias in the predictive model.

For RQ1, our results confirm that EEG-based models can predict response correctness with a promising degree of accuracy. The model achieved stable performance across validation and test datasets, indicating that neural signals capture relevant cognitive patterns. However, the influence of the each phase remains an open question, as further analysis is required to disentangle the contribution of the reasoning phase and the feedback phase. In addition, our findings confirm the scalability of the model, as it achieved better performance when applied to a larger dataset. This suggest the need for continued data collection and model training on increasingly large datasets to fully realise the model's potential.

Regarding RQ2, contrary to initial expectations, our findings did not reveal an improvement when confidence was included as a bias. The confidence-enhanced model achieved slightly better prediction accuracy and AUC compared to the standard model, but performed worse on other metrics. This suggests that confidence in its current configuration does not significantly enhance the predictive ability of our model. This result may be due to participants lacking a clear perception of their own accuracy, which in turn proves that subjective measurements are not reliable.

Nevertheless, while the overall inclusion of confidence did not lead to improvements across all participants, this does not contradict its potential relevance. Instead, our results suggest that its impact may be differ between students, motivating further investigations in future. These results confirm that EEG-based predictions hold promise for real-world applications, despite the need for refinements in leveraging confidence effectively.

Given these findings, our model shows promise for educational applications. By enabling this novel way to assess and enhance students' reasoning abilities, it could inform personalised learning strategies, facilitate early identification of cognitive challenges, and promote metacognitive and self-regulated learning skills. Moreover, the use of cost-effective EEG devices, such as the Muse 2, facilitates broader adoption in educational settings, bridging the gap between cognitive neuroscience and educational practice. One potential issue with the current study is that participants in the extensive dataset may encounter previously seen questions, under which circumstance they might rely on memory to recall correct answers, rather than engaging in the reasoning process. Consequently, this could distort EEG patterns, and negatively impact the prediction performance. Therefore, future research can benefit from including more questions, to avoid the possibility of question repetition. Future work can also focus on a deeper cluster analysis, to determine whether confidence-based modelling can benefit certain subgroups of students more, such as those with well-calibrated self-assessment abilities. Additionally, refining experimental conditions, such as minimising external distractions, and establishing EEG baselines, will help improve data reliability.

6 Conclusion

This study explored predicting abstract reasoning ability from EEG, considering both pre- and post-response brain activity. Our models predicted response correctness with promising accuracy, though the individual contributions of each phase require further study. While self-reported confidence did not consistently improve overall prediction, its impact varies between students. The model demonstrated robustness and scalability with larger datasets. Future work will investigate student-specific confidence effects, refine experimental protocols, and leverage larger datasets for enhanced performance. These future works will reinforce the potential of our current research in personalised feedback and adaptive learning systems, paving the way for future applications in educational settings.

References

1. Abbasimehr, H., Paki, R.: Improving time series forecasting using LSTM and attention models. J. Ambient. Intell. Humaniz. Comput. **13**(1), 673–691 (2022)
2. Al-Nafjan, A., Aldayel, M.: Predict students' attention in online learning using EEG data. Sustainability **14**(11), 6553 (2022)
3. Alhagry, S., Fahmy, A.A., El-Khoribi, R.A.: Emotion recognition based on EEG using LSTM recurrent neural network. Int. J. Adv. Comput. Sci. Appl. **8**(10) (2017)
4. Alsayigh, H.K.S., Khidhir, A.S.M.: Deep learning-based mental task classification using a muse 2 EEG headset. In: AIP Conference Proceedings, vol. 3091. AIP Publishing (2024)
5. Amin, H.U., Malik, A.S., Hussain, M., Kamel, N., Chooi, W.T.: Brain behavior during reasoning and problem solving task: an EEG study. In: 2014 5th International Conference on Intelligent and Advanced Systems (ICIAS), pp. 1–4. IEEE (2014)
6. Apicella, A., Arpaia, P., Frosolone, M., Improta, G., Moccaldi, N., Pollastro, A.: EEG-based measurement system for monitoring student engagement in learning 4.0. Sci. Rep. **12**(1), 5857 (2022)

7. Breuning, M.: The role of analogies and abstract reasoning in decision-making: evidence from the debate over Truman's proposal for development assistance. Int. Stud. Quart. **47**(2), 229–245 (2003)
8. Canizo, M., Triguero, I., Conde, A., Onieva, E.: Multi-head CNN-RNN for multi-time series anomaly detection: an industrial case study. Neurocomputing **363**, 246–260 (2019)
9. Carpenter, P.A., Just, M.A., Shell, P.: What one intelligence test measures: a theoretical account of the processing in the raven progressive matrices test. Psychol. Rev. **97**(3), 404 (1990)
10. Chowdary, M.K., Anitha, J., Hemanth, D.J.: Emotion recognition from EEG signals using recurrent neural networks. Electronics **11**(15), 2387 (2022)
11. Dehais, F., Ladouce, S., Torre-Tresols, J.J., Darmet, L., Callan, D.: Mental workload classification during simulated flight operations based on cardiac and neural dynamics recorded using the muse 2 low-cost system. Neuroergonomics Cogn. Eng. **102**, 171–181 (2023)
12. DiPietro, R., Hager, G.D.: Deep learning: RNNs and LSTM. In: Handbook of Medical Image Computing and Computer Assisted Intervention, pp. 503–519. Elsevier (2020)
13. Du, X., et al.: An efficient LSTM network for emotion recognition from multichannel EEG signals. IEEE Trans. Affect. Comput. **13**(3), 1528–1540 (2020)
14. D'Urso, S., Luongo, R., Sciarrone, F.: Enhancing educational outcomes through EEG-based cognitive indices and supervised machine learning: a methodological framework. In: 2024 28th International Conference Information Visualisation (IV), pp. 1–6. IEEE (2024)
15. Evans, J.S.B.: Thinking and reasoning. In: Companion Encyclopedia of Psychology, pp. 338–357. Routledge (2019)
16. Flores, A., Tito-Chura, H., Apaza-Alanoca, H.: Data augmentation for short-term time series prediction with deep learning. In: Arai, K. (ed.) Intelligent Computing. LNNS, vol. 284, pp. 492–506. Springer, Cham (2021). https://doi.org/10.1007/978-3-030-80126-7_36
17. Fuentes-Martinez, V.J., Romero, S., Lopez-Gordo, M.A., Minguillon, J., Rodríguez-Álvarez, M.: Low-cost EEG multi-subject recording platform for the assessment of students' attention and the estimation of academic performance in secondary school. Sensors **23**(23), 9361 (2023)
18. Gevins, A., et al.: Monitoring working memory load during computer-based tasks with EEG pattern recognition methods. Hum. Factors **40**(1), 79–91 (1998)
19. Heine, S.J., Hamamura, T.: In search of east Asian self-enhancement. Pers. Soc. Psychol. Rev. **11**(1), 4–27 (2007)
20. Klimesch, W., Doppelmayr, M., Russegger, H., Pachinger, T., Schwaiger, J.: Induced alpha band power changes in the human EEG and attention. Neurosci. Lett. **244**(2), 73–76 (1998)
21. Krigolson, O.E., Williams, C.C., Norton, A., Hassall, C.D., Colino, F.L.: Choosing muse: validation of a low-cost, portable EEG system for ERP research. Front. Neurosci. **11**, 243179 (2017)
22. Li, Y., Zhu, Z., Kong, D., Han, H., Zhao, Y.: EA-LSTM: evolutionary attention-based LSTM for time series prediction. Knowl.-Based Syst. **181**, 104785 (2019)
23. Long, F., Zhou, K., Ou, W.: Sentiment analysis of text based on bidirectional LSTM with multi-head attention. IEEE Access **7**, 141960–141969 (2019)
24. Markovits, H., Thompson, V.A., Brisson, J.: Metacognition and abstract reasoning. Memory Cogn. **43**, 681–693 (2015)

25. Miasnikova, A., Troshkov, D., Baklushev, M., Perevoznyuk, G.: Predicting states of abstract reasoning using EEG functional connectivity markers. In: 2019 41st Annual International Conference of the IEEE Engineering in Medicine and Biology Society (EMBC), pp. 2451–2454. IEEE (2019)
26. Mihajlović, V., Grundlehner, B., Vullers, R., Penders, J.: Wearable, wireless EEG solutions in daily life applications: what are we missing? IEEE J. Biomed. Health Inform. **19**(1), 6–21 (2014)
27. Moeller, J.J., Fawns, T.: Insights into teaching a complex skill: threshold concepts and troublesome knowledge in electroencephalography (EEG). Med. Teach. **40**(4), 387–394 (2018)
28. Naderi, M.A., Mahdavi-Nasab, H.: Analysis and classification of EEG signals using spectral analysis and recurrent neural networks. In: 2010 17th Iranian Conference of Biomedical Engineering (ICBME), pp. 1–4. IEEE (2010)
29. Prado, J., Chadha, A., Booth, J.R.: The brain network for deductive reasoning: a quantitative meta-analysis of 28 neuroimaging studies. J. Cogn. Neurosci. **23**(11), 3483–3497 (2011)
30. Raven, J.C., Court, J.: Raven's Progressive Matrices. Western Psychological Services, Los Angeles, CA (1938)
31. Reif, D.M., Motsinger, A.A., McKinney, B.A., Crowe, J.E., Moore, J.H.: Feature selection using a random forests classifier for the integrated analysis of multiple data types. In: 2006 IEEE Symposium on Computational Intelligence and Bioinformatics and Computational Biology, pp. 1–8. IEEE (2006)
32. Richhariya, B., Tanveer, M.: EEG signal classification using universum support vector machine. Expert Syst. Appl. **106**, 169–182 (2018)
33. Saeidi, M., et al.: Neural decoding of EEG signals with machine learning: a systematic review. Brain Sci. **11**(11), 1525 (2021)
34. Sajno, E., Maisetti, M., Luongo, R., Cipresso, P., et al.: Cyberintervention on plant workforce's mental activity for safety. Annu. Rev. Cyberther. Telemed. **20**, 71–77 (2022)
35. Sangeetha, K., Prabha, D.: Retracted article: sentiment analysis of student feedback using multi-head attention fusion model of word and context embedding for LSTM. J. Ambient. Intell. Humaniz. Comput. **12**(3), 4117–4126 (2021)
36. Si, Y., et al.: Predicting individual decision-making responses based on single-trial EEG. Neuroimage **206**, 116333 (2020)
37. Soh, L., Jacobs, K.E.: The biasing effect of personality on self-estimates of cognitive abilities in males and females. Personality Individ. Differ. **55**(2), 141–146 (2013)
38. Speiser, J.L., Miller, M.E., Tooze, J., Ip, E.: A comparison of random forest variable selection methods for classification prediction modeling. Expert Syst. Appl. **134**, 93–101 (2019)
39. Stankov, L.: Noncognitive predictors of intelligence and academic achievement: an important role of confidence. Pers. Individ. Differ. **55**(7), 727–732 (2013)
40. Steinmayr, R., Spinath, B.: What explains boys' stronger confidence in their intelligence? Sex Roles **61**, 736–749 (2009)
41. Sugden, R.J., Pham-Kim-Nghiem-Phu, V., Campbell, I., Leon, A., Diamandis, P.: Remote collection of electrophysiological data with brain wearables: opportunities and challenges. Bioelectron. Med. **9**(1), 12 (2023)
42. Suttidee, A.: Usability of portable EEG for monitoring students' attention in online learning. Ph.D. thesis, Nova Southeastern University (2020)
43. Vasiljevic, G., De Miranda, L.C.: Brain-computer interface games based on consumer-grade EEG devices: a systematic literature review. Int. J. Hum.-Comput. Interact. **36**(2), 105–142 (2020)

44. Wechsler, D.: Wechsler Adult Intelligence Scale. Front. Psychol. (1997)
45. Wen, X., Li, W.: Time series prediction based on LSTM-attention-LSTM model. IEEE Access **11**, 48322–48331 (2023)
46. Wheeler, J.L., Regian, J.W.: The use of a cognitive tutoring system in the improvement of the abstract reasoning component of word problem solving. Comput. Hum. Behav. **15**(2), 243–254 (1999)
47. Xu, H., Liu, Q., van Genabith, J., Xiong, D., Zhang, M.: Multi-head highly parallelized LSTM decoder for neural machine translation. In: Proceedings of the 59th Annual Meeting of the Association for Computational Linguistics and the 11th International Joint Conference on Natural Language Processing (Volume 1: Long Papers), pp. 273–282 (2021)
48. Zhang, L., Cui, H.: Reliability of MUSE 2 and Tobii Pro Nano at capturing mobile application users' real-time cognitive workload changes. Front. Neurosci. **16**, 1011475 (2022)

The Effects of Professional Development Training on Teachers' AI Literacy

Yuki Nagae[1(✉)], Lechen Zhang[2], and Liliana Farias Herrera[3]

[1] Stockholm, Sweden
yuki.nagae@edu.su.se
[2] University of Helsinki, Fabianinkatu 33, 00014 Helsinki, Finland
lechen.zhang@helsinki.fi
[3] Virkesvägen 2, 120 30 Stockholm, Sweden
liliana.farias@hyperisland.com

Abstract. The integration of artificial intelligence (AI) in education is rapidly expanding, yet many teachers lack formal training in AI literacy and its pedagogical applications. This study explores the perspectives of Swedish K-12 teachers who participated in an online AI training program by Sweden's largest AI education provider for schools. Using survey data (N = 206), the study examines teachers' AI attitudes, knowledge acquisition, and classroom applications, guided by UNESCO's AI Competency Framework. Quantitative analysis, including descriptive statistics, correlation analysis, and ANOVA, reveals that over 85% of teachers lacked formal AI education before training, relying on incidental learning. The training significantly improved AI knowledge, particularly in ethics, with the highest mean score across backgrounds. Digital competence positively influenced AI attitudes and knowledge acquisition, while age and teaching experience correlated negatively. Perceptions of AI integration into education were also shown to vary by subject and school level. Summative content analysis of open-ended responses highlights concerns about student misuse, ethical challenges, and institutional barriers to AI adoption. Despite these concerns, teachers viewed AI as beneficial for lesson planning, resource creation, and personalized learning. Special education and language teachers reported distinct advantages, including multimodal learning support and accessibility improvements for non-native speakers. This study contributes to AI literacy discourse by providing empirical insights into how AI training shapes teaching practices and informs policy recommendations for professional development in AI-integrated education.

Keywords: AI Literacy Training · Professional Development · AI Integration in K-12 Education

1 Introduction

The rapid development of artificial intelligence (AI) technology presents both challenges and opportunities for educators. Generative AI (GenAI), which uses machine learning to create high-quality outputs, is transforming educational practices worldwide.

L. Farias—Independent researcher

A. I. Cristea et al. (Eds.): AIED 2025, LNAI 15877, pp. 368–380, 2025.
https://doi.org/10.1007/978-3-031-98414-3_26

However, research on AI literacy in teacher education remains limited, with teachers' professional knowledge often underrepresented or teachers' perceptions inadequately addressed in existing studies [1, 2]. Although global initiatives such as UNESCO's AI frameworks provide valuable guidelines [3], these policies have not yet translated into robust, evidence-based professional development (PD) programs that address the practical challenges educators face [4, 5].

The increasing impact of the technological revolution on education is being observed worldwide. For instance, in Sweden, the integration of digital tools in education has long been a national priority, focusing on promoting digital competence and innovative teaching methods [6, 7]. Digital devices promoted the personalization of learning and especially took advantage in special education. However, there are currently no comprehensive national guidelines for AI competencies in K-12 teacher education or PD programs for all teachers. As Velander et al. [8] pointed out, teachers who acquired their knowledge of AI through "incidental learning" often develop misconceptions and fragmented understanding.

In response to these challenges, various educational programs have been developed to build AI literacy among teachers. One such initiative is a program in Sweden that offers online training courses specifically designed for Swedish K-12 teachers and school leaders to enhance their AI readiness. The training content has been designed in accordance with the UNESCO AI Competency Framework for Teachers (AI CFT), making the program one of the early efforts to translate these global guidelines into a practical training context. Notably, over 20,000 teachers had enrolled in these courses on their platform, and more than 85% of this study's participants reported having no prior AI training—the figures highlighting the increasing demand for structured AI training.

Given that teachers' attitudes, understanding, and practical experiences are pivotal in determining how AI tools are implemented and in shaping educational outcomes, empirical research on PD outcomes is urgently needed. Such research is essential not only for identifying effective elements of AI-focused PD programs but also for guiding policy decisions to ensure that teacher training is both scalable and impactful.

Therefore, this study explores the effects of professional development training in AI on teachers' attitudes towards AI, their knowledge of AI, and their experiences applying AI in pedagogical settings. Using a post-training survey based on UNESCO's AI CFT, our research provides critical insights into how targeted PD programs can enhance teachers' competencies and, ultimately, improve classroom practices in an era of rapid technological change. This study also serves as a unique evaluation of the UNESCO framework's effectiveness in guiding teacher PD programs.

2 Related Work

While AI holds transformative potential for teaching and learning, its successful implementation depends on addressing teachers' attitudes, knowledge gaps, and skill development. Theoretical frameworks from Information and Communication Technology (ICT) research—such as the TPACK and the Will, Skill, Tool model—have been extended to understand AI integration [8–10]. These studies demonstrate that, similar to ICT tools, teachers' attitudes toward AI significantly influence their willingness to adopt new technologies.

However, the shift from ICT to AI introduces additional complexities, as K-12 teachers must navigate ethical, technical, and pedagogical challenges unique to AI. In response to these challenges, initiatives like UNICEF's AI CFT advocate for a comprehensive approach to PD that includes upskilling current educators, incorporating AI into pre-service education, and offering continuous in-service training [3]. The framework also provides concrete guidelines on the specific AI literacy skills teachers need to develop—human-centered mindset, ethics of AI, AI foundation and application, AI pedagogy, and professional development (see Table 2)—in three progression phrases, offering clear direction for the content of training programs. Now, such large-scale teacher training initiatives built upon this framework can develop more with scientific evaluation from teachers' perspectives.

Research on educators' perceptions of AI reveals a duality: while many educators express anxiety and skepticism due to limited AI knowledge, they also recognize AI's potential as a valuable supplemental tool in education [11–13]. Lan [14] identified that teachers' anxiety also often stems from a perceived lack of self-efficacy compared to AI, as well as broader emotional and technical challenges. These emotional barriers highlight the need for PD programs that address both technical competencies and psychological readiness [10]. To ensure teachers feel more confident integrating AI into their professional practices, Hopcan et al. [15] suggested considering factors such as age, gender, and field-specific differences to reduce anxiety and enhance AI competency.

Practical, hands-on experience with AI tools—whether through online courses, seminars, or workshops—has been shown to boost teachers' confidence and mitigate skepticism [16, 17]. Moreover, effective PD programs not only improve technical competencies but also enhance teachers' ability to address the ethical implications of AI, thereby empowering them to integrate AI literacy into their curricula [18]. While top-down frameworks like AI CFT provide an essential policy foundation, bottom-up, empirically driven approaches are critical for identifying the specific competencies that teachers develop and the challenges they encounter [19].

This body of research underscores the necessity of further empirical investigation into the effects of AI training on K-12 teachers. Specifically, it is paramount to understand how PD programs influence teachers' attitudes, enhance their AI-related knowledge, and facilitate the effective application of AI in classroom settings. This study, therefore, aims to evaluate the impacts of AI-focused PD by analyzing the experiences of teachers who have completed an online AI training course. In doing so, we seek to identify both the advantages and the remaining challenges of integrating AI into educational practices.

3 Methods

3.1 Participants

In total, 206 teachers partook and completed the post-training survey. This survey was distributed to the participants via Google Forms after completing the program. Additionally, the analysis focused solely on teachers, including special education teachers at the K-12 school level, whereas responses from other roles in schools, such as technicians or administrators, were excluded. Only data from participants who explicitly consented to participate in the study were included in the analysis. A digital consent form was collected, which explained the voluntary nature and the anonymity of participation. To ensure confidentiality, this survey did not collect names.

Table 1. Summary of Demographic Data.

Age	Frequency	Percentage	Subject	Frequency	Percentage
1 Under 30	17	8.252	1 STEM	43	20.874
2 30-39	44	21.359	2 Social Studies	24	11.650
3 40-49	49	23.786	3 Languages	69	33.495
4 50-59	64	31.068	4 Arts	8	3.883
5 Over 59	32	15.534	5 Preschool	19	9.223
Total	206	100.000	6 Primary School (multiple)	6	2.913
Gender	Frequency	Percentage	7 Special Education (multiple)	6	2.913
1 Female	152	73.786	8 Other	31	15.049
2 Male	50	24.272	Total	206	100.000
3 Other	1	0.485	School Level	Frequency	Percentage
4 Not to say	3	1.456	1 Preschool	20	9.709
Total	206	100.000	2 Compulsory (K0-3)	15	7.282
Teaching Year	Frequency	Percentage	3 Compulsory (K4-6)	37	17.961
1 Under 4	31	15.049	4 Compulsory (K7-9)	37	17.961
2 4-6	13	6.311	5 Upper Secondary	73	35.437
3 7-10	32	15.534	6 Adult Education	16	7.767
4 11-15	41	19.903	7 Vocational Training	4	1.942
5 Over 15	89	43.204	8 Special Education	4	1.942
Total	206	100.000	Total	206	100.000

As shown in Table 1, 152 out of the 206 participants (74%) are female. 145 of them (70%) are 40 years old or older. 89 teachers (43%) have taught longer than 15 years. Some teachers taught more than one subject, but they were asked to select one primary subject. Because preschool education differs from the curriculum of other school levels, and it is normal for one teacher to teach several subjects at the primary and special education schools, their subject was recorded as "multiple subjects" noted with each school category.

3.2 The AI Training Program

The AI training program offered in this study is an online introductory course designed by a private educational technology company in Sweden. The design of this training program was developed based on the acquire level of UNESCO's AI CFT [3], ensuring alignment with global standards of integrating AI into educational practices. Today, this AI education provider is Sweden's largest provider of AI training for schools, further highlighting the widespread adoption of AI and requirement of the structured AI PD programs. The primary aim of the course was to equip teachers and students with foundational knowledge and practical skills to effectively and ethically use AI tools in their teaching and learning.

The AI training program was intended for three groups of audiences. The program tailored its modules primarily for K-12 teachers, for various subjects and grades. Also, this program provided specific examples and tools to special education teachers to support students with diverse learning needs. While school administrators and technicians were excluded from the study, the program was designed to be accessible to all school staff to foster a collaborative approach to AI integration. The training program was delivered online, allowing participants to complete the modules at their own pace. It featured interactive elements such as video tutorials, quizzes, and discussion forums to enhance engagement and ensure knowledge retention.

Table 2. AI Training Content and Conceptual Framework.

Module	Description	UNESCO AI CFT
Introduction to Artificial Intelligence	This module cultivates a basic understanding of AI by covering its history, key concepts, and applications in education and beyond.	Human-Centred Mindset
Ethical considerations & challenges in AI	This module helps teachers identify ethical considerations in AI use, focusing on data privacy, algorithm bias, and ensuring equity.	Ethics of AI
AI tools & resources for teaching	This module explores generative AI tools like ChatGPT for lesson planning, content creation, and admin tasks, with tutorials and case studies.	AI Foundation and Application
AI in pedagogical practice	This module enables teachers to develop strategies for using AI in personalized learning, assessment, and instruction through diverse scenarios.	AI Pedagogy
Future of AI in education	This module supports teachers in acquiring insights into AI's evolving role in education, lifelong learning, and preparing students for the future.	Professional Development

3.3 Data Collection and Data Analysis

The survey measured teachers' self-efficacy and perceptions. Besides teachers' background information, the survey contains four dimensions: experience before the training (T), attitude (A), knowledge (K), and application (P) of AI in education. Dimension T, i.e., technology and AI experience before taking the AI training program, has four items. Dimensions A (six items), K (six items), and P (seven items) were inspired by the AI CFT to understand teachers' perceptions about integrating AI in different educational contexts. The items were formulated as either a 5-point Likert scale, a binary format, or an open-ended question.

This study examines differences in teachers' perceptions and experience of AI after the AI training based on various demographic factors, including age, grade level taught, teaching experience, subject area, and familiarity with technology and AI tools. The descriptive statistics with means and standard deviations illustrate teachers' attitudes, knowledge, and intended AI application after training, followed by Spearman'ρ (rho) correlations to examine relationships between demographic factors (ordinal variables) and these four dimensions. A series of one-way ANOVA was conducted for each independent variable to compare group means on the dependent variables. Post hoc analyses using Tukey's HSD test were performed where significant differences were found. Effect sizes were reported using η^2 (eta squared).

As a supplement to the quantitative analysis, open-ended survey responses in section P were then subjected to Summative Content Analysis, a method of identifying keywords and grouping based on the meaning of the overall data instead of precise coding [20]. The procedure was to identify recurring keywords related to the perceived value and challenges of applying AI to teaching practices while also taking into account the background of the respondents of the data identified.

4 Results

4.1 Descriptive Statistics

The descriptive statistics highlighted that the training program had a positive impact on teachers' AI knowledge and attitudes (Table 3). Over 86% ($N = 179$) of participants reported having no prior AI experience (T1), yet they achieved significantly higher levels of knowledge and increased confidence in applying AI in their teaching after the program. Specifically, all items' measurements post-training reached a moderately high level, with attitude variables overall ranging between 3.1 and 4.3 and knowledge variables ranging between 3.5 and 3.9 out of a 5-point scale. In particular, the high Mean with low SD in A1 indicated that many teachers viewed AI as an important part of future education. They also demonstrated greater interest in and willingness to further develop AI-related skills. High scores on practical applications (P2) indicate that participants found the training directly useful in the classroom, and many reported a strong sense of professional development.

Comparing attitude (A) and knowledge (K) provided more insight for possible improvements in the training program based on what teachers would need. The first comparison is about ethics in A2 and K2: The highest Mean score and lowest SD among the K items was K2, which suggests that the AI training was most effective in teaching teachers about AI ethics. Whereas the Mean score for A2 approached the midpoint with a high SD, it demonstrates diversity of opinion on whether AI should be considered a risk. Secondly, while teachers felt positively about AI's potential usefulness for teaching (A3) and student learning (A4), their scores for knowledge in these areas (K3, K4) were lower. These suggest that PD programs can provide clearer and more concrete information in future design or other forms of training are expected as the next step of teachers' learning on AI.

4.2 Correlation Analysis

The correlation analysis (Appendix 2) revealed several significant relationships between variables. Age was negatively correlated with A2 ($\rho = -0.1555$, $p < .05$), A6 ($\rho = -0.2159$, $p < .01$), and K1 ($\rho = -0.2984$, $p < .001$). This implies that older participants

Table 3. Summary of Descriptive Statistics.

Questions		Mean	SD	Missing	N
T1	Formal Education before AI Training	0.131	0.338	0	206
T2	AI Tool Familiarity before AI Training	2.607	1.098	0	206
T3	Previous Experience of Using Generative AI	0.437	0.497	0	206
T4	Digital Technology Familiarity	4.034	0.805	0	206
A1	AI in Future Education	4.384	0.790	3	203
A2	AI Risks to Education	3.149	1.179	4	202
A3	AI Improving Teaching	4.184	0.917	5	201
A4	AI Helping Students	4.039	0.954	3	203
A5	AI Enhancing Personalized Learning	3.890	1.060	6	200
A6	AI Reducing Teachers' Workload	3.772	1.149	4	202
K1	Understanding AI Principle	3.599	0.968	4	202
K2	Understanding Ethical Principles	3.929	0.889	9	197
K3	AI Usage for Teaching and Assessments	3.464	1.074	10	196
K4	AI Usage for Students' Personalized Learning	3.488	1.096	5	201
K5	AI Usage for Teachers' Professional Development	3.785	1.093	6	200
K6	AI Usage for Administration	3.560	1.163	6	200
P1	Future Expectation	3.961	0.977	0	206
P2	Practical Tools	3.844	1.027	1	205

were less likely to perceive AI as a risk to education, less likely to believe that AI could reduce teachers' workload, and had a lower understanding of AI principles. Years of teaching was negatively correlated with A6 ($\rho = -0.1468$, $p < .05$) and K1 ($\rho = -0.2465$, $p < .001$), indicating that more experienced teachers were less likely to believe that AI could reduce their workload and had a lower understanding of AI principles. T2 was positively correlated with almost all attitude and knowledge variables except A2, A3, and K2. The strongest correlation was observed with K1 ($\rho = 0.5141$, $p < .001$) and K6 ($\rho = 0.3689$, $p < .001$), while the weakest for A4 ($\rho = 0.2088$, $p < .01$). This suggests that familiarity with AI tools before training was associated with a more positive attitude and self-perceived knowledge of AI. Digital Tools Familiarity (T4) also showed positive correlations with almost all attitude and knowledge variables, particularly in the knowledge dimension, such as K1 ($\rho = 0.5284$, $p < .001$) and K5 ($\rho = 0.5205$, $p < .001$). This means that participants who were more familiar with digital tools had a more positive attitude and self-perceived knowledge of AI.

4.3 Anova

The ANOVA results (Appendix 3) indicated some significant differences based on Age, Grade Level, Years of Teaching, Subject Area, and Technology and AI Familiarity. Age had a significant effect on K1 ($F = 4.726$, $p < .001$, $\eta^2 = .108$), K3 ($F = 4.141$, $p = .001$, $\eta^2 = .098$), and K6 ($F = 5.716$, $p < .001$, $\eta^2 = .128$). Younger participants had higher scores on these knowledge variables. Grade Level significantly impacted on A4 ($F = 4.064$, $p = .004$, $\eta^2 = .086$) and K3 ($F = 5.525$, $p < .001$, $\eta^2 = .117$). Secondary school teachers perceive AI as more beneficial compared to primary school teachers. Years of Teaching significantly affected K1 ($F = 3.870$, $p = .002$, $\eta^2 = .090$) and K6 ($F = 2.677$, $p = .023$, $\eta^2 = .065$). More experienced teachers had lower scores on these knowledge variables. Subject Area had a significant effect on K3 ($F = 3.399$, $p = .020$, $\eta^2 = .082$), which also showed that STEM teachers tend to use less AI for teaching and assessment than social science teachers. Technology and AI Familiarity had a significant impact on almost all attitude and knowledge variables, particularly K1 ($F = 25.49$, $p < .001$, $\eta^2 = .279$) and K6 ($F = 26.17$, $p < .001$, $\eta^2 = .286$). Participants with higher familiarity with technology and AI tools had more positive attitudes and greater self-perceived knowledge regarding AI's usage in education.

4.4 Summative Content Analysis of Open-Ended Questions

The most common usage of AI was for creating lessons and teaching materials, followed by lesson planning. Some teachers highlighted its role in their professional development as well. Specific tools were also mentioned, such as chatbots like ChatGPT and Microsoft Copilot for generating ideas and assignments, as well as Gamma for preparing teaching materials, as introduced in the hands-on practice in the training program. AI was valued for saving time, managing information overload, and aiding student assessments.

Teachers across subjects found AI beneficial in different ways. Language teachers used it to provide writing feedback, while special education teachers leveraged AI to adjust text complexity for diverse learners. Though less likely to use AI in instruction, STEM teachers recognized its potential for supporting students. AI's ability to offer multimodal learning formats, like converting from text to audio and translating between languages, was particularly helpful for students who do not speak Swedish as their first language or who have dyslexia. Yet, some teachers were skeptical, raising concerns that AI might encourage shortcuts and reduce students' critical thinking skills, with some viewing its use as a form of cheating. On the other hand, teachers also faced challenges in adopting AI. A major concern was student misuse, prompting calls for ethical guidelines and regulations at both international and local levels. Financial constraints further hindered AI adoption, as many tools required paid subscriptions that schools were unable to afford. Additionally, teachers cited a lack of time and training as barriers to effective AI integration. To address these issues, some suggested professional development initiatives, such as expert-led lectures and collaborative learning opportunities, to enhance AI competency and ensure responsible use.

5 Discussions and Conclusion

This study examined how an AI training program for teachers' professional development impacted teachers' confidence and self-efficacy in integrating AI into their teaching practices. The results demonstrated that the training positively influenced teachers' attitudes, knowledge, and usage of A. With this positive influence of training, teachers grew to acknowledge AI's benefits and viewed it as an asset. This was also confirmed by the open-ended questions responses as teachers' gained confidence and self-efficacy were translated into using AI in their teaching practices.

The findings demonstrated that teachers took advantage of AI's capabilities to enhance and adapt learning experiences and increase student engagement. Their reports point that the training and development of AI literacy resulted in teachers developing pedagogical innovations, for instance, by using AI-generated multimodal content to facilitate differentiated instruction, translate between languages, and create engaging learning materials tailored to students' individual needs. This aligns with previous research (e.g., [15]) suggesting that AI can serve as a tool for pedagogical transformation rather than mere automation. In addition, they started to appreciate AI's other affordances like ideation and content generation, which reduced their workload (effectivization) in lesson planning and administrative tasks, reinforcing their willingness to integrate AI into future teaching practices. Furthermore, as pointed out by earlier studies (e.g., [10, 14, 15]), the lack of training and support on AI in education can lead to anxiety and skepticism among educators. This study provided empirical evidence that teacher professional training can be an effective tool to combat these issues.

Although the results showed the positive effect of the professional training program, they also pointed out possible improvements in the training program. ANOVA results revealed that different teacher groups responded differently to the AI training program, suggesting more effort to diversify professional training opportunities to maximize the effect. For instance, after the training, some groups had a lower self-evaluated level of AI knowledge, while other groups viewed AI more favorably. Differences existed even between subject areas, as STEM teachers, contrary to prior research [21], tended to use less AI for teaching and assessment than social science teachers. This result, while hasty to generalize, suggests that, given that previous research papers related to AI in education has heavily been published in STEM and computer science fields [1, 22], the application of AI may differ among teachers in the process of understanding AI and applying it to educational practice.

Additionally, while teachers gained more understanding through the training program, they expressed growing concerns about AI-related risks and ethical implications, which is an essential element in AI for education [23]. Hence, further program development initiatives could differentiate professional development resources to address the diverse circumstances in the teaching community. Further training programs can focus on challenging topics like cultivating students' critical thinking skills in an AI-enhanced learning environment or subject-specific best practice inspiration.

All the above-mentioned suggest the need for continuous professional development for teachers to deepen their understanding and exploration of responsible and effective AI applications. Another key challenge disclosed by the study was the lack of consistent school policies, leaving teachers unsupported in guiding their practices. As it's suggested in the previous studies (e.g., [1, 2, 22], teachers' perspective and participation in the development of AI tools in teaching and learning is a very important issue for the future of education. More importantly, future AI training programs need to be policy-backed as institutional policies increase the likelihood of more consistent and structured teacher professional development.

While this study offers important insights into teachers' AI literacy development, several limitations must be acknowledged. First, the study relied on self-reported measures of AI knowledge and confidence, which may be subject to biases such as overestimation of abilities. Development of objective assessments of AI literacy would strengthen future evaluations. Second, participation in the survey was voluntary, introducing a potential selection bias; the findings may not generalize to all educators. Third, this study focuses on Acquire, the first stage of the developmental process of teachers' AI competence as outlined in the UNESCO Framework, and does not track the subsequent process of application to practice in classrooms. Future research examining the application of AI literacy to practices for student learning is needed. Future research should incorporate longitudinal designs and mixed methods to capture sustained changes in teachers' AI integration practices.

As concluding remarks, although future studies might need to look at larger samples and different PD initiatives than what was studied here, the findings of this study underscore the strategic importance of AI training for schools and educational institutions. By equipping teachers with AI competencies, schools can enhance teaching quality, reduce administrative burdens, and foster a more engaging learning environment. Investing in AI training is not merely an option but a necessity for schools aiming to prepare both educators and students for the digital age. Given the positive effects of AI training, as demonstrated in this study, school leaders and policymakers should consider professional AI development as a long-term investment in educational quality and innovation.

6 Generative AI Use Declaration

We hereby declare to utilize ChatGPT-4o to proofread the text of this study. While ChatGPT-4o provided valuable suggestions about grammar and structure and enhanced overall readability, we have carefully reviewed all the proposed changes to ensure they align with the intended meaning and context of our original work.

1. Appendix.

Appendix 1. Post-training Survey Questions and Its Format.

T: Technology and AI Experience Before the Training		Response Format
T1	I have received any formal training in AI before this course.	Binary
T2	I was familiar with AI tools before participating in the AI training.	Likert Scale
T3	I have a previous experience with Generative AI before this course.	Binary
T4	I am comfortable with using digital technology in my teaching practice.	Likert Scale
A: Attitude towards AI		
A1	AI will be an important part of the future of education.	Likert Scale
A2	AI poses significant risks and threats to education.	Likert Scale
A3	AI can improve the quality and efficiency of teaching.	Likert Scale
A4	AI can help my students.	Likert Scale
A5	AI can help me personalize the learning experience for students more effectively than traditional methods.	Likert Scale
A6	AI will help reduce my workload as a teacher.	Likert Scale
K: Knowledge about AI		
K1	I have a good understanding of how AI works and can describe its basic principles.	Likert Scale
K2	I have a good understanding of the ethical challenges that can arise when using AI in schools.	Likert Scale
K3	I am confident in integrating AI into lesson planning, teaching, and student assessments.	Likert Scale
K4	I have a good understanding of how AI can be used to individualize student learning.	Likert Scale
K5	I am comfortable using AI tools for my own professional development and learning.	Likert Scale
K6	I am comfortable using AI tools to support my administrative work.	Likert Scale
P: Application of AI		
P1	I will use AI to an even greater extent in my teaching in the future.	Likert Scale
P2	The AI training has given me practical tools that I can use right away in the classroom.	Likert Scale
P3	What extent I have started using AI in any form in your role as a teacher is:	Open-end
P4	What the most valuable ways AI can support you in your role as a teacher are:	Open-end
P5	What the most valuable ways AI can benefit students are:	Open-end
P6	What obstacles could potentially hinder my use of AI in teaching are:	Open-end
P7	What I need to get started with AI usage is:	Open-end

Appendix 2. Correlation Table.

	A1	A2	A3	A4	A5	A6	K1	K2	K3	K4	K5	K6	P1	P2
Age	-0.1093	-0.1555*	-0.1123	-0.1128	-0.1280	-0.2159**	-0.2984***	-0.0336	-0.2505***	-0.1994**	-0.2457*	-0.3171*	-0.1808**	-0.2002**
Teaching Year	-0.0013	-0.1353	-0.0833	0.0224	-0.0438	-0.1468*	-0.2465***	0.0321	-0.1721**	-0.1649**	-0.1923**	-0.2395***	-0.0639	-0.0865
T1	-0.0084	0.1205	-0.0307	-0.0284	-0.0050	-0.0148	0.0808	-0.0681	0.0197	-0.0240	0.0278	0.0777	-0.0134	-0.0074
T2	0.2543***	0.1369	0.1354	0.2088**	0.2181**	0.2555***	0.5141***	-0.0307	0.2759***	0.3167***	0.3288***	0.3689***	0.1914**	0.1655**
T3	0.1398*	0.0968	-0.0073	0.1218	0.0882	0.0597	0.3079***	0.0146	0.1577*	0.1755*	0.2031**	0.2022**	0.0984	0.0255
T4	0.3075***	0.0250	0.282***	0.3579***	0.2589***	0.2832***	0.5284***	0.1798**	0.4094***	0.4184***	0.5205***	0.5134***	0.3665***	0.2666***

Note: N = 205 . *** $p < .001$, ** $p < .01$, * $p < .05$

Appendix 3. ANOVA.

Variables			Mean	SD	F	p-value	η^2
Age	K1	Understanding AI Principle	3.6	0.968	4.726	<.001	0.108
	K3	AI Usage for Teaching and Assessments	3.46	1.074	4.141	0.001	0.098
	K5	AI Usage for Teachers' Professional Development	3.79	1.093	3.453	0.005	0.082
	K6	AI Usage for Administration	3.56	1.163	5.716	<.001	0.128
	P2	Practical Tools	3.84	1.027	4.402	<.001	0.1
School Level	A4	AI Helping Students	4.05	0.976	4.064	0.004	0.086
	A5	AI Enhancing Personalized Learning	3.9	1.082	4.784	0.001	0.1
	K3	AI Usage for Teaching and Assessments	3.52	1.079	5.525	<.001	0.117
	K5	AI Usage for Teachers' Professional Development	3.81	1.097	4.328	0.002	0.092
	K6	AI Usage for Administration	3.58	1.176	4.58	0.002	0.097
Teaching Year	K1	Understanding AI Principle	3.6	0.968	3.87	0.002	0.09
	K5	AI Usage for Teachers' Professional Development	3.46	1.074	2.672	0.023	0.064
	K6	AI Usage for Administration	3.56	1.163	2.677	0.023	0.065
Subject	K3	AI Usage for Teaching and Assessments	3.61	1.03	3.399	0.02	0.082
Digital Technology Familiarity	A1	AI in Future Education	4.38	0.79	6.033	<.001	0.083
	A3	AI Improving Teaching	4.18	0.917	4.976	0.002	0.07
	A4	AI Helping Students	4.04	0.954	9.596	<.001	0.126
	A5	AI Enhancing Personalized Learning	3.89	1.06	6.364	<.001	0.089
	A6	AI Reducing Teachers' Workload	3.77	1.149	5.589	0.001	0.078
	K1	Understanding AI Principle	3.6	0.968	25.493	<.001	0.279
	K3	AI Usage for Teaching and Assessments	3.46	1.074	12.994	<.001	0.169
	K4	AI Usage for Students' Personalized Learning	3.49	1.096	14.254	<.001	0.178
	K5	AI Usage for Teachers' Professional Development	3.79	1.093	25.232	<.001	0.279
	K6	AI Usage for Administration	3.56	1.163	26.176	<.001	0.286
	P1	Future Expectation	3.96	0.977	10.793	<.001	0.138
	P2	Practical Tools	3.84	1.027	6.641	<.001	0.09

References

1. Sperling, K., Stenberg, C.J., McGrath, C., Åkerfeldt, A., Heintz, F., Stenliden, L.: In search of artificial intelligence (AI) literacy in teacher education: a scoping review. Comput. Educ. Open **6**(100169) (2024)
2. Tan, X., Cheng, G., Ling M.H.: Artificial intelligence in teaching and teacher professional development: a systematic review. Comput. Educ. Artif. Intell. **8**(100355) (2025)
3. Miao F., Cukurova, M.: AI competency framework for teachers. UNESCO (2024)
4. Stolpe, K., Hallström, J.: Artificial intelligence literacy for technology education. Comput. Educ. Open **6**(100159) (2024)
5. Chiu, T.K.F., Ahmad, Z., Ismailov, M., Sanusi, I.T.: What are artificial intelligence literacy and competency? A comprehensive framework to support them. Comput. Educ. Open. **6**(100171) (2024)
6. Olofsson, A.D., Lindberg, J.O.: A glimpse of a Nordic model? Policy and practice in the digitalisation of the K-12 school and teacher education in Denmark, Finland, Norway and Sweden: editorial introduction. Educ. Inq. **12**(4), 311–316 (2021)
7. Reis-Andersson, J.: Leading the digitalization in K–12 education at the municipality level. Cogent Educ. **11**(1) (2024)
8. Velander, J., Taiye, M.A., Otero, N., Milrad, M.: Artificial intelligence in K-12 education: eliciting and reflecting on Swedish teachers' understanding of AI and its implications for teaching & learning. Educ. Inf. Technol. **29**(4), 4085–4105 (2024)

9. Polak, S., Schiavo, G., Zancanaro, M.: Teachers' perspective on artificial intelligence education: an initial investigation. In: CHI Conference on Human Factors in Computing Systems Extended Abstracts. New York, NY, USA, ACM (2022)
10. Yang, Y., Xia, Q., Liu, C., Chiu, T.K.F.: The impact of TPACK on teachers' willingness to integrate generative artificial intelligence (GenAI): the moderating role of negative emotions and the buffering effects of need satisfaction. Teach. Teach. Educ. **154**(104877) (2025)
11. Uygun, D.: Teachers' perspectives on artificial intelligence in education. Adv. Mob. Learn. Educ. Res. **4**(1), 931–939 (2024)
12. Konecki, M., Baksa, T., Konecki, M.: Teachers' perception of AI and their attitudes towards AI. In: Proceedings of the 16th International Conference on Computer Supported Education. SCITEPRESS - Science and Technology Publications, pp. 564–568 (2024)
13. Chounta, I.A., Bardone, E., Raudsep, A., Pedaste, M.: Exploring teachers' perceptions of artificial intelligence as a tool to support their practice in Estonian K-12 education. Int. J. Artif. Intell. Educ. **32**(3), 725–755 (2022)
14. Lan, Y.: Through tensions to identity-based motivations: exploring teacher professional identity in Artificial Intelligence-enhanced teacher training. Teach. Teach. Educ. **151**(104736) (2024)
15. Hopcan, S., Türkmen, G., Polat, E.: Exploring the artificial intelligence anxiety and machine learning attitudes of teacher candidates. Educ. Inf. Technol. **29**(6), 7281–7301 (2024)
16. Kitcharoen, P., Howimanporn, S., Chookaew, S.: Enhancing teachers' AI competencies through artificial intelligence of things professional development training. Int. J. Interact. Mob. Technol. **18**(02), 4–15 (2024)
17. Nazaretsky, T., Ariely, M., Cukurova, M., Alexandron, G.: Teachers' trust in AI-powered educational technology and a professional development program to improve it. Br. J. Educ. Technol. **53**(4), 914–931 (2022)
18. Mouta, A., Torrecilla-Sánchez, E.M., Pinto-Llorente, A.M.: Comprehensive professional learning for teacher agency in addressing ethical challenges of AIED: Insights from educational design research. Educ Inf Technol. pp. 1–45 (2024)
19. Mikeladze, T., Meijer, P.C., Verhoeff, R.P.: A comprehensive exploration of artificial intelligence competence frameworks for educators: a critical review. Eur. J. Educ. **59**(3), e12663 (2024)
20. Hsieh, H.F., Shannon, S.E.: Three approaches to qualitative content analysis. Qual. Health Res. **15**(9), 1277–1288 (2005)
21. Ayanwale, M.A., Sanusi, I.T.: Perceptions of STEM vs. Non-STEM teachers toward teaching artificial intelligence, pp. 1–5. In: 2023 IEEE AFRICON. IEEE (2023)
22. Zawacki-Richter, O., Marín, V.I., Bond, M., Gouverneur, F.: Systematic review of research on artificial intelligence applications in higher education – where are the educators? Int. J. Educ. Technol. High. Educ. **16**(1), 1–27 (2019)
23. Akgun, S., Greenhow, C.: Artificial intelligence in education: addressing ethical challenges in K-12 settings. AI Ethics. **2**(3), 431–440 (2022)

MisstepMath: A Diverse Student Mistake Dataset for AI in Mathematics Teacher Training

Shahina Mohd Azam Ansari[1(✉)], James Bywater[2], Sarah Lilly[1], Donald Brown[1], and Jennifer Chiu[1]

[1] University of Virginia, Charlottesville, VA 22903, USA
{dtf8qc,scl9qp,brown,jlc4dz}@virginia.edu
[2] James Madison University, Harrisonburg, VA 22807, USA
bywatejx@jmu.edu

Abstract. Effective teacher training requires exposure to a wide array of student behaviors and learning challenges. This paper introduces MisstepMath (MisstepMath Dataset: https://huggingface.co/datasets/LLMEducation/MisstepMath), a novel semi-synthetic dataset comprising 12,000 categorized student mistakes paired with instructional teacher responses. Designed to enhance AI-driven teacher training, MisstepMath spans mathematics topics and sub-topics from Kindergarten through Grade 8, systematically categorizing errors into conceptual misunderstandings, procedural mistakes, learning disabilities, and language-related difficulties. Developed in three phases—expert brainstorming and categorization, AI-assisted data generation, and expert review and refinement—MisstepMath ensures diverse and contextually rich student simulations. This approach combines human expertise with AI generation to improve coverage of rare errors, reduce bias, and maintain pedagogical quality. The primary goal of MisstepMath is to support the development of AI models capable of generating diverse student interactions, therefore enabling teachers to practice addressing varied learning challenges. It can be used for fine-tuning conversational AI models to produce contextually relevant student responses, as a knowledge base in Retrieval-Augmented Generation (RAG) systems to improve AI-driven educational tools, or as a benchmark for evaluating AI-driven teacher models. By capturing a broad spectrum of student difficulties and instructional strategies, MisstepMath aims to enhance the adaptability and effectiveness of AI models in education, benefiting teacher training programs, intelligent tutoring systems, and adaptive learning platforms.

Keywords: LLMs · Conversational agents · Retrieval Augmented Generation · Data collection · Equity · Inclusion

1 Introduction

Teaching in diverse classrooms requires educators to address a wide range of student challenges, from conceptual misunderstandings and procedural errors to

A. I. Cristea et al. (Eds.): AIED 2025, LNAI 15877, pp. 381–394, 2025.
https://doi.org/10.1007/978-3-031-98414-3_27

difficulties arising from learning disabilities and language barriers. This diversity demands personalized teaching approaches, yet preparing pre-service and in-service teachers to manage such complexities remains a persistent challenge. Traditional teacher training methods often rely on theoretical case studies or scripted role-playing exercises, which fail to capture the variability of real student interactions. This gap highlights the need for structured tools that can enhance teacher training by exposing educators to diverse learning difficulties.

Conversational AI offers a promising solution by enabling teachers to engage with virtual students exhibiting diverse learning challenges [1]. By practicing responses in a low-risk environment, teachers can refine instructional strategies before applying them in real classrooms [2]. However, the effectiveness of such AI-driven tools depends on high-quality training data [3]. Current conversational AI models generate generic student responses, limiting their value as training tools [4]. This limitation arises from the lack of structured datasets that accurately represent student errors and learning challenges [5].

To address this gap, we introduce a semi-synthetic dataset specifically designed for AI-driven teacher training and student modeling. The dataset captures a diverse range of student mistakes across different grade levels and topics, categorizing them by type and teacher response. By incorporating real-world student errors, expert teacher responses and AI-assisted data generation, it ensures diversity, reduces bias, and enhances coverage of rare student errors [6]. This structured approach enables AI models to generate meaningful and contextually rich student interactions.

MisstepMath can be leveraged for fine-tuning AI-driven educational models, supporting Retrieval-Augmented Generation (RAG) systems, and serving as a benchmark for evaluating AI-driven teacher models. We plan to publicly release MisstepMath to support research in AI-driven educational tools and enhance pre-service teacher training through structured student interactions [8]. In this paper, we discuss MisstepMath's design, applications, evaluation, and potential impact on AI-driven teacher training, highlighting how it enhances both model accuracy and teacher preparedness.

2 Related Work

The integration of AI into teacher training has led to the development of conversational models that simulate student interactions. However, the effectiveness of these models highly depends on structured datasets that accurately represent student challenges and teacher interventions. Early Intelligent Tutoring Systems (ITS) [7], such as AutoTutor [8], utilized rule-based methods to engage learners in dialogue. Recent advancements employ large language models (LLMs) like GPT-3 [9] and BERT [10] to generate dynamic responses, though challenges with generic or repetitive outputs persist due to unstructured training data [3]. Our semi-synthetic dataset addresses this limitation by providing structured representations of student mistakes and teacher interventions, enhancing the variability and authenticity of AI-generated student interactions.

Existing educational datasets, including ASSISTments [11] and EdNet [12], offer extensive student response data but often lack detailed annotations of learning challenges. Our dataset explicitly categorizes student challenges—such as conceptual misunderstandings and procedural errors—enhancing AI models' ability to simulate diverse student behaviors. By combining expert-driven categorization with AI-assisted generation, it ensures diversity across grade levels and reduces bias, providing a valuable resource for developing and testing AI-driven educational tools.

Evaluating AI-driven teacher models requires structured benchmarks that reflect effective pedagogical practices. Current evaluation methods involve human ratings and rubric-based assessments. However, there is a lack of datasets tailored for assessing conversational AI in teaching contexts. Our dataset offers a framework for evaluating AI-generated teacher responses by presenting diverse student prompts and comparing outputs to expert reviews, facilitating the development of responsive educational AI systems.

3 Dataset Description

With 12,000 categorized instances, MisstepMath captures a wide range of student mistakes and learning challenges across Kindergarten to Grade 8 in various mathematics topics (Table 1), aligning with research on student misconceptions and error analysis in mathematics education [13]. MisstepMath provides structured annotations of common student failures, misconceptions, and cognitive barriers, supporting the development of AI models that simulate meaningful and contextual rich student interactions [5,14]. MisstepMath categorizes student errors systematically, enhancing adaptive learning and intelligent tutoring systems [11,15].

Table 1. Example data instance from MisstepMath illustrating a common misconception in Grade 5 Data Analysis, showing the structured format of student challenge, mistake, and instructional response.

Dataset parameters	Sample Value
Grade	Grade 5
Topic	Data Analysis
Sub Topic	Solve real world word problems by referring to line plots
Challenge Type	Misconception
Challenge faced	Confusing Mean and Mode
Problem	What is the mode of this data set?
Student's mistake	Calculating the mean instead of identifying the mode.
Teacher's resolution	Explain the difference between mean and mode with simple examples.

The dimensions of the dataset include grade levels, topics, sub-topics, and challenge types. The dataset includes 9 grade levels (Kindergarten to Grade 8), with a fairly even distribution of errors across them (e.g., Grade 1: 12% of the total errors, Grade 5: 14%, Grade 8: 13%). The challenge types are also distributed across categories, with Conceptual errors accounting for 35%, Procedural errors for 28%, and Language barriers for 22%, ensuring a broad representation of different student difficulties.

3.1 Dataset Scope and Diversity

MisstepMath dataset spans arithmetic, fractions, geometry, word problems, and algebraic reasoning, reflecting well-documented student difficulties. It classifies errors into 32 challenge types, including: Conceptual misunderstandings (e.g., misinterpreting place value), Procedural errors (e.g., incorrect application of addition algorithms), Learning disabilities (e.g., attention, memory, dyscalculia), Reading disabilities (e.g., struggling with word problem comprehension), Visuo-spatial learning challenges (e.g., difficulty in geometry visualization), Language barriers (e.g., non-native English speakers misunderstanding problem wording) and Memory-based difficulties (e.g., retention of mathematical facts).

By ensuring diversity in student responses and avoiding repetitive errors, MisstepMath enhances AI-driven teacher training tools, improving their ability to adapt to real-world learning difficulties [16].

3.2 Dataset Creation Process

MisstepMath was developed in a structured, three-phase process, combining expert knowledge and AI-generated augmentation to ensure quality and diversity (as illustrated in Fig. 1).

Phase 1: Expert Brainstorming, Categorization, and Human Data Collection. Two expert mathematics educators, both U.S. nationals with 25 to 30 years of teaching experience, were recruited through educational institutions. The experts helped identify common student failures across different grade levels and math topics. They categorized these mistakes based on their observations, creating a structured taxonomy [17] of failure types and learning challenges across all grades. Next, Fifteen mathematics educators (10 female, 5 male) with 1 to 20 years of teaching experience across elementary, middle, and high school levels were recruited through educational institutions. They contributed problem examples, student mistake prompts, and teacher responses for each identified challenge, forming an initial seed dataset of 500 entries spanning various grade levels.

Phase 2: AI-Assisted Data Generation. Using the expert-curated initial seed data, we leveraged ChatGPT to generate additional student mistakes across various grade levels and topics. The model was prompted to extend identified

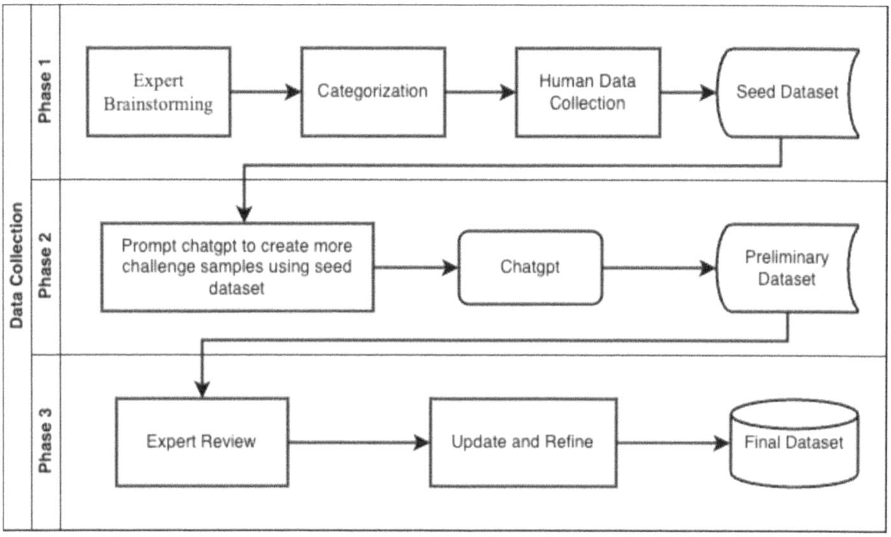

Fig. 1. Overview of the dataset creation process, combining expert input and AI generation in three phases: expert brainstorming and data collection, AI-assisted data generation, and expert review for refinement and alignment with real student misconceptions.

mistake types, simulate diverse student misconceptions, and generate teacher responses aligned with pedagogical best practices [8]. This resulted in a preliminary dataset with broader coverage of real-world errors, supporting AI-driven educational tools.

To support transparency and reproducibility, we publicly release the full set of generation prompts, evaluation forms, expert review protocols, and complete code for dataset generation and evaluation, along with detailed reproduction instructions, on our GitHub repository[1].

Phase 3: Expert Review and Refinement. The preliminary dataset underwent expert review to ensure educational relevance and alignment with real student misconceptions [17]. The expert teachers from Phase 1 evaluated each problem example for age appropriateness, ensuring that student mistake prompts accurately reflected common errors observed in classrooms. They refined teacher responses to align with research-backed instructional strategies and corrected ambiguities or classifications in challenge types.

This rigorous validation process ensured that MisstepMath maintains high quality, and applicability for training AI-driven teacher models [15, 16].

[1] https://github.com/LLMEducation/MisstepMath.

4 Evaluation

Assessing the effectiveness of a dataset designed for AI-driven teacher training and student simulation requires a comprehensive evaluation strategy, aligning with established methodologies in educational AI assessment [8]. Our evaluation approach includes both quantitative and qualitative assessments, including dataset quality analysis, dataset diversity analysis, AI-generated student behavior evaluation, teacher feedback, and benchmarking against baseline models [16].

4.1 Dataset Quality Analysis

To evaluate MisstepMath's quality, five experts were recruited: two math teachers (one female from the U.S. and one male from India, both with over 30 years of experience) and three instructional designers (two females from the U.S. and Canada, and one male from India, all specializing in AI-driven educational tools).

Table 2. Evaluation of Problem and Response Quality. Summary of ratings (1–5 scale) on relevance, diversity, pedagogical quality, clarity, authenticity, and usability for teacher training. Mean ratings and standard deviations (SD) are based on expert evaluations.

Parameter	Mean (±3SD)	Key Observations
Relevance of Problems	4.6 (SD = 0.4)	Problems are well-aligned with curriculum standards.
Diversity of Student Challenges	4.3 (SD = 0.5)	A broad range of challenges and learning difficulties captured.
Pedagogical Quality of Responses	4.2 (SD = 0.6)	Responses address student mistakes effectively.
Clarity and Accessibility	4.4 (SD = 0.4)	Problems are clear and appropriate for the intended grade levels.
Authenticity of Mistakes	4.1 (SD = 0.7)	Mistakes are realistic, reflecting common classroom challenges.
Coverage of Curriculum Standards	4.5 (SD = 0.5)	Comprehensive coverage of key topics and sub-topics.
Engagement and Creativity	4.0 (SD = 0.6)	More dynamic and engaging scenarios could be added.
Usability for Teacher Training	4.3 (SD = 0.5)	Highly valuable for teacher training applications.
Adaptability and Scalability	4.1 (SD = .6)	Flexible enough for different contexts and grades.

The experts were recruited through educational institutions and personal outreach. Their diverse backgrounds in K-8 education and AI applications ensured valuable feedback on MisstepMath's pedagogical alignment [5,15]. Experts assessed 200 randomly selected entries using a 10-parameter rubric including relevance, diversity, clarity, authenticity, and curriculum alignment, scoring each on a 1–5 scale. [11]. MisstepMath received high ratings across all categories, indicating strong alignment with curriculum standards (Table 2) and student cognitive development models. Experts praised the diversity in student challenges, highlighting the capacity of MisstepMath to generate varied and representative learning scenarios and misconceptions.

4.2 Dataset Diversity Analysis

To assess the diversity of student mistakes in MisstepMath, we employed two key metrics: Type-Token Ratio (TTR) [18] and cosine similarity [19], widely used in diversity assessment research [20,21]. TTR measures lexical diversity by dividing the number of unique words (types) by the total number of words (tokens) in a text; a higher TTR indicates more varied language use [22]. In our analysis, MisstepMath achieved a TTR of 0.50, reflecting a rich variety of expressions in student mistake prompts. Cosine similarity, on the other hand, quantifies semantic similarity between two vectors by measuring the cosine of the angle between them; lower cosine similarity scores suggest more diverse and distinct responses. MisstepMath exhibited an average cosine similarity score of 0.34 between student mistake prompts, indicating low redundancy and a wide range of student misunderstandings [23,24]. These metrics confirm MisstepMath's capacity to support AI models in generating varied and contextually relevant student interactions.

4.3 AI Model Evaluation

We evaluated MisstepMath's effectiveness in training AI models for student and teacher conversational agents by comparing three ChatGPT-4 models: a baseline zero-shot ChatGPT-4 model, a fine-tuned ChatGPT-4 model [25], and a ChatGPT-4 model using Retrieval-Augmented Generation (RAG) with the dataset. In the fine-tuned model, the LLM was retrained using 70% of the dataset—updating the model weights based on grade, topic, sub-topic, and target responses (either student prompts or teacher replies)—and then evaluated on the remaining 30%. In contrast, the RAG model did not modify the LLM weights; instead, it retrieved 20 relevant examples from MisstepMath based on the grade+topic+sub-topic combination and appended them to the input prompt during inference to guide the model's generation. Thus, fine-tuning internalizes the dataset within the model, while RAG dynamically augments the prompt with relevant data at runtime. The student and teacher models were evaluated separately for their ability to generate diverse student errors and pedagogically appropriate teacher responses.

For the evaluation, 50 random combinations of grade, topic, and sub-topic were selected from MisstepMath's 30% test set. Both the student and teacher LLM models were tasked with generating 100 responses for each given grade, topic, and sub-topic combination. This resulted in 5,000 responses per model, totaling 15,000 student responses across the three student models (baseline, fine-tuned, and RAG), and an additional 15,000 teacher responses across the three teacher models.

Table 3. Evaluation of teacher and student simulations across different models, showing semantic similarity, lexical diversity (measured by TTR), and the percentage of repeated student mistakes for the zero-shot, fine-tuned, and RAG models.

Model	Teacher Simulation		Student Simulation		
	Semantic Similarity	Lexical Diversity (Avg. TTR)	Semantic Similarity	Lexical Diversity (Avg. TTR)	Percentage of Repeated Student Mistakes
Zero-Shot	0.85	0.08	0.62	0.12	52%
RAG	0.51	0.18	0.48	0.23	33%
Fine-tuned	0.38	0.30	0.35	0.38	21%

Student Response Evaluation. To assess the diversity of student mistakes generated by our models, we evaluated the repetition rate of these errors by first inputting the responses into ChatGPT and prompting it to group similar outputs. Subsequently, a team comprising a 40-year-old male middle school math teacher from the U.S. and a 35-year-old female AI tool expert from Canada reviewed the groupings. The teacher provided educational expertise, while the expert offered insights into AI integration. A higher number of distinct groups indicates a lower repetition rate, reflecting a broader range of simulated student behaviors essential for effective modeling. To further quantify this diversity, we employed semantic similarity and lexical diversity metrics (Table 3). Semantic similarity was calculated using cosine similarity of BERT embeddings [26], where lower scores indicated more varied and distinct responses. Lexical diversity was assessed using the TTR [27], where higher TTR values indicate richer vocabulary use. The baseline zero-shot model had a 52% repetition rate in student mistakes, suggesting limited diversity. The RAG model reduced this repetition to 33%, producing more contextually appropriate errors. The fine-tuned model exhibited the highest diversity, with only 21% repeated mistakes and a TTR of 0.70, demonstrating its capability to simulate a wide array of student errors.

Teacher Response Evaluation. Teacher responses generated by our model were also verified for diversity using TTR and semantic similarity metrics. We assessed the diversity of teacher-generated responses (Table 3) by comparing them with expert resolutions through cosine similarity of BERT embeddings [10]. Lower cosine similarity scores indicated more diverse and distinct responses, which are important for simulating a wide range of teacher feedback. Lexical diversity was evaluated using TTR, where higher values suggested richer vocabulary use [27]. The fine-tuned model demonstrated the highest diversity, with the most varied teacher responses. The RAG model showed improved diversity over the baseline, but with lower lexical richness. The zero-shot model had the lowest diversity, often producing more repetitive responses.

4.4 Human Expert Evaluation

We conducted a human expert evaluation to assess the quality of the models' effectiveness [28] in simulating student interactions and generating teacher responses. A panel of two expert math educators, both from the U.S., one male and one female, each with over 30 years of experience in K-8 education. The experts reviewed 500 student and 500 teacher responses, evenly distributed across the zero-shot, fine-tuned, and RAG models (approximately 167 per model), randomly selected from separate pools of 15,000 responses each, generated during the *AI model evaluation* phase. The evaluation (Table 4) focused on two main criteria: student interaction (Assessing how accurately the student's responses reflected diverse classroom behaviors) and teacher response (Evaluating how effectively the teacher's feedback addressed the student's mistake and provided appropriate guidance).

Table 4. Human expert evaluation of AI-generated student and teacher responses, including average response quality ratings and Cohen's Kappa values for inter-rater agreement across the Zero-Shot, Fine-Tuned, and RAG models

Model	Teacher Simulation		Student Simulation	
	Response Quality (Avg.)	Cohen's Kappa κ	Response Quality (Avg.)	Cohen's Kappa κ
Zero-Shot	3.5	0.80	3.2	0.74
RAG	4.1	0.82	3.7	0.78
Fine-tuned	4.3	0.83	4.2	0.79

Student Interaction Quality. The panel evaluated how closely model-generated student mistakes mirrored diverse classroom behaviors. The fine-tuned model received the highest average score of 4.2 out of 5, indicating its ability to produce diverse and varied student errors. The RAG model followed with a score of 3.7, while the zero-shot model scored 3.2, reflecting more repetitive error patterns.

Teacher Response Quality. In evaluating the quality of teacher responses, the panel assessed responses based on clarity, relevance, and accuracy in addressing students' mistakes. The fine-tuned model outperformed others, achieving an average score of 4.3, indicating its ability to generate contextually appropriate and accurate teacher responses. The RAG model followed with a score of 4.1, while the zero-shot model scored 3.5, often producing more generic feedback less aligned with specific student errors.

Statistical Analysis. To determine the reliability of these evaluations, Cohen's kappa (κ) [29] was calculated for inter-rater agreement. Cohen's kappa is a statistical measure that evaluates inter-rater reliability for categorical items, quantifying the agreement between two raters beyond what would be expected by chance. Values range from -1 to 1, with higher values indicating stronger agreement [30]. The kappa score for student interaction quality was 0.79, and for teacher response quality, it was 0.83, both indicating substantial agreement among evaluators, suggesting high reliability of the evaluations. These findings highlight the dataset's superior performance in simulating diverse student behaviors and generating high-quality teacher responses.

5 Benchmarking the Dataset for Student Response Diversity

To evaluate MisstepMath's effectiveness in capturing diverse student problem-solving approaches and challenge types, we benchmarked it against several LLMs. The assessment focused on student response diversity, measured by TTR and Semantic Similarity, and student challenge type diversity, evaluated using Shannon Entropy [31]—which measures the unpredictability or variety in the distribution of student mistake types—and Pielou's Evenness Index [32], which quantifies how evenly those mistake types are represented, with values closer to 1 indicating a more balanced distribution. These metrics are widely used in natural language generation and diversity assessment research [20,21].

We randomly selected 50 unique (Grade, Topic, Sub-topic) combinations from the MisstepMath test set and generated 100 synthetic student responses per combination using five state-of-the-art LLMs: GPT-4 Turbo [33] (OpenAI, 2024), Claude 3.5 Haiku, Clause 3.5 Sonnet (Anthropic, 2024), and Gemini 2.0 Flash and Gemini 2.0 Flash Lite (Google, 2024) [34]. For each model and MisstepMath dataset, we computed the metrics within each (Grade, Topic, Sub-topic) group and then averaged the results across the 50 combinations (Table 5).

TTR quantifies lexical diversity, indicating the variety of words used. Semantic Similarity (measured via TF-IDF-based cosine similarity) [35] assesses how varied student responses are within each category. Shannon Entropy captures the syntactic variation in challenge types, where higher values indicate greater diversity. Pielou's Evenness Index measures the balance of challenge types, with values closer to 1 indicating a more uniform distribution.

Table 5. Diversity metrics across MisstepMath and LLM-generated responses. TTR and Semantic Similarity measure student response diversity, while Shannon Entropy and Pielou's Index assess student challenge type diversity and balance across categories.

Model/Dataset	Student's Response		Challenge Type	
	TTR	Semantic Similarity	Shannon Entropy	Pielou's Index
MisstepMath (Ours)	**0.50**	**0.34**	**3.3**	**0.81**
GPT-4o-mini	0.12	0.81	0.31	0.10
GPT-3.5 Turbo	0.12	0.74	1.19	0.37
Claude 3.5 Haiku	0.13	0.68	2.88	0.67
Claude 3.5 Sonnet	0.05	0.86	0.65	0.32
Gemini 2.0 Flash	0.15	0.76	1.46	0.38
Gemini 2.0 Flash Lite	0.15	0.75	1.49	0.39

5.1 Results and Analysis

Our evaluation demonstrates that MisstepMath exhibits higher student response and challenge type diversity than LLM-generated responses. Table 4 shows that MisstepMath achieved the highest lexical diversity, with a TTR of 0.50, and the greatest syntactic variation, indicated by a Shannon Entropy of 3.3. These metrics reflect the varied nature of real student mistakes. In contrast, models like GPT-4o-mini and Claude 3.5 Sonnet showed higher semantic similarity scores (0.81 and 0.86, respectively), suggesting more repetitive and less varied responses. Additionally, GPT and Gemini models showed low TTR (0.12–0.15), suggesting limited word diversity. Regarding challenge type diversity, MisstepMath again outperformed the LLMs, achieving the highest Shannon Entropy (3.3) and Pielou's Evenness Index (0.81). These figures denote both a high variety and an even distribution of student challenges. Conversely, GPT-4o-mini recorded the lowest entropy (0.31) and evenness (0.10), indicating a strong bias toward specific challenge types. Among the LLMs, Claude 3.5 Haiku demonstrated relatively higher diversity with a Shannon Entropy of 2.88, while Claude 3.5 Sonnet had the lowest TTR (0.05) and entropy (0.65), suggesting limited syntactic and challenge diversity. These findings highlight the importance of datasets like MisstepMath in training AI models for educational applications. While LLM-generated responses can capture some diversity, they often lack the full range of real-world student mistakes and tend to overfit common error patterns. MisstepMath provides a robust benchmark for evaluating and enhancing the performance of AI systems in capturing diverse student mistakes.

6 Discussion

MisstepMath demonstrates strong potential in advancing AI-driven educational tools, particularly for pre-service teacher training and adaptive tutoring systems. The fine-tuned model trained on MisstepMath significantly outperformed zero-shot and RAG baselines, reducing repeated student mistakes to 21% and achieving the highest lexical diversity (TTR = 0.88), thereby enabling more realistic and varied student simulations [18].

Beyond technical gains, MisstepMath is practically suited for integration into pre-service teacher training platforms. It can support virtual student avatars in simulation-based practice environments [2], enable scenario-specific training for responding to student misconceptions, and enhance adaptive tutoring systems with categorized examples of student difficulties [15]. Its structured taxonomy of conceptual, procedural, linguistic, and cognitive challenges allows educators to design targeted instructional strategies.

To support broader applicability, future work should expand the dataset beyond mathematics, incorporating diverse domains such as science and reading comprehension, as well as international curriculum variants. Additionally, multi-modal enhancements like whiteboard interactions and diagram-based reasoning would help simulate visual and spatial math difficulties. Long-term collaboration with pre-service teacher training programs will be essential to align the dataset with evolving pedagogical practices and curriculum standards.

7 Conclusion

This study presents MisstepMath, a novel semi-synthetic dataset aimed at enhancing AI-driven educational tools, particularly for pre-service teacher training and adaptive tutoring systems. Evaluation results validate MisstepMath's ability to generate diverse, contextually relevant student challenges and support AI models in producing pedagogically sound teacher responses. Notably, MisstepMath enabled fine-tuned model exhibited superior performance in both diversity and factual alignment, highlighting its potential for real-time retrieval and dynamic error simulation.

MisstepMath can serve as a valuable resource for teacher rehearsal tools, retrieval-augmented educational systems, and benchmarking student simulation quality. Expert feedback confirms its alignment with curricular goals and usability in diverse instructional contexts. Future directions include expanding content domains, incorporating multimodal and multilingual data, and working closely with pre-service teacher training programs to ensure MisstepMath remains a practical, scalable resource for preparing educators to respond effectively to student challenges.

Acknowledgments. This material is based upon work supported in part by 4-VA, a collaborative partnership for advancing the Commonwealth of Virginia, by the Robertson Foundation, and by the National Science Foundation under Grant Nos. 2315436 and 2315437. Any opinions, findings, and conclusions or recommendations expressed in this material are those of the authors and do not necessarily reflect the views of 4-VA, the Robertson Foundation, or the National Science Foundation.

Disclosure of Interests. The authors have no competing interests to declare that are relevant to the content of this article.

References

1. Adel, A., Ahsan, A., Davison, C.: ChatGPT promises and challenges in education: computational and ethical perspectives. Educ. Sci. **14**(8), 814 (2024)
2. Berg, C., Dieker, L., Scolavino, R.: Using a virtual avatar teaching simulation and an evidence-based teacher observation tool: a synergistic combination for teacher preparation. Educ. Sci. **13**(7), 744 (2023)
3. Zha, D., et al.: Data-centric artificial intelligence: a survey. ACM Comput. Surv. **57**(5), 1–42 (2025)
4. Atlas, S.: ChatGPT for higher education and professional development: a guide to conversational AI (2023)
5. Shi, F., et al.: Large language models can be easily distracted by irrelevant context. In: International Conference on Machine Learning, pp. 31210–31227. PMLR (2023)
6. Du Boulay, B., Luckin, R.: Modelling human teaching tactics and strategies for tutoring systems. Int. J. Artif. Intell. Educ. **12**(3), 235–256 (2001)
7. Paladines, J., Ramirez, J.: A systematic literature review of intelligent tutoring systems with dialogue in natural language. IEEE Access **8**, 164246–164267 (2020)
8. Graesser, A.C., et al.: AutoTutor: a tutor with dialogue in natural language. Behav. Res. Methods Instrum. Comput. **36**, 180–192 (2004)
9. Brown, T., et al.: Language models are few-shot learners. Adv. Neural. Inf. Process. Syst. **33**, 1877–1901 (2020)
10. Devlin, J.: BERT: pre-training of deep bidirectional transformers for language understanding. arXiv preprint arXiv:1810.04805 (2018)
11. Heffernan, N.T., Heffernan, C.L.: The ASSISTments ecosystem: building a platform that brings scientists and teachers together for minimally invasive research on human learning and teaching. Int. J. Artif. Intell. Educ. **24**, 470–497 (2014)
12. Choi, Y., et al.: EdNet: a large-scale hierarchical dataset in education. In: Bittencourt, I.I., Cukurova, M., Muldner, K., Luckin, R., Millán, E. (eds.) AIED 2020, Part II. LNCS (LNAI), vol. 12164, pp. 69–73. Springer, Cham (2020). https://doi.org/10.1007/978-3-030-52240-7_13
13. Sarwadi, H., Shahrill, M.: Understanding students' mathematical errors and misconceptions: the case of year 11 repeating students. Math. Educ. Trends Res. **2014**(2014), 1–10 (2014)
14. Tan, Z., et al.: Large language models for data annotation and synthesis: a survey. In: Proceedings of the 2024 Conference on Empirical Methods in Natural Language Processing, pp. 930–957 (2024)
15. Koedinger, K.R., Corbett, A.T., Perfetti, C.: The Knowledge-Learning-Instruction framework: bridging the science-practice chasm to enhance robust student learning. Cogn. Sci. **36**(5), 757–798 (2012)
16. Aleven, V., Mclaren, B.M., Sewall, J., Koedinger, K.R.: A new paradigm for intelligent tutoring systems: example-tracing tutors. Int. J. Artif. Intell. Educ. **19**(2), 105–154 (2009)
17. Carpenter, T.P., Fennema, E., Franke, M.L., Levi, L., Empson, S.B.: Children's Mathematics: Cognitively Guided Instruction, vol. 1. Heinemann, Portsmouth (1999)
18. Richards, B.: Type/token ratios: what do they really tell us? J. Child Lang. **14**(2), 201–209 (1987)
19. Rahutomo, F., Kitasuka, T., Aritsugi, M.: Semantic cosine similarity. In: The 7th International Student Conference on Advanced Science and Technology ICAST, vol. 4, no. 1, p. 1. University of Seoul, South Korea (2012)

20. Celikyilmaz, A., Clark, E., Gao, J.: Evaluation of text generation: a survey. arXiv preprint arXiv:2006.14799 (2020)
21. Fergadiotis, G., Wright, H.H., Green, S.B.: Psychometric evaluation of lexical diversity indices: assessing length effects. J. Speech Lang. Hear. Res. **58**(3), 840–852 (2015)
22. Martínez, G., Hernández, J. A., Conde, J., Reviriego, P., Merino-Gómez, E.: Beware of words: evaluating the lexical diversity of conversational LLMs using chatGPT as case study. ACM Trans. Intell. Syst. Technol. (2024)
23. Mikolov, T., Sutskever, I., Chen, K., Corrado, G.S., Dean, J.: Distributed representations of words and phrases and their compositionality. Adv. Neural Inf. Process. Syst. **26** (2013)
24. Pennington, J., Socher, R., Manning, C.D.: GloVe: global vectors for word representation. In: Proceedings of the 2014 Conference on Empirical Methods in Natural Language Processing (EMNLP), pp. 1532–1543 (2014)
25. Wei, J., et al.: Finetuned language models are zero-shot learners. arXiv preprint arXiv:2109.01652 (2021)
26. Lahitani, A.R., Permanasari, A.E., Setiawan, N.A.: Cosine similarity to determine similarity measure: study case in online essay assessment. In: 2016 4th International Conference on Cyber and IT Service Management, pp. 1–6. IEEE (2016)
27. Yang, J.S., Rosvold, C., Bernstein Ratner, N.: Measurement of lexical diversity in children's spoken language: computational and conceptual considerations. Front. Psychol. **13**, 905789 (2022)
28. Shankar, S., Zamfirescu-Pereira, J.D., Hartmann, B., Parameswaran, A., Arawjo, I.: Who validates the validators? Aligning LLM-assisted evaluation of LLM outputs with human preferences. In: Proceedings of the 37th Annual ACM Symposium on User Interface Software and Technology, pp. 1–14 (2024)
29. McHugh, M.L.: Interrater reliability: the kappa statistic. Biochemia medica **22**(3), 276–282 (2012)
30. Warrens, M.J.: Five ways to look at Cohen's kappa. J. Psychol. Psychotherapy **5** (2015)
31. Lin, J.: Divergence measures based on the Shannon entropy. IEEE Trans. Inf. Theory **37**(1), 145–151 (1991)
32. Heip, C.: A new index measuring evenness. J. Mar. Biol. Assoc. U.K. **54**(3), 555–557 (1974)
33. Achiam, J., et al.: GPT-4 technical report. arXiv preprint arXiv:2303.08774 (2023)
34. McIntosh, T.R., Susnjak, T., Liu, T., Watters, P., Halgamuge, M.N.: From google Gemini to openAI Q*(Q-star): a survey of reshaping the generative artificial intelligence (AI) research landscape. arXiv preprint arXiv:2312.10868
35. Chandrasekaran, D., Mago, V.: Evolution of semantic similarity–a survey. ACM Comput. Surv. (CSUR) **54**(2), 1–37 (2021)

More Expert-Like Eye Gaze Movement Patterns are Related to Better X-ray Reading

Pingjing Yang[1(✉)], Jennifer Cromley[1(✉)], and Jana Diesner[1,2(✉)]

[1] University of Illinois Urbana-Champaign, Champaign, IL 61820, USA
{py2,jcromley}@illinois.edu.com
[2] Technical University of Munich, Munich, Germany
jana.diesner@tum.de

Abstract. Understanding how novices acquire and hone visual search skills is crucial for developing and optimizing training methods across domains. Network analysis methods can be used to analyze graph representations of visual expertise. This study investigates the relationship between eye-gaze movements and learning outcomes among undergraduate dentistry students who were diagnosing dental radiographs over multiple semesters. We use network analysis techniques to model eye-gaze scanpaths as directed graphs and examine changes in network metrics over time. Using time series clustering on each metric, we identify distinct patterns of visual search strategies and explore their association with students' diagnostic performance. Our findings suggest that the network metric of transition entropy is negatively correlated with performance scores, while the number of nodes and edges as well as average PageRank are positively correlated with performance scores. Changes in network metrics for individual students over time suggest a developmental shift from intermediate to expert-level processing. These insights contribute to understanding expertise acquisition in visual tasks and can inform the design of AI-assisted learning interventions.

Keywords: Eye-gaze Movement · Time Series Clustering · Network Analysis

1 Introduction

Eye tracking is an established method for studying the allocation of experts' and novices' visual attention in a wide range of domains, e.g., medicine [1], sports [39], transportation [45], and education [16]. At the same time, datasets capturing longitudinal eye tracking data that allow for studying how expertise develops over time are rare, which limits our knowledge about changes in eye-gaze patterns and related learning outcomes. Eye tracking studies often rely on aggregated metrics such as time spent in each Area of Interest (AOI) [30] or the number of fixations per AOI [26]. Some studies have also applied network analysis

A. I. Cristea et al. (Eds.): AIED 2025, LNAI 15877, pp. 395–410, 2025.
https://doi.org/10.1007/978-3-031-98414-3_28

methods to study characteristics of the entire scan path and their relationship with various outcomes, such as performance in flight training simulations [19].

The network metric of the number of nodes, also known as network size, quantifies the number of Areas of Interest (AOIs) fixated on. When applied to eye tracking scanpaths, network size is an indicator of the cumulative number of AOIs that a student has visited. For example, network size is higher for dermatologists trained to do more thorough examinations for skin cancer [10].

The number of edges quantifies the number of saccades (moves) from any AOI to another AOI. When applied to eye tracking, the number of edges indicates the number of moves/transitions/switches that a student has made among AOIs. More transitions between mathematics questions and the representations needed to answer them are associated with higher test scores [44].

The network diameter quantifies the longest yet most graph-efficient distance jumped across AOIs in the scanpath. When applied to eye tracking, the diameter represents the total distance in AOI 'jumps' across the entire stimulus set. The network diameter is significantly positively related to growth in test scores on written answers over time [21].

Degree centrality quantifies the number of edges (saccade) per node (AOI) across all AOIs. When applied to eye tracking, degree centrality indicates how many pieces of visual information (represented as nodes), e.g., AOIs, a node is directly linked to. Higher degree centrality in eye tracking has been associated with better student performance [9].

Eigenvector centrality is a recursive function of degree centrality, thereby indicating the influence of an AOI by considering the degree centrality of a node's neighbors (in our case, other AOIs, in network terms also called alters, that are directly connected to an ego AI). Higher eigencentrality in eye tracking has been associated with better task performance on a web search task [28].

Stationary entropy in networks measures the amount of uncertainty in the spatial distribution of a sequence of fixations. This metric is correlated with expertise in educational development: [7] discovered that stationary gaze entropy (SGE) decreases as students' expertise increases from novice to intermediate and from intermediate to expert in problem solving in physics. Network transition entropy measures the unpredictability of visual scanning patterns. Higher transition entropy suggests a more random pattern of scanning behaviors: [37] found that gaze transition entropy (GTE) is lower for older drivers when completing a subsidiary loading task while driving on a two-lane rural highway. The mentioned studies suggest that entropy-based measures may be relevant for assessing expertise levels in visually demanding tasks.

In this paper, we apply network analysis metrics to an eye tracking data set collected from undergraduate dental students who visually inspected dental X-rays over a semester (with some participating for multiple semesters) and investigate the relationship between characteristics of the scanpath and students' performance on a dental anomaly detection task.

2 Background

2.1 Analyzing Developmental Data

Studying the development of learning—including its component skills, and other learning-related variables such as different aspects of motivation—is usually done by using growth curve modeling, which considers the shape of change in learning-related variables (increasing, decreasing, linear, curvilinear, discontinuous) and predictors of students' initial scores and rates of change [40]. The scores whose change is modeled over time might represent reading comprehension [32], answers to interest questionnaires [34], or other typical summed scales. Researchers have used this approach to analyze changes in physical (e.g., a child's height; [3]) or physiological (e.g., heart rate; [18]) variables. In the present work, we model the change in selected network analytic metrics that capture aspects of a learner's eye tracking scanpaths over time.

We also hypothesize subsets of students with different patterns of change [32] via grouping or clustering methods. These learning patterns are often modeled using a specialized type of growth curve modeling called growth mixture modeling [43]. For example, one subset of students might show positive linear growth on a variable, and a different subset of students might show positive quadratic growth on the same variable, even though these two groups at the final testing point might have (statistically) similar or different scores. Different patterns of change can suggest educational implications, such as fostering a more adaptive trajectory of change or helping instructors understand that different trajectories can result in the same adaptive outcomes, depending on the findings. In other studies, differing growth curves might relate to different student clusters, which indicates that eye-gaze patterns correlate with differences in learning outcomes. In the present research, we test for different trajectories of change in network analysis metrics, which capture aspects of a learner's eye tracking scanpaths.

2.2 Applying Network Analysis to Developmental Data

Despite its limited application in educational research, network analysis has been used to quantify behavioral patterns. [44] found no significant differences in network density or reciprocity between high- and low-performing math-solving groups but identified three triadic structures (003, 021D, and 111U) that significantly differed between the groups. More recently, [29] demonstrated that network metrics—including density, centrality, small-worldness, transitivity, and global efficiency—differentiated scanpath networks of low- and high-ability readers. On the other hand, current studies primarily employ network analysis for between-subject comparisons, using statistical methods such as t-tests [29, 44] to establish correlations between network metrics and learning performance. In the present study, we synthesize existing research to evaluate the predictive power of network metrics in X-ray reading performance. This work advances education performance analysis by incorporating time-series modeling to capture dynamic learning processes.

3 Research Questions

Based on our review of network metrics applied to visual processing, with a focus on expertise development and considering the context of undergraduate dentistry students looking for anomalies in dental X-rays over multiple semesters, we address the following questions:

1. What can we learn about expertise development from the shape of change in various network analysis metrics applied to the students' scanpaths data over time?
2. Are there subsets or clusters of students who show different patterns of change (i.e., different developmental routes)? If so, how do these clusters relate to student performance?
3. What do the patterns of change in network analysis metrics suggest about the novice-intermediate-expert developmental continuum?

This research advances the generally available and validated set of methods and metrics for studying the impact of visual attention allocation on learning outcomes. It also improves our understanding of the potential capabilities of AI technologies for analyzing X-rays: Humans reading X-rays is an instance of a qualitative analysis method applied to qualitative data; a task that requires substantial and domain-specific training to lead to reliable results [2]. How good can AIs be at this task? If human learners advance in their ability to interpret X-rays with continued training and achieve more correct results over time, then using such data to train AI models for X-ray assessment has a chance to result in models that lead to potentially reliable results. If, however, training humans does not lead to sustained improvements in their ability to read X-rays correctly, then we should not assume that AIs such as large vision models have or develop this ability after being trained on any scale of prior data. Our paper also sheds light on this question.

4 Methods

4.1 Data

The dataset we use was collected and made publicly available by a research team headed by Fabian Huettig and Constanze Keutel [4] with funding from the Leibniz-WissenschaftsCampus program Cognitive Interfaces. We downloaded the data from PsychArchives from http://dx.doi.org/10.23668/psycharchives.5681 and additional code from https://github.com/conradborchers/visualsearchopt. Additional clarification was provided by Conrad Borchers (personal communication on June 12 and August 26, 2024).

4.2 Participants and Educational Context

Participants were 107 undergraduate dentistry students from the University of Tuebingen in Germany in 2017–2018. They took part in 90-minute-long session(s) during one or more semesters as early as their 6th semester (middle of 3rd year in the degree program) to as late as their 10th (graduating) semester in the program. At their first time of participation, their average age was 25.25 and they were 64% female. They were paid 15 Euros for each eye tracking session that they participated in [4].

As part of their regular sequence of courses, all students in this program took a 6th-semester course in radiology that involved learning how to read dental X-rays and also included practice reading 100 dental X-rays that did not include the stimuli used in the dataset we analyzed. The general approach to teaching reading of X-rays is top-left to top right (on the X-ray), then bottom right to bottom left [8]. Students might be considered novices at the beginning of the research study [12]. They might be considered intermediates when they had at least five previous semesters of learning about dental anatomy and dental health, including photographic images of healthy gums and teeth, as well as images of gum disease or dental caries, and were taking- or had taken- a radiology course.

4.3 Stimuli Presented to Participants and Performance Task

In each session, students saw a series of ten dental X-rays, were asked to look for dental anomalies in each X-ray, such as evidence of gum disease or dental caries (e.g., cavities), and were eye tracked while examining the X-rays. Students were later asked to use their computer mouse to circle each anomaly in turn. In this paper, we analyze the anomaly detection scores provided in the dataset, and do not use the eye tracking from the marking session. Each anomaly was pre-defined as an AOI in the dataset. Since each X-ray might feature a different number of AOIs, we normalized the performance scores (e.g., finding 50% of the possible anomalies in a particular X-ray) for each X-ray.

4.4 Eye Tracking Methods, Equipment, and Data Collection

The SensoMotoric Instruments RED 250 eye tracker and SMR BeGaze software were are described in detail in the team's publications [4,12–14,33]. After calibration on the mobile eye tracking equipment, each participant's eye gazes were recorded for the duration of the X-ray task session. Data were excluded by the original research team if the tracking rate was below 80%.

4.5 Procedures

After participants provided informed consent, they were seated in front of a computer, put on a pair of eye tracking glasses, and completed the manufacturer's calibration check. They received instructions on how to mark any anomalies they detected. They were then shown the X-rays one at a time, with a 90-second free-exploration phase and a subsequent untimed marking anomalies phase. Subsequently, participants completed a dental conceptual knowledge test and a demographics form, which are not analyzed here.

4.6 Data Analysis

How We Applied Network Analysis Metrics to Scanpaths. Network Analysis is used to represent relational data in a network format (e.g., a graph) and apply network metrics and algorithms to the data. A first step in a network analysis project is to construct a network based on the analytical goals. To this end, we constructed ego networks (one per person per trial) by converting participants' eye-gaze movement data into network representations. In our data, nodes represent participants' focus on individual AOIs (Areas of Interest) as predefined by [4] and edges represent movements or transitions (saccades) between AOIs. Given that prior research has often observed back-and-forth movements between nodes, we used multi-edge directed graphs weighted by cumulative frequency of eye-gaze movements to model these networks. The constructed networks represent the movement of eye-gazing across objects and may provide insights into cognitive processes during tasks. Figure 1 illustrates three network representations for one participant on subsequent study trials. Network representations capture transitions and the temporal order of movements between AOIs.

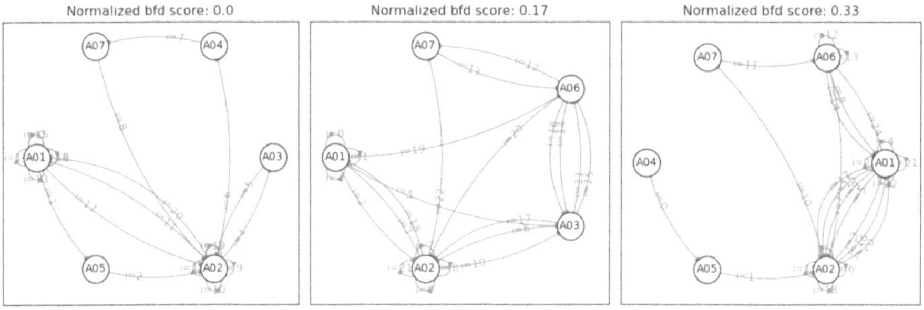

Fig. 1. Network representations of one participant's eye-gaze movements.

Using this definition and representation of eye-gaze networks, we applied mixed linear models to test for correlations between network metrics and measured variables. Figure 1 shows how network representations may correlate with students' performance. The anomaly detection score (normalized BFD score, where BFD refers to "Befund" in German) refers to an adjusted percentage score, scaled from 0 to 1 (lowest to highest performance), which reflects students' performance on the same OPT task that they repeated three times within the same semester. This allows us to form hypotheses, such as whether the number of edges in a network correlates with normalized BFD scores or not.

Based on a literature review [38] of network analysis metrics applied to eye-gaze data such as shifts among AOIs in eye tracking data, shifts between geospatial location by pedestrians, or switches among different tools in virtual environments, we selected the following four categories of network analysis metrics: basic (node and edge count) measures, centrality measures, network-level structural measures, and entropy measures.

Basic measures refer to the number of nodes and edges per network. The number of nodes represents the AOIs a student has explored; the number of edges represents each student's total movements across AOIs. Existing research has shown that a decrease in the number of nodes may suggest higher learning efficiency [41] and a positive correlation between the number of edges with the performance of 8th-grade students during problem solving [44].

Node centralities refer to a collection of metrics that capture different dimensions of the structural importance of individual nodes. Following existing research, we selected degree centrality [9], betweenness centrality [22], closeness centrality [22], eigenvector centrality [35], and pagerank centrality [24].

Structural measures tap characteristics of a network overall, such as the overall interconnectedness of nodes. For example, density, a measure of actual edges in a graph as a proportion of all possible edges, was reported to be positively related to learning outcomes [42]. Reciprocity, a measure of the ratio of back-and-forth movement, can be correlated with better outcomes when it represents integrating information between different sources or locations [27]. Node connectivity is equal to the minimum number of nodes that must be removed to disconnect the parts of a network or render it a disconnected graph [5,15].

Entropy measures [25] are less frequently used than the other mentioned metrics. Prior work has shown that entropy measures are predictive of pilot training performance [11] and correlated with learning under time pressure in an ESL learning context [23]. The present research expands the use of entropy metrics to a longitudinal context. Stationary entropy quantifies aspects of the typical heat map representations of eye tracking by capturing the distribution of eye gazing across different AOIs. Transition entropy measures unpredictability or randomness in the sequence of transitions. Eye tracking research in medical education with intermediate learners and experts has shown that transition entropy decreases with expertise, as does stationary entropy [31].

Analysis of Time Series Data and Data Visualization. When analyzing longitudinal data, methodologists emphasize the importance of inspecting patterns of change visually [40] or quantitatively. In our data, visual inspection of time series plots of all network analysis metrics suggested 1) a general decreasing trend for each metric within each session (examining ten X-rays also known as OPTs), suggesting that eye-gaze patterns were becoming simpler, and 2) increasing trendings of metrics across sessions, indicating that eye-gaze patterns were reverting to more complex patterns, with a great deal of variability in the data. Thus, we decided to use time series analysis to deal with large within-person variability in network metrics at closely spaced measurement times [20]. To implement that, we used a k-means-based time series clustering method to analyze longitudinal eye-gaze data. The k-means-based approach encompasses a family of machine learning algorithms designed to group data points into distinct clusters based on similarity. Each cluster is represented by a "centroid," which is the average position of all points in the group. The k-means-based approach has been widely used for both classification and clustering tasks, demonstrating reliable performance in analyzing behavioral data such as physical exercise and study time [6]. Since our objective is to test for latent classes within time series data, we used unsupervised k-means clustering algorithms to identify groups within the dataset. Specifically, we leverage the tslearn library in Python for time series clustering. Given that our dataset includes time series of varying lengths, we adopt the dynamic time warping (DTW) distance metric to compute averages across participants. DTW has been shown to provide more accurate similarity measurements for time series data than traditional Euclidean distance metrics.

To examine the relationships between network analysis metrics and participant performance, we use a generalized additive model (GAM) to fit a smooth curve to these non-linear data. This approach helps uncover temporal patterns in how network metrics relate to participant performance (i.e., detecting/annotating dental anomalies from the X-rays). GAM extends linear models to accommodate different data types, and facilitates the differentiation of fixed from random effects within a single model, providing flexibility and precision in analyzing complex relationships [17].

5 Results

We first report the time series clustering of students' network representations and the performance on identifying anomalies in the X-rays for students in each cluster. We then present our findings from statistical analyses of the relationship between network metrics and students' performance and explore indicators for varying students' performance.

5.1 Time Series Clustering of Students' Eye-Gaze Network Metrics over Time

Figure 2 presents the results of k-means-based clustering of participants' network metric scores for eleven network metrics. Each subplot illustrates the temporal evolution of a specific network metrics for participants within each identified cluster. The x-axis represents observation moments over time, and the y-axis denotes the normalized values of the respective metric.

Thin black lines in each subplot depict the individual trajectories of participants within the cluster, showing variability in their behaviors over time. The red line is the cluster-level mean trend for the metric, providing a visualization of the general pattern for participants in each cluster on each metric.

The results show distinct patterns in network metrics across clusters. For example, metrics such as Node Connectivity display trends across the three

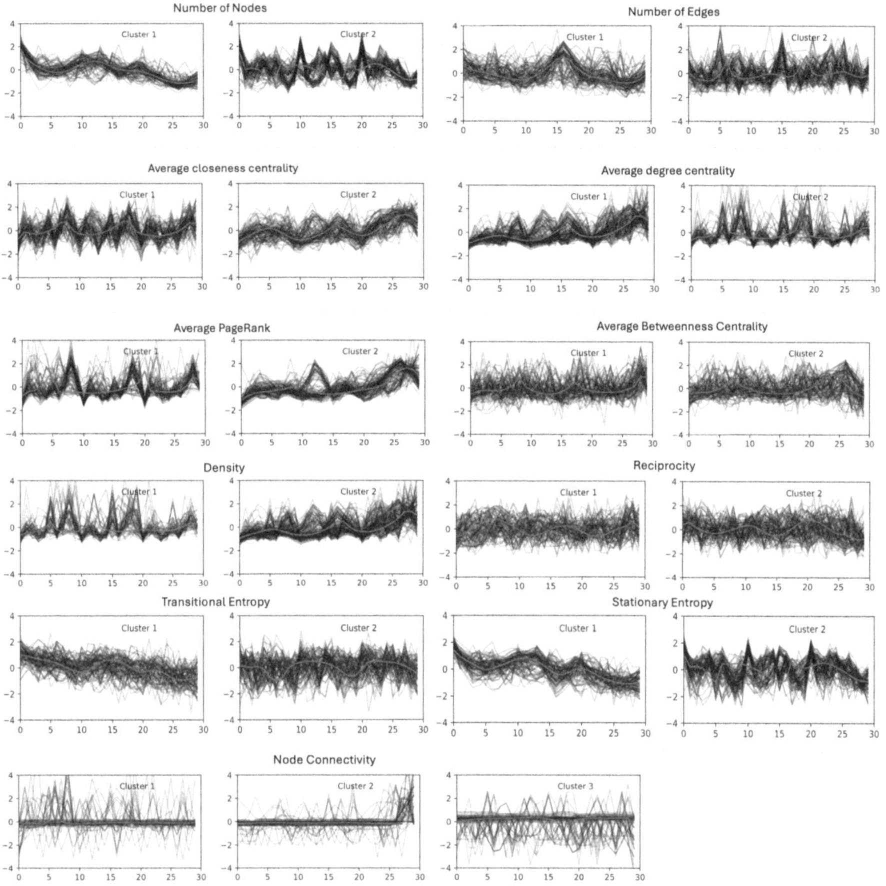

Fig. 2. K-means-based clustering of participants based on eleven network metrics.

clusters: Cluster 1 shows a pattern of decrease over time, Cluster 2 shows an increasing trend, and Cluster 3 shows a relative stable trend in Fig. 2. Cluster numbers are arbitrary and do not imply any ordinal relationship. Similarly, variations in the growth of metrics, e.g., for Reciprocity and Density, suggest potential differences in participants' diagnostic strategies or task engagement, which we will show to be related to performance in Sect. 5.3. Metrics such as the number of nodes and the number of edges demonstrate more similar trends between clusters, but still exhibit observable differences at certain time intervals, suggesting variations in learning processes.

5.2 BFD Performance Comparison Across Time (ANOVA)

Following the clustering of students based on network metrics calculated over networks representing the students' scan paths when visually inspecting X-rays, we compared their post-experiment performance across eleven metrics using an ANOVA (see Table 1 for results). Significant differences were observed for node connectivity ($F = 4.205$, $p = 0.015$) and reciprocity ($F = 4.462$, $p = 0.035$), indicating that students with better performance may exhibit more sophisticated visual exploration strategies and deeper engagement with the task. Specifically, Cluster 1 for node connectivity showed a higher BFD score, and Cluster 2 showed a higher BFD for reciprocity, suggesting that these metrics may play a role in differentiating student performance across groups. However, there were no statistically significant differences between BFD scores among the clusters for the majority of the metrics we considered (see Table 1).

Results suggest that while most network metrics do not vary significantly between clusters, i.e., both patterns of change are equally adaptive in terms of leading to higher BFD scores, structural features such as node connectivity and reciprocity may be important indicators of group differences in post-experiment performance. Further exploration of the correlations of these metrics with learning outcomes could provide deeper insights into their relevance in student clustering and performance outcomes.

5.3 Prediction Models of X-ray Reading Performance Based on Network Metrics

We used regression (mixed linear model) to predict students' BFD scores from network metrics (see Table 2 for results). The analysis included 3,425 observations nested within 165 participants from the original dataset, with a mean group size of 20.8 (range: 10–50). The model successfully converged using the Restricted Maximum Likelihood (REML) estimation method (Log-Likelihood = −416.1442, Scale = 0.0617) using the *statsmodels* package in Python.

Table 1. Comparison of mean BFD scores across groups. N-Mean-1 refers to the mean of the normalized value for the corresponding metric in Cluster 1, and BFD-1 refers to the mean BFD score for Cluster 1. The other columns follow the same rule.

Metric	N-Mean-1	N-Mean-2	N-Mean-3	BFD-1	BFD-2	BFD-3	f-stat	p-stat
number of nodes	−0.0006	−0.0302	na	0.397	0.408	na	0.582	0.446
number of edges	−0.0097	0.0069	na	0.397	0.409	na	0.740	0.390
avg degree centrality	0.0007	0.0040	na	0.399	0.411	na	0.614	0.433
avg closeness centrality	0.0060	0.0014	na	0.403	0.403	na	0.002	0.960
avg pagerank	−0.0003	0.0125	na	0.398	0.407	na	0.385	0.535
avg betweenness centrality	0.0002	0.0170	na	0.407	0.399	na	0.287	0.592
density	0.0005	0.0040	na	0.381	0.412	na	3.723	0.054
node connectivity	−0.0040	−0.0092	0.031	0.398	0.381	0.429	4.205	0.015*
reciprocity	0.0012	0.0078	na	0.419	0.389	na	4.462	0.035*
stationary entropy	−0.0145	−0.0022	na	0.391	0.414	na	2.421	0.120
transition entropy	−0.0027	−0.0003	na	0.397	0.409	na	0.674	0.412

From the fixed effects portion of the model, we can see that the OPT Task Ordered Index ($\beta = -0.030$, $SE = 0.014$, $z = -2.209$, $p = 0.027$) and transition entropy ($\beta = -0.065$, $SE = 0.028$, $z = -2.291$, $p = 0.022$) are significant negative predictors of the normalized BFD score, suggesting that students with better performance tend to exhibit less random scanning paths when completing tasks. Conversely, the number of nodes ($\beta = 0.015$, $SE = 0.006$, $z = 2.761$, $p = 0.006$), number of edges ($\beta = 0.002$, $SE = 0.001$, $z = 3.398$, $p = 0.001$), and average PageRank ($\beta = 0.701$, $SE = 0.192$, $z = 3.651$, $p < 0.001$) were significant positive predictors, suggesting that students with better performance tend to explore more nodes and connections, and place greater visual emphasis on conceptually important AOIs. Other potential predictors, including average degree centrality, density, and reciprocity, were not significant (all $p > 0.05$).

6 Discussion

6.1 Is there a Relationship Between Network Metrics and Earning Performance?

We observe mostly linear changes in students' BFD scores and eye-gaze patterns over time. Among the eleven metrics we examined, transition entropy, number of nodes and edges, and average PageRank were significantly correlated with students' BFD scores. Changes in network metrics, including the number of nodes

Table 2. Predicting students' BFD score using network metrics

	Coef.	Std.Err.	z	P > |z|	[0.025	0.975]
Intercept	0.203	0.129	1.57	0.116	−0.05	0.457
Time	−0.03	0.014	−2.209	0.027	−0.057	−0.003
Stationary Entropy	0.042	0.022	1.93	0.054	−0.001	0.086
Transition Entropy	−0.065	0.028	−2.291	0.022*	−0.12	−0.009
Number of Nodes	0.015	0.006	2.761	0.006*	0.004	0.026
Number of Edges	0.002	0.001	3.398	0.001*	0.001	0.003
Average Degree Centrality	−0.256	0.164	−1.563	0.118	−0.577	0.065
Average Betweenness Centrality	0.115	0.069	1.669	0.095	−0.02	0.251
Average Closeness Centrality	0.082	0.074	1.109	0.267	−0.063	0.226
Average PageRank	0.701	0.192	3.651	0.001*	0.324	1.077
Density	0.509	0.324	1.57	0.117	−0.127	1.145
Reciprocity	0.069	0.045	1.556	0.12	−0.018	0.157
Node Connectivity	−0.004	0.003	−1.428	0.153	−0.009	0.001
Participant Var	1.293	0.94				
Participant x Semester Cov	−0.181	0.131				
Semester Var	0.026	0.018				

and edges, and average PageRank, suggest that participants are transitioning from an intermediate to an expert skill level in reading X-rays. The values of network metrics did not suggest that participants were following the recommended top-left-to-top-right, bottom-right-to-bottom-left inspection patterns [8].

Most of the participants in the dataset we reused could be clustered into one of two or three categories for each of the eleven network metrics, indicating different approaches to the task. However, performance mostly did not differ between clusters. Only node connectivity and reciprocity show significant differences in BFD scores across clusters. As reciprocity measures how likely nodes are interconnected, high reciprocity may be a signal of confusion in individual eye-gaze networks, which aligns with our observation that high reciprocity is associated with low student BFD scores. Higher node connectivity may indicate a higher modularity in the network, suggesting learners tend to organize gaze patterns into well-defined sub-areas of the display.

Transition entropy is low for the very efficient eye-gaze patterns of experts, and here we saw how entropy decreases with instruction. That is, the participants showed more random, exploratory scanpaths in earlier sessions and more directed scanpaths in later sessions, indicative of a shift toward having acquired visual expertise.

6.2 Enabling Personalized Feedback and Learning

As our study finds that certain gaze-based, network analysis metrics are correlated with X-ray reading performance, these metrics could also be adapted to actively intervene in students' learning processes. Without explicit external assessments, these metrics could provide self-assessment feedback to students during the learning process. Additionally, at different stages of learning, these network-based metrics could be used to actively track students' learning progress and enable personalized interventions when necessary. Although some studies have shown that gaze data can be used for AI-generated adaptive interventions to improve student learning outcomes [36], the integration of such interventions into real-time systems remains in its early stages, primarily due to the lack of high-quality data collected through non-intrusive and distraction-free methods. Our clustering and tracking of metrics over time also indicate that network metrics, such as transition entropy, number of nodes, number of edges, and average PageRank, significantly correlate with students' BFD scores. For domain-specific visual tasks, similar approaches could be applied to behavioral data to develop optimized or customized models.

From an instructor's perspective, such network metrics can also provide complementary evidence that may be invisible through traditional assessments, such as tests, to track students' learning progress in visually oriented tasks. Even outside of the context of a specific assignment, changes in students' visual behaviors can serve as a valuable source for evaluating learning progress.

Another consideration for personalized feedback is model transparency. Compared to deep learning-based approaches, our method has lower computational complexity and greater transparency. Network metrics can be traced back to visual network representations, providing an explainable link between NA metrics, BFD scores, and students' behaviors.

7 Limitations and Future Work

As far as we know, this study is the first work to apply network analytic metrics to relationally represented eye-gaze data in a longitudinal setting. There are some improvements to be made in future work. First, we were not able to use the whole dataset due to model restrictions on analyzing varying-length time-series data. Future work should explore a neural temporal encoder approach to analyze the whole dataset. Second, lacking information about the difficulty level of the X-ray tasks may introduce bias into the analyses. Subsequent work should apply IRT scaling to create weights for different OPT tasks. Finally, the expertise level of participants is unknown to us, which makes it difficult to make strong claims in our interpretation of what the changes in network metrics mean. The data we used were anonymized in the original dataset and hence cannot be re-identified. More developmental eye-tracking studies are needed to understand the progression from novice to intermediate to expert.

8 Conclusions

We demonstrated that network metrics calculated on eye-gazing data, such as transition entropy, number of nodes or edges, and average PageRank, are correlated with X-ray reading performance and track the development of visual expertise in dentistry students. Observed changes in these metrics suggest a shift from intermediate to expert-like search patterns, while clustering reveals distinct developmental trajectories. Our findings highlight the potential of using gaze-based metrics for real-time, self-assessment feedback and personalized learning interventions in visual learning tasks.

Acknowledgment. Pingjing Yang is working in the Social Computing Lab, led by Professor Jana Diesner, at the University of Illinois at Urbana-Champaign. This work is conducted under the mentorship of Professor Jennifer Cromley in the College of Education at the University of Illinois at Urbana-Champaign. The research was supported with funds from the US National Science Foundation under Award No. 2225298 to the University of Illinois at Urbana-Champaign. Any opinions, findings, and conclusions or recommendations expressed in this material are those of the authors and do not necessarily reflect the views of the National Science Foundation.

References

1. Ashraf, H., Sodergren, M.H., Merali, N., Mylonas, G., Singh, H., Darzi, A.: Eye-tracking technology in medical education: a systematic review. Med. Teach. **40**(1), 62–69 (2018)
2. Bernard, H.R., Wutich, A., Ryan, G.W.: Analyzing Qualitative Data: Systematic Approaches. SAGE Publications (2016)
3. Black, M.M., Krishnakumar, A.: Predicting longitudinal growth curves of height and weight using ecological factors for children with and without early growth deficiency. J. Nutr. **129**(2), 539S-543S (1999)
4. Borchers, C., Eder, T.F., Richter, J., Keutel, C., Huettig, F., Scheiter, K.: A time slice analysis of dentistry students' visual search strategies and pupil dilation during diagnosing radiographs. PLoS ONE **18**(6), e0283376 (2023)
5. Cela, K.L., Sicilia, M.Á., Sánchez, S.: Social network analysis in e-learning environments: a preliminary systematic review. Educ. Psychol. Rev. **27**, 219–246 (2015)
6. Chang, W., et al.: Analysis of university students' behavior based on a fusion k-means clustering algorithm. Appl. Sci. **10**(18), 6566 (2020)
7. Chanijani, S.S.M., Klein, P., Bukhari, S.S., Kuhn, J., Dengel, A.: Entropy based transition analysis of eye movement on physics representational competence. In: Proceedings of the 2016 ACM International Joint Conference on Pervasive and Ubiquitous Computing: Adjunct, pp. 1027–1034 (2016)
8. Cosson, J.: Interpreting an orthopantomogram. Aust. J. Gen. Pract. **49**(9), 550–555 (2020)
9. Davalos, E., et al.: Identifying gaze behavior evolution via temporal fully-weighted scanpath graphs. In: LAK23: 13th International Learning Analytics and Knowledge Conference, pp. 476–487 (2023)
10. Dhengre, S., Nam, H., Helm, M., Rothrock, L.: Investigating effect of standardized total body skin examination using sequence-networks. Appl. Ergon. **116**, 104219 (2024)
11. Diaz-Piedra, C., Rieiro, H., Cherino, A., Fuentes, L.J., Catena, A., Di Stasi, L.L.: The effects of flight complexity on gaze entropy: an experimental study with fighter pilots. Appl. Ergon. **77**, 92–99 (2019)
12. Eder, T.F., et al.: How to support dental students in reading radiographs: effects of a gaze-based compare-and-contrast intervention. Adv. Health Sci. Educ. **26**, 159–181 (2021)
13. Eder, T.F., Richter, J., Scheiter, K., Huettig, F., Keutel, C.: Comparing radiographs with signaling improves anomaly detection of dental students: an eye-tracking study. Appl. Cogn. Psychol. **35**(4), 909–923 (2021)
14. Eder, T.F., Scheiter, K., Richter, J., Keutel, C., Hüttig, F.: I see something you do not: eye movement modelling examples do not improve anomaly detection in interpreting medical images. J. Comput. Assist. Learn. **38**(2), 379–391 (2022)
15. Esfahanian, A.H.: Connectivity algorithms. In: Topics in Structural Graph Theory, pp. 268–281 (2013)
16. Grub, A.S., Biermann, A., Lewalter, D., Brünken, R.: Professional vision and the compensatory effect of a minimal instructional intervention: a quasi-experimental eye-tracking study with novice and expert teachers. In: Frontiers in Education. vol. 7, p. 890690. Frontiers Media SA (2022)
17. Hastie, T.J.: Generalized additive models. In: Statistical Models in S, pp. 249–307 (2017)

18. Hostinar, C.E., McQuillan, M.T., Mirous, H.J., Grant, K.E., Adam, E.K.: Cortisol responses to a group public speaking task for adolescents: variations by age, gender, and race. Psychoneuroendocrinology **50**, 155–166 (2014)
19. Hua, Y., Fu, S., Lu, Y.: The effect of pilots' expertise on eye movement and scan patterns during simulated flight tasks. In: International Conference on Human-Computer Interaction, pp. 290–299. Springer (2022)
20. Huang, Q., Zhao, C., Zhang, X., Wang, X., Yi, D.: Centrality measures in temporal networks with time series analysis. Europhys. Lett. **118**(3), 36001 (2017)
21. Ifenthaler, D., Masduki, I., Seel, N.M.: The mystery of cognitive structure and how we can detect it: tracking the development of cognitive structures over time. Instr. Sci. **39**, 41–61 (2011)
22. Jayasinghe, A., Sano, K., Rattanaporn, K.: Application for developing countries: estimating trip attraction in urban zones based on centrality. J. Traffic Transp. Eng. (Engl. Ed.) **4**(5), 464–476 (2017)
23. Jónsdóttir, A.A., Kang, Z., Sun, T., Mandal, S., Kim, J.E.: The effects of language barriers and time constraints on online learning performance: an eye-tracking study. Hum. Factors **65**(5), 779–791 (2023)
24. Kakatkar, C., Spann, M.: Marketing analytics using anonymized and fragmented tracking data. Int. J. Res. Mark. **36**(1), 117–136 (2019)
25. Krejtz, K., Szmidt, T., Duchowski, A.T., Krejtz, I.: Entropy-based statistical analysis of eye movement transitions. In: Proceedings of the Symposium on Eye Tracking Research and Applications, pp. 159–166 (2014)
26. Leng, X., Wang, F., Mayer, R.E., Zhao, T.: How to train students to engage in text-picture integration for multimedia lessons. Br. J. Edu. Technol. **55**(3), 1167–1188 (2024)
27. Li, S., Pöysä-Tarhonen, J., Häkkinen, P.: Patterns of action transitions in online collaborative problem solving: a network analysis approach. Int. J. Comput.-Support. Collab. Learn. **17**(2), 191–223 (2022)
28. Loyola, P., Velásquez, J.D.: Characterizing web user visual gaze patterns: a graph theory inspired approach. In: Brain Informatics and Health: International Conference, BIH 2014, Warsaw, Poland, 11–14 August 2014, Proceedings, pp. 586–594. Springer (2014)
29. Ma, X., Liu, Y., Clariana, R., Gu, C., Li, P.: From eye movements to scanpath networks: a method for studying individual differences in expository text reading. Behav. Res. Methods **55**(2), 730–750 (2023)
30. Mason, L., Tornatora, M.C., Pluchino, P.: Do fourth graders integrate text and picture in processing and learning from an illustrated science text? Evidence from eye-movement patterns. Comput. Educ. **60**(1), 95–109 (2013)
31. Mozaffari, S., Klein, P., Viiri, J., Ahmed, S., Kuhn, J., Dengel, A.: Evaluating similarity measures for gaze patterns in the context of representational competence in physics education. In: Proceedings of the 2018 ACM Symposium on Eye Tracking Research & Applications, pp. 1–5 (2018)
32. Pianta, R.C., Belsky, J., Vandergrift, N., Houts, R., Morrison, F.J.: Classroom effects on children's achievement trajectories in elementary school. Am. Educ. Res. J. **45**(2), 365–397 (2008)
33. Richter, J., Scheiter, K., Eder, T.F., Huettig, F., Keutel, C.: How massed practice improves visual expertise in reading panoramic radiographs in dental students: an eye tracking study. PLoS ONE **15**(12), e0243060 (2020)
34. Rotgans, J.I., Schmidt, H.G.: Interest development: arousing situational interest affects the growth trajectory of individual interest. Contemp. Educ. Psychol. **49**, 175–184 (2017)

35. Ryabinin, K., Erofeeva, E., Guseva, K.: Eye tracking data mining based on fuzzy sets of fixations. In: Fuzzy Systems and Data Mining IX, pp. 11–19. IOS Press (2023)
36. Santhosh, J., Dengel, A., Ishimaru, S.: Gaze-driven adaptive learning system with chatGPT-generated summaries. IEEE Access **12**, 173714–173733 (2024)
37. Schieber, F., Gilland, J.: Visual entropy metric reveals differences in drivers' eye gaze complexity across variations in age and subsidiary task load. In: Proceedings of the Human Factors and Ergonomics Society Annual Meeting, vol. 52, pp. 1883–1887. SAGE Publications Sage, Los Angeles (2008)
38. Shiferaw, B., Downey, L., Crewther, D.: A review of gaze entropy as a measure of visual scanning efficiency. Neurosci. Biobehav. Rev. **96**, 353–366 (2019)
39. Silva, A.F., et al.: Differences in visual search behavior between expert and novice team sports athletes: a systematic review with meta-analysis. Front. Psychol. **13**, 1001066 (2022)
40. Singer, J.D., Willett, J.B.: Applied Longitudinal Data Analysis: Modeling Change and Event Occurrence. Oxford University Press (2003). https://doi.org/10.1093/acprof:oso/9780195152968.001.0001
41. Starke, S.D., Baber, C.: The effect of four user interface concepts on visual scan pattern similarity and information foraging in a complex decision making task. Appl. Ergon. **70**, 6–17 (2018)
42. Starke, S.D., Baber, C., Cooke, N.J., Howes, A.: Workflows and individual differences during visually guided routine tasks in a road traffic management control room. Appl. Ergon. **61**, 79–89 (2017)
43. Wickrama, K., Lee, T.K., O'Neal, C.W., Lorenz, F.: Higher-Order Growth Curves and Mixture Modeling with Mplus: A Practical Guide. Routledge (2021)
44. Zhu, M., Feng, G.: An exploratory study using social network analysis to model eye movements in mathematics problem solving. In: Proceedings of the Fifth International Conference on Learning Analytics and Knowledge, pp. 383–387 (2015)
45. Ziv, G.: Gaze behavior and visual attention: a review of eye tracking studies in aviation. Int. J. Aviat. Psychol. **26**(3–4), 75–104 (2016)

Personalizing Explanations of AI-Driven Hints to Users' Characteristics: An Empirical Evaluation

Vedant Bahel(✉), Harshinee Sriram, and Cristina Conati

The University of British Columbia, Vancouver V6T 1Z4, Canada
bahelvedant@outlook.com

Abstract. The paper extends an existing Intelligent Tutoring System (ITS) that supports students' learning via AI-driven personalized hints and can generate explanations to justify why/how the hints were generated. In this work, we investigate personalizing these hint explanations to students with low levels of two traits, Need for Cognition and Conscientiousness in order to enhance their engagement with the explanations, based on prior findings that these students generally do not ask for the explanations although they would benefit from them. We evaluate the effectiveness of the personalized hint explanations with a formal user study. Our results show that the personalization increases our target users' interaction with the hint explanations, their understanding of the hints, and their learning. Hence, this work contributes to exiting initial evidence on the value of Personalized Explainable AI (PXAI) in education.

Keywords: Explainable AI · Personalized Hints · Student Modeling

1 Introduction

There is growing interest in Explainable AI (XAI), namely making AI systems more human-centered by enabling them to explain their actions to their end-users. There is also mounting evidence that the need and effectiveness of these explanations may depend on user characteristics such as personality traits and cognitive capabilities [1–6].

These works suggest that it is important to investigate personalized Explainable AI (PXAI), namely enabling AI systems to personalize explanations of their behaviors to their end-users. In this paper, we contribute to this endeavor by investigating the personalization of the explanations generated by an Intelligent Tutoring System (ITS) to justify its pedagogical actions. The personalization targets two user characteristics: Need for Cognition, which measures one's inclination for engaging in cognitively demanding tasks [7]); and Conscientiousness, a personality trait measuring dedication to goals and effective task management [8].

A. I. Cristea et al. (Eds.): AIED 2025, LNAI 15877, pp. 411–423, 2025.
https://doi.org/10.1007/978-3-031-98414-3_29

To the best of our knowledge, only two other works so far designed and tested personalized explanations of AI behavior. Millecamp *et al.* [9] focused on personalizing explanations for users interacting with a music recommender system, which is arguably a less cognitively demanding task than learning with an ITS. The explanations are relatively simple combinations of texts and graphics. Similar to our work, Hostetter *et al.* [10] personalized the explanations generated by an ITS; however, their explanations consisted of simple one-shot sentences.

We contribute to these existing works by personalizing explanations provided during the cognitively demanding task of learning from an ITS, like in [10] but involving explanations that are much more complex as they span several pages combining text and graphics, that students can access incrementally. Our investigation leverages an existing ITS, the ACSP (Adaptive CSP) applet, which generates personalized hints that helps students learn how to solve constraint satisfaction problems [11] and can provide explanations on why/how each hint is generated. We personalize these hint explanations to students' levels of Need for Cognition (N4C) and Conscientiousness based on the results of previous work [1] showing that:

- Students with low Conscientiousness learned more from the ACSP with hint explanations than with hint without explanations, while the opposite was true for their high Conscientiousness counterparts.
- Students with low N4C showed reduced engagement with the hint explanations compared to their high N4C counterparts.

These results suggest that students with low N4C and low Conscientiousness (LNLC from now on) could benefit from personalization that encourages increased interaction with the ACSP's hint explanations, to counteract their tendency to disregard them (due to low N4C) and potentially improve their learning (due to low Conscientiousness).

We implement this personalization by presenting the hint explanations more proactively to LNLC students and adding prompts encouraging them to stay with the explanations if they try to dismiss them too soon. A preliminary study showed positive results on how users with LNLC benefited from our proposed personalization [12]. In this paper, we formally evaluate the proposed personalization with a controlled user study that compares it with the original non-personalized hint explanations in [1]. The study shows that the personalized explanations significantly increase the interaction of LNLC students with the hint explanations, their perceived understanding of the hints, and their learning from the ACS.

To summarize, this work contributes further evidence on the importance of investigating personalized XAI, namely personalizing explanations of AI behaviors to user differences, looking for the first time at explanations that are interactive, complex, and provided during a cognitively demanding task such as learning from an ITS.

2 Related Work

There is increasing evidence highlighting the impact of individual user differences on XAI effectiveness. Kouki *et al.*, [6] showed that users' preferences for item-centric, user-centric, or socio-centric explanations in a recommender system depend on their levels of the Neuroticism personality trait. Naveed *et al.,* [4] observed that users' decision-making style (rational vs. intuitive) affects their preferences for content-based or item-based explanations of recommendations when purchasing a camera. Schaffer *et al.*, [5] discovered that explanations of an AI agent's suggestions during a decision game benefited only users with low game proficiency. Millecamp *et al.*, [2, 3] investigated the impact of several user characteristics on the effectiveness of explanations for song recommendations. The recommendations were generated based on how well a song fits users' preferences along six song attributes (e.g., popularity and dance-ability), and for each recommendation, the corresponding explanation visualized this fit. Their works found that the effectiveness of these explanations depends on users' levels of openness (one's tendency to be open to new ideas and experiences), N4C, and musical sophistication. Conati *et al.,* [1] (the work that this paper builds upon) uncovered the impact of N4C, Conscientiousness, and Reading Proficiency on the effectiveness of explanations generated to justify the hints generated by the original ACSP applet.

Although the above results provide evidence for the need of personalizing XAI to user characteristics, work on implementing and assessing the effectiveness of personalized explanations is still limited. Kim *et al.*, [13] personalized explanations of the behavior of an AI-driven system (simulated) that helps patients and their clinicians manage a speech impairment. The personalization involved having two different levels of explanation detail, which were both showed to patient and clinicians. Patients preferred the less detailed explanations whereas clinicians preferred the more detailed ones. While this work focused on personalizing explanations to general user groups, Hostetter *et al.,* [10] and Millecamp *et al.*, [9] looked at individual user characteristics (UCs). Hostetter *et al.,* [10] evaluated personalized explanations for the suggestions generated by an ITS that helps students solve probability exercises. The ITS suggestions include solving an exercise independently, in collaboration with the ITS, or having the ITS solve it. The explanations conveyed why it is useful to follow each suggestion, and the explanation content was personalized to the student's learning attitude, namely learning-oriented vs efficiency-oriented. The explanations were conveyed with simple one-shot sentences. The results in [10] showed that these personalized explanations improve student learning.

Millecamp *et al.,* [9] looked at explanations for song recommendations, personalizing them to three user traits that were previously identified as impacting explanation effectiveness in this context, namely N4C, music proficiency, and openness ([2, 3]). The personalization involved both the delivery method (explanations were delivered either upfront with the recommendation or on-demand) and how much detail was included (i.e., just a sentence stating the similarity between the user music preferences and the recommended song vs. adding graphs to visually show the similarity). Their results indicated that users with low MS preferred the text-only explanations and those with low openness preferred the explanations that included the graphs.

The personalization we use in our work is similar to the upfront versus on- demand methods in Millecamp *et al.*, [9], but we investigated it in a very different context, involving both a more complex user task (learning) and much more complex explanations due to the complexity of the underlying AI, described in the following section.

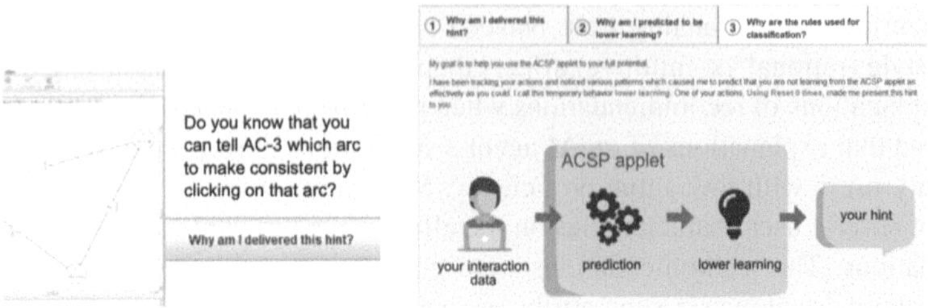

Fig. 1. (Left) An example of ACSP hint; (Right) The first page of the explanation interface that is activated by clicking on "Why I am delivered this hint?" at the bottom of the hint

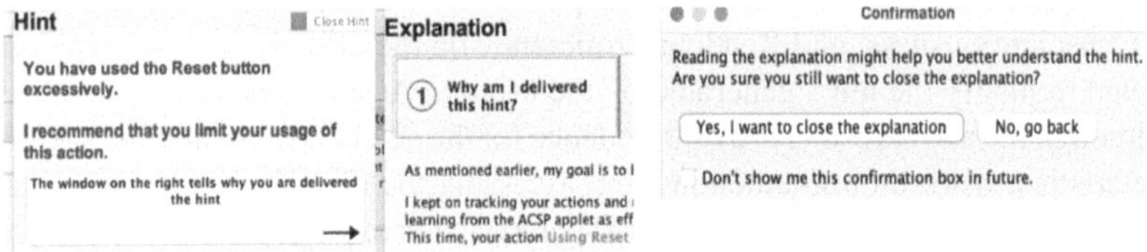

Fig. 2. (Left) Modified hint appearance for the explanation page appearing upfront with the hint; (Right) Confirmation box.

3 The ACSP Applet and Original Explanation Interface

The ACSP applet is an ITS that provides tools and AI-driven personalized hints to explore the workings of the AC-3 algorithm to solve constraint satisfaction problems (CSPs). The personalized hints scaffold a more effective usage of the available ACSP tools. For instance, Fig. 1 (left) shows a hint that suggests to the student a specific applet functionality that they have not used so far. The hints are generated leveraging FUMA (Framework for User Modeling and Adaptation) a framework for modeling and supporting open-ended exploratory interactions that combine several AI modules such as clustering, association rule mining, and rule-based classification [11, 14].

When a student receives a hint, they can access explanations of why and how it was generated by clicking the *"Why am I delivered this hint"* button at the bottom of the hint (Fig. 1, left), which brings up the first of a series of incremental explanations (Fig. 1, right). These explanations are automatically generated from the ACSP user model, and they are structured around 6 pages that explain different aspects of the underlying AI. The first three pages ("why" pages, accessible via the tabs shown in Fig. 1b) justify specific aspects of the rationale for a hint: "*Why am I delivered this hint?*", "*Why am I predicted to be lower learning*?", and "*Why are the rules used for classification?*". From the second why page, the user can access three pages ("how" pages, see Fig. 1c) that detail how specific aspects were computed: "*How was my hint chosen?*", "*How was my score computed*", and "*How was my hint's rank calculated*?". Full details on the original explanation interface can be found in [1].

4 Personalized Explanation Interface

Our goal is to find ways to increase LNLC users' interaction with the ACSP explanation. We do so with modifications to the original explanation interface aimed at increasing (i) access to the interface, and (ii) time spent in it.

Increasing Access: We tried two different approaches to stimulate access to the explanations when a hint is provided. The first approach involved disabling the possibility to close the hint for a brief period, during which the only option users have is to open the explanation interface. The second approach was to have the first page of the explanation interface open automatically when a hint is shown (*upfront delivery*, similar to [9]), instead of waiting for users to explicitly click on the "*why this hint*" button. We compared these approaches in a pilot study, which revealed that users favored the upfront delivery approach. The pilot study also uncovered ways to improve the upfront delivery approach: users indicated that, when the hint and explanation were delivered together, the explanation window was too prominent, causing them to look at it before looking at the hint and resulting in confusion. To address this issue, we enhanced the visibility of the hint by changing its font size and color, and we added a sentence below the hint saying, "The window on the right tells you why you are being delivered the hint" (Fig. 2, left). A follow-up pilot study showed that these minor adjustments helped users first pay attention to the hint and then to its explanations.

Increasing Time Spent in the Explanation Interface: To achieve this objective, we added a confirmation box that appears when a user tries to close the explanation interface too early after accessing it. To determine how early is "too early", we used the median time High N4C users spent in the explanation interface in the previous study [1] (i.e., 27 s) as they were the ones who paid substantial attention to the explanations. The text in the confirmation box conveys the value of reading the explanations and then asks the user if they would still like to close it (Fig. 2, right).

We ran a user study to evaluate whether these changes to the original ACSP explanation interface manage to increase LNLC users' interaction with it and subsequently their learning.

5 User Study

The user study had the same between-subjects design as in [1]. We recruited 39 participants by advertising at our university. Of these, 23 participants (9 females) were assigned to the experimental group where they used the personalized version of the ACSP explanation interface described in the previous section. The remaining 16 participants (9 females) were assigned to the control group who used the original version of the explanation interface. Similar to [1], participants were required to have basic knowledge of graph theory and algebra to learn concepts relevant to CSP. Participants were also required to have low N4C and low Conscientiousness. To find such LNLC participants, we asked those who replied to our advertisement to take standard online tests (also used in [1]) for N4C and Conscientiousness, namely the N4C test [7] (range $\pm$ 36) and the TIPI personality test [8] which includes scales for Conscientiousness (range 1 to 7).

We selected participants who scored below the median for these two tests. The median was computed using the N4C and Conscientiousness values from the 72 subjects in [1], resulting in a median of 0 for N4C and 5.5 for Conscientiousness. Which are consistent with values in the literature that use the same tests [15, 16].

It should be noted that, initially, we aimed to replicate the size of the user groups in [1] i.e., 30 users in the experimental condition and 17 in the control condition. However, our stricter selection criteria (requiring users to be LNLC) reduced the size of our target demographic by 70%, which together with constraints related to the scheduling of the academic terms required us to settle for a slightly smaller sample size for the experimental group.

Items of Usefulness	
E1	I would choose to have the explanations again in the future.
E2	I am satisfied with the explanations.
E3	The explanations were helpful for me.
Items of Intrusiveness	
E4	The explanations distracted me from my learning task.
E5	The explanations were confusing.
E6	I found the explanations overwhelming.

Items of Usefulness	
H1	I would choose to have the hints again in the future.
H2	I am satisfied with the hints.
H3	The hints were helpful for me.
Items of Intrusiveness	
H4	The hints distracted me from my learning task.
H5	The hints were confusing.
Items of Understanding/Trust.	
H6	I understand why hints were delivered to me in general.
H7	I understand why specific hints were delivered to me.
H8	I trust the system to deliver appropriate hints.
H9	I agree with the hints that were delivered to me.
H10	The hints appeared at the right time.

Fig. 3. Questionnaires on perception of the hint explanations (left) and the hints (right)

The study followed the experimental procedure in [1], briefly summarized here. Users first studied a textbook chapter on the AC-3 algorithm, and then they wrote a pre-test on this material. Next, they watched a video on how to use the main functionality of the ACSP applet and then solved three CSPs using their respective versions of the ACSP applet (i.e., either with the personalized or the original explanation interface). After interacting with the ACSP applet, users took a post-test analogous to the pre-test. Finally, users were asked to complete two questionnaires.

The first questionnaire elicited their opinions on the usefulness and intrusiveness of the explanations (Fig. 3 left) to ascertain how the personalized version compared with the original one with respect to these subjective measures. Users in the control group who chose not to open the explanation interface did not fill out this questionnaire as they did not see the explanations. Instead, they were prompted to respond to an open-ended question as to why they did not access the explanations. The second questionnaire elicited the users' opinions on the usefulness, intrusiveness, understanding/trust of the hints (Fig. 3 right) to determine if the personalized explanations affect this perception. Responses were provided on a Likert scale ranging from 1 ('Strongly Disagree') to 5 ('Strongly Agree'). The study took up to 2.5 h and users received monetary compensation.

During the interaction with the ACSP, users' gaze was tracked with a Tobii Pro X3 T-120 eye-tracker, which returns sequences of fixations, namely, points of attention to the screen. Out of the 23 users in the experimental group, 3 did not receive any hints during their interaction with the ACSP and thus they were removed from the data analysis, leaving us with 20 users in the experimental group moving forward.

All users in the control group received at least one hint during the course of their interaction. We evaluate the effectiveness of the personalized explanation interface for LNLC users by looking at: (i) impact on user interaction with the hint explanations; (ii) learning from the pre-test to the post-test; (iii) subjective perceptions of explanations and hints. We use the Shapiro-Wilk test (SW) to test for data normality, the two-sample unpaired t-test to compare data that is normally distributed, and the Mann-Whitney U test otherwise. The Mann-Whitney U test is also used for ordinal Likert-scale data. For all the statistical tests, a p-value of 0.05 was used to determine significance. We remove outliers using U $\pm$ 2SD.

6 Results on Interaction with the Explanations

We evaluate user interaction with the ACSP explanation interface by looking at.

- user access to both individual pages and to the different page types available (i.e. three types of "why" pages and three types of "how pages" as described in Sect. 3), derived from action logs.
- attention to the pages derived from eye-tracking data.

Because the first explanation page is presented upfront to users in the experimental group, they do not need to perform an explicit action to access it, unlike what they have to do to see subsequent explanation pages. To account for this discrepancy, we analyze users' interaction with first and remaining pages separately, where for the first page of the experimental group interaction is analyzed using attention to this page derived from eye-tracking data.

We start by looking at how long participants in the experimental group looked at the first explanation page. This information can be seen in Fig. 4, showing the distribution of fixation durations (in seconds) for all deliveries of the first explanation page to users in the experimental group. 'Dn' refers to the nth delivery of the page for a given user. Looking at the bars in blue (D1), which indicates the fixation duration on the first explanation page the first time it is delivered, we see that all users looked at this page for 5s or longer when they received it together with their first hint, except for one user who glanced at it for 1.6 s. These durations, not surprisingly, are higher for the first few occurrences (D1, D2, and D3) ranging from approximately 40s to 5s, and decrease for the subsequent occurrences (D4, D5, and D6) ranging from 5s to 0.8s.

Out of the 20 users in the experimental group, 14 (70%) accessed explanation pages beyond the first one, and they accessed an average of 5.1 pages (SD = 2.9) and 2.7 page-types (SD = 1.1). In the control group, where the first page of the explanation interface needs to be explicitly opened, 7 out of 16 users (43.8%) opened it. Of these 7, only 3 explored explanation pages beyond the first one. Of these 3 users, one had slightly lower access than the average experimental user (2 pages and 2 page-types accessed), one slightly higher (7 pages and 4 page-types accessed), and one substantially higher (10 pages and 5 page-types accessed). Interestingly, this last user showed negative learning gains. These results show that, overall, the control group had a lower interaction with the explanation pages than the experimental group in terms of access actions. To ascertain how this lower interaction reflects on users' attention to the explanation pages, we compare overall attention to the explanation interface (AE) as defined in [1]:

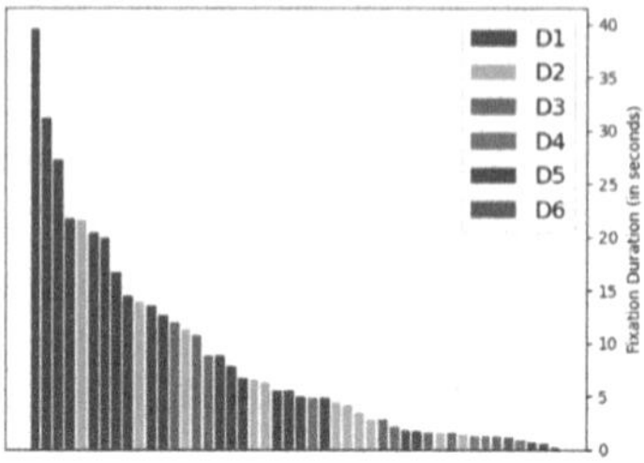

Fig. 4. Distribution of fixation duration (in seconds) for all deliveries of the first explanation page to users in the experimental group.

AE: total fixation duration on any of the explanation pages accessed, divided by the total number of hints received, to account for the varied number of hints received by different users.

For this analysis, we removed 3 users due to ET data loss (all from the experimental group) and 3 users for being outliers (one from the experimental and 2 from the control group), leaving us with 16 users in the experimental group and 14 in the control. The AE data showed a significant departure from normality. Hence, we conducted a Mann-Whitney U test to compare the AE values of the experimental and control groups. The test revealed that the experimental group had a statistically higher AE (M = 34.1 s, SD = 26.3 s) than the control group (M = 6.6 s, SD = 18.4 s) with a large effect size (U (30) = 20, $p = 0.001$, r[1] = 0.70). This result indicates that, overall, users in the experimental group not only accessed more explanation pages but also paid more attention to them. Table 1 reports the statistics for the AE values computed separately for the first explanation page and the following ones.

Table 1. Mean and standard deviation of AE for first and other pages (in seconds).

Condition	N	AE first Page Mean (SD)	N	AE other pages Mean (SD)
Control	6	13 (12.3)	3	139 (108.0)
Experimental	16	12 (8.5)	14	37 (53.0)

The table shows comparable average AE values for the first page between the 6 control users who explicitly accessed it (13s) and the 16 experimental users to whom it was delivered up front (12s). This suggests that showing the first explanation page upfront in the experimental condition elicits similar levels of attention to those shown by users who willingly chose to access the explanations in the control group. The table also shows that the average AE to other pages is much higher for the 3 users in the control group than for the 14 users in the experimental group. However, this large difference is primarily driven by two control group users who have exceptionally large AEs, namely

[1] Effect size range: r: 0.1 (small), 0.3 (medium), 0.5 (large).

171s and 227s respectively, where the latter AE is for the user who showed very high page accesses as discussed earlier. These two users are effectively outliers when AEs to other pages are computed over the experimental and control groups combined, and they both showed very low learning. In summary, the results in this section show that the personalized explanation interface succeeded in increasing LNLC users' interaction with it, in terms of both access and attention.

We also investigated to what extent this increase is due to the confirmation box we added to warn users in the experimental group if they prematurely tried to close the explanation interface. To do so, we analyzed users' responses to this box. Ten out of the 20 users in the experimental group received the confirmation box. Out of these 10, 7 dismissed it, while the remaining 3 stayed in the explanation interface for an additional 10, 20, and 28 s, and accessed 1, 3, and 5 additional pages respectively. These results indicate that, although the confirmation box was impactful for some users, it did not work for the majority who received it, suggesting that the upfront delivery of the explanation interface was the intervention that led to an increase in interaction with the explanations.

Finally, we asked the 9 users in the control group who did not engage with the explanation interface about their reasons and received the following responses: 2 wished to concentrate on solving the CSP problem without being distracted, 3 did not notice the button to open the explanation interface, and 4 did not perceive a need for explanations. The latter two issues could possibly be addressed by the personalized explanation interface that was used by the experimental group where the first explanation page is delivered upfront with the hint, which eliminates the need to click on a button to open the explanation interface and potentially demonstrates the relevance of the explanations to those who don't perceive it a priori.

7 Results on Learning Gains

We measure users' learning using percentage learning gains (PLG) namely, the difference between post-test and pre-test scores, divided by the absolute value of the maximum possible difference between the pre-test and post-test scores. After removing one outlier from both control and experimental groups, the PLG values were found to be normally distributed. A two-sample unpaired t-test to compare the PLG values of the control and experimental groups revealed that the experimental group had a statistically higher PLG ($M = 0.7$, $SD = 0.2$) than the control group ($M = 0.2$, $SD = 0.1$) with a very large effect size ($t(32) = -8.34$, $p < 0.001$, d[2] $= 2.88$) (means shown in Fig. 5).

Together with the increased interaction of the experimental group with the explanation interface, this result indicates a possible relationship between users' amount of engagement with the explanations and their learning. To look more into this possible relationship, we performed a Spearman's rank correlation analysis of the AE and PLG values from all users (irrespective of whether they were from the control or experimental groups), as this correlation should not be affected by the delivery method. The analysis showed a significantly moderate correlation between AE and PLG ($r_s(28)$[3] $= 0.5$,

[2] Effect size range: Cohen's d: 0.2 (small), 0.5 (medium), 0.8 (large), 1.2 (very large).

[3] Correlation range for Spearman's correlation: r_s: 0.4 to 0.59 (moderate), 0.6 to 0.79 (strong), 0.8 to 1 (very strong).

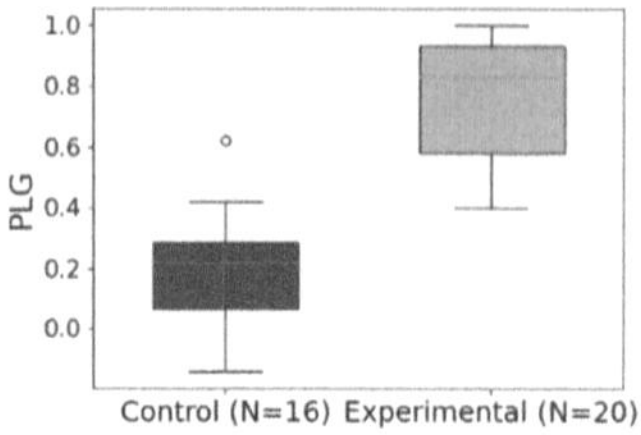

Fig. 5. PLG averages for the users in both the groups.

p = 0.007). Although correlation does not imply causation, this result suggests that it is worthwhile to further investigate whether higher interaction with the explanations (which is the focus of the personalized explanation interface in the ACSP applet) leads to higher learning, by collecting more data to conduct a Structural Equation Modelling (SEM) analysis.

8 Results on Subjective Measures

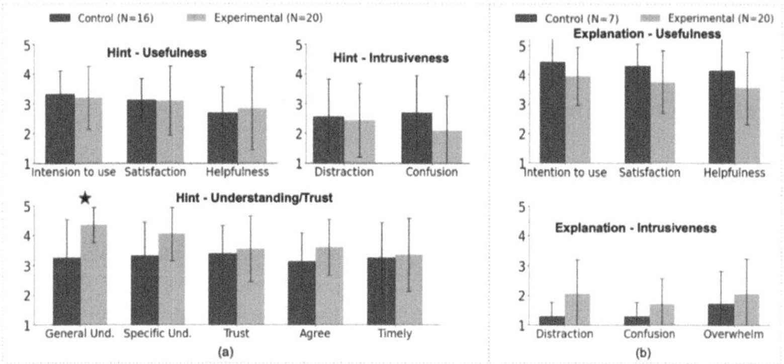

Fig. 6. (Left) Subjective ratings of hints. * Indicates a statistical difference between the control and experimental groups). (Right) Subjective ratings of explanations.

Subjective Ratings of Hints: To evaluate the impact of personalizing the hint explanations on users' perception of the ACSP hints, we compared subjective ratings from the questionnaire on hint perception (see Fig. 3, right) between the experimental and control groups. These ratings are shown in Fig. 6 (left), where they are grouped into three sets of questionnaire items: items related to Usefulness, Intrusiveness, and Understanding/Trust. All comparisons are done with a Wilcoxon-Mann-Whitney test, which is suitable for ordinal ratings. False Discovery Rate corrections are made within each set of questions to account for multiple comparisons. We observe that the ratings for Usefulness and Intrusiveness are generally similar, except for a non-significant trend of lesser confusion on the hints for the experimental group, with medium effect size (r[1] =

0.35). For Understanding/Trust, we find a significant difference with a large effect size for General Understanding ($U = 238.5$, $p = 0.04$, $r^1 = 0.74$) and a non-significant trend with a large effect size for Specific Understanding ($U = 222$, $p = 0.09$, $r^1 = 0.69$), both with higher values for the experimental group.

Subjective Ratings of Explanations: Figure 6 (right) shows the average ratings provided by users in the two groups for the questionnaire (Fig. 3, left) probing users' perception of the explanation interface's usefulness and intrusiveness. The figure illustrates a trend wherein the control group gave better ratings (higher for usefulness and lower ratings for intrusiveness) compared to the experimental group. None of these trends are statistically significant, but there are large effect sizes for confusion ($r^1 = 0.62$) and distraction ($r^1 = 0.69$), which is not surprising because the explanation interface takes up screen space and covers parts of the CSP question being solved. Regardless, the average ratings provided by the experimental group still translate to positive sentiments for all aspects i.e., greater than 3.5 for ratings on usefulness and lower than 2 for intrusiveness.

9 Discussion

Our findings show that personalizing the explanations for AI-drive hints in the ACSP applet for LNLC users significantly increases their interaction with the explanations. Specifically, only about 44% of the 16 control users accessed the explanation interface and only 3 went beyond the first explanation page. In contrast, 70% of the 20 users in the experimental group willingly accessed pages beyond the one presented upfront. Users in the experimental group not only accessed more explanation pages but also paid more attention to them, resulting in higher overall attention to explanation pages compared to the control group. Our results also revealed that the users who worked with the personalized explanations showed significantly higher learning gains compared to the control group, which is of paramount importance as the principal objective of an ITS is to improve learning. Finally, we found that the personalized explanation interface improves users' perceived understanding of the AI-driven hints compared to the original explanation interface, which is consistent with the fact that these users interacted with the explanations more and the explanations justify the reasoning underlying the hints.

The increase in learning gains and perceived hint understanding comes with trends of lower ratings for the personalized explanations, especially for distraction and confusion, although the differences are not significant and the ratings are still positive overall.

To understand the reasons for these trends, at the end of the study we asked the 6 users in the experimental group who gave ratings higher than 3 for confusion and distraction the reasons for these ratings. Two users considered the explanations to be too verbose, 2 deemed the hint to be insignificant and, thus, perceived the corresponding explanations to be not meaningful, and 2 found that the hints and explanation interface appeared too often. The first two reasons relate to the content of the hints and their explanations, which were unchanged between the personalized and the original explanation interface. The concern regarding the frequency of explanations is understandable in the personalized interface, where the delivery of bulky explanations along with the hints can be easily perceived as intrusive. One way to address this concern may be to monitor users' attention to the first explanation page and make the explanations accessible on demand if there is a trend of decreasing attention.

We also investigated the reasons for the limited impact of the confirmation box we added to the personalized explanation interface to warn users who tried to close the explanation interface too quickly. We found that 4 of the 7 users who dismissed the confirmation box had previously accessed the explanation interface for longer than the threshold that makes the box appear (27 s). As these users had already seen the explanations and parts of the explanation content stay the same for different hints, they likely needed less time to process subsequent explanations. Hence, they should not have been asked to stay longer. To address this issue, the threshold for triggering the confirmation box should be adjusted to take into account previous viewing of the explanations.

Finally, we asked the 9 users in the control group who did not engage with the explanation interface about their reasons and received the following responses: 2 wished to concentrate on solving the CSP problem without being distracted, 3 did not notice the button to open the explanation interface, and 4 did not perceive a need for explanations. The latter two issues could possibly be addressed by the personalized explanation interface, since the upfront delivery of the first explanation page with the hint eliminates the need to click on a button to open it and potentially demonstrates the relevance of the explanations to those who don't perceive it a priori.

10 Conclusion and Future Work

In this work, we investigated personalizing the explanations provided by the ACSP tutoring system to justify the hints that it generates to foster student learning. The personalization targets students with low levels of Need for Cognition and Conscientiousness and aims to enhance their engagement with the explanations based on prior findings that these students do not naturally engage with the explanations but they would benefit from them if they do. The personalization consists of delivering a first level of explanation together with the corresponding hint and warn students when they try to leave the explanations too quickly. We showed that the personalized explanations significantly increased users' interaction with the explanations, their perceived understanding of the hints, and their learning.

Although in this paper the personalization is not yet done automatically by the AI, we argue that our results are still significant because they provide new evidence of the benefits of Personalized XAI, showing that personalized explanations can help users with specific traits. Previous work demonstrated these benefits for relatively simple explanations in a less cognitively demanding task (interacting with a music recommender) or, like us, in the more complex task of learning but still involving very simple one-shot explanations.

Moving forward, we will investigate the improvements suggested by our study to reduce the possible distraction/confusion of the upfront delivery and to increase the usefulness of the confirmation box. We also want to dynamically personalize the ACSP explanations by building classifiers that can detect relevant user traits during the interaction, based on existing work on the real-time detection of personality traits and cognitive abilities from multi-modal data such as interface actions (e.g., [17]) and eye-tracking data (e.g., [3]).

References

1. Conati, C., Barral, O., Putnam, V., Rieger, L.: Toward personalized XAI: a case study in intelligent tutoring systems. Artif. Intell. **298**, 103503 (2021)
2. Millecamp, M., Htun, N.N., Conati, C., Verbert, K.: To explain or not to explain: the effects of personal characteristics when explaining music recommendations. In: Proceedings of the 24th International Conference on Intelligent User Interfaces, pp. 397–407 (2019)
3. Millecamp, M., Htun, N.N., Conati, C., Verbert, K.: What's in a user? Towards personalising transparency for music recommender interfaces. In: Proceedings of the 28th ACM Conference on User Modeling, Adaptation and Personalization, pp. 173–182 (2020)
4. Naveed, S., Donkers, T., Ziegler, J.: Argumentation-based explanations in recommender systems: Conceptual framework and empirical results. In: Adjunct Publication of the 26th Conference on User Modeling, Adaptation and Personalization, pp. 293–298 (2018)
5. Schaffer, J., O'Donovan, J., Michaelis, J., Raglin, A., Höllerer, T.: I can do better than your AI: expertise and explanations. In: Proceedings of the 24th International Conference on Intelligent User Interfaces, pp. 240–251 (2019)
6. Kouki, P., Schaffer, J., Pujara, J., O'Donovan, J., Getoor, L.: Personalized explanations for hybrid recommender systems. In: Proceedings of the 24th International Conference on Intelligent User Interfaces, pp. 379–390 (2019)
7. Cacioppo, J.T., Petty, R.E., Feng Kao, C.: The efficient assessment of need for cognition," J. Pers. Assess. **48**(3), 306–307 (1984)
8. Rothmann, S., Coetzer, E.P.: The big five personality dimensions and job performance. SA J. Ind. Psychol. **29**(1), 68–74 (2003)
9. Millecamp, M., Conati, C., Verbert, K.: 'Knowing me, knowing you': personalized explanations for a music recommender system. User Model User-adapt Interact **32**(1–2), 215–252 (2022)
10. Hostetter, J.W., Conati, C., Yang, X., Abdelshiheed, M., Barnes, T., Chi, M.: XAI to increase the effectiveness of an Intelligent Pedagogical Agent. In: Proceedings of the 23rd ACM International Conference on Intelligent Virtual Agents, pp. 1–9 (2023)
11. Kardan, S., Conati, C.: Providing adaptive support in an interactive simulation for learning: An experimental evaluation. In: Proceedings of the 33rd Annual ACM Conference on Human Factors in Computing Systems, pp. 3671–3680 (2015)
12. Bahel, V., Sriram, H., Conati. C.: Initial results on personalizing explanations of AI hints in an ITS. In: Proceedings of the 32nd ACM Conference on User Modeling, Adaptation and Personalization, pp. 244–248 (2024)
13. Kim, M., Kim, S., Kim, J., Song, T.-J., Kim, Y.: Do stakeholder needs differ?-Designing stakeholder-tailored Explainable Artificial Intelligence (XAI) interfaces. Int. J. Hum. Comput. Stud. **181**, 103160 (2024)
14. Kardan, S.: A data mining approach for adding adaptive interventions to exploratory learning environments. University of British Columbia (2017)
15. Thomson, K.S., Oppenheimer, D.M.: Investigating an alternate form of the cognitive reflection test. Judgm. Decis. Mak. **11**(1), 99–113 (2016)
16. Gosling, S.D., Rentfrow, P.J., Swann, W.B., Jr.: A very brief measure of the Big-Five personality domains. J. Res. Pers. **37**(6), 504–528 (2003)
17. Küster, L., Trahms, C., Voigt-Antons, J.-N.: Predicting personality traits from touchscreen based interactions. In: 2018 Tenth international conference on quality of multimedia experience (QoMEX), pp. 1–6 (2018)

"[AI Peers] Are People Learning from the Same Standpoint": Perception of AI Characters in a Collaborative Science Investigation

Soo Hyoung Joo[1] and Eunhye Grace Ko[2(✉)]

[1] Teacher's College, Columbia University, New York, NY 10027, USA
shj2118@tc.columbia.edu
[2] School of Information, The University of Texas at Austin, Austin, TX 78701, USA
eko@utexas.edu

Abstract. While the complexity of 21st-century demands has promoted pedagogical approaches to foster complex competencies, a persistent gap remains between in-class learning activities and individualized learning or assessment practices. To address this gap, studies have explored the use of AI-generated characters in learning and assessment. One such attempt is scenario-based assessment (SBA), a technique that not only measures but also fosters the development of competencies throughout the assessment process. SBA introduces simulated agents to provide an authentic social-interactional context allowing for the assessment of competency-based constructs while mitigating the unpredictability of real-life interactions. Recent advancements in multimodal AI, such as text-to-video technology, allow these agents to be enhanced to AI-generated characters. This explanatory mixed-method study investigates how learners perceived the AI characters taking the role of mentor and teammates in an SBA mirroring the context of performing a collaborative science investigation. Specifically, we examined the Likert scale responses of 56 high school learners' perception of the AI characters, in terms of trust, social presence, and effectiveness. We also analyzed the relationships between these factors and their impact on the intention to adopt AI characters for future learning through PLS-SEM. Our findings indicated that learners' trust shaped their sense of social presence with the AI characters, enhancing perceived effectiveness. Additionally, the qualitative analysis further highlighted factors that foster trust, such as the credibility of materials and alignment with learning goals, as well as the pivotal role of social presence in creating a collaborative context. As an early study examining the role of AI characters in learning, this research contributes to the understanding of key factors influencing engagement with multimodal AI characters adding to the growing body of research on AI-assisted education.

Keywords: AI-based educational avatar · multimodal AI · large language models · Scenario-Based Assessment

S. H. Joo and E. G. Ko—Co–first authors (these authors contributed equally to this work).

A. I. Cristea et al. (Eds.): AIED 2025, LNAI 15877, pp. 424–437, 2025.
https://doi.org/10.1007/978-3-031-98414-3_30

1 Introduction

The complexity of 21st-century demands has led to the development of pedagogical approaches to foster complex competencies such as collaborative problem-solving and critical thinking [1], yet a persistent gap remains between learning activities in class settings and individualized learning or assessment practices [2, 3]. With the advent of Generative AI (GenAI) technology, studies have explored the use of AI-generated characters to promote the development and assessment of these competencies (e.g., [4]).

Given the novelty of this approach, investigation is needed to determine to what extent the interaction with these characters is conducive to learning, and if so, what aspects impact the quality of these interactions. Previous studies have examined various aspects of these characters, such as their voice (e.g., [5]), style of communication (e.g., [6, 7]), familiarity [5], and the credibility of the source materials, and how these factors influence learners' perceptions of AI characters [8] and, in turn, their intent to engage in further AI-driven education. However, many of these studies focus on chat-based interfaces, which—while promising—may limit inclusivity, engagement, and long-term learning effects, particularly for learners with short attention spans shaped by rapid-content platforms [9]. A shift toward multimodal AI can offer a more authentic and immersive learning experience.

One approach where multimodal AI-generated characters are increasingly adopted is scenario-based assessment (SBA), an assessment technique that attempts to both measure and foster the development of real-world competencies throughout the assessment process [10, 11]. Simulated characters play a pivotal role in SBAs, driving the scenario narrative and creating a social-interactional context that necessitates the purposeful deployment of real-life competencies [12]. Traditionally, these characters were represented through static images with voice-overs, which, while effective in structuring interactions, often lacked the realism necessary to fully engage learners [13]. Recent advancements in multimodal GenAI technology offer new possibilities for enhancing SBAs by integrating AI-generated characters. For second language (L2) learners, interaction with these AI characters is critical, as they can serve as valuable scaffolds in addressing the dual challenge of mastering complex scientific concepts while communicating in a non-native language.

As part of a larger effort to develop and validate a scenario-based language assessment for science purposes (SBLA-SP) incorporating multimodal AI-generated characters, this study investigates learners' perceptions of these AI characters in terms of social presence (i.e., the extent to which learners perceive the characters as real and relationally accessible), trust (i.e., the learners' confidence in the characters' reliability and helpfulness), and effectiveness (i.e., the perceived usefulness of the characters in supporting task completion and learning goals). Additionally, learners' intentions to adopt AI-supported learning and assessment in the future were examined. In this study, multimodal AI-generated characters—defined as characters created using Text-to-Video (TTV) technology combining synchronized visual (video) and auditory (voice) outputs —were presented to learners through pre-scripted recordings. 56 high school learners, learning English as an L2 to perform STEM practices, participated in this study. Although this study does not explore AI-generated characters that dynamically adapt to individual differences, it has implications for such contexts by highlighting how AI characters can provide personalized guidance for learning. This study contributes to AI-driven education by examining how trust and social presence shape learners' attitudes toward AI characters in learning and assessment. Accordingly, we explored the following research questions:

- To what extent do Korean high school learners perceive AI characters as facilitative of learning, in terms of their social presence, trust, and effectiveness?
- To what extent do high school learners' perceptions of AI characters' social presence, trust, and effectiveness influence their intention to adopt AI-driven assessments or instructional tools?

2 Related Works

2.1 Scenario-Based Assessment

The increasing emphasis on 21st-century competencies has fueled a growing need for assessments that measure learners' ability to meet competency-driven collaborative goals [11]. As an assessment technique to measure complex, competency-based constructs and support diverse learner populations [2], SBA has been extensively validated across multiple disciplines, including science and L2 [11, 13].

SBAs structure assessment tasks around authentic scenarios— a coherent narrative requiring learners to engage in thematically sequenced tasks that mirror expert cognitive processes and strategies. Central to these scenarios are simulated agents, who can function as mentors, offering instruction, or as collaborative partners, facilitating problem-solving. These simulated agents create a social-interactional context for authentic communication and collaboration. Unlike traditional assessments, which often avoid measuring complex competencies such as collaborative problem-solving due to concerns about reliability, SBA offers a structured yet psychometrically rigorous technique that elicits collaboration while mitigating the unpredictability of real-life interactions [11]. While simulated agents have been accounted for in SBA design in prior research [10, 12], their moderating role has not been systematically validated. Furthermore, previously these agents were presented through images of static chats and voice-overs, but these methods often lacked the authenticity necessary for full learner engagement [13]. Recent advancements in multimodal AI, including Text-to-Video (TTV) technology, allow the enhancement of these pre-scripted agents into AI-generated characters capable of richer interactions [14]. However, understanding learners' perceptions of these AI characters—whether they view these agents as mentors or peers, as intended—can provide insight into their effectiveness as interactive facilitators in assessment and learning. The next section reviews research on AI characters in education.

2.2 AI-Generated Characters in Education

As an attempt to foster engagement and address the diverse learning styles of learners across socioeconomic backgrounds [9], researchers have explored the use of AI-generated characters involving hyper-realistic synthesis of prose, images, audio, and video [4]. Prior research mainly explored how diverse aspects of the voices of the AI characters, generated with text-to-sound technology, influenced learners' learning experiences. Edwards et al. [5] examined how learners' perceptions of AI voice-generated virtual instructors varied by age, while Kim et al. [6] explored how different communication styles (i.e., functional vs. relational) influenced the levels of social presence.

Building on the advancement in multimodal AI, recent studies have e text-to-video, Pataranutaporn et al. [4] explored how familiarity with AI-generated instructors (e.g., historical figures vs. unfamiliar avatars) impacts learning, motivation, and attitudes. Their study underscores the importance of traceability and ethical safeguards in maintaining trust and credibility in AI-generated instructors. Furthermore, they emphasize the need for ethical guidelines, such as consent, transparency, and misinformation screening, to ensure the responsible integration of AI-generated characters in education.

Building on the shift toward multimodal, socially interactive AI characters, our study explores learners' perceptions of AI-generated characters in learning, with a focus on trust and social presence. As prior research highlights the importance of communication style, familiarity, and ethical considerations in AI-driven education, our study aims to further investigate how these factors influence learners' engagement and willingness to adopt multimodal AI characters as learning companions.

2.3 Trust in AI-Based Educational Platforms

Trust is a key driver of technology acceptance and adoption [23], playing a critical role in AI-based educational systems as it directly influences user acceptance and engagement [15]. Qin et al. [15] identified major categories of trust-related factors in AI-based education: (a) Technology-related factors, including functionality, helpfulness, interpretability, dependability, and interaction interface, and (b) individual-related factors, such as perceptions of learning, willingness to interact with teachers, views on AI, and autonomy orientation. These factors highlight the multifaceted nature of trust in AI education, extending technical reliability to include user perceptions and interactions. The importance of learners' perceived trust in AI education is further supported by Kim et al. [7], who found that higher trust in an AI instructor increases the likelihood of learners enrolling in AI-based courses. Similarly, Amoozadeh et al. [16] demonstrate learners with higher trust in GenAI reported greater motivation and confidence in their coursework. Building on these insights, our study explores whether trust serves as a fundamental factor in shaping learners' perceptions of AI characters as learning companions, ultimately influencing engagement, adoption intentions, and learning outcomes.

2.4 Social Presence in AI-Based Educational Platforms

Although definitions of social presence vary, most literature defines it as the perception of being connected with another entity in a mediated environment, where users temporarily overlook the presence of the medium itself [7, 17]. According to Gambino et al. [18], social presence is machines exhibiting more human-like behaviors or appearances that lead users to engage with them similarly to human relationships. In the context of AI-generated pedagogical agents in K-12 learning, social presence is crucial for creating an engaging and interactive learning environment as young learners can benefit from human-like interactions and emotional connection with the AI-generated characters [19]. Specifically, studies show that social presence plays a crucial role in relationship-building with AI instructors [7], and enhancing social presence has been linked to greater emotional engagement in human-AI interactions in teacher education [8]. Building on, our study investigates how social presence impacts learners' experiences with AI-generated characters and explores its influence on the intention to adopt AI characters.

3 Methods

This study employed an explanatory mixed-method associational design [20] to investigate L2 learners' perceptions of AI characters in an SBA and their intention to adopt future AI-driven assessments or instructional tools. This research employed a two-phase approach: (1) a Likert scale questionnaire within an SBA to quantify learners' perceptions and attitudes, and (2) open-ended survey analysis to deepen insights and validate patterns from the quantitative data. The survey examined how learners engaged with AI characters within the SBLA-SP.

3.1 Instrument: SBLA-SP

The instrument was the scenario-based language assessment for science purposes (SBLA-SP), designed to measure specific purpose language ability in the context of performing a scientific investigation. The SBLA-SP is designed to engage learners as part of a group solving a problem with AI characters, mimicking a collaborative process through a scenario aligned with real-life science practices—specifically, planning and carrying out investigations. Learners progress through a scenario narrative, designed to elicit the five key steps of scientific investigation: (1) asking questions, (2) generating hypotheses, (3) designing experiments, (4) collecting and recording data, and (5) analyzing and interpreting data. These steps culminate in the final task: writing a lab report. The SBLA-SP was developed and delivered via Qualtrics.

The AI characters in SBLA-SP serve as mentors and teammates guiding learners through the scenario narrative. The SBLA-SP situates the learners in an online science internship designed for high schoolers. The AI characters include the mentor, Ms. Rosie, guiding the internship, and teammates Anika and Jimmy, collaborating on the science investigation project (Fig. 1). This internship takes place in a virtual science lab, where learners research triboelectric nanogenerators (TENGs)—an energy-harvesting technology that utilizes electric interactions.

AI character videos were created on Synthesia (synthesia.io), a GenAI TTV platform, and embedded into Qualtrics using HTML. Among the repository of available characters and voices in Synthesia, selections were made to ensure that each AI character was representative of their assigned role within the scenario. For example, to reflect the international internship context, characters acting as peers were carefully selected to represent high schoolers of different nationalities and accents. Given that the test was designed for L2 learners, all video outputs were reviewed using an online CEFR analyzer from Cathoven Language Hub (https://nexthub.cathoven.com/cefr) to ensure that the speech was appropriately aligned with the target CEFR B1 (intermediate-low) level for listenability. The AI characters scaffolded lab report writing and facilitated scientific investigations by situating learners in a simulated collaboration through pre-scripted videos, where they co-planned an investigation and co-constructed a lab report. Also, they provided corrective feedback, which was pre-scripted and triggered by learners' selections on multiple-choice questions, offering personalized guidance to support the scientific investigation process (Fig. 1).

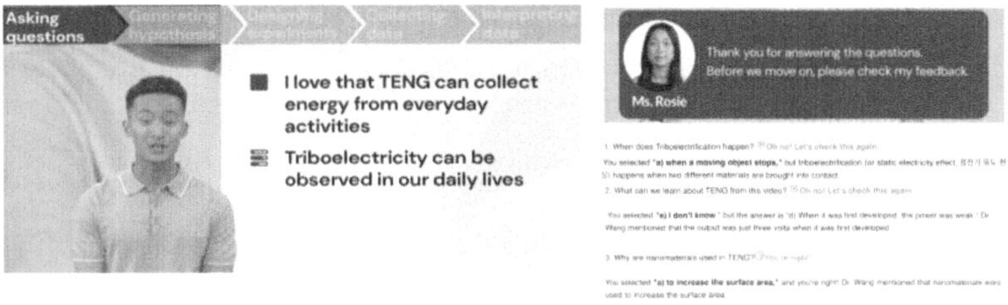

Note: A sample video of the characters can be found at: https://youtu.be/itwGiUIJI2Q

Fig. 1. AI Peer Guiding the Scenario Narrative (Left), Personalized Corrective Feedback Provided by AI Characters (Right). *Note:* A sample video of the characters can be found at: https://youtu.be/itwGiUIJI2Q

Embedded within the SBLA-SP is the perception survey to capture learners' perceptions of the AI characters (Table 1). Each dimension is assessed through 4-point Likert-scale items, adapted from established sources, with a total of 35 items. The survey also includes two open-ended questions for qualitative insights (Table 2).

3.2 Participants

As the SBLA-SP was designed to assess specific purpose language ability within the context of performing STEM tasks, 56 L2 learners pursuing the STEM track were recruited from high schools in South Korea, where English is taught as a foreign language through purposeful sampling [20].

3.3 Data Collection

The SBLA-SP was administered online via Qualtrics during a regular English class, with the teacher proctoring and addressing technical issues, while the researcher remotely monitored and assisted as needed. Before the test, the teacher informed learners that the assessment included simulated agents generated using AI technology, ensuring transparency about its use. The test was conducted on the Chrome browser, with learners using a computer, keyboard, and headphones. Learners were instructed to review and electronically consent to participate in the study. They completed the test within an hour, and the assessment platform automatically recorded their responses. The perception survey was embedded within the SBLA-SP and administered at three points during the test: before the scenario began, during the scenario following feedback, and after the test concluded. Also, the sample size (N = 56) was sufficient to meet PLS-SEM's 10-times rule.

Table 1. Taxonomy of the SBLA-SP perception survey by construct (k = 37)

Construct	Scale	Source	k
Tech Self-efficacy	To what extent are you open to adopting new technologies and tools (e.g., AI characters leading educational activities)?	Nass et al. [25]	3
Social Presence	To what extent did you feel like you were with the mentors and teammates?	Kim et al. [7]	8
Trust	To what extent did you trust the mentors, teammates, and their feedback?	Kim et al. [7]	12
Effectiveness	To what extent did the mentors and teammates help you learn?	Kim et al. [7]	8
Intention to Adopt	To what extent are you willing to take online classes or assessments involving AI characters?	Choi & Ji [24]	4
Total Likert Scale Items			35
Briefly describe how you feel about the mentor (Ms. Rosie) and her feedback			1
Briefly describe how you feel about the teammates (Anika & Jimmy) and their feedback			1
Total including Open-Ended Items			37

Table 2. Reliability analysis and descriptive statistics by construct (N = 56, k = 35).

	k	α	Min	Max	Mean	Median	SD
All Likert Items	35	.96	2.29	4.00	3.42	3.41	0.44
By Construct							
Tech Self-efficacy	3	.86	2.00	4.00	3.18	3.00	0.64
Social Presence	8	.96	1.00	4.00	3.30	3.38	0.70
Trust	12	.89	2.73	4.00	3.51	3.55	0.43
Effectiveness	8	.88	2.11	4.00	3.54	3.56	0.45
Intention to Adopt	4	.96	1.00	4.00	3.36	3.25	0.68

Note: Likert Scale (1 = Strongly Disagree, 4 = Strongly Agree)

3.4 Data Analysis

RQ1. CTT Investigating the Perception of AI Characters. To investigate Korean high schoolers' perceptions of AI characters as facilitative of learning (RQ1), the classical test theory (CTT) analyses followed by qualitative analyses were conducted. First, the descriptive statistics were analyzed on Likert scale responses across three key dimensions: social presence, trust, and effectiveness. These quantitative findings were then complemented and elaborated through thematic analysis of two open-ended survey questions that queried learners' experience with AI characters.

RQ2. SEM Assessing Learners' Intention to Adopt AI Characters. Building on Kim et al.'s [7] model examining how learners' perceptions of an AI instructor's social presence and trust influence their intention to adopt AI character-led education, we built an exploratory model to investigate how trust and social presence impact perceived usefulness and, in turn, influence learners' behavioral intention to adopt AI characters for learning (Fig. 2). To mitigate potential confounding effects from learners' baseline technological confidence, we controlled for technology self-efficacy. The initial model was optimized and the direct influence as well as the interaction of these constructs on the behavioral intention to adopt the AI characters for learning were analyzed utilizing the Partial Least Square Structural Equation Modeling (PLS-SEM) using SmartPLS v.3.3.2.

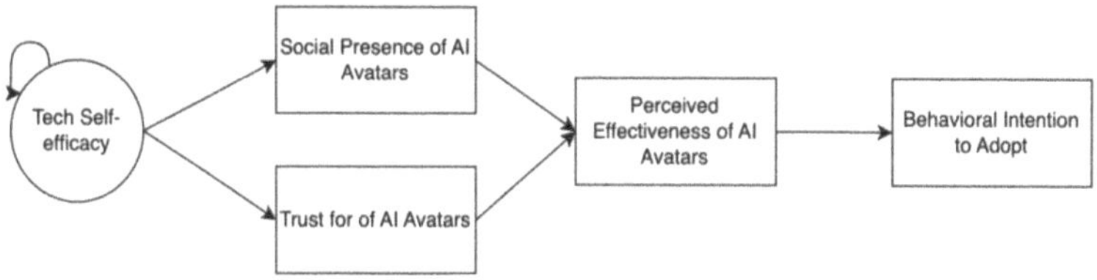

Fig. 2. Initial exploratory model with variables used in the study

PLS-SEM was chosen for its ability to combine ordinary least squares regressions with principal components analysis, which is ideal for emerging fields requiring both exploratory and confirmatory approaches [21] along with its flexibility with small-size data and its capability for causal-predictive modeling [21]. Instead of reporting model fit, which is not suitable for assessing PLS-SEM quality [21], this study validated the optimized model by evaluating construct validity, common method bias, reliability, and convergent and discriminant validity. The structural model's robustness was examined through bootstrapping and t-tests. Technology self-efficacy was measured via the survey and entered as a covariate in the PLS-SEM model, thereby controlling its confounding influence.

4 Results

4.1 RQ1. Perception of AI Characters

To investigate the extent to which Korean high school learners perceive AI characters as facilitative of learning the survey results were analyzed. The reliability analysis demonstrated excellent internal consistency across all constructs (overall $\alpha = .96$).

Analysis of the 4-point Likert scale survey revealed positive attitudes across all measured dimensions. Learners' perceptions of AI characters' effectiveness in facilitating learning were notably positive (M = 3.54, SD = 0.45), with responses trending toward strong agreement. This was closely followed by high levels of trust in AI characters (M = 3.51, SD = 0.43), suggesting learners viewed these digital entities as reliable and trustworthy learning companions. The social presence of AI characters was also perceived positively (M = 3.30, SD = 0.70), indicating that learners somewhat agreed that

AI characters could create a sense of personal connection in the learning environment. Learners demonstrated adequate tech self-efficacy (M = 3.18, SD = 0.64) and showed a positive intention to adopt AI learning (M = 3.36, SD = 0.68). All dimensions supported normal distribution while exhibiting a tendency toward positive ratings within acceptable thresholds. These findings suggest that the learners perceived AI characters as facilitative of their learning, with strong perceptions of trustworthiness, social presence, and effectiveness.

Also, open-ended questions were analyzed through deductive coding methods using social presence, trust, and effectiveness as pillars.

Social Presence (Realism and Naturalness) of AI Characters. Learners perceived AI characters as socially present and realistic. Many addressed the characters as "everyone" or "team members", showing a sense of high social presence. One noted, "As for the team members, even if they are virtual, they are people learning from the same standpoint, so I felt a bit more attached to them compared to the mentor." Others highlighted the immersive nature of the experience, stating, "It felt like actually doing it together," and "It was different because everyone was involved in the experiment." These responses suggest that learners recognized AI characters as active participants, making the experience feel interactive and engaging.

While some found the characters' feedback sufficient, others expressed a need for more bidirectional interaction. One appreciated the AI mentor's feedback, saying, "The fact that I can communicate directly with my AI mentor and that I can get corrections on what I write and apply them makes a big difference." However, others found the lack of two-way communication limiting, stating, "Knowing in advance that they are a virtual character and that it's not possible to have bidirectional communication makes it hard to have human emotions like attachment." Despite this, this learner acknowledged the constructive nature of AI mentor feedback, "However, I am willing to accept the mentor's feedback because it is constructive and practically helpful, and this has led to the formation of trust in the mentor."

Trust for AI Characters. Learners' perceptions of trust in AI characters were shaped by three key factors: trustworthy material provided by the characters, reliable explanations and feedback, and consistent accuracy in information delivery. Learners appreciated the AI characters' ability to retrieve and present relevant materials. One noted, "The materials presented by the team members helped me understand how to set up hypotheses and about triboelectricity, so I think they are trustworthy." Similarly, another highlighted the reliability of the feedback, stating, "It was good because they kindly gave trustworthy feedback." These insights suggest that learners are more likely to trust AI characters when they perceive them as accurate, consistent, and supportive in their learning process.

Effectiveness of AI Characters. Learners found AI characters effective in providing guidance, quality feedback, and learning support, which facilitated their learning experience. They appreciated the instructions AI characters provided, helping them navigate the learning process. One highlighted the effectiveness of feedback, stating, "With the simple explanations and feedback, I was able to better understand and correct my wrong answers." Others emphasized the supportive role of AI characters, with one noting, "It was fascinating and helpful to proceed with the AI avatar that provides assistance."

Additionally, AI characters were seen as helpful in problem-solving, particularly when they asked questions on behalf of learners, as one learner shared, "The way the team members asked the mentor about the difficulties I faced while solving the problem helped in resolving the issue." These insights demonstrate that learners perceive AI characters as valuable learning companions providing structured guidance, high-quality feedback, and interactive support.

4.2 RQ2. SEM Measuring Learners' Intention to Adopt AI Characters

The model validation was confirmed, with details on confirmatory factor analysis, reliability, and validity provided in Appendix A. Figure 3 shows the estimation results of the relationships between constructs in the optimized model, in which the path coefficients of the model are all statistically significant.

Unlike our initial model in Fig. 2, which predicted trust and social presence as simultaneous contributors to effectiveness, the optimized model revealed that trust strongly influenced social presence ($\beta = 0.65$). This underscores that trust in AI characters is a prerequisite for enhancing their perceived social presence. Also, social presence had a very strong effect on effectiveness ($\beta = 0.88$), meaning when learners felt socially engaged with AI characters, they perceived them as highly effective. Effectiveness significantly drove the intention to adopt ($\beta = 0.78$), showing that learners were more likely to embrace AI characters if they found them useful. The moderate (social presence, r2 = 0.44) to high r2 values (effectiveness, r2 = 0.76; intention to Adopt, r2 = 0.65) indicated that a large proportion of the variance was accounted for by the predictors. The non-significant paths of tech self-efficacy confirmed that individual technological confidence did not influence the variables.

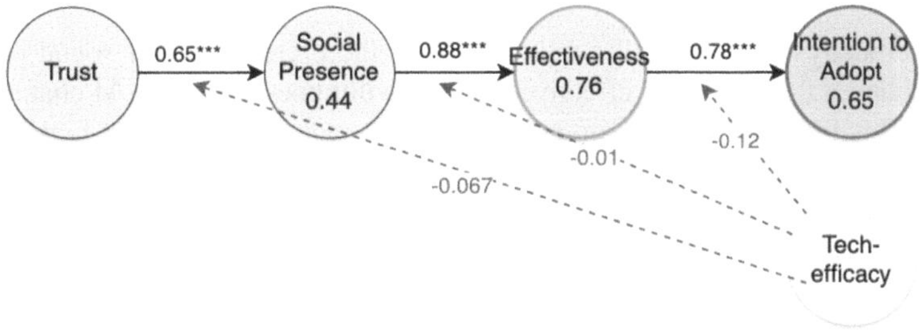

Fig. 3. PLS path model estimation: Bold arrowed lines show valid paths and coefficients, and dotted arrowed lines represent invalid paths. Numbers inside circles indicate r^2 values for constructs (p-values * < 0.05, ** < 0.01, *** < 0.001).

In Appendix B, we report standardized coefficients for direct and indirect effects to provide a comprehensive understanding of relationships in the PLS-SEM model. In sum, the model showed that trust and social presence play a crucial role in shaping learners' perception of AI characters' effectiveness, which in turn strongly influences their intention to adopt education involving AI characters.

Qualitative Responses on Intention to Engage with AI Characters. To further understand learners' intention to engage with AI characters, we analyzed their qualitative responses, revealing two engagement patterns: positive and conditional.

Most learners expressed enthusiasm for future adoption. One noted, "I learned about the technology TENG for the first time, and it was easy to understand as she showed and explained examples that can be found in everyday life. I look forward to activities with the mentor in the future." This suggests that the learner positively perceived the virtual mentor as an actual teaching presence showing high social presence, influenced by the usefulness of the information provided.

Others showed conditional intention, indicating that their engagement depended on improvements in AI interactions. One commented, "It was very unique and innovative….I am excited to see how much it will develop in the future. If there's a slight disappointment, I wish the feedback could be a bit more meticulous and detailed." This response refers to the AI character as "it" suggesting a lower level of social presence, and it highlights the further need for personalized feedback.

Overall, these findings indicate that while learners recognize AI characters' potential, their intention to engage largely depends on the quality of interactions, personalized feedback, and the level of social presence they experience.

5 Discussion

We explored learners' perceptions of multimodal AI characters, extending beyond chat-based interactions. We identified key features that enhance AI characters' effectiveness, offering two main insights for AI characters integration in education.

5.1 Trust as the Foundation for AI Characters in Learning

Our model analysis revealed that trust served as the prerequisite for social presence, which enhances the perceived effectiveness and willingness to adopt AI characters for learning. This finding extends Kim et al.'s [7] study demonstrating that higher trust in an AI voice was associated with a greater likelihood of enrolling in AI-based courses. Because multimodal characters combine synchronized visuals and speech, they naturally amplify social presence and raise users' expectations for human-like interaction—making trust even more pivotal than in text- or voice-only settings. We suggest that no matter how lifelike these characters appear, social presence cannot be fully realized unless trust is established. Thus, for multimodal AIs, trust is the foundation for engagement, effectiveness, and adoption.

To further explore what influences trust, we identified three key factors from the qualitative responses: (1) trustworthy material, (2) reliable explanations and feedback, and (3) accuracy in information delivery. These findings align with prior research by Amoozadeh et al. [16], which found that learners' trust in AI-generated characters declined when responses were incorrect, misleading, or unhelpful, often due to a mismatch in user expectations shaped by prior experiences with human instructors. This suggests that AI characters need to meet human-like instructional expectations to maintain trust. Additionally, Manzini et al. [22] argue that as AI assistants become more human-like, trust is further impacted by the alignment between the AI's objectives and the user's goals. Our findings support this, showing that AI characters were trusted when they provided relevant information aligned with learners' needs. In our study, AI characters had limited autonomy, only delivering human-generated instructions, feedback, and materials. Future implementations with greater AI autonomy, like real-time responses, will require strict safeguards against hallucinations through a combination of verification models, Retrieval-Augmented Generation (RAG), and a human-in-the-loop approach where humans remain accountable for source credibility [3]. Ultimately, we underscore that trust, developed through credible content and meaningful feedback, is a critical factor in AI character adoption, aligning with research on credibility in AI-driven education [23].

5.2 Social Presence and Collaboration with AI Characters for Learning

Our study highlights the importance of social presence, especially in a scenario simulating collaborative science investigation. When social presence was high, learners referred to AI characters as "everyone" or "team members," indicating that they viewed them as active collaborative partners in the learning process. Our learners reported experiencing stronger engagement when AI peers took the same perspective as them or acted on their behalf, mirroring human collaboration in educational settings. We found that the naturalism and realism of AI characters fostered a greater sense of social presence, which in turn enhanced perceived effectiveness. This aligns with prior research in human-AI interaction, which has established social presence as a key factor in relationship-building with AI. Machines exhibiting more human-like behaviors or appearances encourage users to engage with them similarly to human relationships [18]. Furthermore, AI systems that exhibit socially oriented behaviors, such as responsiveness combined with human-like qualities, are perceived as more capable [22]. While most prior research on AI characters has focused on their role as instructors [19], our findings emphasize the need for further investigation into AI agents that provide peer-like, empathetic interactions [7], which is particularly relevant for K-12 learners with shorter attention spans and diverse learning needs [9].

From an assessment development perspective, this study also demonstrates the potential of adopting AI characters to both foster and measure complex competencies such as collaborative problem-solving [1], which traditional assessments often avoid due to difficulties in controlling construct-irrelevant variance. The high social presence of these AI characters in our study suggests that their integration allowed structured yet dynamic social interactions that facilitate the assessment of competency-based constructs such as collaboration and critical thinking, aligning with the increasing demand for 21st-century skills [12]. By incorporating AI characters that facilitate discussion, reflection, and problem-solving, these assessments can enhance both validity and reliability while supporting the development of these crucial competencies.

In sum, our findings underscore that AI characters with high social presence not only enhance engagement and collaborative learning but also offer promising avenues for valid assessment of complex competencies, potentially transforming how we approach both instruction and evaluation in educational settings.

5.3 Limitations and Further Study

Several limitations of this study suggest important directions for future research. First, the AI characters in this study were pre-designed by humans, with the AI functioning only as a delivery mechanism for scripted content rather than dynamically generating responses. Future research should examine GenAI-driven interactive characters that can deliver real-time, adaptive feedback, allowing deeper insights into how trust and social presence evolve during authentic interaction. Second, while this study involved both AI mentors and AI peers, we did not conduct an extensive analysis comparing learner perceptions between these roles and did not isolate potential confounds introduced by role positions. Future studies should explore how assigned social roles influence learner perceptions independently of character behavior, using detailed qualitative analysis to disentangle potential confounds between AI capabilities and social framing. Finally, while this study captured learners' perceptions of AI character effectiveness, analyses of actual learning outcomes—defined as gains in science domain knowledge—will be reported in a future study to allow for a more comprehensive examination of the role of AI characters in promoting learning within the SBLA-SP. Taken together, these directions underscore how findings from this study can inform the thoughtful implementation of AI characters in learning and assessment, ultimately contributing to more responsive, personalized, and effective educational experiences.

References

1. OECD: PISA 2015 Collaborative problem-solving framework (2015)
2. Mislevy, R.J.: Sociocognitive Foundations of Educational Measurement. Routledge (2018)
3. von Davier, A.A.: Computational psychometrics in support of collaborative educational assessments. J. Educ. Meas. **54**(1), 3–11 (2017)
4. Pataranutaporn, P., et al.: AI-generated characters for supporting personalized learning and well-being. Nature Mach. Intell. **3**(12), 1013–1022 (2021). https://doi.org/10.1038/s42256-021-00417-9
5. Edwards, C., Edwards, A., Stoll, B., Lin, X., Massey, N.: Evaluations of an artificial intelligence instructor's voice: social Identity Theory in human-robot interactions. Comput. Hum. Behav. **90**, 357–362 (2019). https://doi.org/10.1016/j.chb.2018.08.027
6. Kim, J., Merrill, K., Jr., Xu, K., Sellnow, D.D.: I like my relational machine teacher: an AI instructor's communication styles and social presence in online education. Int. J. Hum.-Comput. Interact. **37**(18), 1760–1770 (2021). https://doi.org/10.1080/10447318.2021.1908671
7. Kim, J., Merrill, K., Jr., Xu, K., Kelly, S.: Perceived credibility of an AI instructor in online education: the role of social presence and voice features. Comput. Hum. Behav. **136**, 107383 (2022). https://doi.org/10.1016/j.chb.2022.107383
8. Huang, H.-W., Chang, J., Chieh-Y.: Human-AI interactions in teacher education: examining social presence and friendship. In: Proceedings of the 2024 International Conference on Artificial Intelligence and Teacher Education, pp. 64–69 (2024). https://doi.org/10.1145/3702386.3702399
9. Sayed, W.S., et al.: AI-based adaptive personalized content presentation and exercises navigation for an effective and engaging e-learning platform. Multimedia Tools Appl. **82**(3), 3303–3333 (2023)

10. Banerjee, H.L.: Investigating the construct of topical knowledge in second language assessment: a scenario-based assessment approach. Lang. Assess. Q. **16**(2), 133–160 (2019)
11. Bennett, R.E.: CBAL: Results from piloting innovative K-12 assessments (Research Report No. RR-11–23). Educational Testing Service (2015)
12. Purpura, J.E.: A rationale for using a scenario-based assessment to measure competency-based, situated second and foreign language proficiency. In: Masperi, M., Cervini, C., Bardière, Y. (eds.) Évaluation des acquisitions langagières: Du formatif au certificatif. MediAzioni **32**, A54–A96 (2021). http://www.mediazioni.sitlec.unibo.it
13. Purpura, J.E., Joo, S.-H., Beltrán, J., Eskin, D.: Using a Learning-Oriented Assessment Framework to Validate Claims Related to a B1 English Scenario-Based Assessment of Situated English Language Proficiency. Language Assessment Quarterly (2025)
14. Voss, E., Joo, S.-H., Eskin, D., Vafaee, P.: A Learning-Oriented Language Assessment (LOLA) framework argument for artificial intelligence (AI) technologies in scenario-based language assessments (SBLA) Language Assessment Quarterly (2025)
15. Qin, F., Li, K., Yan, J.: Understanding user trust in artificial intelligence-based educational systems: Evidence from China. Br. J. Edu. Technol. **51**(5), 1693–1710 (2020). https://doi.org/10.1111/bjet.12994
16. Amoozadeh, M., et al.: Trust in Generative AI among learners: an exploratory study. In: Proceedings of the 55th ACM Technical Symposium on Computer Science Education V. 1, pp. 67–73(2024). https://doi.org/10.1145/3626252.3630842
17. Lee, K.: Presence, explicated. Commun. Theory **14**(1), 27–50 (2004). https://doi.org/10.1111/j.1468-2885.2004.tb00302.x
18. Gambino, A., Fox, J., Ratan, R.A.: Building a stronger CASA: extending the computers are social actors paradigm. Hum.-Mach. Commun. **1**, 71–85 (2020). https://doi.org/10.30658/hmc.1.5
19. Huang, X., Ruiz-Segura, A., Tan, C., Wang, T., Sharma, R., Lajoie, S.P.: Social presence in technology-rich learning environments: How real we are feeling connected and how does it matter for learning? Inf. Learn. Sci. **124**(11/12), 396–424 (2023). https://doi.org/10.1108/ILS-04-2023-0034
20. Wiersma, W., Jurs, S.G.: Research Methods in Education: An Introduction, 9th edn. Pearson, Boston (2009)
21. Hair, J.F., Risher, J.J., Sarstedt, M., Ringle, C.M.: When to use and how to report the results of PLS-SEM. Eur. Bus. Rev. **31**(1), 2–24 (2019)
22. Manzini, A., Keeling, G., Marchal, N., McKee, K.R., Rieser, V., Gabriel, I.: Should users trust advanced AI assistants? Justified trust as a function of competence and alignment. In: Proceedings of the 2024 ACM Conference on Fairness, Accountability, and Transparency, pp. 1174–1186 (2024). https://doi.org/10.1145/3630106.3658964
23. Pitardi, V., Marriott, H.R.: Alexa, she's not human but… Unveiling the drivers of consumers' trust in voice-based artificial intelligence. Psychol. Mark. **38**(4), 626–642 (2021). https://doi.org/10.1002/mar.21452
24. Choi, J.K., Ji, Y.G.: Investigating the importance of trust on adopting an autonomous vehicle. Int. J. Hum.-Comput. Interact. **31**(10), 692–702 (2015). https://doi.org/10.1080/10447318.2015.1070549
25. Nass, C., Moon, Y., Fogg, B.J., Reeves, B., Dryer, D.C.: Can computer personalities be human personalities? Int. J. Hum. Comput. Stud. **43**(2), 223–239 (1995). https://doi.org/10.1006/ijhc.1995.1042

Designing Effective LLM-Assisted Interfaces for Curriculum Development

Abdolali Faraji(✉), Mohammadreza Tavakoli, Mohammad Moein, Mohammadreza Molavi, and Gábor Kismihók

Leibniz Information Centre for Science and Technology (TIB), Hanover, Germany
{abdolali.faraji,reza.tavakoli,mohammad.moein, mohammadreza.molavi,gabor.kismihok}@tib.eu

Abstract. *Large Language Models* (*LLMs*) have the potential to transform the way a dynamic curriculum can be delivered. However, educators face significant challenges in interacting with these models, particularly due to complex prompt engineering and usability issues, which increase workload. Additionally, inaccuracies in LLM outputs can raise issues around output quality and ethical concerns in educational content delivery. Addressing these issues requires careful oversight, best achieved through cooperation between human and AI approaches. This paper introduces two novel User Interface (*UI*) designs, *UI Predefined* and *UI Open*, both grounded in *Direct Manipulation* (*DM*) principles to address these challenges. By reducing the reliance on intricate prompt engineering, these UIs improve usability, streamline interaction, and lower workload, providing a more effective pathway for educators to engage with LLMs. In a controlled user study with 20 participants, the proposed UIs were evaluated against the standard ChatGPT interface in terms of usability and cognitive load. Results showed that *UI Predefined* significantly outperformed both *ChatGPT* and *UI Open*, demonstrating superior usability and reduced task load, while *UI Open* offered more flexibility at the cost of a steeper learning curve. These findings underscore the importance of user-centered design in adopting AI-driven tools and lay the foundation for more intuitive and efficient educator-LLM interactions in online learning environments.

Keywords: User-centered design · LLM user interface · Curriculum development

1 Introduction

Online learning has become indispensable in modern education, revolutionizing the way knowledge is accessed and disseminated. Its popularity has surged in recent years due to several factors. The convenience of learning at one's own pace and from any location has made it particularly appealing to busy individuals and those with limited access to traditional educational institutions [8]. Moreover, the demand for rapid access to up-to-date information on various topics, including skills, tasks at hand, and hobbies, has made online learning a highly effective

A. I. Cristea et al. (Eds.): AIED 2025, LNAI 15877, pp. 438–451, 2025.
https://doi.org/10.1007/978-3-031-98414-3_31

and efficient educational method [22]. This highlights the importance of dynamic up-to-date curriculum development in the context of online learning [21]. Maintaining curricula dynamically to align with the rapid pace of societal changes and learning needs poses significant challenges [21]. The burden on teachers to continuously update their content is substantial, as it requires extensive time and effort [6]. Additionally, accessing high-quality, valid information from the vast amount of available online resources is also challenging, making it difficult to ensure the accuracy and relevance of the curriculum content [1].

The emergence of LLMs has sparked optimism for addressing the challenges associated with dynamic curriculum development [15]. Despite the potential of LLM-based methods, they are questionable in terms of the output quality [2,6] (i.e. inaccurate, wrong, or even ethically questionable outputs). This has led to a growing interest in investigating the collaborative Human-AI approaches that combine the strengths of LLMs with human expertise [21]. Such collaboration between AI and human educators enables a sustainable, future-ready approach to curriculum development [19].

One of the primary limitations of LLM usage by experts lies in their text-based UIs, which are often not user-friendly and impose a higher cognitive load [7]. Interacting with these text-based UIs relies heavily on textual prompts that need to be optimized. This technology-centered method (in contrast to the user-centered method) requires *careful wording* and *precise references* to the object of interest, which results in more difficult optimization [4]. This leads to challenges like 1) *indirect engagement* due to limited direct access to the object of interest, 2) *semantic distance* in expressing intent in written form, and 3) *articulatory distance* between prompts and their intended actions [14]. Addressing these challenges through user-friendly LLM interfaces is essential to facilitate content development and maximize AI's potential [6,14].

This paper proposes two novel UI designs to address the challenges of LLM-based curriculum development, specifically those related to their interfaces. These proposed UIs aimed to optimize the interaction between educators and LLMs, potentially surpassing the capabilities of existing interfaces. Furthermore, by conducting a comprehensive evaluation, we sought to determine whether these UI solutions could enhance the efficiency and effectiveness of curriculum development processes in terms of usability and workload. Therefore, our main contributions are:

- Designing and prototyping UIs for LLM, specifically ChatGPT, which aim at enhancing the usability of LLMs for educators, when it comes to curriculum development
- Conducting an experiment to evaluate the proposed UIs against the default ChatGPT UI in terms of usability, effectiveness, and cognitive load

2 Related Work

In this section, we cover the related research, which influenced key components of our conceptual and technical work. We begin by discussing AI-based curricula development. Next, we explore the development of LLM-based UIs. Finally, we examine the research on human-computer interaction within the context of AI systems, focusing on how to optimize the user experience.

2.1 Curricula Development

Previous research has explored the integration of AI algorithms into curriculum development. For instance, [13] used an adaptive AI algorithm to create real-time curricula for robot-assisted surgery using simulators, based on learners' feedback. Although the number of participants was limited, their results demonstrated improved learning outcomes for students using these AI-generated curricula. Additionally, both [10,16] employed *Latent Dirichlet Allocation (LDA)* to extract covered topics from educational resources to support curriculum development processes. Moreover, [21] utilized various traditional machine learning models (e.g., LDA and Random Forest) to assist human experts in developing curricula by recommending learning topics and related educational resources. It can be observed that previous research efforts primarily relied on traditional machine learning methods, limiting their focus to specific educational domains.

2.2 LLM-Based UIs

To address the challenges of interacting with LLMs, researchers have explored various UI approaches. For instance, [14] proposed the *DirectGPT* UI to enhance the usability of LLMs by providing features like continuous output representation and prompt control. Through a user study with 12 experts, they demonstrated that *DirectGPT* users achieved better task completion times and reported higher satisfaction compared to traditional interfaces. Additionally, [5] explored the impact of different slider types on user control over generative models, highlighting the importance of UI design for effective interaction.

Beyond general-purpose LLMs, researchers have also investigated LLM-based UI applications in specific domains. [12] developed *SPROUT*, a tool designed to assist users in creating code tutorials using LLMs. Their study found that SPROUT significantly improved user satisfaction and the quality of generated content. Furthermore, [23] demonstrated the potential of LLMs in video editing workflows, emphasizing the need for intuitive UIs to facilitate this process.

2.3 Human-Computer Interaction for AI Systems

While AI solutions, particularly LLMs, have opened up numerous possibilities that were previously unimaginable, the development of many AI-based systems continues to be hindered by a "technology-centric" approach rather than a "user-centric" approach [18,25].

As already mentioned in the introduction, interaction with LLMs usually happens using textual prompts which introduce different challenges (i.e. indirect engagement, semantic distance, and articulatory distance). These challenges closely resemble issues that caused the shift from command-line interfaces to *Direct Manipulation (DM)* interfaces (like graphical user interfaces) in the 1980s [9]. Shneiderman [20] defined DM interfaces with four key traits:

(DM1). Continuous representation of the object of interest
(DM2). Physical actions (e.g. movement and selection by mouse, joystick, touch screen, etc.) instead of complex syntax
(DM3). Rapid, incremental, reversible operations whose impact on the object of interest is immediately visible
(DM4). Users should recognize the actions they can do instead of learning complex syntax

We use the term *DM* in our paper to refer to these four pillars in the user interface.

2.4 Lessons Learned

As discussed in the Curricula Development subsection, there is a clear need for developing and evaluating more advanced and up-to-date AI-driven solutions (such as those based on large language models) for curriculum development, given their demonstrated potential in these educational contexts [6]. However, as we highlighted, these solutions must be complemented with user-friendly interfaces, as text-based interaction with LLMs can be less than ideal for users [14]. Consequently, UI principles (e.g., DM), as explored earlier, should be carefully considered when designing such interfaces for LLM-based curricula development.

3 Method

To address text-based interface challenges, we applied DM principles to UIs designed for *course outline creation*, assisting educators in defining course titles, learning outcomes, and related topic lists. Below, we describe the two developed UIs, the prompt engineering techniques used, and the control group's standard ChatGPT UI.

3.1 UI 1: Predefined Commands

UI Predefined offers educators clickable buttons with predefined commands in a familiar graphical user interface (*GUI*) layout. These commands, curated from expert inputs in European Union educational projects[1], support key tasks in creating and refining course outlines. Commands in *UI Predefined* are organized into four functional groups, presented as clickable actions, as depicted in Fig. 1. The first group includes commands for modifying course-level information (i.e. the course title and learning outcome). The second group comprises batch actions, which are activated upon selecting multiple topics. The third group focuses on

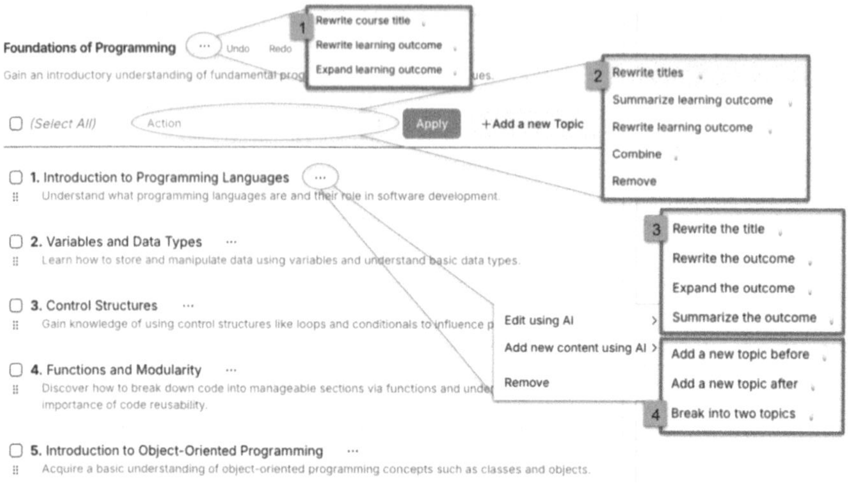

Fig. 1. An example of a course outline representation in *UI Predefined*. Four groups of predefined commands are visible: *group-1)* course-related commands, *group-2)* batch commands, *group-3)* single-topic refinement commands, and *group-4)* content generation with respect to a single topic.

actions for refining individual topics, while the fourth group facilitates the generation of new content based on a single topic.

As it is visible in Fig. 1, the course outline representation in *UI Predefined* is enhanced with an interactive table format (aligned with DM1) which replaces static text, improving clarity and interaction. Command execution is transparent, with only the updated outline sections displaying a loading effect. A meatball menu next to each item supports contextual actions (DM2, DM4), while checkboxes enable batch operations (DM3). Users can directly edit course titles or outcomes, rearrange topics with drag-and-drop, and add/remove topics, aligning with DM2 and DM4. Undo/redo functionality supports rapid, reversible interactions consistent with DM3.

3.2 UI 2: Open Commands

UI Open was developed as an alternative to *UI Predefined*, retaining its core visual structure (as shown in Fig. 2) while addressing key limitations, particularly the lack of direct user interaction with the LLM. To overcome this limitation, a dynamic command mechanism was introduced, allowing users to engage directly with the LLM. These command functions include three key enhancements: (1) automatic integration of the course outline context, ensuring LLM awareness of

[1] Project details can be found here: https://www.tib.eu/en/research-development/research-groups-and-labs/learning-and-skill-analytics/projects.

the structure; (2) a drag-and-drop interface for associating commands with specific course elements; and (3) the ability to save and reuse commands, reducing repetition and improving time-efficiency.

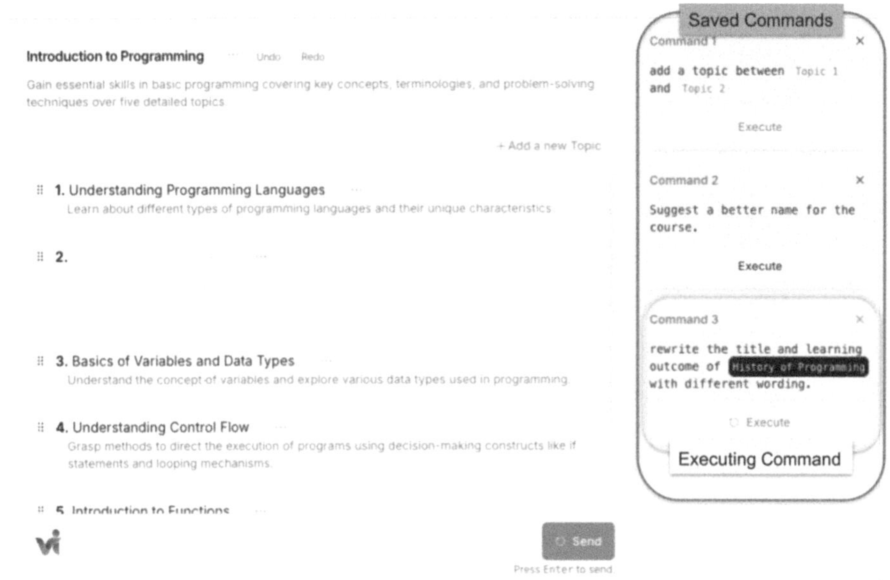

Fig. 2. An example of a course outline being developed by a user with dynamic commands in *UI Open*. In this figure, Command 3 is being executed on Topic 2.

To enhance user-friendliness, *UI Open* incorporates a chat box at the bottom of the course outline interface. The outline representation remains largely unchanged (DM1), allowing manual edits via a click-based interface (DM2). Unlike *UI Predefined*, it removes predefined buttons, offering a more flexible approach. The chat box enables users to input, execute, and save dynamic commands for reuse, supporting DM2 and DM3. Commands can be global (affecting the entire outline) or local (applied to specific sections), adjusted by dragging topics into the chat box (DM2), as shown in Fig. 3.

3.3 Prompt Engineering

To achieve the desired results from an LLM in our UIs, prompts were tailored based on OpenAI's best practices for prompt engineering [17]. To be more specific, using the `gpt-4o-2024-08-06` model (the latest model at the time of the experiment), a system prompt was applied to (1) define the LLM's persona, (2) delimit prompt components, (3) specify the task (course outline curation), and (4) establish the output format. Moreover, the current course outline and

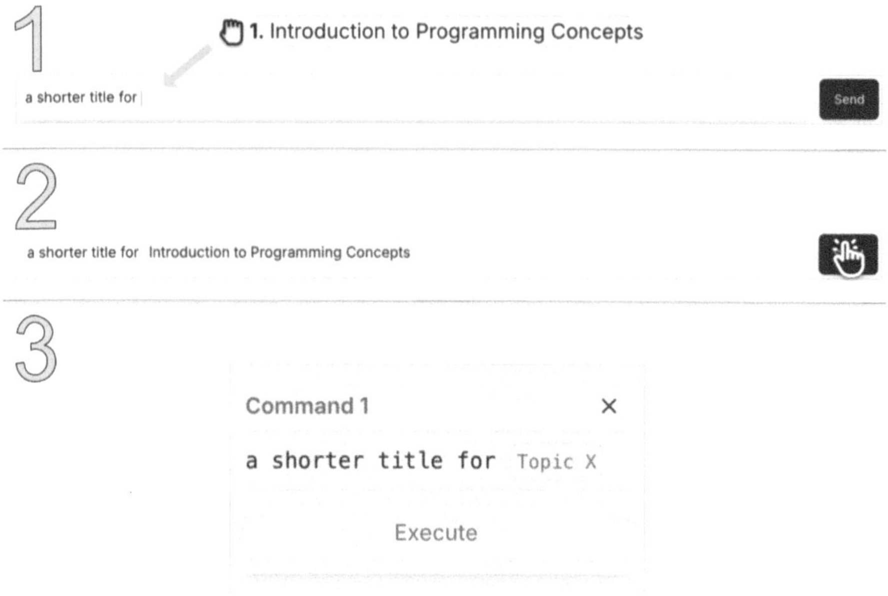

Fig. 3. *UI Open*: *1)* User is creating a command while dragging a topic for localization *2)* Command is executed and saved *3)* Any other topic can be dragged to the saved command.

user-issued commands were always included in prompts, allowing the LLM to respond within context. The output format adhered to a defined structure, translated by the UI engine for display. To ensure consistency, each topic generated by the LLM was assigned an identifier, enabling precise referencing throughout interactions.

3.4 ChatGPT Replica Tool

To establish a control application for comparison with *Predefined* and *Open* UIs, we required a tool that emulated the ChatGPT interface. Direct usage of ChatGPT was unsuitable, as it did not allow for monitoring user interactions, nor did it guarantee the use of the same model utilized in our UIs. After exploring alternatives, we opted for `open-webui`[2], an open-source project designed for interacting with LLMs. This tool offers an experience closely comparable to the original ChatGPT interface, making it a suitable choice for our experiment.

[2] Open WebUI repository: https://github.com/open-webui/open-webui.

4 Evaluation

We conducted a user study to evaluate the effectiveness and usability of the UIs: *UI Predefined*, *UI Open*, and a control interface replicating *ChatGPT*[3]. Participants from diverse educational backgrounds used each UI and completed a questionnaire capturing their experience and background. Below, we detail the experimental design, procedures, and analytical methods.

4.1 Participants

The study involved 20 participants, with teaching experience ranging from 1 to 21 years, providing a broad spectrum of perspectives on the usability and effectiveness of the UIs. They were evenly distributed by gender, with an equal number of females and males. Each participant had a minimum of five years of professional experience across diverse fields, including but not limited to Computer Science, Mathematics, Nursing, and Soft Skills. Additionally, participants exhibited varying degrees of familiarity with *ChatGPT*, ranging from low to very high proficiency. This range of teaching and technological backgrounds enabled us to collect feedback that reflects a diverse set of educational contexts. The demographic distribution of the participants is depicted in Fig. 4.

4.2 Questionnaire

The evaluation focused on two primary objectives: (1) assessing perceived workload and (2) measuring interface usability. We used the *Raw NASA Task Load Index* (NASA RTLX) to quantify task load and the *System Usability Scale* (SUS) to evaluate usability, both established methods in HCI research [3,11]. *NASA RTLX* measures perceived workload in the dimensions of mental demand, physical demand, temporal demand, performance, effort, and frustration. *SUS* on the other hand, covers the ease of use, efficiency, consistency, and learnability. Data was collected through a three-step questionnaire: participants first completed the NASA RTLX to assess workload, followed by the SUS for usability evaluation, and finally answered an open-ended question for additional feedback. This approach combined quantitative and qualitative insights into the UIs' effectiveness and usability.

4.3 Experiment Steps

Each participant followed a structured process to evaluate the three AI-powered UIs for course outline development:

1. **Study Introduction (≈10 min).** Participants were briefed on the study's objectives, focusing on the workload and usability of the UIs.

[3] Demo of the experiment, including different steps, is available under: https://figshare.com/s/faa7fcea8bbf9d93ad1f.

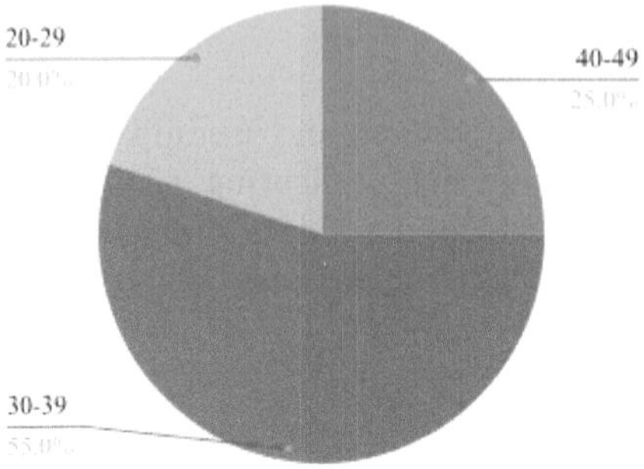

(a) Age

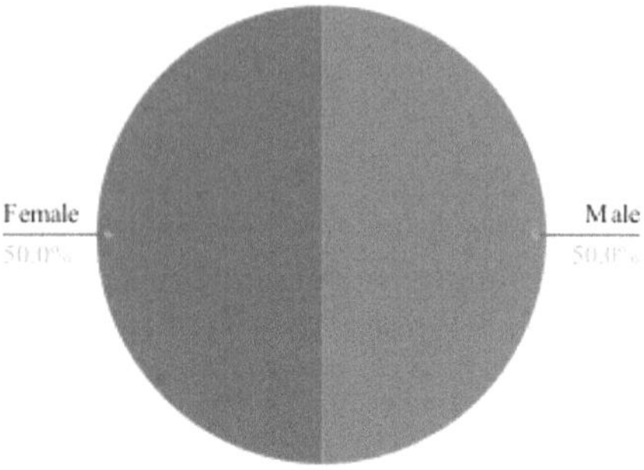

(b) Gender

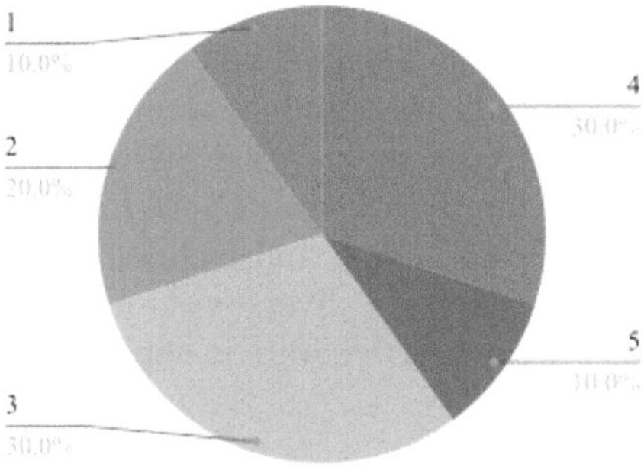

(c) LLM Experience - self rated from 1 (least) to 5 (most)

Fig. 4. Background information of the participants.

2. **Background Information (≈5 min).** Demographic data, including teaching experience and prior *ChatGPT* familiarity, were collected.
3. **Reference Course Outline (≈30 min).** Participants created a baseline course outline in their teaching subject for comparison with different UI outputs.
4. **Curriculum Development with UIs (3 rounds, ≈30 min each).** Participants used each of the three UIs in randomized order, for a fair evaluation, spending 20 min per UI to create course outlines, followed by completing an evaluation form.
5. **Final Evaluation (≈5 min).** Participants provided suggestions for improvement and shared challenges.

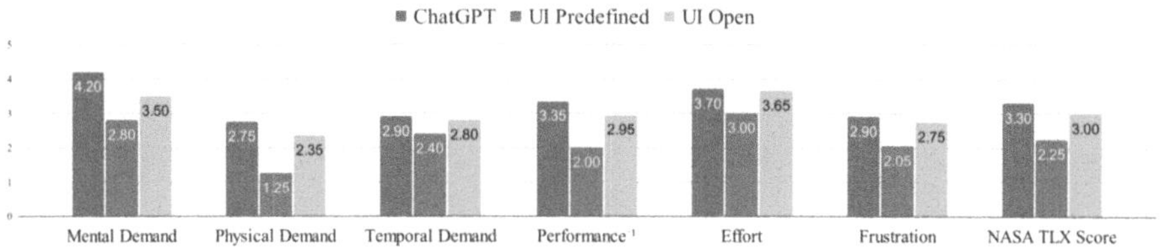

Fig. 5. The average results for each metric in NASA RTLX. Lower values mean a lower workload. (Performance^{-1} is defined as 8 – Performance)

Table 1. Workload Comparison.

Comparison		|Difference|	*p-value*
UI Predefined 2.25	ChatGPT 3.30	1.05	<0.03
UI Predefined 2.25	*UI Open* 3.00	0.75	<0.02
UI Open 3.00	*ChatGPT* 3.30	0.30	–

5 Results and Discussion

5.1 Results

All 20 participants completed the study[4]. Results showed *UI Predefined* significantly outperformed *ChatGPT* in workload, usability, and efficiency, while *UI Open* ranked second with a non-significant improvement over *ChatGPT*. We used the *Wilcoxon signed-rank test* [24] to analyze differences in workload and usability, with statistical analysis conducted in *Python* 3.12 using *scipy*. *p-values* were reported to assess significance.

Workload and Performance. To compute the NASA RTLX scores, we transformed the *Performance* dimension into *Performance*$^{-1}$ by subtracting the original value from 8, ensuring lower scores indicated better performance (Performance^{-1} would be between 1 to 7 like other dimensions). *UI Predefined* had the lowest workload with a mean score of 2.25, followed by *UI Open* (3.00) and *ChatGPT* with the highest workload (3.30). The adjusted *Performance* metric further emphasized the efficiency gap, with *ChatGPT* showing a consistently higher workload compared to both developed UIs. These findings highlight the superior efficiency and reduced cognitive load of *UI Predefined* and *UI Open* over the control. Detailed results and *p-values* are presented in Table 1 and visualized in Fig. 5.

[4] The raw data, including the background information of the participants, the questionnaires, and the participants' answers, is available at: https://figshare.com/s/76c780adbae8f3d22f07.

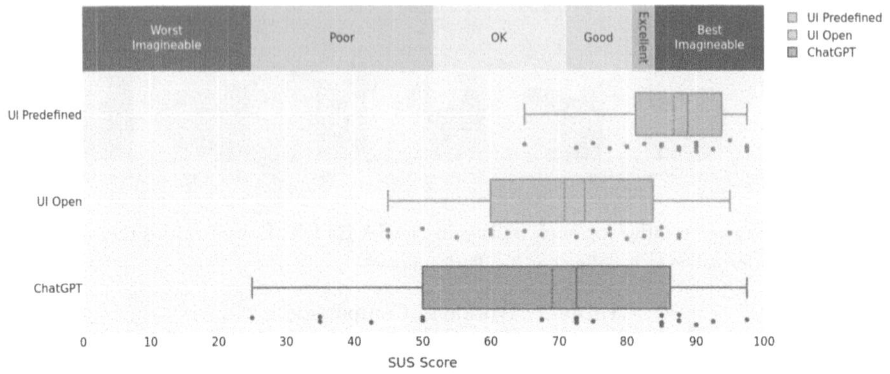

Fig. 6. UIs' SUS Scores. Min, max, 1st, 2nd, and 3rd quartiles are shown. The dotted lines are *mean*.

Table 2. SUS Comparison.

Usability Comparison		|Difference|	*p-value*
UI Predefined 86.75	ChatGPT 69.00	17.75	<0.009
UI Predefined 86.75	UI Open 70.75	16.00	<0.002
UI Open 70.75	ChatGPT 69.00	1.75	–

Usability. The System Usability Scale (SUS) results show *UI Predefined* achieving the highest usability score of 86.75, well above the "Excellent" threshold [3]. In comparison, *UI Open* scored 70.75, and *ChatGPT* scored 69.00, both within the "OK" category. These findings highlight the superior ease of use and participant satisfaction with *UI Predefined*. Detailed *p-values* are in Table 2, with results visualized in Fig. 6.

5.2 Discussion

Our findings indicated that the UI with predefined commands outperformed the others in both usability (SUS) and workload (NASA RTLX) dimensions. This superiority was attributed to its ability to streamline the course outline creation process. Eight participants specifically noted that predefined commands significantly reduced their typing burden, while ten emphasized the overall ease of use.

While the UI with open commands also received positive feedback for its flexibility, participants acknowledged a steeper learning curve. This suggests that a hybrid approach, combining predefined and open commands, might offer the optimal balance of usability and adaptability. Although the ChatGPT UI received some preference due to participants' familiarity, all participants agreed that features like command definition, reuse, and better output presentation were essential for enhancing their overall experience.

Despite the promising results of our study, there are limitations that must be acknowledged. The experiment was constrained to controlled environments, which may not accurately reflect the dynamic and diverse settings in which educators interact with LLMs in real-world scenarios. On the other hand, the study was conducted on a limited number of educators, potentially limiting its diversity. However, we tried to mitigate this limitation by inviting educators from diverse areas, ensuring representation across different backgrounds and demographics. These limitations suggest that future research should encompass a wider range of user backgrounds and real-world testing to enhance the applicability and robustness of UI designs in practical educational contexts.

6 Conclusion

In conclusion, this paper highlighted the growing role of online learning and the potential of LLMs in education. While LLMs enhance accessibility and personalization, they also pose challenges, particularly for educators. Key concerns include (1) the accuracy of LLM outputs and (2) the complexity of effective interaction. To address these, we proposed and evaluated two user interfaces, *UI Predefined* and *UI Open*, designed with DM principles to simplify educator interaction. These interfaces reduce reliance on prompt engineering and improve usability. Additionally, they mitigate the risks associated with output quality by fostering Human and AI collaboration, integrating a human check to ensure accuracy and alignment with the teacher standards.

Our findings revealed that the UI Predefined significantly outperformed ChatGPT, showcasing its potential to streamline educational interactions with a set of expert-derived commands that reduce cognitive load and enhance efficiency and usability. Although UI Open also showed improvements over ChatGPT by allowing more direct, context-rich interactions for educators, it did not exhibit a statistically significant advantage.

Building on our findings, future research should explore a hybrid approach that integrates elements of both UI Open and UI Predefined, balancing structured guidance with open-ended interaction. Additionally, expanding the study to a more diverse group of educators across various real-world settings will enhance the generalizability of the results. Finally, the impact of different UI designs on the learning processes should be investigated. This will help to improve learning as the ultimate goal of educational applications.

References

1. Abdi, S., Khosravi, H., Sadiq, S., Demartini, G.: Evaluating the quality of learning resources: a learner sourcing approach. IEEE Trans. Learn. Technol. **14**(1), 81–92 (2021)
2. Bahrami, M., Sonoda, R., Srinivasan, R.: LLM diagnostic toolkit: evaluating LLMs for ethical issues. In: 2024 International Joint Conference on Neural Networks (IJCNN), pp. 1–8. IEEE (2024)
3. Bangor, A., Kortum, P.T., Miller, J.T.: An empirical evaluation of the system usability scale. Intl. J. Hum.-Comput. Interact. **24**(6), 574–594 (2008)
4. Chen, B., Zhang, Z., Langrené, N., Zhu, S.: Unleashing the potential of prompt engineering in large language models: a comprehensive review. arXiv preprint arXiv:2310.14735 (2023)
5. Dang, H., Mecke, L., Buschek, D.: GANSlider: how users control generative models for images using multiple sliders with and without feedforward information. In: Proceedings of the 2022 CHI Conference on Human Factors in Computing Systems, pp. 1–15 (2022)
6. Denny, P., Khosravi, H., Hellas, A., Leinonen, J., Sarsa, S.: Can we trust AI-generated educational content? Comparative analysis of human and AI-generated learning resources. arXiv preprint arXiv:2306.10509 (2023)
7. Feng, K., Liao, Q.V., Xiao, Z., Vaughan, J.W., Zhang, A.X., McDonald, D.W.: Canvil: designerly adaptation for LLM-powered user experiences. arXiv preprint arXiv:2401.09051 (2024)
8. Gros, B., García-Peñalvo, F.J.: Future trends in the design strategies and technological affordances of e-learning. In: Learning, Design, and Technology: An International Compendium of Theory, Research, Practice, and Policy, pp. 345–367. Springer (2023)
9. Hutchins, E.L., Hollan, J.D., Norman, D.A.: Direct manipulation interfaces. Hum,-Comput. Interact. **1**(4), 311–338 (1985)
10. Kawamata, T., Matsuda, Y., Sekiya, T., Yamaguchi, K.: Analysis of computer science textbooks by topic modeling and dynamic time warping. In: 2021 IEEE International Conference on Engineering, Technology & Education (TALE), Wuhan, Hubei Province, China, pp. 865–870. IEEE (2021). https://doi.org/10.1109/TALE52509.2021.9678834
11. Kosch, T., Karolus, J., Zagermann, J., Reiterer, H., Schmidt, A., Woźniak, P.W.: A survey on measuring cognitive workload in human-computer interaction. ACM Comput. Surv. **55**(13s), 1–39 (2023)
12. Liu, Y., Wen, Z., Weng, L., Woodman, O., Yang, Y., Chen, W.: Sprout: an interactive authoring tool for generating programming tutorials with the visualization of large language models. IEEE Trans. Vis. Comput. Graph. (2024)
13. Mariani, A., Pellegrini, E., De Momi, E.: Skill-oriented and performance-driven adaptive curricula for training in robot-assisted surgery using simulators: a feasibility study. IEEE Trans. Biomed. Eng. **68**(2), 685–694 (2021)
14. Masson, D., Malacria, S., Casiez, G., Vogel, D.: DirectGPT: a direct manipulation interface to interact with large language models. In: Proceedings of the CHI Conference on Human Factors in Computing Systems, pp. 1–16 (2024)
15. Moein, M., Molavi, M., Faraji, A., Tavakoli, M., Kismihók, G.: Beyond search engines: can large language models improve curriculum development? In: 19th European Conference on Technology Enhanced Learning, EC-TEL 2020, Krems, Austria, 16–20 September 2024. Springer (2024)

16. Molavi, M., Tavakoli, M., Kismihók, G.: Extracting topics from open educational resources. In: Addressing Global Challenges and Quality Education: 15th European Conference on Technology Enhanced Learning, EC-TEL 2020, Heidelberg, Germany, 14–18 September 2020, Proceedings 15, pp. 455–460. Springer (2020)
17. OpenAI: Prompt engineering - openAI API (2024). https://platform.openai.com/docs/guides/prompt-engineering. Accessed Sept 2024
18. Ozmen Garibay, O., et al.: Six human-centered artificial intelligence grand challenges. Int. J. Hum.-Comput. Interact. **39**(3), 391–437 (2023)
19. Padovano, A., Cardamone, M.: Towards human-AI collaboration in the competency-based curriculum development process: the case of industrial engineering and management education. Comput. Educ. Artif. Intell. **7**, 100256 (2024)
20. Shneiderman, B.: Direct manipulation: a step beyond programming languages. Computer **16**(08), 57–69 (1983)
21. Tavakoli, M., Faraji, A., Molavi, M., T. Mol, S., Kismihók, G.: Hybrid human-AI curriculum development for personalised informal learning environments. In: LAK22: 12th International Learning Analytics and Knowledge Conference, pp. 563–569 (2022)
22. Tavakoli, M., Faraji, A., Vrolijk, J., Molavi, M.d., Mol, S.T., Kismihók, G.: An AI-based open recommender system for personalized labor market driven education. Adv. Eng. Inform. **52**, 101508 (2022)
23. Wang, B., Li, Y., Lv, Z., Xia, H., Xu, Y., Sodhi, R.: LAVE: LLM-powered agent assistance and language augmentation for video editing. In: Proceedings of the 29th International Conference on Intelligent User Interfaces, pp. 699–714 (2024)
24. Woolson, R.F.: Wilcoxon signed-rank test. Encycl. Biostat. **8** (2005)
25. Xu, W., Dainoff, M.J., Ge, L., Gao, Z.: Transitioning to human interaction with AI systems: new challenges and opportunities for HCI professionals to enable human-centered AI. Int. J. Hum.-Comput. Interact. **39**(3), 494–518 (2023)

Author Index

A. I. Cristea et al. (Eds.): AIED 2025, LNAI 15877, pp. 453–455, 2025.
https://doi.org/10.1007/978-3-031-98414-3

The manufacturer's authorised representative in the EU is Springer Nature Customer Service Centre GmbH, Europaplatz 3, 69115 Heidelberg, Germany. If you have any concerns regarding our products, please contact ProductSafety@springernature.com

Printed and bound by CPI Group (UK) Ltd, Croydon, CR0 4YY
30/09/2026
02225560-0016